FROM ASIAN TO GLOBAL FINANCIAL CRISIS

This is a unique insider account of the new world of unfettered finance. The author, an Asian regulator, examines how old mindsets, market fundamentalism, loose monetary policy, carry trade, lax supervision, greed, cronyism, and financial engineering caused both the Asian crisis of the late 1990s and the current global crisis of 2007–2009. This book shows how the Japanese zero interest rate policy to fight deflation helped create the carry trade that generated bubbles in Asia whose effects brought Asian economies down. The study's main purpose is to demonstrate that global finance is so interlinked and interactive that our current tools and institutional structure to deal with critical episodes are completely outdated. The book explains how current financial policies and regulation failed to deal with a global bubble and makes recommendations on what must change.

Andrew Sheng is currently the Chief Adviser to the China Banking Regulatory Commission and a Board Member of the Qatar Financial Centre Regulatory Authority, Khazanah Nasional Berhad and Sime Darby Berhad, Malaysia. He is also Adjunct Professor at the Graduate School of Economics and Management, Tsinghua University, Beijing, and at the Faculty of Economics and Administration at the University of Malaya, Kuala Lumpur. Mr Sheng was Chairman of the Securities and Futures Commission of Hong Kong from 1998 to 2005. A former central banker with Bank Negara Malaysia and Hong Kong Monetary Authority, between 2003 and 2005 he was Chairman of the Technical Committee of IOSCO, the International Organization of Securities Commissions, the standard setter for securities regulation. He is a columnist for *Caijing Magazine*, the largest and most widely read finance journal in China. He edited *Bank Restructuring: Lessons from the 1980s* (1996) and holds an honorary doctorate from the University of Bristol.

From Asian to Global Financial Crisis

*An Asian Regulator's View of Unfettered Finance
in the 1990s and 2000s*

ANDREW SHENG

CAMBRIDGE UNIVERSITY PRESS
Cambridge, New York, Melbourne, Madrid, Cape Town, Singapore,
São Paulo, Delhi, Dubai, Tokyo

Cambridge University Press
32 Avenue of the Americas, New York, NY 10013-2473, USA

www.cambridge.org
Information on this title: www.cambridge.org/9780521134156

First published 2009

Printed in the United States of America

A catalog record for this publication is available from the British Library.

Library of Congress Cataloging in Publication data
Sheng, Andrew.
From Asian to global financial crisis : an Asian regulator's view of unfettered
finance in the 1990s and 2000s / Andrew Sheng.
p.   cm.
Includes bibliographical references and index.
ISBN 978-0-521-11864-4 (hbk)
1. Finance–Asia.   2. Financial crises–Asia.   I. Title.
HG187.A2S54 2009
330.95′0429–dc22   2009027826

ISBN 978-0-521-11864-4 Hardback
ISBN 978-0-521-13415-6 Paperback

*This book is dedicated to my mother, Chuen Mo Jhen, and my wife,
Lim Suan Poh, whose infinite patience, encouragement
and support made this work possible.*

Contents

Figures

Tables

Acknowledgements

This book could not have been written without acknowledging my huge debt to all my friends, colleagues, teachers and mentors, past and present, who are too numerous to mention. My time at Bank Negara Malaysia, World Bank, Hong Kong Monetary Authority, Hong Kong Securities and Futures Commission, IOSCO, and the China Banking Regulatory Commission (CBRC) all shaped my thinking and sharpened my analysis. Specific gratitude must go to guidance and support by the late Tun Ismail Mohd Ali, Tan Sri Aziz Taha and Tan Sri Lin See Yan; Tan Sri Zeti Aziz in Bank Negara; Millard Long and Alan Gelb at the World Bank; Sir Donald Tsang, Rafael Hui, Joseph Yam and David Carse in Hong Kong; and Chairman Liu Mingkang and his colleagues in CBRC. I am grateful to Malcolm Knight and his colleagues at the Bank for International Settlements for the sabbatical I spent with them in the winter of 2005 researching this book. In academia, the Tun Ismail Ali Professorship offered me the opportunity to work at the Faculty of Economics and Administration in the University of Malaya, funded by Bank Negara Malaysia. I also had the privilege of working with colleagues at the Tsinghua University Graduate School of Economics and Management, as well as spending time at the London School of Economics, Stanford Center for International Development. Charles Goodhart was particularly helpful with his insightful comments.

The meticulous research work for this book was done cheerfully and ably by Ms Sharmila Sharma, who patiently slogged at the drafts, data and analyses, despite my hectic schedule. The ideas in this book were first tested in a series of articles on the Asian and current crisis that was published in Chinese by *Caijing Magazine*, with translation by my able Tsinghua assistant Cheng Jiuyan and polished elegantly by CBRC colleague Su Xinming. I am particularly grateful to Ms Tan Gaik Looi and Michael Pomerleano, who were the first to comment on raw chapters of this book.

At Cambridge University Press, Scott Parris and Adam Levine and three anonymous readers all gave incisive comments and contributions that helped this book to come to fruition. To all I am eternally grateful. They have the credits; I alone bear all debits and personal responsibility for any errors, omissions and opinions.

Introduction

The story of the boom and crash of 1929 is worth telling for its own sake. Great drama joined in those months with a luminous insanity. But there is the more sombre purpose. As protection against financial illusion or insanity, memory is far better than law. When memory of the 1929 disaster failed, law and regulation no longer sufficed. For protecting people from the cupidity of others and their own, history is highly utilitarian.
   ~ *John Kenneth Galbraith,* The Great Crash 1929, *Preface to the 1975 Edition*

In December 2008 I received a text message on my phone which must have been passed through a million hands:

1 year ago RBS paid \$100 bn for ABN AMRO. Today that same amount would buy: Citibank \$22.5 bn, Morgan Stanley \$10.5 bn, Goldman Sachs \$21 bn, Merrill Lynch \$12.3 bn, Deutsche Bank \$13 bn, Barclays \$12.7 bn, and still have \$8 bn change … with which you would be able to pick up GM, Ford, Chrysler and the Honda F1 Team.

If I had told anyone even six months ago that the current crisis would have resulted in governments owning one quarter of the capital of the Western banking system, most people would have thought me mad.

When friends asked me Why another book on the Asian and global financial crises? I gave four reasons. First, I was a ringside audience to the Asian crisis, as Deputy Chief Executive of the Hong Kong Monetary Authority (HKMA) in charge of external affairs and reserves management from 1993 to 1998. I was present during some of the key discussions over policy and the international architecture. Most of the key actors were personal friends or colleagues, central bankers and policymakers whom I had grown up with through my early days as Chief Economist and Assistant Governor (Bank and Insurance Regulation) of Bank Negara Malaysia. Principal actors, such as Larry Summers, Stan Fischer and Joe Stiglitz, I had worked with when

I was seconded to the World Bank between 1989 and 1993. Others, such as Tim Geithner, former President of the New York Federal Reserve and Treasury Secretary under the Obama Administration, Eisuke Sakakibara (Mr Yen) and Masahiro Kawai, I got to know during the crisis, as we shared both the agony and the drama that deserve to be told, even though the story had been told many times.

It is useful to remember that after the Asian crisis and the dot-com bubble of 2000 the world underwent the most thorough overhaul of accounting, corporate governance, regulation and national financial architecture since the 1930s. As former Chairman of the Hong Kong Securities and Futures Commission, I participated actively in the design of that architecture, being one of the few Asian representatives with an emerging market background. I co-chaired with Bank of England Governor (then Deputy Governor) Mervyn King the Working Group on Transparency and Accountability, which was established by the Group of Twenty-Two in 1998. I also chaired the Financial Stability Forum's Task Force on Implementation of Standards in 1999. As Chairman of the Technical Committee of the International Organization of Securities Commission (IOSCO), the international standard setter on securities regulation, from 2003 to 2005, I worked with luminaries such as former SEC Chairman Arthur Levitt, Arthur Docters Van Leeuwen, former Chairman of the Netherlands Authority for Financial Markets and the Committee of European Securities Regulators, Sir Andrew Crockett, former General Manager of the Bank for International Settlements and Chair of the Financial Stability Forum, Sir Howard Davies, former Chairman of the U.K. Financial Services Authority, Michel Prada, former Chair of the French securities regulator and both the Technical Committee and Executive Committee of IOSCO, and many others to push forward reforms in accounting and securities regulatory standards. None of these was enough to stem the present crisis. Some of them may have contributed to the crisis. *Mea culpa.*

A PERSONAL ASIAN VIEW

Second, there are very few books on the Asian crisis by senior Asian officials who were in place during the crisis. Perhaps we had neither the time nor the inclination to write about our perspectives and experiences. Since we had no good theories to explain the Asian Miracle, we had even less incentive to explain the Asian bust. But for posterity's sake, the Asian side of the story deserves to be told.

At the outset I need to stress that even though this is one Asian's view of financial crises, I am not a proponent of Asian values, because I sincerely believe that the accepted values of hard work, thrift, loyalty and social conscience are universal and not unique to Asia. During the crisis, a number of Western analysts, including Francis Fukuyama explored whether Asian values were associated with authoritarian, corrupt, crony capitalism.[1] Alas, not only have we not reached the end of history, but also financial crises are common to both authoritarian and democratic societies, and both suffer from crony capitalism of different forms.

Hubris always ends up as humbug. Nothing proves the universality of this truth better than the fact that everything that is being done to deal with the current crisis is exactly what the Washington Consensus told us that we should not do during the Asian crisis. The list includes intervention in markets, blanket deposit guarantees, lower interest rates, loosened fiscal discipline, letting banks fail to stop moral hazard, stopping short selling and blaming market manipulation.

Saying 'I told you so' gets us nowhere because I would be the first one to say that if Asia does not get its act together in certain areas, it may suffer the next crisis in the next decade or so. What we need to realize is that we are all fallible, vulnerable and in the same boat.

The global nature of the present U.S. crisis can be seen in the following context. At the end of 2007, the United States had gross domestic product (GDP) of US$13.8 trillion, compared with Japan (US$4.4 trillion) and China (US$3.2 trillion). The United States had gross and net international liabilities of US$16.3 trillion and US$2.5 trillion,[2] respectively (data at end of 2006). On the other hand, Japan and China together held half of the total U.S. government treasury securities at the end of July 2007.[3] At the end of June 2007, foreigners owned 56.9 percent of marketable U.S. Treasury securities, 24 percent of corporate and other debt, 21.4 percent of U.S. government agency paper and 11.3 percent of total U.S. stock market capitalization.[4]

In other words, whatever pain the United States feels, the rest of the world will also share. No one is gloating.

Personally, this book is my attempt at unravelling the *Rashomon* of financial crises. When I first saw Japanese director Akira Kurosawa's film as a

---

[1] See Fukuyama (1998).
[2] Data from www.bea.gov.
[3] Data from www.ustreas.gov/tic/mfh.txt.
[4] Data from www.ustreas.gov/tic/shl2007r.pdf.

student in the 1960s, I realized that there are many sides to truth. The story is about a nobleman and his wife who are attacked by a brigand in an isolated wood. Each version of the story as it unfolds during the trial (including the victim's story as told by a medium) demonstrates that truth is in the eyes of the beholder. I shall try to tell in each chapter the drama from both the perspectives of the crisis economies and the major players, quoting where possible from different personal, official and public sources.

THE SECOND COMING

The third reason is simply the eruption of the current financial crisis. In the summer of 2007, even as I was putting finishing touches to the book, I was reminded eerily of the summer of 1996. Things looked too good to be true. Stock markets and property prices were at record levels. The world was flush with liquidity and risk premiums had declined to record lows. There was just too much hubris in the air. I was reminded of W. B. Yeats' poem 'The Second Coming':

> Things fall apart; the centre cannot hold;
> Mere anarchy is loosed upon the world,
> The blood-dimmed tide is loosed, and everywhere
> The ceremony of innocence is drowned;
> The best lack all convictions, while the worst
> Are full of passionate intensity.

In 1996 the Asian crisis crept up on East Asia, flush with more than a decade of prosperous high growth and low inflation. Almost everyone saw large capital inflows and low-risk premiums as votes of confidence, rather than harbingers of disaster. In July 1997 the Thais floated the baht, and by October Malaysia, Indonesia and Hong Kong were already in crises. In December South Korea, a member of the Organisation for Economic Co-operation and Development (OECD), had to call in the International Monetary Fund (IMF). The miracle economies of East Asia were pummelled with escalating bad news one after another, until in August 1998 Hong Kong intervened in the stock market, Malaysia introduced exchange controls and Russia defaulted on its debt obligations. The failure of long-term capital management (LTCM) and the subsequent lowering of interest rates by the U.S. Federal Reserve (the Fed) in September was the signal that the centre now took the crisis seriously as one of global proportions.

The Asian economies recovered because the centre and main engine of global growth, the U.S. economy, was fundamentally strong in 1998. Ten years later the tables have been turned. Asia, including the Middle East oil producers, as a whole has become a major creditor to the U.S. economy. In contrast, the U.S. economy is running large twin deficits as current account deficits surpassed 5 percent of GDP since 2004, whilst the fiscal deficit had grown in the face of the costs of the Iraq war and growing demands for tax cuts and social services. From 2005 onwards the U.S. dollar began its depreciation of more than 20 percent in real effective exchange rate terms. Initially there was no apparent impact on the rest of the world, but as gold, commodity, food and energy prices began to rise for a variety of reasons, the world moved from the decade of Great Moderation to a period of grave uncertainty.

Like its Asian predecessor, the subprime crisis crept into global awareness almost by stealth. Even though two Bear Stearns hedge funds investing in subprime mortgages had failed in February 2007, there was no awareness of the ferocity and speed of the deterioration. By summer 2007 the subprime crisis that began with the decline in housing prices in the United States had started to unwind. In August the European Central Bank and the Fed injected over US$300 billion into their interbank markets to ease liquidity. The Bank of England, concerned with the risks of moral hazard, was initially more reluctant to follow suit. But by September it had to intervene in the run against Northern Rock, the first bank run in the United Kingdom for 189 years, stopped by a blanket guarantee of all deposits. The Fed responded to the subprime crisis by lowering interest rates.

Just like the second half of 1997, the summer of 2008 erupted like a volcano, with events every month escalating in size and intensity. In March the fifth largest U.S. investment bank, Bear Stearns, was taken over by JP Morgan with US$29 billion worth of Fed support. By July the U.S. Treasury had to mount a rescue for Fannie Mae and Freddie Mac, the government-sponsored mortgage corporations, which together held or guaranteed more than US$5 trillion worth of mortgages. In the first week of July, the price of oil rocketed to a peak of US$147 per barrel, sparking fears of global inflation in the midst of possible financial collapse. By 7 September the Treasury had to put both Fannie Mae and Freddie Mac into conservatorship, de facto nationalizing them. In the following two weeks, the world as we knew it changed.

As pressure mounted on the four remaining U.S. investment banks, Merrill Lynch found refuge after agreeing to be taken over by Bank of America over the weekend of 14 September. The next day Lehman Brothers failed with over US$613 billion in debt. The same day the largest insurance company in the world, AIG, received a US$85 billion loan support from the Fed in exchange for a 79.9 percent equity stake. It had provided US$446 billion of credit default swaps and had become too big to fail. On 17 September the money market funds were facing large institutional withdrawals, forcing the U.S. Treasury to announce a US$50 billion guarantee for them. If these funds failed, more than US$3.4 trillion of funds were at stake.

It was by now clear that piecemeal solutions would not solve the crisis in confidence. On the weekend of 20 September, U.S. Treasury Secretary Paulson announced a US$700 billion rescue package to buy toxic mortgage assets and unclog the system. On 23 September the Fed allowed Goldman Sachs and Morgan Stanley, the last two remaining investment banks, to become bank holding companies.

On Wednesday, 24 September, President Bush admitted that the United States was in the midst of a crisis, as he tried to get Congress and Senate to pass his rescue proposal. To the shock of the markets, the U.S. Congress voted down the rescue package, reflecting huge anger of Main Street towards Wall Street.

By the end of 2008 it was clear that the meltdown in global financial markets had severely shocked the real economy. The United States was officially declared to have been in recession at the end of December 2007, whilst the rest of the world prepared for the worst. Everyone expected that 2009 and beyond could be the toughest economic conditions since the Great Depression.

What went wrong? Were the lessons of the Asian crisis and the subsequent reforms insufficient? Despite huge advances in theory and understanding of institutions and markets, have we missed something?

A FRAMEWORK FOR ANALYSIS

The fourth justification for this book therefore is a framework for thinking about the role of financial regulation in financial stability and crises.

No financial crisis is exactly alike, but there are common elements that would, I hope, help us identify and mitigate the next one. All crises start with excess liquidity, followed by speculative manias, culminating in a bubble and subsequent crash. History is replete with such bubbles and crashes, but the intellectual debate about their causes and their resolutions continue. If the 1994 Mexican crisis was 'the first financial crisis of the 21st century' as famously dubbed by Michel Camdessus, then Managing Director of the IMF,[5] the 1997–1998 Asian crisis was the harbinger of the present crisis.

---

[5]   Camdessus (1995).

The problem of describing the Asian and current crises is that they cannot be seen as static country-by-country analyses, but rather as dynamic, complex interactions between a group of Asian countries, Japan included, and their relationship with the United States, their largest customer and trading partner. The Asian crisis was a structural crisis of the Asian global supply chain, which had not one currency standard, but two, the U.S. dollar and the Japanese yen, emerging into a globalized world of growing imbalances, awash with huge capital flows. The volatility erupted into crisis. No one anticipated how quickly contagion could spread.

Ten years later, after a period of great global prosperity with low inflation, the developed world also slipped into crisis. Again, the usual suspects were questioned – large capital flows, misaligned exchange rates, excess liquidity and leverage, greedy bankers, hedge funds and inadequate supervision. Influential *Financial Times* columnist Martin Wolf coined the phrase 'unfettered finance' in a prescient piece in May 2007 on how capitalism has mutated: 'While the new world of unfettered finance has many friends and foes, all are concerned about the possibility of serious instability'.[6]

But for all its tragedy, the Asian crisis was a crisis at the periphery, when the centre was strong. Today we are witnessing a financial crisis at the centre, and its shocks are spreading worldwide like a tsunami, in both financial and real economy terms.

Consequently the signal difference between the Asian crisis and the current crisis is not just one of size, but in essence, complexity. Because of complexity, we must try to reduce the multidimensional origins and causes into simpler understandable components. Using an institutional and evolutionary perspective,[7] we approach both financial crises at three levels: the lens of history, the macro-view and the micro-issues.

Jerry Corrigan, former President of the New York Fed and arguably one of the most perceptive, brilliant and incisive thinkers and practitioners in global financial markets today, taught me that you need to look at a problem from 30,000 feet up, zoom down to ground level and then slowly rise to 300 or 3,000 feet until you get a much clearer perspective of the issues and the problem.

When you are at 30,000 feet up, you have an overview of the context and the relativity of issues. At 3,000 feet, there is a clearer macro-perspective of the scale of the problem, but the devil is in the details that you might be able

---

[6] Wolf (2007a), 15.
[7] For an overview of Complexity Economics, see Beinhocker (2007).

to examine only at ground level. Hence one must also have a grasp of the complex issues at the micro-institutional level of what led to the crisis.

This book starts from the premise that markets are an essential part of social institutions that have a symbiotic relationship with governments. We will examine the complex institutional interaction between markets and governments to consider how financial crises emerge.

To encompass such complexity, we must be eclectic in approach, but there is an underlying theme woven into the fabric of our approach. Markets are what sociologist Manuel Castells called part of the Network Society.[8] They function to trade and exchange ideas, goods and services. Successful markets all share three key attributes: the protection of property rights, the lowering of transaction costs and the high transparency. Financial markets are interlocking networks that exchange money, equity, bonds and derivatives.

But the more networks evolve, the more complex they become, so that shocks or failure in one hub can easily be transmitted to other parts of the network through contagion. The cascading waves of institutional failure can be seen as network failure, whereby hubs (read: investment banks) have to shut down if only to isolate the damage to the rest of the network. Contagion is like viral transmission of disease. You have to quarantine the infected quickly, so that the rest of the network remains healthy. In that sense crises are only one stage of evolution of markets.

There is, however, another level of history that is more powerful than the history of events – the history of economic thought. Since the fall of the Berlin Wall in 1989, the power of free market fundamentalism has been on the ascendant. Ironically, free market fundamentalists viewed the Asian financial crisis as proof that government fettering financial markets was futile, because Asian governments were impotent before the forces of global markets.

The free market philosophy powerfully encouraged financial innovation, particularly in derivatives that created new profits and reputedly improved risk management. There is no doubt that the flowering of derivative markets in the 21st century was a marvel to wonder at. From 2001 to 2007 global GDP increased by 75.8 percent from US$31 trillion to US$54.5 trillion.[9] Over the same period, global bonds, equities and bank assets grew by 53.1 percent from US$150 trillion to US$229.7 trillion. In contrast, the notional amount of outstanding contracts of global over-the-counter (OTC) derivatives market rose 536.5 percent from US$111.1 trillion to US$596 trillion.

---

[8]   Castells (2000).
[9]   IMF, *Global Financial Stability Report* (2003, 2008).

In other words, the derivative book rose 10.1 times faster than traditional financial assets and 7.1 times faster than real economy activity.

Unfortunately, as the current financial crisis showed, unfettered finance also leads to instability and destruction, not all of it creative. U.S. Treasury Secretary Hank Paulson summed it up best in September 2008 in explaining the bailout: 'raw capitalism is a dead end'.[10]

At the other end of the spectrum, state intervention in markets is seen as necessary to deal with distributional justice and the protection of property rights. This was fundamentally the Asian view of development. The tragedy is that, taken to its authoritarian extreme, overregulation and state intervention has also been disastrous.

The complex reality, as Asian philosophy has argued, is a golden mean, somewhere in the fuzzy wuzzy middle, a dynamic and complex interaction and interdependence between creative disorder in the market and the rigid order of bureaucracy, and between individual freedom and social responsibility. A reality is that whilst national governments may have in the past been successful in managing development within national borders, it does not mean that they can be successful in managing shocks emanating from the borderless world of unfettered finance.

Unfettered globalization has also been accused of creating social inequality and wanton destruction of the environment for short-term gains. As Dani Rodrik and other development economists have noted, we should not get into the facile debate between market fundamentalism's 'just let the market work' and institutional fundamentalism's 'just get governance right'.[11] The view of 'letting the market work' is mostly right, but not always. On the other hand, the institutional view of 'getting governance right' is necessary but not sufficient, because many times crises have been the result of bad policies and weak governance. Nobel Laureate Michael Spence,[12] in the recently published Growth Commission Report, rightly emphasized that no generic formula exists for successful economic development or governance.

Herein lies the flaw of globalization. We have today a global financial system with almost unrestricted capital flows, but macroeconomic policies and regulation are conducted within national borders. We often ignore the externalities of our national policies on the rest of world. National crisis is about the failure of domestic markets, policies or institutions, but global

---

[10] Quoted in Gunther and Easton (2008), 53.
[11] Rodrik (2008).
[12] Spence (2008).

crisis is about the breakdown transmitted through the interdependence of economies in a networked world. National policymakers and regulators have grossly underestimated not only the size and nature of global flows and our interdependency, but also our ability to coordinate and execute appropriate responses.

In other words, we have been blind to emerging crises because we have too many mental, legal and bureaucratic silos operating in social disciplines and policymaking and execution, each with their blind spots. If it is bad at the national level, it is disastrous at the global level.

A POTTED HISTORY OF ASIAN AND GLOBAL FINANCIAL CRISES

London Business School Professor John Kay insightfully observed that markets are social institutions that are self-organized and path dependent. No one designed the market economy, but one of the principal participants is the government, as owner, regulator and protector (in some cases predator) of property rights.[13] This path dependency is why we need to look at history, if only to remind us of our own follies.

History is a river of the timelines of life. There is a cycle of boom and bust, order and disorder, memory and dementia. No crisis is identical to the previous one, but there are general principles that apply, which we forget at our peril.

Crisis is an event, but as Nobel Laureate Douglass North has noted, development is a process.[14] All human activity is an unending process of man's control over his environment and vice versa. Therefore, the ultimate test of economic success is not natural resource endowment or geography, but the quality of governance.

Seen from the longer perspective of macro-history,[15] the Asian crisis was a defining moment in the resurgence of Asia after nearly two centuries of decline. At its height in 1820, Asia accounted for 57 percent of global GDP in purchasing power terms, but its outmoded feudal system could not compete with the march of Western markets and technology. By 1950 Asia's share of global GDP had fallen to 18 percent. Applying this path-dependent analysis of economic change, the Asian story from Miracle to Crisis can be encapsulated into how Japan led the way in mental and institutional

---

[13] Kay (2004).
[14] North (2005b).
[15] Huang (1998) first used this term.

transformation from an agricultural and feudal society into an industrial powerhouse. In the postwar era Japan led Asia out of decay into a period of strong growth. By 1998 Asia's share of world GDP had risen back to 37 percent, and by 2030 it is expected to rise to 53 percent, with Western Europe, the United States and other Western offshoots falling back to 33 percent.[16]

But Asia cannot rise to its rightful share in world governance without passing the test of markets and crises. This perspective cannot be divorced also from the history of global money. Monetary historians also understand all too well how wrong adherence to the gold standard created the deflation that led to the Great Depression in the 1930s. Historically we are now in an era in which we are moving from a single dominant reserve currency (U.S. dollar) into a bi-currency or multicurrency model, in the same way that in the 19th century the bimetallic (gold-silver) arrangement changed to a gold standard. We all know that such tectonic shifts come together with traumatic financial crises. Currency arrangements shift in the same direction as global financial power.

Japanese economic historians have depicted the Asian growth process as a theory of Flying Geese, in which the lead goose, Japan, successfully industrialized, then shed, its labour-intensive industries to the Four Dragons (South Korea, Taiwan, Hong Kong and Singapore), the Four Tigers (Indonesia, Malaysia, Philippines and Thailand) and then China. Together, they formed the global supply chain, geared towards supplying the markets of the West, using essentially the U.S. dollar as the benchmark currency.

But there was a fundamental flaw in the Japanese model. It remained essentially a two-track growth path, with a protected weak financial and service sector, and a strong manufacturing and export sector. It was as if the body was fit and lean, but the heart, the banking system, was not designed at the same level of efficiency.

That dualism was soon put to severe test. The rise of Japan as the second largest economy in the world in the late 1980s created a situation in which the yen posed a possible challenge to the U.S. dollar. The U.S.–Japan trade dispute led to the Plaza Accord of 1985 that resulted in a massive upward revaluation in the yen, an associated Japanese balance sheet bubble and then years of decline.

The Japanese fought the post-bubble deflation by exporting more capital and shifting their production to East Asia, in an effort to create a yen zone in East Asia. The zero interest rate policy gave rise to the yen carry

---

[16] Maddison (2007).

trade. In hindsight, that huge inflow of liquidity into East Asia replicated the Japanese bubble on a smaller scale.

The Asian policymakers did not fully realize the implications of this capital inflow. They thought they could have their cake and eat it too – enjoy capital flows and unending prosperity, even whilst maintaining their soft pegs to the U.S. dollar. The Asian banking system was a dollar-based system without a dollar lender of last resort, because the Fed and the IMF could not or would not act in that role.

Thus, when the Mexico crisis erupted in 1994 and Latin American currencies devalued, it was the East Asians' turn to feel the pressures of overvalued exchange rates, current account deficits, fragile financial systems, weak corporate balance sheets and capital outflows that ultimately led to the Asian crisis.

The matter was worsened when the Japanese economy went further into deflation in 1996 and its financial system also had its first failures. The volatility of the yen-dollar relationship, pulling back bank loans to Asia and the reversal of the carry trade all formed part of the complex interactive relationship between Japan and the Asian crisis economies.

Most Westerners were unable to understand the depth of the pain and shame of proud Asians ceding their hard-earned sovereignty to the IMF during 1997–1998. When Fed Chairman Alan Greenspan said in 1999 'East Asia had no spare tires',[17] he was basically saying that despite years of strong growth, Asia had a weak banking system, without sufficient foreign exchange reserves and a strong capital market to absorb shocks.

The relationship between the Asian crisis and the current crisis can now be made clear. Since Asian markets were inadequate to intermediate their excess savings, they built up their savings and foreign exchange reserves and placed that spare tire largely with the U.S. markets. They were willing to do so because the United States was the world's engine of growth. The Dooley–Garber–Folkerts-Landau school argued that this arrangement was mutually beneficial, a 'total equity return swap' between Asia and the United States that swapped fundamentally cheap credit in return for labour employment.[18]

As Gourinchas and Rey have argued, the United States has moved from being the world's commercial banker to an investment banker.[19] It borrowed cheap funds from Asian surplus countries and reinvested them back in Asia

---

[17] Greenspan (1999b).
[18] Dooley, Garber and Folkerts-Landau (2004).
[19] Gourinchas and Rey (2005).

and elsewhere to earn higher returns, but on a leveraged basis. From a net creditor position of 10 percent of GDP in 1952, the United States moved to a net debtor position of 22 percent of GDP by 2004. The United States could afford to do so because it had an 'exorbitant privilege' as the reserve currency country and 'banker of the world'. In addition, unlike East Asia, which could not print money to repay foreign debt, most of the U.S. debt was denominated in dollars, so dollar depreciation could transfer the burden of adjustment to holders of such debt.

But it was not sustainable.[20] As the national savings rate declined because of higher levels of consumption, the United States became more and more leveraged. By 2007 the nonfinancial sector debt rose to 226 percent of GDP, compared with 183 percent a decade ago. The financial sector debt nearly doubled from 64 percent of GDP to 114 percent of GDP during the same period. The decline in savings was manifested in the large current account deficit, which rose to US$857 billion (6.5 percent of GDP) in 2006.

The pendulum has swung, but adjustment has now to be done at the centre. But since Asia is a large creditor, it cannot escape a large part of the burden sharing of the U.S. adjustment.

MACRO-STORY – GREAT MODERATION CREATED GREAT COMPLACENCY

Descending from 30,000 feet to, say, 3,000 feet, we are now able to put the macro picture into perspective.

The free market ideology reached its apogee in 1989, the year Japan had its mega-bubble and the Berlin Wall fell, releasing three billion new workers and consumers into global markets.[21] The supply-side shock of new labour coming from China, India and formerly state-planned economies created the period of high growth and low inflation called the Great Moderation. Many central bankers attributed this to their improvement in their monetary policy tools and success of the financial liberalization model. But as former U.S. Treasury Secretary Robert Rubin said, 'what almost nobody saw was the confluence of factors that turned out to be something of a perfect storm – low interest rates, reaching for yield, the increased use of financial engineering, and triple-A ratings for certain subprime securities'.[22] Leaders like Rubin should have seen that the low interest rate–induced

[20] Xafa (2007).

[21] Prestowitz (2005).

[22] Quoted in Kassenaar (2008).

excess leverage was almost a repeat of what happened in Japan in the late 1980s – a bubble in the property market.

From 2001, when the Fed Funds rate was reduced to an all-time low of 1 percent per annum, to the end of 2007, the real estate value of U.S. households and the corporate sector increased by US$14.5 trillion to US$31.3 trillion, equivalent to 226.4 percent of GDP, compared with 163.5 percent of GDP at the end of 2001.[23] The growth in real estate value was 86.4 percent over this period. But during the same period, the U.S. household sector debt increased by US$6.1 trillion, indicating that consumption was increasing sharply due to the wealth effect.

After the Fed started tightening monetary policy in 2005–2006, real estate prices began to fall, with subprime mortgages already showing signs of defaults in 2007. The defaults began to affect severely the liquidity in the asset-backed securities (ABS) market, which was a major source of liquidity for the banking system. What was totally unexpected was that instead of risks being spread through securitization to long-term risk holders, such as insurance companies and pension funds, these investors sold them back to the market to avoid credit risks, causing sharp decline in prices that seized up the interbank market, the lifeblood of modern wholesale banking. This illiquidity forced the banks to write down their assets, causing calls on capital that shook confidence in the financial markets.

In the period 2007 to mid-2008, the banks wrote off over US$500 billion in asset losses, which kept on escalating. In April 2008 the IMF estimated the global bank losses at US$945 billion, but by September this was increased to US$1.4 trillion. One month later the Bank of England had doubled the estimate to US$2.8 trillion. Nouriel Roubini, on the other hand, claimed that the losses for the U.S. banking system alone would be US$3.6 trillion, which would wipe out the total capital of the U.S. banking system of US$1.5 trillion. It was clear that the damage was no longer one of financial losses, but credit losses due to the credit crunch spreading to the real economy.

How did the U.S. banking system get into such a fragile situation? We need to understand that it was the blend of high global liquidity, lax monetary policy, permissive financial regulation and financial engineering that created a derivative crisis of a higher order. Just as the Asian crisis had its origins in excess leverage and regulatory arbitrage, the present crisis had its origins in the creation of an underregulated 'shadow banking system', a term coined by PIMCO CEO Bill Gross.[24]

---

[23] Federal Reserve Bank of Kansas City (2008).
[24] Gross (2008).

This shadow banking system comprised the dynamic trading entities such as hedge funds, investment banks and securities houses that thrived in the world of unregulated financial engineering. These entities were allowed by accounting and regulatory standards to move liabilities off balance sheets through special investment vehicles (SIVs), so the true market leverage was not apparent to investors or regulators. As one money-manager graphically explained, 'allowing investment banks to be leveraged to the tune of 30:1 is like Russian roulette with five out of six chambers loaded'.[25]

The scary part of the shadow banking system was that it was sustained by a series of assumptions built on shifting sands. AAA ratings by the rating agencies to the new collateralized debt obligations (CDOs), plus mortgages insured by undercapitalized monoline insurers, plus credit risks underwritten by credit default swaps (CDSs) all gave investors the illusion of investment-grade paper that turned out to be toxic. The panic that we witnessed when everyone crowded for the exit resulted in the global meltdown in the second half of 2008.

THE MICRO-INSTITUTIONAL MESS

Now that we have looked at the history and the big picture of what led us to where we are, how do we sort out the complex and conflicting details?

Those who look for sensationalism would love for crises to be a tale of conspiracies. During the unfolding of the crisis, I often asked myself whether I could have personally done more to stop the tide of events in the Asian crisis. But the more I studied markets, the more I realized that market events are of a spontaneous order. There is no single architect – there may be many conspiracies or plots trying to influence the tide one way or the other, but it is the interaction amongst all parties – some deliberative, some calculated, others random – that cause events to unfold like a tsunami. Not even the most brilliant minds in the world, nor the largest economy in the world, could stop the force of the crises, which became not just economic, but political, in nature.

After working for more than 12 years in Hong Kong, the most free market economy in the world, I decided to immerse myself in the theory and practice of regulatory work in China, working as Chief Adviser to the China Banking Regulatory Commission. Here I began to appreciate the complexities of institutional change in a continental economy that was both old and dynamic. In order to communicate better with my students at the Tsinghua

[25] Quoted in Plender (2008), 12.

University, I went back to ancient Chinese classics on governance in a comparative study with modern regulation theory.

As early as 2,200 years ago, the Chinese Legalist philosopher Han Feizi had already outlined the modern analysis of governance. Governance or the Ruler's Way comprises only two levers – reward and punishment, namely, the *incentive structure*. The key problem of all governance is that the interests of the ruler and the officials are not aligned, an early identification of the *principal-agent problem*. The biggest problem is one of *transparency*, or what the classics understood as form and substance. In order to determine the right amount of reward and punishment, the ruler needs clear *standards* to measure performance, and to differentiate between form and substance.

The clarity of Han Feizi's thinking was amazing. Governance stems from three factors: law, the enforcement process and ultimately individual will. Laws and processes are all theory until put into practice. What ultimately determines whether policies are implemented or pushed through is the individual will. In all matters of governance, the best policies are useless if the leader is unwilling to push unpleasant reforms through huge obstacles, including the entrenched bureaucracy. For example, it took Japan more than seven years to achieve social consensus to act on the bank losses. The United States acted much more pragmatically and quickly because of will and pragmatism. All said and done, in the face of bubble or panic, ultimately it is the personal courage and will of leaders to act decisively for what they believe is right, despite enormous opposition, that shapes the course of destiny.

These ancient insights, combined with the new institutional approach of Nobel Laureates Douglass North, Joseph Stiglitz and others, led me to break down the complex issues into a framework of thinking, comprising the policy and institutional elements of markets.

To sum up, if development and change is a process, comprising many processes of policy and institutional evolution, we need a process to manage these complex processes. We need a Windows operating system to manage different software programmes. Because each economy or society is different and so complex, we cannot find a one-size-fits-all solution. There is nevertheless a common search and browse process to arrive at common principles, common goals and desired outcomes.

All institutions or human organization share eight common elements that are in constant change and evolution. These comprise *values, information, incentives, standards, structure, process, rules and property rights*. We can depict this as a Tree of Life drawing, with values as the roots (Figure A). Human beings join organizations with common values to protect their property rights, reduce risks and transaction costs. Trading in information

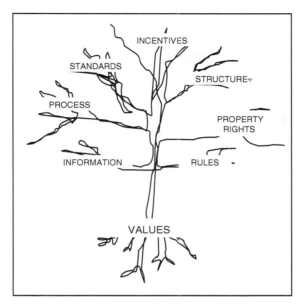

Figure A. Institutional Tree of Life

and property rights is the lifeblood of the institution. Transparency has been an important element of human institutions, because it is the access to information and knowledge that determines whether the system is fair, efficient and progressive. Without transparency, property rights can be stolen or misused, leading to injustice, ignorance and, ultimately, social stagnation, inequality and fragility. As the tree grows, it must have structure, processes and rules, using standards, knowledge and incentives. But we must understand that each institutional tree grows within its own context, and it competes with other trees for air, water and nutrients.

This Darwinian view of the crisis and survival of institutions suggests that when things go wrong, as happens in financial crises, it is defects in these elements, between the people, the institutions or the complex interaction between institutions and markets, that create disorder. Markets and institutions must be viewed in their entire (network) context. Fed Chairman Ben Bernanke admitted to this blind spot when he called for a system-wide approach to supervisory oversight at the August 2008 Jackson Hole Conference.[26]

---

[26] Bernanke (2008).

How is all this linked to the Asian and ongoing global credit crisis?

The Asian crisis is fascinating because it was a test of Asian governance as the region emerged into the borderless world of large capital flows, complex derivatives and changing world order. The crisis revealed the total nakedness of policymakers and financial regulators, trapped in mindset of increasingly irrelevant national boundaries. But the crisis caused Asia to move from being net borrowers to net savers, whilst Japan was the first to experiment with a zero interest rate policy. The extra liquidity at near zero funding costs was a massive catalyst to the explosion of financial engineering and leverage, which could happen only with lax monetary policy and financial oversight.

Seen in that context, the current crisis that started with subprime woes is also a test of global governance, in which national central banks and regulators struggle with global flows and shocks that are outside their ken. My perception is that the Fed arguably did not perceive that it was not just the central bank for the dollar, the currency of the most powerful nation on earth, but that it also had the moral responsibility of setting the tone for the rest of the world.

If the United States is to enjoy sustainable financing of the current account deficit by the foreign community, it has to ensure that the banking and financial system in the United States is sound. But having allowed the U.S. financial system to become highly leveraged through complex financial innovation, further allowing excessive low interest rates created the U.S. property bubble that fed also excessive consumption. By not tackling the property bubble promptly, almost exactly the same mistake that the Japanese and the rest of Asia made in the 1990s, the stage was set for the most serious financial crisis since the Great Depression. It is illuminating to note that Hong Kong suffered a similar bubble from 1994 to 1997, but the banking system survived the financial crisis because the banks and the Hong Kong Monetary Authority together lowered the loan-to-value ratio to cushion the banks from the property bubble, despite huge protests from the property developers. It is amazing that the United States did not use the same tool to restrict speculative financing of real estate or cushion banks from the potential damage.

STRUCTURE OF THE BOOK

This book is structured in three parts. Chapter 1 provides a quick timeline for the Asian crisis. Chapter 2 looks at the role of Japan in the East Asian crisis, because as the largest economy in Asia and key hub for the global supply chain, Japan had a role that could not and should not be ignored. Japan's was the first economy to go to balance sheet deflation, the first to experiment with zero interest rates. This gave rise to the yen carry trade, which had massive implications for financial engineering, leverage and capital flows.

Chapter 3 examines the evolution of the East Asian mindset that was unable to comprehend that the global ballgame had changed. Chapter 4 examines the weakest link in the network of East Asian economies, the banking system. Chapter 5 considers the role of the Washington Consensus and the IMF in the resolution of the crisis.

Chapters 6 through 11 examine more closely the individual country cases, starting with Thailand and ending with China, the emerging giant. The chapters examine in more detail why each crisis economy had nuanced differences in context that led to its crisis and therefore responded differently. Chapter 12 looks at the losses from the crises and efforts at regional integration.

Chapters 13 through 16 examine the emergence of the current crisis. Chapter 13 explores the new world of financial engineering and how the modern banking system evolved into its present state. Chapter 14 critiques how financial regulation allowed the crisis to happen. Chapter 15 compares and contrasts the Asian crisis with the current crisis. Chapter 16 concludes with thoughts on key lessons for Asia, particularly its governance structure. A chronology of events is given at the end to help the reader identify key dates and events.

In the conclusion of his book *The Great Crash 1929,* John Kenneth Galbraith said something that resonates seven decades later:[27]

There seems little question that in 1929, modifying a famous cliché, the economy was fundamentally unsound. This is a circumstance of first-rate importance. Many things were wrong, but five weaknesses seem to have had an especially intimate bearing on the ensuing disaster. They are:

1. The bad distribution of income.
2. The bad corporate structure ... a kind of flood tide of corporate larceny.
3. The bad banking structure.
4. The dubious state of the foreign balance.

---

[27] Galbraith (1954), 194–202, 210.

5. The poor state of economic intelligence. … The economic advisers of the day had both the unanimity and the authority to force the leaders of both parties to disavow all the available steps to check deflation and depression. In its own way this was a marked achievement – a triumph of dogma over thought. The consequences were profound.

Has all that much changed? Did all of us refuse to see what was going wrong because of greed, pride, vested interest or regulatory capture?

During the debate on the US$700 billion bailout plan, the Democratic Speaker of the House of Representatives, Nancy Pelosi said, 'We've sent a message to Wall Street that the party is over'.

In this regard, I am of the old school of central bankers who believe that central bankers are appointed precisely because our job is to lean against the wind or, as former Fed Chairman William McChesney Martin used to say, to take away the punch bowl just when the party gets interesting.

The Chinese have a saying, 'Fortune is made by one generation, conserved by the next and spent by the third'. The old Kondratieff cycle was roughly 60 years, but it has been 79 years since the Great Crash. It is perhaps no coincidence that this baby boomer generation, to which I belong, has an average life expectancy of around that age. We had our party, and we now need to pay for it. To find who is to blame, we only have to look in the mirror.

Beijing, Penang and **Ubud**
December 2008

ONE

Things Fall Apart

The only cause of depression is prosperity.
~ Clement Juglar

Towards midnight on 30 June 1997, even the heavens cried for Hong Kong. The searing rain drenched me as I arrived at the brand-new new wing of the Hong Kong Convention and Exhibition Centre (HKCEC), where we watched an impeccably dressed white-uniformed People's Liberation Army soldier unfurling the red Chinese flag. Outside, HM Yacht *Britannia,* with Prince Charles and the last Governor Chris Patten on board, sailed out of Victoria Harbour against gusty winds and choppy waves.

The next day was one of celebration amidst an eerie calm as Hong Kong's citizens began to adjust to the return to Chinese sovereignty after 156 years of British colonial rule. Three days earlier, on 27 June, the Hong Kong Hang Seng stock market index (HSI) rose to a peak of 15,196. The rally was led by the euphoria surrounding shares of companies with Mainland China interests, known as Red Chips and H-shares. Property prices too were at a record high. Even the most optimistic of forecasters did not envision the buoyant sentiments the return of Hong Kong to China would evoke. As China promised, 'There will be a better tomorrow'.

Things, however, began to fall apart.

WEDNESDAY, 2 JULY 1997

At around 4.30 A.M. on Wednesday, 2 July 1997, the Bank of Thailand (BoT) began calling top local and foreign bankers for an important announcement. The Thai baht, which was pegged at around B 25 to the U.S. dollar for more than a decade, would be allowed to float. By the end of that day, the baht lost about 14 percent of its value in onshore trading and 19 percent in offshore trading, causing the central bank to call on the IMF for technical assistance.

It took awhile for the significance of the unpegging of the Thai baht to sink in. My first thought was – here comes the pressure on the other Asian currencies. I anticipated that the Hong Kong dollar would be a prime target as it was pegged at HK$7.80 to the U.S. dollar. As Deputy Chief Executive of the HKMA, the de facto central bank of Hong Kong, I was in charge of reserves management and external affairs. At that time my hands were already full with the preparations for the 52nd joint annual meetings of the IMF and the World Bank that were to be held in Hong Kong between 17 and 25 September 1997, when the world financial crème de la crème would converge to celebrate Hong Kong's peaceful and successful return to China. It was an occasion that could not go wrong. The quip by former U.S. Secretary of State Henry Kissinger that 'a crisis can't happen – my schedule is already full' came to mind, but we were already in the midst of a tsunami that was about to sweep first Asia and then the world.

Only six weeks earlier, on 24 May 1997, I had attended a key meeting in Bangkok to discuss the Thai baht crisis that had been ongoing before July 1997. The Bank of Thailand had invited key officials of the EMEAP[1] central banks and monetary authorities to exchange ideas on market speculation and techniques in the defence of local currencies. My good friends at the BoT, led by its Deputy Governor Chaiyawat Wibulswasdi, briefed us. Chaiyawat is a quiet and effective MIT-trained economist also well known for his books on Winnie the Pooh in the Thai language. The meeting was deadly serious – very much akin to a war-room briefing.

In early May a Goldman Sachs research note had predicted a devaluation of the baht to help export competitiveness. On 8 May there was a widespread rumour circulating in London that the exchange rate band for the baht would be widened on 13 May. Indeed, between 13 and 15 May, there was a large speculative attack against the Thai baht with huge selling orders on the currency in the London and New York markets. The BoT called for intervention assistance from the regional central banks. It also engineered a liquidity squeeze on the offshore market by prohibiting local banks from supplying baht to foreign companies. Overnight interest rates on baht lending to foreigners shot up to 1,000–1,500 percent, and the hedge

[1] EMEAP stands for Executives' Meeting of East Asia–Pacific Central Banks. As of July 1997, the members of EMEAP are central banks and monetary authorities from Australia, China, Hong Kong, Indonesia, Japan, Malaysia, New Zealand, the Philippines, Singapore, South Korea and Thailand.

funds had reportedly suffered losses of up to US$300 million as a result. The *Wall Street Journal* on 22 May[2] identified the key players as hedge funds run by George Soros' key lieutenant Stan Druckenmiller, Julian Robertson, Bruce Kovner and Lee Cooperman, as well as trading operations at dealers such as BZW, JP Morgan, Citibank and Goldman Sachs. It was rumoured that the hedge funds were targeting devaluations of around 20–25 percent, and they were not deterred by the 3 percent costs in defending their short positions.

The speculators on the Thai baht funded themselves by borrowing yen, which had an interest cost of around 3 percent per annum in the early to mid-1990s, whereas they could invest in baht deposits earning overnight bank rates of around 17 percent per annum engaging in what the business called the 'carry trade'. However, the yen had strengthened by 12 percent against the U.S. dollar since 1 May 1997, increasing speculators' cost of financing the carry trade. A 22 May *Wall Street Journal* article proclaimed 'Traders Burnt in Thailand's Battle of Baht', but it was already the third major speculative attack on the baht since the Mexican crisis spillover in January 1995, the last two attempts being in July 1996 and January/February 1997.

The tense 24 May meeting reflected the central bankers' nervousness about the markets. Those of us who monitor the markets very carefully, such as Hong Kong and Singapore, understood that the carry trade was playing a major role in market volatility. In particular, volatility in the U.S. dollar–yen rate had significant implications in Asian markets. Thailand was most vulnerable to the yen carry trade because about 55 percent of its external debt was in yen. Since mid-1996 our Japanese central bank and Ministry of Finance friends had already hinted loudly that Asian central banks should abandon the fixed exchange rate against the U.S. dollar and adopt a basket of currencies, implying that the weight of the yen should be increased. Since the U.S. dollar was the anchor of most of the Asian currencies, few people, including myself, fully understood what they were hinting.

Why were we all caught off-guard? The collapses of the European Monetary System in 1992 and the Mexican peso in 1994–1995 were recent reminders of the dangers of contradictions between domestic fundamentals and overvalued exchange rates.[3] Since my return to central banking in Hong Kong in 1993, I had worked hard to understand fully the dangers of speculative attacks against pegged exchange regimes,

---

[2] Sesit and Jereski (1997).
[3] Krugman (2000).

particularly with the rising use of derivative instruments. We were aware how hedge funds, led by such colourful fund managers as George Soros, had even humbled the Bank of England in 1992. We had several regional conferences with our Mexican central bankers to understand how speculation against the peso was engineered. The general conclusion was that economic fundamentals were crucial to the defence of the currency and that previous failures to defend the currency pegs were due to weaknesses in the underlying fundamentals. We thought Asian fundamentals were strong, but we grossly underestimated the power of markets and the underlying fragilities.

TIGERS WOUNDED

Tsunamis and earthquakes tend to occur at the weakest fault line, with the shock effects spreading in widening circles of declining magnitude. On 14 May 1997 Goldman Sachs issued a research report: *Malaysia and Philippines: Thailand in the Making?* Speculative attention then turned to the Philippine peso and the Malaysian ringgit.

On the same day the Thai baht floated, the Philippine peso was also savagely attacked, forcing the central bank, Bangko Sentral ng Pilipinas (BSP), to spend US$543 million to defend the currency that day. According to BSP Governor Gabby Singson in an interview with *Asiaweek* journalists in mid-July 1997, the central bank ultimately spent US$1.58 billion – nearly one-eighth – of its international reserves in just the first 10 days of July.[4] On 11 July the BSP bowed to the inevitable and allowed the peso to float. In a matter of hours the peso nose-dived by more than 10 percent against the U.S. dollar to Php29.45 to the dollar. The Philippines requested help from the IMF, which on 18 July promised about US$1 billion in financial support. That same day, to preempt attacks on the Indonesian rupiah, Bank Indonesia, the Indonesian central bank, voluntarily widened its official intervention band from 8 to 12 percentage points.

The Malaysian ringgit came under attack on 8 July. About a week later, on 14 July, the Malaysian central bank, Bank Negara Malaysia (BNM), opted to allow the ringgit to depreciate against the U.S. dollar but did not request for help from the IMF.

Central bankers tend to be quite reticent about their comments to the public, understanding market sensitivities. However on 24 July, then Prime

---

[4]   Saludo and Lopez (1997).

Minister of Malaysia, Dr Mahathir Mohamad, was angry enough to claim at the 30th ASEAN[5] Ministerial Meeting held in Malaysia:

Presently we see a well-planned effort to undermine the economies of all the ASEAN countries by destabilising their currencies. Our economic fundamentals are good yet anyone with a few billion dollars can destroy all the progress that we have made. We are told we must open up, that trade and commerce must be totally free. Free for whom? For rogue speculators. For anarchists wanting to destroy weak countries in their crusade for open societies, to force us to submit to the dictatorship of international manipulators. We want to embrace borderlessness but we still need to protect ourselves from self-serving rogues and international brigandage.[6]

It was a first salvo against the speculative hordes, but its immediate effect was further pressure against all ASEAN currencies.

REGION'S CENTRAL BANKERS MEET

Markets behave very much according to the law of the jungle. They are merciless against the weak, culling those who are unprepared for their ferocious animal spirits. The speculators pick on the weakest and most vulnerable in the pack, and in spite of the threatening noises of the leader of the herd, eventually the weakest will fall to the predators. This ensures the survival of the fittest. Calling in the big white game warden like the IMF to fend off the wolves would not necessarily defend the herd.

On 25 July 1997 the shepherds of Asian currencies, the central bank governors, gathered in Shanghai for the Second EMEAP Governors' Meeting, chaired by Governor Dai Xianglong of the People's Bank of China (PBoC). The governors understood the significance of the meeting, with the world watching their response to market turbulence. Would they stand together against the market's animal spirits, or would they call in the game warden?

Central bankers generally understand the importance of economic fundamentals to currency markets. After over 30 years of strong growth, Asian fundamentals were basically good, with high growth and savings, but there were signs that asset prices were getting overheated. Some of the countries, such as Thailand, were running current account deficits of nearly 8 percent of GDP by 1995, but with a fiscal surplus of around 2 percent of GDP in

---

[5]   ASEAN stands for the Association of Southeast Asian Nations. As of July 1997, the members of ASEAN were Brunei, Indonesia, Lao PDR, Malaysia, Myanmar, Philippines, Singapore, Thailand and Vietnam.

[6]   Mohamad (1997a).

1995–1996 and external debt then estimated at nearly 50 percent of GDP,[7] these numbers were not wildly inconsistent with the European Maastricht standard debt limits of 60 percent of GDP. What most analysts did not fully appreciate was the fragility of the Thai financial system, of which an SBC Warburg report in March 1997 had presciently warned, 'The Economy is Tanking; the Financial System is a Ticking Bomb'.

The tools available to central banks in turbulent foreign exchange markets were limited. Even though collectively Asian foreign exchange reserves were not small (approximately US$700 billion in June 1997), no formal mechanism was available to pool these reserves. ASEAN did have a currency swap arrangement amongst the five original members pursuant to the ASEAN Swap Arrangements (ASAs) of 5 August 1977,[8] but at US$200 million then, it was too small to be convincing. If Soros could single-handedly humble the august Bank of England with speculative profits of reputedly over US$1.1 billion, what chance did the smaller Asian central banks have?

I had estimated from market sources that the BoT had expended US$8–11 billion in defending the baht. Afterwards an investigation of the baht crisis[9] revealed that between 1 and 14 May 1997 the BoT actually suffered a net decline in reserves of US$21.7 billion.

The other tool, raising interest rates to defend the exchange rate, was counterproductive given the vulnerabilities in Asian financial systems. Even fiscal tools were not very helpful. If markets could be rattled with a relatively small fiscal deficit of around 0.3 percent of GDP, as was the case in Thailand in 1996–1997, how much more fiscal surplus would be necessary to convince the market of sound fundamentals? It was clear that markets were nervous and were willing to sell at the slightest sign of bad news.

So what were the alternatives available to the EMEAP central banks in July 1997? Even if we could agree on an institutional arrangement to pool reserves, which institution would be able to undertake the necessary surveillance and disbursements? The Shanghai meeting therefore was significant in that all central bank governors knew that they had to show solidarity in the face of adversity. I worked almost all night behind the scenes to try and stitch together some kind of agreement, as many governors privately met with Bank of Thailand Governor Rerngchai to try and understand what happened. By midnight almost all central banks and monetary authorities agreed to commit some funds to be placed with the IMF under

---

[7] In hindsight, however, Thailand's external debt was higher at around 60 percent of GDP in 1995–1996.

[8] Original members of ASEAN are Indonesia, Malaysia, Philippines, Singapore and Thailand.

[9] The report is entitled 'The Nukul Commission Report: Analysis and Evaluation on Facts Behind Thailand's Economic Crisis'.

its New Arrangements to Borrow (NAB). We wanted to call it the Asian Arrangements to Borrow. It was also agreed that a study group at the deputy governor level would be convened quickly to study the operational and implementation details.

This was an important agreement in the true spirit of central bank solidarity, but with typical central bank modesty and understatement, the communiqué issued was extremely bland, only hinting at what the EMEAP governors wanted to do. The communiqué stated, '[T]hey welcomed the initiatives to strengthen the financial position of the Fund through the New Arrangements to Borrow (NAB) and urged that the NAB become operational as soon as possible'.

With such bland understatement, it was not surprising that the markets concluded that the central bank meeting did not come up with any constructive measures, and market volatility continued.

On the same day the EMEAP governors met, Thailand and Malaysia sought Japan's help in the creation of a regional rescue fund. But as the pressure from the markets mounted, on 28 July 1997, Thailand called in the IMF. In less than two weeks, as part of the IMF's suggested policies for a rescue package, Thailand unveiled an austerity plan and complete revamp of the finance sector. Thus, on 6 August 1997 the BoT suspended an additional 42 Thai finance companies, bringing the total number under suspension to 58.

FIRST ATTEMPT AT EXPLAINING THE ASIAN CRISIS

Back in Hong Kong, I was working frantically to prepare for the oncoming tsunami, making sure that ample research was being done on what was happening in Asian markets. I was also up to my ears in the preparation for the September IMF/World Bank Annual Meetings.

As it happened, I had promised my mother, who lived in the town of Sandakan in Sabah on the East Coast of the Island of Borneo, to deliver a speech to a local Chinese school. I was therefore away when the IMF and the Japanese Ministry of Finance (MoF) decided to call a meeting in Tokyo on 11 August 1997 to discuss the Thai situation. HKMA Chief Executive Joseph Yam headed the Hong Kong delegation instead.

At the school speech on 10 August I made my first attempt to try and analyse the unfolding of Asian currency turmoil.[10] My views, in a nutshell, were as follows:

The irony of the turmoil was the fact that the global economy was enjoying good growth. The U.S. economy was in its sixth year of straight growth; the

[10]   Sheng (1997a).

Japanese economy was recovering by 3.5 percent in 1996; world trade volumes were still projected to increase by 7.3 percent in 1997; and the Chinese economy was growing at a remarkable 9.5–10.0 percent per annum.

The obvious suspect for the currency turmoil was the large capital flows into Asia. At the beginning of the 1990s, net private capital flows to emerging markets were US$46 billion. This figure increased four times in six years to US$239 billion in 1996. Within the total, over 40 percent came to Asia, about half of which were in the form of foreign direct investment (FDI). Another one-fifth was in the form of portfolio investment.

Contrary to a widely shared view, Asians did not spend all the foreign capital inflows. In fact, 70 percent of the inflows went towards reserve accumulation. The Guidotti-Greenspan rule holds that countries should hold liquid reserves equal to their foreign liabilities coming due within a year. At the brink of the 1997–1998 Asian crisis, Asian central banks held about 40 percent of the world's foreign exchange reserves. Indeed, by the end of 1996, five of the top six foreign exchange holders in the world were Asians, whereby Japan, China, Hong Kong, Taiwan and Singapore together held about US$600 billion of reserves.

But the reasons for the vulnerability were also clear. The combined current account deficits of South Korea plus the ASEAN-4 economies affected by the crisis[11] rose to a cumulative US$128.1 billion between 1993 and 1996, of which US$111.5 billion or 87 percent of the cumulative deficit was financed by external bank borrowing, largely in the form of short-term credits. Unfortunately, several central banks within the region did not fully meet the Guidotti-Greenspan rule, partly because, as in the case of South Korea, they were not aware that their corporations had built up short-term debt in offshore markets.

Looking back, I had missed the true degree of banking fragility at that time. Although we knew there were Thai banks in trouble, we had not focused on banking problems in Indonesia, South Korea and Japan. Little did I foresee then that by the end of the year, the whole of East Asia would be swept into crisis.

One question that was being debated in 1997 was whether the turmoil reflected a de-linking of Asian currencies with the U.S. dollar, hinting towards the formation of a yen-bloc.[12] There were four interrelated issues. First, the reversal of the carry trade had the impact of rapid capital withdrawal from Asian currencies whenever interest or exchange rates in the

[11] Indonesia, Malaysia, Philippines and Thailand.
[12] See, e.g., Kwan (1997).

United States or Japan threatens to rise. Second, high global liquidity led to the sharp compression of credit spreads. Third, Asian issuers also took advantage of these favourable conditions to borrow in foreign currency, exposing themselves to foreign exchange and maturity mismatches and the risk of capital flow reversals. Fourth, after the Mexican crisis of 1994, the sharp devaluation of the Latin American currencies led to a shift in the balance of trade in their favour, and Asian countries began to run current account deficits.

I was of the view that the deterioration in Asian trade balances also reflected partly the lagged impact of the sharp depreciation of the yen vis-à-vis the U.S. dollar since mid-1995, when the yen reached ¥80 to the dollar. From April 1995 to July 1997, the yen depreciated more than 30 percent against the U.S. dollar, moving from around ¥80 to the dollar to around ¥118 to the dollar during this period. In the first month after de-pegging, Asian currency movements were relatively minor, ranging from around 3 percent depreciation against the U.S. dollar for the Singapore dollar to 25 percent for the Thai baht. Thus I felt that the Asian currency turmoil was a reflection of the large waves (that is, the U.S. dollar–yen movements) making small waves. This was not the same as the 1994 Mexican crisis, when the peso fell about 50 percent against the U.S. dollar between December 1994 and March 1995.

In hindsight, I was thinking in the right direction, but wrong as to the magnitude of the waves. A tsunami was coming that even the IMF could not stop.

THAILAND'S RESCUE PACKAGE

Following the IMF convened meeting on 11 August in Tokyo, on 20 August, the IMF announced a rescue package for Thailand, amounting to around US$17 billion of pledges from the IMF (US$4 billion) and other multilateral and bilateral contributors. What was remarkable was the extent of Asia-Pacific solidarity. Australia, China, Hong Kong, Malaysia and Singapore all pledged US$1 billion each towards that pool. Japan contributed the largest share of US$4 billion, whilst Indonesia and South Korea pledged US$500 million each. It was remarkable that the United States and Europe did not contribute at all but still insisted on the principle of transparency that the Bank of Thailand had to reveal its forward foreign exchange commitments. In contrast, the IMF package in 1995 for Mexico was three times larger at US$50 billion, with the United States pledging another US$20 billion of financial assistance.

In Sandakan, before the days of the Internet and Blackberrys, I was cut off from the news of the IMF package. On my return to Hong Kong, I quickly realized that the IMF had a smooth ride in getting regional help to put together the funding because the bulk of the background work was already done in Shanghai. But the outcome was also very ominous. The ministries of finance, led by Dr Eisuke Sakakibara, then Japanese Vice-Minister of Finance for International Affairs, and Tim Geithner, then U.S. Treasury Assistant Secretary, had taken over the negotiations, with the Asian central banks being sidelined. Any hope of discussing the Asian Arrangement to Borrow was dashed.

A quick study of the Tokyo package revealed a fatal flaw. There was no bank standstill, a common measure taken during the Latin American crisis. Under the principle that markets should be kept open as long as possible, the foreign bank lenders to Thailand were not told to 'standstill', that is, not to seek immediate repayment or cut their exposure to Thailand. I called my good friend Dr Chaiyawat, who had become Governor of the BoT on 31 July, to ask him why there was no standstill. He replied that one of the conditions of the package was that there be no standstill. I explained over the phone the inconsistency of the package. The total amount pledged was around US$17 billion, but the U.S. Treasury had insisted as a matter of transparency that the BoT had to disclose its forward and swap commitments, which at their peak in June 1997 was around US$29 billion.[13] It did not take a genius to figure out that the package was totally inadequate to meet Thailand's foreign exchange needs, particularly since there was no bank standstill. The market reaction of anyone holding exposure to Thailand would be to get out as fast as possible, with the IMF money funding those who could get hold of foreign exchange fastest.

I decided to call Dr Sakakibara, much more famous as 'Mr Yen', because I had gotten to know him through my earlier visits to Japan. His reaction was that the decision of G7 members[14] at the Ministerial level was that the IMF should be in charge and that Japanese banks had committed to a standstill vis-à-vis Thailand, but he could not enforce standstills on either the

---

[13] By the end of 1997, the BoT had remaining swap obligations totaling US$18 billion and had incurred losses due to swap contracts amounting to B 241.92 billion or about US$5.12 billion at the year-end 1997 exchange rate of B 47.25 to the U.S. dollar. See Commission Tasked with Making Recommendations (1998; hereafter Nukul Commission Report), para. 236.

[14] The G7 consists of Canada, France, Germany, Italy, Japan, United Kingdom and United States.

European and American banks. I followed up with a call to Stan Fischer, who was not only a teacher of Chaiyawat's at MIT, but also my former boss as Chief Economist of the World Bank when I worked there between 1989 and 1993. Stan explained that the IMF had no legal standing in negotiating a bank standstill. Clearly the powers that be believed that the credibility of the IMF alone, with Asia standing behind Thailand, would be enough to stem the bleeding.

It dawned on me then that we Asians were in big trouble.

STORM IN THE MAKING

That same week as the IMF-sponsored meeting in Tokyo, on 13 August, the Indonesian rupiah hit a historic low of Rp2,682 to the U.S. dollar, forcing Bank Indonesia to give up the fight and allow the rupiah to float the next day. How people underestimated the scale of the contagion could be judged from the fact that when the IMF announced the disbursement of the support package for Thailand on 20 August, the then IMF Managing Director, Michel Camdessus, was reputed to have said the next day, 'The worst of the crisis is behind us'. *Après moi, le déluge.*

It was a relentless summer. On 28 August the Kuala Lumpur Stock Exchange (KLSE)[15] banned short selling of index stocks in Malaysia, only for its benchmark index, the Kuala Lumpur Composite Index (KLCI), to shed 12 percent in less than a week. Malaysia, Indonesia and Philippines were all forced to cut back on fiscal expenditure and investments to stem the loss of market confidence, but the bleeding continued.

Throughout the summer the G7 members were busily debating the correct strategies to manage the Asian crisis. What became clear was that the United States would not be able to commit funds to help any crisis, mainly because the U.S. Congress would not allow the U.S. Treasury to bail out any country, after the United States helped Mexico. Robert Rubin, U.S. Treasury Secretary during the period of the Asian crisis, confirmed in his memoirs[16] that after the Mexican crisis the U.S. Congress practically forbade the use of its Exchange Equalization Fund for any international rescue. Politically, it meant that the U.S. Fed could not be the lender of last resort in U.S. dollars, and it became clear that the IMF was neither designed nor willing to take that role. Certainly its major shareholders would not want it to act in that role.

---

[15] Now Bursa Malaysia following demutualisation of the stock exchange in 2004.
[16] Rubin and Weisberg (2003).

In the meantime the IMF/World Bank Annual Meetings took centre stage in the financial calendar, as the HKMA was the implementation agency for the hosting of the Meetings in Hong Kong. Logistically it was perfect. But a perfect storm was brewing. Ironically, the 1997 Meetings were supposed to be a landmark meeting to endorse the capital account liberalization movement, one of the cornerstones of the Washington Consensus, then not yet a catch phrase. The Meetings, however, will be remembered for two separate dramatic events.

WAR OF WORDS

On 26 July Dr Mahathir had accused George Soros, who ran the Quantum hedge fund, as being the person responsible for leading the attack on the Southeast Asian currencies, which Soros promptly denied. Dr Mahathir subsequently branded Soros a 'moron'. The World Bank had invited Dr Mahathir to give a keynote address on 'Asia as Opportunity' at the Program of Seminars that was organised in conjunction with the Annual Meetings. The organizers did not anticipate the fireworks that were to come.

As Meetings organizer and a Malaysian, I had to make sure that Dr Mahathir and his entourage would be properly escorted to the lecture theatre. I already had word that the Prime Minister had asked where Andrew was when he arrived at the Convention Centre. I had worked for Dr Mahathir's brother-in-law, the legendary BNM Governor Tun Ismail Mohd Ali, back in the 1980s. Indeed, I have also accompanied Dr Mahathir on several of his overseas trips when he was Deputy Prime Minister and later Prime Minister. He was Chairman of the Bumiputra Foundation when I was the secretary to the working party that formulated the strategy on distributing the wealth from the growing securities market to the Bumiputra community. This was to be done through a national mutual fund, today one of the largest funds in the world in terms of membership. Knowing him, I had suspected that the speech would be unusual.

Standing at the back of the packed hall that evening of 20 September, I listened intently as Dr Mahathir addressed the audience of bankers, fund managers, diplomats and currency traders:

We have always welcomed foreign investment, including speculation. … But when the big funds use their massive weight to move shares up and down and make huge profits by their manipulation, it is too much to expect us to welcome them. … I know I am taking a big risk to suggest it but I am saying that currency trading is unnecessary, unproductive and immoral. It should be stopped. It should be made illegal. We don't need currency trading. We need to buy money only when we want to finance real trade. Otherwise we should not buy or sell currencies as we sell commodities.[17]

I looked at my old friend, the late Tan Sri Dr Noordin Sopiee, who was one of Dr Mahathir's principal advisers and speechwriters. He winked back at me. I knew immediately that the speech was vintage Mahathir, straight from the heart. The next day Soros retorted, 'Dr. Mahathir suggested banning currency trading. This is such an inappropriate idea that it doesn't deserve serious consideration. Interfering with the convertibility of capital at a moment like this is a recipe for disaster. Dr. Mahathir is a menace to his own country'.[18]

These two antagonists publicly made up in December 2006 when Soros was in Malaysia to promote his book *The Age of Fallibility*.

ASIAN MONETARY FUND

The other showstopper at the Annual Meetings was the proposal by the Japanese Ministry of Finance on the creation of the Asian Monetary Fund (AMF) at the G7-IMF meetings in Hong Kong. In August 1997 news had reached us at the HKMA that Dr Sakakibara had been travelling to Indonesia, Malaysia and Thailand to canvas support for such an idea. However, word on the grapevine was that the U.S. Treasury and the Europeans were sceptical. Obviously such a fund could challenge the role of the IMF.

Back in June 1997 both Dr Sakakibara and Haruhiko Kuroda were promoted to Vice-Minister of Finance for International Affairs and Director-General of the International (Finance) Bureau, respectively. They began to push for the idea of the AMF, which probably was floated earlier by the Institute for International Monetary Affairs, headed by another former Japanese Vice-Minister, Toyoo Gyohten, as early as late 1996 or early 1997. If so, the Japanese had some inkling that a crisis was coming, but the signals we received were mostly to abandon the U.S. dollar peg and be more flexible.

By late August 1997 the AMF was envisioned as a US$100 billion fund composed of 10 members from the region – Australia, China, Hong Kong, Indonesia, Japan, Malaysia, Philippines, Singapore, South Korea and Thailand. The proposed fund excluded the United States and Europe, which had not contributed to the Thai rescue. According to Sakakibara's

[17] Mohamad (1997b).
[18] Friedman (1997).

memoirs,[19] published only in Japanese, then U.S. Deputy Treasury Secretary Larry Summers called him at midnight at his residence to protest against the AMF. The United States was angry because it was not consulted and invited to participate. Moreover, the AMF would create both moral hazard and competition with the IMF.

Whilst it was obvious that the possible recipients of assistance from the AMF might welcome an alternative source of funding, the other players in Asia were not so sure. First, there was not enough information on how the fund would operate. Would it be operated through the IMF as a supplementary fund, or would the Japanese decide its disbursement? Second, the Japanese clearly thought that they could get an Asian consensus after the successful Thai rescue package that was shaped in Tokyo on 11 August 1997.

What they did not realize was that the proposal stirred up too many political undertones. If Taiwan were willing to contribute to the AMF, how would China react? Hong Kong was also facing a new set of issues after July 1997. The new Legislative Council was much more willing to question the new Hong Kong Special Administrative Region (HKSAR) Government on whether it had the authority to contribute to any regional rescue operations. This was fundamentally the same reason why the United States could not contribute to the Thai rescue.

As the debate continued, the Indonesians decided to call in the IMF on 8 October 1997 after the rupiah had fallen by over 30 percent since July. On 24 October the Thais established a Financial Sector Restructuring Authority (FRA) to review the rehabilitation plans of the 58 suspended finance firms. Subsequently an asset management corporation was established for the impaired assets of the finance companies. However, a political crisis was looming as Prime Minister Chavalit Yongchaiyudh's coalition government began to fall apart. By end of October 1997, the currencies of Indonesia, Malaysia, Philippines, Singapore and Thailand had depreciated between 9 percent (Singapore dollar) and 40 percent (Thai baht) relative to the U.S. dollar since July 1997. Furthermore, around this time the epicentre of the currency panic began to widen throughout Asia.

DRAGONS IN TURMOIL

Warning signs that the Dragon economies of Hong Kong, South Korea and Taiwan would soon be engulfed by the ongoing tsunami had emerged in

---

[19] Quoted in Lipsey (2003), 95–96. Sakakibara's memoirs are entitled *Nihon to Sekai ga Furneta Hi* (The Day That Rocked Japan and the World).

August 1997, when the New Taiwan dollar came under speculative attack. On Friday, 15 August, the HKMA raised short-term interest rates sharply to fend off speculative attacks on the Hong Kong dollar. The HSI began to fall from its peak of 16,673 on 7 August to 15,477 on 17 August. In South Korea there were increasing signs that that the country's banking sector was badly affected by a series of corporate failures.

Having spent an estimated US$7 billion in reserves between August and October 1997 to defend the New Taiwan dollar, on Friday, 17 October, the central bank of Taiwan announced that the New Taiwan dollar, which had been averaging around NT$26–27 to the U.S. dollar for the past decade, would be allowed to float. This marked the second phase of the Asian crisis. This announcement caught the markets by surprise because the Taiwan economy had 'massive foreign exchange reserves and little evidence of serious market pressure. With this act, developments in Asia took on the aura of competitive devaluation, with no limits to its potential scope'.[20]

The Hong Kong dollar came under intense pressure soon after. Hong Kong's currency board system is an automatic adjustment mechanism. If there are capital outflows, interest rates rise and the supply and demand for Hong Kong dollars adjust around the exchange rate. In other words, the exchange rate is fixed, and the real economy adjusts around the exchange rate.

As a result of fears over rising interest rates due to the intense pressure on the Hong Kong dollar, the Stock Exchange of Hong Kong (SEHK) suffered four consecutive days of massive losses. On 21 October, James Tien, then Chairman of the Hong Kong General Chamber of Commerce, was reported by *Asiaweek* to have called for a rethink of the peg in two months,[21] probably not the most astute of public comments given the public nervousness.

Matters came to a boil on 'Black Thursday', 23 October, when the overnight Hong Kong Interbank Offered Rate (HIBOR) went to as high as 280 percent for a few hours at one point. The HSI fell about 1,211 points or more than 10 percent to close at around 10,426, the HSI's biggest ever one-day point decline.[22] On the same day, HSBC, Hong Kong's largest bank, took the unusual step of invoking its right to restrict early redemption of time deposit accounts. In a matter of 10 days, between 17 and 28 October 1997, the HSI fell by more than 33 percent or 4,541 points, closing at around 9,060 on 28 October.

[20] Lipsky (1998), 12.
[21] *Asiaweek* (1998).
[22] On 5 November 2007, the HSI dropped by 1,526 points.

By this time even the U.S. markets had begun to wake up to the depth of the Asian crisis. On 27 October the Dow Jones Industrial Average (DJIA) declined 554 points or over 7 percent, closing at 7,161. This was one of the Dow's single-biggest point losses ever. Fortunately, the U.S. economy remained robust. That week, in Bangkok to present a lecture, I noticed that the traffic jams that plagued Thailand's capital had disappeared. Instead, gloom and doom were everywhere as friends were busy coping with the ongoing crisis in economics and politics. At that lecture I spelt out what everyone today recognized as the fundamental 'double mismatch' in Asia: the banking systems were running the risks of financing long-term assets by short-term deposits (a maturity mismatch), whilst the private sector borrowed foreign exchange to finance investments in local currency (the foreign currency mismatch). There were simply inadequate foreign exchange reserves or liquidity to meet demands for repayment.[23]

A CRISIS OF POLITICS

As autumn approached, the pace of events began to accelerate like a runaway train in a Hollywood action drama.

On 3 November 1997 Thailand's Prime Minister Chavalit announced that he would resign from office amidst street protests and rumours that the military was restless. The weak Chavalit coalition government was replaced by another coalition led by Democratic Party leader Chuan Leekpai.

On 5 November 1997 the IMF announced a US$23 billion financial support package for Indonesia, of which US$10 billion came from the IMF and the remaining US$13 billion was to come from the World Bank, the Asian Development Bank (ADB), Asian nations, the United States and Indonesia's own external assets.

Indonesia's IMF funding came with some stringent reform conditions, including the closure of 16 privately-owned banks that were considered to be unviable. President Suharto's close relatives owned three of these banks. The Indonesian technocrats and the IMF seriously miscalculated the resistance to reforms that was to come.

South Korea was gearing up for a presidential election to be held later in December 1997. Political discontent was so widespread that, for the first time, there was a real possibility that an opposition leader would take over as president.

---

[23] Sheng (1997d).

ASIAN GIANTS STUMBLE

As the Korean elections loomed, global attention began to turn towards Seoul. In October 1997 a senior vice president of the New York Fed came through Hong Kong on a regional scouting event. In Singapore he heard for the first time that South Korea was the next Asian economy to go under. His reaction was incredulity. South Korea had been the second Asian member after Japan to join the club of developed countries, the Organisation for Economic Co-operation and Development, in 1996. The Korean external debt to GDP ratio was less than 30 percent of GDP, and its balance of payments and fiscal situation was nowhere as serious as the rest of the Asian crisis economies.

Coming through Hong Kong, he sought our views. I told him that during a period of contagion and market nervousness anything was possible. The problem was that Korean companies were highly leveraged relative to other Asian corporations. The Korean development model followed that of Japan, except that the Koreans took even higher risks. The average debt-to-equity ratio of the top 30 *chaebol*, the dominant industrial groups, was over 500 percent. As the yen depreciated, Korean exporters were the first to be hurt, because the Korean won had been stable at around W 750–800 to the U.S. dollar for the last decade.

Excess capacity in manufacturing production, worsening trade conditions and a somewhat inflated asset market all created conditions for the pricking of the Korean bubble. Korean investment banks and commercial banks decided to seek liquidity abroad through their branches in Singapore and Japan, drawing on interbank funding. As the Asian crisis worsened, foreign banks refused to roll over the short-term debts of Korean financial institutions, forcing them to sell won to finance their repayments in foreign exchange.

By early November 1997 at least eight *chaebol*, recipients of huge bank loans, were in deep trouble. Reflecting this, Standard & Poor and Moody's downgraded South Korea's long-term sovereign debt ratings and the credit ratings of four major Korean banks, respectively. Between 5 and 8 November the Korea Composite Stock Price Index (KOSPI), the benchmark index of the Korean stock market, plunged over 10 percent to close at 496, 55 percent below its peak almost exactly two years before.

Because the Bank of Korea foreign exchange reserves were depleting very fast, officials from Japan, the United States and the IMF were quietly contacted to secure emergency financing. On 16 November Michel Camdessus was invited to visit Seoul secretly for discussions.[24]

[24] Independent Evaluation Office (2003), 36.

To make matters worse, on 3 November Sanyo Securities, a medium-sized Japanese securities house, suspended operations. On 17 November Japan's Hokkaido Takushoku Bank failed, the first of Japan's big banks to collapse under the weight of bad loans. The weaknesses of the Japanese financial institutions were finally unravelling after nearly seven years of deflation. Instead of being able to help other Asian economies, the Japanese authorities were now facing an internal crisis of confidence at home.

In life, the political diary and the economic calendar often converge to create a crisis atmosphere. South Korea was now in a political limbo, as the elections were being held in December 1997 and the outgoing administration tried to keep the dam from bursting until a new administration could take charge.

On 18 November 1997, amidst strong protests from labour unions, the Korean National Assembly refused to pass a package of financial reform bills. In a matter of days the South Korean Finance and Economy Minister, Kang Kyong Shik, and the president's Chief Economic Secretary, Kim In Ho, resigned, and South Korea turned to Japan and the IMF for help. Monday, 24 November, was 'Seoul's Black Monday'. The Korean won continued its slide downwards, falling by 2.3 percent against the U.S. dollar to around W1,085 to the dollar, and the KOSPI closed at a 10-year low when it fell by 7.2 percent to 451.

MANILA FRAMEWORK

As events unfolded like a tragedy, the Japanese authorities continued to fight a rear-guard action to launch the AMF despite pressure from both the United States and Europe to abandon the idea. My informal polling of my central bank friends in Southeast Asia, Taiwan and South Korea suggested that they were inclined to support the AMF. China was deafening in its silence.

Things came to a head on 23–24 November when the EMEAP, European Union (EU) and U.S. central bank deputies together with the MoF deputies met in the grand Manila Hotel, famous for being occupied by General Douglas MacArthur when he was U.S. Viceroy in the Philippines in the prewar period.

As we gathered for pre-dinner drinks, there was the usual caucus in the corridors, with my old friends exchanging gossip and notes. Larry Summers came in, as did Eisuke Sakakibara. I introduced them to Fong Weng Phak, then Deputy Governor of BNM and several ASEAN friends. From an idle nervous chat, we inevitably moved to confront Sakakibara on the status of the AMF as he was reputed to be the principal architect. We had heard that the Japanese economy was slowing much faster than expected and that the Japanese parliament, the Diet, was concerned whether Japan could afford to raise US$60–100 billion to assist Asia whilst their own banks were in trouble. Sakakibara reluctantly admitted that the money might not be forthcoming. That delivered the coup de grâce to that idea.

From that moment onward, the only alternative was the U.S.-led solution, basically called the Manila Framework. As the first line of defense, the IMF would be at the core of any rescue programme, and all assistance would be tied to IMF conditionality. The Manila Framework was a second-tier, bilateral financing arrangement for the crisis economies and was more a forum for regional economic surveillance and cooperation. It covered 14 economies, three from the Group of Seven (G-7) including the United States and Japan, the five worst crisis-hit economies of Indonesia, Malaysia, South Korea, Philippines and Thailand, Australia, Brunei, China, Hong Kong SAR, New Zealand and Singapore and the IMF. As a talk shop, it was useful, but its bilateral funding arrangements were never activated.

In the meantime, on 24 November, Yamaichi Securities Co. Ltd., the third largest securities house in Japan, failed. As Japan's financial system appeared to be increasingly fragile, the Bank of Japan (BoJ) announced that it would provide unsecured loans to Yamaichi to protect the assets of the securities firm's clients. The next day the yen fell to ¥127.45 to the U.S. dollar, and the Nikkei-225 index plunged a little over 5 percent, closing at 15,868.

Then on 26 November a second Japanese bank, Tokuyo City Bank, failed. With depositors forming long queues at banks to withdraw their money, the Japanese Finance Minister, Hiroshi Mitsuzuka, and the Governor of the BoJ, Yasuo Matsushita, had to issue an extraordinary joint statement later in the day appealing for calm. BoJ official Hiroshi Nakaso who led the team dealing with the Japanese banking crisis recalled, 'It was as though the financial system was starting to melt. ... This was probably the day that Japan's financial system was closest to a systemic collapse'.[25]

A DRAMATIC END TO THE YEAR

Unfortunately November 1997 was only a prelude to a frantic December, when the won, rupiah, baht and ringgit all crashed to all-time lows against the U.S. dollar.

---

[25] Nakaso (2001), 11.

In South Korea, on 2 December, nine technically insolvent Korean merchant banks were suspended. On 3 December Korean officials signed a Letter of Intent (LOI)[26] to the IMF accepting conditions and policies in exchange for financial support from the IMF. Many Koreans consider this day as South Korea's 'Second National Humiliation Day', the first being that of its colonization by the Japanese. The next day, 4 December, the IMF announced a financial package for South Korea worth around US$55 billion, one of the largest packages ever given. The IMF would provide US$21 billion; the World Bank and ADB were to lend US$14 billion, whilst the remaining funds would come from bilateral sources.

Despite the IMF package, however, time was running out in South Korea. The IMF Independent Evaluation Office (IEO) later revealed that

At the start of the negotiations with Korea in late November 1997, the staff estimated the country's financing gap during the years 1998 and 1999 at US$25 billion, of which US$20 billion was for the first year. ... No financing need was envisioned for 1997. These assumptions had to be revised radically almost as soon as the IMF team arrived in Korea. ... It was discovered that Korea's usable reserves – that is, official reserves, minus the amount that had been deposited at overseas bank branches to cover short-term payments – were around US$11 billion, and falling very fast. ... The debt, in turn was far larger than initially thought. ... [S]hort-term external debt (bank and non bank) was estimated at around US$86 billion at end-September 1997, of which banks owed US$62 billion. It was this component that triggered the crisis.[27]

On 9 December, five Korean merchant banks were suspended, whilst the Korean government took majority stakes in two major banks to stem their losses. On 11 December Moody's downgraded the Korean sovereign debt rating but also the credit rating of 31 Korean issuers. The effects of this sequence of events were unmistakable. The Korean won could not be defended, and by 16 December South Korea shifted to a free float.

Things were equally gloomy in Southeast Asia. In Indonesia the rupiah plunged below Rp 4,000 to the U.S. dollar by early December, half its value against the dollar only six months before, on rumours of President Suharto's ill health. On 12 December the rupiah crashed to Rp 5,000 against the dollar.

The Japanese were not doing much better. On 17 December Prime Minister Ryutaro Hashimoto announced a special ¥2 trillion (about US$15.7 billion)

---

[26] A Letter of Intent is IMF jargon for documents that describe the policies that a country intends to implement in the context of its requests for financial support from the IMF and is effectively the result of negotiation between the government of the country and the IMF.

[27] Independent Evaluation Office (2003), 187–189.

cut in personal income taxes to ease Japan's faltering economy. Two days later Japan witnessed one of its largest postwar bankruptcies with the failure of foodstuffs trader Toshoku Ltd. In April 1998 the Japanese Prime Minister would announce a ¥16 trillion (about US$120 billion) fiscal stimulus package aimed at reviving the economy.

Back in Seoul on 18 December Kim Dae-Jung did indeed win the presidential elections, the first time in Korean history that power was peacefully transferred to a democratically elected opposition victor. Despite uncertainty whether he would follow orthodox policies, the new President reaffirmed that he would abide by the agreements with the IMF.

However, on 22 December both Standard & Poor's and Moody's stunned the markets by downgrading the long-term sovereign debt ratings of South Korea to below investment grade. On 23 December the Korean won broke through the W 2,000 to the U.S. dollar psychological barrier, the KOSPI closed at 366, down by more than 7 percent from the previous day's close, and market interest rates shot up to as high as 40 percent. Something had to be done to stop the bleeding.

A RESTLESS CHRISTMAS

As I was about to leave for a much-needed break for Christmas, I had a call on Christmas Eve from Ted Truman, then Director of the International Finance Division of the U.S. Fed, asking whether Hong Kong would be able to join in providing funding for South Korea. I took the call on my mobile phone, walking in the crisp evening air in a garden so as not to disturb my dinner hosts. I explained that it was unlikely that the Hong Kong Legislative Council would support any further funding for South Korea, which was after all an OECD country, far stronger than Hong Kong.

On that Christmas Eve a deal was struck between South Korea, the IMF and the G7 economies for a US$10 billion emergency financing programme, which included a coordinated private sector rollover of debt. For the first time in the Asian crisis, the Big Powers recognized that official aid alone would not suffice. The world's major banks had to 'bail-in', and they were asked to roll over Korean short-term debt of about US$100 billion, of which US$15 billion was due by 31 December and another US$15 billion by the end of January 1998.

At last, the powers that be came to their senses that in a panic everyone had to bail-in, because up to then, any official aid allowed only the banks and other investors to bail out. As David Hale, a leading strategic analyst, perceptively pointed out, the United States had almost without fail

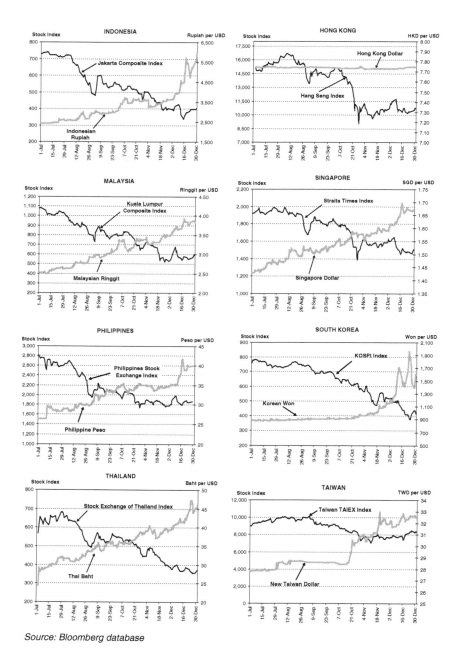

Source: Bloomberg database

Figure 1.1. Asian Dragons and Tigers: Currency and Stock Exchange Indices, July–December 1997

helped those countries where it had troops (the previous crisis country being Turkey), and South Korea had 35,000 U.S. troops guarding the 38th Parallel, the dividing line between the two Koreas.

I recall that it was a restless Christmas break between the Christmas Eve and New Year. By the end of December 1997, the currencies of crisis-hit Asian economies had lost between 15 and 55 percent of their value whilst their stock markets had plunged between 10 and 50 percent since the flotation of the Thai baht in July 1997 (Figure 1.1).

TRACING IT HOME

How did Asia get into such a mess? To understand Asia's failings, one has to go deeper back to the roots of the region's successes and weaknesses that were forgotten during the Asian Miracle years.

In 1996, on a visit to Tokyo for a regional meeting, a leading Japanese academic, known to be close to the Japanese MoF, asked me in a casual conversation whether the Hong Kong dollar would be de-pegged if the yen went to ¥150 to the U.S. dollar. I knew the question was significant, but I had not appreciated how significant. The yen had peaked at ¥80 to the U.S. dollar in April 1995, and the Japanese economy was enjoying a small recovery, with the yen trading at roughly ¥115–120 to the U.S. dollar.

I knew from experience that Asian prosperity was inextricably tied to Japan and the behaviour of the yen against the U.S. dollar. We shall therefore analyse the Japanese role in the Asian crisis in the next chapter.

TWO

Japan and the Asian Crisis

Success is 99 percent failure.
~ Soichiro Honda, founder of Honda Motor Company

The Chinese Qing Dynasty statesman and philosopher Zeng Guofan used to say, 'In life, start at the big picture, but work at the details'. No understanding of the 1997–1998 Asian crisis could be complete without understanding Japan, which had a GDP and total financial assets about double those of the rest of Asia[1] put together in 1996, the year before the Asian crisis began. Indeed, the fate of the Asian economy was inextricably tied to that of Japan, because it was the first Asian economy to become a member of the industrial countries. The largest economy in Asia is the second largest economy in the world, next to the United States and excluding the EU as a common national entity.

There are two common critiques of the Asian crisis, typically focussing on the four worst crisis-hit economies of Indonesia, Malaysia, South Korea and Thailand. The first is that the victims are to blame, due to their own mistakes of bad risk management and crony capitalism. Notably, this was a predominant view in Washington, especially at the beginning of the crisis. The second is that Asia suffered a banking panic. Both views have elements of truth, but we need to take a step back into history to see how the big picture reflects the small details.

JAPAN: ASIA'S LARGEST ECONOMY

In its Annual Survey on Japan in 1995, the *Economist* described Japan as 'a riddle, wrapped in a mystery, inside a trauma. Japan has always been an

---

[1] Asia in this chapter is generally defined as the original Four Dragons (Hong Kong, Singapore, South Korea and Taiwan) and Tigers (Indonesia, Malaysia, Philippines and Thailand) and China.

enigma, especially to outsiders.[2] Today, it is common to forget that Japan used to enjoy fast economic growth in the 1960s and mid-1970s, and that despite the rise of China and India, it still plays a formidable role in the Asian and global economy. Indeed, the story of the Asian Miracle in the 1990s cannot be divorced from Japan as the first nation to reach industrial country status nearly two decades ahead of the next, South Korea. In the spring of 1986, Harvard Professor Ezra Vogel wrote an influential article called 'Pax Nipponica?' in *Foreign Affairs*, in which he raised the fear of Japan becoming No. 1 in the world.[3] For a brief moment in 1990 the Japanese stock market overtook the U.S. market as the largest stock market in the world in terms of market capitalization, but it was to come crashing down, signalling a deflation of the Japanese economy that was to last almost 17 years.

Popular Western descriptions of the Asian Miracle tend to focus mainly on the post–Second World War period, when Asian economies began to industrialize and enjoy fast growth. But in reality, the Asian emergence from colonialism came in 1868 with the Meiji period, 15 years after U.S. Admiral Perry forced open Japanese ports to foreign trade. At this time, when China was still reeling from the devastation of the Opium Wars and the Taiping Rebellion, Japan embarked on major institutional and industrial reforms that were to transform it into a major military power with its naval defeat of China in 1894 and the defeat of Russia in 1904.

There were three major characteristics of Japanese long-term growth.[4] First, Japan actively imported foreign technology to upgrade industrial capacity that was initially focused on import substitution but eventually moved to exports. Second, growth was financed in the prewar period largely by domestic savings, with limited dependence on foreign capital, although Chinese historians have not forgotten that reparations from China for its defeat in 1894 amounted to ¥138 million, equivalent to 6 percent of Japan's Gross National Product (GNP) in 1899 and more than financed its balance of payments drain between 1885 and 1899. Third, the growth of agriculture, through both improvements in crop production and technology, enabled the release of surplus labour to propel industrialization.

Japan's present economic and financial structures, however, also have much to do with the so-called 1940s economic system, set up between 1937 and 1945 to mobilize for war.[5] This involved a cartel of selected *zaibatsus*

---

[2] *The Economist* (1995), 15–16.
[3] Vogel (1986).
[4] Teranishi and Kosai (1993).
[5] Hartcher (1998b) quotes the wartime model to a study by Yukio Noguchi and Eisuke Sakakibara in 1977 that was part of the book by Noguchi in Japanese entitled *1940-nen*

or conglomerates, supported by the main bank system, tied in with life-time employment. The cartels were protected from international competition, so that they could invest in heavy armaments and shipbuilding to extend Japan's military power. The *shogoshosha* or trading companies such as C. Itoh and Marubeni were specialist import-exporters that extended Japan's distribution network for required imports and penetrating export markets. In the postwar period the industrial combines became *keiretsu* groups such as Mitsubishi, Sumitomo and Mitsui, loosely affiliated in legal terms, but bound together by cross-holdings centred on a major bank or insurance company.

The Japanese were able to develop the model of manufacturing export-led growth, supported by a technology/export-friendly bureaucracy and financed by low interest rates provided by the banking system. This approach of picking winners led by the Japanese Ministry of International Trade and Industry (MITI) with the main bank system[6] proved so successful that South Korea, Taiwan and other Asian countries tried to imitate the system, with varying degrees of success.

FLYING GEESE MODEL

The model of geese flying in V-shape formation was developed by Japanese economists Kaname Akamatsu and others to describe the copy, learn, produce and export mode of development. Akamatsu's ideas about the flying geese pattern moved through three cycles. The first cycle in the 1930s concerned the process of moving from import substitution to production for export. Later on in the second cycle, he used the model to describe interindustry migration or integration through shifting comparative advantages. The third and last cycle, widely publicized by Saburo Okita and others in the 1980s, described the Asian stages of development, showing how Asian countries followed Japan in their development path.[7]

To me, the flying geese model is a graphic and intuitively attractive way of describing Asia's pathway to becoming the world's manufacturing powerhouse that it is today. In 1970 Asian manufacturing output made up merely 16 percent of the world's manufacturing output. Fast forward to 2006, about four decades later, and the region's manufacturing output made up 36 percent of the world's manufacturing output.

Taisei, translated as 'The 1940 System', published in Tokyo by Tōyō Keizai Shimpōsha.
[6]   Vittas and Wang (1991).
[7]   Akamatsu (1961).

The flying geese model illustrates how Asia achieved its economic transformation from labour-intensive agriculture and manufacturing to state of the art technology in manufacturing and services in two ways.

First, on a macro-level, the flying geese model graphically depicts the Asian economic growth model of copying a successful leader, ultimately forming the Asian global supply chain. The lead goose in V-shaped pattern is Japan, followed closely by the Four Dragon economies of Hong Kong, Taiwan, Singapore and South Korea and then the ASEAN Tiger economies of Indonesia, Malaysia, Philippines and Thailand. The last group consists of China and Vietnam, with China moving rapidly to become a leader just behind Japan. The crucial thread that binds this V-shaped pattern together is the fact that the leading economy has an incentive to support and shift production to followers due to rising costs, land shortages, pollution costs and the desire to develop market share.

Second, on a micro-level, the flying geese model also graphically illustrates the evolution that took place in the Asian global supply chain. As the leader moves up the value-added chain, it sheds the low-value-added industries to the followers, who in turn pass them down to others as they themselves become more advanced and prosperous.

Technology has radically transformed the global supply chain. First, the standardization of manufacturing products, components and processes enabled Japanese engineers to gain huge efficiencies of scale through lower transaction costs, just-in-time inventory control and order-to-delivery processes. Second, with the emergence of the Internet, production could be outsourced to where it is most efficient to produce. This became a single global supply chain, located mostly in Asia, but sourced on a worldwide basis, dominated by Japanese and American multinationals. Their network of affiliates, subsidiaries and related companies, together with regional partners and suppliers, probably account for about 45 percent of global trade.

The emergence of global networks had a tremendous impact on international trade. Between 1970 and 2007 the value of world trade increased dramatically from US$650 billion to around US$28 trillion, growing at twice the speed of world GDP. At the same time, intra-Asian trade also doubled from about one-quarter of all trade in the region in 1970 to about half in 2006. China has emerged as the aggregator of Asian trade and production for reexport to the West. In 2007 China ran trade surpluses of US$163.2 billion with the United States and US$132 billion with the EU, but the country had trade deficits with South Korea (US$47.9 billion), Japan (US$31.8 billion), ASEAN (US$14.1 billion) and Australia (US$7.8 billion).

ONE SUPPLY CHAIN, TWO CURRENCY STANDARDS

In 1999 Toyoo Gyohten, one of the most eminent Japanese thinkers in finance and former Vice Minister of Finance, drew two key lessons from the East Asian crisis: 'First, we need to have an emergency financing mechanism to cope with the onset of a financial crisis. Second, we need to have greater stability of exchange rates between major trading currencies'.[8] What Gyohten saw clearly was that

[the] 10-year weakening of the dollar between 1985 and 1995 [mainly against the yen] brought about a windfall trade surplus for the affected countries. Then the sharp reversal started in 1995 erased their excessive price advantage and weakened their current account position, which in turn undermined market confidence and prepared a feeding ground for a crisis. In other words, it was not the dollar-peg system per se, which is to blame. *It was the unheeded fundamental disequilibrium in the countries' economies and the wild fluctuation of the dollar-yen exchange rate.*[9]

The aim of this chapter is to demonstrate that the East Asian economies had no clue that they could be killed by U.S. dollar–yen volatility. East Asian economies adopted essentially a dollar peg, because the U.S. dollar was the dominant global currency and the buyer of last resort, with no ostensible credit risks. They benefited in two ways from the strengthening of the yen between the Plaza Accord in 1985 to its peak in 1995 – both in trade diversion and from the large capital flows from Japan.

What they could not comprehend was that when the yen began to weaken, they had double trouble. The trade account swung into deficit, and their balance sheets were already fragile, subject to double mismatches, borrowing short to invest long and borrowing foreign currency in domestic assets. The large capital inflows created a boom in stock and real estate markets that domestic banks lent to fuel. The capital reversals after 1995 drained the system and broke the soft pegs. The fragile banking systems broke, and the economies went into a tailspin. It was both a banking and currency crisis without a lender of last resort. The supply chain had a power surge when the dollar-yen rose and plunged, and it blew the fuse.

Japan's economic growth model was essentially a dual economy structure. A McKinsey study on the Japanese economy in 2000[10] revealed that the best Japanese industries – autos, steel, machine tools and consumer electronics – accounted for only 10 percent of GDP but had productivity

[8] Gyohten (1999).
[9] Gyohten (1999).
[10] Kondo et al. (2000).

levels 20 percent above global competitors. In contrast, 90 percent of Japan's GDP were in the nonexport sectors of domestic production and services, but these sectors had productivity levels 63 percent below that of the United States.

The 1997–1998 Asian crisis starkly brought to fore the fact that the network effects that accompanied the Asian global supply chain were a sharp double-edged sword. Whilst the networks that operated within the Asian global supply chain enabled the region to boom and prosper, lurking in the background was a fundamental flaw in the system – it was a supply chain with two financial standards, the U.S. dollar and the Japanese yen. An engineer, for instance, would understand that a system would not function well if it used two conflicting standards. Indeed, the fundamental weakness of the Asian global supply chain was that it was, and in some ways still is, operating on two conflicting standards.

The Asian crisis of 1997–1998 is thus a tale that cannot be told in isolation. Specifically, we must use the wider perspective of international financial balance sheets and trade flows to examine the interconnectedness of the individual countries within the regional network. It is this complex interconnectivity that was a precursor to the current crisis. In the rest of this chapter, I use recently available international balance sheet data and trade statistics to shed light on the events that unfolded in the region and how they were interlinked with Japan. The data used are sourced from the Japanese Ministry of Finance, Bank for International Settlements (BIS) and Lane and Milesi-Ferretti (2006).

POST-PLAZA: RISE OF JAPAN'S TIES WITH ASIA

The Pacific Ocean divides two of the largest national economies in the world: the United States and Japan. The economic relations between these two nations have been, at the very least, rather volatile. Until the emergence of China and the Middle East oil producers, the United States was the largest deficit and debtor country and Japan the largest surplus and creditor country. As C. Fred Bergsten of the Peterson Institute for International Economics pointed out, in the lead-up to the Asian crisis, the U.S. dollar–yen relationship was experiencing violent fluctuation: 'from 360:1 as recently as 1971 to 80:1 in early 1995 before weakening again to about 130:1 [in June 1998]'.[11] During and after the Asian crisis, the United States had

---

[11] Bergsten (1998). For some additional perspective on Japan's exchange rate issues during the 1980s, see Eichengreen (2007).

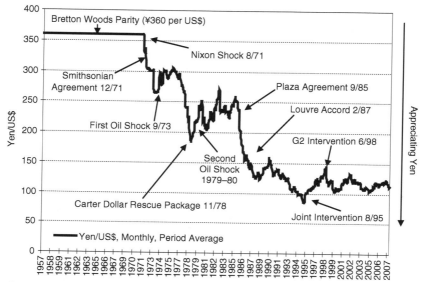

Sources: IMF International Financial Statistics database and McKinnon and Ohno (2005)

Figure 2.1. Monthly Fluctuations in Yen–U.S. Dollar Exchange Rate, 1957–2007

been pushing Japan hard to reflate because it was felt that the East Asian crisis could not be resolved without a pickup in Japanese growth, whilst Japanese yen weakness would also worsen the trade imbalance.

One of the main characteristics of the 1997–1998 Asian crisis was the disruptive cross-border capital flows and how the contagion effects were transmitted rapidly from one country to another. The interconnectivity of the Asian economies was both the boon and the bane of these economies.

We have to begin our tale of the Asian crisis by keeping in mind the U.S.-Japan relationship. Japan was the lead goose in Asia, but the United States was not just Asia's major trading partner. It also provided military security and served as an important source of both FDI and foreign portfolio investment (FPI) in the region. Since the United States was and still is the largest economy in the world, it was not surprising that much of the trade and financial flows across the Pacific was conducted in U.S. dollars.

As can be seen from Figure 2.1, Japan commenced its dramatic industrialization in the postwar era with a fixed exchange rate of ¥360 to the U.S. dollar. This rate was not abandoned until the dollar left the gold standard in 1971. Thereafter the yen appreciated against the U.S. dollar almost continuously until 1979, when the sharp increase in interest rates by the U.S.

Fed to deal with domestic inflation caused the U.S. dollar to strengthen and overshoot. As Japan has run persistent trade surpluses of an average of over US$50 billion annually with the United States since the 1980s, the dollar-yen relationship was a constant sore point in the bilateral relationship. To stop the U.S. dollar from strengthening too much back in the mid-1980s, Japan agreed, following the Plaza Accord of September 1985, to allow the yen to appreciate drastically against the dollar. In less than 2½ years, the yen moved from roughly ¥240 to the dollar in September 1985 to as low as ¥120 in December 1987.

The Plaza Accord shock was to have considerable impact not only on the Japanese domestic economy, but also on its whole industrial policy, particularly with respect to its Asian neighbours.

First, the initial shock from the doubling of the yen, a period called *endaka* or 'high yen crisis', put considerable pressure on Japanese exporters and caused Japan's economic growth rate to drop from 5.1 percent in 1985 to 3 percent in 1986. The BoJ responded by cutting interest rates five times between 1986 and early 1987. By February 1987 the Japanese official discount rate reached a postwar low of 2.5 percent per annum.

Second, in order to maintain global market share despite a strong yen, Japan took an even bolder decision to upgrade productivity and shift production to countries that not only welcomed Japanese FDI but also had cheap land and labour. The advantages of shifting production overseas when the yen was strong were apparent from several perspectives. First, the bilateral Japan-U.S. trade surplus could be reduced as it was shifted to neighbouring countries, thus relieving protectionist pressure against Japan. Second, the upward pressure on the yen could be alleviated through capital outflows. The third advantage was widening Japanese political influence in its neighbourhood. Thus began the rise in Japan's economic and financial linkages with the rest of Asia in the immediate period after the Plaza Accord. Japanese FDI in Asia increased nearly sixfold from about US$1.4 billion in 1985 to around US$8.1 billion in 1989. The major hosts of Japanese FDI during this period were the Four Dragons (Figure 2.2).

The massive Japanese direct investments into the rest of Asia turned the region into an integrated production base for Japan. By the late 1980s, Japan had become the single largest source of FDI for the fast-growing emerging Asian economies. This trend was particularly clear when another surge of Japanese FDI into Asia took place between 1993 and 1997, with Japanese FDI rising nearly twofold from US$6.5 billion to US$11.1 billion during this period. This time the major hosts of Japanese FDI were the Four Tigers (Figure 2.2). Thailand, for example, became the 'Detroit of Asia', as Japanese

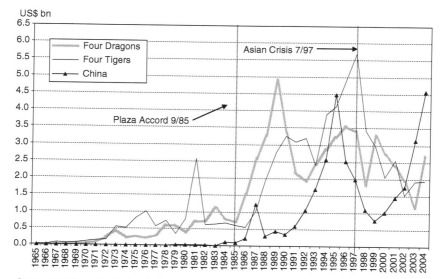

Source: Japan External Trade Organization (JETRO) based on MOF, Japan data and author's estimates
Four Dragons: Hong Kong, Singapore, South Korea and Taiwan
Four Tigers: Indonesia, Malaysia, Philippines and Thailand
Figures based on report and notifications

	1965–1984 Average	1985–1992 Average	1993–1997 Average	1998	1999	2000	2001	2002	2003	2004
Four Dragons	0.3	2.6	3.1	1.8	3.3	2.7	2.4	2.0	1.2	2.7
Four Tigers	0.5	2.1	4.2	3.4	3.0	2.0	2.6	1.5	1.9	1.9
China	0.0	0.5	2.6	1.1	0.8	1.0	1.5	1.8	3.1	4.6
Total	0.9	5.2	10.0	6.3	7.0	5.8	6.4	5.2	6.2	9.2

Figure 2.2. Japanese Foreign Direct Investment to Asia, US$ billion, 1965–2004

car manufacturers, together with their component suppliers, converged into Thailand to establish a regional centre for car production. After the 1997–1998 Asian crisis, Japanese FDI pattern in Asia altered again, and since 2003 China has become the largest host of Japan's FDI amongst Asian countries (Figure 2.2).

Apart from the increase in Japanese private capital flows into Asia during the decade of *endaka*, Figure 2.3 shows that Japanese official aid and market loans, in the form of soft loans, export credits and yen-denominated debt, also increased markedly during this period to 1997. Between 1994 and 1997, for instance, officially recorded net financial flow into emerging economies from Japan averaged US$35 billion annually, approximately four times greater than current flows.

Third, Japanese trade with Asia grew in tandem with the increase in overseas investment flows. Japanese exports to the region rose significantly from approximately 26.4 percent of total Japanese exports in 1985 to 30.1 percent

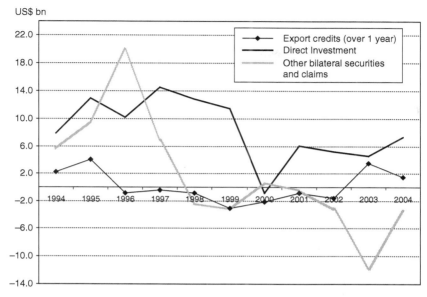

US$ bn

Source: MOF, Japan
Excluding flows to Eastern European countries, more advanced developing countries and European Bank of Reconstruction and Development

	1994	1995	1996	1997	1998	1999	2000	2001	2002	2003	2004
Export credits (over 1 year)	2.3	4.0	−0.8	−0.4	−0.8	−3.1	−2.0	−0.8	−1.6	3.5	1.5
Direct investment	7.9	12.9	10.1	14.5	12.8	11.4	−0.8	6.0	5.2	4.6	7.3
Other bilateral securities and claims	5.6	9.5	20.0	6.8	−2.4	−3.1	0.7	−0.4	−3.1	−11.8	−3.4

Figure 2.3. Japan's Net Financial Flows to Developing Countries, US$ billion, 1994–2004

in 1989 mainly because of capital investment equipment, whilst Japanese imports from Asia increased from 28.7 percent of total Japanese imports in 1985 to 31.0 percent in 1989, as component imports and raw material purchases rose. As Japanese FDI into Asia again surged between 1993 and 1997, Japanese exports to Asia rose sharply from 37.7 percent to 42.1 percent of total Japanese exports whilst Japanese imports from Asia rose from 34.7 percent to 37.2 percent of total Japanese imports. In 2007 Japanese exports to the region stood at 48.2 percent of total Japanese exports, whilst Japanese imports from the region amounted to 43.3 percent of total Japanese imports.

Thus, whilst the decade of *endaka* from 1985 to 1995 spelled trouble for the Japanese domestic economy, it signalled a boom period for the rest of Asia. The region grew rapidly as they became the recipient of large Japanese

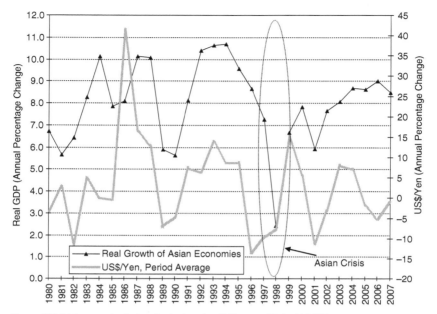

Source: IMF databases and author's estimates based on McKinnon and Schnabl (2005)
Asian economies comprise China, Hong Kong, Indonesia, Malaysia, Philippines, Singapore,
South Korea, Taiwan and Thailand

Figure 2.4. Growth Rates of Asian Economies and Changes in the Yen–U.S. Dollar
Exchange Rate, 1980–2007

direct and financial flows. Keen observers like Ronald McKinnon[12] pointed
out that a clear pattern emerged – the stronger the yen, the more prosperous was Asia (Figure 2.4). In flying geese terms, the stronger the lead goose
flaps, the greater the uplift for the rest of the followers. The stronger the yen,
the more Japan would transfer production to its cheaper neighbours and
lend or invest in the region to prevent further yen appreciation. The more
liquidity and investment inflows, the more the Asian economies boomed,
because they were on a 'soft peg' to the U.S. dollar. On the other hand, the
reverse situation would occur if the yen were to depreciate.

1987–1990: JAPANESE BUBBLE ECONOMY SOWS SEEDS
OF ASIAN CRISIS

Over the period 1987–1988, the Japanese economy recovered with a growth
rate of 6.8 percent. However, the BoJ was initially reluctant to raise interest

[12] McKinnon and Schnabl (2005).

rates to pre-*endaka* levels, partly due to U.S. pressure to make Japan an engine of global growth following the New York stock market crash of 19 October 1987, and partly because the low domestic inflation misled Japanese authorities to go 'in the wrong direction'.[13] Moreover, raising interest rates in a period of higher growth would only attract more capital inflows, thus pushing the exchange rate higher. Thus, the BoJ began to increase interest rates only in 1989, with the official discount rate peaking at 6 percent by August 1990 following five rate increases between May 1989 and August 1990. In hindsight, however, the reluctance of the central bank to raise interest rates proved to be a huge miscalculation.

The prolonged low interest rate environment in Japan following the Plaza Accord created one of the largest domestic asset bubbles in the world. As explained by Yoshio Suzuki of the Nomura Research Institute:

The emergence and bursting of the bubble in the Japanese asset market was neither a result of financial reform nor of financial deregulation. It was the international policy coordination carried out in the latter half of the 1980s that led to these events. Because of coordinated cuts in interest rates decided upon in the Louvre Accord of February 1987, Japan's ODR was cut to 2.5 percent, an historical low. ... Therefore, in compliance with the Louvre Accord, Japan was obliged to continue its easy monetary policy, keeping its interest rates at the lowest level ever through May 1989. As a result a mistaken notion spread in the Japanese market between 1988 and 1989 that Japan would not be able to raise interest rates lest she create a dollar crisis. This assumption of permanent low interest rates was responsible for the bullish sentiment that caused asset prices to surge beyond the level justified by economic fundamentals, thereby creating the bubble.[14]

Valuations in both the stock and property markets reached staggering levels. By 1989 the value of real estate in Japan was roughly US$24 trillion. This was four times the value of real estate in the United States, although Japan had half the population and only 60 percent of U.S. GDP.[15] The Nikkei-225 reached a peak of 38,916 in December 1989 with a price-earnings ratio of around 80, compared with roughly 15 in the United States. At the height of the euphoria, the capitalized value of the Tokyo Stock Exchange stood at 42 percent of world stock market value, and Japanese real estate accounted for about 50 percent of the value of all the land on the face of the earth, whilst representing less than 3 percent of its total area. It was rumoured that the square mile of land containing Tokyo's Imperial Palace was worth more than the entire state of California.[16]

[13] Kuroda (2002).
[14] Suzuki (1994), 447–448.
[15] Hartcher (1998a), 70.
[16] Krugman (2000), 64.

In 1988 I vividly recall being invited to a regional insurance regulators' meeting in Tokyo, where we were all taken to the highest art gallery in the world, located at Yasuda Marine and Fire Insurance's glass and steel building in Shinjuku. There we viewed in awe the gem in the gallery, Van Gogh's *Still Life: Vase with Fifteen Sunflowers*, for which Yasuda paid a record price of US$40 million. A member of staff proudly told us that one Managing Director was sent to Europe and told to bid for the painting and not to return without it. I did not know whether it was madness or sheer folly.

The Japanese asset bubbles were identical to other asset bubbles in the sense that they were essentially inflated by credit. Banks lent to highly leveraged developers to buy real estate against inflated collateral values, which then fuelled the bubble further. Asset prices bore no realistic relationship to their return on capital, particularly since cost of funding was exceptionally low. The minute the credit stopped, the bubble began to deflate, and the main victims were the banks themselves.

Why did Japanese bankers, normally staid and conservative individuals, go overboard in this bubble? There were two standard explanations.

First, the liberalization of the Japanese financial markets was probably mismanaged in terms of both its pace and scope. Although Japanese credit management was generally good, market risk management was weak because the banks operated in an environment of long market stability, including price stability. Regulation did not keep pace with market changes. Accounting and disclosure standards lagged behind Europe and the United States. The Japanese even actively participated in devising a Tier 2 capital adequacy ratio for the Basel Capital Accord of 1988 that turned out to have terrible consequences for the banking system.[17] As the Japanese economy became flush with liquidity in the boom period to 1990, banks competed actively for loans in an environment of declining interest rate margins, so that they responded by expanding into riskier lending.[18]

Second, Japanese banks became victims of their own lack of corporate accountability. As the core of the *keiretsu* system of interlocking shareholding between banks, insurance companies and industrial and trading groups, they felt obliged to lend to failing affiliated companies. From the beginning, minority shareholders other than interlocking group investors had little

---

[17] I shall describe this technical issue later.

[18] See Ueda (1999) and Kawai (2003). Among the policies which created difficulties for banks include allowing housing finance companies (*Jusen*) and other real estate investments to invest freely.

say in exercising their corporate governance rights.[19] Indeed, foreign investors felt that the exceptionally high price-earning ratios were a formidable
defence against takeovers or mergers by foreigners. This lack of corporate
accountability of Japanese banks, combined with the lack of experience in
dealing with market and international risks, proved almost fatal to their
status as a pillar of Japan's economic strength.

To an emerging market bank supervisor like myself, who had admired
the rise of Japan as a superpower, this was a riddle that had no satisfactory
explanation. How did an advanced OECD country, the second richest in
the world, get into such a banking mess, despite OECD-level bank supervision and the fact that Japanese bankers were by and large very honest and
dedicated individuals?

In their own fields, Japanese bankers were highly trained to understand
their business risks. Their information sources and comprehension of specific
businesses were far superior to that of other Asian bankers. When I grew up
in Sabah, formerly one of the leading timber producers in Asia, the Japanese
bankers I knew understood every aspect of the timber business. They always
huddled amongst themselves, drinking nightly with the timber traders, and
they had no qualms about going directly to the timber yards and the jungle
to check out the situation first hand before confirming any letters of credit.
Working with Japanese bankers on one of their investments in a shipyard
in Malaysia taught me a great deal about how much homework they did in
checking and rechecking the business proposition and all the business details.
Japanese bankers prided themselves that they were the ones responsible for the
turnaround of various failed industrial projects, both in Japan and abroad.

In 2002 I happened to visit Tokyo and decided to try to get an answer for
myself. Talking to old friends and doing a bit of digging, I finally unravelled
one side of the story that exposed one dark side of the Japanese bubble.
I do not pretend that it is the whole story, but it explained well enough
to me why it was not just policy blunders, political errors and bad bank
management that were responsible for the bubble.

AMAKUDARI: THE OLD BOYS CLUB

One of the pillars of the Japanese ascent to industrial power was the cohesiveness, determination and integrity of the elite, particularly the bureaucracy,
centred mostly in Japan's MoF, but also in its BoJ and MITI. This cream of the
crop was mostly educated at the University of Tokyo or similar elite Japanese

---

[19] See Ito (1996), Ueda (1999), Krugman (2000), Kanaya and Woo (2000) and Kawai (2003).

universities, entry into which depended on a stringent series of examinations. All this was reminiscent of the Eton/Oxbridge dominance of the British civil service. Japanese civil servants were frequently rotated through many different jobs, including postings overseas with embassies as financial attachés or seconded to the IMF and OECD, for example, to give them a well-rounded training. Many of them received a master's degree at foreign elite universities, such as the Sorbonne, Harvard and the London School of Economics. A few, such as Eisuke Sakakibara, received their doctorates. Those whom I have met were sophisticated, worldly individuals, fluent in English or French, with exquisite tastes in Western art, classical music or Bordeaux wines.

There was, however, one crucial difference with the British civil service. I was told that as each level of civil servants rose in the elite, it was the responsibility of the most successful person in that batch to find a job for those in his cohort who had to drop out because top posts became scarce as one moved higher up in the hierarchy. The descent of high-ranking Japanese MoF officials into financial institutions is called *amakudari,* or descent from heaven.[20]

The obligation of finding employment by the official who stays and rises in the bureaucracy for his former colleagues 'placed' or descended into a bank became a symbiotic power relationship. The official who remains in the bureaucracy exercises enormous influence on the financial system through the *amakudari* system, because it is an unofficial channel of government influence on the business sector. The retired former colleagues enjoy power and patronage because their new employers in the financial sector can now have access to the highest levels of government through this unofficial channel and perhaps get approvals and support denied to others without the *amakudari* connection. Prime Minister Junichiro Koizumi, who served as Japanese Prime Minister from 2001 to 2006, stopped the practice in 2002, after public opinion turned sharply against this system as a source of corruption. *Amakudari* was associated with the 1993 general contracting scandal and the *jusen* or mortgage bank scandal of 1995–1996, where the *jusens* were found to have approximately ¥6.41 trillion (around US$63.2 billion)[21] in bad debt.

Amakudari was dangerous precisely because the downward integration of officials into the financial sector intersected with the upward integration of Japanese gangsters or *yakuza* into the real estate business. Fans of Japanese film noire by Juzo Itami would recall that the *yakuza* became strong-arm men for property developers to get rid of squatters and inconvenient tenants for

[20] Suzuki (2001), 447–448.
[21] Converted at the exchange rate of ¥101.45 to the U.S. dollar, the average exchange rate for the 1995–96 period.

property development. They soon found that property developers depended on bankers to fund their projects, and once property deals became gangster ridden, it was almost impossible for government officials to take action against problem banks, where the senior bank officials may have been former colleagues through the *amakudari* connection. According to a former head of Japan's organized crime division of the police, 'The key issue today is that a substantial portion of the existing bad loans cannot be recovered solely by bankers because the original loans involved politicians, bankers and *yakuza*'.[22]

This *yakuza* tale is poignant because one BoJ official whom I knew personally, Tadayo Honma, committed suicide just after he became the President of Nippon Credit Bank in 2000. I knew him as an able Executive Director of the BoJ, who dealt with the failure of Yamaichi Securities in December 1997 and later helped to nationalize Nippon Credit Bank when it failed in 1998. The tragedy was that it was rumoured that Nippon Credit Bank was involved in lending to the *yakuza*.[23]

1991–1995: THE EMERGENCE OF THE YEN CARRY TRADE IN ASIA

The Asian crisis is a story intermeshed with the after-effects of the Japanese asset bubbles. After 1991 there were essentially three basic responses to the post-bubble deflation in Japan.

The first was the fiscal pump-priming in construction expenditure. From having the healthiest fiscal position amongst OECD countries in 1990, Japanese tax cuts and fiscal expenditure led to annual fiscal deficits of nearly 6 to 7 percent of GDP, creating a huge gross public debt of about 195 percent of GDP in 2007.

Second, complementing a loose fiscal policy was loose monetary policy. Between July 1991 and September 1995, the BoJ progressively brought interest rates to 0.5 percent and by 1999 operated a zero interest rate policy. This was the golden opportunity for the 'carry trade', described later.

Third, because Japan wanted to reflate its own economy and to keep the yen from being overvalued, after 1985 there were large outflows in FDI, portfolio investments, bank loans and official aid. From April 1990, when the yen bottomed at around ¥160 to the U.S. dollar, it continued to appreciate until April 1995, when it peaked at around ¥80 to the U.S. dollar. It was this outflow of Japanese bank loans, FDI and portfolio investments that

---

[22] Kattoulas (2002), 12.
[23] Chemko (2002).

created the conditions for the bubble in Asia and the subsequent crisis in 1997–1998.

One of the distinct characteristics of Asian development is that there is a natural tendency for Asians to try to grow out of a problem. Hence, what happened after the Japanese bubble in 1990 was not a drastic cutback in excess capacity domestically, but a deliberate policy to expand into Asia to create an Asian region with Japan at its centre. Part of this was a response to relentless Japan bashing or U.S. pressure for Japan to play a larger role in global affairs, including burden sharing in security and other matters. Japan alone underwrote US$13 billion for the cost of the first Iraq war of 1991 and began funding a whole series of studies and research on the Japanese model of development, including the famous 1993 World Bank Asian Miracle study, which I had the privilege to work on during my stint at the Bank.

As the Japanese economy slowed and competition between Japanese banks for business intensified, the banks followed their manufacturing customers into non-Japan Asia in earnest (Figure 2.5). Between the latter

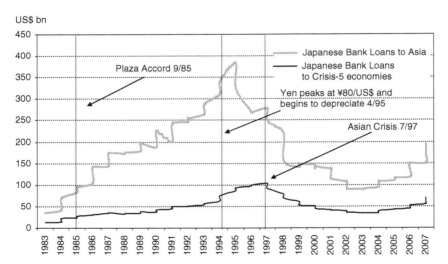

Source: BIS and author's estimates
Asia comprises China, Hong Kong, Indonesia, Malaysia, Philippines, Singapore, South Korea, Taiwan and Thailand
Crisis-5 economies comprise Indonesia, Malaysia, Philippines, South Korea and Thailand

	1983–1984 Average	1985–1992 Average	1993–1997 Average	1998–2001 Average	2002	2003	2004	2005	2006	2007
Crisis-5	17.7	38.6	82.8	51.4	34.9	34.2	39.8	43.9	52.9	69.1
Asia	52.4	188.2	293.8	140.6	90.9	90.8	107.7	116.4	149.9	195.3
Figures for table are based on end-of-period data										

Figure 2.5. Japanese Banks' Consolidated Foreign Claims on Asian Economies, US$ billion, 1983–2007

half of the 1980s and the mid-1990s, partly to finance Japanese subsidiaries operating in the region, Japanese banks were the major lenders in Asia, with banks and branches opening up in Hong Kong and Singapore and in every Asian capital. From 1985 to 1997 Japanese banks supplied over 40 percent of the total outstanding international bank lending to Asia in general as well as to the Crisis-5 economies of Indonesia, Malaysia, Philippines, South Korea and Thailand. During this period outstanding international bank lending by Japanese banks to Asia in general peaked at US$383 billion in June 1995 whilst outstanding international bank lending by Japanese banks to the Crisis-5 countries peaked at US$103 billion in June 1997.

The massive expansion in Japanese bank lending, in both yen and foreign currency, created huge capital flows globally. Because Japanese interest rates were also low, it created what is now commonly known as the Yen Carry Trade. The yen carry trade is essentially an arbitrage trade – you borrow yen at very low interest rates and invest in currencies with higher-yielding interest rates such as the U.S. dollar or the Thai baht. An investor earns the difference in spread between the return on dollar or baht assets and the cost of carrying the yen liability – hence the name, carry trade. If the yen depreciates against the U.S. dollar, one scores a double win – higher interest differential and lower repayment in dollars.

To prevent deflation in Japan, the BoJ's low interest rate policy was a 'gift' to all who wanted to engage in the carry trade. After April 1995 when the yen peaked at ¥80 to the U.S. dollar until it bottomed at ¥147 in August 1998, hedge funds and professional investors who engaged in the yen carry trade made huge profits.

Based on BIS data, international yen-denominated bank lending[24] went through two important phases in the lead-up to the Asian crisis. The first was from September 1985 to September 1990, when total outstanding yen lending went from US$100 billion to roughly US$580 billion, mostly to the developed markets. International lending in yen peaked when yen interest rates reached their post-Plaza peak of 6 percent in August 1990, and then declined to US$400 billion by mid-1993. Thereafter, in spite of the rise in yen to ¥80 to the U.S. dollar in April 1995, the outstanding yen-denominated foreign bank lending rose to US$920 billion by March 1998, an increase of US$520 billion. This time a fair share went to Asia.

---

[24] This is referred to as total international yen-denominated bank lending, with adjusted exchange rate valuation and excluding domestic lending in Japan so as to abstract the issue of domestic demand for yen.

A crude estimate of the carry trade during this period was US$200–350 billion.[25]

Since the spread between the U.S. Fed Funds target rate and the BoJ official discount rate was roughly 5 percent during those years, the average interest spread from the average increase in the yen carry trade alone was US$13 billion per year (5 percent spread on an average volume of US$260 billion of carry trade) or US$39 billion over three years. However, since the yen depreciated by about half between April 1995 and August 1998, the average gain in having an exposure in the yen liability was US$130 billion. In other words, the 'gift' in the carry trade in those three years would conservatively be US$169 billion (US$130 + US$39 billion). Those who engaged in such trade and took profits during this period made huge fortunes. Hedge funds became rich by leveraging up in the carry trade and took large calculated risks in emerging markets, particularly countries like Thailand that had high interest rates and a soft peg against the U.S. dollar.

These huge numbers illustrate how profitable it was for nimble investors that took advantage of the carry trade, pushing capital from Japan and other developed markets to emerging markets. Investors from the developed markets benefited from the portfolio diversification to emerging markets and from the policy mistakes of post-bubble deflation Japan. Thus, the combination of outflow of capital from Japan to its neighbours in Asia and the attraction of these growing markets led to the bubble in Asia. Of course, this would not have happened if the Asian markets had not made the fundamental risk management mistake of the 'double mismatch'. In other words, they were on the other side of the yen carry trade – borrow short, invest long and borrow foreign currency (dollar or yen) and invest in local currency. For every bad lender, there is a bad borrower.

1995–1999: JAPANESE BANKS IN TROUBLE BACK HOME

Although hedge funds got the blame for taking speculative positions, the bulk of the funds outflow from the Asian region was the result of the withdrawal of Japanese banks from the region for their own valid reasons. The banks were in deep trouble, mainly because of their domestic nonperforming loans (NPLs).

---

[25] Although a rough estimate, this is close to the size quoted by major market participants in New York and Tokyo of US$200–300 billion at its peak in mid-1998 (de Brouwer 2001, 42).

As in the case of most crises, problems occur not necessarily at the centre, but at the periphery of organizations. In the case of Japan, problems in its banking system surfaced as early as December 1994, when two Tokyo-based credit cooperatives failed with almost US$1 billion in bad loans,[26] mostly because of lending to real estate companies. Japanese banks traditionally carried lower core capital than their Western counterparts whilst Japanese corporations were also more highly leveraged. This was the legacy of the main bank system in which Japanese banks supported Japanese trading houses and manufacturers to invest and export abroad using cheap domestic loans. The main or lead city clearing bank acting as the leader of a convoy was supported by regional banks, which were in turn supported by related credit cooperatives. The regional banks and credit cooperatives were most vulnerable to real estate loans, and when they failed, the main banks also began to suffer.

In 1995 two events shook Japanese confidence – on 17 January the earthquake struck Kobe, and on 19 April the yen appreciated to ¥80 to the U.S. dollar and thereafter began to depreciate. As the yen depreciated, there was an export stimulus, and the Japanese economy had a minor recovery in 1996. The real economy grew by 2.6 percent in 1996, a slight increase from 1.9 percent the previous year. Despite this improvement in the Japanese real economy, however, Japanese banks became increasingly weak because domestic NPLs continued to increase, reaching levels that could no longer be hidden, because of weak property prices. In April 1997 Japan misjudged the recovery and raised its value added tax from 3 to 5 percent, causing the fragile Japanese economy to slump till 1999. By November 1997 the first serious Japanese bank failure occurred following the downfall of Hokkaido Takushoshu Bank.

Amidst this series of domestic events that was taking a toll on the Japanese banking system, Japanese banks were also taking a beating on the external front. First, the 1995 Daiwa banking scandal in New York increased the Japan premium, the rate at which Japanese banks could fund themselves overseas. Second, and perhaps more importantly, the decline of the yen against the U.S. dollar between 1996 and 1997 was also beginning to have a devastating effect on Japanese banks by a quirk of historical fate. Because there was no Glass-Steagall prohibition against Japanese banks owning shares in nonfinancial companies, Japanese banks had over the years accumulated a massive amount of corporate shares that were understated on their accounts. Japanese banks could outlend their European and American competitors because of their superior capital position, only if the unrealized value of their share portfolio was included as capital. Accordingly, when the Basel

---

[26] Bruell (1994).

Capital Accord was negotiated in 1988, the Japanese authorities fought hard to include a Tier 2 capital category, which would allow banks to use part of their unrealized profits on their share portfolio to count as bank capital.

This meant that the capital base of the Japanese banking system was hostage to the level of the stock market, just as European and U.S. bank capital 10 years later became hostage to mark to market accounting in derivatives priced to illiquid markets.

This technical quirk meant that Japanese banks suffered from two vicious deflationary pressures. First, overall share prices fell in 1996–1997 as the economy slowed down and foreigners began cashing out of the Japanese stock exchange. Share prices also fell when the weaker banks had to sell their shares in order to prop up their capital base because of the write-off of their rising NPLs. The lower the share price, the lower the Tier 2 capital.

Second, the decline in capital base from lower share prices came at a time when the weak yen increased the yen value of the Japanese banks' foreign currency loans.

These twin pressures had the net effect of reducing the ability of Japanese banks to meet the minimum 8 percent BIS capital adequacy ratio. This could not have come at a worst time, when the banks were beginning to feel the after-effects of the Japanese deflation. The sharp drop in real estate prices meant that much of the collateral of their loans were shrinking in value. A declining stock market meant that raising capital through rights issues would have been costly. The only way to meet their capital adequacy ratio was to reduce their overseas foreign exchange loans. Indeed, as the yen continued on its depreciating path against the U.S. dollar, slowly inching towards the ¥150 to the U.S. dollar level in August 1998, the Nomura Research Institute estimated that Japanese banks would have to reduce their loans by ¥56 trillion (around US$400 billion) if the yen remained at ¥140 to the U.S. dollar and the stock market stayed at 15,000. This would be equivalent to a contraction of 11 percent of Japan's GDP.[27]

Consequently, by mid-1995 following the depreciation of the yen against the U.S. dollar, Japanese bankers began to ask themselves where they could cut their lending, and it was obvious that they should reduce their commitments in other Asian economies, including their interbank activities in Hong Kong and Singapore. Hence between June 1995 and June 1997, that is, just before the Thai baht devaluation on 2 July 1997, Japanese bank loans to Asia in general dropped by about 27 percent from its June 1995 peak of US$383 billion to US$278 billion, but Japanese banks continued to

[27] Koo (1998), 9.

lend to the Crisis-5 economies, with Japanese bank loans to these economies increasing from US$86.4 billion in June 1995 to its June 1997 peak of US$103.3 billion (see Figure 2.5).

With the surprise devaluation of the Thai baht, however, the yen carry trade began to unwind in a most disorderly manner.[28] Japanese banks also accelerated their withdrawal from Asia. This time they also withdrew from the Crisis-5 economies (see Figure 2.5). Therefore, with the unwinding of the yen carry trade post-Thai baht devaluation coupled with the considerable Japanese bank lending withdrawals, Asia had a bank run, but domestic central banks did not have enough foreign exchange reserves to meet that run on foreign currency.

Japanese bank lending withdrawals were staggering. Between the June 1997 peak and 1999, Japanese banks withdrew US$51.2 billion from the Crisis-5 economies, amounting to almost 6 percent of their GDP during that period, and a total of US$235.2 billion from Asia in general between the June 1995 peak to 1999, mostly from Singapore and Hong Kong. This amounted to almost 10 percent of Asia's GDP during that period. Even healthy countries cannot withstand a liquidity shock of that scale.

Hence, a slump in Japan with a fragile banking system and a bloated Asian economy with a bubble in asset prices that was funded by foreign short-term capital, including short-term bank loans, created the ripe conditions for the dam to break in July 1997. Most economists were focused either on Asia exclusive of Japan or on Japan. Few put both pieces of the puzzle together, but some hedge funds that engaged in the carry trade were already beginning to smell a massive opportunity.

THE YO-YO YEN: ASIA'S KEY VULNERABILITY

There is a common saying amongst foreign exchange traders that 'dollar-yen goes up by the stairs and down by the lift'.[29] Why has the yen been so volatile against the U.S. dollar? After all, since Japan was persistently running a trade surplus with the United States, one would have expected that the yen would gradually appreciate against the U.S. dollar, rather than experiencing sudden sharp appreciations against the dollar only to depreciate again.

---

[28] Although it is widely acknowledged that the unwinding of the massive yen carry trade is a major contributor to the events that unfolded in Asia in 1997–1998, the impact is by no means isolated to Asia.

[29] Breedon (2001), 151.

In 1996 I attempted to explain this in a seminar in Tokyo with fellow central bankers and Japan MoF officials.[30] I attributed the volatility to four factors.

First, as a result of running a persistent current account surplus, Japan has become a major creditor nation. With the recent release of data on the international balance sheet position of member countries by the IMF in 2006,[31] it is now possible to determine just how large a creditor nation Japan was back in the 1990s. By the end of 1995, Japan's gross foreign assets amounted to US$2.6 trillion whilst its net international investment position (NIIP), the difference between foreign financial assets and liabilities, was US$816 billion, equivalent to about 15.5 percent of 1995 GDP. Net foreign assets meant that Japan suffered foreign exchange if the yen appreciated.

Second, there was a large pool of yen debtors, because Japan was also a major exporter of capital, particularly official and private debt denominated in yen. World Bank external debt data showed that at the end of 1995 developing countries had US$265 billion worth of yen-denominated debt or 12.8 percent of their total debt denominated in yen, with countries in the East Asia and Pacific region having US$111.1 billion worth of yen-denominated debt or 30.2 percent of their debt denominated in yen. An appreciation of 25 percent in the yen rate would have added nearly US$28 billion to their debt burden.

Developing countries with U.S. dollar debt did not generally have to worry about dollar fluctuations because the bulk of their income was in U.S. dollars. However, the flip side of this was that the yen debtor countries amongst the developing countries could not hedge their yen liabilities well. In a period of ever-rising yen, Japanese exporters tended to export in yen and pay for their imports in U.S. dollars. Thus, in Japan's trade with Southeast Asia, for example, yen-denominated trade accounted for 52.5 percent of exports in 1993 and only 25.7 percent of imports. This meant that yen debtors had to buy yen for both their imports and also to service their yen debt.

Third, Japanese exporters also hedged their U.S. dollar export income into yen by buying yen forward or purchasing options to sell dollars and buy yen. At the same time, the financial institutions on the other side of the hedging contracts also hedged their exposures on a dynamic basis, but did not hedge fully.

Fourth, as professional risk managers like to say, 'The only perfect hedge is in a Japanese garden'. Hedging strategies generally would work only if

---

[30] Sheng (1996).
[31] Lane and Milesi-Ferretti (2006).

there were rough balance between supply and demand in the market. With an overhang of U.S. dollars and shortage of yen unless there were continuous outflows of capital from Japan, any sharp appreciation of the yen would create a huge amount of dynamic hedging as market participants rush to cover their yen liabilities.

All these factors led to great volatility in the currency. The currency would overshoot because borrowers in yen would not hedge as they gained from yen depreciation, whilst those who engaged in carry trade benefited not only from the positive interest spread, but also an appreciation of foreign exchange holdings in yen terms. The carry trade encouraged capital outflows but at the expense of high currency volatility. This explains why in recent years the yen has continuously depreciated against the U.S. dollar despite Japan's running a continuous current account surplus amounting to 2.8 of percent of GDP annually since 1985, the year of the Plaza Accord.

The 1997–1998 Asian crisis brought to the fore the sort of adverse impact a volatile yen-U.S. dollar relationship may have on Asia in terms of both trade and finance and ultimately on the real economy as a whole. Unfortunately, the volatility of the yen against the U.S. dollar would persist as long as Japanese interest rates were significantly different from those of the major currencies. Its direction would be determined not by trade flows, but by capital flows induced by the carry trade. This volatility exists because fundamentally there is an imbalance in the trade and capital accounts. Unless these are addressed structurally, the potential volatility due to sudden swings in the reversal of the carry trade would remain one of the key vulnerabilities of the Asian global supply chain.

A FINAL NOTE: THE INTERNATIONAL BALANCE SHEET PERSPECTIVE

The data on the international balance sheet position of member countries that was first released by the IMF in 2006[32] is particularly revealing because they provide valuable insights that were not obvious from looking at flow data alone and present a balance sheet picture that was not previously available to investors, policymakers and bankers. Had the balance data been extensively available back in the early to mid-1990s,

---

[32] Lane and Milesi-Ferretti (2006). This paper comprehensively updated and extended the authors' initial contribution in this area, which included estimates for the external portfolios of only 67 countries and only over the period 1970–1998 (see Lane and Milesi-Ferretti, 2001).

Table 2.1. *Selected Asian Economies: Net International Investment Positions*

	1996 NIIP (US$ Billion)[1]	1996 NIIP (% of GDP)[1]	1997–98 Nominal GDP (% Change)[2]	1997–98 Exchange Rate (% Change)[3]	Remarks
Japan	+890.0	+19.0	−9.2	−7.6	
China	−122.9	−14.4	+7.0	+0.1	Protected by exchange control
Hong Kong	+69.2	+43.5	−5.3	+0.0	Currency Board System
Indonesia	−127.4	−50.8	−55.8	−70.9	
Malaysia	−55.9	−55.4	−27.9	−28.3	
Philippines	−41.6	−49.2	−20.5	−27.9	Already under IMF program in 1997
Singapore	+80.2	+87.0	−14.0	−11.3	Contagion effect
South Korea	−50.2	−9.0	−33.9	−32.1	Bank run causing exchange overshoot
Taiwan	+172.2	+59.5	−8.1	−14.2	
Thailand	−101.8	−55.9	−25.9	−24.2	

Source: IMF, Lane and Milesi-Ferretti (2006) and author's estimates
[1] + means net assets position; − means net liabilities position
[2] Nominal GDP in U.S. dollar terms
[3] U.S. dollar per national currency, period average

it would have been obvious that several countries were maintaining foreign exchange balance sheets that were highly vulnerable to exchange rate shocks.

Table 2.1 shows that economies with negative NIIP or external financial liabilities exceeding external assets of more than 50 percent of GDP got into crisis. The exception was China, which was protected by exchange control. South Korea also got into difficulties, although its negative NIIP was only 9 percent of GDP. This was clearly a serious liquidity crisis, as the Bank of Korea did not have sufficient foreign exchange reserves to meet the large outflows that arose out of the banking panic South Korea experienced at the end of 1997.

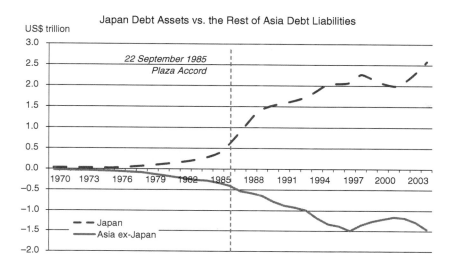

Japan Debt Assets vs. the Rest of Asia Debt Liabilities

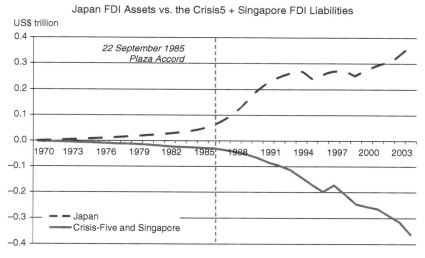

Japan FDI Assets vs. the Crisis5 + Singapore FDI Liabilities

Source: Lane and Milesi-Ferriti (2006)
Liabilities are plotted as negative

Figure 2.6. Japan Debt Assets vs. the Rest of Asia Debt Liabilities

Table 2.1 also demonstrates that the sharp fall in nominal GDP in U.S. dollar terms over the period 1997–1998 in most Asian countries could be explained by their respective sharp currency exchange rate devaluation against the U.S. dollar. Since Singapore and Japan had large surplus NIIP as well as current account surpluses, it was surprising that their currencies also depreciated. Singapore's case could be explained by contagion from its neighbours, but clearly the yen depreciation against the U.S. dollar was an important factor in the spread of the crisis.

Notably, the dramatic changes that occurred during the period leading up to the Asian crisis could be distinctly and neatly summarised in the balance sheet positions of the countries involved. As shown in Figure 2.6, Japanese gross FDI and debt, which includes loans and trade credit, assets increased steeply after 1985, and this was clearly mirrored by the FDI and debt liabilities build-up for the rest of the region, underlining the interconnectedness of the countries in the region and the pivotal role that Japan played in driving this interconnectivity.

In sum, we cannot examine the Asian crisis without looking at the problems of Japan. Japan's banking withdrawal from the region arising from its own problems exacerbated the crisis. This was not intentional, but the effects were nevertheless catastrophic.

Next, we will look at how the way we look at the world exposed our vulnerabilities to crises.

THREE

The Beam in Our Eyes

The human mind is like an umbrella – it functions best when open.
~ Walter Gropius, German architect

There is an old Malay saying, 'When elephants fight, the mouse deer gets trampled'. This is similar to the African saying that when elephants fight, the grass gets trampled. But a cynic will also say that the grass also gets trampled when elephants make love.

Marc Faber, the famous market analyst based in Hong Kong, has a very graphic way of explaining macroeconomic conditions, money and financial markets.[1] Think about the world's money like water in a giant half spherical tank (like a rice bowl without a foot) sitting on a field that represents world markets. Into the tank go the world's savings, and the central banks control the tap that lets the liquidity (monetary savings) go out. The world's investors are like elephants pushing on different sides of the tank of water. If the tank tilts, the water flows out, and in the areas where water flows, the market will rise, whereas in the areas where no water flows, it will be dry and the markets will fall. If a lot of water falls in one spot, there may be a bubble. When one day the investors push in a different direction and another market rises, the old bubble will collapse for lack of liquidity.

Large governments, multinational businesses, banks and fund managers are like the elephants that push all the time in different directions, and small markets and retail investors are like the grass or mouse deer that prosper or suffer when global liquidity rushes in or out. Global markets are also a food chain. When the largest elephant falls or steps into a pond, what are small waves to the elephants are tsunamis to the smaller creatures feeding near the pond.

[1] Faber (2002).

PRACTICAL MEN ...

Before I go further into what and why of the Asian financial crisis, it is perhaps useful to spend a bit of time on the power of economic thought on practical men. Why is it that Asians, and the best minds in the IMF, World Bank and other international financial institutions (IFIs) responsible for global financial stability, were caught like animals transfixed before an oncoming tsunami, or the bright headlights of an oncoming train? Could the crisis have been avoided?

In his famous book that changed the landscape of economic theory and policy in the 1930s, the *General Theory of Employment, Interest and Money*, the English economist Lord Keynes said, 'The ideas of economists and political philosophers, both when they are right and when they are wrong, are more powerful than is commonly understood. Indeed, the world is ruled by little else. Practical men, who believe themselves to be quite exempt from any intellectual influences, are usually the slaves of some defunct economist.'[2]

The Asian financial crisis and the current crises are final proof that we were badly served by flawed economic theory. As I was also trained in that tradition, let me confess that I made the same analytical and judgemental mistakes. What follows is a personal explanation as to what went wrong with our reading of the crisis as it unfolded.

... AND NEO-CLASSICAL FLAWS

The mainstream economic theory, defined as 'the economics one finds in university textbooks, discussed in the news media and referred to in the halls of business and government',[3] preached that governments should get out of business to allow markets to thrive. The more they liberalized, the more the markets will move into stable equilibrium. The naive version of the theory taught that it was the incomplete markets with incomplete information, as well as moral hazard or government intervention, that cause crises and instability. Liberalize, level the playing field and prosperity will come with stability.

In his magnum opus on economic development in South Asia in the 1960s, *Asian Drama*, Swedish economist and Nobel Laureate Gunnar Myrdal had this to say about economists: 'Economic theorists, more than

---

[2]   Keynes (1942) [1936], 383.
[3]   Beinhocker (2006).

other social scientists, have long been disposed to arrive at general propositions and then postulate them as valid for every time, place and culture'.[4] In other words, economic theories are only as good as their assumptions. If the assumptions are false, the conclusions are false. Myrdal pointed out, using the biblical metaphor, that we have *a beam in our eyes*, seeing what we choose to see or what we are trained to see, and we may ignore the most important details.

What had happened is that the rise of economics as a quantitative science had taken the discipline along a route that neglected the institutional underpinning of economic life. By the mid-1970s the ideas of free market monetary economists such as Milton Friedman led to the rejection of Keynesian ideas that governments can fix economic problems. The free market ideas of Friedrich Hayek, implemented through the policies of Margaret Thatcher in the United Kingdom and Ronald Reagan in the United States, became more influential. It was a rejection of government intervention and a glorification of the market.

The ideal of the free market, of course, goes all the way back to 18th-century Scottish philosopher and economist Adam Smith, who expounded that where the entrepreneur 'in such manner as its produce may be of the greatest value, he intends only his own gain, and he is in this, as in many other cases led by an invisible hand to promote an end which was no part of his intention'.[5] In other words, capitalism is the belief that the combined individual acts of greed by market participants end up to create the greatest good.

This naive version of capitalism and free markets was adopted for former Soviet economies when the Berlin Wall fell. As Nobel Laureate Milton Friedman admitted of the disaster, 'What do these ex-communist states have to do in order to become market economies? And I used to say: "You can describe that in three words: privatise, privatise, privatise." But, I was wrong. That wasn't enough. The example of Russia shows that ... the rule of law is probably more basic than privatisation'.[6] It took the collapse of the Soviet Union and hyperinflation to prove that free market dogma was irresponsible and dangerous in the hands of naive policymakers and their advisers who forgot that policies work only with effective institutions. The government has a central role, and it has to function well if markets are to function well. It does take two hands to clap.

---

[4]   Myrdal (1968), 17.
[5]   Smith (1976) [1776], 454.
[6]   See Friedman (1998).

Ironically, the Asian Miracle happened precisely because the government had a large hand in the economy and helped to foster markets where there were none.

It is strange that East Asians who are good at development are not that good at explaining how they do it. So far, there has only been one Asian Nobel Laureate in Economics, Amartya Sen from India. Thus far, no one from East Asia, the region that houses most of the so-called miracle economies, has been able to win a Nobel Prize in economics, despite their success in taking their economies out of poverty.

This does not mean that Asians in general and East Asians in particular are not capable of thinking[7] or undertaking sound theoretical work, because many East Asian economists were trained in the best universities in the West. The fact that Marxian theory was dominant in China, Vietnam and North Korea, and Fabian socialism was highly influential in former British colonies, testifies to the power of Western ideas. Indeed, U.S.-trained academics turned bureaucrats were responsible for much of the successes of the South Korean, Taiwanese and Indonesian economies.

There is, however, a fundamental difference between the East and West in their worldview. Western economists are by and large deductive, trying to construct a theory of the real world through deduction from fundamental principles and making very basic assumptions. East Asians, on the other hand, tend to be more inductive. Perhaps they come from civilizations with a long memory that mistrust bad ideology and bad governance. East Asians tend to trust only things that are proven to work. Indeed, East Asians tended to be bold in their industrial policies and yet curiously conservative in their fiscal and financial policies. By and large, they copied what worked and were more than likely to reject good ideas or bold visions as untested, or rather they would prefer that someone else be the first to try the experiment.

MY PERSONAL JOURNEY IN ECONOMIC DEVELOPMENT

It may be useful to share the evolution of my own thinking about development. I come from a family of refugees from China. I grew up in what was then British North Borneo, one of the most beautiful states in Malaysia, in the shadow of the highest mountain in Southeast Asia, Mount Kinabalu. Sabah, as the state is now known, has some of the best tropical forests and coral reefs in the world. Jesselton, as Kota Kinabalu, the present capital

---

[7]   Mahbubani (1998).

of Sabah, was then called, was a sleepy town of only 10,000 people when we arrived, with one weekly ship from Singapore that brought ice cream. I went to school in one of the first government secondary schools to compete with the missionary schools, the first to provide science classes and chemistry labs. We had English headmasters, Indian chemistry teachers and American-trained Chinese that taught in Borneo only because they sought refuge in a quiet corner of the world. My parents' generation had a sense of failure as they encountered not just the Second World War but also the Chinese Revolution. Since education was the traditional East Asian path out of poverty, they poured their knowledge into the young.

Nineteen of my class of 24 went abroad for further studies, many provided by Colombo Plan scholarships to universities in Kuala Lumpur, Singapore, Australia, New Zealand, Canada and the United Kingdom. A few went off on their own funds to the United States. My classmates went on to become important local politicians, bureaucrats and leading professionals overseas.

I went to England in 1965 and experienced for the first time the intellectual ferment that was going on as Britain shed its role as a dominant colonial power and struggled with the loss of its industrial power to a rising Japan and Germany. We were part of the baby boomer generation of 1968, the hippie generation of the Beatles and flower power who loved protesting against nuclear armament and the Vietnam War. Whilst I was curious about the ideas of Herbert Marcuse and Noam Chomsky, which were the rage at the University of Bristol where I took my first degree, I chose, like 90 percent of my cohort from Asia, to be trained as a lawyer, accountant, engineer or a doctor. Rather than going to London School of Economics to do further research but under a small Bristol University scholarship in 1969, I chose instead to be trained as a chartered accountant in London with Arthur Andersen & Co, then one of the best U.S. accounting firms, which uniquely offered an irresistible six-week training course in Paris as starters. Pragmatism won over idealism.

The idea that one should contribute to nation building did not, however, leave me. After qualification and my return to Malaysia in 1972, I chose to leave a lucrative but boring position in the auditing profession for a job as a senior economist in the Malaysian central bank, Bank Negara Malaysia. I was inspired to join public service by the legendary governor, Tun Ismail Mohd Ali, a Cambridge-educated lawyer and economist who studied under Keynes. Widely respected for his integrity and professionalism, he single-handedly built up a strong institution, gathering around him the best professionals of that generation. He sent one of his most brilliant economists, Tan Sri Dr Lin See Yan, to Harvard University for his doctorate to build up the economic and monetary policy formulation area. Fellow alumni of BNM went on to be major institution builders in Malaysia, providing amongst bankers and others the first Chief Executive of Petronas, the national oil corporation, Cagamas, the national mortgage corporation, and the first Chairman of Permodalan Nasional Berhad, the national investment corporation that today runs one of the largest mutual funds in emerging markets.

The late Tun Ismail not only had a passion for nation building, but he was also committed to regional cooperation. Through his friendship with fellow central bank governors in ASEAN, he helped initiate the first ASEAN swap arrangements and the Southeast Asian Central Banks (SEACEN) Training Centre in Kuala Lumpur.

Through that tutelage, I had first-hand experience with policy formation in emerging markets, working under that illustrious first generation of post-independence Malaysian civil servants, who not only had a national view, but also a good understanding of the impact of the industrial countries on small export-oriented countries like Malaysia. There was an esprit d'corps amongst the civil servants, not only because they were committed to nation-building but also to prove to their former colonial powers that they could run a country as well, if not better, because there was now ownership.

One could almost say that the 1970s and 1980s were a golden age for developing countries in Asia, not only because of their fast growth and economic achievements, but also because of the excellent dialogue with the IMF, World Bank and other First World institutions, such as the BIS. Every year Tun Ismail would attend the IMF/World Bank meetings in Washington, DC, the Commonwealth Central Bank Governors' meeting hosted by the Bank of England in London as well as the BIS Annual Meetings in Basel to ensure that he understood what was happening globally. Regionally there was excellent rapport with fellow central bankers in Southeast Asia, through the SEACEN Centre activities. As Chief Economist at BNM in 1981, I literally grew up learning about monetary policy and financial institutions through regular meetings with fellow Directors of Research from the ASEAN central banks. Many of them rose to become governors, prominent bankers and even Ministers of Finance, some to play crucial roles during the Asian crisis.

Following in Tun Ismail's footsteps and working closely under his successors, Tan Sri Aziz Taha and Tan Sri Jaffar Hussein, both superb chartered accountants, I also became a bank regulator, cutting my teeth in the first serious financial crisis in Malaysia – the failure in 1986 of 24 deposit-taking cooperatives that led to bank runs in some finance companies and banks. It was the wise Tan Sri Aziz Taha who told me that since I was part of the team that devised the tight monetary policies to slow the economy from over-heating in the boom of 1981–1982, it was my job to deal with the banking system before it suffered the consequences of macroeconomic adjustment. That foresight saved the banking system from considerable grief, because we amended the banking law just in time to allow the central bank to inter-vene to prevent bank failure.

In dealing with the failed deposit-taking cooperatives, I had the great fortune to work together with the most dedicated team of colleagues and professionals in BNM, the accounting profession, the police and the Attorney-General's chambers. We initiated a 'war room' to deal quickly and decisively with the bank runs and problems of the failed cooperatives, which had as many as 500,000 depositors. Their failure was essentially one of mismanagement, as a few rapacious entrepreneurs captured the coopera-tive movement and used the resources for their own purposes. One memo-rable element of that episode of what today would be called bad corporate governance was the line 'Never let monkeys look after bananas'. Lessons from an incident involving political negotiation over loss allocation never left me.

Fate was to step in, because Millard Long at the World Bank invited me to join the Bank in 1989 for a sabbatical to do a study of bank failure in the developing world. Millard was a quintessential academic turned develop-ment banker. He was interested in development finance and was shocked to find that the orthodoxy of 'finance for growth' was failing throughout the developing countries. He gathered around him in the Financial Policy and Systems Division of the World Bank a seminal group of academics, bankers, bank supervisors, capital market and pension fund professionals that thought through the lessons of bank failure. This group produced such luminaries in the 'finance for growth' field as Alan Gelb, Jerry Caprio, Ross Levine, Patrick Honohan, Yoon Je Cho, Dimitri Vittas, Aristobulo de Juan and Asli Demirgüç-Kunt.

My contribution to the research effort was my book *Bank Restructuring in the 1980s*, the culmination of travels to more than 24 countries work-ing on financial crises and adjustment programmes from Argentina to Hungary. After succeeding Millard as Division Chief in the Financial Policy and Systems Division of the Bank, I participated in discussions on the famous Asian Miracle study, led by John Page, and the debates on financial reform in the transitional economies, from Hungary to Russia. It was very intellectually rewarding to work with the finest minds in development and financial economics, because Stan Fischer, Larry Summers and Joe Stiglitz all worked during this period as Chief Economist at the World Bank. Stan later moved to the IMF as Deputy Managing Director and is now Governor of the Bank of Israel, whilst Larry became U.S. Treasury Secretary, President of Harvard University and currently Economic Advisor to President Obama. Joe Stiglitz went on to win his Nobel Prize in Economics.

In 1993 fate was to take me to Hong Kong, when founding Chief Executive Joseph Yam hired me as his deputy in the newly established Hong Kong Monetary Authority, Hong Kong's equivalent of a central bank that would be responsible for the tricky but important transition of Hong Kong financial markets in 1997, when Hong Kong's political sovereignty would return to China. It was a dream team – Joseph Yam as Chief Executive, David Carse from the Bank of England as the bank supervisor, and fully backed by Donald Tsang, then the first Hong Kong Chinese to become Financial Secretary. Donald became the Second Chief Executive of the Hong Kong Special Administrative Region in 2005.

After 4½ years in Washington, I was delighted to be back in Asia and participating actively in Asian central banking again, working closely with colleagues from the Bank of Japan in the EMEAP forum and renewing my acquaintances with friends from the ASEAN central banks and reserve banks of Australia and New Zealand.

In the HKMA my education in central banking became complete when I was given the responsibility to manage Hong Kong's external reserves and, through that experience, getting to know fund managers, understanding the need for derivatives to hedge risks and, most of all, beginning to appreciate the power of market forces. As Chairman of the Market Practices Committee in Hong Kong, I worked regularly with the banking and foreign exchange professionals on the intricacies of foreign exchange markets, from trading, clearing and settlement to the importance of market rules and behaviour. From Joseph and other friends in Hong Kong, I learnt not only the wisdom and power of free markets, but also their ferocity and unpredictability.

In the period leading up to 1997, the Japanese actively urged the Asian central banks to make their exchange rates more flexible against the U.S. dollar. It was a message that was not easy to read. First, Japan was the largest economy in Asia, and from a geopolitical point of view, those who suffered during the Second World War were wary of Japanese hegemony through a yen zone. Second, Asians understood that their biggest trading partner was ultimately the United States, and whichever way one calculated the basket of currencies, the U.S. dollar remained the most important international currency for trade and investments. Third, there was reluctance to change the systems that had worked well in the past.

From the risk point of view, it was also difficult to envisage how volatile the foreign exchange markets could be, although the 1994 Mexican crisis had already presaged the dangers of capital flows. I was busy working on Hong Kong market issues, preparing for the volatility that could arise from shocks due to the return of Hong Kong to China. There were enough seminars on the rise of derivative trading strategies and their impact on foreign exchange markets. Given its strong fundamentals, I was more confident that Hong Kong would be able to weather the coming storm.

After talking to my old friends in the regional central banks through the EMEAP network, I had the sense that there was some vulnerability in some countries, but I trusted their judgement and technical abilities. But I had not understood the weaknesses that were hidden by the bubbles that emerged since 1993, or the interconnectivity between Japan and Asia.

When I was appointed Chairman of the Securities and Futures Commission of Hong Kong in October 1998, I entered a whole new world of governance and regulation that I had previously grossly underappreciated. Although I had direct experience as a banking and insurance regulator, and had dealt with the directors of deposit-taking cooperatives, some of whom were linked with criminal activities, I had not realized how complex it was to deal with one of the most active markets in the world.

The Hong Kong stock exchange was run and controlled by over 600 brokers, ranging from the small family firms that are still active as traders in penny stocks to some of the largest investment banks in the world. Behind these financial intermediaries were the listed companies that were run by respectable blue-chip executives, self-made tycoons or flashy characters of dubious integrity. A handful of them had no qualms manipulating the shares of the companies that they controlled. Some of them were, as my Australian colleagues colourfully labelled them, the scumbags of capital markets. It was a journey into the real world of corporate governance. I counted myself lucky to be cursed to be living in interesting times.

This period was particularly interesting because we were witnessing the rise of China and India, approximately 40 percent of mankind, taking them out of poverty.[8] Up until 1979, when China began its journey towards markets, the developing world operated in two worlds, divided by the Cold War and the Iron Curtain. Behind one was central planning and relatively

---

[8] For an excellent overview, see Prestowitz (2005).

closed economies. The other was dominated by the United States, which was rapidly globalizing American values and technology through trade, investments and media.

Once China and the former centrally planned economies decided to join global trade, the whole ballgame changed. At the same time, the confluence of technology, financial engineering, information sciences and demography had changed the landscape of financial markets and the geopolitical economic order. In Hong Kong, a major international financial centre with its free markets and free media, I was lucky to be in the eye of that geopolitical shift. The difficulty was first to recognize that shift and then to change one's own mindset about how to adjust to it.

THEORY AND PRACTICE

It was perhaps the combination of innate conservatism and distrust of markets that caused most Asians not to recognize that the ball game had changed. This was not unique to Asians. Even at a global institution such as the World Bank, which I joined in 1989 just in time to experience the fall of the Berlin Wall, it was very difficult to challenge the institutional orthodoxy.

The World Bank comprised over 10,000 professionals (including full-time consultants), ranging from economists, engineers and sociologists to project planners, former politicians and senior bureaucrats. They comprised some of the finest minds in the world, with the best country experiences. I learnt a lot because within the Bank I could always find someone who was a specialist in a field, from the most obscure to the most profound. Being essentially a democratic organization that was a development institution with an academic bent, as the President of the Bank was always an American, the Bank encouraged free intellectual debate. It was stimulating and mentally invigorating, but trying to reach consensus from opposing views, elegantly argued, meant the preparation of member country reports became in the end a drafting exercise. The compromises and recommendations covered everything under the sun, with lots of technical advice that would have been possible under perfect conditions but was, in many cases, difficult if not impossible to implement bureaucratically or politically. Intellectual perfectionism became enemy of the good. There was lots of wishful thinking and less prioritization of what could realistically be implemented in stages. Very often, much of the macroeconomic advice did not take into consideration what was really happening on the ground, partly because it was almost impossible to reconcile ground-level reality with the politics of large bureaucracies. The end product was not necessarily what happened on the ground but country reports that were drafting compromises of different views that ended up being far too complex for many developing countries to implement fully.

One of the oddities of the Bank as a development institution was the anomaly that it preached free markets, but there were few professionals with strong financial market experience in the front line. It was not as if the Bank did not have strong market professionals who managed the Bank's own liquidity and investments. But that group of professionals was not part of the inner circle of theoreticians that dominated policy formulation at the Bank. The finance group gave good technical assistance on reserves and debt management to member country central banks, but that was the limit of their policy advice. In the finance area, the IMF then was dominated by macroeconomists who had even less experience in financial markets, an issue that was not resolved until the creation of the capital markets group after the Asian crisis.

To me, the frustrating part was that most of the people working in these institutions were dedicated professionals who personally cared a lot about development issues and devoted their entire lives to trying to fight inequality and poverty. Many preferred to work in the field, rather than fighting bureaucracy in Washington. I was always amazed that such dedication always seemed to cancel the various attributes out, so that good ideals came out with weak execution or even huge inertia.

The simple reason why the Bank was lesser than the sum of the whole was because large bureaucracies operate with an institutional orthodoxy that is always difficult to change. Because the Bank was involved in 150 plus countries, it was nearly impossible to arrive at 'one size fit all' solutions, but the broad orthodoxy was the neoclassical theory that bureaucrats fell back on during uncertainty. Free markets, small governments and good macro-policies were the 'mother's pie' mantras that were difficult to refute logically.

Unfortunately, sometime in its history, the Bank had decided that politics was too sensitive to deal with and that the Bank's job was to lend for development. Hence, the real problems of governance, private or public, were neglected, or it was assumed that they would be taken care of by the United Nations or elsewhere, whilst the Bank focused on lending. Initially the Bank lent through clones of itself around the world, and development banks were created all over the world in the same way that it is a must for a developing country to have a brand new airport. This carried on for nearly 30 years until the end of the 1980s, when Millard Long did some checking on the ground and found that not only were most development banks in developing countries bust because of nonperforming loans, but the commercial banking systems in many countries were also in crisis.

When I landed in Buenos Aires in 1989 as part of the Bank team to look at the Argentinean crisis, it did not take me long to figure out, even though I did not speak Spanish, that the banking system there was in deep trouble. This was basically because inflation was an accepted way of life to reduce one's real debt. Until inflation was removed from the mindset, it was difficult to create sound banks. Similarly, when I worked on the Kenyan banking system in 1990, I quickly came to the conclusion that we were really dealing not with a banking crisis, but a crisis of politics. Since the previous Kenyatta regime had dished out a number of bank licenses to its supporters who treated the banks like their ATM cash boxes to fund their political activities, no one should have been surprised that these banks would fail over time. An interesting by-product of that work in Nairobi was the opportunity to meet Peter Eigen, then resident director of the Bank in Kenya, who left the Bank and founded Transparency International. Thus, he created a successful NGO to deal with governance and corruption issues in development, which the Bank could not then confront officially.

I soon came to realize that many professionals in the Bank or Fund in Washington also had a 'silver bullet' mindset, meaning that they were unconsciously driven to find elegant, simple solutions to complex and messy problems in the real world. The IMF technocrats were terrific technicians, and their worldview was blinkered with their 'two-gap' models, finding all the ills in either a fiscal gap (too much government spending) or a balance of payments gap (current account deficit). The remedy was simple: cut government expenditure, raise taxes, devalue, raise interest rates and lend in the short term. The World Bank could not argue with the Fund on the latter's turf, and instead devoted its energy to infrastructure projects or projects that allowed the Bank to meet its lending targets. This did not avoid much of the bureaucratic in-fighting over many of the country programmes.

The Bretton Wood institutions, the IMF and the World Bank, were in essence lending machines, founded in 1946 on the intuitively right but simplistic idea that the developing world was short of funds, and therefore their fundamental tool was the power to lend or withdraw funds. The funding gap was, of course, true immediately after the Second World War when many countries suffered foreign exchange shortage. But the whole theory of economic development cannot be blind to the fact that in most developing parts of the world, many countries were rich in natural resources, human talent and opportunities. It was never about the shortage of money or savings, but the quality of governance that differentiated the rich from the poor. South Korea is perhaps the best example of strong governance that dragged the country from rags to riches, whereas Myanmar went from one of the richest and well-educated countries in Asia in the 1950s to become one of the poorest in the region.

To put it bluntly, I came to the realization that the neoclassical framework was an excellent excuse for the Bretton Wood bureaucracies to concentrate on coming up with country strategies and macroeconomic policies, because it was so much easier to talk about policies in air-conditioned comfort. The real world outside was much more messy and complicated. During the period when developing economy technocrats were still grappling with the challenges of development and the daily grind of being underpaid, underresourced and fighting vested interests all the way, what the Bretton Wood institutions offered was both intellectual comfort and logic. In truth, the institutional context of development was intrinsically hard and unrewarding, if not dirty work. This was not to deny that many Bretton Wood bureaucrats were dedicated idealists who cared personally and passionately about development.

The incentive structure of bureaucracies therefore caused many economists to see policy as an end in itself, spending considerable time figuring out what is the right policy, forgetting that the best policy is the one that can actually be implemented. Moreover, without the right institutional framework, many ideal policies cannot be implemented at all, or, at least, implemented with tragic results.

Institutional reform is hard because no one likes to have to sack people, with all the bureaucratic in-fighting, cleaning up of corruption and confronting powerful vested interests. The refusal to deal with the hard problems of governance and politics was like the psychoanalyst's favourite tool of 'the elephant in the room'. We always like to deal with the easy things first, rather than tackling head-on the hard part. To his credit, Jim Wolfensohn, the former President of World Bank, was perceptive in pointing out corruption as the real issue confronting the Bank and development, but he was not able to convince his bureaucracy how to institutionally confront bad governance.

Fortunately, there is an emerging body of work in behavioural economics and institutional research that is much more realistic and pragmatic. Thanks to the pioneering work of Nobel Laureate Douglass North and others, the new institutional economics is beginning to integrate various disciplines of physical and social sciences to try and explain complex systems and their behaviour.

Nobel Laureate Kenneth Arrow, who was responsible for much of the theoretically underpinning of neoclassical theory, has undertaken work on the logic and agenda of organizations that have only recently been taken more seriously.[9] Arrow also recognized that information or knowledge is like a fixed capital investment, with depreciating value. Once codes or knowledge is acquired, it is very costly to shift to another code or institutional process or system. This explains the innate conservatism of institutions.

As North explained in his work *Understanding the Process of Economic Change*, 'It is the complex interplay between the stock of knowledge, institutions, and demographic factors that shapes the process of economic change.'[10] Further, 'The key to understanding the process of change is the intentionality of the players enacting institutional change and their comprehension of the issues'.[11]

THE BEAM IN OUR EYES

To sum up, the Asian crisis was a tragedy that was perhaps inevitable. It was not just the fact that concrete conditions were ripe for a crisis, but how Asians, their advisers in Washington and market participants reacted to the crisis depended very much on their perception and response as well as 'reflexivity' of action and counter-action with each other. That perception, or the beam in our eyes, was coloured by our individual and collective education and our experience. And if we misread the situation, we could neither prevent the crisis nor mitigate it. Indeed, our misreading could exacerbate the crisis.

For bureaucrats who have to deal with daily problems, trust in the invisible hand generated an inherently passive strategy. If markets will adjust to some stable equilibrium level, then we need not act (read 'intervene'). The greatest hazard of neoclassical thinking is to believe that in the long run the market will always correct. As Lord Keynes aptly quipped, 'In the long run, we are all dead'.

The other problem with modern education and technical training is that we have created silos of specialists, each arguing with each other from their own specialization and narrow points of view. Perhaps we should go back to history and philosophy as it was taught in the days of Aristotle and Sun-tzu, a more panoramic view of global and local events and trends, as well as the failings of human beings and their institutions.

---

[9] Arrow (1974).
[10] North (2005b), 78.
[11] North 2005b, 3.

By virtue of their success, Asians developed beams in their eyes that blinded them to pitfalls in their road to globalization. They stuck to tried and tested ways, hoping against hope that government intervention and the model of imbalanced growth that worked before would work again.

Nowhere was this more obvious than in Japan. Even stalwarts such as Mr Yen, Eisuke Sakikabara, have been frustrated enough with Asian inertia to say that 'it is not simply that macro policies and financial supervision have failed the economy, but rather that the whole structure or institution has become dysfunctional'.[12]

The history of East Asia has been one of huge cycles of growth and decay. Chinese historians remember all too well that the dilemma of a large central kingdom was either internal corruption or external invasion. Bureaucrats with deep institutional memory understood that internal dissension created gridlocks that could not be resolved without external pressure. But as Asians became wealthier, vested interests demanded more and more protection of the status quo. Unfortunately, the advance of technology and global competition meant that the status quo was no longer viable. As always, the greatest threat to change is a closed mind.

Failure to understand this was to have very costly consequences, particularly on the banking system, which will be discussed in the next chapter.

[12] Sakakibara (2003), xi.

FOUR

Banking: The Weakest Link

One thing is certain, that at particular times a great of deal of stupid people have a great deal of stupid money. ... At intervals, from causes which are not to the present purpose, the money of these people – the blind capital, as we call it, of the country – is particularly large and craving; it seeks for someone to devour it, and there is a 'plethora'; it finds someone, and there is 'speculation'; it is devoured, and there is 'panic'.
~ Walter Bagehot, Essay on Edward Gibbon

Was the Asian crisis a classic currency crisis or was it a banking crisis? Currency crises are about flight of capital, both domestic and foreign, and they arise because central banks do not have enough foreign currency to defend their national exchange rate. Nobel Laureate Paul Krugman was amongst the first to question the validity of the Asian Miracle by asserting that Asian growth was more a product of perspiration than inspiration. In January 1998[1] he was also amongst the first to point out that any analysis of the Asian crisis 'needs to focus on two issues normally neglected in currency crisis analysis: the role of financial intermediaries (and of the moral hazard associated with such intermediaries when they are poorly regulated), and the prices of real assets such as capital and land'. In other words, the Asian crisis was a banking crisis on top of the currency crisis, where asset bubbles and moral hazard played important roles. This is also true for the current crisis.

MANIAS, PANICS AND CRASHES

The Asian crisis confirmed Charles Kindleberger's dictum that financial crisis is a hardy perennial.[2] The Kindleberger classic on financial manias,

[1]   Krugman (1998a).
[2]   Kindleberger (1996) [1978].

panics and crashes, recommended reading for all Finance 101 courses, noted in the first half of the 19th century the spacing of crises 10 years apart (1816, 1826, 1837, 1847, 1857 and 1866). Towards the end of the 20th century and going into the 21st century, we are witnessing three crises 10 years apart – the stock market crash of 1987, the Asian crisis of 1997 and the subprime crisis of 2007–2008.

History often repeats itself, although in different forms. Financial crises in the first half of the 20th century stemmed not just from banking problems on both sides of the Atlantic, but also from the gradual replacement of gold, and then sterling, by the U.S. dollar as the key global currency. Just as Kindleberger presciently pointed out that financial crises have international origins and connections, one could easily hypothesize that the Asian crisis was a precursor to a larger crisis in the U.S. dollar as the preeminent sovereign currency. But analysis of that hypothesis would have to await a later chapter.

The Asian crisis followed the topography of a Minsky-Kindleberger model of financial crisis that goes through roughly five stages – displacement, monetary expansion, overtrading, revulsion and discredit.[3] Stage one, displacement, is an exogenous or outside shock to the macroeconomic system. This changes the outlook, increasing opportunity for profits, and a boom is underway. The boom and optimism spreads to the banking system, which begins to lend. The credit expansion is not just through the banking system but through financial innovation that encourages leverage, increasing profits as well as risks. Stage two of monetary expansion gives way to the third stage of overtrading, when borrowers begin to speculate and 'euphoria' begins.

Minsky identified three types of debt financing – hedge, speculative and Ponzi financing. Hedge financing is when a firm borrows against relatively assured cash flow. This is self-financing and generally stable. Speculative financing is defined as borrowing when cash flow is uncertain and the firm depends on renewal of old debt or new sources. Risks increase but are manageable under normal circumstances. Ponzi financing is defined as a situation 'in which debt can be paid off only if the firm succeeds in selling an asset at an appreciated price'.[4] This smacks of fraud and desperation and usually comes to grief. The irony is that at or near the top of the boom, irrational exuberance and greed are such that hardly anyone questions Ponzi financing behaviour when it emerges.

[3] Kindleberger (1996) [1978], 17.
[4] Minsky (1982).

Ponzi schemes deserve much more academic study because they work on crowd behaviour of pyramiding. They are momentum trades, in which the earlier players are attracted by greed, but it stops when the perpetrator can no longer continue the game, either because he finds it harder and harder to find new suckers or because they wise up to the fraud and he has to exit before then.

In the fourth stage, the market begins to top, smart money cashes out and there is a period of 'financial distress'. Investors and creditors show uneasiness that some of the overtrading firms or financial institutions will fail, and when they do, everyone tries to rush out the door. Prices decline, revulsion occurs and illiquidity is the order of the day. Discredit occurs when even supposedly blue-chip institutions begin to lose their reputation, as stories of fraud and misfeasance emerge. In the fifth and final stage, there may be panic that feeds on itself, so that normal conditions are restored only when either prices fall so low that buying returns or a lender of last resort convinces the market that liquidity will be available to meet normal cash flow.

Astute readers will note that the boom-bust cycle always starts with a bubble, defined by Kindleberger as an upward price movement over an extended period that then implodes. In the Asian crisis the bubble in East Asia began with the Japanese bubble of 1989–1990. In the current subprime crisis, the worldwide dot.com bubble of 2000 preceded the housing bubble of 2003–2006. In each bubble, bank credit expansion played a major role.

But what was the displacement in the 1980s that created the Japanese bubble in the first place? Some would argue excessive appreciation of the yen arising from the famous Plaza Accord of September 1985. Others feel that long periods of prosperity and low interest rates led Japan to forget its traditional prudence and go on a spending spree. Nothing succeeds like excess, nor fails so catastrophically.

We can therefore see how loose monetary policies, excessive global liquidity and low interest rates create bubble conditions. But at the core of the financial bubble lies the banking system.

A BRIEF HISTORY OF BANKING IN ASIA

Modern banking was not an Asian invention, even though the Chinese invented paper money in the 1st century A.D. Instead, commercial banking arrived in Asia with Western trade and colonialism.

To understand Asian banking, one has to appreciate that Asians basically viewed banking as a tool to serve national economic development. Early

Asian reformers saw banks as mobilizers of savings to be controlled, guided or even nationalized to ensure that scarce funds were channelled towards financing industrialization and export trade. Asian elites understood the importance of banking to politics and business, and banking licenses remained highly coveted and protected. Many Asian conglomerates started with banks as part of their private cash machine or were financed heavily by the banking system.

Over time, however, the smartest of the tycoons understood that to own a bank was a chink in their corporate armour. The richest Hong Kong tycoons, for example, rarely owned banks, having learned the lesson in the 1980s that owning banks during financial crises was a liability, not an asset. They understood that if they owed the bank billions, it would be the bank that would be held ransom, rather than themselves as borrowers.

Nevertheless, the mindset of banks as private or public jewels in the crown did not change even as Asian economies became industrialized. The price was a model of growth that was basically imbalanced. Long-term investments were funded not by long-term capital markets but by banking systems that relied on short-term bank deposits. Bank financing was cheap and convenient, especially if the elites controlled the banks, but it was flawed.

Commercial banking evolved in Western Europe and underwent a number of crises before the authorities figured out its strengths and weaknesses. Early on, Western capitalism understood that efficient banking or financial systems can support growth, but the health of the banks depends ultimately on the health of the real sector. Banks cannot completely cushion themselves from problems in the real sector, but as the Asian crisis has shown, they can amplify real sector weaknesses.

Banks have three structural characteristics. First, they operate the savings, credit and payment systems, which are networks and therefore vulnerable to contagion that spreads through the network. They provide a crucial public good or utility, the failure of which could have systemic or catastrophic consequences. Second, they are notoriously opaque because their main assets are loans to diverse borrowers, and they are also privy to confidential credit and deposit information. Third, they run a fundamental maturity mismatch, with short-term deposits funding long-term loans.

All three characteristics make banks vulnerable to runs. Since depositors do not have sufficient information to be aware of large banking losses, they are prone to withdraw their deposits at the slightest hint that the banks may fail. In the 19th century and as late as the 1930s, widespread bank runs caused large-scale bank failures in Europe and the United States before the emergence of central banks as lenders of last resort, stringent bank supervision rules and deposit insurance stabilized the banking system.

The shape of Asian banking was formed by competition between three major groups of banks – foreign banks, domestic indigenous or family-owned banks and government-owned or -controlled banks.[5]

Three major observations may be made in relation to the region's banking landscape in the prewar colonial era. First, foreign banks in Asia that initially dominated the financial sector were geared more towards international trade than to domestic financing needs. These banks were part of the colonial trading system that recycled liquidity from colonies which supplied commodities to the 'mother country', which in turn reexported manufactures to the colonies. Any colonial balance of payments surplus was reinvested in the London, Paris or New York capital markets, in the form of gilts or bonds. That liquidity was recycled back to Asia in the form of long-term bonds, colonial loans and foreign investments in manufacturing, agriculture, mines and trading companies. Liquid assets were invested largely in silver, gold, sterling bonds or deposits with other foreign banks.

Thus, British banks such as Hong Kong and Shanghai Banking Corporation and Chartered Bank followed the colonial trade and had branches from the Middle East and India to Shanghai. French banks were dominant in Indochina, and Dutch banks were dominant in Indonesia. Citibank has operated in Asia for more than 100 years, with branches in the key trade ports and the Philippines, which was an American colony.

Second, before 1950 domestic indigenous banks tended to be small relative to the foreign banks, as local entrepreneurs lacked capital and foreign exchange to compete. In China, for example, the moneychangers that flourished in the 19th century collapsed when state-owned banks were created around the turn of the 20th century. Japanese banks tended to evolve with their clan industry groups, and several large banks emerged as core institutions within these groups, such as Mitsubishi, Sumitomo, Mitsui and others. They had the support of the Japanese government, particularly in the financing of foreign trade and industrial investment lending.

Third, bitter rivalry existed between 'native' banks and foreign banks. Native banks, despite their local knowledge, were unable to compete with foreign banks that had superior capital, market information and human skills. Much of the rivalry that took place dates back to the 1930s when foreign banks dominated the trade and bills exchange business. In 1934–1935 the sharp rise in silver prices caused monetary deflation in China, where

---

[5] Goodstadt (2007).

silver was still the official currency. The role of the foreign banks in that crisis, and the failure of native banks had some enduring impact on negative local attitudes towards Western banks.[6]

Asia's banking landscape began to gradually change in the postwar period in three major ways. First, nationalist financial systems emerged to serve the national interest. Many foreign- and family-owned banks were nationalized in Burma, India, China, Indonesia and Vietnam, whilst state-owned banks were established in Malaysia, Singapore and Thailand, giving the state control over financial resources to implement the national policy of 'planned catching-up development'.

Second, although there was no deliberate policy to imitate the Japanese model, banking in Asia by and large followed the Japanese mercantilist model. This model operated on 'mild financial repression', which used the domestic banking system to provide subsidized or low-cost financing to domestic industries and services engaged in competitive manufacturing export sectors.[7] The banks paid positive real deposit rates, and Asian banks benefited from the foreign exchange business. Communist China and Vietnam followed the Russian model with a monobank model, based on a single central or commercial bank and a foreign trade bank.

By and large the Japanese financing model led to bank-dominated financial systems throughout East Asia (Table 4.1). The banking systems were also highly concentrated, with total resources held by a handful of large banks. In 1997 nine city banks, one Post Office Bank, and 129 regional banks accounted for 85 percent of Japanese bank assets. The Japanese system was also unique in that it operated a 'main-bank system', described in Chapter 2.

Third, family-owned or private sector banks were established by local tycoons or grew out of clan business networks throughout Asia. Early entrepreneurs all sought to have banks in their networks, because growth depended on scarce financing. Unfortunately, in the days before formal bank supervision, there was no law banning bankers from being borrowers at the same time. For every good banker, there was always the bad one, especially if he was also the bad borrower.

As former Filipino central banker Gregario Licaros insightfully pointed out in the 1970s, 'The average Filipino banker is in banking not for banking profits; he uses his bank for allied purposes'.[8] Although most thought that

---

[6] I am grateful to an anonymous referee for this point. For a history of the silver crisis, see Einzig (1935).

[7] World Bank (1993).

[8] Quoted by Studwell (2007), 103, originally quoted in the *Far Eastern Economic Review* (1978).

Table 4.1. *Selected Asian Economies: Financial Structure (% of GDP)*

	Bank Assets[1]		Equity Market[2]		Bond Market[3]		Insurance Market[4]	
	1990	2006	1990	2007	1990	2005	1990	2005
Japan	226.8	154.7	122.6	106.4	86.4	191.5	8.5	10.6
China	100.3	165.1	2.4[6]	137.8	5.9	34.1	0.8	2.7
Hong Kong	145.6[5]	156.1	105.2	1,284.1	1.5	27.7	3.0[6]	9.9
Indonesia	41.9	32.9	4.5	48.9	0.1[5]	20.3	0.9	1.5
Malaysia	103.0	117.4	100.7	174.4	69.9	90.5	3.0	5.6
Philippines	23.4	40.3	20.6	71.5	25.8	38.9	2.0	1.5
Singapore	89.0	114.8	95.9	334.2	27.7	57.8	3.0	8.8
South Korea	50.7	101.6	48.2	117.3	44.3	102.0	11.0	10.5
Taiwan	–	236.4	104.6	173.2	16.6	55.9	–	14.2
Thailand	84.6	99.0	29.2	80.2	9.8	41.3	1.7	3.6
Memo items								
Germany	109.6[6]	133.2	21.2	63.4	50.4	75.7	5.7	7.1
United States	62.3	62.8	57.5	143.9	121.7	160.8	8.3	9.2

Sources: Central Bank of the Republic of China (Taiwan), World Federation of Exchanges, Beck, Demirgüç-Kunt and Levine (2000), revised 13 August 2007 and author's estimates

[1] Deposit money bank assets
[2] Stock market capitalization
[3] Public and private bond market capitalization
[4] Life and non-life insurance volume
[5] 1991 data
[6] 1992 data

Dash means data not available

banks were cheap sources of funds, the more voracious of local bankers made fortunes by treating banks as opportunities to prey on those of their borrowers who had fallen on bad times. Good assets during hard times were bought up cheaply by the banker for his own account, usually with funding by the bank. The colourful story of how Asian tycoons emerged, their financing by local and foreign banks and their interrelationship with politics has recently been told by Joe Studwell and will not be repeated here.[9]

Not all family-controlled banks were bad. Some of these banks used outside professional talent and became the largest banks nationally, but their scale rarely reached regional or international status. Others fell by the wayside or were merged into larger entities when their family members running the banks were incompetent and made bad banking judgements. The consolidation of family-based banks into larger banks became more obvious after the Asian crisis. In Malaysia, for example, out of nearly 40 Chinese-owned banks or finance companies that existed in the 1970s, only two family-owned banks survive today.

Fourth, in some countries state-owned or -controlled banks competed actively with family-owned and foreign banks for the share of business. The record of state-owned banks, unfortunately, has not been good. The Singapore government-sponsored bank, DBS (formerly the Development Bank of Singapore), remains highly successful. However, it is an exception rather than the rule. Instead, a number of Southeast Asian state-owned banks have had to be rescued several times during the last two decades. State-owned banks tended to be subject to more political influence and weakly managed because their managers were badly paid.

In fact, in the 1970s to mid-1980s, many Asian banks, especially the state-owned or -controlled ones, still practiced priority lending, namely, policy-directed credit policies that channelled lending to industrialization, trade financing and social development. For example, before its privatization in the 1980s, South Korea had a government-controlled banking system that essentially channelled consumer savings to fund the industrial program led by a handful of industrial groups or *chaebol* that were the rough equivalent of Japanese *keiretsu*. These banks financed essentially 60 institutions, of which 30 were family-owned *chaebol* and another 30-odd state-owned giants, mainly in the utilities or infrastructure area. Eight large banks accounted for roughly 75 percent of total banking loans in South Korea.

Only when the middle class emerged in the mid-1980s did many banks follow Citibank's lead in moving towards consumer credit. Some state-owned

[9] Studwell (2007).

banks became important housing and infrastructure finance institutions. Policy-based lending retarded development in the equity and bond markets because 'planners' were more inclined to be exercising control over bank lending than developing capital markets as the engine of growth. Indeed, bond financing was not a priority, because emerging Asia had a young population and rising household savings and enjoyed overall fiscal surpluses. Retirement funds were mainly state sponsored, and given the young population, these funds were normally used to finance fiscal needs. The insurance sector comprised mainly state and foreign firms. The securities markets tended to be speculative, which reinforced ownership and control by the ruling elites.

Today, despite some progress, Asia is still dependent on bank financing (Table 4.1). Can this be sustained? My personal view is that Asia's present imbalanced growth and funding strategy is increasingly unsustainable in a globalized environment. Bluntly speaking, the Asian crisis marked the failure of the 'finance for development or growth' strategy.

ASIA'S CHANGING DEMOGRAPHIC ENDOWMENT

To understand why the bank-dominant system has to change, one needs to understand the changing structure of the East Asian economies. Asian economies started with many advantages: low wage and surplus labour, stable political environment with an educated elite, high savings rate, prudent fiscal management and a friendly global environment with declining trade barriers which gave East Asia huge export opportunities. Most economic analysts missed the important demographic endowment of a young labour force in the post–Second World War period (Figure 4.1).

Having suffered large population losses in the Second World War, there was a large birth 'bulge' after the war, so that from roughly 1945 to 1980 there was a period of 'youth demographic burden' when the Asian economies had to import savings, as there was a huge need for infrastructure development and imports of machinery and technology. As the labour force came of age, their productivity increased substantially because the openness to foreign trade and investment meant that Asian economies were able to exploit their cheap labour and access modern technology and management skills. The blend of stable government, commitment to prudent fiscal policies and a strong commitment to education and good social infrastructure meant that Asian economies began to enjoy high growth and high savings.

As explained in Chapter 2, the dualist mercantilist model with a highly efficient export sector financed by protected services sectors was flawed. The shortage of savings in the early period of development created a

Growth rate of real GDP per capita

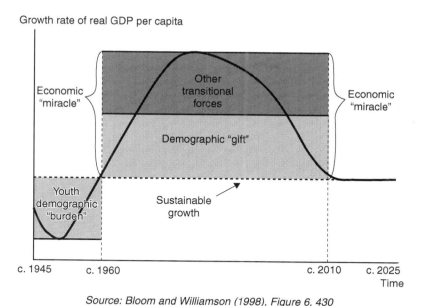

Source: Bloom and Williamson (1998), Figure 6, 430

Figure 4.1. Stylised Model of Economic Growth and Demographic Transition in East Asia, 1945–2025

deeply ingrained 'fish-trap' mindset that welcomes the inflow of capital (FDI and FPI) but restricts or delays the outflow of capital by imposing capital controls or liberalizing very slowly capital account transactions by its residents.

This model of development focused on the banking system as the dominant channel of finance, and less on the capacity of the capital markets to manage risks for corporations and investors alike. Unfortunately, if there were flaws in the banking system, these weaknesses would extract a high cost that may have to be borne in later generations.

We now review these inherent weaknesses of the Asian banking system, relative to their key functions.

FUNCTIONS OF FINANCIAL SYSTEMS

Financial systems have essentially four major functions: resource allocation, price discovery, risk management and corporate governance. The Asian crisis was an excellent example of how these four functions were not performing well in Asian markets.

Table 4.2. *Selected Asian Economies: Pre-crisis Conditions of Banking Sector, 1997*

Item	Indonesia	Malaysia	Philippines	South Korea	Thailand
Major financial institutions (early 1997)	228 banks 10 foreign banks	35 banks 39 finance companies 7 discount houses 13 foreign banks	53 commercial banks 117 thrift banks	26 commercial banks 30 merchant banks 52 foreign banks	15 banks 91 finance companies 14 foreign banks
Capital adequacy ratio	8% target 87% of banks complied	8% target 11.4% actual average	10% target 16.0% actual average	8% 7.3% actual average	8.5% target 9.8% actual average
Banking sector profitability (1996)	1.2% ROA 16.3% ROE	1.2% ROA 18.4% ROE	2.1% ROA 16.3% ROE	0.2% ROA 4.5% ROE	1.1% ROA 12.9% ROE
Interest rate spread[1]	1.8%	1.8%	6.1%	1.1%	3.1%
NPL (% of total loans) (end 1997)	7.2%	4.1%	4.7%	6.0%	22.6%
Foreign liabilities of banks (% of total liabilities)	15.0%	7.4%	31.5%	55.2%	27.4%
Loans (% of GDP)	60.0%	152.0%	65.0%	87.3%	150.0%
Corporate debt (1998)	US$118.0 billion	US$120.2 billion	US$47.5 billion	US$444.0 billion	US$195.7 billion
Bankruptcy law	Outdated, 1908	Modern	Outdated	Modern	Outdated, 1940
Deposit insurance (guarantee)	None (explicitly unlimited in Jan. 1998)	None (unconditional and unlimited in Jan. 1998)	Yes	Yes (explicitly unlimited and unconditional in Nov. 1997)	None (explicitly unlimited in Aug. 1997)

Sources: World Bank, ADB (2000), Kawai (2002) and Delhaise (1998)

[1] Interest Rate Spread = Lending Rates – Deposit Rates

NPL = nonperforming loans; ROA = return on assets; ROE = return on equity

Broadly speaking, most developing countries have bank-dominated financial systems, but as they mature, they will need a full range of money, equity, debt and derivative markets, as well as a complete spectrum of institutional and financial services to meet the needs of a modern economy. By and large, other than perhaps Hong Kong and Singapore, which are still relatively small compared with London and New York as international financial centres, the other Asian financial centres function primarily as domestic financial centres. Table 4.2 illustrates the conditions of the banking sectors in the five worst crisis-hit economies in or around 1997.

Resource Allocation

The Asian 'finance for growth' policy meant that resource allocation had for a long time been 'policy or state-directed', whereby the protected banking system channels resources to 'priority sectors' such as exports, industrialization and infrastructure. In a study by Chun Chang,[10] for example, family-controlled conglomerate or *chaebol*, used as vehicles of Korean export industrialisation policy, enjoyed negative real interest rates or below curb market rates of 40 percent in the 1960s and 1970s. The highly diversified structure of *chaebol* included unrelated industries. Profitable affiliates extended loans to loss-making affiliates to keep the entire group afloat. Gains were privatized and losses were socialized, because the state either bailed the banks out or directly bailed the conglomerates out. It was a cosy but effective triad between state, banks and conglomerates.

Because banks were the primary source of funding, they became 'captive sources' that had negative but mutually reinforcing consequences. First, the more the banks supplied credit to the larger borrowers, the more they lost their capacity to evaluate the quality of projects objectively. Their borrowers became 'too large to fail', and therefore banks lost the incentive to develop a strong independent credit culture. They stuck with bad projects and bad corporations through thick and thin, resulting in large NPLs. When five of the 30 largest *chaebol* went bankrupt before the crisis hit South Korea, their bad loans amounted to almost two-thirds of the total capital of Korean commercial banks.[11]

The 'finance for growth' policy in essence gave preference to the interest of enterprises over that of savers. But economic rents create vested interests that become hard to remove.

---

[10] Chun Chang (2000).
[11] Lee (2000).

Table 4.3. *Selected Asian Economies: Cost of Crisis in the 1990s*

Economy	Systemic Banking Crisis (Starting Date)	Nonperforming Loans[1] (% of Total Loans)	Gross Fiscal Cost of Crisis[2] (% of GDP)	Lowest Real GDP Growth Rate during Crisis (%)	Estimated Output Loss[3] (% of GDP)
Japan	1997	35.0	24.0	–2.0	17.6
China	1998	20.0	18.0	+7.6	36.8
Hong Kong	1997	5.3	Nonsystemic banking crisis. One large investment bank failed in 1998.	–5.5	–
Indonesia	1997	32.5	56.8	–13.1	67.9
Malaysia	1997	30.0	16.4	–7.4	50.0
Philippines	1997	20.0	13.2	–0.6	n.a.
South Korea	1997	35.0	31.2	–6.9	50.1
Thailand	1997	33.0	43.8	–10.5	97.7
Memo items					
United States	1988	4.1	3.7	–0.2	4.1
Sweden	1991	13.0	3.6	–1.2	30.6

Source: Laevan and Valencia (2008) and HKMA

[1] At peak

[2] Fiscal cost is the cost to the government of paying depositors or other debtors or nationalized debt and recapitalization of banks

[3] IMF's definition of the term

Dash means data not available

Second, since banks were the most important sources of public savings, they themselves became 'too large to fail' from a public policy point of view. Before the Asian crisis, of the five worst crisis-hit Asian nations, only the Philippines and South Korea had explicit deposit insurance schemes.

However, the moral hazard of governments standing implicitly behind banks meant that banks undertook risks that would not have existed without such backing. There is truth in the view that ownership creates responsibility. Under the laissez-faire philosophy of the colonial Hong Kong government in the 1980s, there was no certainty that the Hong Kong government would support banks in Hong Kong.[12] As the main clearing bank and note-issuing bank in Hong Kong, the Hong Kong and Shanghai Banking Corporation behaved like a central bank and maintained very careful credit and liquidity standards because it realized that its dominant position gave it extra responsibilities during times of financial instability. The private-owned banks without explicit deposit insurance understood that to survive crises they needed to take more prudent measures than state-owned bank managers who could always rely on the state to bail them out of their mistakes.

The cost of bad resource allocation in Asia has been enormous. The fiscal costs of resolution of NPLs in Asia, for instance, ranged from 13.2 percent in the Philippines to as high as 56.8 percent in Indonesia (Table 4.3), representing a huge waste of national savings. Ultimately these losses were borne by savers through growing public sector debt burden, future taxation, higher inflation or lower interest rates. In other words, the savers and taxpayers ultimately pay for the policy mistakes and excessive debt of the corporate sector.

Price Discovery

Asia generally maintains openness to trade, thus enjoying traded goods at competitive global prices. Hence, there has been generally little consumer price inflation in Asia. But capital controls and supply distortions associated with lending and listing rules have distorted key financial prices. Thus, prices of bonds and equity, for instance, often do not reflect true market supply and demand forces partially because of shortages of quality assets relative to demand as well as demand restrictions due to exchange controls that restrict investing abroad or portfolio restrictions on pension and other funds that prevent asset diversification.[13]

[12] For an excellent history of banks in Hong Kong, see Goodstadt (2007).
[13] See Cabellero (2006).

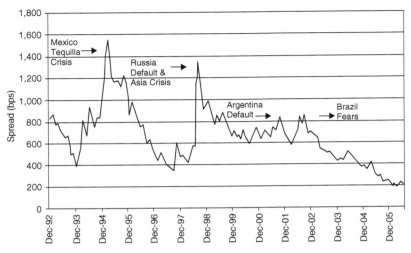

Source: Sargen (2006) based on JP Morgan's Emerging Market Bond Index (EMBI) data
EMBI spread through 1997; EMBI Global spread thereafter

	1990	1991	1992	1993	1994	1995	1996	1997	1998	1999	2000	2001	2002	2003	2004	2005	2006
EMBI + spread in basis points	1,111	631	831	396	1,039	1,044	537	510	1,151	824	756	731	765	418	351	244	171

Source: IMF
Figures for table are based on end-of-period data

EMBI spread through 1996; EMBI + spread through 1999; EMBI Global thereafter
JP Morgan Emerging Market Bond Indices are popular benchmarks for money managers who deal with emerging market debt

Figure 4.2. Emerging Market Credit Spreads, 1990–2006

The cost of such mispricing of risks in financial assets is that many Asian economies still plough huge amounts into fixed investments and real estate that yield low returns. For example, Asian bank spreads[14] of 1.5 to 2 percent when NPLs are running at levels of over 10 percent of total assets mean that many banks are inherently not pricing risks adequately. Furthermore, bond spreads have also recovered close to or below pre-Asian crisis levels, mainly because of excess savings (Figure 4.2).

In the equity market, price distortion is reflected in historically high price-earning ratios (PE ratios) relative to global norms. A structural feature of many Asian markets is the small free float that inherently fuelled stock prices. For instance, Mainland China's PE ratio peaked at around 63 in 2000–2001 because, until the reforms in 2006, nearly two-thirds of the stock market capitalization remained in the hands of nontradable state or

---

[14] Average lending rate less deposit rate less administration costs, before provisions.

Table 4.4. *Selected Asian Economies: Capitalization and Turnover of Stock Markets, July 2008 (US$ terms)*

	Market Capitalization (US$ Billion)	% Change over Last 12 Months	Market Turnover[1] (US$ Billion)	% Change over Last 12 Months	Market Capitalization (% of 2007 GDP)	Price-Earning Ratio
Japan	3,925.6[2]	–16.0	3,685.6	–6.4	89.5	16.6
China	2,658.2[3]	0.9	2,744.7	–23.4	81.8	22.5
Hong Kong	2,121.8	–4.8	1,089.0	18.1	1,026.5	13.2
India	1,117.4[4]	0.0	728.5	51.7	101.7	14.4
Indonesia	198.1	10.4	83.4	45.8	45.7	16.1
Malaysia	262.2	–13.4	69.0	–37.5	140.6	12.7
Philippines	73.3	–22.1	11.0	–36.4	50.8	11.6
Singapore	468.5	–8.7	179.3	–15.6	290.3	10.4
South Korea	875.7	–24.4	947.7	–11.1	91.5	12.4
Taiwan	582.7	–16.8	604.1	7.6	152.0	11.4
Thailand	159.8	–18.6	80.1	25.4	65.0	10.5
Memo items						
Euronext	3,358.2	–17.8	2,920.2	–9.1	83.8	10.4
Germany	1,764.2	–7.3	2,548.8	1.3	53.1	12.7
United Kingdom	3,173.5	–19.5	4,565.7	–30.1	114.5	10.5
United States (NYSE)	13,418.2	–18.3	20,545.8	30.4	96.9	14.0

Source: World Federation of Exchanges, Bloomberg and author's estimates

[1] Year to date
[2] Tokyo Stock Exchange
[3] Shanghai and Shenzhen Stock Exchange
[4] Bombay Stock Exchange

legal shares. In other Asian stock markets, the bulk of the shares of listed companies are in either family or state hands. Recently, however, most major Asian stock markets are trading at more sober PE ratios, as local and foreign investors weighed the impact of the 2007–2008 U.S. subprime crisis and rising inflationary pressures on corporate profits (Table 4.4).

High PE ratios indicate that the cost of funds to Asian corporations has been low, whilst the high prices tend to deter hostile takeovers. The illiquidity of listed stocks in Asia, due to the low float, has also deterred global fund managers who are otherwise eager to participate in Asian markets from actually investing in the region.

Risk Management

Banks are supposed to help their savers and borrowers diversify their risks. But the Asian crisis demonstrated that there was a lack of risk diversification as Asian savings were concentrated in the banking system and residents were not encouraged to hold foreign assets. In general, late capital account liberalization meant that retail and institutional investors lacked the ability and experience to invest abroad to diversify domestic risks. Volatile exchange rates have also deterred retail investors from overseas portfolio diversification. This was compounded by the high moral hazard risk created through the provision of explicit or implicit deposit insurance that allowed NPLs to grow whilst banks maintained relatively low capital.

By definition, imbalanced growth meant weak risk management. Bank-dominated financial systems already meant that risks were concentrated in the banks. By concentrating on 'priority sectors', policymakers never developed a national risk management strategy to assess risk concentrations, diversify sources of financing and growth, and build domestic capacity for absorbing internal and external shocks. But one should not put all the eggs in one basket – namely, the domestic economy.

Corporate Governance

In many cases, banks have not been good at guarding against poor corporate governance. If the institutional investors and lenders do not exercise their powers as creditors and owners, then corporate behaviour will not change. Banks will not exercise restraint on corporate behaviour if they are captive in terms of ownership or political influence. As leaders in the financial and business community, banks can contribute significantly to reinforcing the credit culture and building up the property rights infrastructure.

The importance of segregating borrowers from lenders cannot be underestimated. Time and again, I have witnessed the failure of banks or finance companies because of connected lending. Not only does connected lending impair the credit decision, but the whole culture of imprudence spreads throughout the system. When I was cleaning up the failed finance companies in Malaysia in the mid-1980s, I uncovered entrepreneurs who swapped loans through finance companies controlled by each other. This was cleverer than 'ever-greening', which was the technique of disguising bad loans by issuing new loans to pay off bad ones. Since regulators frowned on loans to shareholders, it was difficult to detect loans given to seemingly nonrelated entrepreneurs. The only sign was that these loans always seemed to be repaid just before they went bad, often with a loan from another entrepreneur-controlled finance company. We quickly put a stop to that practice.

A major reason the financial centres of Hong Kong and Singapore escaped the Asian financial crisis was the fact that not only were the banks highly capitalized and professionally run, but there was continuous market pressure to improve the credit culture and banking environment. Credit discipline is an anchor of sound corporate governance. Unfortunately, in many parts of Asia, the protection of domestic interests such as the legal and accounting professions, as well as restricted entry of foreign financial institutions, delayed corporate governance reforms. There is now greater awareness that proper accounting, auditing and disclosure standards and practices are important checks and balances in preventing poor corporate governance.

WHITHER ASIAN BANKING?

There are a number of studies that suggest that Asian banking has improved considerably since the Asian crisis.[15] McKinsey partner Dominic Barton identified five key improvements since the crisis: in external policies, in fiscal and monetary management, in corporate governance and leverage, in banking health and profitability, including supervision, and finally, in – so far – avoiding asset bubbles. These strengths were also noted by Philip Turner, Ramon Moreno and Madhusudan Mohanty,[16] of the BIS, based on survey data on Asian banks.

---

[15] Barton (2007).
[16] Turner (2007); Moreno (2006); Mohanty (2006).

Specifically, Barton and others have suggested that the underlying strength and resilience of banks across Asia have improved significantly after the crisis; they pointed out that the return on assets now exceed 1 percent, the average global norm. State control of bank assets has been reduced and foreign participation has increased substantially, notably in South Korea and Indonesia. Moreover, concentration in banking systems across Asia has increased, with better capital adequacy, more professional management and better risk management systems. The market share of the top four banks in China, Hong Kong, Malaysia, Singapore, South Korea and Thailand now exceeds 50 percent.

Commensurate with the market concentration was the improvement in credit and risk management skills. Almost all East Asian banking systems now have capital asset ratios at the double-digit level,[17] well above the minimum of 8 percent of risk assets. NPL rates have declined, partly because of improvements in credit management and evaluation technology, but also because of revival in corporate profits and lower leverage ratios. NPL levels remain at double digits in Indonesia, Philippines and Thailand,[18] as bad debt resolution still remains a problem with certain corporate borrowers. Credit bureaus have been established, although their effectiveness remains uneven. There is greater use of rating agencies to evaluate credit risks, and the wider availability of credit risk data globally has helped banks and regulators to benchmark credit quality.

There is also no doubt that the quality of bank regulation and supervision has improved since the crisis. A major contributor to this was the reforms made globally, described in the next chapter.

A further area of financial sector reforms is the effort to shift towards greater capital market development to reduce the emphasis on bank-dominated systems. The success of this remains debatable. Efforts in this area are described in Chapter 12. As access to capital market and bond financing improved, the leverage ratios of the Asian corporate sector have declined. Corporate leverage ratios were over 200 percent in Indonesia, South Korea and Thailand, coming down to below 100 percent in recent years.[19]

One area that has received considerable improvements is the underlying financial infrastructure, due partly to improvements in technology that are readily available on a commercial basis, and partly to standardization to common standards. For example, real time gross settlement (RTGS)

---

[17] Mohanty (2006), table 1.
[18] Mohanty (2006), table 1.
[19] Pomerleano (2007).

payment systems became widely available throughout Asia, whilst stock exchanges implemented trading and clearing systems that are increasingly integrated with each other and can interoperate with other exchanges and payment systems. The work of the Group of 30 (G-30) and the Committee on Payment and Settlement Systems (CPSS) has also helped to standardize operational and robustness capacity.

As latecomers in utilizing technology to deliver financial services, Asian economies are amongst the fastest to improve their broadband services, as well as credit card and electronic payment systems. Several countries are also innovating and experimenting with banking services using mobile phone technology. These are aspects that could improve Asian banking services in advance of developed markets.

Despite these improvements, what other areas of reform would be necessary to further strengthen the Asian banking system to prevent the next crisis?

Michael Backman,[20] an eloquent critic of Asian governance practice, suggests that substantive reforms are necessary in the following areas:

- Pay public servants decently
- Enforce bankruptcy laws
- Reform bank ownership
- Reform accounting and auditing
- Ensure greater protection for minority shareholders
- Ban *Amakudari* and
- Reform media ownership.

What Backman looked for was a more Anglo-Saxon model of greater checks and balances in the system, including greater transparency. Since his book was written, the Japanese Government has already banned *amakudari*. Furthermore, bankruptcy laws, accounting and auditing standards and greater protection for minority shareholders are all being reformed throughout Asia, with varying degrees of seriousness. Moreover, issues relating to pay for civil servants, bank and media ownership and reform of the political and judicial systems are getting more serious attention in many parts of Asia. Nevertheless, the fact remains that, for a variety of reasons, reforming governance systems is an uphill task.

In the end, it is external pressure that pushes for faster change. The threat of Financial Sector Assessment Programs (FSAPs) would put domestic systems under greater scrutiny and, ultimately, disclosure. Within the

---

[20] Backman (2001).

region, the emergence of China, India and Vietnam as competitors in manufacturing and FDI destinations is putting considerable pressure on the rest of the Asian economies to raise their game.

However, my opinion is that the World Trade Organization (WTO) pressure for opening up has also begun to drive change because of the arrival of foreign banks, fund managers and financial service providers at all levels. First, in terms of foreign competitiveness, the region still has a long way to go relative to Latin America. For example, the average foreign ownership of banks in Latin America in 2005 was 38 percent, compared with 6 percent in Asia and Oceania. Despite the Asian crisis, which allowed many foreign banks to acquire stakes in banks in Indonesia, South Korea and Thailand, the change in market share of foreign banks increased by only one percentage point since 1995.[21] A survey of cross-border activity[22] of the 90 largest banks by region indicates that Asia and Pacific banks are the most locally oriented, with 86 percent of their assets within their home territory, compared with North America (77 percent) and Europe (55 percent).

Second, the Asian banking sector is also vulnerable to exposure to the household sectors. As at the end of 2005, the average household-credit-to-GDP ratio in emerging market countries was 18 percent, with emerging Asia having the highest levels at 27.5 percent of GDP, followed by emerging Europe (12.1 percent) and Latin America (9.2 percent).[23] Whilst this is still below that of mature markets that have an average household-credit-to-GDP ratio of 58 percent, banks suffered severe credit card losses in Hong Kong (2002–2003), South Korea (2003–2004) and most recently Taiwan (2006–2007).[24]

The advantage of letting in foreign institutional investors and intermediaries is that they impose stronger discipline on domestic players through competition or the threat of additional competition. This was clearly the policy intention when three of China's big four banks were opened to partial public and foreign ownership through their 2005–2006 IPOs in Hong Kong.

The other advantage of allowing foreign institutional players is the importation of global skills in financial product and risk management, as well as the training provided for locals to learn such skills. In this regard, some of the strongest bank professionals in Asia came from Citibank and JP Morgan, because they provided excellent training for their local staff.

---

[21] International Monetary Fund (2007a), table 3.2.
[22] International Monetary Fund (2007a), table 3.3.
[23] International Monetary Fund (2006b), fig. 2.1.
[24] See Kang and Ma (2007).

Large markets like Mainland China, which have over two million employees in the banking sector alone, would have difficulty developing in-depth management skills in banking, securities and asset management fast enough using their own domestic institutions. China's opening up under the WTO would hasten the absorption of market discipline into commercial operations that, in turn, would lend greater support to the institutional infrastructure development that is needed for the protection of property rights. The change in mindsets to a truly market economy is critical for China to maintain its growth story. This is true for Asia as a whole.

An urgent issue facing Asian banks is their role in the rapidly changing demographics. Asian economies have generally neglected to prepare for the needs of an aging population for efficient retirement schemes. North Asia is aging with slowing growth, thus requiring real returns and cash flows from its citizens' retirement funds. For example, McKinsey studies estimate that Japan's retirees are expected to equal the number of working adults by 2051, compared to four working adults supporting one retiree in 2001 and a ratio of two to one by 2021. This reflects the expected decline in population from 125 million in 2000 to less than 115 million by 2020. Consequently, Japan's pension and health insurance systems are expected to record a combined annual deficit of about US$300 billion, more than twice the total annual government deficit in 2002.[25]

Employee pension funds in Japan cover on average only 62 percent of the payments they need to pay their pensioners, compared with 103 percent in the United States and 98 percent in the United Kingdom.[26] If banks and pension funds continue to provide only low interest yields, it is not surprising that Asian excess savings have to be parked outside the region in the search for yield.

Another challenge going forward for banks in Asia and globally is the reputational risk suffered from inadequately protecting the interests of bank clients, particularly through private wealth management. There is sufficient evidence that senior bank management and financial regulators have not paid enough attention to the need for higher investor education, as well as strengthening the quality of bank financial planning advice and controls in their wealth management business. The result is a lot of misselling of risky financial products to clients who had insufficient understanding of the risks.

---

[25] Bowers, Gibb and Wong (2003), exhibit 1.4, 38.
[26] Greenwich Associates, quoted in Jopson (2003).

RETHINKING ASIA'S GROWTH STRATEGY

We need to rethink the benefits and costs of 'finance for development'. Extracting resources from savers to subsidize growth and infrastructure may have been appropriate during the 'catching-up' growth phase of emerging markets. But it is not fair to the consumer and the saver to continue such imbalanced growth strategies.

In my mind, Asian economies have reached the stage of 'middle growth', when they must pursue a balanced growth strategy. The failure of the wholesale banking model, which is described in Chapter 13, means that Asian bankers cannot copy Western models without understanding what risks are entailed. Not only must the banking system deal with the problem of protecting property rights for an aging population and an increasing affluent middle class, but it must also serve the needs of the changing Asian real sector.

If, as I believe, the Asian economic structure may have to be very different from being just a supply chain, in which domestic consumption and balanced growth that is equitable and environmentally sustainable play a greater role, the Asian financial system will be very different in the years to come.

In the face of present risks, bankers today will do well to remember what former U.S. Securities and Exchange Commission Chairman Arthur Levitt gave succinctly as a health warning for all investors: 'know your risks, know your counter-party, know your market, and know your contracts'.[27]

Next, we shall look at the role of the Washington Consensus.

[27] Quoted in Sheng (1999d), 420.

FIVE

Washington Consensus and the IMF

The Consensus is that there is no Consensus.
~ Anonymous

If we were to look at all the actors on the Asian financial crisis drama, we cannot ignore the role of Japan. But on a global scale, the real superpower is undisputedly the United States. In 1996 the U.S. GDP was US$7.8 trillion, nearly 60 percent larger than Japan's and nine times larger than China. Asia's rise and fall had a lot to do with the United States, as the single largest Asian trading partner. Asia relied so much on the U.S. economy that it used to be said that if the United States were to sneeze, Japan would catch a cold and the rest of Asia would catch pneumonia.

The world was fortunate that when Asia got into trouble in 1997, the U.S. economy was strong and prosperous. In 1950 the United States accounted for over 27 percent of world GDP and as much as 38 percent of world exports. In the postwar era, the United States was such a dominant economic and military power that the U.S. dollar accounted for more than 55 percent of global transactions. Like Rome, all roads lead to Washington, where the Federal Reserve System, the World Bank and the IMF are based. The World Bank and IMF were established in 1944 under the Bretton Woods Agreements that created the international financial order after the Second World War. The United States is also the largest shareholder of the Bretton Wood institutions, accounting for over 16 percent of their voting power.

THE WASHINGTON CONSENSUS

In the 1990s there evolved what became known as the Washington Consensus, a phrase attributed to former World Bank staff member John

Williamson[1] in 1987–1988 as the consensus set of views or recommendations of the Washington-based institutions, the IMF, World Bank and U.S. Treasury, on managing the global economy. There were broadly 10 key recommendations, not unlike the Ten Commandments, with motherhood advice to developing countries:

1. Maintain prudent fiscal discipline
2. Remove subsidies and concentrate public expenditure on social infrastructure, such as education, health services and basic infrastructure needs
3. Reform taxation to be more equitable and reward entrepreneurship
4. Maintain market based interest rates that are positive in real terms
5. Leave exchange rates to be determined by the market
6. Liberalize trade, through removing trade protection measures and lower tariff barriers
7. Liberalize capital flows, especially foreign direct investments
8. Privatize state-owned enterprises and get government out of business as much as possible
9. Allow overall deregulation to let market forces work, except for prudential regulations on financial institutions and
10. Maintain legal protection for private property rights.

Between 1989 and 1993 I worked in Washington at the World Bank and got to appreciate how the Washington Consensus evolved. The Washington Consensus was not so much a strategy as a way of looking at the world. James Fallows, in his famous book on the U.S. views on Asia, *Looking at the Sun*,[2] the sun representing Asia, said there were three mental habits when Westerners look at the rest of the world: a desire to convert them to Western values, an assumption of superiority and a misplaced faith in science, particularly economics.

Philosophically, the Washington Consensus was based on the neoliberal free market model. This view was pushed on the rest of the world through global institutions, such as the OECD, WTO, IMF and World Bank. The view was spread also through the Anglo-Saxon universities, where many of the elite of the developing world were educated. Nevertheless, as Nobel Laureate and former World Bank Chief Economist Joseph Stiglitz pointed out, 'The most successful countries, those in East Asia, had not followed this strategy;

---

[1]　Williamson (2002) [1990].
[2]　Fallows (1995).

government had played an active role, not just in promoting education and savings and distributing income but also in advancing technology'.[3]

It was not so much the success of the Washington Consensus, but rather the failure of central planning and excessive government intervention that gave it empirical support. Liberalization of trade, investments, capital, information and know-how spread in the late 1980s. The irony was that the free market experiment was tried in the Soviet Union in the late 1980s by naïve Soviet economists under Gorbachev. This failed miserably despite considerable aid and technical assistance from the West.

Just as market fundamentalism was reaching its apogee, in the early 1990s, the Japanese mounted an intellectual attack through financing the Asian Miracle study by the World Bank, which I participated in reviewing as Chief of the Financial Policy and Payments Division at the Bank. The Japanese authorities sought to strengthen the underpinning of the Japanese model of development, which worked because of their strong government intervention in the markets. Caught between its own dominant philosophy and one of its largest donor, the World Bank fudged by concluding that Asian governments succeeded in getting the fundamentals right, mimicked market prices and selectively intervened in areas where governments should intervene, such as education, public health and social infrastructure. No one side was completely satisfied, but at least the role of government in development was acknowledged. Nevertheless, the liberalization momentum was so strong within the Bretton Wood institutions that even as late as the IMF Annual Meetings in Hong Kong in 1997, the big debate was whether there should be further liberalization of the capital account globally.

RECONSIDERING THE WASHINGTON CONSENSUS

When the Asian crisis occurred, there were two broad schools of explanation. The Krugman story argued that bad Asian policies created moral hazards and bubbles that combined with underregulated financial institutions to create a crisis. This school, which included the IMF, basically blamed the crisis on the crisis countries themselves. The other school, led by Harvard Professor Jeffrey Sachs, felt that a banking panic would have brought down even sound economies. Then World Bank Chief Economist Joe Stiglitz argued one step further that IMF policies which emphasized further fiscal tightening and higher interest rates worsened the crisis. This position reflected views within the World Bank that IMF policies did not take into

---

[3]   Stiglitz (2003), 230.

account the balance sheet fragilities in the Asian corporate and financial sectors, but the Fund was the lead agency during the crisis, and the Bank's views were largely ignored.

In his memoirs Robert Rubin[4] revealed that the U.S. intervention in the Mexican crisis of 1994 had created such opposition in the U.S. Congress that the U.S. Administration's hands were tied during the Asian crisis. The democratic process in the United States meant that Congress had to approve the use of any U.S. Government funds for international aid. Since the views of Congressmen and Senators were exceptionally powerful, even if they may agree about policy direction with the U.S. Government, they may impose conditions that would not have been acceptable to the countries concerned. Nevertheless, the view that the Asian crisis was an opportunity to further democratization and the free market was quite strong within the Washington Beltway.

Since the United States had the largest single bloc of votes in the Bretton Wood institutions, it could also influence strongly the conditions under which the Bretton Wood institutions could lend to a particular country. Consequently the fundamental philosophy of the Washington Consensus was projected in the rescue programmes designed by the Bretton Wood institutions. During the crisis, negotiations on country assistance programmes and the attached conditions became complicated not only by trying to reconcile the views of important members, such as the Europeans, but also between the Bretton Woods bureaucrats, the U.S. Treasury and Congress. The Japanese authorities tried hard to represent the Asian views, but often they were outvoted on the Board and had to go with the majority. As Chapter 2 also explained, the weakening of the Japanese economy during this period also undercut the Japanese negotiating position. For domestic political reasons, therefore, the United States was unable initially to participate in financial aid to Thailand, a strong ally during the Vietnam War. Financial aid was forthcoming only through the Bretton Wood institutions or bilateral aid.

To Asians, the refusal of the United States to help bilaterally signalled the limitations of its friendship. The United States was refusing to help directly what was essentially a dollar zone. The U.S. Fed categorically refused the role of lender of last resort in U.S. dollars, whilst the IMF was not equipped for that role. Unlike the Latin American crisis in the 1980s, when the IMF took an active role in 'bailing in' the lending banks, the whole liberalization philosophy gave the IMF a 'hands-off' approach in working with the banks.

[4]   Rubin and Weisberg (2003).

'Bailing in' involved standstills – that is, the lending banks would not pull out their funds, which would buy time for resolution of the crisis. With strong market fundamentalism and their own vested interest in bailing out quickly, the American and European lending banks were not likely to agree to any standstill without strong political pressure. The fear was that any IMF involvement in 'bailing in' private sector involvement (PSI), would engender moral hazard, and that was a Washington Consensus no-no. Consequently, for Thailand, no bank standstill was put in place, so that investors and lending banks were free to flee in Thailand and Indonesia.

It was perhaps naïve to think that the IMF brand name would give the vote of confidence for investors and lenders to stay. Any banker would understand that if no 'standstill' was in place, it was far safer to take your money and run, rather than to wait for the IMF to apply its medicine. As a result, as higher interest rates and cuts in fiscal expenditure worsened the deflation, the crisis spread from Thailand to Indonesia and Malaysia and then infected South Korea. In the meantime the Japanese idea of an Asian Monetary Fund to help Asians was essentially vetoed by the United States and Europe in order not to compete with the IMF. The bank standstill was only brought in for South Korea very late into the day, when it was clear to all, especially the U.S. and European lending banks themselves, that if the contagion were not stopped there, it would have had greater global damage, including to American investments and European lenders. But the damage of contagion had already been done.

In June 1998, when the yen was falling towards ¥150 to the dollar and putting huge pressure on the regional currencies, the U.S. Fed intervened only when it became clear that if China devalued with the yen, the global economy could be on the brink of a competitive exchange rate war. By August Malaysia refuted the Washington Consensus by imposing exchange controls and proved that under the right policies this can work to stop a crisis.

My own reaction after reading Rubin's memoirs was the confirmation of Lord Acton's dictum that there are no permanent enemies or permanent friends, only permanent interests. Every country should look after its own interests and reform before a crisis gives its sovereignty to others. China's Vice Minister of Finance Lou Jiwei recently had the most perceptive comment on the Washington Consensus – it confused an ideal outcome with the process of getting there.[5] It was natural that everyone would want sound macroeconomic policies, freer trade and finance, good governance and sound regulation without distortions. But how does each country get

---

[5]   Lou Ji Wei (2007).

there, given the legacies of history, culture, social, political and institutional structures that are far from ideal? The process to achieve development is not easy, and we all make mistakes. Indeed, most countries cannot achieve reform or progress without a crisis. No pain, no gain.

THE ROLE OF THE IMF

The Fund's defence of its role in the crisis has been explained many times. As the leading international agency that coordinated aid during the crisis, the IMF provided technical assistance and advice, as well as direct loans of about US$36 billion to support Indonesia, South Korea and Thailand, roughly one-third of the total of around US$100 billion of international aid provided to the three crisis countries that called for IMF aid. The Philippines was already under an IMF programme when the crisis broke, and Malaysia refused any IMF funds.

Perhaps the most widely available explanation of the IMF's role in the Asian crisis was in the June 1998 issue of *Finance & Development*, a leading magazine of the Fund. Rereading it 10 years later revealed both the organization's strengths and weaknesses. In defending the IMF's role in the crisis, then Deputy Managing Director Stanley Fischer argued that the IMF had a changing role, but it saw itself as an important agency in promoting international cooperation, international trade and exchange rate stability through its surveillance role and in lending to member countries in need: 'The IMF is typically called in only in a crisis, which is often a result of the government's having been unwilling to take action earlier'.[6] In other words, it is the member's fault.

It is useful to summarize the IMF staff view of the causes and cures of the crisis. According to the IMF staff, the causes of the Asian crisis were attributed to both domestic and external factors:[7]

- A build-up of overheating pressures, evident in large external deficits and inflated property and stock market values
- The prolonged maintenance of pegged exchange rates, in some cases at unsustainable levels
- A lack of enforcement of prudential rules and inadequate supervision of financial systems, coupled with government-directed lending practices that led to a sharp deterioration in the quality of banks' loan portfolios

---

[6]   Fischer (1998b), 4.
[7]   IMF Staff (1998), 18–19.

- Problems resulting from the limited availability of data and lack of transparency
- Problems of governance and political uncertainties, which worsened the crisis of confidence
- International investors had underestimated the risks as they searched for higher yields when investment opportunities appeared less profitable in Europe and Japan
- Since several exchange rates in East Asia were pegged to the U.S. dollar, wide swings in the dollar-yen exchange rate which contributed to the build-up in the crisis through shifts in international competitiveness that proved to be unsustainable
- International investors – mainly commercial and investment banks – may, in some cases, have contributed, along with domestic investors and residents seeking to hedge their foreign currency exposures, to the downward pressure on currencies.

Note that in the above laundry list, the interaction between different economies and the channels of contagion was missing as a culprit. At the same time, the fundamental cures to restore confidence included the standard strategies:[8]

- *Monetary policy* must be firm enough to resist excessive currency depreciation
- *Financial sector weaknesses* are at the root of the Asian crisis and require particularly urgent attention
- *Governance* must be improved in the public and corporate sectors, and transparency and accountability strengthened
- *Fiscal policies* will need to focus on reducing countries' reliance on external savings and take account of the costs of restructuring and recapitalizing banking systems.

Perhaps the most illuminating views were those of John Lipsky, current Deputy Managing Director of the IMF, who was Chief Economist at Chase Manhattan Bank when he made them in 1998.[9] His views, many of which I concur with and are italicized below, included the following:

- The virulence of the crisis, and the speed with which it spread throughout the region, was unanticipated, indicating that *the importance of preexisting regional linkages was not adequately recognized.*

---

[8]   IMF Staff (1998), 19–20.
[9]   Lipsky (1998).

- *The economic damage and financial disorder resulting from the crisis were not inevitable and were exacerbated by policy errors* that sapped investor confidence.
- *The role of fixed or pegged exchange rate policies in precipitating the currency crisis has been exaggerated.* The critical failure in the crisis countries was in following inconsistent policies – albeit in difficult circumstance – that progressively lost credibility.
- The catalytic role of external capital flows in triggering the crisis has been overestimated – in essence, treating symptoms of deeper problems as if they were the problems themselves. At the same time, *the critical importance of capital flight from the crisis countries has been underestimated.*
- The reluctance of the crisis countries to tighten their monetary policies to stem capital flight – and their attempts to shield domestic firms and wealth holders from the impact of market discipline – proved to be self-defeating.
- The economic and financial challenges differ substantially from country to country. The Japanese economy's stagnation throughout the 1990s, the Chinese economy's transformation, and the maturing of the Association of Southeast Asian Nations (ASEAN) economies all represent distinct – although linked – issues, requiring individually tailored approaches.
- Any solution to the ongoing crisis necessarily will rely on private funding.

Note specifically that in the current crisis, massive public funding is already an active ingredient in the solution of the crisis.

Economist Jeff Sachs, amongst the brightest of the current generation of economists and someone who taught many of the best economists working in Asia and in the IFIs, was correct when he said, 'In the past, when an IMF program has collapsed in the midst of social chaos and economic distress, the IMF has simply chalked it up to the weak fortitude and ineptitude of the government. Finally, that approach is beginning to change'.[10]

THE IMF'S CRISIS OF CREDIBILITY

Rodrigo de Rato, who was Managing Director of the IMF until October 2007, reviewed the lessons of the Asian crisis 10 years later.[11] He thought

[10] Sachs (2005), 74.
[11] de Rato (2007).

there were primarily three. First, everyone has learned to guard against capital market disruptions. Asian countries have moved to flexible exchange rates and strengthened their macroeconomic policies. The Fund has introduced new instruments, increased its financial resources to deal with future crises and now appreciates the risks associated with capital flows.

The second is that contagion can be quick and damaging, and interlinkages between sectors and countries must be taken into account. The Fund has now formally adopted balance sheets analysis into its surveillance work, complemented by its FSAP reviews of country vulnerability. With the adoption of global standards and codes, endorsed by the Financial Stability Forum in 1999, there are now uniform standards to judge vulnerabilities on a comparable and consistent basis.

Third, the Fund has finally admitted that it needs to listen more to its members in order to have ownership, prioritization and effective implementation of Fund programmes. It appreciates that it needs to deal with civil society and that social stability would support macroeconomic stability and growth. Finance is only one dimension of crisis resolution.

These are important admissions of the Fund's need to correct its role to prevent future crises. To be more transparent and credible, the Fund established in 2001 an Independent Evaluation Office (IEO) to examine its work more objectively. The IEO published in 2003 a frank analysis of the role the Fund played in addressing the capital account crises of Indonesia, Korea and Brazil.[12]

In Indonesia, the Report concluded that the Fund did identify the vulnerabilities in the banking sector, but it underestimated its severity and the macroeconomic risks it posed. Specifically, a comprehensive bank restructuring strategy was absent.

Indeed, perhaps the most controversial part of the IMF's role in the Indonesian crisis related to the handling of the emerging bank crisis. The IEO Report treaded this area carefully:

The report considers the issue of whether a blanket guarantee, instead of the partial guarantee actually offered, should have been introduced in November 1997. It concludes that the banking crisis was not yet systemic in November, so that the partial guarantee was appropriate. The problem in bank restructuring was more with the initial lack of a comprehensive and well-communicated strategy, and not the nature of the guarantee.[13]

---

[12] Independent Evaluation Office (2003).
[13] Independent Evaluation Office (2003), Executive Summary.

What was omitted in the Report was the fact that there were considerable disagreements between the World Bank, which had been providing technical assistance on bank supervision in Indonesia prior to the crisis, and the Fund staff who were called in at short notice to put a comprehensive support programme together. The debate whether there was mishandling of the closures of Indonesian banks will be examined in depth in Chapter 9.

Apart from underestimating the severity of the emerging banking crisis in Indonesia, according to the IEO Report, the Fund also 'misjudged the extent of ownership at the highest political level and underestimated the resistance to reform likely to be posed by vested interests'.[14] This was due to the earlier failure of surveillance to recognize the impact of corruption and cronyism. In short, it did not pay enough attention to the political dimensions of crisis and reform.

In South Korea, 'IMF surveillance failed adequately to identify the risks posed by the uneven pace of capital account liberalization and the extent of banking sector weaknesses, owing to the adoption of a conventional approach that focused on macroeconomic variables. There were gaps in the data needed to make a full assessment, though available data on short-term debt and financial market indicators were not fully used ... the IMF was optimistic until virtually the last minute'.[15]

The Office's assessment was very illuminating. It concluded that 'the IMF's role as confidential advisor was not very effective in persuading countries to modify their policies even when key vulnerabilities were identified'.[16] 'Surveillance reports were insufficiently candid about potential vulnerabilities, especially those related to governance issues'.[17] In other words, the Fund's surveillance role had little practical influence on policy. Countries would ignore them until a crisis forced their hand.

In regard to another of the Fund's pet medicines, the Report concluded that 'the experience of the three countries with monetary policies varies and does not provide a definitive answer on the effectiveness of high interest rates in stabilizing the exchange rate'.[18] This somewhat vindicates Stiglitz's charge that high interest rates in a situation of high leverage were worsening the crisis, rather than curing it. There is no single medicine that works all the time.

---

[14] Independent Evaluation Office (2003), 13.
[15] Independent Evaluation Office (2003), 13.
[16] Independent Evaluation Office (2003), 15.
[17] Independent Evaluation Office (2003), 85.
[18] Independent Evaluation Office (2003), 16.

The Report also considered that in order to restore confidence, an IMF program must include a strategy to communicate the logic of the program to the public and the markets. Failure to convince the market and the public will lead to confusion and weak outcomes. For example, the size and format of the first package for Korea was considered inadequate relative to the short-term debt exposure, because 'usable reserves' had fallen to around US$7.3 billion by early December 1997. Since there was no agreement on a private sector standstill, money still flowed out. Only by Christmas were the foreign banks arm-twisted to roll over their interbank debt. This stopped the bleeding.

On the controversial question of Fund loan conditionality, the Report urged prioritization rather than trying to tackle too many fronts with too many conditions, some of which are structural and could not be fulfilled quickly. For example, it concluded that the 'proliferation of structural conditionality may also have led to lack of ownership at the highest political level and non-implementation, both of which damaged confidence'.[19] In plain language, President Suharto did not buy into Fund conditions that undermined his own political standing and therefore was not whole-hearted in supporting these reforms.

The Report correctly identified that the crises in Indonesia and South Korea were 'twin crises', with a balance-of-payments crisis taking place at the same time as a banking crisis. In both cases Fund surveillance 'failed to signal alarm because the crisis occurred against the background of sound macroeconomic fundamentals, including good export growth performance, relative price stability, and broad fiscal balance'. The common vulnerabilities in the form of financial sector weaknesses, highly leveraged corporate balance sheets, weak public and corporate sector governance, and rising short-term unhedged external indebtedness were in varying degrees identified in IMF surveillance, but *their seriousness or their implications were not adequately appreciated*. This was because these vulnerabilities in the private sector were not yet core areas of IMF surveillance.[20]

In other words, silo mentality in IMF methodology prevented the Fund staff from looking at financial crises from different perspectives, notably the failure in balance sheet analysis and the interactive contagion channels between sectors and countries as well as a political economy angle. There was a lack of appreciation of the interaction between the politicians and the

---

[19] Independent Evaluation Office (2003), 19.
[20] Independent Evaluation Office (2003), 23.

bureaucracy in the formulation and implementation of policies, particularly during the crisis.

In the debate on the Report in Asia,[21] there was clear consensus that the IMF should be reformed. As a result of the criticism that the IMF did not have enough market expertise, the International Capital Markets Department was created in March 2001, which provided the IMF with better understanding of rapid changes in global markets. This was subsequently merged with the Monetary Affairs and Exchange Department, which provided technical expertise to central banks. The merged Monetary and Capital Markets Department prepares the half-yearly Financial Stability Reports that are useful surveys of financial stability issues on a regional and global basis.

The other area that was beefed up significantly was the recruitment of senior bank supervisors who had first-hand experience in handling banking crises. Advice on crisis management is clearly not something to be left to staff, however well trained, which understood events only second hand. The issues of blanket guarantees, standstills, and bank closures were not only complicated, but timing was everything. Even mature markets, such as the United Kingdom, gave blanket guarantees in the case of Northern Rock in 2007, when faced with a run on a mortgage lender. These issues will be discussed in Chapter 9 on Indonesia and Chapter 12 on financial stability.

Much of the IEO conclusions could well apply to the other crisis-hit economies not covered in the Report, such as Malaysia and Thailand. It also reminded me of the inability to implement the idea of the Asian Monetary Fund during the crisis. Can a new fire engine be successfully built during a fire? The answer must be no. Not only must the fire engine be designed before a fire, there is also a need to train the firemen how to use the fire engine correctly. One had therefore to rely on the existing fire engine, whether it was ready or not. A fire engine that is designed for one type of fire is useless when a new type of fire is started.

FROM WASHINGTON TO GLOBAL CONSENSUS?

The Asian crisis therefore was also a crisis that faced the IMF itself as the fire engine operating in a global financial crisis. The crisis revealed also the weaknesses of the IMF in a new and complex multipolar global world that is rapidly changing. What is the exact role of the IMF in this new world?

Mervyn King, Governor of the Bank of England, reminded us that Lord Keynes, in the first meeting of the Fund in 1947, said that the Bretton

---

[21] Institute for International Monetary Affairs (2003).

Woods twins should have three attributes: universalism (in that they belong to the whole world), an energy and fearless spirit to solve issues and 'a spirit of wisdom ... so that their approach to every problem is absolutely objective'.[22]

Has the IMF lost its way? Sixty years ago there was shortage of foreign exchange, and the international monetary system evolved around fixed exchange rates. Today's environment is one where international capital is no longer scarce, exchange rates are more flexible and sovereign wealth funds can easily supplant the IMF as a lender of last resort.

The IMF is now too small in size relative to modern financial markets. As of February 2008, the Fund's one-year forward commitment capacity (FCC), that is, its estimated resources available for new loans in the coming year, is US$206 billion. In 2006 the net increase in international credit was four times larger. The Fund cannot borrow directly from financial markets. It has to obtain capital from the shareholders, the national governments, who may not always agree on a capital increase during a crisis. The process of capital increase is complex and time consuming. Today the Asian economies have reserves that are about 15 times larger than the IMF's capital resources.

From a resource point of view, the Bretton Wood institutions are increasingly less relevant. Until the recent crisis, emerging markets have been repaying their loans, so that the amount outstanding to the Fund at the end of March 2007 was only SDR7.3 billion[23] (US$11 billion). If we add up all the resources of the Bretton Wood institutions, including the BIS, the total resources of US$945 billion in early 2007 would be less than 0.5 percent of total global financial assets of US$194.5 trillion.[24] Currently China lends more to Africa than the World Bank.

The second issue is if the IMF is not a central bank of central banks and not a lender of last resort, does it have a role to play? King thinks that the IMF's role should be to support national policymakers by providing expert analysis about external risks to their domestic monetary policy. Effectively, the Fund should look after the global externalities generated by national policies. It should be a producer of global public goods, being an independent and respected voice to support global monetary policy, with a global

---

[22] King (2006).

[23] Special Drawing Rights (SDRs) are an international reserve asset, created by the IMF in 1969 to supplement the existing official reserves of member countries. The SDR also serves as the unit of account of the IMF, and its value is based on a basket of key international currencies.

[24] International Monetary Fund (2008), appendix table 3.

surveillance role and 'a forum for national authorities to discuss risks to the world economy'.[25]

But to do so, the Fund must have focus, independence and legitimacy. But from an emerging market perspective: Whose focus? Independence from whom? And whose legitimacy? The *realpolitik* of the world is that there are global markets, but also national governments, which are loath to cede that power to any global government.

So the crux of the issue lies in the fact that no one is running global monetary policy, and no one wants to pay for the consequences of each other's mistakes. Even Jean-Claude Trichet,[26] President of the European Central Bank, acknowledged that the game is changing far too fast for the existing architecture to cope. The power balance is shifting, but there is neither a roadmap nor remit on how to change the global financial architecture to meet future needs. Like the Boston Tea Party that crystallized the issue: how do we ensure global taxation or action in any area when there is no adequate representation?

What about the Fund's preventive or surveillance role? Surveillance can be effective only if the IMF has an enforcement role. In reality, the Fund cannot exercise effective surveillance because it cannot enforce its recommendations or views against member countries that do not need to borrow from it. Moreover, enforcement can be effective only if the global organization has legitimacy.

In the area of global surveillance, there was some progress. In recognition that there was insufficient representation, the G-10 deputies created a wider group in April 1998, initially called the G-22,[27] which later was formalized into the Group of 20 (G-20). The G-22 recommended the establishment of the Financial Stability Forum in April 1999, which brought together not only representatives of the ministries of finance, central banks and supervisory agencies, but also the heads of standard-setters to promote international financial stability through information exchange and greater cooperation in financial supervision and surveillance. By meeting regularly, the Forum brings together national authorities responsible for financial stability from

---

[25] King (2006).

[26] Trichet (2007).

[27] The Group comprises the Group of Seven (Canada, France, Germany, Italy, Japan, United Kingdom and United States), plus Argentina, Australia, Brazil, China, Hong Kong SAR, India, Indonesia, Malaysia, Mexico, Poland, Russia, Singapore, South Africa, South Korea and Thailand. Meetings were attended by the heads of the BIS, World Bank, IMF, OECD and World Bank, as well as the chair of the Interim Committee (later International Monetary and Financial Committee), as observers.

12 significant international financial centres, international financial institutions, sector-specific international groupings of regulators and supervisors as well as committees of central bank experts.[28]

Since 1999 there has been significant improvement in global standards and codes, as well as stronger surveillance through the implementation of the Financial Sector Assessment Programmes. The objective of the FSAP, which is a comprehensive review of a member country's financial system strengths and weaknesses by the World Bank and IMF jointly, is to make financial systems more resilient to shocks and help design appropriate policy responses. Up to the end of October 2007, the IMF and the World Bank had conducted and completed 114 FSAPs out of a total of 197 member economies or 57.9 percent. However, the largest countries, such as the United States, China and India, had not yet been subject to FSAPs, although the last two countries are preparing for them. Interestingly, the Asia-Pacific region had done the least number of FSAPs, completing only 10 out of a possible 40 members or 25 percent.

In a 2006 review of the effectiveness of FSAPs, the IEO of the IMF considered that the FSAP represented a distinct improvement in the IMF's ability to conduct financial sector surveillance and in understanding the key linkages between financial sector vulnerabilities and macroeconomic stability. The FSAP work has helped to deepen the IMF's understanding of the financial sector, prompted better discussions with authorities and helped support policy and institutional changes. Specifically, the FSAP permits an integrated approach to assessing financial sector vulnerabilities and development needs that could not be achieved by the Fund's own ad hoc assessments.

Nevertheless, the current international architecture lacks focus, independence and legitimacy precisely because it has been difficult to resolve the problem of changing power in terms of financial resources, the most obvious being the dramatic shift of the emerging markets from net debtors to net creditors.

The IMF has two dominant groups of shareholders, the United States and the European bloc, who have great influence on the appointment of staff and the formulation of policies. Even though Japan has a significant share, it

---

[28] Comprising Australia, Canada, France, Germany, Hong Kong SAR, Italy, Japan, Netherlands, Singapore, Switzerland, United Kingdom, United States, BIS, IMF, World Bank and OECD, as well as Chairs of Basel Committee on Bank Supervision, IOSCO, IAIS and IASB. The Chairs of the Committee for Payment and Settlement Systems (CPSS) and Committee for Global Financial Systems (CGFS) plus the President of the European Central Bank also attend. The secretariat is provided by the BIS.

could not persuade the IMF to follow its views without strong support from the other emerging market members. If there were no consensus support from the others, it would be very difficult to change the views of the dominant shareholders. In other words, rules are obeyed because members agree that violation carries a moral authority of legitimacy and therefore grant the enforcer real teeth and legal powers to take enforcement action. Without legitimacy and power to act, including a fair and transparent dispute resolution mechanism, no global institution can be effective.

The present difficulties in power sharing stem from the fact that Europe has become a single political entity, but international representation is still through a number of the smaller EU members. These countries are reluctant to diminish their roles or their shareholding in the Bretton Wood institutions in order to accommodate the rise of the emerging members. As pointed out by fund manager Mohamed El-Erian, a former IMF staff member, 'the Fund's governance structure is outmoded and feudalistic'.[29] Belgium, with a population of 10 million, has almost the same voting power (2.13 percent) as China with 1.3 billion people (2.94 percent) and Brazil and Mexico combined (2.61 percent and 300 million people).

The most obvious instance in the lack of consultation with the emerging markets was the nomination process for the heads of the Bretton Wood institutions. When Paul Wolfowitz announced his resignation as President of the World Bank in May 2007, the United States immediately nominated its own candidate, Robert Zoellick, to fill the post, as was the status quo convention. Even though Mr Zoellick was eminently qualified, there was no open, transparent selection process to find out whether there would be candidates from other countries. Similarly, when IMF Managing Director Rodrigo de Rato, a Spaniard, resigned weeks after the resignation of Wolfowitz, the Europeans quickly closed ranks and nominated Dominique Strauss-Kahn of France to succeed him. The immediate question that both heads of the Bretton Wood twins has to deal with is resources: will the emerging markets and the new sources of wealth be willing to fund the activities of the twins, in which they do not have yet much say?

So what can and should the Bretton Wood institutions do?

Two obvious roles can immediately be ruled out. The first is whether the Fund should be the world's policeman in global financial markets, acting, as Lord Eatwell and others have suggested, as a World Financial Authority.[30] There can be no agreement on this because neither national supervisory

---

[29] El-Erian (2008), 44.
[30] Eatwell and Taylor (2000).

authorities nor current international supervisory standard setters are willing to cede power to the IMF.

The second role, as lender of last resort, is also ruled out, because no central bank, especially the G-10 members, is willing to cede this to an international body. Without an international lender of last resort, global monetary policy will continue to be held hostage to different national interests.

From the perspective of emerging markets, there is perhaps general consensus that the IMF should provide the international public goods, in such areas as national and global market statistics, information exchange, technical assistance, technical research and a forum for discussion of international issues. There is also general consensus that the Bretton Woods institutions do provide good work in the surveillance work such as FSAPs. Given limited resources, the Fund can play only a coordinating role during financial crises. This is a role where there is still considerable ambiguity. How and through what channels should the IMF work with the financial markets (where private sector resources dominate) to resolve future crises? Or is this still the remit of national central banks?

The second controversial issue is whether the Fund should get involved in the surveillance on the appropriateness of exchange rate valuation. Since exchange rates are relative prices, it would be most difficult to assess objectively whether any particular exchange rate was overvalued or undervalued. No country is willing to admit that its exchange rate is overvalued or undervalued. If there was disagreement, should this be resolved on a bilateral level or multilateral level?

The brutal conclusion from this brief survey is that the international financial architecture will continue to lack clarity, because so far no national government is willing to cede any powers to an independent body to coordinate and somehow allocate the losses. If there is one thing that the Asian crisis demonstrated, it is that the losses were fundamentally borne by the crisis countries themselves; ironically, the weaker the country, the greater the losses. The IMF or any other global institution can work only if it is demonstrated that it can fulfil a useful role to ameliorate and share the losses from any crisis on a global basis. Ideally, it should prevent crises, or provide advice to countries on how to do so.

In the next few chapters, we discuss the four crisis economies of Thailand, South Korea, Malaysia and Indonesia.

SIX

Thailand: The Karma of Globalization

Don't try to catch a tiger with bare hands.
~Thai proverb

The law of karma states that each and everyone will reap the fruit of his karma, either good or bad, in due time, with certainty and in its entirety.[1] The predominantly Buddhist Kingdom of Thailand was where the Asian crisis officially began on 2 July 1997. Amongst the worst crisis-hit economies, Thailand is perhaps the prime example of a middle-income country that enjoyed and then succumbed to the vicissitudes of globalization, where strong and effective institutional governance in economic and political life is crucial to sustainable prosperity. It was the karma of globalization that could not be avoided by any emerging country, whether good or bad.

In hindsight, Thailand got into trouble mainly because, first, on the macroeconomic side, it suffered from incompatible policy targets. In particular, in the period leading up to the crisis, it was confronted with an increasingly difficult dilemma of the Impossible Trinity, that is, how to reconcile having a near-fixed exchange rate, free capital movements and an independent monetary policy all at the same time. Second, on the structural side, Thailand suffered from an inadequate risk management regime that led to excessive private sector debts, which fuelled a massive stock and property bubble. Both were perhaps signs of a flawed decision process, a consequence of bad politics.

SOUTHEAST ASIA'S STAR PERFORMER

In the early to mid 1990s, Thailand was one of Southeast Asia's star performers, transforming from a rice exporter to a leader in light manufacturing and

---

[1]   Prieb (2004).

tourism. Between 1990 and 1995, its GDP grew around 9.1 percent annually, the government was running a budget surplus of around 3.2 percent of GDP per year and its domestic savings were high at about 35 percent of GDP per year (Table 6.1). With a GDP of US$168 billion in 1995, Thailand was Asia's seventh largest economy and Southeast Asia's second largest after Indonesia. Prosperity was so evident that in the early 1990s Thai bankers were famed for their Chateau Petrus wine collections and heavy Audemars Piguet Royal Oak watches.

True, there were some concerns about the Thai economy around early to mid-1995. These concerns, however, focused not on Thailand's institutional weaknesses but on the economy's macroeconomic stability. In particular, there were reservations as to whether the accelerating inflation and current account deficits were sustainable. Between 1990 and 1995, inflation averaged around 5 percent per annum whilst the Thai current account deficits for the same period averaged 6.6 percent of GDP per year (Tables 6.1 and 6.2). When the Mexican peso crisis erupted in December 1994, there was much debate as to whether Thailand would go down the Mexican route.

As is commonly claimed, the Thai baht was on a 'soft peg' to the U.S. dollar. Officially pegged to an undisclosed basket, the baht was very stable at roughly B 25 against one U.S. dollar since 1984. Soft pegs became vulnerable to attack from specialist macro-hedge funds after George Soros played a key role in forcing the Bank of England to devalue sterling in 1992. However, the Thai baht was able to survive the first speculative attack in January 1995 immediately following the Mexican crisis for two key reasons.

First, the conventional wisdom was that Asia, including Thailand, was different from Mexico. The Thai macroeconomic problems were not considered that serious by emerging market standards, and from a macro-perspective, the economy in general still appeared robust. As Masaru Yoshitomi, a former senior Japanese Ministry of Finance official, recalled in October 1997:

In 1994–95, when the Mexican peso crisis took place, we all discussed whether a contagious run could hit the Thai baht. Many people, including those at the IMF and the World Bank, concluded that all Thailand's macroeconomic fundamentals were quite good: low inflation, a balanced budget, a high saving rate, and a high potential growth rate. Inflation may have been accelerating, but from 5 percent to at most 7 percent. So we were satisfied with the stability of the baht.[2]

Second, as Thailand's economic institutional weaknesses were somewhat hidden by its rapid pace of economic growth, there was still a high level of

[2]   Yoshitomi (1999), 183.

Table 6.1. *Thailand: Selected Real Economy Indicators*

	1990	1991	1992	1993	1994	1995	1996	1997	1998	1999	2000
GDP US$ billion	85.6	96.2	109.4	121.8	144.3	168.0	181.9	150.9	111.9	122.6	122.7
GDP per capita US$	1,518	1,687	1,899	2,084	2,442	2,826	3,038	2,496	1,829	1,985	1,967
Real GDP Annual % change	11.6	8.1	8.1	8.3	9.0	9.2	5.9	-1.4	-10.5	4.4	4.8
Unemployment rate % of total labour force	2.2	3.1	2.9	2.6	2.6	1.7	1.5	1.5	4.4	4.2	3.6
Inflation Annual % change	5.9	5.7	4.2	3.3	5.1	5.8	5.9	5.6	8.1	0.3	1.6
Fiscal balance % of GDP	4.8	4.3	2.6	1.9	2.7	3.0	0.9	-1.5	-2.8	-3.3	-2.2
Central government debt % of GDP	13.6	9.9	8.0	6.2	4.3	3.4	3.8	5.1	10.8	20.7	22.2
Gross domestic capital formation % of GDP	41.4	42.8	40.0	40.0	40.3	42.1	41.8	33.7	20.4	20.5	22.8
Gross domestic savings % of GDP	34.3	36.1	36.0	35.0	34.7	34.1	33.8	32.9	33.3	30.7	30.4
Manufacturing production index 2000 = 100	52.6	57.7	65.5	73.4	79.2	83.7	91.4	91.9	83.4	93.7	100.0

Sources: Bank of Thailand, ADB, IMF and Jaimovich and Panniza (2006)

Table 6.2. *Thailand: Selected Currency and Current Account Indicators*

	Currency Indicators*										
	1990	1991	1992	1993	1994	1995	1996	1997	1998	1999	2000
Baht to U.S. dollar Period average	25.6	25.5	25.4	25.3	25.2	24.9	25.3	31.4	41.4	37.8	40.1
Baht to U.S. dollar End of period	25.3	25.3	25.5	25.5	25.1	25.2	25.6	47.2	36.7	37.5	43.3
Baht nominal effective exchange rate 2000 = 100	–	–	–	–	132.3	131.8	135.8	89.6	107.1	101.2	95.7
Baht real effective exchange rate 2000 = 100	–	–	–	–	119.2	123.0	128.7	89.1	108.2	101.4	95.2
Yen to U.S. dollar Period average	144.8	134.7	126.7	111.2	102.2	94.1	108.8	121.0	130.9	113.9	107.8
Yen to U.S. dollar End of period	134.4	125.2	124.8	111.9	99.7	102.8	116.0	130.0	115.6	102.2	114.9
Yen nominal effective exchange rate 2000 = 100	–	–	–	–	87.2	85.4	77.9	78.3	86.5	102.0	98.5
Yen real effective exchange rate 2000 = 100	–	–	–	–	104.9	97.0	85.3	84.9	91.0	104.0	97.0

(continued)

Table 6.2. *(continued)*

	Current Account Indicators[†]										
	1990	1991	1992	1993	1994	1995	1996	1997	1998	1999	2000
Terms of trade 2000 = 100	118.5	117.6	120.0	119.8	121.6	116.0	114.4	115.1	108.2	107.4	100.0
Exports US$ billion	22.9	28.3	32.2	36.6	44.7	55.7	54.7	56.7	52.9	56.8	67.9
Exports growth Annual % change	15.1	23.6	13.8	13.4	22.1	24.8	−1.9	3.8	−6.8	7.4	19.5
Imports US$ billion	32.7	37.8	40.1	45.1	53.4	70.4	70.8	61.3	40.7	47.5	62.4
Imports growth Annual % change	29.8	15.6	6.1	12.3	18.4	31.9	0.6	−13.4	−33.8	16.9	31.3
Trade balance US$ billion	−9.8	−9.5	−7.9	−8.5	−8.7	−14.7	−16.1	−4.6	12.2	9.3	5.5
Current account balance US$ billion	−7.1	−7.2	−6.0	−6.1	−7.8	−13.2	−14.4	−3.1	14.3	12.5	9.3
Current account balance % of GDP	−8.3	−7.5	−5.5	−5.0	−5.4	−7.9	−7.9	−2.1	12.8	10.2	7.6

Sources:
* BIS and IMF
[†] Bank of Thailand, IMF, UNCTAD and author's estimates

Dash means data not available

confidence in the Thais' good track record of macroeconomic management. The Bank of Thailand was particularly respected as a strong central bank, a development that many attributed to the visionary late Dr Puey Ungphakorn, who served as its governor for more than 12 years between June 1959 and August 1971. Dr Puey developed the Bank by giving scholarships to the best students from all walks of life and sending them to the best academic institutions in the West, gaining both intellectual and professional depth and respect of both the Thai people and foreigners.[3] The BoT had a staff that was the envy of other central banks, filled with top graduates, chartered accountants and MBAs, technically strong and a match for the best macroeconomists sent from the IMF or World Bank. The BoT handled the baht devaluation and the banking crisis in the early 1980s with finesse, and I personally learnt a lot as a central banker on monetary policy and bank supervision from my Thai colleagues.

Sentiments however began to change around mid-1995 and into 1996 when the Thai economy showed increasing signs of trouble. Notably, Thailand had

- A rising external debt, particularly short-term debt. Total external debt rose from 45 percent of GDP in 1994 to 60 percent in 1995 with short-term debt rising from 45 percent of total external debt in 1994 to 52 percent in 1995.
- A notable appreciation in the real effective exchange rate of the baht between 1995 and 1996.
- A sharp decline in exports, the Thai economy's main engine of growth. Whilst exports grew by 24.8 percent between 1994 and 1995, there was a contraction in Thai exports by 1.9 percent between 1995 and 1996.
- An increasingly and persistently large current account deficit of about 8 percent in both 1995 and 1996, up from 5.4 percent in 1994.
- A slowing economy, with real GDP growing at 5.9 percent in 1996, a sharp fall from 9.2 percent in 1995.
- A deteriorating fiscal balance. Although the Thai government remained in the black, its budget surplus fell sharply from 3 percent of GDP in 1995 to 0.9 percent in 1996.
- Declining asset prices, particularly in terms of the Thai stock and property markets. Property prices peaked in 1992 whilst the stock market peaked in 1994; and
- Increasing difficulties in the financial sector, particularly with ailing finance companies by 1995–1996.

---

[3] Nukul Commission (1998), para. 426.

As a result, the international banking and investment community began to reassess the Thai economy more closely. Pressures on the Thai baht reemerged in late 1996, building up further in the first half of 1997. At the same time, the SET Index, the benchmark index of the Thailand stock exchange, fell from its peak of 1,754 on 4 January 1994, to close at 527 on 30 June 1997, about one-third of its 1994 peak. An oversupply in the property market became noticeable after 1994 with Bangkok experiencing 17.7 percent office vacancy rates by June 1997.[4]

THE MEXICAN CRISIS REDUX?

It may be useful to compare the Thai crisis with the Mexican crisis. Before the devaluation of the peso in 1994, Mexico had two key points of vulnerabilities. First, Mexico's current account deficit, which was 7 percent of GDP in 1994, was significantly funded by short-term dollar-indexed government securities called *Tesobonos*. In comparison, Thailand's current account deficits of about 8 percent in 1995 and 1996 were larger than those of Mexico, although its deficits were mainly financed by short-term private sector external borrowings.

Second, the Mexican financial system was going through financial liberalization, including bank privatisation and the removal of foreign exchange controls in 1991, all preconditions for Mexico to join the OECD in 1994. Thailand also went through financial liberalization with the opening up of the Bangkok International Banking Facility (BIBF) in 1993, which exposed the Thai financial system to an inflow of liquidity that it did not manage well. As credit rating analyst Philippe Delhaise noted,

At various meetings and seminars that Thomson BankWatch was holding in 1995 and 1996, [t]he rating agency warned its clients in no uncertain terms about the dire consequences for Thailand's banking system if either the baht was attacked, as happened briefly in the wake of the Mexican peso crisis, or the international financial community cut down their huge US dollar funding lines.[5]

Guillermo Ortiz, current Governor of the Bank of Mexico, pointed out that these two main vulnerabilities coupled with an unstable political environment led to the collapse of currencies in both Mexico and Asia.[6]

The Mexican crisis, however, was stemmed relatively quickly because the United States gave decisive and solid support. The IMF rescue package

---

[4] See Siamwalla (2000) and Koh et al. (2004) citing report by JP Morgan.
[5] Delhaise (1998), 93.
[6] Martinez (1998).

amounted to US$50 billion, with the United States pledging to provide up to US$20 billion of financial assistance. This was followed by tough reforms, including a devaluation of the peso against the U.S. dollar of about 50 percent between 20 December 1994 and mid-March 1995. Consequently, although the other Latin American economies were affected by the Mexican crisis, they did not suffer significantly from contagion.

Just as Mexico had the tequila effect of contagion, the Asian version was what former Thai Foreign Minister Surin Pitsuwan termed the ' "Tom Yum Koong Syndrome", like the famous Thai hot shrimp soup – very spicy and dangerous for those who come unprepared'.[7]

WHAT HAPPENED TO THAILAND IN THE MID-1990S?

The Thai explanation of the crisis may be centred on two broad areas – excessive private sector debt and mistaken policy decisions,[8] the former somewhat encouraged by the latter.

Victim of Its Own Success

To some extent, Thailand's difficulties resulted from its earlier economic success. In the early 1990s, foreign capital poured into Thailand (Table 6.3). In 1990 Thai net capital inflows amounted to about US$9.7 billion or 11.3 percent of GDP. By 1995 they increased by about 126 percent to US$21.9 billion or 13 percent of GDP. Of the US$21.9 billion, approximately 95 percent were private capital flows, 51 percent took the form of bank credit, 19 percent took the form of portfolio investments and 5 percent took the form of FDI. Between 1990 and 1995, more than 60 percent of Thailand's international bank borrowings took the form of short-term loans denominated in foreign currencies.

Thailand's massive influx of foreign capital, particularly between 1993 and 1995, was the result of several coincidental developments. First, there was ample liquidity in the developed markets. Initially there was loose monetary policy due to the weak growth in Japan and Europe and a savings glut due to the aging population. The low interest rates in Japan in particular fuelled the lucrative yen carry trade. Stanley Fischer, then First Deputy Managing Director of the IMF, noted that these factors together with 'an imprudent search for high yields by international investors without due

---

[7] Pitsuwan (2000).
[8] Nukul Commission (1998), 5.

Table 6.3. *Thailand: Selected Foreign Capital Indicators*

					Capital Flows*						
	1990	1991	1992	1993	1994	1995	1996	1997	1998	1999	2000
Net FDI flows US$ billion	2.4	1.4	1.5	1.6	0.9	1.2	1.4	3.3	7.4	5.7	3.4
Net portfolio investment flows US$ billion	0.5	0.0	0.5	5.5	2.2	4.2	3.7	4.6	0.3	−0.1	−0.7
Net other flows, including bank credit US$ billion	6.9	9.9	7.6	3.5	9.1	16.6	14.4	−12.2	−17.4	−13.5	−12.9
Net total capital flows US$ billion	9.7	11.3	9.7	10.5	12.2	21.9	19.5	−4.3	−9.7	−7.9	−10.3
Net private capital flows US$ billion	11.0	10.3	8.0	10.3	12.0	20.8	18.2	−7.6	−15.5	−13.5	−9.8
Net bank credit flows US$ billion	–	−0.3	1.9	3.6	13.9	11.2	5.0	−5.7	−12.7	−10.6	−6.6

	Other Indicators[†]										
	1990	1991	1992	1993	1994	1995	1996	1997	1998	1999	2000
Total foreign bank borrowings US$ billion	16.2	22.3	26.2	34.4	49.6	68.3	77.6	73.5	58.1	46.9	43.2
Short-term international bank loans[1] US$ billion	8.8	13.0	15.8	21.4	31.0	43.6	45.7	38.5	24.0	14.2	10.3
Japanese bank lending to Thailand US$ billion	8.9	12.5	14.5	18.7	29.7	39.0	39.5	35.1	24.0	15.5	12.8
Direct investments from Japan[2] US$ billion	1.2	0.8	0.7	0.6	0.7	1.2	1.4	1.9	1.4	0.8	0.9
Net external wealth position[3] US$ billion	−26.6	−34.4	−40.2	−61.0	−66.4	−94.8	−101.8	−96.0	−97.9	−92.6	−66.0
Net external liabilities position % of GDP	31.1	35.8	36.8	50.1	46.0	56.4	55.9	63.6	87.5	75.5	53.8

Sources:
* Bank of Thailand, ADB and author's estimates
[†] BIS, Japan External Trade Organization (JETRO), Lane and Milesi-Ferretti (2006) and author's estimates
[1] Foreign currency denominated loans of up to and including one year
[2] Based on report and notifications
[3] Negative means net liabilities position; positive means net assets position

regard to potential risk',[9] drove a massive amount of private capital flows to emerging markets. Thailand, with its high growth rates and generally prudent macroeconomic management, was particularly attractive to foreign investors. Furthermore, the carry trade was especially profitable in Thailand because of the interest rate differentials of about 6 percent between the U.S. dollar and the Thai baht and about 8 percent between the Japanese yen and the Thai baht (Table 6.4). The depreciation of the yen since April 1995 made that trade even more profitable.

The second factor, as noted by Thirachai Phuvanatnaranubala, former Deputy Governor of the Bank of Thailand and currently Secretary-General of the Securities and Exchange Commission of Thailand, 'The 1990s saw dramatic changes in the liberalisation and internationalisation of emerging market economies'.[10] The Thai financial system followed this trend beginning in 1990, when Thailand felt confident enough to accept its obligations under Article VIII of the IMF, which lifted all controls on all foreign-exchange transactions on the current account.[11] In line with the Bank of Thailand's plan to develop Bangkok into a regional financial hub, there was a gradual opening of the capital account with the launching of the BIBF in 1993. It was a bold move designed to encourage foreign financial institutions to set up operations in Thailand and upgrade the Thai financial system. The effect of the BIBF status was to allow domestic banks to conduct offshore transactions.

In 1996, however, net total capital flows into Thailand fell by 11 percent to US$19.5 billion or 11 percent of GDP, the first time a decline was noted since 1986. The net outflows reflected investor nervousness. By mid-1996 the confidence was shaken by a series of internal and external events, including the Bangkok Bank of Commerce (BBC) scandal in May 1996 and the downgrade of Thailand's short-term debts credit by Moody's on 3 September 1996.

An Overheated Economy

The foreign capital that flooded Thailand initially created excess liquidity and faster economic growth. Real GDP growth in 1994 and 1995 rose to 9 and 9.2 percent, respectively, up from an average of 8.2 percent between 1991 and 1993 (Table 6.1).

---

[9] Fischer (1998a).
[10] Phuvanatnaranubala (2005), 269.
[11] Siamwalla (2000).

Table 6.4. *Thailand: Selected Interest Rate Differentials (% per Annum)*

	1990	1991	1992	1993	1994	1995	1996	1997	1998	1999	2000
Thailand money market rate (TMR)	12.9	11.2	6.9	6.5	7.3	11.0	9.2	14.6	13.0	1.8	1.9
U.S. effective federal funds rate (FFR)	8.1	5.7	3.5	3.0	4.2	5.8	5.3	5.5	5.4	5.0	6.2
Euro overnight index average (EONIA)	–	–	–	–	5.2	5.6	4.0	4.0	3.1	3.0	4.8
Switzerland call rate (SCR)	8.9	7.6	5.9	4.4	3.6	2.3	1.8	1.0	1.0	1.4	3.5
Japan call rate (JCR)	8.2	6.3	3.9	2.4	2.3	0.5	0.5	0.4	0.3	0.0	0.2
Interest rate differential (TMR – FFR)	4.8	5.5	3.4	3.5	3.0	5.1	3.9	9.1	7.7	–3.2	–4.3
Interest rate differential (TMR – EONIA)	–	–	–	–	2.0	5.3	5.2	10.6	9.9	–1.3	–2.9
Interest rate differential (TMR – SCR)	4.0	3.5	1.0	2.1	3.7	8.6	7.4	13.6	12.0	0.4	–1.6
Interest rate differential (TMR – JCR)	4.6	4.8	3.0	4.1	5.0	10.5	8.7	14.2	12.8	1.7	1.7

Sources: U.S. Federal Reserve Board, IMF, OECD and author's estimates

Table 6.5. *Thailand: Financial Structure (% of GDP)*

	1990	1991	1992	1993	1994	1995	1996	1997	1998	1999	2000
Assets of deposit money banks	84.6	91.7	98.3	108.2	120.5	131.7	142.9	159.2	173.5	155.8	131.6
Assets of other financial institutions	22.1	24.3	27.2	31.6	35.8	39.6	44.4	47.0	47.8	37.9	29.3
Stock market capitalization	29.2	30.4	42.2	75.7	90.9	81.5	67.0	41.2	26.1	38.1	36.2
Bond market capitalization	9.8	9.5	9.3	9.1	8.7	8.5	9.2	9.5	15.3	22.6	25.4
Insurance premium volume	1.7	1.8	1.9	2.2	2.4	2.4	2.5	2.5	2.3	2.3	2.5

Source: Beck, Demirgüç-Kunt and Levine (2000), revised 13 August 2007

Thailand was also a bank-dominated financial system. In 1995–1996, for instance, assets of Thai banks and other financial institutions amounted to 170–180 percent of GDP (Table 6.5) with the bulk of business being concentrated in the hands of 15 banks and the major finance companies. In contrast, Thai stock market capitalization was about 60–80 percent of GDP whilst the size of the Thai bond market was a mere 8–9 percent of GDP.

At the same time, the banking sector was ill prepared to take on its starring role of financial intermediation. In 1998 the Thai Government appointed a 'Commission Tasked with Making Recommendations to Improve the Efficiency and Management of Thailand's Financial System', headed by former Bank of Thailand Governor Nukul to examine the crisis. The Nukul Commission Report argued that when the BIBF was established, the supervision and regulation of the Facility was not sufficient.[12] In particular, as there were no restrictions as to the geographic distribution of bank lending, most of the lending was in the form of offshore lending to onshore, rather than mostly offshore to offshore, that being the objective of the BIBF (Table 6.6). By the end of 1996, BIBF offshore credit to onshore banks increased to more

[12] Nukul Commission (1998), para. 4.

Table 6.6. *Thailand: Bangkok International Banking Facilities Credits (Billions of Baht)*

End of Period	1993	1994	1995	1996	1997	1998	1999	2000
Out-In	**197.0**	**456.6**	**680.5**	**807.6**	**1,411.4**	**767.0**	**487.1**	**387.0**
Thai banks	126.7	189.8	254.6	330.0	514.1	213.5	100.1	62.2
Foreign banks with full branch(es) in Thailand	50.8	102.2	152.4	222.8	690.4	431.9	304.2	253.1
Other BIBF units	19.6	164.6	273.6	254.8	206.9	121.6	82.8	71.7
Out-Out	**3.8**	**100.8**	**517.0**	**482.6**	**471.1**	**148.5**	**63.7**	**44.1**
Thai banks	2.6	11.6	10.8	16.3	35.4	29.0	20.1	15.1
Foreign banks with full branch(es) in Thailand	0.3	2.0	4.8	9.4	264.3	89.1	33.5	23.3
Other BIBF units	0.9	87.2	501.4	456.9	171.4	30.4	10.1	5.8
Total	**200.8**	**557.5**	**1,197.6**	**1,290.2**	**1,882.4**	**915.5**	**550.8**	**431.1**
Thai banks	129.3	201.4	265.4	346.4	549.4	242.5	120.2	77.3
Foreign banks with full branch(es) in Thailand	51.1	104.2	157.2	232.2	954.8	521.1	337.7	276.3
Other BIBF units	20.4	251.8	775.0	711.7	378.2	152.0	92.9	77.5

Source: Bank of Thailand

than 60 percent of total BIBF credits, prompting Philippe Delhaise to remark, 'the BIBF will go down in the history books as a Trojan Horse invading the banking sector: a gift it should have refused'.[13]

In itself, a massive amount of foreign loans need not be damaging if there was prudent and efficient risk management. Unfortunately, flushed with foreign money, the Thai banking system relaxed their loan requirements and expanded lending rapidly, simultaneously taking on greater risks.

The apparent lackadaisical attitude towards risk management was due mainly to two factors. First, as noted by Thirachai, 'the huge capital flows coming into the country overwhelmed the risk management capacity of banks. This fed through to banks' lending policies, leading them to "overlend" to sectors, which they might not have done under normal circumstances'.[14]

Second, the risky loans were made based on a number of morally hazardous assumptions. The first assumption was that the cost of foreign capital was considered cheap because of the historical stability of the baht against the U.S. dollar. The second assumption was that the Thai authorities would not allow Thai banks and other financial institutions to go under because they were 'too big to fail'.

Thus, greed fed into speculation and then into Ponzi-type financing. Projects were launched in expectation that they could be listed in the stock market so that the promoters could take an instant profit in the bull market. In a rising market, financial institutions agreed to provide short-term bridge loans repayable on successful listing. When the bull run stopped, the projects stopped, and the banks were left with bad loans on their books.

The euphoria in the stock market also permitted Thai *jao sua* (tycoons) who engaged in the carry trade to amass huge wealth. In July 1998 the *Nation*, a Thai English daily, reported that at the height of his fortune before July 1997, the liquor tycoon Charoen Sirivadhanabhakti's net worth was about B 100 billion or about US$4 billion,[15] much of it tied to the stock market:

Charoen got most of his cash from arbitraging the interest differentials between his U.S. dollar borrowings and Thai baht deposits. Leveraged from his massive assets, Charoen borrowed US$4 billion (about B 100 billion) at 7 or 8 percent and converted it into Thai baht deposits to enjoy an interest rate differential of 4 or 5 percent

---

[13] Delhaise (1998), 83.
[14] Phuvanatnaranubala (2005), 271.
[15] Converted at the exchange rate of B 25.3 to the U.S. dollar, the average rate between 1990 and 1995.

a year. It was an article of faith that the Thai currency peg system would be there forever, and there would be no foreign exchange risks.[16]

Between January 1990 and its peak in January 1994, the Stock Exchange of Thailand (SET) index rose by about 95 percent from 900 to 1,754, whilst at roughly the same time property stock prices rose as much as 285 percent, supported by a construction spree and a property boom. However, when the crisis hit Thailand, the wealth contraction from the fall in the market capitalization of the stock market between 1995 and 1997 was roughly US$113 billion or 68 percent of GDP (Table 6.7). Charoen's fortune plunged to a mere B 10 billion or about US$242 million.[17]

Thailand's Achilles Heel

As Ammar Siamwalla, former President of the Thai Development Research Institute pointed out, whilst it was the stock market that was especially speculative, the property bubble was more significant due to the large exposure of the Thai banking sector to the property sector: 'Bank of Thailand data indicate that the banks' share of real estate lending in their overall portfolio went up from 6.3 percent at the end of 1988 to 14.8 percent at the end of 1996. Over the same period, the share of real estate in the portfolios of the finance companies went up from 9.1 percent to 24.3 percent'. In reality, as most of bank loans were collateralized by property, the exposure of the financial system to the property bubble was larger than what was shown.

By 1996 it was clear that the private sector had become highly overleveraged, with private credit by financial institutions alone amounting to 137.4 percent of GDP, nearly double that of 72.4 percent in 1990 (Table 6.8). In stark contrast, central government debt was only 3.8 percent of GDP (Table 6.1).

At the same time Thailand's external debt rose sharply to US$108.7 billion or about 60 percent of GDP, of which US$47.7 billion or 44 percent was short term (Table 6.9), and more than US$90 billion or over 80 percent was borrowed by the private sector. In particular, bank borrowings of US$41.9 billion made up 39 percent of Thailand's total external debt. Of these bank borrowings, US$28.9 billion or 69 percent were short term. Borrowings by private enterprises that amounted to US$50.1 billion made up 46 percent

---

[16] *The Nation* (1998), 10.
[17] Converted at the exchange rate of B 41.4 to the U.S. dollar, the 1998 average rate.

Table 6.7. *Thailand: Selected Asset Prices*

	1990	1991	1992	1993	1994	1995	1996	1997	1998	1999	2000
Stock Market Indicators*											
SET index End of period	612.9	711.4	893.4	1,682.9	1,360.1	1,280.8	831.6	372.7	355.8	481.9	269.2
Domestic market capitalization US$ billion	20.8	37.5	57.3	127.5	125.6	135.8	95.9	22.8	34.1	57.2	29.2
Stock Exchange of Thailand Price-earning ratio	13.8	15.6	16.3	26.1	19.5	19.8	12.0	6.6	10.0	14.7	5.5
Real Estate Indicators†											
Land price index 1991 = 100	–	100.0	119.4	138.0	140.5	150.6	155.1	163.4	153.1	135.5	144.9
Land price index Annual % change	–	–	19.4	15.6	1.8	7.2	3.0	5.4	–6.3	–11.5	6.9
Single detached house index Land included, 1991 = 100	–	100.0	113.5	124.7	124.4	132.4	135.2	144.0	141.0	127.1	131.2
Single detached house index Land included, annual % change	–	–	13.5	9.9	–0.2	6.4	2.1	6.5	–2.1	–9.8	3.2

Sources:
* World Federation of Exchanges and Bloomberg
† Bank of Thailand

Table 6.8. *Thailand: Selected Financial Sector Indicators*

	1990	1991	1992	1993	1994	1995	1996	1997	1998	1999	2000
Narrow money (M1) Annual % change	11.9	13.8	12.3	18.6	17.0	12.1	9.1	1.2	3.0	30.2	–8.6
Broad money (M2) Annual % change	26.7	19.8	15.6	18.4	12.9	17.0	12.6	16.4	9.5	2.1	3.7
Private sector credit by financial institutions[1] % of GDP	72.4	81.3	89.4	100.1	113.2	125.7	137.4	154.1	166.0	143.4	116.6
Lending rates % per annum	14.4	15.4	12.2	11.2	10.9	13.3	13.4	13.7	14.4	9.0	7.8
Deposit rates % per annum	12.3	13.7	8.9	8.6	8.5	11.6	10.3	10.5	10.7	4.7	3.3
Interest rate spreads % per annum	2.2	1.7	3.3	2.5	2.4	1.7	3.1	3.1	3.8	4.3	4.5

Sources: Bank of Thailand, World Bank, Beck, Demirgüç-Kunt and Levine (2000), revised 13 August 2007 and author's estimates
[1] Deposit money banks and other financial institutions

143

Table 6.9. *Thailand: Selected Foreign Reserves and External Debt Indicators*

	1990	1991	1992	1993	1994	1995	1996	1997	1998	1999	2000
Foreign exchange reserves (FER) US$ billion	13.2	17.3	20.0	24.1	28.9	35.5	37.2	25.7	28.4	33.8	31.9
FER growth Annual % change	40.0	30.5	15.8	20.3	20.0	22.8	4.9	−30.9	10.7	18.9	−5.5
Total external debt US$ billion	29.3	37.9	43.6	52.1	64.9	100.8	108.7	109.3	105.1	95.1	79.7
Total external debt % of GDP	34.2	39.4	39.9	42.8	45.0	60.0	59.8	72.4	93.9	77.5	65.0
Short-term external debt US$ billion	10.4	15.4	18.9	22.6	29.2	52.4	47.7	38.3	28.4	19.5	14.7
Short-term external debt % of total external debt	35.5	40.6	43.4	43.4	45.0	52.0	43.9	35.0	27.1	20.6	18.4
Short-term external debt % of FER	78.6	89.0	94.5	94.0	101.0	147.8	128.4	149.0	100.0	57.8	46.0

Sources: Bank of Thailand, IMF and author's estimates

of Thailand's total external debt. Of these borrowings, US$18.8 billion or 38 percent were short term. What was serious was the fact that the short-term debt of US$48 billion was larger than the foreign exchange reserves of US$38 billion, a worrying trend observable since 1994 (Table 6.9).

All in all, the economy was clearly vulnerable, but it was not obvious to those caught up in the heady days of 1996. The most obvious indicator of vulnerability was the Net External Wealth Position, which was negative US$101.8 billion or 55.9 percent of GDP in 1996 (Table 6.3), a clear sign that the country was overextended in foreign exchange terms in terms of both liquidity and solvency. Unfortunately, such data were not extensively available until 2006, when the IMF first published them.

Thus, by mid-1995 and clearly by 1996, overleveraging and bubbles became the Achilles' heel of Thailand. As both phenomena were created on the back of short-term foreign loans, Thailand's fate hung on volatile capital flows.

A Yen for Trouble

To add to Thailand's misfortunes, around about the time when the Thai economy was looking increasingly overheated and vulnerable, the yen began to depreciate against the U.S. dollar.

Japan was Thailand's main foreign investor and lender. Between 1990 and 1995 Japanese FDI into Thailand averaged about 30 percent of Thailand's FDI. Japanese manufacturers, attracted by Thailand's tax incentives, friendly but hard-working people and its potential as a stepping stone into the ASEAN market, helped Thailand build up its light engineering capacity. At the same time, during the same 1990–1995 period, Japanese bank lending to Thailand averaged about 56 percent of Thailand's total international bank borrowings.

The implications of the depreciating yen and Japan's strong economic and financial presence in the Thai economy were spelt out by Masashi Namekawa, former economic adviser to the Japanese government who was based in Thailand between 1994 and 1996:

More than half of Thailand's long-term debt is denominated in yen [see Table 6.10], and about 20 percent of its trade is settled in currencies other than the dollar. It is therefore necessary to observe the fluctuation of the baht not only vis-à-vis the dollar but also vis-à-vis other currencies, especially the yen. The baht had continued to depreciate vis-à-vis the yen by approximately 8 to 9 percent annually from 1990 to 1995. This trend came as a surprise, given the rapid appreciation of the yen in

Table 6.10. *Selected Asian Economies: Currency Composition of Long-Term External Debt, 1996 and 1997 (%)*

	US$		Yen		Multiple Currency		Others	
	1996	1997	1996	1997	1996	1997	1996	1997
China	65.0	74.6	15.9	11.8	15.9	10.8	3.2	2.8
Indonesia	24.3	27.2	34.5	32.9	24.7	23.3	16.5	16.6
Malaysia	55.6	55.8	28.2	26.5	11.5	15.0	4.7	2.7
Philippines	29.8	33.9	38.1	36.8	26.0	24.1	6.1	5.2
South Korea	47.8	59.9	32.4	22.9	8.8	5.4	11.0	11.8
Thailand	32.4	47.0	44.7	38.8	17.7	10.8	5.2	3.4

Source: World Bank (2001)

those years. However, in 1996 the value of the baht turned around as a result of the depreciation of the yen vis-à-vis the dollar and of the practically pegged rate of the baht to the dollar. The baht appreciated from 3.7 yen per baht to 4.5 yen per baht in 1996, a trend that continued until the first half of 1997. This appreciation restricted Thai exports to Japan, made Thai goods less competitive, stimulated imports from Japan, and raised the cost of Japanese investment.[18]

In other words, as the spearhead of Japanese investment in the Asian global supply chain, Thailand was most vulnerable to the one supply chain/ two currencies volatility. Between 1995 and 1996 Thailand's export growth sank sharply, contributing to the growing current account deficits in 1995 and 1996 and its slower real GDP growth in 1996. In addition, Japanese capital began to withdraw from Thailand in 1996. Whilst Japanese FDI continued to flow into Thailand, it was at a slower pace. More importantly, the depreciating yen provided Japanese banks, already having to deal with problems back home, with the impetus to accelerate their withdrawal from international lending. Thus, Thailand soon found that Japanese bank credit, an important source of funding of the Thai boom, was drying up. Whilst Japanese bank lending grew by about 31 percent between 1994 and 1995, it slowed to a mere 1.2 percent between 1995 and 1996, resulting in a massive 56 percent drop in net bank credit flows into Thailand in the same period (Table 6.3).

[18] Namekawa (1998).

THE BUBBLE DEFLATES

The liquidity crunch in the late stages of a deflating bubble worked through declining cash flows and falling asset prices. As exports declined, export cash flow weakened. Exporters or manufacturers who had diverted their cash flow into property or stock market speculation found themselves in a double bind. In a falling market, they could sell their stocks or property only at sharply lower prices, whilst those who speculated on margin were exposed to increased margin calls or 'forced sold'. Either way, the speculators found their losses increasing as cash flow dried up.

As the bubbles began to deflate, the weaker finance companies and banks that financed the bubbles began to feel the lagged impact through their growing loan losses. As their nonperforming loans and losses mounted, reducing their capital adequacy, the Bank of Thailand began to take regulatory action. In 1996 scandals surrounding the BBC and the Bangkok Metropolitan Bank (BMB) broke, providing a glimpse of the banking crisis that was to come in 1997.

The BBC was taken over by the Bank of Thailand in May 1996, prompting a no-confidence motion in Parliament against then Prime Minister Banharn Silapa-archa's Government that month. The Banharn Government survived the motion, but the debate revealed disturbing lending practices that created a bank run against BBC. Public nervousness began to spread.

According to *Asiaweek* magazine, the parliamentary debate revealed that the BBC had disbursed about US$3 billion of doubtful loans, nearly half of the bank's assets. Of the US$3 billion loans, only 18 percent of their value was secured by collateral assets, and even then much of the collateral was overvalued land in faraway provinces. Huge loans amounting to millions of U.S. dollars were disbursed to senior BBC executives and other individuals with inadequate or no collateral. In the week of such revelations, BBC depositors withdrew more than US$430 million from the bank.[19] Vijit Supinit, the Bank of Thailand Governor since October 1990, resigned shortly afterwards, and Rerngchai Marakanond, a Deputy Governor, was appointed in his stead.

Then at the end of July 1996, the U.S. branch of the BMB was targeted by the U.S. regulatory authorities for 'questionable loans to individuals associated with the bank'.[20] The *New York Times* reported that the BMB was

---

[19]   Healy and Gearing (1996).
[20]   Delhaise (1998), 94.

ordered to close its banking operations in the United States and was fined US$3.5 million.[21]

BBC and BMB signalled the deepening malaise amongst Thai financial institutions. In particular, the Thai banking sector suffered a double mismatch of borrowing short term in foreign currency but lending long term in local currency. Many of these loans, especially to the property sector, were already nonperforming because of falling collateral prices.[22] A JP Morgan report estimated that 16 percent of Thailand's real estate loans were nonperforming by 1996.[23] When the Thai crash came in 1997–1998, leading to a massive 50 percent fall in the value of the baht, a 70 percent fall in share prices, a 50 percent fall in property prices and a sharp contraction in the Thai economy, the bad debt problem exploded.

With a banking system that was estimated to be exposed 30–40 percent in property, the damage was enormous, with nonperforming loans peaking at 47 percent of total loans (nearly B 2.7 trillion or US$65.2 billion) in mid-1998.[24] Many of the banks and finance companies that failed in 1997 were BIBF participants as the rapid deterioration in the quality of their loans correlated with the sharp fall in the value of the baht.[25]

Also, the weakest links were the finance companies and smaller banks, many of which were family owned, badly run and financing the asset bubble. The Bank of Thailand first moved on some of the worst cases on 3 March 1997, when it asked 10 finance companies to increase their capital. Then in May 1997 Finance One, Thailand's largest finance company, collapsed. On 27 June 1997 the operations of 16 finance companies, including the 10 mentioned earlier, were suspended. Finally on 5 August 1997 another 42 finance companies were suspended, bringing the total number of suspended finance companies to 58.

POLITICS + BAD ECONOMY = CRISIS

Just as capital inflows led to an overheating of the economy with asset bubbles in the stock and property markets, there were tumultuous political changes in Thailand between 1996 and 1997 that led to a succession of three Prime Ministers and six Ministers of Finance. Politically, there was a transition from a history of military coups and authoritarian governments before

---

[21] *New York Times* (1996).
[22] Siamwalla (2000).
[23] Cited in Koh et al. (2004).
[24] Converted at the exchange rate of B 41.4 to the U.S. dollar, the 1998 average rate.
[25] Siamwalla (2000).

the 1980s to a more democratic multiparty parliamentary system under a constitutional monarchy, accompanied unfortunately by money politics. It was a time of great social change, as new grassroots and business leaders were edging old elites aside. One coalition government succeeded another, and by the end of 1996 Thailand had a new coalition government that was confronted immediately with a major policy decision: whether or not to abandon its economic and financial anchor, the baht exchange rate, which had been stable at around B 25 to the U.S. dollar since late 1984.

This was not an easy decision to make, both politically and economically. In early 1997 most of Asia except Japan was in an effective U.S. dollar zone, with each currency being stable against each other and against the U.S. dollar. Stability against the dollar offered many advantages, because there was no trade war through devaluation. Competitiveness was fought through increases in productivity, not through devaluation.

Moreover, it was the stability of the currency that enabled the country to benefit from capital flows. As everyone benefited from the rising asset prices that were the consequence of the stable exchange rate, no one wanted to change to an unknown floating system.

In addition, it was not at all clear whether a one-time devaluation against the U.S. dollar would solve the prevailing trade deficit because if other competing Asian currencies were to devalue by the same amount, the trade deficit might not be eliminated. Consequently a devaluation or float would have to be accompanied by other measures to cure the deficit, such as tough expenditure cuts or higher interest rates. Weak political governments might not be willing to take such tough decisions, hence the danger of maintaining the status quo and getting deeper and deeper into trouble. In other words, there was innate fear of floating.

There was no simple answer to this dilemma.

Mundell-Fleming[26] was the first to highlight the 'Impossible' Trinity, which is the dictum that policymakers can have a choice of only two out of the three options of full capital account liberalization, flexible exchange rates and monetary independence. Dutch econometrician Jan Tinbergen won a Nobel Laureate reminding everyone that for every policy target you need a policy tool. Common sense tells you that you cannot have your cake and eat it too. In a two-dimensional market, you control either the quantity or the price, but you cannot control both.

The choice of an exchange rate regime can be starkly put as a choice of disciplines. A fixed exchange regime means that the economy adjusts to the

---

[26] Mundell (1961), 657–665; Fleming (1962), 369–379.

exchange rate, which means that all policies are subordinate to that policy. Conversely, a flexible exchange rate regime allows the exchange rate to adjust to the economy. If the economy is inflexible, then a flexible exchange rate helps the economy to adjust. The Hong Kong dollar peg demonstrated this dilemma par excellence.

Strictly speaking, the criticism that Asian currencies were 'soft pegs' was debatable. In theory, other than the Hong Kong dollar, which was truly fixed, every other Asian economy was technically and legally a 'managed float'. The Thai baht was pegged to a currency basket of undisclosed composition, but everyone noted that the currency hardly moved against the U.S. dollar.

The Asian currencies were meant to be flexible, but in practice, they were forced through competitive pressures to be roughly in parity with each other and to be benchmarked against the U.S. dollar. For example, before the crisis there was a rough parity of 10:1 between the Thai Baht, the Filipino peso and the Taiwan dollar to the Malaysian ringgit, so that when the ringgit–U.S. dollar was 2.5 to 1, the other currencies hovered around 25 to 1. The stability of East Asian currencies to each other facilitated intra-regional trade,

As discussed in Chapter 2, none of them expected that the dollar-yen relationship would become so volatile, nor that capital flows could be so large. But if you share the same pond as an elephant, there is no way that you can avoid the waves if it starts moving around in the pond.

To make matters worse for Thailand, when the working environment for public institutions is infected by uncertain political change and volatile financial flows, the outcome is often tragic. Former Bank of Thailand Governor Chatu Mongol Sonakul, who was tasked with restoring the image of the BoT in 1998, remarked bluntly in a retrospective on the Asian crisis: 'Certainly in Asia it was not a case of being mainly a financial collapse. The collapse arose from bad politics and bad elections, thereby installing bad government, who therefore made the traditionally strong Asian civil service bad'.[27]

Therefore, when it came to making the crucial decision on whether to change the exchange rate regime, the Nukul Commission Report noted that in the first half of 1997, although top-ranking finance ministry and Bank of Thailand officials were aware of the need for a clear decision, their various meetings 'did not [lead] to any substantive policy change because the two key decision makers, [then finance minister] Amnuay Viravan and [then

---

[27] Sonakul (1999).

BoT governor] Rerngchai were not decisive. Whilst Amnuay waited for a BOT proposal, Rerngchai waited for a consensus from the top management of the BOT, which did not materialise'.[28]

By June 1997 the situation had become untenable. Net available foreign reserves fell from US$6–7 billion at the beginning of the month to US$4–5 billion between 20 and 26 June and collapsed to US$2.8 billion on 30 June.[29] Forced into action, the decision-making process inside the Bank of Thailand finally changed, and on Saturday, 21 June, a meeting was held amongst high-ranking central bank officials without the presence of the Governor. In the meeting they decided amongst themselves to adjust the exchange. After the meeting Chaiyawat Wibulswasdi, the Deputy Governor who headed the meeting, called Governor Rerngchai 'to tell him that the meeting had reached a consensus that the system should be changed … preparation was made for a managed float system'.[30]

On 22 June 1997 Thanong Bidaya was summoned by Prime Minister Chavalit to act as the Finance Minister, after the resignation of Amnuay. A longtime banker, Thanong 'could sense the financial sector falling apart, with rumours and massive withdrawals of deposits from the finance companies' and 'vividly remembered the advice of Dr Amnuay … to look closely into the matter of currency management'.[31] When he finally had the chance to call a meeting of the Bank on Thursday, 26 June, he decided to change the exchange policy.[32] Recalling the decision, Thanong noted in a *Bangkok Post* review on the Thai crisis ten years later:

The report I heard about Thailand's foreign exchange position was much worse than I expected. There was practically no other choice for me except to devalue the baht, one way or the other.

I had to make the bitter decision and told the central bank governor to proceed to find the best measure for devaluation and prepare all the procedures as well as all the measures needed to contain a financial crisis. I myself would take all the responsibility for the decision.

At first we wanted to announce the flotation of the baht as soon as we could. We considered making an announcement on Sunday, June 29, with official implementation on Monday June 30.

But we felt that doing so would result in all Thai banks facing sudden currency losses for their first-half balance sheets, to the extent that many banks would be made immediately insolvent.

[28] Nukul Commission (1998), 7.
[29] Nukul Commission (1998), para. 206.
[30] Nukul Commission (1998), para. 207.
[31] Bidaya (2007).
[32] Nukul Commission (1998), para. 208.

Fortunately, the first of July was a bank holiday, so we secretly prepared to make the announcement in the early morning of July 2 and tell the world that Thailand had resorted to floating the currency and would seek assistance from the International Monetary Fund to provide financial support to contain the upcoming financial crisis.

The two major tasks were to negotiate with the IMF to draft the first letter of intent and to design appropriate measures to contain the financial crisis.

The negotiations with the IMF in the first two weeks were the toughest moments in my life. The IMF representatives came with a 'cookbook' of solutions that demanded the opening up of Thailand's economy, especially the financial sector, to foreign investors to create a competitive financial market situation.

They also demanded the total privatisation of state enterprises, the closure of weak financial institutions, the liquidation of all bad assets as well as a disciplined fiscal policy and balanced budget for the government.

All of us who were involved in the negotiation team were so stressed during the two weeks after the currency was floated. But in the end we had to bite the bullet to get the financial support needed to withstand the call of foreign debt payments that totalled higher than US$100 billion.

...

In addition to the funds from the IMF, I also had to request further financial assistance from Japan. It should be remembered that most of the financial assistance was obtained from Asian friends, with Canada, Australia and Japan taking the lead and the largest burden.

We did not receive direct support from the United States or European countries. It's only during times of crisis and need that we find out who are our 'friends'.[33]

BELEAGUERED INDIVIDUALS AND INSTITUTIONS

Any financial crisis has its share of scapegoats and those to be blamed. Unfortunately, rightly or wrongly, individuals and institutions cannot escape that responsibility, with only history as the ultimate judge. Since many of the individuals concerned are my personal friends, it would be neither fair nor objective for me to comment on whether they were right or wrong. The Nukul Commission Report made severe criticism of key people and the central bank for its policies relating to financial liberalization and the handling of major events leading up to the crisis.

In the area of supervision and regulation following the liberalization of the capital market, for example, the Nukul Commission Report suggested that although the Bank of Thailand recognised that financial institutions 'must be strengthened so that they meet international standards, particularly in the areas of capital base adequacy, asset quality, management

[33] Bidaya (2007).

efficiency and database development', measures to achieve these goals were 'apparently never achieved'. In fact, the central bank relaxed rather than tightened measures that would have led to the strengthening of local financial institutions.[34]

Herein lies the inherent dilemma of a central bank trying to manage both a banking crisis and a currency crisis. Even today, the global view on whether a central bank should maintain both the role as a lender of last resort and a bank regulator remains controversial. On the positive side, the fact that the central bank has the financial resources to be the lender of last resort means that it has great power to exercise financial regulation and supervision over the banking system. Since the central bank also runs the payment system, it has superior knowledge and understanding as well as leverage over the banking system that it supervises.

On the other hand, financial institutions are not devoid of political and vested interests, especially when governments are politically weak. Banks and owners of banks are likely to protect their interests through money politics, putting considerable political pressure on central banks to relax bank supervision (namely, regulatory forbearance), or to lend to help the banking system. The business community will also put pressure on governments to relax monetary policy or not to raise interest rates to ease the pain of recession. The danger of a soft peg is therefore that pressure for bank regulation and supervision to be relaxed comes at a time when both should be tightened to manage the huge credit and market risks arising from deflating asset bubbles.

The basic principles of the Lender of Last Resort role of central banks to stem financial panic was first enunciated by Walter Bagehot in his 1873 classic *Lombard Street*. In a financial panic the central bank must lend freely at penalty interest rates against good collateral.[35] But the central bank cannot exercise the role of lending freely during a currency attack, particularly in trying to defend a fixed exchange rate. In a situation of open capital flows, the only defence of a fixed exchange rate is through higher interest rates. However, if the corporate sector is already overleveraged and the banking system fragile, then raising interest rates is in fact no defence. Higher interest rates would only worsen the financial position of the corporate sector and the banking system, leading also to bank runs.

It was this vulnerability that the hedge funds understood perfectly.

Hence, a precondition of the defence of a fixed exchange rate is not only prudent fiscal policy, but also low leverage in the corporate and banking

---

[34] Nukul Commission (1998), paras. 3 and 4.
[35] Bagehot (1991) [1873].

sectors. If the central bank had to pump in liquidity to rescue a bank during a currency attack, it would be fuelling the liquidity that can easily be borrowed by speculators to buy scarce foreign currency from it. In other words, the central bank cannot defend both a currency attack and a bank panic at the same time.

Thus, my personal opinion is that it is perhaps too much to expect a central bank to try and manage financial stability and financial supervision all on its own, especially if there are inconsistencies in macro- and prudential policies that are not all within the central bank's control. In a complex world of global capital flows, a market economy will need a whole array of institutions and policies, properly coordinated, in order to manage financial market volatility. The current trend globally to separate the bank supervision function from the central bank therefore is an attempt to share the institutional burden of financial stability. The bank supervisor looks after individual institutional stability, and the central bank looks after systemic stability.

Even in developed markets, this division of labour is not easy to operate, as the run on the Northern Rock episode in the United Kingdom revealed in the third quarter of 2007. The ultimate decision on whether to intervene in the United Kingdom rested with a Tripartite Agreement between the Treasury, the Bank of England and the supervisor, FSA. Clearly there are likely to be differences of opinion between the central bank (which is lender of last resort and therefore wants to avoid moral hazard), the supervisor (which would prefer intervention to prevent systemic contagion) and the Ministry of Finance (which is concerned with the political fallout and possible fiscal costs).

Some, but not all, of the above policy and institutional inconsistencies were present in the Thai crisis. When the market is going through an economic boom and bubbly exuberance, no one wants the central bank or any other institution to take away the punch bowl or spoil the party. But when the time comes to clean up, everyone wants the central bank to ease the pain. There is, however, no free lunch. The price of institutional and policy neglect, and, indeed, lack of tough action, is financial crisis and pain.

Of all the policies and actions by the Bank of Thailand leading up to the crisis, it was its decision to defend the baht, which was pegged to the U.S. dollar (about 80–90 percent of the combined international currencies in the basket), right up to the very end that came under intense fire. The Nukul Commission Report had this to say of the episode:

The Bank of Thailand (BOT) had the option not to liberalise the capital market in 1990, but it chose to do so. … Having decided to liberalise the capital market, the

BOT should have adopted a more flexible exchange rate policy, but it preferred to maintain a narrow trading band for the baht instead. ... Having decided to maintain the narrow trading band for the baht, the authorities needed to pursue a particularly conservative aggregate demand policy, particularly after 1994. While fiscal policy remains the responsibility of the Finance Ministry and of the Parliament, the BOT did not push forward the need for conservative fiscal policy aggressively. The BOT's own deflationary policy was generally ineffective, as it was negated by the inflow of foreign money. Unable to constrain effectively the fiscal and monetary policies, the BOT could have imposed policies to control large capital inflows. When it finally did so, they were too late and ineffective. By that time, the stock of debt was already excessive.

...

The Commission concludes that BOT's insistence on adhering to its position, that the basket currency system was appropriate for Thailand, led to a baht defence which cost the country large amounts of its foreign reserves. BOT continued with this position despite the realisation that the slowing economy, declining export growth, weak financial institutions and property market collapse, were destroying foreign investors' confidence in the Thai economy, and putting pressure on the baht. However, in trying to rectify the problem, the BOT gave priority to problems that would take a long time to resolve, such as tighter monetary and fiscal policies, and resolving debt and property market problems, before attacking the foreign exchange regime. On the other hand, from the point of view of foreign investors and speculators the exchange rate is the most crucial variable affecting the profitability of their investments, and is the point that is most amenable for them to attack. Consequently the fixed exchange rate regime became the most vulnerable point of the economic system.[36]

The Nukul Commission Report noted that the Bank of Thailand did reconsider its policy of maintaining the baht peg to the U.S. dollar in April 1996. But, particularly after May 1996 when the double-mismatch vulnerabilities within the Thai financial system were increasingly obvious to all, the central bank was in a no-win situation. Furthermore, since the market did not hedge its foreign debt, any devaluation of the baht could be costly to Thai corporations with net exposure to foreign exchange risk.

There was a very delicate balance between the balance sheet effects of devaluation with its flow impact. Theoretically, an improvement in the trade balance from a devaluation should be able to offset a balance sheet loss, but not if the net external liability made many of the key corporations insolvent and therefore the banking system insolvent with it. Since good balance sheet data was not readily available, no one was able to judge the true net impact of devaluation on the economy as a whole.

[36] Nukul Commission (1998), 5–6.

In the process the central bank dug itself into a deeper and deeper dilemma as foreign reserves depleted rapidly. By July 1996 the IMF, which in its annual summary reports since 1994 had been quietly advising more exchange rate flexibility, stepped up its calls for the Bank of Thailand to do so. Then in May 1997 the IMF suggested a devaluation of around 10 to 15 percent accompanied by a float.[37]

In the meantime, however, by January 1997 the hedge funds had already smelt that the Bank of Thailand was vulnerable. Speculation against the baht accelerated, and with limited reserves the Bank of Thailand could defend itself only by intervening in the forward market, which hid the extent of reserves loss. By July, when the devaluation occurred, the amount of forward commitments was about US$29 billion, bringing the net reserves almost to zero. Without any foreign exchange to defend the baht, Thailand had no option but to call in the IMF on 28 July.

A NATION SOBERED

From 1998 Thailand followed the IMF medicine diligently, but the crisis cost the country two years of deflation and nearly 35 percent of GDP to clean up the banking system. The baht devalued from B 25 to the U.S. dollar just before the crisis to B 56 in January 1998, setting back GDP per capita from US$2,496 in 1997 to US$1,829 in 1998. Nominal GDP fell over US$70 billion during the crisis. Even today the stock market index is roughly half the value of its 1994 peak. An unemployed banker ended up as a well-known sandwich seller.

Thailand signed altogether eight letters of intent with the IMF between August 1997 and September 1998. The first IMF package amounted to around US$17 billion, with US$10 billion from Asia, US$2.7 billion from the World Bank and the ADB and the balance from the IMF. As noted by former Minister of Finance Thanong Bidaya, Europe and the United States did not provide any direct funding. Compare this with US$50 billion for the Mexican crisis and around US$55 billion for the South Korean crisis. The tight monetary policy and fiscal tightening that was imposed as conditionality by the IMF ran from August 1997 to May 1998, resulting in a contraction in the economy of 10.5 percent in 1998. Only after the publication of its Independent Evaluation Office report in 2003 did the Fund finally acknowledge that its first phase policy recommendations had compounded the pain in the early part of the rescue package.

[37] Nukul Commission (1998), paras. 45, 47, 82–86 and 202.

Thailand has done quite a bit of soul searching since the crisis. Nevertheless, out of the pain rose courageous and remarkable leadership. Former Prime Minister of Thailand Chuan Leekpai, who took over the helm of the Thai Government in November 1997 and whose coalition government was faced with the task of stabilizing the Thai economy, reflected:

What went wrong? During the period of rapid economic growth, we were too complacent. In the good times, we forgot many important truths and neglected many important tasks.

- We opened up our economy, but our stated plans to pursue discipline were not followed up;
- We attracted massive flows of cheap foreign capital, which we did not always spend or invest with enough prudence in spite of our original plans to channel funds to productive investments;
- We created wealth but were perhaps negligent in creating competitiveness;
- We were successful in our economic performance, so much as that we did not examine the fundamentals of our politics and governance or tackle issues such as the bureaucratic inefficiency, lack of transparency and lack of accountability;
- We became a part of the globalized world and felt proud to belong to the twenty-first century, while much of our law and governance and many of our instruments for macroeconomic, financial and business management are waiting to be modified, modernized, and upgraded to international standards and practices.

There is immunity in success. As long as we continued to succeed, this complacency could go unpunished. But once the cracks appeared, we compounded the mistakes by committing much of our fiscal reserve to shore up insolvent finance companies and our foreign currency reserve to defend the baht. Naturally, we were quickly and severely disciplined by the market.

...

The most crucial component of reform is, of course, political reform. Clean politics is wise politics. It enables the country to avoid costly mistakes and to revive and sustain market confidence.[38]

The quiet Finance Minister, Tarrin Nimmanhaeminda, who served from November 1997 to February 2001 with the Leekpai Government, probably had the most incisive comments:

One key lesson emerged. To avert a crisis, monetary policy must strike a correct balance between these three elements [exchange rate regime, domestic interest rates and the control of capital flows into and out of a country]. Monetary policy

---

[38] Leekpai (1998).

must be flexible and not biased towards any one position over the other. As all three elements are interrelated, no single element can be pursued independently.

...

The public sector is a critical instrument in formulating development policy of the country. Therefore, public sector management must be efficient, transparent, and free from manipulation by vested influences and focused on the benefits of the public at large.[39]

The key lesson from Thailand is that one should avoid bubbles in the asset sector, which could cause serious fragilities in the private sector balance sheets that result in a crisis in the financial sector. Just as individuals must manage their personal risks, nations must manage their total risks; if they fail, global flows could punish these mistakes very severely. One could blame the volatile capital flows due to circumstances outside one's control, such as the volatile dollar-yen rate, but the responsibility of sound macroeconomic management and risk management has to rest with the country itself. In other words, globalization tests the quality of national governance at all levels, from the corporate to the political level.

It is perhaps fitting to close this chapter with the words of Pin Chakkaphak, former President of the failed Finance One and the poster boy of the go-go era of Thai banking, reportedly maintaining a fleet of four Ferraris, a Porsche and a Honda NSX at the height of his success:

Ten years already? Has Thailand moved on?[40]

Next, we shall discuss the case of South Korea, the country that had a strong real economy but a fragile financial sector.

---

[39] Nimmanhaeminda (2007).
[40] Chakkaphak (2007).

SEVEN

South Korea: Strong Body, Weak Heart

Korea's banking industry was an industry 'managed' to be weak.
~ Dominic Casserley and Greg Gibb

Amongst the economies that were worst hit by the Asian crisis, the South Korean experience is probably the best example of the interdependence between the real and financial sectors. South Korea's high economic growth levels could not last too long because the real economy lacked a strong financial base. The Korean experience demonstrated that failure of the financial system could be devastating on the real sector. This was like a strong body but a weak heart. You ignore the fragility of the financial sector at your peril.

MIRACLE IN THE LAND OF THE MORNING CALM

South Korea is the best example of the Asian Miracle. In the early 1950s, it was a poor farming nation with no natural resources. The country was devastated by a bitter Korean civil war that was fought between 1950 and 1953. Not many observers then were optimistic about South Korea's poverty-stricken economy. In 1962, when the Park Chung Hee Government launched the first Five-Year Economic Development Plan, South Korea was an economy with a GDP of about US$2.3 billion and a per capita income of around US$87.

The South Korean economy, however, went through a remarkable transformation in the three decades leading up to the 1997–1998 Asian Crisis (see Table 7.1). Between 1962 and 1996 the economy grew at an average of 8.6 percent annually on the back of a massive industrialization and export drive, which ballooned from a mere US$55 million in 1960 to US$130 billion in 1996. In 1996, with a GDP of US$558 billion, South Korea's was the world's 11th largest

Table 7.1. *South Korea: Selected Real Economy Indicators*

	1990	1991	1992	1993	1994	1995	1996	1997	1998	1999	2000
GDP US$ billion	263.8	308.3	329.9	362.2	423.5	517.2	558.0	527.3	348.5	445.5	512.0
GDP per capita US$	6,155	7,120	7,542	8,195	9,486	11,470	12,258	11,474	7,528	9,558	10,891
Real GDP Annual % change	9.2	9.4	5.9	6.1	8.5	9.2	7.0	4.7	−6.9	9.5	8.5
Unemployment rate % of total labour force	2.5	2.5	2.5	2.9	2.5	2.1	2.1	2.6	7.0	6.6	4.4
Inflation Annual % change	8.6	9.3	6.2	4.8	6.3	4.5	4.9	4.4	7.5	0.8	2.3
Fiscal balance % of GDP	−0.6	−1.8	−0.7	0.3	0.1	0.3	0.2	−1.4	−3.9	−2.5	1.1
Central government debt % of GDP	13.0	12.1	11.9	11.2	10.1	8.9	8.2	10.3	14.8	16.9	17.4
Gross domestic capital formation % of GDP	37.5	39.7	37.3	35.7	37.0	37.7	38.9	36.0	25.0	29.1	31.0
Gross domestic savings % of GDP	37.3	37.6	36.7	36.7	36.3	36.5	35.7	35.8	37.9	35.8	33.9
All industry production index 2000 = 100	43.1	47.3	50.0	52.2	58.0	64.9	70.4	73.7	68.9	85.6	100.0

Sources: Bank of Korea, ADB, IMF and Jaimovich and Panniza (2006)

economy, and on 12 December 1996, the country joined the OECD. South Korea, with a land area of 98,480 square kilometres and 47 million people, was the second country in East Asia to be an industrial nation.

In fact, despite facing increasingly intense competition in terms of international trade from its Asian neighbours, the Korean economy looked in pretty good shape just before the Asian crisis. In 1996 the economy grew strongly by 7 percent, and the fiscal budget was broadly in balance, whilst its external debt ratio of 28.2 percent of GDP was considerably lower than many OECD countries. Although inflation was slightly high at 4.9 percent per annum and the current account deficit was 4.1 percent of GDP, no one took serious notice.

First, South Korea had a record of strong economic management. The nation's outstanding economic success, after all, had often been attributed to its government-guided economic framework and model.

Second, by 1996 South Korea had developed leading positions in several major industries. It was the largest shipbuilding nation, edging out Japan, the largest manufacturer of DRAM chips in the world, the sixth largest steel producer and the fifth largest producer and exporter of automobiles.

Third, South Korea had by 1996 become a more consumer-oriented society with considerable purchasing power. Between 1970 and 1996 employees' share of GDP increased significantly from a third in 1970 to almost half by 1996.

However, by early 1997 South Korea was confronted with the issue of how to restructure its industrial policy. The economy needed to reform and rethink the systems and institutions that had propelled the country to great heights for the last three decades. In April 1997 Korea's top research institutes and companies commissioned a major study entitled *Revitalising the Korean Economy toward the 21st Century* that made five major propositions:[1]

- The Korean economic miracle was over. South Korea's economic dynamism was being sapped by an increasingly debilitating set of systemic impediments and a dramatic managerial and technology knowledge gap.
- There was a stalemate, precipitated by a lack of agreement on the nature and severity of the problem, lack of a vision and strategy to guide the changes, fear of some apparently insurmountable transition risks and lack of appropriate institutions to manage the change process.
- South Korea could become an entrepreneurial economy, without government intervention, by acting as a nerve centre for Northeast Asia and bringing to bear the best of global managerial and technical knowledge.

---

[1]   Booz, Allen and Hamilton (1997), 6–7.

- The strategy for change should concentrate initially on breaking the core systemic impediments whilst resolving the main transitional issues. The key was to focus on the changes needed to create an entrepreneurial and externally-oriented economy.
- The agenda for change should concentrate on progressively restructuring the roles of the government as the transition towards a market economy progresses.

The study also highlighted two major points. First:

Korea has become a victim of its own success. It has followed the Japanese model of government-led industrial growth, drawing on the technical knowledge of others, to create a strong global position in several industries. Today, however, Korean companies find themselves in a competitive nutcracker between the knowledge and technology advantages of countries such as Japan, and the emerging cost-based competitors such as China. The government-led system has today become the major impediment to responding to the competitive nutcracker. At the same time the managerial and technical knowledge gap is becoming increasingly serious. Both these gaps will become more serious over the coming years without dramatic changes. Without a radical restructuring of the economy, of the government role, and of Korea's economic relationship with the outside world, the economy faces severe unemployment, and relegation to the status of a second-class economic power.[2]

Second, there were serious concerns in terms of the financial sector, particularly with regard to the Korean banking system, which was suffering from 'shaky accounts'.[3]

It was clear that although leading elites in South Korea were aware of the challenges facing the economy, even as late as October 1997 no one dreamt that South Korea would find itself a victim of the tsunami that was tearing apart its Southeast Asian neighbours. Indeed, the prevailing IMF view at that time, 'shared by many (though not all) other public and private-sector observers', was that 'while Korea faced problems in its financial sector that were potentially very serious and that needed to be addressed promptly, there was no risk that this would lead to a loss of confidence and crisis-inducing capital account outflows'.[4] Leading Korean economist Professor Park Yung-Chul probably accurately described the consensus view at that time when he said, 'Korea's financial crisis has been as dramatic as it has been unexpected'.[5] The Land of the Morning Calm was about to witness the calm before the storm.

---

[2] Booz, Allen and Hamilton (1997), 22.
[3] Delhaise (1998), 115.
[4] Independent Evaluation Office (2003), 159.
[5] Park (1998), 25.

THE MAKING OF KOREA INC.

South Korea built its economy through sheer hard work and determination. A Japanese colony from 1910 to 1945, South Korea copied the Japanese industrialization and export model with great success, perhaps giving credence to the observation that 'Koreans learned the Japanese way of doing business and managing the economy, and remain the Asians who understand Japan best'.[6]

In a nutshell, following the Japanese model, the Korean economy operated like a single company, Korea Inc. The development model called for a concentration of efforts in government-inspired specialization that linked the government and the big business groups, with the banks playing the important middlemen. The Korean government, through the Economic Planning Board, targeted specific industries for development. Many of the industries chosen by the government were the same as the ones also chosen earlier by the Japanese, specifically, textiles, toys, apparel, footwear, petrochemicals, shipbuilding, steel, automobiles, consumer electronics and semiconductors.

Exactly like the Japanese, 'champions' from existing firms were selected for spearheading these industries. In exchange, they received preferential treatment, including business licenses, protection from foreign investors and imports as well as access to cheap financing channelled through largely government-controlled banks. This pattern resulted in the growth of a small number of very large mainly family-owned business conglomerates or *chaebol* such as Samsung, Hyundai, Daewoo and LG. By 1996 the top 30 *chaebol* were reputed to control as much as 85 percent of industrial output and 50 percent of Korean assets.[7] The market concentration ratio was thus higher in South Korea than in Japan, where growth was based on a significant number of very large firms as well as a large number of small firms.

FINANCING KOREA INC.

Three decades of strong economic growth propelled South Korea's financial market into Asia's second largest by the mid-1990s. Financial assets totalled about US$1.4 trillion in 1997, up from US$243 million a decade earlier.

I first visited South Korea in 1992, when I was at the World Bank, to study its financial system in preparation for the country's membership in

---

[6] Harvie and Lee (2003), 267.
[7] Delhaise (1998), 102; Akaba, Budde and Choi (1998), 70.

the OECD. Briefly, the Korean financial system had four main characteristics that lasted until the early 1990s.

First, as with its Asian neighbours, the Korean financial system was dominated by banks (Table 7.2). Assets of banks and other financial institutions amounted to 115 percent of GDP. In comparison, the Korean stock market was only 29 percent of GDP, and the bond market was only 50 percent of GDP in 1996.

Second, as observed by Cambridge University political economist Chang Ha-Joon, 'it will be difficult to make sense of Korea's financial system before the mid-1990s without recognising that the government basically saw finance as a servant to industry'.[8] Being the dominant source of financing for Korean economic activity, the banking system was 'managed to be weak', meaning the government intervened heavily by segmenting financial markets, placing artificial ceilings on interest rates and directly allocating credit amongst enterprises. As a result, the Korean banking system suffered from five main weaknesses: poor profit orientation and performance, inadequate regulation and supervision, excessive industry fragmentation, insufficient credit assessment and management skills and limited product and service innovation, all of which are often seen as symptoms of financial repression, which was viewed as 'necessary for national development'.[9]

The McKinsey Study on Asian banking[10] found that the return on assets of all Korean domestic banks in 1995–1997 was a mere 0.16 percent, less than one-tenth the earnings of world-class banks. According to the Study, Korea's approach to bank regulation and supervision left much to be desired, falling short in eight areas of public disclosure, accounting and legal framework, asset classification systems and loan portfolio concentration limits, government involvement, connected lending, capital adequacy requirements, incentive-compatible safety nets and consolidated supervision. 'The supervisory style of the MOFE (Ministry of Finance) and BOK (Bank of Korea) was perceived to be ad hoc and at times discriminatory by players in the industry'.[11]

Third, despite liberalization of the financial sector since early 1980s that included the privatization of commercial banks and unrestricted entry of other financial institutions, the Korean banking system was nevertheless still heavily influenced by the government either directly through complete or

---

[8]   Chang (2006), 263.
[9]   Chang (2006), 263.
[10] Casserley and Gibb (1999), 324.
[11] Casserley and Gibb (1999), 325.

Table 7.2. *South Korea: Financial Structure (% of GDP)*

	1990	1991	1992	1993	1994	1995	1996	1997	1998	1999	2000
Assets of deposit money banks	50.7	51.3	52.0	49.1	49.0	48.6	50.7	55.3	66.4	69.6	76.5
Assets of other financial institutions	43.0	43.9	48.6	53.1	57.7	60.0	64.1	68.3	82.0	75.5	59.4
Stock market capitalization	48.2	33.8	30.9	34.1	39.1	36.4	29.0	18.0	24.2	57.8	56.2
Bond market capitalization	44.3	43.2	47.8	51.1	50.6	49.0	50.2	42.6	66.8	75.7	73.0
Insurance premium volume	11.0	11.1	11.6	11.1	11.1	11.6	11.5	13.2	12.5	11.6	11.8

Source: Beck, Demirgüç-Kunt and Levine (2000), revised 13 August 2007

partial ownership or indirectly through approval of key executive appointments and lending 'recommendations'. It was not dissimilar to the Japanese system of 'window guidance'.

Directed credit or 'policy loans' were a key instrument in the Korean model of economic development. Like the Japanese main-bank system, a specific bank was designated to supervise the utilization of these loans by the respective players. The banks effectively underwrote the large industrial projects, made with government blessing and implicit support. Consequently, 'these conglomerates were able to take business and financial risks that they otherwise could not have afforded. Many of these big bets paid off and thus drove Korea's rapid economic growth'.[12]

The overall effect was a Korea Inc. that was highly leveraged. At the end of 1997, private sector credit was 121 percent of GDP (Table 7.3), and the 30 largest Korean conglomerates had an average debt-to-equity ratio of 519 percent, a sharp contrast with 193 percent in Japan, 154 percent in the United States or 86 percent in Taiwan.[13] Even though the proportion of new policy loans to new total credit had dropped steadily from a high of 100 percent in the 1970s to between 60 and 80 percent in the 1980s, they nevertheless remained a prominent feature in the period leading up to the Asian crisis, amounting to around 15 percent of new credit. Indeed, even up to 1992 the ratio of policy loans to bank assets was as high as 30 percent.[14]

Fourth, tight capital controls existed on both inflows and outflows, with the level of controls dictated mainly by developments in the current account. Unlike Japan, which had had a structural trade surplus since the 1960s, South Korea suffered from a chronic current account deficit, caused by its need to import all raw materials, parts and machinery required for the production of export goods on a large scale.[15] In order to obtain the foreign exchange required to assist the financing of such chronic current account deficits, 'the Korean authorities alternately liberalized and restricted both inward and outward capital account transactions'.[16]

Fundamentally, South Korea chose to shun FDI even in the manufacturing sector, preferring to rely on domestic ownership, external borrowing and technology licensing to fill the funding gap (Table 7.4). According to the 1997 study *Revitalizing the Korean Economy*, 'This import and localization of foreign-originated technology has, however, been achieved at

---

[12] Booz, Allen and Hamilton (1997), 24.
[13] Park Jae-Joon (1998), 56.
[14] Adelman and Song (1999).
[15] Harvie and Lee (2003), 263.
[16] Independent Evaluation Office (2003), 155.

Table 7.3. *South Korea: Selected Financial Sector Indicators*

	1990	1991	1992	1993	1994	1995	1996	1997	1998	1999	2000
Narrow money (M1) Annual % change	23.7	22.8	19.5	17.2	15.2	16.2	12.9	12.3	−5.6	40.2	15.3
Broad money (M2) Annual % change	25.3	19.5	21.5	17.4	21.1	23.3	16.7	19.7	23.7	5.1	5.2
Private sector credit by financial institutions[1] % of GDP	89.7	91.4	97.1	99.1	103.8	106.0	112.4	121.0	144.6	139.8	129.9
Lending rates % per annum	10.0	10.0	10.0	8.6	8.5	9.0	8.8	11.9	15.3	9.4	8.6
Deposit rates % per annum	10.0	10.0	10.0	8.6	8.5	8.8	7.5	10.8	13.3	8.0	7.9
Interest rate spreads % per annum	0.0	0.0	0.0	0.0	0.0	0.2	1.3	1.1	2.0	1.5	0.6

Sources: Bank of Korea, World Bank, Beck, Demirgüç-Kunt and Levine (2000), revised 13 August 2007 and author's estimates
[1] Deposit money banks and other financial institutions

Table 7.4. *Selected Asian Economies: Inward Foreign Direct Investment Stock (% of GDP)*

	1980–1985 Annual Average	1986–1990 Annual Average	1991–1994 Annual Average	1995	1996	1997	1998	1999	2000–2003 Annual Average	2004–2006 Annual Average
Japan	0.3	0.3	0.4	0.6	0.6	0.6	0.7	1.1	1.6	2.3
China	0.9	3.7	9.3	13.9	15.0	16.2	17.2	17.2	15.1	12.0
Hong Kong	78.5	65.0	48.8	49.2	50.7	141.4	134.9	248.2	241.9	324.2
Indonesia	5.1	7.1	7.9	9.2	10.7	13.2	29.6	19.0	8.1	5.4
Malaysia	21.1	21.4	28.8	32.3	35.7	42.3	62.4	61.9	44.0	36.4
Philippines	6.0	7.9	8.0	8.1	8.7	10.1	14.0	15.0	15.6	14.8
Singapore	52.5	72.6	76.1	77.9	81.1	78.0	105.4	124.1	144.0	159.3
South Korea	2.1	2.2	2.0	1.8	2.1	2.7	5.5	6.5	8.2	8.3
Taiwan	5.0	5.5	5.6	5.7	6.1	6.6	7.3	7.7	9.9	12.6
Thailand	4.0	6.9	11.1	10.5	10.8	8.8	22.8	25.4	29.4	33.0

Sources: IMF, UNCTAD and author's estimates

great cost to Korea's international image. Almost without exception, it is viewed as the most difficult market in Asia'.[17] '[The] Korean business community was seen as unreliable and xenophobic' and 'the most unprincipled partners in the region' because of barriers to investment by foreign businesses, an unwillingness to offer foreign companies access to Korean markets whilst expecting other countries to do so, questionable business ethics, at least in international dealings, and an ideologically motivated drive to expand aggressively into markets irrespective of global supply and demand balances.[18]

Foreign direct investment or participation in the Korean financial system was even more limited. In the banking system, foreign participation was severely restricted, with foreign bank held assets accounting for just 2.1 percent of total bank assets in 1996.[19] The stock market was directly opened to foreign investors in 1992, but there were restrictions on the amount of shares foreigners could hold in individual stocks. Foreigners were eligible only to purchase a limited number of corporate bond issues, and it was announced in August 1996 that the full opening of the bond market would be delayed until the differential between Korean and overseas interest rates, which was about 6 to 7 percent, narrowed to two percentage points.[20]

In 1993 there was a concerted push towards deregulation and liberalization of the Korean financial system. This was the result of a combination of factors, including South Korea's burgeoning current account deficit, conditions for joining OECD and lobbying by the business community, which wanted to take advantage of the relatively low short-term interest rates in the global markets. Domestic real interest rates in South Korea were substantially above world markets during this period as a result of the tightening of Korean monetary policy in face of higher inflation (see Table 7.5). Before the crisis the nominal interest rate was about 12 to 13 percent annually, whilst real interest was about 7 to 8 percent. In comparison, the world-market nominal rate was about 6 to 7 percent, whilst real rates were about 3 to 4 percent. However, according to the IMF IEO Report:

In spite of the overall commitment to freeing capital flows, this process had not moved very far by 1997. Korea still maintained substantial controls on many capital account transactions, particularly on the external issuance of long-term bonds and long-term commercial loans by financial and non-financial entities. ... Joining

---

[17] Booz, Allen and Hamilton (1997), 28.
[18] Booz, Allen and Hamilton (1997), 31.
[19] Cull and Martínez Pería (2007).
[20] Noland (1996).

Table 7.5. *South Korea: Selected Interest Rate Differentials (% per Annum)*

	1990	1991	1992	1993	1994	1995	1996	1997	1998	1999	2000
South Korea call rate (KCR)	–	16.8	13.5	11.5	14.1	11.0	12.5	21.3	7.0	4.8	5.3
U.S. effective federal funds rate (FFR)	8.1	5.7	3.5	3.0	4.2	5.8	5.3	5.5	5.4	5.0	6.2
Euro overnight index average (EONIA)	–	–	–	–	5.2	5.6	4.0	4.0	3.1	3.0	4.8
Switzerland call rate (SCR)	8.9	7.6	5.9	4.4	3.6	2.3	1.8	1.0	1.0	1.4	3.5
Japan call rate (JCR)	8.2	6.3	3.9	2.4	2.3	0.5	0.5	0.4	0.3	0.0	0.2
Interest rate differential (KCR – FFR)	–	11.2	10.0	8.5	9.8	5.1	7.2	15.8	1.7	−0.2	−0.9
Interest rate differential (KCR – EONIA)	–	–	–	–	8.8	5.3	8.4	17.3	3.9	1.7	0.5
Interest rate differential (KCR – SCR)	–	9.2	7.6	7.1	10.5	8.6	10.7	20.3	6.0	3.4	1.8
Interest rate differential (KCR – JCR)	–	10.5	9.6	9.1	11.8	10.5	12.0	20.9	6.7	4.7	5.1

Sources: Bank of Korea, U.S. Federal Reserve Board, OECD and author's estimates
Dash means data not available

the OECD was seen as an important political goal and as a way to reduce borrowing costs, but in the accession talks the authorities resisted efforts to bring Korea's capital account regulations in line with those of other OECD members. In taking this stance, the authorities cited their concern about the consequences of a sharp increase in capital inflows, given prevailing interest rate differentials. The policy of permitting short-term borrowing and restricting long-term flows allowed the authorities additional flexibility vis-à-vis OECD's rules, which grant members the right to 'roll back' previously adopted liberalization measures with respect to most short-term capital movements but not those regarding long-term movements.[21]

The policy of liberalizing short-term capital inflows rather than long-term FDI translated to a South Korean investment boom that was supported by foreign short-term credit obtained through domestic financial institutions. In particular, Korean merchant banks, mostly owned by *chaebol*, found a profitable niche. They were able to take advantage of the easier rules on overseas borrowing because they were less regulated than their traditional commercial banks as they were established to facilitate the 'curb market', meaning serving borrowers who require cash urgently or are unable to procure bank financing because of lack of creditworthiness. Therefore, Korean merchant banks were at the forefront of Korean institutions that accessed the international short-term capital money for funding and onward lending or investing. They also borrowed in U.S. dollars. In reality, the commercial banks were were happy to let the merchant banks take some of the risks.[22]

In addition to funding Korean companies, Korean merchant banks were also active players in the yen carry trade and international arbitrage business. However, because their funding costs were higher, they took higher risks by investing in high-yield Russian and Brazilian bonds. These opportunities proved to be so lucrative that 24 new merchant banks were established between 1994 and 1996, and by 1995–1996 a number of Korean merchant banks together with Korean commercial banks and securities houses, opened branches in the offshore financial centres of Hong Kong and Singapore specifically to tap the international banking market for funds.

Consequently, South Korea's short-term external debt increased sharply immediately following the liberalization of short-term capital flows. Between 1990 and 1996 it shot up by almost more than 158 percent, from US$29.4 billion to US$75.9 billion (Table 7.6). By July 1997 South Korea had total external debts of US$177.4 billion, of which US$80.5 billion, or more than 45 percent, were short term. Bank borrowings were US$110.2

---

[21] Independent Evaluation Office (2003), 156–157.
[22] Park Yung-Chul (1998), 30.

Table 7.6. *South Korea: Foreign Reserves and External Debt Indicators*

	1990	1991	1992	1993	1994	1995	1996	1997	1998	1999	2000
Foreign exchange reserves (FER) US$ billion	14.5	13.3	16.6	19.7	25.0	31.9	33.2	19.7	52.0	73.7	95.9
FER growth Annual % change	−3.5	−8.0	25.1	18.4	27.0	27.5	4.1	−40.7	163.6	41.8	30.1
Total external debt US$ billion	49.5	58.8	63.8	72.1	89.8	119.8	157.4	174.2	163.8	152.9	148.1
Total external debt % of GDP	18.8	19.1	19.3	19.9	21.2	23.2	28.2	33.0	47.0	34.3	28.9
Short-term external debt US$ billion	29.4	33.7	36.1	39.4	38.5	54.9	75.9	63.8	39.6	43.1	49.7
Short-term external debt % of total external debt	59.4	57.3	56.6	54.6	42.9	45.8	48.2	36.6	24.2	28.2	33.6
Short-term external debt % of FER	203.3	253.3	216.9	200.0	153.8	171.9	228.4	323.7	76.2	58.5	51.8

Sources: Bank of Korea, IMF and author's estimates

billion, making up more than 62 percent of South Korea's total external debt, borrowings of nonbank financial corporations were US$1.7 billion or around 1 percent of total debt, whilst private corporation borrowings were US$52.5 billion, just under 30 percent of South Korea's total external debt. Of the US$80.5 billion in short-term debt, US$64.7 billion or more than 80 percent were short-term borrowings by Korean banks.[23]

It is interesting to note that South Korea's long-term external debt was nearly 60 percent in U.S. dollars, with 23 percent in yen (Table 6.10). This contrasted with Thailand, where the comparable ratios were 47 percent and 39 percent, respectively. The high level of debt in U.S. dollars meant that when the won depreciated against the U.S. dollar, the borrowing corporations suffered both large foreign exchange losses and higher borrowing costs.

WHAT WENT WRONG?

Korean explanations for the crisis centre around three broad areas: the yen-dollar exchange rate, the mismanagement of the financial and capital account liberalization process and the loss of investors' confidence. Both external and internal forces, together with the transition to a change in administrations due to the elections in December 1997 partially paralysing critical decision making, created the environment for crisis.

The Yo-Yo Yen Strikes Again

Like the exchange rate issue in Thailand, the yen-dollar exchange rate affected South Korea in two ways. First, when the yen depreciated from ¥80 to the U.S. dollar in April 1995 to around ¥127 in April 1997, Korean goods lost their competitive edge, because the Korean won was a managed float against the U.S. dollar. To add to the woes of Korean exporters, there was a sharp drop in the world prices of computer chips, ships, automobiles and garments, affecting over 50 percent of South Korea's exports.

The first overt signs of trouble were evident when the current account deficit widened from 2 percent in 1995 to 4 percent in 1996, but, worse, exports growth dropped sharply from a phenomenal 30 percent to 4 percent during this period, triggering a fall in real GDP growth from 9.2 percent in 1995 to 7.0 percent in 1996 (Tables 7.1 and 7.7). However, as observed by Professor Park Yung-Chul:

[23] For South Korea's currency composition of long-term external debt see Table 6.10.

The reason for the Korean policymakers' reluctance to devalue the won during this period was not altogether clear. It is speculated however, that the policymakers, who were then preoccupied with industrial restructuring, believed that a strong won would help facilitate the shifting of resources away from those industries such as light manufacturing, where Korea was losing its competitiveness. If this was indeed their policy objective, much of the effect of a strong won was more than offset by a large increase in foreign capital inflows facilitated by the deregulation of capital account transactions.[24]

The sharp fall in exports growth meant trouble for Korean exporters, who depended critically on their export cash flow to keep their leverage sustainable.

Following market liberalization efforts, which, like financial liberalization, also began in earnest in 1993 as a prelude to South Korea's membership in the WTO in January 1995, *chaebol* were able 'to do whatever they believed was in their best interest'[25] as the South Korean government, in a change from previous decades, suddenly found that it was unable to control or coordinate their investment activities. Thus, a McKinsey Report in 1998 noted:

Intense rivalry between the chaebol led their owners to invest in many areas that had growth potential but did not necessarily provide good returns. ... [I]n the chemicals industry, South Korea added almost as much new capacity between 1990 and 1997 as the whole of Western Europe, even though world markets for many products were already glutted. ... Although revenue soared, the chaebol were not earning the cost of their debt, let alone the weighted average cost of capital.[26]

Therefore, squeezed on cash flow and corporate profits, by January 1997 weaker *chaebol* began to fail. On 23 January 1997, Hanbo Steel, the fourteenth largest *chaebol* in terms of assets, went bankrupt with US$6 billion of debt. According to Kim Kihwan, the government economic policy team then in office refused to bail out the group because 'the team truly believed that in an economy run on market principles, a *chaebol* group should stand on its own feet'.[27]

The consequence was a string of corporate debt crises. In March 1997 the Sammi group, South Korea's twenty-sixth largest conglomerate, failed. In early April the Ssangyong automobile group, the sixth largest conglomerate, revealed that it was more than US$3 billion in debt and in an

---

[24] Park Yung-Chul (1998), 29, 30.
[25] Park Yung-Chul (1998), 33.
[26] Akaba, Budde and Choi (1998), 70.
[27] Kim (2006).

Table 7.7. *South Korea: Selected Currency and Current Account Indicators*

					Currency Indicators*						
	1990	1991	1992	1993	1994	1995	1996	1997	1998	1999	2000
Won to U.S. dollar Period average	707.8	733.4	780.7	802.7	803.4	771.3	804.5	951.3	1,401.4	1,188.8	1,131.0
Won to U.S. dollar End of period	716.4	760.8	788.4	808.1	788.7	774.7	844.2	1,695.0	1,204.0	1,138.0	1,264.5
Won nominal effective exchange rate 2000 = 100	148.6	140.1	136.3	131.6	127.3	129.5	123.6	75.8	90.0	95.6	95.2
Won real effective exchange rate 2000 = 100	112.5	111.8	110.8	110.6	110.9	116.5	114.0	73.2	89.6	95.3	95.6
Yen to U.S. dollar Period average	144.8	134.7	126.7	111.2	102.2	94.1	108.8	121.0	130.9	113.9	107.8
Yen to U.S. dollar End of period	134.4	125.2	124.8	111.9	99.7	102.8	116.0	130.0	115.6	102.2	114.9
Yen nominal effective exchange rate 2000 = 100	66.1	70.4	75.3	88.4	93.7	89.9	81.8	80.3	86.2	101.8	98.4
Yen real effective exchange rate 2000 = 100	80.6	84.3	88.1	101.2	105.1	98.0	86.9	85.1	90.8	103.8	97.1

(continued)

Table 7.7. (*continued*)

	1990	1991	1992	1993	1994	1995	1996	1997	1998	1999	2000
						Current Account Indicators[†]					
Terms of trade 2000 = 100	133.3	134.2	134.2	132.4	137.3	138.5	125.9	121.9	117.2	114.9	100.0
Exports US$ billion	65.0	71.9	76.6	82.2	96.0	125.1	129.7	136.2	132.3	143.7	172.3
Exports growth Annual % change	4.2	10.5	6.6	7.3	16.8	30.3	3.7	5.0	−2.8	8.6	19.9
Imports US$ billion	69.8	81.5	81.8	83.8	102.3	135.1	150.3	144.6	93.3	119.8	160.5
Imports growth Annual % change	13.6	16.7	0.3	2.5	22.1	32.0	11.3	−3.8	−35.5	28.4	34.0
Trade balance US$ billion	−4.8	−9.7	−5.1	−1.6	−6.3	−10.1	−20.6	−8.5	39.0	23.9	11.8
Current account balance US$ billion	−2.0	−8.4	−4.1	0.8	−4.0	−8.7	−23.1	−8.3	40.4	24.5	12.3
Current account balance % of GDP	−0.8	−2.7	−1.2	0.2	−1.0	−1.7	−4.1	−1.6	11.6	5.5	2.4

Sources:

* BIS and IMF

† Bank of Korea, IMF, UNCTAD and author's estimates

unprecedented move was looking for a foreign buyer. In short order, the Jinro Group (nineteenth largest), the Dainong retail chain, and the car manufacturer Kia (eighth largest conglomerate) all required emergency loans. A perfect storm was brewing just as Thailand got into trouble.

The bank-dominated financial system bore the brunt of the financial risk. Philippe Delhaise, former President of Thomson BankWatch Asia Pacific, remarked,

The exposure of each of the major banks to the large corporate problems of 1997 would illustrate a sorry fact: that the concentration of exposure to single names would have been enough to send some of the banks to intensive care. ... When KIA collapsed in 1997, three merchant banks were found to have lent over 120% of their own capital to the group. ... When the crisis hit, what had been a shaky situation turned into a disaster.[28]

Second, the depreciation of the yen against the U.S. dollar caused a reversal of Japanese funds from South Korea (Table 7.8). When the yen began depreciating in 1995, Japanese manufacturers shifted production back to Japan and cut back FDI. Japanese FDI into South Korea fell by 31.3 percent between 1997 and 1998. In addition, Japanese bankers, whose loans constituted about 30 percent of South Korea's foreign bank borrowings by the early to mid-1990s, cut back their foreign lending to South Korea by 14.1 percent between 1997 and 1998. Thus, Korean businesses and banks were facing a double liquidity squeeze from a huge slowdown in export income and a cut in Japanese bank lending. To worsen matters further, other foreign lenders were also cutting back lending.[29]

By October 1997 the crunch came. First, it was revealed that the Korean banks had offshore short-term borrowings of more than US$60 billon that were not reported to the Bank of Korea. Then, in the same month, Standard & Poor and Moody's began sharp downgrades of South Korea's sovereign credit ratings as well as those of Korean banks and financial institutions. Foreign financial institutions thus refused to roll over loans to Korean banks and provide new loans, and Korean banks had no alternative but to borrow in won to exchange for foreign exchange to repay their foreign debt, causing short-term interest rates to rise to over 20 percent per annum. The higher interest rates caused the stock exchange to fall, whilst foreign institutional investors began to exit the market. Both the Korean won and the stock market came under intense pressure.

[28] Delhaise (1998), 115, 116.
[29] Park Jae-Joon (1998), 54.

Table 7.8. *South Korea: Selected Foreign Capital Indicators*

	1990	1991	1992	1993	1994	1995	1996	1997	1998	1999	2000
Capital Flows*											
Net FDI flows US$ billion	-0.3	-0.3	-0.4	-0.8	-1.7	-1.8	-2.3	-1.6	0.7	5.1	4.3
Net portfolio investment flows US$ billion	0.1	3.1	5.8	10.0	6.1	11.6	15.2	14.3	-1.9	8.7	12.0
Net other flows, including bank credit US$ billion	3.1	4.0	1.6	-6.0	6.3	7.5	11.1	-10.8	-2.2	-11.4	-3.6
Net total capital flows US$ billion	2.9	6.8	7.0	3.2	10.7	17.3	24.0	1.9	-3.4	2.4	12.7
Other Indicators†											
Total foreign bank borrowings US$ billion	34.0	40.6	44.3	47.8	64.0	85.8	108.0	107.2	79.6	80.1	76.8
Short-term international bank loans[1] US$ billion	20.4	23.9	26.6	29.3	40.1	54.3	67.5	58.8	29.7	35.1	32.8

Japanese bank lending to South Korea US$ billion	10.2	12.3	12.1	13.0	18.6	22.8	25.7	21.3	18.3	13.5	11.0
Direct Investments from Japan[2] US$ million	284	260	225	246	400	449	416	442	304	980	817
Net external wealth position[3] US$ billion	−15.3	−20.1	−19.4	−24.4	−30.8	−38.2	−50.2	−55.2	−38.9	−52.3	−10.7
Net external liabilities position % of GDP	5.8	6.5	5.9	6.7	7.3	7.4	9.0	10.5	11.2	11.7	2.1

Sources:

* Bank of Korea and author's estimates

[†] BIS, Japan External Trade Organization (JETRO) and Lane and Milesi-Ferretti (2006)

[1] Foreign currency denominated loans of up to and including one year

[2] Based on report and notifications

[3] Negative means net liabilities position; positive means net assets position

The financial problems also coincided with the looming Presidential elections. The outgoing government, which had been in power since the Korean War, was reluctant to undertake unpopular measures that were necessary to stem the crisis, hoping against hope that after the elections a new government would make that decision.

But by early November 1997 the Bank of Korea was forced into a classic bind – either to relieve domestic liquidity to lower interest rates or to intervene to defend a sliding won. The Korean won was allowed to depreciate as the daily band of exchange fluctuations widened from 2.25 percent to 10 percent on November 20. However, the more the won fell, the more the corporations and the banks lost on their net foreign exchange liabilities.

By the end of November 1997, the Korean central bank had about US$7.3 billion of usable reserves, versus a total short-term external debt bill that amounted to US$88.9 billion, ultimately forcing South Korea to officially seek the assistance of the IMF on November 21. It was a classic liquidity crisis, caused by the overleveraged corporate sector and excessive reliance on short-term foreign debt. Significantly, the United States and Europe joined in providing aid when South Korea and the IMF signed an agreement for a financial aid package totalling around US$55 billion on 4 December 1997. It was the largest loan ever made by the IMF.

Liberalization Out of Sync

The second explanation for the Korean crisis was the mistake in the sequencing and pace of the 1993 financial and capital account liberalization process. It was a classic case of an economy 'not being adequately prepared for financial market opening'.[30] In the 2003 evaluation of the South Korean crisis, the IMF IEO Report noted that the Korean financial institutions, businesses and authorities were not sufficiently prepared to face up to the risks of financial and capital account liberalization.

First, domestic financial institutions lacked the relevant knowledge and risk management skills to manage credit and foreign exchange risks. They were used to collateralized lending with real estate and full backing by the government. Korean merchant banks, especially the 24 that were established in the 1990s, acted with 'uncontrollable madness',[31] as they believed that in the spirit of Korea Inc., 'the government would not allow financial institutions to fail'.[32]

---

[30] Park Yung-Chul (1998), 34.
[31] Delhaise (1998), 115.
[32] Park Jae-Joon (1998), 55.

Second, corporate governance and risk management at the *chaebol* were also weak, because they have always survived with their extremely high debt-to-equity ratios, including foreign debt prominently in their books. The idea that 'conglomerates will never go broke' was considered 'unwritten law'.[33]

Third, there was inadequate understanding of the vulnerabilities of balance sheet fragility and global market volatility by government circles. Capital account liberalization risks should have been contained through tighter, not looser, prudential regulation and financial supervision. Indeed, the problems were compounded by the mistake of liberalizing short-term capital flows ahead of long-term capital flows. According to Kim Kihwan:

> Indeed, the government in effect discouraged long-term foreign borrowing by business firms as it required detailed disclosure on the uses of the funds as a condition for its permission. On the other hand, short-term borrowing was mainly regarded as trade-related financing requiring no strict regulation. These de facto incentives for short-term borrowing led banks and business firms to finance long-term investments with short-term foreign borrowings.[34]

Although the government tried to draft various policies to overcome the looming economic difficulties in 1997, they were frequently ineffective because of inappropriate timing and confusing inconsistencies. Unlike Thailand, South Korea did not maintain a hard peg against the U.S. dollar. It operated a daily fluctuation band of the exchange rate, using a market average foreign exchange rate system that was adopted in 1990. Despite widespread expectation of a depreciating Korean won due to the widening current account deficit, the band was kept fairly narrow, so that the won was continually bumping against the floor. It was probable that the authorities wanted to maintain exchange rate stability in the run-up to Presidential elections and to avoid large devaluation losses for foreign debt borrowers.

It is now recognized that the premature financial and capital account liberalization coupled with inherent moral hazard in the South Korean financial system was a major breakdown in market discipline. As a result, it suffered from the same three key problems as the other Asian crisis economies.

First was the maturity mismatch, with South Korean banks and other financial institutions borrowing short to invest long. Approximately 80 percent of short-term foreign debts were financing 70 percent of long-term assets.[35] Korean financial institutions, particularly the merchant banks,

---

[33] Park Jae-Joon (1998), 55.
[34] Kim (2006).
[35] Kim (2006).

became vulnerable to foreign lenders not rolling over their short-term debts and had a liquidity crisis almost immediately when this happened.

Second was the foreign currency mismatch, with Korean banks borrowing foreign currency in dollars and yen and lending in domestic currency. This mismatch was essentially borne by their borrowers, but banks cannot survive without a lender of last resort. In the South Korean case, the Bank of Korea also ran out of U.S. dollars.

The third is the classic lender-borrower relationship: borrowers, because of the inherent conflict of interest, must never control lenders or banks. Many of the merchant banks were controlled by the *chaebol*, who were also 'too big to fail' for the commercial bank lenders.

In essence, the Korean financial institutions and *chaebol* situation bore similarities with those in Thailand and in Indonesia, so it was not surprising that contagion spread when international investors and lenders began to reassess their exposures to South Korea after July 1997. The rest is history.

With the benefit of hindsight, premature financial liberalization to meet OECD membership conditions was a major risk. However, the incumbent President Kim Young-Sam's Government felt that joining the OECD was a sign of 'legitimacy and popular support'.[36] Pride comes before a fall.

Crisis of Confidence

Third, Korean commentators pointed out that the 'country's loss of confidence in the eyes of international investors'[37] was a primary cause. This was attributed to a pendulum swing of emotions from one of 'irrational exuberance' during the Asian Miracle years to one of 'irrational panic' during the crisis. South Korea therefore was a victim of contagion.

In the Korean case, the loss of confidence was perhaps worsened by inadequate transparency, a market fundamental that was little understood or appreciated in the go-go years. Foreign investors had little understanding of the fragilities of the Korean banks and *chaebol* because of the lack of conformance to international accounting and disclosure standards. The complex accounting arrangements within *chaebol* and possible overstatement of profits due to intercompany transactions were not transparent, because South Korea had not adopted international accounting standards by 1996.

The Korean problem was not one of national solvency. The net international investment position was only negative 9 percent of GDP in 1996

---

[36] Adelman and Song (1999).
[37] Park Jae-Joon (1998), 54.

(Table 7.8), by no means critical compared to the negative 50 percent for Thailand, Malaysia and Indonesia. Investors were caught by surprise by the extent of the weakness in the Korean economy, in addition to the fact that the Korean central bank had insufficient reserves to repay these short-term liabilities. The mad rush out of Korean investments and loans was a classic bank panic run and a liquidity crisis without a lender of last resort.

South Korea was also the channel whereby contagion was transmitted to the rest of the emerging markets. When the Korean banks liquidated their portfolio of emerging market bonds in the first half of 1998, the prices of Russian and Brazilian bonds collapsed, triggering crises in these markets that culminated in the meltdown of Russia in August 1998. But that is another story.

RECOVERY AND RESURGENCE

Looking back, no one can deny that the South Korean government succeeded in building up Korea Inc. by strong window guidance in economic management. However, by the mid-1990s the structures and systems had reached the end of their useful life. The 1997 study *Revitalizing the Korean Economy* listed four primary causes for the policy paralysis on the way forward before the crisis: a lack of agreement on the nature and severity of the problems, an inability to agree on a shared vision of what the future Korean economy should look like, a failure to identify and launch the fundamental changes that would naturally trigger/enable other needed actions and a lack of appropriate institutions and leadership to overcome transition risks, which had become highly politicized. This analysis would have been appropriate for the other crisis economies as well, including Japan.

The South Korean policy paralysis reached a climax in November 1997 when the government tried to restore foreign confidence by pushing a financial reform bill package through the legislature. But,

afraid of possible adverse effects of passing such a reform package on the forthcoming presidential election, however, all the political parties, including the Democratic Liberals, the party then in power, refused to act on the reform package. This was literally the proverbial last straw that broke the camel's back. The withdrawal of foreign funds accelerated even more, forcing the government to officially request help from the IMF on November 21.[38]

---

[38] Kim (2006).

The 'inflexibility' of South Korea's economic structure was not only confined within the government sector. It was also prevalent in the corporate sector. As usual, Professor Park Yung-Chul was most insightful when he identified the rigidities of mindsets. First, 'the rigid and bureaucratic management system, where the decision-making was concentrated at the top, made it difficult for the *chaebol* to adjust their investment and production to changes in market conditions as rapidly as they should'. Second, 'unable to lay off workers, the *chaebol* were unwilling to adjust their production and hoped that the government would come in at a certain stage to rescue them'.[39] However, by the end of 1998, 14 of the top 30 *chaebol* as of April 1996 were either bankrupt or nearly bankrupt, and the collapse in July–August 1999 of Daewoo Group, South Korea's fourth largest conglomerate, which was in debt by about US$80 billion, was one of the biggest corporate failures in the world.

Perhaps the crisis was 'a blessing in disguise for the Korean economy'.[40] The remarkable aspect of the Korean crisis was the speed by which Korea recovered from the crisis. By mid-1999 it was already obvious that the worst was over. Once South Korea opened up the financial system and overhauled its corporate governance and accounting and disclosure standards, foreign investment poured in, picking up and restructuring failed banks and corporations. They were not fixing systems that were broken, but systems that needed fixing, with OECD level skills and knowledge. There is nothing like a crisis to change mindsets.

Most of the credit can be attributable to the resilience of the Korean people in general and the workers in particular. Throughout the crisis there were pictures of Korean housewives donating their jewelry to help reduce the national debt. Although Korean workers did protest in the streets for the loss of jobs, by and large, the nation pulled together and worked as tirelessly for recovery as it had worked for growth.

There is also no doubt that credit should be paid to the then incoming President Kim Dae-jung, an opposition leader who had spent over 30 years in the political wilderness with no experience of government and thus had to make crucial decisions to restructure and save the nation during one of its darkest hours. On his election in December 1997, he made the vital decision to go ahead with reforms and accept IMF conditionality.

Why did President DJ Kim choose this path of painful reforms? A brilliant analysis by Professor DH Kim of South Korea's Chung-Ang University

---

[39] Park Yung-Chul (1998), 32, 40.
[40] Park Jae-Joon (1998), 54.

using cognitive maps of policymakers, comparing DJ Kim in Korea with Dr Mahathir of Malaysia, goes into how different leaders perceive the problem shaped their decision making. First, he built cognitive maps based on an analysis of the two leaders' speeches. He found that the Korean President

approached the financial crisis from the perspective of internal factors, while Mahathir approached it from the external factors. DJ attributed the cause of the financial crisis to the failure of domestic financial institutions and national competitiveness that resulted because of lack of democracy. Mahathir, on the other hand, attributed the cause of financial crisis in Malaysia to the speculative investment of foreigners who exploit countries with low wealth.

While President DJ saw national credibility as a defense against speculative behaviour Mahathir did not find any solace in it. President DJ perceived that the balancing loop of restructuring the financial and industrial institutions could take care of the problem, Prime Minister Mahathir did not see any option but breaking the vicious cycle of national credibility versus speculative behavior by shunning off Malaysian currency trade.[41]

This contrast in decision making confronting two leaders facing the same financial crisis is illuminating. Both choices reflected the contradictions within Asians. One is the tradition of Asians looking inward to seek solutions within oneself in order to meet the problems of the world. The other is to blame others, especially foreigners, for problems of globalization beyond one's control. It was not just a clash of civilizations, but also the clash between state-led mindsets versus unfettered financial markets. The different solutions come from different perceptions of the world. The outcomes would have far-reaching consequences.

The biggest lesson from the Korean crisis is that a strong industrial base is not enough for stable growth. For nations to grow stably, their industrial base must be supported by a sophisticated financial system with good risk management and strong governance. The markets will punish mistakes of policy, risk management or the underestimation of market reaction to policy changes, such as what happened in Thailand in December 2006. The Thai stock market was reported to have lost about US$21 billion or 15 percent of its value on 18 December 2006 when the Thai authorities announced their intention to impose capital controls aimed at preventing the baht from appreciating.[42]

In the case of South Korea, it took Koreans more than three decades to build their economy to where it was just before the Asian crisis. However, in

---

[41] Kim (2005), 34, 37.
[42] *Financial Times* (2006).

a matter of a year between 1996 and 1997, the Korean won lost more than 50 percent of its value whilst the Korean stock exchange lost US$97.2 billion or almost 70 percent of its market capitalization. This was equivalent to about 18 percent of GDP. Then between 1997 and 1998, GDP fell by about US$180 billion and GDP per capita fell by around US$3,900. Between 1996 and 1998 the Korean economy experienced a sharp reversal of US$27.4 billion worth of foreign capital or about 6 percent of GDP, with an inflow of US$24 billion in 1996 but an outflow of US$3.4 billion in 1998.

In short, a crisis comes when the body has grown into an adult, but the mind has not adapted to the fact that both body and environment have changed. South Korea paid a high price for that complacency, but it became more ready for globalization after the crisis.

Next, we shall discuss the case of Malaysia, the country that did not follow the IMF's advice.

EIGHT

Malaysia: The Country That Went Its Own Way

Malaysia Boleh (Malaysia Can Do).
~ National slogan

If you felt that the maelstrom would also catch you, would you contribute US$1 billion to assist Thailand as part of the US$17 billion IMF aid package in August 1997? The fact that Malaysia did so without hesitation was an indication that the Malaysian authorities had little inkling that contagion from the Thai crisis would hit the country so badly and so quickly.

STRONG MACROECONOMIC FUNDAMENTALS

Malaysia is one of the richest countries in Southeast Asia, with a population of 27 million and 330,000 square kilometres in area, roughly the same size as Vietnam with one-third its population and eight times in terms of per capita GDP. Malaysia is rich with oil and gas resources and is one of the world's leading producers of palm oil and natural rubber. Malaysia is also one of the most open economies in the world, with a total trade to GDP of more than 200 percent, whilst foreign banks account for more than 20 percent of banking system assets. Foreign capital had helped build Malaysia into one of the leading exporters of electronic chips and products, accounting for half of exports.

Malaysia successfully overcame the recession of the mid-1980s at the same time as the country was embarking on a voluntary structural adjustment programme that shifted the primary engine of growth from the public to the private sector. This shift was implemented as Malaysia was confronted with unsustainable twin deficits, with a fiscal deficit peaking at 16.6 percent of GDP whilst the current account deficit reached a high of 13.2 percent of GDP in 1982.

Having risen to the challenges of the 1980s, the Malaysian economy looked much more resilient than those of its neighbours (Table 8.1). Between 1990

187

Table 8.1. *Malaysia: Selected Real Economy Indicators*

	1990	1991	1992	1993	1994	1995	1996	1997	1998	1999	2000
GDP US$ billion	44.0	49.1	59.2	66.9	74.5	88.8	100.9	100.2	72.2	79.1	90.3
GDP per capita US$	2,432	2,681	3,153	3,419	3,703	4,294	4,764	4,623	3,254	3,485	3,844
Real GDP Annual % change	9.0	9.5	8.9	9.9	9.2	9.8	10.0	7.3	−7.4	6.1	8.9
Unemployment rate % of total labour force	5.1	4.3	3.7	3.0	2.9	3.1	2.5	2.4	3.2	3.4	3.0
Inflation Annual % change	3.0	4.4	4.8	3.6	3.7	3.2	3.5	2.7	5.3	2.7	1.6
Fiscal balance % of GDP	−2.9	−2.0	−0.8	0.2	2.3	0.8	0.7	2.4	−1.8	−3.2	−5.5
Central government debt % of GDP	79.6	73.4	64.2	55.8	47.7	41.2	35.3	31.9	36.4	37.2	36.6
Gross domestic capital formation % of GDP	32.4	37.8	35.4	39.2	41.2	43.6	41.5	43.0	26.7	22.4	26.9
Gross domestic savings % of GDP	34.4	34.1	36.7	39.1	39.6	39.7	42.9	43.9	48.7	47.4	44.0
Manufacturing production index 1993 = 100	70.4	80.2	88.6	100	114.9	131.2	147.3	165.6	148.6	167.8	209.7

Sources: Ministry of Finance, Malaysia, ADB, IMF and Jaimovich and Panniza (2006)

and 1996, the country's average annual growth rate was 9.5 percent per annum, the savings rate averaged 38 percent of GDP annually and inflation and unemployment rate averaged a low 3.7 and 3.5 percent per year, respectively.

Furthermore, Malaysia consolidated its public finances, bringing the share of public expenditure down from a peak of 44 percent of GDP in 1982 to 21 percent in 1997, mainly as a result of privatization. At the same time central government debt was substantially reduced to 32 percent of GDP in 1997 from a peak of 103 percent in 1986. Between 1993 and 1997 the federal government budget enjoyed a surplus.[1]

In addition, Malaysia succeeded in reducing poverty whilst maintaining ethnic peace in a multiracial and multireligious society. The level of absolute poverty declined to 6.8 percent of total households in 1997 from 17.3 percent in 1987 (1970: 49.3 percent) whilst the incidence of urban and rural poverty declined to 2.4 and 11.8 percent, respectively.[2]

In sum, in 1996, with a GDP of US$100.9 billion, Malaysia was Southeast Asia's third largest economy, after Indonesia and Thailand. It was dubbed one of Asia's 'miracle' economies and was thus a popular destination for not only foreign direct investment but also foreign equity investors.

Possibly the only glaring concern was the deteriorating current account balances over the period 1990–1997 (Table 8.2), due to strong imports, following the high rate of investment. However, in comparison with the other crisis economies, there were three marked differences.

First, unlike Thailand and South Korea, which saw continued deterioration in their current account deficits in 1995–1996, Malaysia's current account deficit fell from 9.7 percent of GDP in 1995 to 4.4 percent in 1996, mainly because of deliberate government action to correct the imbalance, by cutting back the implementation of large infrastructure projects. In fact, the government expected the current account deficit to improve further in 1997.

Second, in contrast to its Asian neighbours, Malaysia's current account deficits were not financed by short-term external borrowings that were vulnerable to outflows. Instead, Malaysia's current account deficits were financed mainly by long-term capital flows in the form of FDI and long-term borrowing from abroad. In fact, in 1996 Malaysia's net private long-term capital inflow of US$5.1 billion, made up of mainly FDI, was more than sufficient to finance the current account deficit of US$4.5 billion (see Tables 8.2 and 8.3).

---

[1] Vijayaledchumy (2003), 173.
[2] Bank Negara Malaysia (1999), 17, 18.

Table 8.2. *Malaysia: Selected Currency and Current Account Indicators*

	Currency Indicators*										
	1990	1991	1992	1993	1994	1995	1996	1997	1998	1999	2000
Ringgit to US$ Period average	2.70	2.75	2.55	2.57	2.62	2.50	2.52	2.81	3.92	3.80	3.80
Ringgit to US$ End of period	2.70	2.72	2.61	2.70	2.56	2.54	2.53	3.89	3.80	3.80	3.80
Ringgit nominal effective exchange rate 2000 = 100	115.6	114.6	123.7	128.4	127.5	127.6	131.2	126.8	98.7	98.4	100.0
Ringgit real effective exchange rate 2000 = 100	120.7	117.9	126.1	127.4	122.5	122.7	127.0	122.6	97.9	98.7	100.0
Yen to US$ Period average	144.8	134.7	126.7	111.2	102.2	94.1	108.8	121.0	130.9	113.9	107.8
Yen to US$ End of period	134.4	125.2	124.8	111.9	99.7	102.8	116.0	130.0	115.6	102.2	114.9
Yen nominal effective exchange rate 2000 = 100	52.2	58.2	63.2	79.3	89.5	95.6	83.3	79.2	81.1	92.0	100.0
Yen real effective exchange rate 2000 = 100	77.3	83.3	85.9	101.4	106.5	108.2	90.7	85.3	85.3	94.8	100.0

Current Account Indicators[†]

	1990	1991	1992	1993	1994	1995	1996	1997	1998	1999	2000
Terms of trade 2000 = 100	102.7	109.2	109.1	108.6	110.2	108.5	112.1	111.2	107.0	105.1	100.0
Exports US$ billion	28.6	33.5	39.6	46.0	56.6	71.7	76.9	77.4	71.8	83.9	98.2
Exports growth Annual % change	16.3	17.1	18.1	16.1	23.0	26.6	7.2	0.7	–7.3	16.9	17.0
Imports US$ billion	26.0	33.0	36.2	42.8	54.9	71.6	72.8	73.7	54.1	61.2	77.2
Imports growth Annual % change	28.5	26.9	9.8	18.1	28.3	30.5	1.7	1.2	–26.6	13.0	26.2
Trade balance US$ billion	2.6	0.5	3.4	3.2	1.7	0.0	4.0	3.7	17.6	22.8	21.0
Balance on services US$ billion	–3.6	–4.8	–5.7	–6.5	–6.5	–7.7	–7.3	–8.1	–5.7	–8.5	–10.7
Current account balance US$ billion	–0.9	–4.2	–2.2	–3.1	–5.6	–8.6	–4.5	–5.9	9.5	12.6	8.5
Current account balance % of GDP	–2.1	–8.6	–3.7	–4.6	–7.6	–9.7	–4.4	–5.9	13.2	15.9	9.4

Sources:
* IMF

[†] Bank Negara Malaysia, IMF, UNCTAD and author's estimates

Table 8.3. *Malaysia: Selected Foreign Capital Indicators*

					Capital Flows*						
	1990	1991	1992	1993	1994	1995	1996	1997	1998	1999	2000
Net official long-term capital flows US$ billion	−1.0	−0.2	−1.1	0.4	0.3	2.5	0.3	1.7	0.5	1.8	1.0
Net private long-term capital flows US$ billion	2.3	4.0	5.2	5.0	4.1	4.2	5.1	5.1	2.2	1.6	1.9
Net long-term capital flows US$ billion	1.3	3.8	4.1	5.4	4.4	6.6	5.4	6.8	2.7	3.3	2.9
Net private short-term capital flows US$ billion	0.5	1.9	4.7	5.4	−3.2	1.0	4.1	−4.6	−5.3	−9.9	−9.2
Net total capital flows US$ billion	1.8	5.6	8.7	10.8	1.2	7.6	9.5	2.2	−2.5	−6.6	−6.3

											Other Indicators[†]
	1990	1991	1992	1993	1994	1995	1996	1997	1998	1999	2000
Total foreign bank borrowings US$ billion	9.4	10.4	11.9	17.4	17.5	21.0	29.8	34.0	27.9	37.1	49.9
Short-term international bank loans[1] US$ billion	2.1	3.0	4.1	7.4	6.6	7.9	11.2	14.4	9.3	7.7	7.0
Japanese bank lending to Malaysia US$ billion	4.6	4.6	5.1	5.5	6.0	7.3	9.2	9.3	7.4	6.8	6.4
Direct investments from Japan[2] US$ million	725	880	704	800	742	575	572	791	521	527	232
Net external wealth position[3] US$ billion	–8.0	–12.3	–14.8	–25.0	–42.6	–48.8	–55.9	–49.9	–34.4	–40.3	–34.7
Net external liabilities position % of GDP	18.1	25.0	25.0	37.4	57.1	55.0	55.4	49.8	47.7	50.9	38.4

Sources:

* Bank Negara Malaysia and author's estimates
[†] BIS, Japan External Trade Organization (JETRO), Lane and Milesi-Ferretti (2006) and author's estimates
[1] Foreign currency denominated Loans of up to and including one year
[2] Based on report and notifications
[3] Negative means net liabilities position; positive means net assets position

Third, Malaysia's total external debt was relatively low at US$38.7 billion or 38.4 percent of GDP in 1996 (Table 8.4). Crucially, in 1996, amongst the crisis-hit countries, Malaysia had the lowest short-term external debt of US$10 billion or about 26 percent of total external debt, as compared to US$75.9 billion or 48 percent for South Korea and US$47.7 billion or 44 percent for Thailand. With relatively large foreign exchange reserves of US$26.2 billion, Malaysia's short-term debt to foreign exchange reserves ratio in 1996 was around 38 percent, small beer compared with the vulnerable ratios of South Korea (228 percent) and Thailand (128 percent).

Malaysia's prudent external debt management was a lesson learnt from the country's experiences with a severe banking crisis in the mid-1980s that resulted from the recession and stock market collapse in the first half of the 1980s. At that time nonperforming loans, defined on a six-month basis, had reached more than 30 percent of the banking system lending portfolio.[3] The central bank, Bank Negara Malaysia (BNM), consequently was much more cautious in financial liberalization than were other regional central banks.

In the period leading up to the crisis, Malaysia had a healthier external debt profile, due to a deliberate policy in the late 1980s of prepaying the more expensive external loans as part of its efforts to contain the nation's external debt. At the same time, private sector foreign currency borrowings were subject to stringent regulations and prudential criteria. For example, external borrowings had to be utilized to finance productive activities, which excluded external borrowing to finance the purchase of properties or shares. Therefore, private sector foreign currency borrowings in general were by and large fairly hedged.[4]

A COMPARATIVELY RESILIENT FINANCIAL SYSTEM

In addition to having relatively stronger macroeconomic fundamentals, the Malaysian financial system was also comparatively more robust, with the single exception of the stock market.

Like the rest of Asia, the Malaysian financial system also had a dominant banking sector, with assets of banks and other financial institutions amounting to 172 percent of GDP in 1996 (Table 8.5). However, the Malaysian financial system had two features that made it more resilient.

---

[3]   Jomo (2005).
[4]   Bank Negara Malaysia (1999), 34.

Table 8.4. *Malaysia: Selected Foreign Reserves and External Debt Indicators*

	1990	1991	1992	1993	1994	1995	1996	1997	1998	1999	2000
Foreign exchange reserves (FER) US$ billion	9.3	10.4	16.8	26.8	24.9	22.9	26.2	20.0	24.7	29.7	27.4
FER growth Annual % change	26.2	11.7	61.1	59.8	−7.2	−7.8	14.0	−23.5	23.6	20.0	−7.5
Total external debt US$ billion	17.0	18.7	21.4	25.6	28.8	33.4	38.7	43.9	44.7	42.7	42.4
Total external debt % of GDP	38.6	38.1	36.2	38.3	38.6	37.6	38.4	43.8	62.0	53.9	46.9
Short-term external debt US$ billion	1.6	2.6	5.0	6.4	5.6	6.4	10.0	11.1	9.4	5.9	4.6
Short-term external debt % of total external debt	4.2	6.9	13.9	16.7	14.4	16.9	25.9	25.4	15.2	10.9	9.9
Short-term external debt % of FER	17.5	25.3	30.0	23.9	22.4	27.8	38.1	55.5	38.1	19.9	16.9

Sources: Bank Negara Malaysia, IMF and author's estimates

Table 8.5. *Malaysia: Financial Structure (% of GDP)*

	1990	1991	1992	1993	1994	1995	1996	1997	1998	1999	2000
Assets of deposit money banks	103.0	76.5	96.4	108.7	108.3	116.1	129.6	146.0	164.2	152.4	136.0
Assets of other financial institutions	3.7	4.5	4.8	4.7	5.7	40.8	42.4	48.0	52.1	45.1	38.5
Stock market capitalization	100.7	109.2	129.0	234.5	282.4	238.5	263.4	201.7	133.4	154.2	146.4
Bond market capitalization	69.9	69.4	63.3	61.4	64.6	65.6	67.4	65.4	82.6	81.1	78.4
Insurance premium volume	3.0	3.2	3.5	3.6	3.9	4.1	4.6	4.3	4.1	4.1	4.7

Source: Beck, Demirgüç-Kunt and Levine (2000), revised 13 August 2007

First, in terms of long-term funding, Malaysia has a large employees' provident fund (EPF) that provided stable long-term funding equivalent to more than 40 percent of GDP.

Second, by and large, in the lead-up to the crisis, the Malaysian banking sector was also relatively healthy. In 1996 the banking system had a risk-weighted capital-adequacy ratio of 10.7 percent, higher than the Basel-recommended minimum level of 8 percent. Nonperforming loans, albeit defined on a six-month basis, were around 3.7 percent of total loans, whilst the ratio of loan provisions to NPLs was at 96.6 percent.

The Malaysian banking sector was reasonably sound because, following the 1980s banking crisis, the central bank had introduced a series of prudential reforms that forced the banks to identify, recognize and provide for bad loans. As rating analyst Philippe Delhaise noted:

Bank Negara Malaysia has its critics. The most vocal accused the institution of having gambled away billions of dollars in foreign exchange transaction in the 1980s. Indeed, Bank Negara Malaysia was moving markets at the time. Unsettling was a more appropriate word for their activities, and legend has it that some central banks around the world warned them in vain that it was a dangerous game to play. Granted, Bank Negara Malaysia was not an astute foreign exchange player, but the mid-1980s crisis brought two lessons that made it one of the best bank regulators in Asia: you must apply the rules strictly and you must be transparent. Rules in Malaysia may not be good enough yet, but banks are strongly invited to follow them.[5]

Given this backdrop of relatively strong macroeconomic fundamentals and a comparatively resilient financial system, Dr Mahathir Mohamad, who had been the Malaysian Prime Minister for nearly 16 years by 1997, had reasons to be surprised when Malaysia was also hit by currency speculation. In 1997 the ringgit came under two speculative attacks. The first attack took place in mid-May around the time of the 'Battle of the Baht', causing interest rates to shoot up to 18.75 percent. Pressure on the ringgit, however, subsided quickly, and interest rates drifted downwards again. The second round of speculative attacks occurred in July 1997 soon after the devaluation of the Thai baht.

Dr Mahathir pointed out that even as late as 17 June 1997, IMF Managing Director Michel Camdessus listed the strengths of the Malaysian economy in great detail when he addressed the World Affairs Council of Los Angeles:[6]

Malaysia is a good example of a country where the authorities are well aware of the challenges of managing the pressures that result from high growth and of

---

[5]   Delhaise (1998), 146.
[6]   Tourres (2003), 26.

maintaining a sound financial system amid substantial capital flows and a booming property market. … It is the kind of attitude that fully justifies the confidence of the markets on the positive prospects of countries persevering in such endeavours.[7]

BUT VULNERABILITIES LURKED

Behind Malaysia's relatively strong fundamentals were emerging vulnerabilities. There were essentially three: a domestic economy that was overheating, the massive influx of short-term foreign capital that was fuelling the emerging asset bubbles and a chronic current account deficit.

An Economy on the Boil

According to the Malaysian government's *White Paper on the Status of the Malaysian Economy*, which was released on 6 April 1999 one of the main concerns in the domestic economy in the lead-up to the Malaysian crisis was that 'Since 1991, the economy consistently grew above its potential output'.[8] Although inflation remained low because of monetary restraint, all signs pointed to overheating.

A key driver of Malaysia's high GDP growth in the lead-up to the 1996–1997 Asian crisis was excessive investment spending. In the public sector, investments were poured into building infrastructure facilities, into mega projects such as highways, light railway transit, Kuala Lumpur International Airport and the Westport seaport infrastructure. As a result, public investment grew at an average rate of 15.8 percent per annum between 1988 and 1997.[9] In 1996 the total cost of the various infrastructure projects under construction was estimated to be about US$62 billion.[10]

During the same period, private sector investment grew at an even higher rate, averaging 22.8 percent annually. The building frenzy reflected the philosophy of 'Malaysia Incorporated', pushed by Dr Mahathir, who unveiled in 1991 a development strategy to achieve developed nation status by 2020. As a result, by 1994 Malaysia's gross domestic capital formation exceeded 40 percent of GDP, up from 32 percent in 1990 (Table 8.1). The country's level of investment activities in the early to mid-1990s was thus one of the highest in the region.

---

[7] Camdessus (1997).
[8] Government of Malaysia (1999).
[9] Bank Negara Malaysia (1999), 8.
[10] Athukorala (2000), 25.

On the surface Malaysia Inc. did not look as highly leveraged as Korea Inc. On average the debt-to-equity ratio of Malaysia Inc. was about 118 percent in 1996.[11] But averages often do not tell the full story. Diversified holdings listed on the Kuala Lumpur Stock Exchange between 1992 and 1996 consisting mainly of conglomerates heavily engaged in property and construction, for instance, had an average debt-to-equity ratio exceeding 500 percent.[12]

Thus, in tandem with the high level of private investment, Malaysia experienced a private sector credit boom. The strong growth in investment activity and private consumption injected RM 330.6 billion (US$126 billion) worth of credit to the private sector between 1990 and 1997, equivalent to 173 percent of GDP. As such, going into 1997, Malaysia's private sector credit by banks and other financial institutions was 124 percent of GDP (Table 8.6), lower than Thailand's (137 percent) but higher than South Korea's (112 percent). This was almost double the level in 1991 of 70 percent of GDP, which was far lower than both South Korea (91 percent) and Thailand (81 percent). Consequently the Malaysian private sector had one of the fastest credit build-ups in the region.

Ironically, the private sector credit boom was also an unintentional result of the 1994 prudential reforms by the central bank to consolidate the banks into two tiers. The Two-Tier Regulatory System (TTRS) was designed to create a core of strong and competitive domestic institutions, but it led to 'shareholders resorting to heavy short-term borrowings, banking institutions adopting aggressive loan growth strategy, and double leveraging which increased the risk of the banking system as a whole'.[13]

Growing Asset Bubbles

Exactly like Thailand and to a lesser extent South Korea, Malaysia experienced growing asset bubbles in the lead-up to the Asian crisis.

The Malaysian stock market, however, stood out for its speculative element, earning the label 'a giant casino',[14] which rose by more than 140 percent between 1990 and 1996 (Table 8.7).

The stock market speculation was accompanied by speculation in the real estate market, even though Malaysia was not short of land. Between 1990 and 1996, the property market witnessed housing prices rising by more

---

[11] Claessens, Djankov and Lang (1998). See also Table 9.6.
[12] International Monetary Fund (1999c), table IV.4, 82.
[13] Bank Negara Malaysia (1999), 210.
[14] Delhaise (1998), 149.

Table 8.6. *Malaysia: Selected Financial Sector Indicators*

	1990	1991	1992	1993	1994	1995	1996	1997	1998	1999	2000
Narrow noney (M1) Annual % change	14.1	11.0	13.0	37.5	11.2	11.7	16.7	4.6	−14.6	35.7	6.5
Broad money (M2) Annual % change	12.8	14.5	19.1	22.1	14.7	24.0	19.8	22.7	1.5	13.7	5.2
Private sector credit by financial institutions[1] % of GDP	78.7	69.7	89.5	102.2	103.7	111.4	123.9	139.5	155.3	142.9	127.5
Lending rates % per annum	7.2	8.1	9.3	9.1	7.6	7.6	8.9	9.5	10.6	7.3	6.8
Deposit rates % per annum	5.9	7.2	8.0	7.0	4.9	5.9	7.1	7.8	8.5	4.1	3.4
Interest rate spreads % per annum	1.3	1.0	1.3	2.0	2.7	1.7	1.8	1.8	2.1	3.2	3.4

Sources: Bank Negara Malaysia, World Bank, Beck, Demirgüç-Kunt and Levine (2000), revised 13 August 2007 and author's estimates
[1] Deposit money banks and other financial institutions

Table 8.7. *Malaysia: Selected Asset Prices*

	1990	1991	1992	1993	1994	1995	1996	1997	1998	1999	2000
Stock Market Indicators*											
Kuala Lumpur Composite Index End of period	505.9	556.2	644.0	1,275.3	971.2	995.2	1,238.0	594.4	586.1	812.3	679.6
Domestic market capitalization US$ billion	47.9	56.7	91.5	219.8	190.2	213.8	306.2	93.2	95.6	139.9	113.2
Bursa Malaysia Price-earning ratio	25.5	24.2	22.8	48.2	28.5	24.5	28.6	10.3	-130.6	-32.4	22.1
Real Estate Indicators†											
All houses price index 1990 = 100	100.0	125.5	140.7	147.5	159.3	188.5	212.8	216.8	196.4	191.8	–
All houses prices Annual % change	4.1	25.5	12.2	4.9	8.0	18.4	12.9	1.9	-9.5	-2.4	–
Value of property transaction RM billion	15.2	17.3	20.3	22.4	29.7	39.9	49.0	53.2	27.9	34.4	41.3
Value of property transaction Annual % change	–	14.2	17.0	10.7	32.4	34.2	22.9	8.6	-47.6	23.4	20.0
Volume of transaction Thousands	148.2	164.0	168.3	178.1	217.5	251.9	270.5	274.8	186.1	225.9	240.1
Volume of transaction Annual % change	–	10.7	2.6	5.8	22.2	15.8	7.4	1.6	-32.3	21.4	6.3

Sources:
* World Federation of Exchanges and Bloomberg
† National Property Information Centre
Dash means data not available

than 100 percent, with double-digit growth in terms of both transactions and housing prices in 1994–1995 (Table 8.7).

Malaysia's asset bubbles were fuelled by two main factors. First, like the Japanese experience in the 1980s, bank credit poured into stocks and property like a giant Ponzi scheme. By end-June 1997, 31.9 percent of all credit generated by the banking system was to the broad property sector, whilst 9.8 percent was used in the purchase of securities, with loans by merchant banks in this regard being as high as 22.5 percent (Table 8.8). Like Thailand, the Malaysian banks' exposure to both property and shares was probably higher than these statistics suggest because the majority of bank loans to other sectors of the economy were secured by either of these assets.[15]

To the credit of the central bank, since 1995 measures had already been taken to slow the pace of bank lending to the asset markets to address the issue of overheating. When the measures did not seem effective enough, they were tightened in April 1997, albeit with significant exemptions. But by then the measures were perhaps too little too late.

The momentum to keep borrowing remained strong. Loans to the property sector continued to grow at an average of 30 percent for most of 1997, whilst loans for the purchase of shares between 1993 and 1997 grew at an average rate of 38 percent.[16]

Second, apart from bank credit, the stock market boom was also fuelled by foreign funds. Hubris always begins with flattery, and foreign portfolio inflows are the best form of flattery to an emerging market. In the first half of the 1990s, the Malaysian stock market was a darling of emerging markets, resulting in massive foreign portfolio equity investment flooding the Malaysian equity market.

Traditionally, foreign capital inflows to Malaysia have been dominated by FDI, with net FDI stock in Malaysia growing relatively in line with GDP.[17] FDI is stable because these are long-term investments in plant and equipment, and their funding could be serviced largely from the manufacturing exports.

However, in the early to mid-1990s, there was a concerted push by Malaysia to develop its domestic capital markets, particularly the equity and bond markets. The most significant move to promote the domestic equity market was the delisting of Malaysian-registered companies from the Stock Exchange of Singapore (SES) and vice versa, taking effect on 1 January 1990. Together with greater capital account convertibility, there was a massive influx of foreign portfolio equity investment into Malaysia (see Table 8.9).

---

[15] Government of Malaysia (1999).
[16] Government of Malaysia (1999).
[17] See Sheng and Ng (2006).

Table 8.8. *Malaysia: Selected Banking System Loans by Type and Sector, End of June 1997 (% of Total Loans)*

	Manufacturing	Real Estate	Broad Property Sector				Purchase of Securities		
			Construction	Residential Property	Nonresidential Property	Total	Stock-brokers	Individuals	Total
Commercial banks	19.5	4.6	9.4	12.6	7.1	33.7	1.3	4.0	8.6
Finance companies	4.3	3.9	7.0	11.9	4.4	27.3	0.2	6.7	10.0
Merchant banks	12.4	9.4	18.2	0.3	2.9	30.7	4.2	2.6	22.5
Total	**15.2**	**4.7**	**9.3**	**11.7**	**6.2**	**31.9**	**1.2**	**4.6**	**9.8**

Source: Bank Negara Malaysia and author's estimates

Table 8.9. *Crisis Economies: Net Portfolio Equity Liabilities*

	1990	1991	1992	1993	1994	1995	1996	1997	1998	1999	2000
Indonesia											
Net portfolio equity liabilities US$ billion	0.3	0.1	0.1	2.9	3.8	5.6	9.0	6.3	4.5	17.7	5.9
Net portfolio equity liabilities % of GDP	0.2	0.1	0.1	1.6	1.9	2.5	3.6	2.6	4.3	11.5	3.6
Net portfolio equity liabilities % of FER	3.7	1.6	1.4	26.1	31.8	42.3	50.7	38.9	20.1	67.6	20.9
Malaysia											
Net portfolio equity liabilities US$ billion	2.1	2.3	4.5	21.7	20.5	21.8	29.3	16.0	7.5	17.2	12.4
Net portfolio equity liabilities % of GDP	4.8	4.6	7.7	32.5	27.6	24.5	29.1	16.0	10.4	21.7	13.8
Net portfolio equity liabilities % of FER	22.7	21.6	27.0	81.1	82.5	94.9	112.0	80.1	30.3	58.0	45.3

South Korea

Net portfolio equity liabilities											
US$ billion	0.9	0.8	3.6	12.5	18.8	21.5	16.1	3.9	19.0	53.5	32.7
% of GDP	0.3	0.3	1.1	3.5	4.4	4.2	2.9	0.7	5.5	12.0	6.4
% of FER	6.3	6.1	21.8	63.7	75.2	67.5	48.5	19.7	36.6	72.6	34.1

Thailand

Net portfolio equity liabilities											
US$ billion	6.2	7.4	10.3	26.0	22.6	24.1	16.0	9.1	10.5	16.9	8.1
% of GDP	7.3	7.7	9.4	21.3	15.7	14.3	8.8	6.0	9.4	13.8	6.6
% of FER	47.1	42.8	51.3	107.8	78.4	67.9	43.0	35.4	37.0	49.9	25.4

Source: IMF; Lane and Milesi-Ferretti (2006) and author's estimates

The foreign equity capital flooded the Malaysian stock market, with foreign investors' participation on the local bourse increasing sharply from 15 percent of total trading by value in 1993 to 27 percent in 1998.

What attracted the foreign investors was the Malaysian super bull run of 1993, which broke all records. Total turnover in 1993 surpassed the combined total turnover in the preceding 20 years from 1973 to 1992. In one year the market increased 98 percent to reach an all-time high of 1,275.3 points at the end of 1993, a level not touched again until 2007.

The Second Board, designed as an entry into the stock market for smaller enterprises, also turned out to be a riskier and more speculative market. It was said that some fancy Kuala Lumpur houses were built by issuers and punters who made their killing on the Second Board. The Second Board Index rose 352 percent from 127.5 in 1991 to 576.3 in 1996. In February 1997 it recorded the highest price-earnings ratio of 57.7.[18] Thus, going into 1997, Malaysia had a stock market capitalization of 263 percent of GDP (Table 8.5), far larger than South Korea (29 percent) and Thailand (67 percent), a bubble of grave vulnerability.

The trouble with all bull runs is that sooner or later they must end. Amongst investors familiar with Asian markets, two important indicators point to irrational exuberance. The first is the *amah* (domestic maid) syndrome. When *amahs* get into the market, that is the time to get out. This is because they usually have no clue what they are buying and are always the last to sell. Their losses are almost always tragic, but since their collective savings are small relative to the size of the market, the impact is not systemic.

The second systemic indicator is when businessmen begin to neglect their businesses and begin to punt heavily in the market. Asian businesses have traditionally been built by the hard work and sweat of their entrepreneurs, many of whom made their small fortunes through exports, manufacturing and trading. Making money through hard labour, by definition, has never been easy, but when they discover an easier alternative, such as speculating on the stock market, the core business gets neglected, and surplus cash is diverted to speculation.

When the market reverses, the entrepreneur often finds his core business in shambles due to neglect whilst his stock market and property investments become black holes. If speculation was done with leverage, the reversal comes with vengeance. He is caught in a classic bind of banks calling for more collateral on his loans, whilst his core business is also a cash drain.

---

[18]　Bank Negara Malaysia (1999), 20.

Forced sales of good assets further drive down the asset markets, thus sending the speculator into insolvency.

Perhaps every generation of investors need to learn their own lessons. The influx of foreign investors was too good to be true, and everyone enjoyed the ride up. The downside of overdependence on foreign portfolio equity capital was the risk of exit and contagion.

Following the super bull run experience, the Malaysian central bank recognized this vulnerability, and in 1994 it imposed selective capital controls to restrict inflows in order to stabilize the financial system. These measures only temporarily halted the inflows and were grossly unpopular with the punters. When the controls were lifted in 1994 and 1995, foreign portfolio equity capital returned to Malaysia with a vengeance. By 1996 net foreign portfolio equity capital in Malaysia amounted to US$29.3 billion, equivalent to 29.1 percent of GDP, the highest amongst the crisis-hit Asian nations (Table 8.9). The Malaysian stock market capitalization of 263 percent of GDP was also almost double that of developed markets such as the United Kingdom (133 percent of GDP) and United States (99 percent GDP). Crucially, by 1996 Malaysia's net foreign portfolio equity liabilities exceeded the size of foreign exchange reserves by 12 percent, indicating that any sharp withdrawal would have severe foreign exchange consequences.

According to George Soros, the Soros Fund Management had already begun to speculate on both the Thai baht and the Malaysian ringgit early in 1997, noting that 'If it was clear to us in January 1997 that the situation was untenable, it must have been clear to others'.[19]

The formula of trading in small emerging markets is simple: since foreign funds already account for around one-third of the market, their arrival can drive up the market. If a short-selling mechanism is available, the foreign buyer can hedge the position by buying in the cash market and selling the same amount in the futures market. Since local retail buyers are mostly momentum players, they will follow when the foreigners pile in. Once the foreign investors consider that the market is overvalued relative to other markets, they will quietly exit, leaving the locals to hold the baby. The local syndicate players also know whether the foreigners are in or out, so that, more likely, the ordinary retail investor is in for a double whammy.

Of course, foreign investors also faced foreign exchange risk on their ringgit assets even under benign circumstances. However, foreign fund managers, such as hedge funds, could borrow the local currency from

---

[19] Soros (1998b), 136–137.

Table 8.10. *Malaysia: Foreign Direct Investment and Net Portfolio Investment (RM Billion)*

	Jan	Feb	Mar	Apr	May	Jun	Jul	Aug	Sept	Oct	Nov	Dec	Total
						1997							
Foreign direct investment	1.5	1.4	1.5	0.9	0.7	1.5	1.0	1.0	0.9	0.9	0.9	1.4	13.4
Net portfolio investment	0.7	1.1	0.0	−3.8	−3.9	−0.9	−3.9	−5.3	−7.0	−3.2	−4.2	1.5	−29.1
						1998							
	Jan	Feb	Mar	Apr	May	Jun	Jul	Aug	Sept	Oct	Nov	Dec	Total
Foreign direct investment	0.8	0.6	0.8	0.9	0.9	0.9	1.0	1.0	1.1	2.8	0.9	1.0	12.7
Net portfolio investment	0.2	4.1	1.2	−1.3	−0.6	−1.5	−1.4	−0.4	−1.9	−0.4	−0.4	0.0	−2.2

Source: Government of Malaysia (1999)

either domestic banks or foreign banks that had surplus ringgit. They could easily hedge their ringgit assets against such ringgit liabilities. Once speculative attacks on the currency began in early 1997, all that the speculators had to do was to short their equity holdings, that is, sell such stocks forward by borrowing the stocks through the stock borrowing and lending programme, and at the same time sell their ringgit forward. This was the classic double play, described in Chapter 10 on Hong Kong.

By February–March 1997, following the first major attack on the Thai baht in January–February of that year, foreign investors began to withdraw from the Malaysian stock exchange (Table 8.10). The withdrawal escalated in April–May with the first attack on the ringgit along with the second attack on the Thai baht in mid-May. By June, as the situation in Thailand became increasingly untenable, foreign fund managers began to withdraw capital from the whole region, including Malaysia.

The Kuala Lumpur Composite Index, having reached a post-1994 capital controls peak of 1,272 points on 25 February, fell by more than 15 percent to close at 1,077 points by 30 June, 1997. This was not yet a rout. But

Table 8.11. *Selected Asian Economies: Stock Market Collapse*

	2 July 1997	Lowest after 2 July	Date of Lowest Point	% Fall in Value
Hong Kong: Hang Seng Index	15,055.7[1]	6,660.4	13 August 1998	55.8
Indonesia: Jakarta Composite Index	730.2	256.8	21 September 1998	64.8
Malaysia: Kuala Lumpur Composite Index	1,084.9	262.7	1 September 1998	75.8
Philippines: Philippine SE IDX Index	2,764.9	979.3	24 October 2001	64.6
Singapore: Straits Times Index	1,921.8	805.0	4 September 1998	58.1
South Korea: KOSPI Index	777.3	280.0	16 June 1998	64.0
Taiwan: Taiwan TAIEX	8,996.7	3,446.3	3 October 2001	61.7
Thailand: SET Index	568.8	207.3	4 September 1998	63.6
Memo item				
Japan: Nikkei-225	20,196.4	7,607.9	28 April 2003	62.3

Source: Bloomberg
[1] 3 July 1997

the repatriation of capital started putting pressure on the Malaysian ringgit when the crunch came in July 1997. As Malaysia had the highest exposure to foreign portfolio equity capital amongst the crisis-hit nations, the country experienced the biggest stock market plunge (Table 8.11).

In hindsight, the numbers are illuminating. Between 1990 and 1996 net foreign portfolio equity liabilities rose by US$27.2 billion (Table 8.9), more than inflows of bank borrowings of US$20.4 billion (Table 8.3). But in 1997 alone portfolio outflows reversed to RM 29.1 billion (US$10.4 billion) (Table 8.10), whereas net bank borrowings still increased by US$4.2 billion (Table 8.3).

Furthermore, between 1996 and 1997 the Malaysian stock exchange lost US$213 billion or about 70 percent of its market capitalization, equivalent to 212 percent of GDP (Tables 8.1 and 8.7). Since the banking system was exposed by 31.9 percent to the property market and 9.8 percent to the stock market (Table 8.8), it was not surprising that there was also a banking crisis.

Was This a Currency Story?

Malaysians have tended to point towards currency speculation as the obvious culprit for the crisis. As noted by Bank Negara:

> Malaysia was among the first countries to highlight the role of currency speculators and highly leveraged institutions in the crisis. ... [L]arge market players, such as highly leveraged institutions (HLIs) and hedged funds, could manipulate developments, particularly in small, emerging markets, given the size of their position taking and the influence they have on other market participants.[20]

The question then becomes, What triggered the currency speculation? Soros had another story:

> The most immediate cause of trouble was a misalignment of currencies. The Southeast Asian countries maintained an informal arrangement that tied their currencies to the US dollar. ... But the arrangement came under pressure, partly from the undervaluation of the Chinese currency in 1996, and partly from the appreciation of the US dollar against the yen. The balance of trade of the countries concerned deteriorated, although the trade deficits were at first offset by continuing substantial inflows on capital accounts. Nevertheless, by the beginning of 1997 it was clear to us at Soros Fund Management that the discrepancy between the trade account and the capital account was becoming untenable. We sold short the Thai baht and the Malaysian ringgit early in 1997 with maturities ranging from six months to a year. Subsequently Prime Minister Mahathir of Malaysia accused me of causing the crisis. The accusation was totally unfounded. We were not sellers of the currency during or several months before the crisis; on the contrary we were buyers when the currencies began to decline – we were purchasing ringgits to realize the profits on our earlier speculation (much too soon, as it turned out).[21]

In other words, Soros was actually doing exactly what he did to sterling in 1992. When the baht and the ringgit devalued, the hedge funds made a killing. Unfortunately for Soros, his funds took profits too early, as the crisis-hit Asian currencies continued to plunge.

Should Malaysia have used greater flexibility of the exchange rate to free up monetary policy to tackle the asset bubbles? Meigs and others have argued that the Mexican crisis suggested that 'a currency crisis could be avoided by permitting the exchange to *rise* when capital flows *in*'.[22]

There were three reasons why the exchange rate tool was not used in Malaysia. First, the fear was that any appreciation of the exchange rate would

---

[20] Bank Negara Malaysia (1999), 564.
[21] Soros (1998b), 136–137.
[22] Meigs (1998). I am grateful to an anonymous referee for pointing this out.

invite more capital inflows, thus negating any monetary policy tightening. Second, in the absence of exchange control, any increase in the interest rate would also increase capital inflows. Third, the ringgit was actually floating upward from 2.70 to one U.S. dollar in 1990 to 2.50 in 1995. That foreign exchange reserves did not change materially from around US$20 billion from 1993 to 1997 indicated that the market flows were determining the exchange rate, rather than through central bank intervention.

FREE FALL

When the ringgit came under the second round of speculative attack in July 1997, Bank Negara initially intervened through allowing higher interest rates to rise sharply. On 10 July the overnight interest rate rose to 40 percent from 7.5 percent the previous day. However, after spending nearly 12 percent of reserves to defend the ringgit, the central bank allowed the ringgit to freely depreciate on 14 July.

The freefall in the ringgit began and the stock market plunged. By December 1997 the ringgit was trading at RM 3.89 to the U.S. dollar, falling by 34 percent since 14 July. Over the same period, the KLCI fell 41 percent to close at 594 points on 31 December.

The Malaysian corporations with net foreign exchange liabilities suffered massively from the ringgit depreciation. In mid-November there was a bailout of two well-connected public-listed companies: United Engineers Malaysia (UEM) and the Renong Group.[23]

Throughout most of 1998 the ringgit and the KLCI suffered with the region. The ringgit hit a historic low of RM 4.88 to the U.S. dollar on 7 January 1998, and the stock market index plunged another 20 percent from end-December 1997 to close at 477 points on 12 January 1998. After a Chinese New Year surge on 3 February of over 23 percent in a single day, the KLCI continued its downward trend, falling to 538 points at the end of May.

Exacerbating the uncertainty was the debate about the correct medicine for the crisis. Should Malaysia follow the IMF prescription that was being applied in Indonesia, South Korea and Thailand? The policy dispute was underpinned by an increasingly tense political battle between Dr Mahathir and his Deputy Prime Minister, Anwar Ibrahim, concurrently Finance Minister. On 21 May 1998, President Suharto had to step down after 32 years in power as a result of political pressure and riots. Would Dr Mahathir, who

---

[23] Tourres (2003), 77.

had been Prime Minister since 1981 and was visibly uncomfortable with the IMF approach, follow?

By June 1998 the continued depreciation of the Japanese yen to a low of ¥140.57 to the U.S. dollar added to the pressure. By this time it was feared that both the Malaysian real economy and the financial system were on the brink of collapse. In the first quarter of 1998, the economy contracted by 2.8 percent with another contraction of 6.8 percent in the second quarter.[24] Around this time total NPLs in the banking system had risen to RM 74 billion (US$17.7 billion) or 15.7 percent of total loans by the end of 1998, rising to RM 100 billion (US$24.0 billion) or 19.7 percent by the end of 1999.[25]

Clearly something had to be done. But what was the right course of action?

The IMF was willing to provide financial assistance, but Malaysia was not willing to accept conditionalities that impinged on its sovereignty. Furthermore, Dr Mahathir believed that the IMF did not understand the complexities of Malaysia's multiracial society and was concerned that the Washington-based institution would prescribe policies that could threaten the country's social fabric. 'Since the IMF is not an option for Malaysia we had to think of something home grown',[26] he said. The 'something home grown' would soon shock the world.

FROM ORTHODOXY TO HERESY

Malaysia's initial response to the crisis was fairly orthodox. The country followed the IMF's standard prescription without entering into a formal loan programme, which was essentially a combination of tight fiscal and monetary policies accompanied by financial sector reforms. Interest rates were kept high, and mega-projects were cancelled or postponed. However, as there were signs within Malaysia and in other countries that these measures did not restore confidence, Malaysia began to change its course.

In November 1997 the late Tan Sri Noordin Sopiee, one of the foremost intellectuals in Malaysia, recommended to Dr Mahathir the establishment of the National Economic Action Council (NEAC), comprising a group of leading market professionals and economists to deal with the crisis. The

---

[24] Government of Malaysia (1999).
[25] National Economic Action Council (1998), 12.
[26] Mohamad (1999a).

'hands-on-24-hour crisis team', modelled on the Operations Room that acted decisively to handle the Malayan Emergency period in the 1950s, was to identify priorities and concrete action plans. The NEAC was formally established in 7 January 1998.

The group came up with a National Economic Recovery Plan (NERP). Tan Sri Noordin, whom I knew as a brilliant student leader in London in the 1960s, was succinct in his analysis of the situation, as he told me then, 'During a crisis, don't deal with all problems. Deal only with the top three'. The NERP report had six core objectives, 40 lines of action and over 580 detailed recommendations; it was officially launched on 23 July 1998.

By this time Bank Negara, which had already begun to ease monetary policy in February 1998, began to aggressively ease monetary policy further.[27] On 13 July the Malaysian government announced a fiscal stimulus package amounting to RM 7 billion (US$1.69 billion) and projected a budget deficit of 3.7 percent for 1998, the first budget deficit in five years.

The official launching of the NERP was followed up in August 1998 with the creation of three vehicles: the Corporate Debt Restructuring Committee, the national Asset Management Corporation (Danaharta) and an agency for the recapitalisation of banks (Danamodal) to spearhead corporate debt restructuring and bank restructuring and recapitalization.

Indeed, August 1998 was a momentous month. On 14 August Hong Kong dropped the bombshell by intervening heavily in the market. The Russian crisis erupted shortly afterwards, and on 26 August the Governor and Deputy Governor of Bank Negara resigned.

Then, on 1 September 1998 the Malaysian authorities shocked the world by announcing the introduction of selective capital controls. On 2 September the ringgit was fixed at RM 3.80 to the U.S. dollar. On the same day Deputy Prime Minister Anwar Ibrahim was sacked from the government and subsequently arrested on charges of sodomy that were later overturned in the courts.

CHILE INFLUENCE; CHINA MODEL

Although it was the NEAC where the idea of capital controls was to emerge, the idea of capital controls germinated during Dr Mahathir's four-nation tour of the Caribbean and South America in late September 1997 when he was briefed on the Chilean experience with exchange controls. According to

---

[27] Bank Negara Malaysia (1999), 177.

Marie-Aimée Tourres, author of the book *The Tragedy that Didn't Happen*, documenting Malaysia's crisis management:

[D]uring his two days in Argentina, he summoned Bank Negara's former foreign exchange department head Nor Mohamed Yakcop to Buenos Aires to brief him on the financial situation in general and on the nuts and bolts of foreign exchange and the peculiar off-shore currency markets for the ringgit in particular. ... Mahathir wanted answers to the following: How exactly do people trade? Why are investors panicking?; What are the psychological factors motivating them?; Where are the loopholes in the system?; and so on. He was also extremely concerned about where the foreigners sourced their ringgit. One of the key points that surfaced during that discussion was that in currency trading, currency traders would borrow their ringgit from residents/banks through external accounts in order to sell short. Mahathir was struck by how damaging offshore markets for the ringgit and the existence of external accounts could be. From this crucial meeting, Mahathir formed a strategic plan to fight the currency speculators.[28]

Tan Sri Nor Mohamed Yakcop, currently Malaysia's Second Finance Minister, was well experienced in the foreign exchange market, having been Assistant Governor in charge of reserves management at Bank Negara during the sterling crisis of August 1992.

As the crisis worsened, Dr Mahathir became increasingly convinced that the only way for the economy to recover was to stabilize the ringgit and protect the stock market from further attacks.[29] In his opinion, he had to frustrate the currency speculators through currency controls:

When Britain failed to join the European Monetary Union we lost almost two billion Ringgit. We got out but we learnt valuable lessons which stood us in good stead when our Ringgit was attacked by currency traders. We knew what they were doing and how they were doing it. We studied their activities closely and were finally able to frustrate them and save our currency.[30]

Consequently, a technical plan had to be devised to curb the offshore markets for both the ringgit and the securities listed on the KLSE. Both offshore markets operated from Singapore, although some was traded in London, New York and Hong Kong. The offshore market for Malaysian stocks took place through an 'over-the-counter' market known as the Central Limit Order Book (CLOB) that was established in Singapore on 2 January 1990 following the KLSE-SES split that year.

---

[28] Tourres (2003), 84–85.
[29] Mohamad (1999a).
[30] Mohamad (1999a).

Even though Chile inspired the notion of capital controls, it was China that was the role model. As long as China had exchange controls, it was shielded from the currency attacks. As Tan Sri Noordin Sopiee put it when addressing a business forum in Shanghai on 22 September 1998: 'From 1 September 1998, until normalcy returns to the international financial system, my country unfortunately will be running a currency convertibility regime that is completely modelled on the China model. It is unfortunate because it's not a good policy, it's not the best policy, but it seems to be the necessary policy at this point in time'.[31]

UNANIMOUS CONDEMNATION

The immediate reaction was almost unanimous condemnation from the West and the IMF. Then U.S. Federal Reserve Chairman Alan Greenspan called it 'decidedly mistaken' as 'the obvious consequence of confiscating part, or all, of foreign investors' capital and/or income, is to ensure a sharp reduction in the availability of new foreign investment in the future'.[32] Michel Camdessus was reported to have said that capital controls 'were not desirable, or even feasible, in today's globalised economy'.[33]

More importantly, rating agencies such as Moody's all downgraded Malaysia's credit and sovereign risk ratings. At the same time, the major stock market index providers, such as MSCI and FT-S&P, removed Malaysian stocks from their indices.[34] As investors tried to exit the market, the KLCI plunged to an all-time low of 262.7 on 1 September 1998. It took more than a decade for the KLCI to recover beyond its 5 January 1994 peak of 1,332.

The good news was that the imposition of exchange control allowed Malaysia to regain control over monetary policy and paved the way for lower interest rates. Within a week, daily interbank interest rates had fallen back to 5.5 percent per annum. The government was able to fund a fiscal stimulus program through the sale of government bonds on the domestic market. Economic recovery began, and the stock market index nearly doubled during the first week of the controls.

The exchange control regulations were complex and sophisticated, attempting to distinguish short-term outflows from long-term outflows.[35]

---

[31] Tourres (2003), 180.
[32] Greenspan (1998b).
[33] Quoted in Tourres (2003), 201.
[34] International Monetary Fund (1999c), 7–9.
[35] Abdelal and Alfaro (2003), 46–47.

The central bank even created a 24-hour hotline to answer questions on the controls. Later the IMF had to acknowledge that the measures were found to be in conformity with Malaysia's obligations under IMF's Articles of Agreement.[36]

As an official of the HKMA in 1998, I could not comment publicly on the exchange controls, but I quietly defended the decision to IMF friends as follows: Morally, if a patient who is bleeding could not obtain blood from his doctor, did he not have the right to tie a tourniquet to stop the bleeding? As a sovereign nation, Malaysia had every right to do what it felt was right to do. However, external bleeding was only a symptom, not the sickness that caused it. Hence, Malaysia had to undertake the necessary surgery to cure its sickness. Today even the IMF admits that the exchange controls worked and Malaysia was able to regenerate growth.

There were three factors that contributed to the success of Malaysia's capital controls.[37] First, the controls were feather-light. The commercial banks were made the operational authority for administering the selective capital controls instead of the central bank. Therefore, red tape for approving requests for sending money out of the country was reduced to the minimum, and approvals were generally the norm since the banks were eager to assist their clients. Malaysians were able to buy goods from abroad, as long as such payments were legitimate and justified.

Furthermore, each Malaysian was allowed to take a maximum of RM 10,000 in cash out of the country, whilst credit card use overseas was specifically exempted from this RM 10,000 limit. Potentially these two features were tremendous loopholes because of the high movement of people across the borders with Singapore and Thailand. However, in practice, the leakage was not significant.

Second, the Malaysian ringgit was deliberately pegged at a relatively cheap rate of RM 3.80, which minimized the risks of a black market for the currency. Since the bulk of Malaysia's exports were denominated in U.S. dollars, the stable exchange rate encouraged the resumption of trade and contributed to the strong inflow of liquidity especially in the fourth quarter of 1998.

Third and critically, a change in the base year for paying income taxes was announced in 1998. After deciding to impose selective capital controls, a major concern was that exporters would delay repatriating their export earnings back to Malaysia. There were worries that the exporters would also

---

[36] International Monetary Fund (1999c), 9.
[37] I am grateful to Ms Tan Siok Choo for pointing out these reasons.

under-invoice export proceeds and over-invoice import bills. To prevent such practices, a change in the tax assessment system was made to avoid two sets of taxes being paid in a single year. The year 1999 was declared a tax-free year, with losses in that year allowed to be carried forward. This was an ingenious move. To gain maximum advantage of the tax-free year, exporters had to maximise their profits, reducing their likelihood of under-invoicing exports and overbilling imports. At the same time, in terms of actual tax collection, the impact was neutral, because in 1999 taxes would be paid based on 1998 income, whilst in 2000 taxes would be paid based on 2000 income.

The above shows that Malaysian policies were pragmatic and used market practice to the country's advantage.

EXTRAORDINARY CIRCUMSTANCES; EXTRAORDINARY SOLUTIONS

Since February 1999 Malaysia has gradually relaxed its selective capital controls, and by 2003 most of the capital controls introduced in September 1998 were either removed or liberally relaxed. Furthermore, on 21 July 2005, the ringgit peg to the U.S. dollar was abolished.[38] The Malaysian central bank's announcement came on the same day as the People's Bank of China announced that the renminbi would operate under a managed floating exchange rate regime.[39] Nevertheless, Malaysia's decision to impose exchange controls will be debated for years to come.

Whether the experience of Malaysia can be emulated elsewhere or not, the lesson from Malaysia is that it is easy to give policy advice, but it is harder to judge what is right or wrong in a crisis. Henry Kissinger used to say that during a crisis the most dangerous option is usually the safest. Malaysia took the unorthodox way out, proving that even the best brains in Washington were wrong to rule this out. But it was not necessarily the medicine that could work for Indonesia, the country that suffered the most during the crisis and the subject of the next chapter.

[38] Bank Negara Malaysia (2005).
[39] People's Bank of China (2005).

NINE

Indonesia: From Economic to Political Crisis

Jang Harus Dibabat dan Harus Dibangun (What to Clear Away and What to Build).
~ Indonesian author Pramoednya Toer (1962)

If the Asian Crisis was an accident, Indonesia must be the worst casualty. From 1 July 1997 to its lowest point in June 1998, the Indonesian rupiah fell 85 percent against the U.S. dollar, much more than the Thai baht (56 percent), the Korean won (55 percent) and the Malaysian ringgit (48 percent) at their respective worst points. Furthermore, in 1998 Indonesian GDP fell 13.1 percent, the worst Asian decline compared with Thailand (10.5 percent), Malaysia (7.4 percent) or South Korea (6.9 percent).

The Indonesian tragedy is that it was the Asian crisis shocks that exposed a banking crisis that in turn precipitated a political crisis that ultimately led to the end of President Suharto's 32 years of rule on 21 May 1998. The country's IMF programmes, officially initiated on 8 October 1997, ended nine years later following Indonesia's early repayment of all its debts to the Fund in October 2006, but not before four Indonesian Presidents had come and gone.

Above all, it was the Indonesian people who suffered the most from this tragedy. I first visited Indonesia in the mid-1970s when it was still very poor. Indonesia is my favourite country to visit because of its long history, diverse culture and the fact that I admired how the nation steadily grew out of poverty. Throughout my many visits as an intrepid tourist to the remotest parts of Indonesia, especially the islands east of Bali, I had always been impressed by the people's warmth, friendliness and generosity.

Sadly, the crisis set back real GDP per capita by about 14.4 percent in 1998, and the poverty rate rose to a peak of 37 percent in September 1998[1]

---

[1] Islam (2002).

as inflation rose by 58 percent, by far the highest amongst the crisis-hit economies. It was not surprising that riots occurred in many cities in reaction to the sharp increases in fuel and food prices that the poor just could not afford. Resentment against the targeted Indonesian Chinese community arose from the fact that although they numbered only approximately seven million out of a country of 237 million, the ethnic Chinese minority had a major influence in running the distribution and manufacturing parts of the economy. It was reported by Crosby Corporate Advisory that in 1998 there were nearly 2,000 student demonstrations, 1,300 rallies by nongovernment groups, 500 strikes and 50 riots.[2]

FROM RAGS TO RICHES

By any standards Indonesia is an important nation, Southeast Asia's largest economy and Asia's fifth largest in 2007. The country has the fourth largest population in the world, after China, India and the United States. Sitting on an estimated 3.99 billion barrels of proven crude oil reserves in 2007, outside the Middle East, Indonesia is also Asia's only member of the Organization of Petroleum Exporting Countries (OPEC), the 'big boys' club of oil exporters. Furthermore, half of the world's shipping passes through its waters, and with more than 17,000 islands, Indonesia has an exotic culture that blends together the largest Muslim population in the world with sizable Christian, Hindu and Buddhist communities and indigenous traditions. Indonesia is also home to some of the world's most primitive jungles, reefs and rare botanical species.

In the mid-1960s, when Indonesia's first president, the charismatic Sukarno, was nearing the end of his leadership, the country suffered from serious macroeconomic neglect. Domestically the government ran large budget deficits that were financed by printing money. As a result, annual inflation was as high as 635 percent in 1966.[3] Externally, Indonesia's foreign debt of 50 percent of GDP in 1965 made the country almost bankrupt, as it was unable to service the debt because of weak exports earnings. During a period of bad governance, partly due to nationalization of major industries, the economy was in disarray. In 1965, for instance, non-oil exports made up a mere 4 percent of GDP.[4]

Indonesia's transformation came in the mid- to late 1960s when General Suharto, from Central Java, ascended to power following a failed coup

[2] Quoted in Djiwandono (2000), 51. For an excellent survey of reasons see Sidel (2006).
[3] Feridhanusetyawan and Pangestu (2003), 130.
[4] Jomo et al. (1997), table 6.1, 124–126.

attempt against President Sukarno. On 27 March 1968 Suharto was formally sworn in as Indonesia's second president. Under his *Orde Baru* (New Order), Indonesia soon became a model developing country. President Suharto provided not only political stability to the country but also prosperity as he was well served by able and loyal U.S.-trained technocrats who worked continuously as a group for over 30 years. This group of dedicated civil servants became famous as the 'Berkeley Mafia' because some of its more prominent members, including Professor Widjojo Nitisastro, the recognised intellectual leader,[5] had studied at the University of California, Berkeley.

Between 1968 and 1996 the country enjoyed high economic growth rates that averaged about 7 percent per annum. Rapid growth was achieved on the back of rapid industrialization and growing trade, with oil and timber producing windfall income. The stable political and macroeconomic environment also translated into a better standard of living for the Indonesian people. GDP per capita rose from US$70 per capita in 1968 to US$1,264 in 1996, and the poverty rate fell from around 60 percent to 18 percent over the same period. The World Bank lauded Indonesia's achievement as 'one of the most "pro-poor growth" in the economic history of any country'.[6]

In 1996 the Indonesian economy looked generally in good shape. It had a fiscal surplus of 1 percent of GDP, central government debt was brought down to 23.2 percent, the savings rate was high at 30.1 percent of GDP and unemployment for such a large country was only 4.9 percent (Table 9.1). In addition, although Indonesian trade competitiveness also fell following the yen depreciation against the U.S. dollar in mid-1995, its current account deficit was only 2.9 percent of GDP (Table 9.2), much lower than Thailand's 8 percent, Malaysia's 4.4 percent and South Korea's 4.1 percent. Moreover, Indonesia was a staunch supporter of the West in terms of foreign policy and was a favourite amongst foreign investors and creditors seeking higher yields in emerging markets.

Ironically, as a result of the current account deficit and the high rate of capital flows into Indonesia that led to inflationary pressures, according to J. Soedradjad Djiwandono, former Governor of Bank Indonesia, the technocrats at the World Bank and the IMF were divided as to whether the Indonesian rupiah should be strengthened instead of weakened.[7] Unlike Malaysia or Thailand, Indonesia operated a flexible exchange regime, floating around a band, which was abandoned on 14 August 1997 after the rupiah

5   Boediono (2005), 318.
6   World Bank (2006), x.
7   Djiwandono (2005), 36.

Table 9.1. *Indonesia: Selected Real Economy Indicators*

	1990	1991	1992	1993	1994	1995	1996	1997	1998	1999	2000
GDP US$ billion	125.7	140.8	152.8	174.6	195.5	223.4	250.7	238.4	105.5	154.7	165.5
GDP per capita US$	699	770	822	923	1,017	1,144	1,264	1,184	516	746	807
Real GDP Annual % change	7.2	7.0	6.5	6.8	7.5	8.2	7.8	4.7	-13.1	0.8	5.4
Unemployment rate % of total labour force	2.5	2.6	2.7	2.8	4.4	7.2	4.9	4.7	5.5	6.4	6.1
Inflation Annual % change	7.8	9.4	7.5	9.7	8.5	9.4	7.0	6.2	58.0	20.7	3.8
Fiscal balance % of GDP	-0.9	-0.7	-1.1	-0.5	1.0	3.0	1.0	0.5	-1.7	-2.5	-1.1
Central government debt % of GDP	39.2	34.7	36.6	34.8	35.4	29.0	23.2	23.7	79.3	91.8	100.0
Gross domestic capital formation % of GDP	30.7	32.0	32.4	29.5	31.1	31.9	30.7	31.8	16.8	11.4	22.2
Gross domestic savings % of GDP	32.3	33.5	35.3	32.5	32.2	30.6	30.1	31.5	26.5	19.5	31.8
Manufacturing production index 2000 = 100	67.6	73.8	82.4	91.6	107.7	119.8	125.7	115.9	94.7	96.5	100.0

Sources: ADB, IMF and Jaimovich and Panniza (2006)

221

Table 9.2. *Indonesia: Selected Currency and Current Account Indicators*

							Currency Indicators*					
	1990	1991	1992	1993	1994	1995	1996	1997	1998	1999	2000
Rupiah per U.S. dollar Period average	1,843	1,950	2,030	2,087	2,161	2,249	2,342	2,909	10,014	7,855	8,422
Rupiah per U.S. dollar End of period	1,901	1,992	2,062	2,110	2,200	2,308	2,383	4,650	8,025	7,085	9,595
Rupiah nominal effective exchange rate 2000 = 100	–	–	–	–	317.3	301.6	305.8	171.1	103.9	112.2	90.8
Rupiah real effective exchange rate 2000 = 100	–	–	–	–	151.8	151.9	158.5	95.4	101.0	109.5	94.8
Yen to U.S. dollar Period average	144.8	134.7	126.7	111.2	102.2	94.1	108.8	121.0	130.9	113.9	107.8
Yen to U.S. dollar End of period	134.4	125.2	124.8	111.9	99.7	102.8	116.0	130.0	115.6	102.2	114.9
Yen nominal effective exchange rate 2000 = 100	–	–	–	–	87.2	85.4	77.9	78.3	86.5	102.0	98.5
Yen real effective exchange rate 2000 = 100	–	–	–	–	104.9	97.0	85.3	84.9	91.0	104.0	97.0

Current Account Indicators[†]

	1990	1991	1992	1993	1994	1995	1996	1997	1998	1999	2000
Terms of trade 2000 = 100	94.9	91.3	88.6	88.3	84.9	90.4	97.3	99.0	81.8	66.3	100.0
Exports US$ billion	25.7	29.1	34.0	36.8	40.1	45.4	49.8	53.4	48.8	48.7	62.1
Exports growth Annual % change	15.9	13.5	16.6	8.4	8.8	13.4	9.7	7.3	−8.6	−0.4	27.7
Imports US$ billion	21.8	25.9	27.3	28.3	32.0	40.6	42.9	41.7	27.3	24.0	33.5
Imports growth Annual % change	33.5	18.5	5.5	3.8	12.9	27.0	5.7	−2.9	−34.4	−12.2	39.6
Trade balance US$ billion	3.8	3.3	6.7	8.5	8.1	4.8	6.9	11.8	21.5	24.7	28.6
Current account balance US$ billion	−3.2	−4.4	−3.1	−2.3	−3.0	−6.8	−7.3	−3.8	4.0	5.8	8.0
Current account balance % of GDP	−2.5	−3.1	−2.0	−1.3	−1.5	−3.0	−2.9	−1.6	3.8	3.7	4.8

Sources:

* BIS and IMF

† ADB, IMF; UNCTAD and author's estimates

Dash means data not available

was attacked like the currencies of other countries. Consequently, when the financial panic hit Indonesia via contagion in July 1997, Indonesian policy-makers generally believed that the economy would be able to weather the coming storm. The opposite turned out to be true.

For the more discerning observers, four fault lines laid beneath Indonesia's relatively benign macroeconomic indicators. These vulnerabilities were already evident long before the crisis erupted, but they were 'swept under the carpet'[8] amidst the euphoria of a booming economy. But when the tsunami spread from Thailand to Indonesia, these weaknesses came together to form a 'perfect storm', causing Indonesia to plunge into a deep and prolonged crisis.

POWER POLITICS

The first vulnerability was political succession. When the crisis hit Indonesia in July 1997, President Suharto had ruled Indonesia for 31 years. At 76 years of age and ailing, he had no clear successor strong enough to lead such a large and complex country.

Concerns surrounding President Suharto's leadership surfaced following the passing of his wife, Siti Hartanah, popularly known as Ibu Tien, on 28 April 1996. Ibu Tien was President Suharto's partner for 49 years, a politically astute pillar of support and a power in her own right.

As Indonesia has a history of Hindu civilization, the Javanese outlook in life bears a cosmic element. Power in a leader is believed to be endowed through cosmic forces on either the leader or someone close to him. Many believed that President Suharto's bequest or *wahyu* was bestowed on Ibu Tien, a minor princess of the Solo royal family. Therefore, when she passed away, many believed that President Suharto would not be able to retain power: 'Whatever the Javanese believed, the fact remains that President Suharto stepped down just two years after her death'.[9]

Since Indonesia's 'miracle' economic growth had been heavily dependent on the nation's political stability, doubts regarding President Suharto's leadership began to spill over to the foreign exchange market. The business community still remembered the violent history of leadership change 30 years before.

By July 1996, just as the Thai baht experienced its first major speculative attack, the rupiah too came under intense pressure. That month, whilst

[8]   Djiwandono (2005), 30.
[9]   Abdulgani-Knapp (2007), 30, 31, 193.

President Suharto travelled to Germany for a health checkup, the headquarters of the Indonesian Democratic Party (PDI) headed by former President Sukarno's daughter, Megawati Soekarnoputri, was the target of arson, and in the aftermath riots broke out in Jakarta on Saturday, 27 July. The foreign exchange market, which has always been a barometer of confidence in Indonesia, reflected the uncertainty.

The value of the rupiah is also influenced heavily by the yen-U.S. dollar exchange rate,[10] because 40 percent of the country's public debt was denominated in yen, whilst 80 percent of Indonesia's exports were priced in U.S. dollars. Consequently, in July 1996 Bank Indonesia had to sell US$800 million to stabilize the rupiah in the wake of the riots. The last time the Bank had to intervene this heavily had been in January 1995 in the aftermath of the 1994–1995 Mexican crisis.[11] The riots also affected the Indonesian stock market, with the Jakarta Composite Index (JCI) falling by almost 4 percent on Monday, 29 July, when the market resumed trading.

Given this backdrop, the political climate took a turn for the worst when President Suharto was rumoured to be gravely ill in December 1997. Market confidence was badly shaken, not only because of uncertainties as to presidential succession, but also because 'those lacking close ties to the family – including the economic team – were effectively cut off from access to the President'.[12] It was a crisis of governance, as no one emerged to take decisive leadership in the absence of the President during a time of riots and turmoil. It was revealed later that in December 1997 President Suharto had suffered his first stroke.[13]

CRONY CAPITALISM

The second vulnerability was the close links between business and government, labelled derogatively 'crony capitalism'. Indonesia always had a number of state-run monopolies and franchises in oil, rice, cloves and imported material that kept prices above world prices, even in the Dutch colonial days. In a country where public servants and armed forces were poorly paid, monopolies and franchises were sources of revenue for the elite to retain power by distributing favour and rewarding loyalty. Since power in Indonesia was concentrated in the President and the armed forces, crony

---

[10] Banker (1996); Djiwandono (2005), 24.
[11] Djiwandono (2005), 24.
[12] Independent Evaluation Office (2003), 30.
[13] Djiwandono (2005), 268.

capitalism was largely charged against the Suharto children, various generals and an elite group of businessmen close to the centre of power. The Suharto family knew how to exercise such power by delicately balancing different factions and regional interests, using the largesse skilfully.

However, keen observers of Indonesian political economy have noted that when Ibu Tien passed away in April 1996, Suharto's many children and relatives were no longer restrained in their demands for business privileges.[14] As noted by the IMF IEO Report:

Indonesia's vulnerability to crisis was greatly increased by the increase in corruption and its changing nature. … Originally, corruption in Indonesia was akin to a tax on the cost of a project, charged by and paid through established channels to maintain the stability of the political system. … Even such corruption raises moral and equity concerns, but its impact on efficiency was said to be limited by the certainty and relatively low levels of the charge. In the early 1990s, however, the media began to see a change in the system of corruption, and to draw links with the empire building of the President's children and well-connected businessmen. Corruption was being transformed into an ever-widening system of deliberate rent-creation for the well connected, including the creation of monopolies and monopsonies, and exclusive rights to large industrial or infrastructure projects, such as the National Car Project.[15]

Nevertheless, however damaging crony capitalism was to the economy, it would be difficult to argue that crony capitalism was the trigger or the cause of the Asian crisis. What was interesting was that the IMF had imposed reform conditions that were wide-ranging. They included reforms in banking, monopolies in cloves and plywood, trade barriers on wheat flour, soybeans and garlic, the suspension of large infrastructure projects and the opening of previously closed sectors to foreign investment. Indeed, the second IMF Letter of Intent signed personally by President Suharto on 15 January 1998 included 'over fifty action points and would later become a poster child for those criticizing the IMF's conditionality excesses in the 1990s'.[16]

Stephen Grenville, former Deputy Governor of the Reserve Bank of Australia and an acknowledged expert on the Indonesian economy, noted that 'the content of the IMF program in Indonesia was influenced, above all, by the view that the situation was not serious and could quickly be restored by sufficiently firm demonstration of policy probity on the part of

---

[14] See Abdulgani-Knapp (2007), 193; Lee (2000), 309.
[15] Independent Evaluation Office (2003), 108–109.
[16] Martinez-Diaz (2006), 402.

the authorities, together with support from the international community'.[17] If this was the true intention, then the IMF and the U.S. Administration, possibly egged on by the Indonesian economic team, viewed the crisis as an opportunity for reform to restore the loss of market and public confidence and eliminate crony capitalism. The strategy backfired.

The attempt to confront head-on the power to allocate domestic largesse by an outside force led to a highly publicised impasse between President Suharto and the IMF. Suharto knew that the IMF had the full backing of the United States, which he considered a key ally. But, in practice, the President was only half-hearted in 'the sincerity of his commitment'[18] in implementing the tough IMF structural reform conditions that would cut his own political influence. Tragically, the rupiah acted as a public barometer of the President's indecisiveness. In addition, the Indonesian stock market lost 76 percent of its market capitalization between 1996 and 1999, amounting to about 35 percent of GDP (Table 9.3).

President Suharto and the IMF first publicly crossed swords on 1 November 1997, a day after the first IMF LOI was signed, when 16 privately owned banks were closed. Amongst the banks closed were three connected with the President's family.[19] As if in defiance, President Suharto's son bought a small bank and on 23 November started a banking business on the former premises of a closed bank, Bank Andromeda.

As these events took place, within five months from July to December 1997, the rupiah fell 55 percent from Rp 2,400 to Rp 5,400 to the U.S. dollar. The crisis was moving rapidly from a collapse of confidence in the banking system to a collapse in the value of the domestic currency. In a situation where there was no exchange control and with inflation rising and banks failing, the only alternative for depositors was capital flight. During the same period the JCI fell 45 percent, from 731 points on 1 1, 1997 to 402 points on 30 December 1997.

The situation deteriorated further in 1998 as President Suharto's authority began to slip away. On 6 January 1998 the President announced an expansionary budget that was contrary to IMF demands for a budget surplus. On the announcement of the 6 January budget, the Indonesian currency plunged 25 percent from Rp 7,500 to the U.S. dollar to Rp 10,000 to the dollar on 8 January, breaking a crucial psychological barrier. In the same week, the JCI fell about 14 percent from 402 points to 347 points.

---

[17] Grenville (2004a), 78.
[18] Sadli (1998), 273.
[19] Independent Evaluation Office (2003), 127.

Table 9.3. *Indonesia: Stock Market Indicators*

	1990	1991	1992	1993	1994	1995	1996	1997	1998	1999	2000
Jakarta Composite Index End of period	417.8	247.4	274.3	588.8	469.6	513.8	637.4	401.7	398.0	676.9	416.3
Domestic Market Capitalization US$ billion	8.1	6.8	12.0	32.8	47.2	66.5	90.9	29.1	22.1	64.0	26.8
Jakarta Stock Exchange Price-earning ratio	–	–	14.3	28.6	31.8	21.6	19.6	10.6	4.1	9.5	5.9

Sources: World Federation of Exchanges and Bloomberg

Dash means data not available

At this juncture social and political unrests broke out. On 8 January, fearing hyperinflation and food shortages, 'in a frenzy of panic buying, crowds in Jakarta had cleaned out all shops and supermarkets to get rid of their melting rupiah and to stock up'.[20]

Following the riots, on 15 January, there was another public outcry, this time in connection with the publication of a famous picture showing Michel Camdessus, standing like a school master over President Suharto with his arms folded whilst the President meekly signed the second IMF LOI. The aura of the invincible Hindu God-King was broken. According to Retnowati Abdulgani-Knapp, the author of Suharto's authorised biography, 'On the same day, a group of retired military officers and national figures called for Vice-President Try Sutrisno to take over from President Soeharto at the end of his term in March'.[21]

Although President Suharto subsequently tried to restore confidence by announcing the resumption of the National Car Project without state funding, he was already caught in a serious political dilemma. His reelection was due in March 1998, and the economy was collapsing around him. Thus, when his allies persuaded him that the Argentinean experiment with a currency board could stabilize the exchange rate, President Suharto toyed with the idea between January and February 1998 in a desperate attempt to find a quick fix. The economic team and the IMF desperately tried to dissuade him from this flirtation, but their own medicine did not appear to be working either. By the end of January 1998, the Indonesian rupiah had plunged further to Rp 13,000 to the U.S. dollar.

Calls for a change in leadership grew stronger from this point onwards. As inflation hit a record of 12.8 percent in February 1998,[22] riots erupted because of rising prices, and on 19 February students from the University of Indonesia carried out their first demonstration.[23] A sign of the President's desperation at this point was the firing of the central bank Governor, Soedradjad Djiwandono, who was related to the President by marriage, ostensibly for not supporting the currency board idea.

As if to spite the foreign community, on his reelection as Indonesia's president on 10 March, President Suharto appointed his eldest daughter and close friends to his new cabinet, which elicited further student protests, this time outside the campus.

---

[20] Lee (2000), 311.
[21] Abdulgani-Knapp (2007), 209.
[22] Pangestu (1998).
[23] Abdulgani-Knapp (2007), 209.

In early May President Suharto was forced to raise petroleum product prices and electricity rates, as part of conditionality imposed by the IMF.[24] Between 13 and 16 May 1998, riots and demonstrations reached a peak following the shooting of four students on 12 May by security forces outside the campus of Trisakti University. During this time President Suharto was in the Middle East to attend a conference in Cairo. Although he returned a day early in order to calm the situation, it was already too late. Calls for his resignation came even from former loyalists and, crucially, the armed forces. He threw in the towel. At 9 A.M. on Thursday, 21 May 1998, he handed power to his Vice President, B. J. Habibie.[25]

The end of President Suharto's rule, however, did not mean the end of Indonesia's troubles. The markets remained depressed, as the nation plunged deeper and deeper into a multidimensional crisis. In June 1998 the rupiah collapsed to its lowest point with an exchange rate of just under Rp 17,000 to the U.S. dollar, coinciding with the sharp weakening of the yen against the dollar. On 21 September 1998 the JCI closed at its lowest point at 257 points, at around the same time as global markets were reeling from the Russian crisis and the Malaysian capital controls. By this time it was clear that Indonesia had entered a deep economic crisis as a result of the ongoing financial, social and political upheavals.

In the first quarter of 1998 the Indonesian economy contracted by 7.9 percent, and by the second quarter had contracted by 16.5 percent, with no clear indications whether the economy had hit rock bottom. In the meantime government estimates suggested that about 20 million people would become unemployed by the end of the year, up from 14 million earlier in the year. As a result of rising prices – by then food prices had increased by more than 100 percent – and declining incomes, there were estimates that about 79.4 million Indonesians had fallen into poverty.[26]

In his memoirs Singapore Minister Mentor, Lee Kuan Yew, had this to say about President Suharto:

I did not understand why his children needed to be so rich. But for their excesses he [Suharto] would have had a different place in Indonesia's history. ... I watched a telecast of his resignation. He deserved a more graceful exit. Suharto had concentrated his energies on stability and the economy. His policies created the conditions for strong economic growth from the 1970s to the 1990s in all Asean countries. They were golden years for Southeast Asia.[27]

---

24 Independent Evaluation Office (2003), 32.
25 Abdulgani-Knapp (2007), 211, 214, 215.
26 Pangestu (1998).
27 Lee (2000), 318–319.

FRAGILE FINANCIAL SYSTEM

The third vulnerability that exposed the fragility of Indonesia's political and business structures was the Indonesian financial system. Like its crisis-hit Asian neighbours, the Indonesian banking sector was the weakest link in the system (see Table 9.4).

In retrospect, Indonesia's vulnerable banking sector mainly resulted from the financial liberalization and deregulation that began in October 1988 with the *Paket 27 Oktober* (Pakto) banking reforms. These reforms were well intentioned but got taken captive by vested interests. The liberalization reminded me of my work at the World Bank looking at the Kenyan banking system in the late 1980s, when the outgoing Kenyatta government issued banking licenses liberally to favoured politicians who had no clue how to run banks.

Briefly, in the lead-up to the Asian crisis, three features of the Indonesian banking system stood out. First, the deregulation allowed the establishment of new private domestic banks and foreign and joint venture banks to compete against the state-owned banks that were nationalized during Independence and dominated the Indonesian banking scene. Between 1988 and June 1997 the number of state-owned banks remained at seven, whilst the number of foreign and joint venture banks increased from 11 to 44. However, during the same period the number of private domestic banks increased dramatically from 66 to 160, with 1,537 branches and 2,469 sub-branches by the end of 1997. In 1988 state-owned banks accounted for 70 percent of the banks' combined assets, with private national banks making up a little more than 20 percent. By mid-1997 the share held by state banks had fallen by half, with their loss in market share taken up by private domestic banks.[28]

Second, competition in the banking system changed the incentive structure. Before deregulation, state banks were seen principally as 'agents of development' channelling funds into areas considered high priority by the authorities.[29] Following deregulation, both state and private banks competed actively for household deposits and commercial loans that resulted in deterioration in credit and governance standards. This is a classic banking problem: credit growth at the expense of credit quality.

Third, ironically, the shift from public to private sector banks was supported by aid agencies and the foreign community as a positive step in

---

[28]   Bank Indonesia; Djiwandono (2005), table 4, 53; Grenville (2004b), 308.
[29]   Grenville (2004b), 308.

Table 9.4. *Indonesia: Financial Structure (% of GDP)*

	1990	1991	1992	1993	1994	1995	1996	1997	1998	1999	2000
Assets of deposit money banks	41.9	47.1	47.4	48.1	50.1	51.4	53.9	56.3	55.3	48.1	43.7
Assets of other financial institutions	–	–	–	–	–	–	–	–	–	–	–
Stock market capitalization	4.5	5.8	6.8	14.2	22.7	28.2	34.8	28.1	26.9	30.7	27.9
Bond market capitalization	–	0.1	0.4	0.9	1.2	1.3	2.1	2.6	5.6	19.7	31.3
Insurance premium volume	0.9	0.8	0.9	0.9	1.1	1.2	1.2	1.2	1.2	1.1	1.2

Source: Beck, Demirgüç-Kunt and Levine (2000), revised 13 August 2007
Dash means data not available

dealing with the inefficiencies of the state-banking sector.[30] Given the dominance of the state-owned banks, it was unclear whether prudential oversight of state banks fell under the jurisdiction of Bank Indonesia as the bank supervisor or the Ministry of Finance as the shareholder.[31] Unfortunately it was the poor governance in the private sector banks that contributed significantly to the banking crisis in Indonesia.

Given the environment of cronyism, many of the newly established privately owned banks were politically connected and owned by favoured conglomerates.[32] These banks expanded rapidly without professional expertise and lent indiscriminately. Related party lending, namely, credit facilities to persons or companies associated with the bank owners, was so common that Philippe Delhaise described it as a 'national pastime' and 'the one aspect that distinguishes the Indonesian banks from most of the rest of Asia.'[33] It was a tragedy waiting to happen. To quote Stephen Greenville, 'Indonesia's banking sector exchanged one set of undesirable qualities (those associated with government allocation of credit) for another (those associated with insider relationships).'[34]

The end result was a massive growth in private credit by banks, from 22.3 percent of GDP in 1988 to 51.2 percent in 1996 (Table 9.5), with the Indonesian corporate sector having the third highest debt-to-equity ratios in the region, next to South Korea and Thailand (Table 9.6).

Many Indonesian corporations used the loans they obtained from the banks 'to engage in reckless expansion in the nontradable sectors, such as shopping malls, real estate and housing projects, office buildings, hotels and even golf courses.'[35] Many of the projects were also politically related.

The lapse of judgement in lending was not confined to Indonesian bankers. For example, the largest of Hong Kong's local investment houses, Peregrine, collapsed in January 1998 when it lent nearly one-third of its capital to an Indonesian taxi cab company whose chairperson was the daughter of President Suharto. Peregrine thought that the bridging loan would be repaid through a subsequent initial public offering (IPO) or bond issue, banking on the strength of the Suharto relationship. Peregrine failed because it seriously misjudged the risks inherent in relationship banking.

---

[30] Independent Evaluation Office (2003), 107.
[31] Grenville (2004b), 309.
[32] Enoch et al. (2003), 76.
[33] Delhaise (1998), 129, 130.
[34] Grenville (2004b), 308.
[35] Sadli (1998), 275.

Table 9.5. *Indonesia: Selected Financial Sector Indicators*

	1990	1991	1992	1993	1994	1995	1996	1997	1998	1999	2000
Narrow money (M1) Annual % change	18.4	10.6	9.3	27.9	23.3	16.1	21.7	22.2	29.2	23.2	30.1
Broad money (M2) Annual % change	44.2	17.1	20.2	22.0	20.2	27.6	29.6	23.2	62.4	11.9	15.6
Private sector credit by financial institutions % of GDP	38.0	43.4	43.6	44.8	47.3	48.9	51.2	53.5	52.6	33.9	17.7
Lending rates % per annum	20.8	25.5	24.0	20.6	17.8	18.9	19.2	21.8	32.2	27.7	18.5
Deposit rates % per annum	17.5	23.3	19.6	14.6	12.5	16.7	17.3	20.0	39.1	25.7	12.5
Interest rate spreads % per annum	3.3	2.2	4.4	6.0	5.2	2.1	2.0	1.8	−6.9	1.9	6.0

Sources: Bank Indonesia, World Bank, Beck, Demirgüç-Kunt and Levine (2000), revised 13 August 2007 and author's estimates

Table 9.6. *Selected Asian Economies: Average Corporate Leverage (% of Total Debt over Equity)*

	1988	1989	1990	1991	1992	1993	1994	1995	1996	1988–96
Hong Kong	183.2	231.1	178.3	204.7	183.5	175.8	227.3	198.0	155.9	190.2
Indonesia	–	–	–	**194.3**	**209.7**	**205.4**	**166.1**	**211.5**	**187.8**	**195.1**
Japan	299.4	284.3	287.1	202.9	204.2	205.7	219.3	236.7	237.4	230.2
Malaysia	72.7	81.0	101.0	61.0	62.7	70.4	99.1	110.3	117.6	90.8
Philippines	–	–	–	83.0	118.6	117.5	114.8	115.0	128.5	112.9
Singapore	76.5	92.2	93.9	88.7	85.6	110.2	86.2	103.7	104.9	93.6
South Korea	282.0	264.4	310.5	322.1	337.3	363.6	353.0	377.6	354.5	346.7
Taiwan	–	–	–	67.9	88.3	86.6	89.4	79.6	80.2	82.0
Thailand	160.2	190.5	215.9	201.0	183.7	191.4	212.6	222.4	236.1	200.8
Memo items										
United States	79.8	84.8	90.4	97.2	105.9	105.1	106.6	109.9	112.5	103.4
Germany	153.5	155.2	158.2	159.4	150.7	153.4	151.2	148.5	147.2	151.4

Source: Claessens, Djankov and Lang (1998), table 6, 9
Dash means not available

The first major bank problem emerged as early as 1990, following the bail-out of Bank Duta, which in one year had lost US$420 million or twice its capital in foreign exchange transactions.[36] Three of President Suharto's charitable foundations held majority shareholdings in Bank Duta, each with about 27.5 percent.[37] Then, Bank Summa, a relatively major private domestic bank, with liabilities of US$750 million, was liquidated in December 1992.[38] The bank faced serious financial problems as a result of the deteriorating quality of its loans – most of them in the real estate sector and held by related parties. Related party lending rules limited such loans to no more than 10 percent of the bank's equity. However, when Bank Summa failed, 'it was rumoured that the bank was found to have 55% of total loans to related parties'.[39]

In the early 1990s, the IMF and the World Bank were well aware that the Indonesian banking system was fragile, and there were already considerable aid and technical efforts to strengthen supervision and help restructure problem banks. As Division Chief of the Financial Policy and Systems Division of the World Bank till September 1993, I sent one of our strongest bank supervisors to be based in Jakarta to help with the efforts. Unfortunately bank restructuring is most problematic when it has a political dimension. As former Bank Indonesia Governor Djiwandono pointed out, as early as May 1993, there was a leaked report to President Suharto 'containing a list of names of Indonesian corporations and individuals that had debt problems with their respective banks. This list looked like a *Who's Who* of Jakarta'.[40]

The question then becomes: Why were the weaknesses allowed to perpetuate? Governor Djiwandono attributed these to four related factors, of which the last was in my opinion decisive:[41]

- First, the lack of transparency hid the weak governance in the banking community
- Second, there was an element of moral hazard, as the public were easily lured to unnaturally high deposit rates by a number of banks
- Third, the central bank that was also the bank supervision authority had a variety of limitations due to its lack of autonomy and lack of professional skill
- Finally, the government policy of not being willing to liquidate insolvent banks was putting Bank Indonesia in an impossible position.

---

[36] Visser and van Herpt (1996), 303.
[37] Abdulgani-Knapp (2007), 179.
[38] Encoh et al. (2003), 76.
[39] Delhaise (1998), 130.
[40] Djiwandono (2005), 27.
[41] See Djiwandono (2005), 59.

I also agree wholeheartedly with his observation that there was an underlying flaw in the analysis of economic fundamentals before the Asian crisis:

A question that I was kept being asked was, if our fundamentals were strong how come Indonesia suffered so much? ... Only after the Asian crisis did economists explicitly acknowledge that the soundness of the banking sector should be included in the analysis of a national economy. ... The point I am making here is that the awareness of the need for a national economy to have a sound banking system for effective macroeconomic policies came too late for countries caught up in the Asian crisis. Macroeconomists like myself should have the intellectual humility to acknowledge this flaw.[42]

The recognition of the importance of the banking system on the health of the Indonesian economy did indeed come too late. In April 1997 Bank Indonesia had resubmitted an earlier proposal made in December 1996 to President Suharto to liquidate seven problem banks that did not have good prospects of rescue. President Suharto approved the proposal, but decided that the liquidation of the seven banks was to be delayed until after the elections in March 1998.[43]

However, by July 1997 the financial crisis severely impacted the balance sheets of Indonesian corporations. Even good businesses got into trouble as a result of their foreign exchange debt exposure, as the rupiah exchange rate increased over fourfold, making servicing foreign debt and interest costs highly costly. Many corporations defaulted, and the NPLs of Indonesia banks escalated dramatically, with several banks experiencing NPLs as high as 70 percent of their total loans.[44]

In October 1997 the IMF team collaborating with teams from World Bank and the ADB carried out a detailed assessment of the Indonesian banking sector. According to the IMF IEO Report:

The combined team identified 50 vulnerable banks, of which 34 banks were judged insolvent, including 26 private banks, 2 state banks, and 6 regional development banks. ... According to MAE [Monetary and Exchange Affairs Department, IMF], the 34 banks identified as insolvent accounted for about 15 percent of total banking sector assets, with the 26 private banks alone accounting for 5 percent.[45]

In hindsight, even that report severely underestimated the scale of Indonesian banking sector problem.[46]

---

[42] Djiwandono (2005), 28–29.
[43] Djiwandono (2005), 128.
[44] Nasution (2000), 151.
[45] Independent Evaluation Office (2003), 126.
[46] Independent Evaluation Office (2003), 126.

A crucial decision had to be made as to whether the authorities ought to close the insolvent banks. In November 1997 the IMF conditionality was that 16 out of the 26 insolvent private banks would be closed, including the original seven that were identified in April 1997.[47] Tragically, instead of winning back market confidence, the closure of the 16 banks caused a complete collapse in confidence in the Indonesian banking industry. By mid-December 1997, 154 banks, representing half of the total assets of the system, faced at least one episode of depositor runs.[48]

In hindsight, the closure of the failed banks created not only bank runs and flight to quality, but also capital flight. The Indonesian central bank faced exactly the same problem as the Thai central bank. A massive emergency liquidity support that Bank Indonesia was pumping into the banking system – Bantuan Likuiditas Bank Indonesia (BLBI) – which 'skyrocketed from 10.9 trillion rupiah in July 1997 to 62.9 trillion rupiah at the end of 1997, 96 trillion rupiah at the end of February 1998, 173.4 trillion rupiah in 1998 and 178.6 trillion in 1999'[49] was also leaking out into the foreign exchange market, as depositors sold rupiah and bought dollars; and if this could not be done, they bought real goods, creating hyperinflationary pressures.

Thus by the end of 1997/beginning of 1998, there was increasing recognition that a critical design flaw in terms of the bank closures was not installing a blanket guarantee, meaning a generalised guarantee for depositors and creditors. As such, on 26 January 1998 the blanket guarantee was officially introduced together with a comprehensive bank restructuring plan and the creation of the Indonesian Bank Restructuring Agency (IBRA) as a combined bank restructuring and centralized public asset management agency. Following the announcement of the blanket guarantee, there was relative calm in the Indonesian banking sector.

Why was the blanket guarantee not introduced sooner? In providing the insider story, Governor Djiwandono wrote:

During the discussions that led to the decision to liquidate the banks, IMF staff never brought up a *blanket guarantee*. The IMF staff only mentioned the *limited* guarantee for small depositors, which was in fact formulated by the Indonesian team. The agreement was documented in point 26 of the first LOI.

It was only after the devastating effects of the bank closures became apparent that the IMF came up with the proposal for Indonesia to adopt a blanket guarantee. In fact, this discussion was only conducted after the signing of the second LOI of 15 January 1998 and implemented on 26 January 1998.

---

[47]   Djiwandono (2007), 174.
[48]   Enoch et al. (2003), 78.
[49]   Djiwandono (2005), 175.

As in the case of private debt, the adoption of a blanket guarantee, if one accepts it as a proper policy, came definitely too late, at least in comparison to Thailand and Korea. ...

The fact that blanket guarantees were adopted by practically all countries severely affected by the Asian crisis has made me wonder why the IMF did not suggest that Indonesia adopt the scheme prior to, or together with, the bank closures in November 1997. ...

Why did Indonesia not adopt a blanket guarantee? I myself am not familiar with a blanket guarantee scheme, which was why I never suggested it. In fact, I first learnt of it when Dr. Bijan B. Aghevli wrote a memo on 18 January 1998 and another one in 23 January 1998, both about the banking sector crisis and proposed measures to deal with it. In the first memo, he mentioned the need to introduce a generalized guarantee for depositors and creditors of banks, which later became known as a blanket guarantee. ...

However, the Fund argued that the crisis was becoming systemic and without immediate drastic action the banking sector as a whole could be technically bankrupt. Ultimately, the Monetary Board agreed to adopt the scheme, and after getting approval from the President, the blanket guarantee was officially introduced on 26 January 1998.[50]

The calm in the Indonesian banking sector was short lived, however, as it came to an abrupt end following the May 1998 riots. By this time 'the blanket guarantee could do little about the crisis of confidence in the entire economic and political system ... let alone the ability of the government to honour that guarantee.'[51] Consequently the Indonesian banking sector went into complete disarray. In addition to bank runs, there was also a complete collapse of credit discipline: 'Most borrowers just stopped servicing their loans, regardless of their ability to repay. The few who did continue to pay asked for, and obtained, concessional interest rates.'[52]

Both the liquidity support by Bank Indonesia (BLBI) and the blanket guarantee came with a huge price. Following the restructuring of the Indonesian banking system, the government had taken over around 85 percent of the assets of the banking system.[53] The government took over the banks' losses by issuing various types of new bonds to cover three types of costs – compensation to Bank Indonesia for the liquidity support extended to banks, compensation to those banks taking over the liabilities of the banks that have been closed and recapitalisation of those banks that are undercapitalised and stay open.[54]

---

50 Djiwandono (2005), 122–123.
51 Independent Evaluation Office (2003), 128–129.
52 Frécaut (2004), 39.
53 Feridhanusetyawan and Pangestu (2003), 133–134.
54 Enoch et al. (2003), 84.

From practically zero domestic public debt from 1966 to 1998, domestic debt stood at US$76.8 billion at the end of 2006,[55] or about 22 percent of GDP. In addition, foreign public debt amounted to US$67.7 billion or about 19.2 percent of GDP as of 2006. In effect, the Indonesian government nationalized the mistakes of the private banking and corporate sectors that primarily resulted from its own policy mistakes.

At the heart of the controversy over blanket guarantees is the dilemma of all central banks acting in a banking crisis under conditions of grave uncertainty and rapid change. Here there are almost no good theories to guide the practitioner. In my experience only three rules of thumb are helpful: the Bagehot rule, the De Juan Rule and the French Hospital Rule.

Walter Bagehot's dictum states that in a banking crisis the central bank must lend freely against good collateral.[56] It does so to ensure that a liquidity crisis does not escalate into a full-scale solvency crisis, when asset prices collapse because of the lack of liquidity. This was essentially the rationale for the injection of liquidity during the Indonesian crisis, and also the response of G-3 central banks during the subprime crisis.

Central bank intervention unfortunately gives rise to the risks of moral hazard, which is the danger that all banks would take unnecessary risk because they would also consider themselves 'too big to fail'. The complex issue of moral hazard will be discussed in more detail in Chapter 12.

Unfortunately, the reality facing most decision makers during a financial crisis is that estimations of current costs and losses are almost always imperfect, and if no decision is taken, the crisis could escalate into a systemic crisis that could create huge losses. Hence, the decision maker must trade off the hazard of not making a present decision with the moral hazard costs in the future. In practice, therefore, and this was confirmed in the recent subprime crisis, moral hazard concerns were thrown out the window, and the EU and Fed central banks all intervened with massive amounts of liquidity. They did so in confirmation of what I call the modified De Juan rule.[57]

Former Bank of Spain bank supervisor Aristobulo De Juan's rule evolved from his experience in the Spanish banking crisis. It is what is known as the 'double loss' rule. In a financial crisis the losses are double what is originally estimated. Hence, the external auditors' estimates of loan loss provisions are double that of the bank management, the bank examiner's estimates are double those of the auditors and in liquidation, the actual losses are likely to

---

[55] Feridhanusetyawan and Pangestu (2003), 133; World Bank (2007b).
[56] Bagehot (1991) [1873].
[57] De Juan (2003). An earlier version of this article was written in 1989.

be at least double those of the bank examiners. In other words, actual losses are likely to be significantly worse than you think. Under such conditions it is not surprising that central bankers chose to intervene, for the consequences of not intervening could be considerable larger.

In hindsight, a primary mistake was not to assess the gravity of the situation accurately, as the IMF IEO Report admitted in 2003: 'This assessment [in October 1997] turned out to be a serious underestimation of the true state of the banking sector. The reality at the time was that, except for foreign banks, state banks, and a few large private banks, much of the rest of the banking system was illiquid and possibly on the verge of insolvency.[58] 'The Report stated clearly 'the extent to which the IMF missed the scale of the problem is obviously crucial in making an ex post evaluation'.[59]

Given the drain on illiquidity through capital flight, not providing liquidity was also not an option, because if the whole system (including the corporate sector) seized up, the losses would have become even larger. Unlike Malaysia, where capital controls could work, 'the Indonesian authorities told the evaluation team that they had never considered introducing capital controls, knowing that there was no infrastructure to administer such a system effectively. They also pointed out that one of the reasons for abolishing controls in the 1970s in the first place had been their ineffectiveness due to corruption'.[60]

Since capital controls were ruled out, would a blanket guarantee have helped? Initially a partial guarantee was provided, but it was clearly not enough to restore confidence. As the handling of the U.K.'s Northern Rock case in late 2007 showed, lack of clarity in explaining government measures in a crisis could worsen the crisis, forcing an escalation of measures. Since the initial partial guarantee in November 1997 did not work, a blanket guarantee was implemented subsequently in January 1998. In for a penny, in for a pound: 'Many, including IMF staff, have increasingly come to accept the view that the decision not to install a blanket guarantee was the critical mistake of the November 1997 bank closure'.[61]

What about the controversial BLBI, which has since been shrouded with controversy because of its magnitude? The IEO criticized the IMF for 'the failure to follow up on the close monitoring of BLBI (bank liquidity from Bank Indonesia) undertaken by the staff on the field. IMF staff was monitoring liquidity support bank by bank on a daily basis and keeping senior

---

[58] Independent Evaluation Office (2003), annex I, 74.
[59] Independent Evaluation Office (2003), 74.
[60] Independent Evaluation Office (2003), 72.
[61] Independent Evaluation Office (2003), 75.

staff at headquarters informed'.[62] The liquidity support reached as much as 5 percent of GDP or 100 percent of base money by the end of January 1998. The Report recognized that the central bank had either to close the bank or provide liquidity support. As the President did not want any more banks to close, the liquidity support was the only option forward.

Here the French Hospital Rule is useful as a guide to understand the moral dilemma involved. In the First World War French doctors found that given the unending stream of wounded flowing into the hospitals on the front line and the limited number of beds, doctors and medicine, a decision rule had to made on whom to save. The decision was that only those still fit to fight would be treated, because if the war was lost, all would have been lost. This illustrated that there was no good decision to be made, given infinite demands and limited resources. Once the decision of central bank intervention was made, the moral choice of whom to provide liquidity and under what circumstances was a moral and governance question that has no simple answer.

Hence, blaming the IMF, the speculators, the borrowers or the bureaucrats involved in the crisis would not help in the resolution of the crisis. If it were the weakness of the complete governance structure that exposed the country to the vicissitudes of global contagion, there would inevitably be many victims, innocent or otherwise, to that crisis.

GOOD-BYE FINANCIAL REPRESSION, HELLO FINANCIAL CRASH

The fourth vulnerability was the increasing volume of volatile capital flows that entered Indonesia in the period leading up to the crisis.[63]

The issue of capital account liberalization in Indonesia is a controversial one. Unlike its neighbours, many of whom retained capital controls until the mid-1980s, Indonesia was one of the first to open up its capital account completely. Indeed, Indonesia reversed the sequence of liberalizing its trade and financial sectors: 'Liberalization of the capital account was completed in 1971 long before the liberalization of the current account transactions began in the second half of the 1980s'.[64]

It was a pragmatic decision and one that served the country well initially. First, with a free port and financial centre like Singapore sitting at its border, there was little ability to enforce exchange controls. Second, because

---

[62] Independent Evaluation Office (2003), 79.
[63] The title of this section is attributed to Diaz-Alejandro (1985).
[64] Nasution (2000), 153.

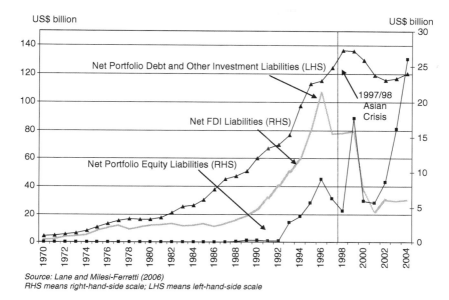

Source: Lane and Milesi-Ferretti (2006)
RHS means right-hand-side scale; LHS means left-hand-side scale

Figure 9.1. Indonesia: Net Foreign Liabilities, 1970–2004

there were few reputable Indonesian companies that were able to access the international financial markets, the open capital account did not cause too much problems. Third, since there was no international portfolio flows to speak of in the 1970s, there were very few volatile short-term capital flows, in or out. Indonesia relied largely on FDI, particularly from Japan, as well as public external debt, including aid flows, to finance its current account deficit with the rest of the world.

Things changed in the 1990s. Large amounts of short-term and portfolio capital inflows entered the Indonesian financial system, particularly in the form of external debt (Figure 9.1).

It was a qualitative change, both domestically and internationally. As a new generation of Indonesian businessmen grew up, they were more willing to borrow externally and experiment with new types of funding. With domestic interest rates being higher than global rates (Table 9.7), partly because of higher inflation, these businessmen were willing to borrow off-shore. Foreign banks were willing to lend to Indonesia to take advantage of the carry trade.

Indonesia was ideal for the carry trade, because even though the exchange rate floated within a band, average annual depreciation rate of the rupiah was between 4 and 5 percent per annum before the crisis. The rupiah-yen interest rate spread was 13.5 percent in 1996, which was very attractive even

Table 9.7. *Indonesia: Selected Interest Rate Differentials (% per Annum)*

	1990	1991	1992	1993	1994	1995	1996	1997	1998	1999	2000
Indonesia call money rate (ICR)	14.0	14.9	12.0	8.7	9.7	13.6	14.0	27.8	62.8	23.6	10.3
U.S. effective federal funds rate (FFR)	8.1	5.7	3.5	3.0	4.2	5.8	5.3	5.5	5.4	5.0	6.2
Euro overnight index average (EONIA)	–	–	–	–	5.2	5.6	4.0	4.0	3.1	3.0	4.8
Switzerland call rate (SCR)	8.9	7.6	5.9	4.4	3.6	2.3	1.8	1.0	1.0	1.4	3.5
Japan call rate (JCR)	8.2	6.3	3.9	2.4	2.3	0.5	0.5	0.4	0.3	0.0	0.2
Interest rate differential (ICR – FFR)	5.9	9.2	8.5	5.6	5.5	7.8	8.7	22.4	57.4	18.6	4.1
Interest rate differential (ICR – EONIA)	–	–	–	–	4.5	8.0	9.9	23.8	59.7	20.5	5.5
Interest rate differential (ICR – SCR)	5.1	7.3	6.1	4.3	6.2	11.3	12.2	26.8	61.8	22.2	6.8
Interest rate differential (ICR – JCR)	5.7	8.6	8.1	6.2	7.4	13.2	13.5	27.4	62.5	23.6	10.1

Sources: U.S. Federal Reserve Board, IMF, OECD and author's estimates

taking into consideration the depreciation of the rupiah within the band (Table 9.7).

Consequently, Indonesia's external debt increased sharply in the 1990s, reaching over 50 percent of GDP, up from 39.7 percent in 1985.[65] Most of the increase in debt took the form of short-term debt (Table 9.8). Again, Japan was Indonesia's significant source of foreign currency. Japanese FDI in Indonesia was one of the highest within the Asian region, amounting to 5.0 percent of Japan's total outward investment in 1996, higher even than Thailand (3.0 percent) and four to five times the amount to Malaysia (1.2 percent) or South Korea (0.9 percent). Moreover, between 1990 and 1996 Japanese bank lending to Indonesia averaged about 53 percent of total Indonesian foreign bank borrowings (Table 9.9).

By June 1997 Indonesia had a total external debt of approximately US$140 billion, of which US$80 billion or 57 percent of total external was private sector debt. Of the US$80 billion private sector debt, some US$60 billion or 75 percent was incurred by the corporate sector and US$20 billion or 25 percent by the banking sector. About US$33 billion or 41 percent of private sector external debt was maturing in one year or less.[66] Crucially, by 1994 Indonesia's net external liabilities were more than 50 percent of GDP (Table 9.9), and by 1995 short-term external debt was nearly double that of Indonesia's foreign exchange reserves (Table 9.8). Like its crisis-hit neighbours, Indonesia was therefore extremely vulnerable to capital outflows by the mid-1990s.

Added to this mixture of fragility in the foreign exchange liquidity mismatch at the national level was the double mismatch at the corporate level, common to all the Asian crisis economies.

First, similar to the loans that were obtained from Indonesian banks, most of the external debt was used to finance projects in the nontradable sector, such as real estate, because only these paid such high returns during an economic boom.

Second, most of the Indonesian corporate sector did not have export income to hedge against their foreign currency borrowings, because they were invested in domestic currency projects. The risks went straight from the corporations to their lending or guaranteeing domestic banks, which had to fund their foreign currency shortage by borrowing from foreign banks. As soon as foreign banks cut their lines to domestic banks, the only way to repay their foreign debt was to sell rupiah for dollars, thus exacerbating the

---

[65] Feridhanusetyawan and Pangestu (2003), 133.
[66] Sadli (1998), 274; Djiwandono (2005), 106.

Table 9.8. *Indonesia: Selected Foreign Reserves and External Debt Indicators*

	1990	1991	1992	1993	1994	1995	1996	1997	1998	1999	2000
Foreign exchange reserves (FER) US$ billion	7.4	9.2	10.2	11.0	11.8	13.3	17.8	16.1	22.4	26.2	28.3
FER growth Annual % change	37.2	24.5	11.3	7.9	7.6	12.6	33.9	−9.7	39.2	17.2	7.8
Total external debt US$ billion	69.9	79.5	88.0	89.2	107.8	124.4	128.9	136.3	151.3	151.3	144.2
Total external debt % of GDP	55.6	56.5	57.6	51.1	55.2	55.7	51.4	57.2	143.5	97.8	87.1
Short-term external debt US$ billion	11.1	14.3	18.1	18.0	19.5	26.0	32.2	32.9	20.1	20.0	22.6
Short-term external debt % of total external debt	15.9	18.0	20.5	20.2	18.0	20.9	25.0	24.1	13.3	13.2	15.7
Short-term external debt % of FER	151.4	156.4	177.4	163.7	164.6	195.2	180.9	204.3	89.8	76.3	80.0

Sources: ADB, IMF and author's estimates

Table 9.9. *Indonesia: Selected Foreign Capital Indicators*

	Capital Flows*										
	1990	1991	1992	1993	1994	1995	1996	1997	1998	1999	2000
Net FDI flows US$ billion	1.1	1.5	1.8	2.0	1.5	3.7	5.6	4.7	-0.2	-1.9	-4.6
Net portfolio investment flows US$ billion	-0.1	0.0	1.1	1.8	3.9	4.1	5.0	-2.6	-1.9	-1.8	-1.9
Net other flows, including bank credit US$ billion	3.5	4.2	3.2	2.0	-1.8	2.3	0.2	-2.5	-7.5	-2.3	-1.4
Net total capital flows US$ billion	4.5	5.7	6.1	5.8	3.6	10.1	10.8	-0.5	-9.6	-5.9	-7.9

	Other Indicators†										
	1990	1991	1992	1993	1994	1995	1996	1997	1998	1999	2000
Total foreign bank borrowings US$ billion	26.4	28.9	30.1	32.9	37.5	48.1	59.6	64.2	49.6	46.8	44.7
Short-term international bank loans¹ US$ billion	13.4	15.1	17.2	18.8	21.3	27.6	34.2	35.1	23.7	19.0	20.1

(*continued*)

Table 9.9. *(continued)*

						Other Indicators[†]					
	1990	1991	1992	1993	1994	1995	1996	1997	1998	1999	2000
Japanese bank lending to Indonesia US$ billion	15.8	17.5	17.7	17.6	19.6	22.5	23.5	22.8	17.0	13.1	10.9
Direct investments from Japan[2] US$ billion	1.1	1.2	1.7	0.8	1.8	1.6	2.4	2.5	1.1	1.0	0.4
Net external wealth position[3] US$ billion	−57.8	−64.5	−67.7	−78.3	−100.9	−120.6	−127.4	−129.4	−133.8	−143.4	−114.1
Net external liabilities % of GDP	45.9	45.8	44.3	44.9	51.6	54.0	50.8	54.3	126.8	92.7	68.9

Sources:

* ADB and author's estimates

[†] BIS, Japan External Trade Organization (JETRO), Lane and Milesi-Ferretti (2006) and author's estimates

[1] Foreign currency denominated loans of up to and including one year

[2] Based on report and notifications

[3] Negative means net liabilities position; positive means net assets position

downward depreciation of the rupiah. The more the rupiah devalued, the more the net foreign exchange borrowers became insolvent.

Consequently, even though Indonesian bankers and borrowers were used to floating interest rates and flexible exchange rates, they could not envisage the extent to which they were held hostage to the exchange rate devaluation: 'The long and short of this is that Indonesia experienced the not unusual combination of "Good-bye financial repression, hello financial crash".[67] The two critical vulnerabilities coming out of the history of financial deregulation were, first, very large and potentially volatile foreign capital inflows and, second, a fragile domestic financial system'.[68]

OLD MEDICINE THAT DID NOT WORK

The Indonesian structural fragility in terms of its domestic financial system and its external accounts meant that past successful actions to stabilize the rupiah could not work after July 1997.

First, as with previous occasions when the rupiah came under attack, Bank Indonesia widened the band rates for the intervention band. This time, on 11 July, the same day the Philippine peso was allowed to float, the band was widened from 8 percent to 12 percent or from Rp 192 to Rp 304 to give more room for manoeuvre. However, this time around it did not work because the capital flight was region-wide, and Indonesia was not spared.

As Indonesia formed part of the ASEAN class of assets, fund managers and hedge funds dumped their ASEAN assets for dollars. Thus, net total capital flows flipped from an inflow of US$10.8 billion in 1996 to an outflow of US$0.5 billion in 1997 (Table 9.9). In addition, foreign creditors including Japanese and other bankers not only stopped giving out new loans; they also refused to roll over existing loans and began to withdraw credit lines.

As described in Chapter 2, Japanese bankers, facing their own domestic problems, already began to reduce their exposures throughout Asia by mid-1995. In Indonesia, although Japanese bank lending still increased over the period 1995–1996, it grew only by 4.4 percent, a sharp drop from the growth rate of 14.9 percent over the period 1994–1995 and 11.4 percent over the period 1993–1994.

In Indonesia Japanese bank lending dropped by about US$619 million or around 3 percent over the period 1996–1997 (Table 9.9). They realized that since they had the largest exposure in the region, the correct strategy was to cut their exposure everywhere before.

---

[67] Diaz-Alejandro (1985).
[68] Grenville (2004b), 311.

As soon as the banking lines were cut, domestic corporations had to sell rupiah to cover their unhedged foreign currency borrowing, and when the rupiah plunged, all these led to a panic flight to dollars. Once the rupiah was allowed to free float on 14 August 1997, the Indonesian business community woke up to a reality that they were staring into the abyss. They thought that in a floating exchange rate regime, they could have their cake and eat it too. Their unhedged foreign debt became their demise.

The second 'tried and tested' initial response to stabilize the rupiah was to cut domestic liquidity and raise interest rates. Thus, by the end of August 1997, base money was abruptly reduced by around 20 percent.[69]

Whilst the 'shock therapy' of massive liquidity withdrawal worked in the past, it could not work in 1997 in the face of frail banks and overleveraged borrowers. The borrowers were hit with the double whammy of higher borrowing costs and rising foreign debt as the rupiah plunged. The banks could not raise enough foreign currency to repay their foreign bankers, who had cut their lines and wanted repayment.

Bank Indonesia was thus caught in a Catch-22 situation of providing liquidity in the banking system, as the lender of last resort, or to retain tight monetary stance through high interest rates to support the currency. The more it provided liquidity to the banks, the more that liquidity leaked out to push the rupiah down. The higher it increased interest rates, the faster the borrowers failed. Either way was no win. By September 1997 amidst the lobbying by the business sector, pundits and the press for lower interest rates, Bank Indonesia began to ease interest rates in stages.[70]

However, the continued outflow of foreign exchange meant that Indonesia found that it had insufficient reserves to defend the currency. Thus, there was no alternative except to call in the IMF in October 1997. The IMF staff worked under incredible time pressure to put together a quick package, but it quickly became clear to the markets that, exactly like the Thai package, the US$23 billion package, which included US$5 billion of Bank Indonesia's own reserves, was insufficient to meet Indonesia's immediate foreign exchange requirements, particularly the approximately US$30 billion short-term debt that needed to be rolled over. Since there was no bank standstill (which did not become an IMF tool until after the Korean crisis in December 1997), the failure of the first IMF program was inevitable.

The Indonesian crisis also demonstrated that the IMF, however well intentioned, was not geared to be a lender of last resort. Matters were made

---

[69] Grenville (2004b), 311.
[70] Djiwandono (2005), 62.

worse because the IMF money was tranched rather than heavily front-loaded, with US$3 billion available immediately and a similar amount not to be disbursed until mid-March 1998: 'So, the central problem was analogous to a traditional bank run, but the resources available to the Fund were inadequate to provide the traditional solution'.[71] The combination of bad politics, bad banking and inadequate resources to stem the crisis meant that Indonesia sank deeper and deeper into crisis.

OF GOVERNANCE AND INSTITUTIONS

The Indonesian economy took the longest of those discussed in this book to recover, and the effects are still being felt today. As mentioned, despite improvements, Indonesia currently still carries a huge public debt that was incurred to sort out the banking and corporate mess. Furthermore, even today, despite a good recovery with the rest of region, the social impact of the crisis is still felt. In 2007 the rate of unemployment, though falling, stood at 9.1 percent, whilst the poverty rate was 15.4 percent as of March 2008.

The Indonesian crisis story illustrates vividly the dictum that the core difference between a nation being rich or poor is the quality of the governance. President Suharto gave Indonesia political stability and prosperity, but by not managing his own political succession and not removing excessive corruption from the system, he opened Indonesia to vulnerability when the winds of globalization came blowing.

As former Minister of Finance and current Vice President Dr Boediono noted with great frankness and typical Indonesian modesty:

The crisis brought not only an acute awareness of how treacherous it can be to live in an interconnected world, but also a growing realisation that institutions of society and the way they are run (governance) matter a great deal in such a world. Many now have come to accept that the reason for our defencelessness in the face of the crisis, and the extended ordeal that we have had to endure, is our weak institutions and their poor governance. The recent focus on how to improve them is a move in the right direction. ...

Of the many exercises in institution building and reform, none is more fundamental, or promises a greater payoff, than those in the legal sphere, including the judiciary and other aspects of law enforcement. For here is where society's rules of the game are actually played out. ... As in other areas, the government has to take a strong lead. Greater support, and perhaps also pressure, from the international

---

[71] Grenville (2004a), 80.

community may help speed up the process, but the main force for change must be home-grown.

Next in terms of urgency is civil service reform, for herein lies the hope for more effective government and better implementation of policies. ... Over the years, the service was expanded rapidly out of necessity, while the damaging influence of politics was allowed to creep in, leading to a fateful decline in performance, service quality and the integrity of its corps. ... A complete overhaul is long overdue, but no government since independence has had the resolve to take up this challenge seriously. ...

Indeed, the success of the current democratic experiment hinges on success in managing the economy.[72]

In the next chapter we shall therefore discuss how Hong Kong surprised many when it decided to intervene in the stock market one fateful day in August 1998.

[72] Boediono (2005), 321–322.

TEN

Hong Kong: Unusual Times Need
Unusual Action

If small fortune does not go out, large fortune will not come in.
~ Hong Kong tycoon

In late 1996 one of the managing directors of Soros Management, Arminio Fraga, read an article by Professor Carmen Reinhart from the University of Maryland on the vulnerabilities of the East Asian economies. He passed the article to George Soros. In his book *The Crisis of Global Capitalism*, Soros admitted that his fund management company anticipated the Asian crisis at least six months before it happened. The fund sold short the Thai baht and Malaysian ringgit early in 1997 with maturities ranging from six months to a year.

PLACING YOUR BETS IN CURRENCY BATTLES: CENTRAL BANKS OR THE HEDGE FUNDS?

Hedge funds were invented in 1949, reputedly by Alfred Winslow Jones, who first leveraged his investments, sold short positions, had a limited partnership to avoid having greater regulation and took 20 percent of profits as performance fees. Initially they were slow to grow, but George Soros made hedge funds famous when his funds took a US$10 billion short position against the Bank of England. On the famous Black Wednesday, 16 September 1992, the Bank of England had to abandon the exchange rate mechanism (ERM) after it spent US$15 billion to support the pound and raised interest rates to as high as 15 percent to prevent sterling devaluation. Soros was reputed to have made about US$1.1 billion from this trade. His former partners in Quantum Fund included such legendary investors such as Jim Rogers, Victor Niederhoffer, Stan Druckenmiller and Arminio Fraga, who later made his reputation as a Governor of the Central Bank of Brazil.

In the 1990s as the Bank of Japan began to reduce interest rates, the rise of hedge funds and other highly leveraged institutions (HLIs) were helped by the yen carry trade because they were able to earn a good spread or 'carry' by borrowing Japanese yen cheaply and buying high-yielding assets in both the developed and emerging markets. The Asian side of the carry trade has been reported to have started in 1991–1992 by international money centre banks in Malaysia, and by 1993 carry trade activities had shifted from Malaysia to Thailand and Indonesia, where interest rates were higher relative to yen rates.[1]

Hedge funds often see crises as an opportunity. In particular, if they see an unsustainable asset bubble looming on the horizon, shorting the overvalued assets and the related currencies becomes an easy profit, especially if the funds are large players relative to the central banks defending the currencies. In hindsight, it is amazing that the Bank of England had spent US$15 billion defending the sterling, and Soros had admitted taking a US$10 billion short position. If this position was taken in the equity market, and not the foreign currency market, it would have been considered market dominance, if not cornering, because the rest of the other short positions put together amounted to only US$5 billion.

Cornering of commodity markets is technically illegal, but this does not appear to be the case in foreign exchange markets. This is puzzling because the stock market has tight regulation and oversight because it is largely domestic in nature. Historically, because the foreign currency market is an OTC market, with many foreign and domestic buyers and sellers, it is largely unregulated. To my knowledge, no central bank has ever taken enforcement action on market manipulation or abuse behaviour in the foreign currency market. The fact that the leading foreign exchange market in the United Kingdom did not take umbrage or action against such speculation even after the U.K. Treasury admitted that it cost the government £3.4 billion was to have immense consequences for emerging markets.

Hedge funds, of course, do not operate on their own, with their funding coming from their prime brokers, the major commercial and investment banks, who also hold proprietary positions on foreign exchange. There is supposed to be segregation from the deals of their hedge fund clients by Chinese walls, but given the thinness of Chinese walls and the fact that investors tend to herd in one direction, the amount of firepower that short sellers can mount against individual currencies is formidable. If the Bank of

---

[1]   Asia-Pacific Economic Cooperation Study, University of Hong Kong and China Centre for Economic Research (2000).

England could not withstand massive currency speculation against sterling, what chance did the smaller emerging market central banks have? This was a question that Asian central banks asked themselves immediately after the Mexican peso crisis.[2]

THE HONG KONG DOLLAR LINK

During some failed experiments in flexible exchange rates between 1974 and 1983, the Hong Kong dollar had been pegged against either silver, sterling or the U.S. dollar, using a currency board arrangement. Indeed, in reviewing the history of Hong Kong banking from 1935 to 1985, former Hong Kong civil servant and journalist Leo Goodstadt considered that 'the currency board offered a simple but effective defence against the damage done by misguided and ill-informed monetary decisions executed by officials who lacked professional expertise'.[3]

Prior to the Hong Kong dollar's current peg to the U.S. dollar, Hong Kong experimented with a floating rate for nine years between 1974 and 1983 (Table 10.1). As noted by the HKMA,

Although the first two years went fairly well, the experience of a floating rate regime was not a comfortable one. The then prevailing monetary policy framework was too rudimentary to replace the external monetary anchor. There was no clear monetary policy objective, let alone the tools to pursue such objectives. As a result, this was a period of high volatility on almost all fronts. Real GDP growth dropped to 0.3% in 1975 and climbed to 16.2% in 1976. Inflation swung sharply from 2.7% in 1975 to 15.5% in 1980. The value of the Hong Kong dollar moved from HK$5.13 in 1981 to HK$9.60 to the US dollar in 1983. The depreciation of the Hong Kong dollar was made worse by speculative attacks and by the escalating crisis of confidence over the future of Hong Kong, which came to a head in 1983. The record low point of HK$9.60 in September 1983 was reached after a drop of 13% in just two days.[4]

After consulting the Bank of England and the U.K. Treasury, the Hong Kong Government adopted on 17 October 1983 the currency board regime at the fixed rate of HK$7.80 to one U.S. dollar.

The lesson of currency volatility for small open economies, such as Hong Kong's, was that for those economies that did not have sufficient foreign exchange or market power to avoid volatility, there was no choice but to peg to one's main trading partner. A small economy 'borrows' credibility

---

[2] See Chapter 1.
[3] Goodstadt (2007), 184.
[4] Hong Kong Monetary Authority (2005), 34.

Table 10.1. *Hong Kong: Exchange Rate Regimes*

Date	Exchange Rate Regime	Reference Rate
1863–November 4, 1935	Silver standard	Silver dollars as legal tender
December 1935–June 1972	Link to sterling	£1 = HK$16 (December 1935–November 1967)
	Link to sterling	£1 = HK$14.55 (November 1967–June 1972)
6 July 1972	Link to the U.S. dollar with ±2.25% intervention bands around a central rate	US$1 – HK$5.65 (July 1972–February 1973)
14 February 1973	Linked to the U.S. dollar	US$1 = HK$5.085 (14 February 1973–November 1974)
25 November 1974	Free float	Exchange rates on selected dates: US$1 = HK$4.965 (25 November 1974) US$1 = HK$9.600 (24 September 1983)
17 October 1983	Link to U.S. dollar	US$ = HK$7.80

Source: Hong Kong Monetary Authority (2005)

from its larger trading partner, the larger and more stable the better. To protect the currency peg, the Hong Kong government could not run a fiscal deficit,[5] and monetary policy was basically delegated to the U.S. Federal Reserve Board.

Why was the peg to the U.S. dollar and not the yen? First, the United States was the major trading partner and dominant reserve currency. Second, anchoring to the yen would have meant that the Hong Kong dollar would be similarly volatile.

The mechanics of foreign currency speculation was easy – you simply borrowed local currency and sold it forward in the market. If a futures market existed in the local stock market, it made the speculation easier because you could short the stock market at the same time you shorted the currency market. This was known as the double play and was prevalent in Hong Kong during the crisis.

---

[5]   For a discussion on whether a currency board system could have a fiscal deficit, see page 277.

From a speculative point of view, the Hong Kong dollar Link to the U.S. dollar was the perfect setup for the double play. A cynic would say that in a poker game, the biggest potential victim is the player with the largest chips. As at the end of 1997, at US$92.8 billion, Hong Kong had one of the largest foreign exchange reserves in the world.

During the Asian crisis, the role of currency boards became controversial, because Professor Steve Hanke tried to recommend it to Indonesia as a bulwark against currency speculation.[6] There were also accusations that departures from currency board 'orthodoxy' diluted countries' efficacy in defending a fixed exchange rate regime. The principal argument was that it was the automaticity of the currency board arrangement that carried market credibility. Hanke specifically argued that deviations from orthodoxy allowed monetary and exchange rate policies to conflict with one another.[7] Indeed, the credibility of the currency board arrangements in Hong Kong was severely tested during the Asian crisis.

Although small movements took place in the Hong Kong dollar in the aftermath of the Thai baht devaluation on 2 July 1997, the first serious attack on the Hong Kong dollar Link was launched on 23 October 1997, when overnight interest shot up to nearly 300 percent at one point. The Hang Seng stock market index fell from peak to trough by more than 60 percent to a low of 6,660 on 13 August 1998. Property prices, which had risen to bubbly heights in 1997, also took a dive of about 50 percent from pre-crisis levels before bottoming out in September 1998.

The significant negative wealth effects from the sharp pull-back in asset prices sent the Hong Kong economy spiralling into a recession. In 1998 GDP deflated by 5.5 percent, whilst unemployment rate shot up to 4.7 percent (Table 10.2). By comparison, Singapore suffered relatively mildly in real GDP contraction of 1.4 percent in 1998, whilst Taiwan still grew by 4.5 percent in GDP. The impact on Hong Kong thus turned out to be deeper than was anticipated.

SOUND FUNDAMENTALS WITH VULNERABILITIES

At first sight, in terms of pure fundamentals, Hong Kong should not have been a victim of the Asian crisis. First, the real economy was robust, growing at a relatively healthy rate of 5.1 percent in 1997. Second, fiscal policy was prudent, as exemplified by the budget surplus of 6.4 percent of GDP in

---

[6]   See Chapter 9 on Indonesia and Hanke (2002).
[7]   Hanke (2002), 204.

Table 10.2. *Hong Kong: Selected Real Economy Indicators*

	1990	1991	1992	1993	1994	1995	1996	1997	1998	1999	2000
GDP US$ billion	76.9	88.8	104.0	120.0	135.5	144.2	159.0	176.3	166.9	163.3	168.8
GDP per capita US$	13,368	15,276	17,666	20,001	22,149	23,003	24,583	27,055	25,353	24,600	25,144
Real GDP Annual % change	4.0	5.7	6.5	6.3	5.6	3.9	4.2	5.1	−5.5	4.0	10.0
Unemployment rate % of total labour force	1.3	1.8	2.0	2.0	1.9	3.2	2.8	2.2	4.7	6.2	4.9
Inflation Annual % change	10.3	11.3	9.5	8.8	8.8	9.0	6.3	5.8	2.8	−3.9	−3.7
Fiscal balance % of GDP	0.7	3.3	2.7	2.1	1.0	−0.3	2.1	6.4	−1.8	0.8	−0.6
Gross domestic capital formation % of GDP	27.0	26.8	28.0	27.1	31.2	34.1	31.6	34.0	28.9	24.8	27.5
Gross domestic savings % of GDP	35.7	33.7	33.3	33.9	32.5	29.6	30.1	30.7	29.4	30.1	32.0
Manufacturing production index 2000 = 100	119.9	120.6	123.0	122.3	122.0	123.1	118.6	117.6	107.4	100.5	100.0

Sources: ADB and IMF

Table 10.3. *Hong Kong: Foreign Reserves and External Wealth Indicators*

	1990	1991	1992	1993	1994	1995	1996	1997	1998	1999	2000
Foreign exchange reserves (FER) US$ billion	24.6	28.8	35.2	43.0	49.3	55.4	63.8	92.8	89.6	96.2	107.5
FER growth Annual % change	–	17.3	22.1	22.2	14.6	12.5	15.2	45.4	−3.4	7.4	11.7
Net external wealth position[1] US$ billion	154.0	122.9	101.9	−24.8	100.5	115.2	69.2	229.8	254.9	183.9	221.8
Net external wealth position[1] % of GDP	200.2	138.4	98.0	−20.7	74.2	79.9	43.5	130.3	152.7	112.6	131.4

Sources: IMF, Lane and Milesi-Ferretti (2006) and author's estimates
[1] Negative means net liabilities position; positive means net assets position
Dash means data not available

1997 with zero sovereign debt. Third, the economy operated largely under free market discipline and was flexible and responsive to market forces. Fourth, official reserves were ample at just under US$100 billion, the third largest in the world after Japan and mainland China (Table 10.3). Fifth, Hong Kong's linked exchange rate system had a high degree of credibility as its reserves provided nearly 800 percent backing for the currency in 1997,[8] and the Hong Kong dollar link operated on a rules-based monetary system. Sixth, Hong Kong had a strong banking system, well capitalized and well supervised. Much of Hong Kong's enviable position was attributable to the hard work done in preparing the Hong Kong economy for a smooth and successful return to China on 1 July 1997.

In retrospect, however, there was a glaring vulnerability in the Hong Kong economy. It took the form of growing asset bubbles both in the real estate sector and in the stock market that were fuelled by two main factors.

---

[8] Yam (1998a).

First, like its regional peers, Hong Kong also benefited from the large private international capital inflows into Asia. It was particularly successful in attracting foreign capital because of its position as an international financial and business centre. In the early 1990s there was a large influx of Japanese and South Korean banks to fund the regional business. Eighty of the world's top 100 banks had offices and branches in Hong Kong.

Second, in the lead-up to the Asian crisis, Hong Kong witnessed skyrocketing real estate prices that were the result of strong demand and low supply. Hong Kong was a property developer's dream market. The exchange rate was stable, but when the domestic market boomed, interest rates that were pegged to U.S. dollar rates because of the Link became negative in real terms when inflation rose higher than that in the United States (see Tables 10.2 and 10.4).[9] The middle class and property developers piled into real estate as a hedge against inflation. By 1997 the real estate sector (construction, real estate and ownership of premises)[10] was the largest sector in the Hong Kong economy, contributing about 26.8 percent to GDP, followed by trade (20.7 percent) and finance (10.3 percent). The stock market was dominated by property and banking stocks, and stock market speculation was essentially another play on the property market. As Philippe Delhaise noted,

Hong Kong is a microcosm that encompasses everything good and bad about Asia, and the very same lunacies that drive *amahs* and taxi drivers to bid up the price of an obscure firm operate everywhere in Asia with the same devastation. Markets, like people are often manipulated. Asia is a huge gambling den where among other minor aspirations to become happy, educated or caring, the central ambition is to get rich.[11]

Consequently, both the large influx of foreign capital and the rising dominance of the property sector in Hong Kong fuelled an unprecedented boom in the stock and property markets, with the Hang Seng Index closing at a peak of 16,673 points on 7 August 1997, and the property market also peaking around that time (Table 10.5). Indeed, according to an *Asiaweek* report, by 1997 Hong Kong was the second most expensive city in the world in U.S. dollar terms after Tokyo,[12] causing concerns that the SAR was losing

[9] Asia-Pacific Economic Cooperation Study, University of Hong Kong and China Centre for Economic Research (2000), 110.
[10] Imputed rental charge for owner-occupied premises.
[11] Delhaise (1998), 12.
[12] Bacani (1998).

Table 10.4. *Hong Kong: Selected Financial Sector Indicators*

	1990	1991	1992	1993	1994	1995	1996	1997	1998	1999	2000
Narrow money (M1) Annual % change	13.3	19.5	21.1	20.6	−1.2	2.8	14.2	−4.3	−5.0	13.9	8.3
Broad money (M2) Annual % change	22.4	13.3	10.8	16.2	12.9	14.6	10.9	10.1	11.6	8.8	7.8
Private credit by financial institutions % of GDP	–	143.0	127.1	124.3	131.7	143.5	147.0	156.2	176.7	164.0	150.6
Lending rates % per annum	10.0	8.5	6.5	6.5	8.5	8.8	8.5	9.5	9.0	8.5	9.5
Deposit rates % per annum	6.7	5.5	3.1	2.3	3.5	5.6	4.6	6.0	6.6	4.5	4.8
Interest rate spreads % per annum	3.3	3.0	3.4	4.3	5.0	3.1	3.9	3.5	2.4	4.0	4.7

Sources: ADB, World Bank, Beck, Demirgüç-Kunt and Levine (2000), revised 13 August 2007 and author's estimates
[1] Deposit money banks and other financial institutions
Dash means data not available

its competitiveness as the region's international financial and commercial centre.

As the April 1998 Hong Kong Government Report on Financial Market Review to examine Hong Kong's currency defence following the October 1997 major attack frankly admitted,

This region which is stricken by the financial turmoil was the region that was hailed not too long ago for its strong growth and economic dynamism. The crux of the problem, in many cases, lies in the structural and systemic weaknesses. ...

Hong Kong generally has little such structural and systemic problems. However, through a period of exceptional buoyancy in the economy and highly bullish outlook for the future, the stock and property markets in Hong Kong had gone to excessive heights. For example, residential property prices rose on average by as much as 80% to the peak during the two years prior to October 1997. The HSI gained by 1.4-fold to reach the record high in August 1997 in slightly more than

Table 10.5. *Hong Kong: Selected Asset Prices*

	1990	1991	1992	1993	1994	1995	1996	1997	1998	1999	2000
Stock Market Indicators*											
Hang Seng Index End of period	3,025	4,297	5,512	11,888	8,191	10,073	13,452	10,723	10,049	16,962	15,096
Domestic market capitalization US$ billion	83.4	121.9	172.0	385.0	269.5	303.7	449.2	413.3	343.6	609.1	623.4
Hong Kong exchanges Price-earning ratio	9.9	13.0	13.1	21.6	10.7	11.4	16.7	12.1	10.7	26.7	12.8
Real Estate Indicators†											
Private domestic (overall) Price index (1999 = 100)	47.3	73.2	85.7	100.8	110.1	103.9	134.5	155.0	104.6	95.7	81.8
Private retail (overall) Price index (1999 = 100)	54.1	75.0	101.7	119.1	129.8	125.9	144.5	165.3	102.7	95.5	92.4
Private office (overall) Price index (1999 = 100)	102.9	109.7	149.2	184.1	235.2	183.8	217.2	173.3	106.6	95.5	84.9

Sources:
* World Federation of Exchanges and Bloomberg
† Hong Kong Rating and Valuation Department

2½ years. At that record high, the P/E ratios for Blue Chips surged to an average of 17 times, while those for Red Chips and H-shares[13] were even more dramatic, at 52 and 30 times respectively. In retrospect, while the fundamentals of the economy at that time remained generally and basically sound, the sharp escalation in asset prices to unsustainable levels did expose a substantial weakness making our financial sector open to assault. It was against this background that the heavy speculative attack on the Hong Kong dollar took place in the latter part of October 1997. The subsequent adjustments, painful though they were, in hindsight were perhaps not only unavoidable but even necessary.[14]

HONG KONG'S BLACK THURSDAY

The Asian crisis that claimed consecutive victims in Southeast Asia reached Hong Kong in August 1997. On 19 August overnight interest rates rose to an intraday high of 10 percent, in the first of the speculations against the Hong Kong dollar. The currency board mechanism kicked in and markets stabilized, but interest rates remained high at 6–7 percent for the rest of the third quarter.

Initially, the Hong Kong stock market adjusted only between 15 and 20 percent from its 7 August 1997 peak of 16,673. However, Hong Kong's day of reckoning came in October 1997 about a month after Hong Kong hosted the September 1997 IMF/World Bank Annual Meetings, when the world's bankers gathered to assess what happened to Asia.

On Friday, 17 October 1997, the Taiwan dollar was allowed to float. This was despite the fact that the Taiwan economy was actually still strong and there were exchange controls in place. During the week of 20 October speculators, having tasted blood after Taiwan gave up the defence of its dollar, took up huge short positions against the Hong Kong dollar. On 21 and 22 October many banks sold substantial amounts of Hong Kong dollars to the HKMA for U.S. dollars, and as the HKMA was obliged to redeem Hong Kong dollars for U.S. dollars, a Hong Kong dollar liquidity crunch became inevitable.

Settlement day came on Thursday, 23 October 1997, subsequently known as Hong Kong's 'Black Thursday'. The banks that sold Hong Kong dollars would be short of Hong Kong dollars to fund their Hong Kong

---

[13] Red Chips are shares of mainland China-owned companies, registered outside China, whereas H shares are Chinese-registered companies, both being listed on the Stock Exchange of Hong Kong.

[14] Financial Services Bureau (1998), Executive Summary, xi.

dollar commitments. On that day, as reported by the HKMA 1997 Annual Report,

To discourage the use of the Liquidity Adjustment Facility (LAF)[15] to fund a short Hong Kong dollar position, the HKMA issued a circular on the morning of 23 October reminding banks that they should organise their Hong Kong dollar funding prudently and not be overly dependent on the LAF for last resort liquidity support. The circular also warned them that the HKMA might impose penal LAF rates for repeated borrowers.[16]

In other words, the banks could not rely on the HKMA to provide them with Hong Kong dollars to fund speculation against the Hong Kong dollar.

There was a wild scramble for Hong Kong dollars, causing an acute shortage of interbank liquidity. The banks had collectively sold more Hong Kong dollars to the HKMA than they could settle by using their credit balances in their clearing accounts with the HKMA. Since the banks did not wish to resort to the LAF on a repeated basis, interbank interest rates shot up, with overnight HIBOR rising from around 9 percent to 280 percent for a few hours. Interest rates eased slightly to around 100 percent at the close of 23 October as banks sold U.S. dollars back to the HKMA to obtain Hong Kong dollars as hedges against high interest rates, which, again, the HKMA took passively in accordance with the discipline of the currency board system.

The reaction was mostly on the stock exchange, where the Hang Seng Index dropped by 10.4 percent. Although it rebounded by 6.9 percent the next day when the overnight HIBOR returned to around 5 percent, the world woke up to the fact that the Asian crisis had now hit one of the strongest economies in Asia. Contagion rapidly spread to global markets. On 27 October the Dow Jones Industrial Average lost 554 points, one of its biggest point drops in its history. Equity markets in Brazil, Argentina and Mexico also saw their biggest single-day losses. As if there was a feedback effect from global markets, the Hang Seng Index nosedived by 13.7 percent on 28 October to close at 9,060 points.

After the October 1997 shock, interest rates remained relatively high and volatile, particularly at the longer end. Hong Kong was beginning to pay a risk premium in terms of interest rates. Although banks were flushed with liquidity, they were somewhat reluctant to lend longer-term money in the interbank market as they sought to conserve liquidity for fear of another liquidity squeeze. Facing tight liquidity and higher interest rates,

---

[15] The Liquidity Adjustment Facility (LAF) is Hong Kong's equivalent to the discount window.
[16] Hong Kong Monetary Authority (1997).

the politically influential property developers started criticizing the HKMA for relying solely on interest rates to defend the Hong Kong dollar and not injecting liquidity into the system.

University of Hong Kong Professor Y. C. Jao, a member of the Hong Kong Exchange Fund Advisory Committee (EFAC), the de facto board of the HKMA, defended the HKMA:

Some people seem to think that high interest rates can be suppressed if the HKMA provides cheap credit on demand through LAF. But this was precisely the mistake made by such countries as Thailand, Indonesia and Korea. ...

The last thing the HKMA should do is to relax its prudential supervision, and to provide cheap credit on demand. Last but not least, historical experience has clearly shown that, as long as the monetary and banking system remains sound and robust, then after the painful period of adjustment, the real economy will bounce back. In 1982–83, for instance, we went through a much graver crisis. Indeed, on 'Black Saturday', September 24, 1983, the whole financial system nearly went under. But once the linked rate system gained its initial, though still fragile, credibility, the real economy recovered eventually. The same conclusion will hold true for Hong Kong in the current Asian crisis.[17]

To restore public confidence after the October 1997 attack, the Hong Kong SAR Government undertook an official review of the currency defence, published in the April 1998 Report on Financial Market Review.[18] After carefully reviewing the whole speculative attack, the Hong Kong Government put forward a 30-point programme with a view to strengthening the discipline and transparency of the markets. The measures covered specific areas such as short-selling activities, system improvement, risk management, rule enforcement, intermarket surveillance and contingency powers. These laid the groundwork for the future intervention.

RUMOURS, RUMOURS, RUMOURS

In November 1997 the Asian crisis deepened when even Japan and South Korea began to falter. In Japan the financial system stumbled visibly with the failures of Hokkaido Takushoku Bank, Yamaichi Securities and Tokuyo City Bank. In South Korea the Bank of Korea had to seek financial assistance from the IMF on 21 November. These factors clearly affected confidence in Hong Kong.

The underlining nervousness led to all sorts of quirky runs. There was a 'cake run' on St. Honore Cake Shop, a leading bakery chain, seeking to

---

[17] Jao (1998), 43–45. See also Jao (2001).
[18] Financial Services Bureau (1998), Executive Summary, ii–iii.

redeem thousands of coupons that it had sold to its customers for future purchases Another run occurred at the Whimsy amusement arcades, which rewarded winners with tickets that could be exchanged for toys and cheap electrical goods. It was a sign of the times.

The speculative attacks continued throughout 1998. In the first two weeks of January 1998, following the sharp fall in the Indonesian rupiah, the Hong Kong dollar also came under intensified selling pressure. The greatest shock to domestic pride came on 12 January 1998, when Hong Kong's largest domestic investment bank, Peregrine, failed because of a miscalculated funding of an Indonesian taxi company, called Steady Safe, linked to the daughter of Indonesian President Suharto. The Hang Seng Index lost 8.7 percent of its value that day to close at 8,121 points. On 19 January CA Pacific Securities, a midsized stockbroker with more than 10,000 retail accounts, voluntary suspended operations.

There was a brief spell between February 1998 and May 1998, when speculative attacks on the Hong Kong dollar abated somewhat. Short-term interest rates fell, and the Hang Seng Index recovered by around 20 percent from its January 1998 levels to the 10,000 level trading range. However, the 'Asian premium', the interest differential between the Hong Kong dollar and the U.S. dollar, widened to as high as five percentage points.

In mid-June 1998 a second speculative attack on the Hong Kong dollar took place. Currency markets were nervous as the Japanese yen continued to decline. It did not stop depreciating to an eight-year low of nearly ¥150 to the U.S. dollar in August 1998, despite the 17 June joint intervention by the U.S. Fed and the Bank of Japan. Nevertheless, as interest rates rose as interbank liquidity tightened, the stage was set for the showdown at the end of the summer.

THE BULWARK OF HONG KONG'S STRENGTH

Although Hong Kong was more affected by the Asian crisis than its closest competitors, why didn't its economy collapse like the other crisis-hit Asian economies? The answer is the strength of Hong Kong's banking sector (Table 10.6) and the low debt level of the corporate sector. Despite the capital outflow, Hong Kong's financial sector remained essentially sound, and foreign exchange reserves stood at a high level of US$96.5 billion at end June 1998. Thus, instead of being the weakest link during the crisis, it was the banking sector that proved to be the bulwark of Hong Kong's strength.

The reason was quite obvious. Hong Kong's banks and corporate sector had learnt their lessons from the mistake of the 1980s, when they went

Table 10.6. *Hong Kong: Financial Structure (% of GDP)*

	1990	1991	1992	1993	1994	1995	1996	1997	1998	1999	2000
Assets of deposit money banks	–	145.6	130.1	129.0	139.4	151.0	153.5	165.3	187.9	176.2	164.5
Assets of other financial institutions	–	–	–	–	–	–	–	–	–	–	–
Stock market capitalization	105.2	115.6	141.5	232.1	242.9	199.6	237.4	245.6	227.4	291.5	367.4
Bond market capitalization	1.5	2.3	3.6	5.1	8.9	14.1	18.1	21.3	24.7	26.2	26.2
Insurance premium volume	–	–	3.0	3.1	3.3	3.6	3.5	3.5	3.9	4.4	4.7

Source: Beck, Demirgüç-Kunt and Levine (2000), revised 13 August 2007
Dash means data not available

on a property binge. The crash of 1987 had taught the bankers and the corporate sector an important lesson. Supervision was tightened significantly, particularly when David Carse, a canny Scottish bank supervisor on loan from the Bank of England, came in 1988, just in time to handle the failure of the Hong Kong operations of the infamous Bank of Credit and Commerce International (BCCI). The highest leverage of the blue-chip–listed property companies was a mere 40 percent of their equity base. Hong Kong banks were very careful to be highly collateralized in their lending to the corporate sector. Thus, both banks and borrowers were able to cope with the high interest rate movements necessary under the currency board arrangement.

When the crisis hit in 1997, the local banks' capital adequacy was about 17.5 percent, whilst overdue loans were about 1.81 percent of total loans, clearly one of the strongest banking systems in the region (Table 10.7). That prudence and robustness served the banking system well throughout the crisis.

Thus, even though overdue loans rose to around 5.12 percent in 1999, the banks were nevertheless strong enough to withstand large withdrawals by the Japanese and South Korean banks in 1997–1998. From July 1997 to June 1998, these withdrawals amounted to US$123 billion.

Table 10.7. *Selected Asian Economies: Summary Measures of Bank Strength, 1997*

	Total Score	Capital Position	Loan Classification	Foreign Ownership	Liquidity	Operating Environment
Singapore	16	1	6	2	5	1
Hong Kong	**21**	**3**	**9**	**1**	**2**	**2**
Malaysia	41	5	9	8	8	3
South Korea	45	7	9	10	11	3
Philippines	47	4	6	7	7	11
Thailand	52	7	12	12	8	6
Indonesia	52	7	8	9	12	8

Source: IMF (2001) based on Caprio (1998)

The score for each category represents the relative ranking of the country among a group of 12
Lower total score signals relatively stronger position

Furthermore, although before and during the crisis about 40 percent of domestic bank loans were directly exposed to the property sector, the banking system was cushioned against deflation in the property bubble because the banks had progressively reduced the loan-to-value (LTV) ratio from 70 percent against collateral to 50 percent as property prices rose. The creation of the Hong Kong Mortgage Corporation Limited in March 1997 to buy mortgages from banks also eased their liquidity and maturity mismatch problems. Banks that had liquidity problems went quietly to the Mortgage Corporation to obtain liquidity in exchange for mortgages in the normal course of business, without having to draw on the LAF from the HKMA. This also avoided the stigma of banks having to borrow from the lender of last resort.

The prudent lending of Hong Kong banks reinforced prudent business practices in Hong Kong. Where mistakes were made by both sides were in bank lending to imprudent Mainland state-owned enterprises, such as the failure of the Guangdong Investment and Trust Company (GITIC) in October 1998 to honour its US$200 million bond. The Chinese Government decisively sent a former Deputy Governor of the People's Bank of China, Mr Wang Qishan, to Guangdong as Executive Vice Governor to resolve the crisis.

Nevertheless, as the crisis deepened, the failure of CA Pacific Securities, which had taken shares pledged by clients to finance its own equity margin financing, emerged as an area of vulnerability. To prevent loss of investor confidence, the Government and the regulatory bodies had agreed to relax the current compensation rules and the upper limit of compensation per retail customer to HK$150,000 each. Until then the compensation rules stipulated a maximum total payout of HK$8 million per broker failure. To fund the payout, the Stock Exchange and the SFCHK would each inject HK$150 million into the Compensation Fund immediately, and, if necessary, another HK$150 million would be further injected by each party. The government would also top up the Compensation Fund should it fall below a prudent level.

However, despite efforts by the government to shore up confidence, by August 1998 the Hong Kong economy was feeling the heat of high interest rates. The greatest threat to the banking system was the default on mortgages, because homebuyers had to live with higher mortgage rates. Although data for 1997–1998 are not available, the middle class was being severely hammered as the economy, which began contracting in the fourth quarter of 1997, continued to contract by about 5 percent in 1998 – the worst recession since the early 1960s.[19] By August 1998 the unemployment rate stood at around 4.8 percent.

By this time it became a test of wills between the political determination of the Hong Kong authorities to maintain the Link and the speculators who bet that the Link would break as the recession worsened. As long as the Hong Kong Government had no external debt, theoretically only the Hong Kong people could abandon the Link, but the speculators wanted to test their pain threshold.

But more than just a test of wills was at stake. The real problem for floating exchange rates for small economies, as experience elsewhere had shown, is that they can be driven to very low equilibrium levels, well below 50 percent, even though on a trade-weighted basis the best estimate for devaluation would be between 15 to 20 percent. Since Hong Kong had an external trade to GDP ratio of more than 250 percent, a devaluation of such order could destroy the SAR as an entrepot centre and financial centre. Furthermore, for China to allow a newly returned territory to be subject to speculative attacks was politically unacceptable. A financial crisis in Hong Kong would have contagion effects way beyond the borders of China.

A MATTER OF SURVIVAL

The psychological warfare almost reached the breaking point by early August as the Japanese yen hovered around the ¥146 to the U.S. dollar level.

[19] Tsang (1998).

By this same time, rumours that the Chinese renminbi would devalue and Hong Kong would abandon the linked exchange rate increased by the day. Numerous media articles in July and the first half of August 1998 predicted a possible renminbi devaluation, leading various research houses to predict that the Link would soon be broken. The Hong Kong perspective looked bleak, but on the other side of the world, the growing instability in Russia and Latin America was about to come to the boil.

The fundamental problem, like an itch that would not go away, was the efficacy of the double play. As explained earlier, the combination of a short on the currency together with a short on the stock market was very profitable. Shorting the currency alone had an interest rate cost. If the currency did not devalue, the speculator would have to pay a higher interest cost for borrowing the currency. However, shorting the stock market at the same time by selling Hang Seng Index futures was profitable, because when interest rates rose, the stock market fell.

This was where Hong Kong's sophisticated stock and futures market helped speculation. There was no restriction on short selling. Moreover, there were sophisticated swap markets whereby the speculators could swap U.S. dollar bonds for Hong Kong dollars and therefore get their hands on Hong Kong dollars to sell. Furthermore, they also discovered that the stock borrowing and lending programme operated by several custodian banks allowed them to borrow blue chip stocks at interest rates below market rates. The custodian banks had persuaded the institutional investors, during calmer days, that they could earn at least 1 percent above their dividend rate by lending their stocks held by custodians to short sellers to facilitate clearing and settlement operations. Institutional investors did not mind this, because they earned extra income and there are relatively little credit risks involved when you are dealing through prime quality custodian banks. Only later did the institutional investors catch on that they were lending the speculators to drive their own share prices down. The withdrawal of such stock from lending would later help to slow the speculation.

Consequently Hong Kong's own market sophistication allowed the double play to increase in intensity with each speculative attack, with handsome profits for the hedge funds. Before August 1998 the media complained openly that Hong Kong was an ATM machine for the hedge funds, which took money out every time there was a speculative scare.

In the lead-up to August 1998, the double play involved three simple steps. First, from the beginning of 1998 to the middle of August, whenever the Hong Kong dollar interest rates were relatively stable, hedge funds pre-funded themselves with Hong Kong dollars in the debt market. They swapped U.S. dollars for Hong Kong dollars with multilateral institutions that raised Hong Kong dollars through the issue of debt paper. Such paper amounted to over HK$30 billion by mid-August 1998 with an interest cost of around HK$4 billion a day.

Second, at the same time, the speculators accumulated large short positions in the stock index futures market, with gross open interest in the spot Hang Seng Index futures rising from 70,000 contracts in June to some 92,000 contracts in early August 1998. The Hong Kong authorities estimated that speculators held about 80,000 short contracts, so that for every fall of 1,000 points in the Hang Seng Index, they would have made a profit of HK$4 billion.[20]

Third, the speculators waited patiently for the opportune moment to dump the Hong Kong dollars that they had borrowed, to drive up interest rates and send a shock wave through the stock market. The Hong Kong authorities estimated that 'If they could have engineered that fall within 1,000 days they would have broken even. If they could have achieved it within 100 days they would have netted HK$3.6 billion.'[21]

Obviously the Hong Kong authorities could not stand by idly and watch the speculators and hedge funds create a vicious circle involving the stock market, the currency and interest rates. On 13 August 1998 the Hang Seng Index traded at its lowest post-crisis point of 6,660. The Hong Kong authorities reacted. Between Friday, 14 August, and Friday, 29 August, the expiration date of the August stock futures contracts, in an unconventional, unprecedented and unpredicted move, the Hong Kong Government used its official reserves to intervene in the stock and futures markets to buy the 33 constituent stocks of the Hang Seng Index. In total, it spent around US$15 billion.

Donald Tsang, then Financial Secretary of Hong Kong and now Hong Kong's Chief Executive, explained the rationale on 14 August, the first day of the intervention:

In order to achieve their objectives in undermining the Hong Kong dollar, speculators have deployed a whole host of improper measures which are clear to all. These measures include spreading vicious rumours on the delinking of the Hong Kong dollar with the US dollar, devaluation of the Renminbi, as well as the instability of our banks which led to bank runs. We have recovered from each of these speculative attacks. We have also demonstrated our resolve in maintaining our linked

---

[20]   Yam (1998d).
[21]   Yam (1998d).

exchange rate. However, the sharp rise in interest rates created by speculative attacks has clearly hurt our economy and the public at large.

In order to deter such manipulation, I have exercised my power under the Exchange Fund Ordinance and asked the HKMA to draw upon the resources of the Exchange Fund to mount appropriate counter activities in the stock and futures markets. The Exchange Fund Advisory Committee, which I have formally consulted, supports this course of action. Accordingly, the HKMA mounted counter activities earlier today.

The decision to intervene in the stock and futures markets did not come easily because failure was not an option. First, the intervention was potentially damaging for an economy that had thrived on the reputation of free markets. Second, the intervention also raised problems of conflicts of interest, with the government acting as both a regulator and shareholder in 33 of the economy's largest companies. However, the Hong Kong Government knew that if incentives for currency speculators were not removed, Hong Kong would be headed down a vicious spiral of economic collapse. As Donald Tsang wrote in the 1998 *Hong Kong Yearbook*, 'The incursion was a matter of survival to preserve local community confidence, protect the integrity of the linked exchange rate to the US$ as well as restore a level-playing field to the stock and money markets'.[22] There was no question that it took courage to make that decision.

Both the Hong Kong authorities and hedge funds understood the dangers of the intervention perfectly. Joseph Yam noted, 'This was not a decision that we enjoyed taking. It involved many risks, not least among them the risk of being misunderstood'.[23] Stanley Druckenmiller, Manager of the Soros Quantum Fund, was quoted to have said in the *Hong Kong Standard* on 16 August 1998, 'Unfortunately, if they're wrong on the fundamentals, all they'll be doing is providing profits for speculators. ... From our perspective no matter what they want to do in their market, when they wake up Monday morning they're still going to be in a depression'.[24]

London School of Economics Professor Charles Goodhart, formerly with the Bank of England and an architect of the Hong Kong Link, has coauthored the authoritative study on the intervention.[25] Although it would be difficult to speculate where the Hang Seng Index would have bottomed out, the Goodhart-Lu study had a model suggesting that the Index might have declined to as low as 5,393 by 28 August, instead of rising to 7,830 after the

---

[22] Hong Kong SAR Government (1998), 4.
[23] Yam (1998d).
[24] Quoted in Goodhart and Dai Lu (2003), 1.
[25] Goodhart and Daily (2003).

intervention.[26] The authorities clearly feared that the HSI would go as low as 2,000 to 3,000 points,[27] but they were also aware that at 8,000 points, the PE ratio was around eight, indicating that the market was good value. The trouble was that if confidence did not return, it would be almost completely a seller's market.

Fortunately for Hong Kong, the intervention worked, because the stock market stabilized and the speculators closed out their positions, realizing that the tide had turned against them. Hong Kong dollar interest rates came down from 12 percent per annum to around 5 percent, the level around July 1997, with much of the Asian premium disappearing. Goodhart and Dai Lu estimated that the losses inflicted on the speculators amounted to as much as HK$1.3 billion or US$166 million.

FROM CONDEMNATION TO TACIT ACCEPTANCE

Initially there were severe criticisms of this unconventional move. As Joseph Yam admitted in Singapore in October 1998,

Internationally, the initial response has been hostile, to put it mildly. The foreign press has been critical, almost as critical as it was about the imposition of exchange controls in Malaysia. Sadly, my most respected Nobel Laureate Milton Friedman, who has been most supportive of the free market philosophy so diligently practised in Hong Kong, thought that we had simply gone crazy.[28]

Opinion on the August 1998 intervention, however, changed soon after it was condemned. In August and September 1998, Russia and Brazil went into crisis, triggering the LTCM failure where the New York Fed had to intervene through moral suasion to unravel the mess. Alan Greenspan, when explaining why the Federal Reserve Bank of New York intervened on behalf of LTCM before the Committee on Banking and Financial Services of the U.S. House of Representatives in October 1998, said:

While the principle that fire sales undermine the effective functioning of markets may be clear, deciding when a potential market disruption rises to a level of seriousness warranting central bank involvement is among the most difficult judgments that ever confront a central banker. In situations like this, there is no reason for central bank involvement unless there is a substantial probability that a fire sale

---

[26] Goodhart and Dai Lu (2003), table 7.5, 170.
[27] *South China Morning Post* (1988), quoted in Goodhart and Dai Lu (2003), 164.
[28] Yam (1998c).

would result in severe, widespread, and prolonged disruptions to financial market activity.

It was the judgment of officials at the Federal Reserve Bank of New York (FRBNY), who were monitoring the situation on an ongoing basis, that the act of unwinding LTCM's portfolio in a forced liquidation would not only have a significant distorting impact on market prices but also in the process could produce large losses, or worse, for a number of creditors and counterparties, and for other market participants who were not directly involved with LTCM.[29]

In other words, Greenspan was still defending the 'no intervention as much as possible', leaving the New York Fed to make the judgement call as to the systemic implications of no intervention. As Charles Kindleberger puts it succinctly, 'General rules that the central bank should always intervene or that it should never intervene are both wrong. ... Markets generally work, but occasionally they break down. When they do, they require government intervention to provide the public good of stability'.[30] The Hong Kong Government had to intervene in a period of grave uncertainty to ensure that public confidence in Hong Kong was not lost. The cost of the intervention was judged lower than the cost of the alternative of Hong Kong spiralling into a massive crisis.

In central banking technical terms, the key to understanding the Hong Kong intervention is that it was classic central bank intervention in the tradition of Bagehot to inject liquidity in an unstable market situation. Bagehot, Kindleberger and other experienced central bankers understood that at certain moments during a crisis, the unwillingness of the banks to lend would create a situation of illiquidity that would drive the crisis deeper. Total illiquidity and inability of the market to price securities because of innate fear is a time-honoured event, not a theoretical impossibility. This was exactly what was experienced in the subprime crisis of 2007–2008. When investors could not value their holdings of asset-backed securities, their only escape from further loss was flight, a refusal to buy or sell. Unfortunately, the collective effect was total illiquidity and further decline in asset prices. No single bank dared to lend freely without itself being caught in an asset bind. In such a situation of market illiquidity, the Bagehot dictum applies – the central bank must lend freely, but against good security.

Conventionally, central bank intervention in markets is achieved through buying or selling bonds, but in the Hong Kong case the unconventional part was the intervention in stocks. For the ordinary investor in Hong Kong,

[29] Greenspan (1998e).
[30] Kindleberger (1996) [1978], 2–3.

the Hang Seng Index was not only an index of market confidence, but also a measurement of liquidity. The Hang Seng Index component stocks comprised 33 blue chips that carried high liquidity and low credit risks. By intervening to stem the price decline, the government achieved two strategic aims. First, it stemmed any possible panic by being 'the buyer of last resort'. Second, it told the whole world that it did not believe that Hong Kong was a bankrupt state with fire sale assets. It could do this only because the government did not have any foreign currency debt. It bought back good assets and did not need to borrow to buy such assets. In essence, it restored confidence in the Hong Kong dollar by willingness to buy during a period of panic selling. The liquidity injection also brought down interest rates and therefore relieved the deflationary pressure on the Hong Kong economy.

UNUSUAL TIMES, UNUSUAL ACTION

Hong Kong's action in August 1998 marked the trough of the Asian crisis. As David Hale, then of the Zurich Group, noted in October 1998, 'In an ironic twist of fate, the global financial contagion which began with the New York hedge funds' attack on the Thai baht in the spring of 1997 had gone full circle back to a near collapse of the New York markets themselves'.[31] The Asian crisis had become global following the Russian, Brazilian and LTCM crises, and there was increasing recognition that something had to be done to plug the loopholes in the international financial architecture that was creating havoc in domestic capital markets.

The crisis that seemed to be spiralling out of control began to ease in September 1998, following a number of positive developments. Crucially, the yen began to appreciate sharply against the U.S. dollar beginning September 1998, thus taking the downward pressure off the other Asian currencies. David Hale was amongst the first to elaborate on the role of the yen carry trade and its unwinding on global events:

During the past two years, it was popular for hedge funds to borrow yen and redeploy their cash in higher yielding debt markets. ...

But the gyrations in the value of the yen are a further illustration of the changing character of interdependence in global financial markets. The hedge funds are massively short the yen through a mixture of both loans and calls in the future markets. The fact that they are now deleveraging themselves is therefore creating a surge of

---

[31] Hale (1998f).

demand for the yen which has little to do with traditional economic factors such as output growth and interest rates.[32]

In Hong Kong the August 1998 intervention was followed through with various measures to strengthen the monetary and financial systems. On the monetary side, technical measures were implemented to modify the currency board arrangements then existing to make it less susceptible to manipulation. On the securities side, a series of reforms was introduced to lessen the potential of market dislocation. At the same time, the Exchange Fund Investment Limited (EFIL) was established in October 1998 to advise the Hong Kong Government on the orderly disposal of the substantial portfolio of Hong Kong shares it acquired.

The Hong Kong economy began to show some signs of recovery towards the end of 1998. By 1999 the economy staged a significant turnaround, and the stock market entered on a steady path to recovery. Thus, toward the second half of 1999, the Hong Kong Government thought it timely to dispose of the shares that it had acquired in August 1998. In November 1999 the Tracker Fund of Hong Kong (TraHK), an Exchange Traded Fund, was launched as the first step of the government's share disposal programme. This route was chosen because it was thought to be a stock-neutral solution to the disposal of the shares, it would create minimal disruption to the market and it would add depth to Hong Kong's capital markets. With an issue size of HK$33.3 billion (approximately US$4.3 billion), the Tracker Fund's IPO was the largest IPO ever in Asia outside Japan at the time of launch.[33]

Happily, the August 1998 intervention has turned out to be a very profitable investment for the people of Hong Kong. By September 1999, that is, just before the launch of TraHK, the value of the portfolio had increased to US$26 billion or more than 70 percent, prompting Joseph Yam to quip, 'too bad there are no bonuses for those responsible for acquiring the portfolio', whilst stressing that huge profits was not the primary purpose of the August 1998 intervention.[34]

The Hong Kong experience taught me two important lessons. The first is that preventive action should be done 'the sooner the better' and 'the problems are always worse than expected'. Second, the August 1998 intervention taught me that unusual times always call for unusual action. During a period of crisis, the most daring move is also the least risky.

---

[32] Hale (1998f).
[33] See TraHK web site at http://www.trahk.com.hk/eng/index.asp.
[34] Yam (1999b).

We cannot end this chapter without considering whether Hong Kong had deviated from the currency board orthodoxy and therefore made it vulnerable to attack. My personal view is no. The key issue during the speculation attack was the psychological element. The only people who could break the Link were the people of Hong Kong, who held the bulk of the currency. If they lost confidence in the Link, the currency board arrangement was gone, orthodox or not. To me, there are no such things as perfect currency arrangements. The protagonist for currency boards, Steve Hanke, argued that the currency board arrangement could allow fiscal deficits or foreign exchange banking in excess of 115 percent of issue.[35] These are finer points of detail that the man in the street (the holders of Hong Kong dollars) did not consider material during moments of grave uncertainty. When confidence is shaken, any news can be interpreted as bad news.

The key, which Hong Kong leaders read correctly, was that in periods of uncertainty, the public expected leaders to act decisively. Hong Kong had no fiscal deficits or sovereign debt in the hand of foreigners. It had nothing to fear but fear itself if the Hong Kong people were behind the currency. But if the public lost confidence, all was lost. Leaders are paid to make judgements in times of crisis, right or wrong. No theory, however perfect, will guide them during those dark hours.

Next, we shall discuss China, a country that played a crucial role during the Asian crisis.

---

[35] See Hanke (2002).

ELEVEN

China: Rise of the Dragon

Chinese history since the Opium War is a series of continual efforts at readjustment to meet this challenge [of] a merger of China's cultural tradition, developed on a huge continent, with this oceanic influence [of Western capitalism].
~ Ray Huang

What was China's role during the Asian crisis?

In May 2007 a *Financial Times* editorial stated that the real lesson of Asia's financial crisis was that China's rise meant that ASEAN never fully recovered from the 1997–98 Asian crisis.[1] The editorial noted that with the exception of South Korea, the crisis-hit economies have been growing at about two percentage points lower than they did before 1997. It was thought that this was due to the rise of China as 'a vast new competitor with an almost limitless capacity to sell at a lower price'.

This is a familiar story surrounding the Asian crisis – either blame the victim (an internal cause) or blame the global architecture (the external story). The truth is not so simple, because both internal and external causes interacted to create the crisis. China had a role in the Asian crisis, but it was a positive one, not negative. The big picture would tell the story.

CHINA COMPARED WITH THE CRISIS:
FIVE OBSERVATIONS

Taking a 30,000 feet high-level observation, five observations may be made with regard to China in the period leading up to and during the crisis.

The first observation is that China was indeed emerging as an important member of the global manufacturing supply chain that was forming in the

[1] *Financial Times* (2007).

Asian region in the period leading up to the crisis. Thus, apart from rising inflation, as with the crisis-hit economies, China's macroeconomic outlook appeared robust. Between 1990 and 1996, China's real GDP grew at 10.7 percent annually, unemployment rate was low at 2.6 percent, central government budget was slightly in deficit and domestic savings rates were high at 37.4 percent of GDP (Table 11.1). In 1996 China's GDP of about US$856 billion was the second largest in Asia after Japan.

However, at the outbreak of the crisis, China's role in the supply chain was relatively small relative to the crisis-hit economies. To illustrate this point:

- Although China's GDP was the second largest in Asia in 1996, it was only around a fifth the size of Japan (US$4.6 trillion) and roughly 35 percent *smaller* than South Korea plus the ASEAN economies put together (US$1.3 trillion).[2]
- Although China's 1996 GDP was around 1.2 times that of the ASEAN nations (US$740 billion), in trade the ASEAN nations' total exports were about 2.2 times larger than China's exports of US$151 billion.
- Total exports of the ASEAN nations plus South Korea, at US$469 billion, were about 3.1 times that of China's. This also happened to be 1.1 times larger than Japanese exports of US$411 billion.

The second observation is that the emergence of China as an increasingly important member of the Asian global supply chain was only part of the Asian crisis story. As explained earlier, since China unified its currency, the renminbi (RMB) in 1994, almost all Asian currencies maintained broad parity with each other against the U.S. dollar, but there was one important outlier – the Japanese yen, which was also the most volatile currency against the dollar. As the dollar-yen relationship was highly volatile in the lead-up to the 1997–1998 crisis, pressure emerged within the supply chain in the form of asset bubbles, corporate overleverage and fragile banking systems.

The broad pattern of the Asian supply chain was that yen strength added to Asian prosperity, and a weak yen witnessed lower growth in Asia excluding Japan. The reason was simple: a strong yen meant more production and investment was shifted to the cheaper labour production markets outside Japan, and vice versa. Second, Asia's major competitor for the U.S. market, South America, had higher inflation and was losing competitiveness

---

[2]   In 1996, the members of ASEAN were Brunei, Indonesia, Malaysia, Philippines, Singapore, Thailand and Vietnam.

Table 11.1. *China: Selected Real Economy Indicators*

	1990	1991	1992	1993	1994	1995	1996	1997	1998	1999	2000
GDP US$ billion	387.8	406.1	483.0	613.2	559.2	728.0	856.0	952.6	1,019.5	1,083.3	1,198.5
GDP per capita US$	339.2	350.6	412.3	517.4	466.6	601.0	699.4	770.6	817.1	861.2	945.6
Real GDP Annual % change	3.8	9.2	14.2	14.0	13.1	10.9	10.0	9.3	7.8	7.6	8.4
Unemployment rate % of total labour force	2.5	2.3	2.3	2.6	2.8	2.9	3.0	3.1	3.1	3.1	3.1
Inflation Annual % change	3.1	3.4	6.4	14.7	24.1	17.1	8.3	2.8	-0.8	-1.4	0.4
Fiscal balance % of GDP	–	-2.2	-2.3	-2.0	-2.7	-2.1	-1.6	-1.8	-3.0	-4.0	-3.6
Central government debt % of GDP	8.7	8.7	8.6	8.0	10.1	10.1	10.5	11.4	17.8	20.9	22.8
Gross domestic capital formation % of GDP	36.1	36.1	37.5	44.5	42.2	41.9	40.4	37.9	37.1	36.7	35.1
Gross domestic savings % of GDP	35.2	35.3	36.1	38.0	39.3	39.6	38.3	39.0	38.9	38.0	38.0

Sources: ADB, IMF and Jaimovich and Panniza (2006)
Dash means data not available

relative to the region. Eastern Europe did not emerge as a major exporter until later in the game.

However, in 1994 the formation of NAFTA and a massive devaluation of the Mexican peso as well as other Latin American currencies caused U.S. imports to be diverted partly from Asia to other NAFTA countries. Thus, after 1994 the crisis-hit Asian economies experienced current account deficits.

In sum, the role of China as a growing member of the Asian supply chain cannot be viewed in isolation from the other important events that also played a part in the Asian crisis.

The third observation is that the Chinese economic success story follows that of the flying geese pattern of export growth, explained in Chapter 2. As a latecomer, China also developed its special export and industrial zones and concentrated on welcoming foreign direct investment and manufactured exports. If China had not emerged, some other cheap labour economies such as Vietnam or South Asia would have risen sooner or later to compete against the ASEAN economies.

Indeed, in the lead-up to the Asian crisis, many of the weaknesses that characterised the crisis-hit economies could easily have described China. As with the crisis-hit economies, China's financial system was dominated by the banking sector with underdeveloped stock and bond markets (Table 11.2). Furthermore, China also suffered from poor corporate governance, a highly leveraged corporate sector, high nonperforming loans, weaknesses in financial supervision and the lack of transparency. McKinsey estimated that 'by 1998, the Chinese central, provincial and municipal governments had controlling interests in more than 300,000 companies. ... Of the 100,000 largest SOEs [State-Owned Enterprises] in 1998, about 46 percent were expected to lose money. The SOE sector consumed more than 80 percent of China's new loans, but contributed less than 30 percent of the nation's total output. ... The most generally accepted number (in early 1998) of nonperforming loans was around US$250 billion or about 30 percent of the total loans of the Chinese banking system ... concentrated in China's four large state banks'.[3]

Despite these vulnerabilities, China was relatively unaffected by the Asian crisis. In 1998 China's real economy continued to grow by 7.8 percent in contrast to the huge contraction in the real economies of the crisis-hit nations. Critically, the RMB was stable whilst the crisis-hit economies witnessed huge depreciation and extreme volatility.

---

[3]   Casserley et al. (1999), 343.

Table 11.2. *China: Financial Structure (% of GDP)*

	1990	1991	1992	1993	1994	1995	1996	1997	1998	1999	2000
Assets of banking sector	100.3	105.1	102.0	116.0	106.8	104.4	112.7	122.7	133.6	141.3	145.8
Stock market capitalization	–	–	2.4	6.7	7.5	5.9	9.1	16.8	21.5	26.0	38.1
Bond market capitalization	5.9	5.5	5.5	6.1	5.4	5.4	6.3	7.6	10.3	13.3	15.1
Insurance premium volume	0.8	0.9	0.9	1.0	1.1	1.1	1.2	1.5	1.6	1.7	1.8

Sources: IMF, Beck, Demirgüç-Kunt and Levine (2000), revised 13 August 2007 and author's estimates
Dash means data not available

Why was China shielded from the 'run' in 1997–98? There were two main reasons.

The first reason is that China's capital account was closed. Without a freely convertible currency coupled with controls on capital outflows, it was virtually impossible to bet against the RMB. The second and more important reason is that although the country suffered from internal weaknesses, China ran prudent external financial policies (Table 11.3). In particular, it limited foreign borrowing to its capacity to repay. Hence, going into 1997 China's external debt was around 15 percent of GDP, compared to 28 percent for South Korea, 38 percent for Malaysia, 51 percent for Indonesia and 60 percent for Thailand.

Significantly, in 1996 China's short-term external debt to foreign exchange reserves ratio at 24 percent was far lower than that of Malaysia (38 percent), Thailand (128 percent), Indonesia (181 percent) and South Korea (228 percent). Much of China's foreign exposure was not short-term loans but long-term funds and direct investments. Furthermore, in 1996 China's net external liabilities were a mere 14.4 percent of GDP in contrast to the more vulnerable ratios of Thailand (55.9 percent), Malaysia (55.4 percent) and Indonesia (50.8 percent).

Table 11.3. *China: Foreign Reserves and External Debt Indicators*

	1990	1991	1992	1993	1994	1995	1996	1997	1998	1999	2000
Foreign exchange reserves (FER) US$ billion	28.6	42.7	19.4	21.2	51.6	73.6	105.0	139.9	145.0	154.7	165.6
FER growth Annual % change	68.0	49.2	−54.4	9.0	143.5	42.5	42.7	33.2	3.6	6.7	7.0
Total external debt US$ billion	55.3	60.3	72.4	85.9	100.5	118.1	128.8	146.7	144.0	152.1	145.7
Total external debt % of GDP	14.3	14.8	15.0	14.0	18.0	16.2	15.0	15.4	14.1	14.0	12.2
Short-term external debt US$ billion	9.3	10.8	13.8	15.3	17.5	22.3	25.4	31.5	17.3	15.2	13.1
Short-term external debt % of total external debt	16.8	17.9	19.0	17.8	17.4	18.9	19.7	21.4	12.0	10.0	9.0
Short-term external debt % of FER	32.6	25.3	70.8	72.2	33.9	30.3	24.2	22.5	12.0	9.8	7.9

Sources: ADB, IMF and author's estimates

The fourth observation is that China played a globally responsible role because of its decision to keep the RMB stable during the crisis. This resolve by China at the height of the crisis contributed to the calming of markets at a time when there were real concerns that a devaluation of the RMB could lead to yet another round of competitive currency devaluations.

It must be understood that this decision took great courage, as there were many pundits arguing for devaluing the RMB to maintain export competitiveness with the other countries, particularly since the currency of the largest export competitor, Japan, was depreciating as well.

The fifth observation is the reforms made to the exchange rate system in 1994. Before 1994 China had a two-tier exchange rate system with a fixed official rate of RMB 5.80 to the U.S. dollar, and a more depreciated market-driven rate, the so-called swap rate that stood at RMB 8.70 to the dollar. In January 1994 the official and swap rates were unified, and the official rate of the RMB was devalued by about 33 percent from RMB 5.80 to RMB 8.70 to the dollar. Many analysts thus claimed that China had devalued competitively first in January 1994, thereby triggering the subsequent Asian export slowdown in the period 1995–1996. However, a study by the Monetary Authority of Singapore in October 1998 showed that 'the impact of the devaluation may have been overstated'[4] for three main reasons.

First, by 1994 about 80 percent of foreign exchange transactions were already taking place at the market-determined swap rate. The devaluation in January 1994 of the official rate to the swap rate was thus 'merely the next logical step in phasing out the increasing irrelevant official rate'.[5] According to Richard Margolis and Xu Xiaonian, then of Merrill Lynch, the weighted-average exchange rate of the RMB before the 1994 reunification was around RMB 8.10 to the U.S. dollar. Thus, weighting the RMB by the value of transactions at the official and swap rates, the RMB was devalued by about 7.4 percent in nominal terms against the dollar in January 1994.[6]

Second, even if China's exports had become more competitive because of the devaluation of the RMB in nominal terms in January 1994, these gains were quickly wiped out by the country's high inflation. Over the period 1994–1996, China's inflation averaged about 17 percent. As a result, China's real effective exchange rate began to appreciate back to its level in the early 1990s (Table 11.4).

[4] Monetary Authority of Singapore (1998), para. 2.3.
[5] Monetary Authority of Singapore (1998), para. 2.3.
[6] See also Margolis and Xu (1998).

Table 11.4. *China: Selected Currency and Current Account Indicators*

				Currency Indicators*							
	1990	1991	1992	1993	1994	1995	1996	1997	1998	1999	2000
Yuan per U.S. dollar Period average	4.8	5.3	5.5	5.8	8.6	8.4	8.3	8.3	8.3	8.3	8.3
Yuan per U.S. dollar End of period	5.2	5.4	5.8	5.8	8.4	8.3	8.3	8.3	8.3	8.3	8.3
Yuan nominal effective exchange rate 2000 = 100	142.9	129.4	114.5	91.9	83.2	82.2	86.0	92.5	100.6	98.4	100.0
Yuan real effective exchange rate 2000 = 100	98.9	88.2	79.3	70.1	76.0	84.7	93.2	100.4	105.7	99.9	100.0
Yen to U.S. dollar Period average	144.8	134.7	126.7	111.2	102.2	94.1	108.8	121.0	130.9	113.9	107.8
Yen to U.S. dollar End of period	134.4	125.2	124.8	111.9	99.7	102.8	116.0	130.0	115.6	102.2	114.9
Yen nominal effective exchange rate 2000 = 100	52.2	58.2	63.2	79.3	89.5	95.6	83.3	79.2	81.1	92.0	100.0
Yen real effective exchange rate 2000 = 100	77.3	83.3	85.9	101.4	106.5	108.2	90.7	85.3	85.3	94.8	100.0

(continued)

Table 11.4. (continued)

					Current Account Indicators[†]						
	1990	1991	1992	1993	1994	1995	1996	1997	1998	1999	2000
Terms of trade 2000 = 100	102.1	101.0	103.1	101.0	102.0	101.9	105.9	110.2	110.6	104.1	100.0
Exports US$ billion	62.1	71.9	84.9	91.7	121.0	148.8	151.0	182.8	183.7	194.9	249.2
Exports growth Annual % change	18.2	15.8	18.1	8.0	31.9	23.0	1.5	21.0	0.5	6.1	27.8
Imports US$ billion	53.3	63.8	80.6	104.0	115.6	132.1	138.8	142.4	140.2	165.7	225.1
Imports growth Annual % change	−9.8	19.6	26.3	29.0	11.2	14.2	5.1	2.5	−1.5	18.2	35.8
Trade balance US$ billion	8.7	8.1	4.4	−12.2	5.4	16.7	12.2	40.4	43.5	29.2	24.1
Current account balance US$ billion	12.0	13.3	6.4	−11.9	7.7	1.6	7.2	37.0	31.5	15.7	20.5
Current account balance % of GDP	3.1	3.3	1.3	−1.9	1.4	0.2	0.8	3.9	3.1	1.4	1.7

Sources:
* IMF
† IMF, UNCTAD and author's estimates

Third, China's export growth over the period 1993–1995 did not appear to come at the expense of the export growth of the crisis-hit economies. To illustrate this point:

- Over the period 1994–1995, the crisis-hit economies in fact experienced export booms, with South Korea's exports growing by 30.3 percent, Malaysia's by 26.6 percent, Thailand's by 24.8 percent and Indonesia's by 13.4 percent. Over the same period, China's exports grew by 23.0 percent, but down from 31.9 percent over 1993–1994.
- China's high exports growth over the period 1994–1995 was also partly due to the reduction in tax rebates offered to exporters in July 1995 and again in January 1996, which prompted them to frontload exports to the first half of 1995.
- The subsequent downturn in exports in 1996 was much more severe for China than for the crisis-hit countries. Over the period 1995–1996, China's exports grew by 1.5 percent, Indonesia's by 9.7 percent, Malaysia's by 7.2 percent and South Korea's by 3.7 percent. 'This suggests that common factors, such as the cyclical downturn in electronics were more likely the cause of the 1996 downturn than a competitive devaluation by China'.[7]
- Although their currencies were sharply lower against the U.S. dollar between mid-1997 and 1998, ASEAN exports in U.S. dollar terms actually contracted in 1998. Over the period 1997–1998, Indonesia's exports contracted by 8.6 percent, Malaysia's by 7.3 percent. Thailand's by 6.8 percent and South Korea's by 2.5 percent. 'This poor performance ran contrary to the export boost that was first expected when their currencies were devalued'.[8]

RISE OF THE DRAGON

Fortune belongs to the brave. The decision not to devalue and to maintain a stable rate against the U.S. dollar was not without its risks. However, the decision proved to be a crucial catalyst for China's economic success story today as it forced structural adjustments throughout the country, making reforms in the tax system and the restructuring of state-owned enterprises and the banking system more urgent. As a result, China embarked on an ambitious set of reforms in 1998 and beyond, laying the firm foundations

---

[7] Monetary Authority of Singapore (1998), para. 2.7.
[8] Monetary Authority of Singapore (1998), para. 2.8.

for the next step in its transition to a market economy. As Mr Zhu Rongji said in his first press conference as Chinese Premier on 19 March 1998, 'The financial crisis in Asia will not affect the agenda and schedule for China's financial [and SOEs] reform'.[9]

The most important step taken during this period was the decision to abide by the conditions for the accession of China into the WTO in 2001. The decision, controversial within China at that time, was taken to open up further, despite nationalist sentiment that China should take its time in opening up. However, this bold and decisive action at one stroke laid down both the direction and the timetable for opening up to external competition. It reaffirmed the correctness of Deng Xiaoping's decision on the Four Modernizations: the modernization of agriculture, industry, science and technology and national defence. Only by opening up to world knowledge and competition could China emerge as a competitive and efficient economy.

In other words, by the second half of the 1990s China's leaders had already a clear vision that for China to emerge as a major player in the global economy, the corporate and banking systems must be transformed in terms of their governance, encouraged to be listed in global capital markets subject to global standards and made to compete on a global scale. The Chinese leaders understood from the Asian crisis that the banking sector was the biggest point of vulnerability in times of financial turmoil.

CHINA TRANSFORMS

China's transformation from a poor centrally planned economy with US$200 per capita income in 1978 to the present economic powerhouse with US$2,461 per capita GDP in 2007 is one of the wonders of the 20th century. There are many reasons for China's peaceful transition into the global economy. Chief amongst these are global security stability, China's own political stability, the opening of global trade and financial markets, the rise of technology and China's willingness to learn and open up to the rest of the world.

Nevertheless, China does share many of the characteristics of the Asian growth miracle. First, China's rapid growth in the last 25 years is a demographic endowment, with a large increase in the working age population. China's high growth rate, due to high savings and investments, comes from the growing number of young people in the work force relative to the

[9]   *China Daily* (1998), 1.

dependent population – the very young and the retirees. Between 1990 and 2007 China's gross domestic savings rate rose by 13.4 percentage points to 48.6 percent of GDP, whilst investment rate rose by 8.1 percentage points to 44.2 percent of GDP, mainly as the active labour force ratio grew.

Indeed, China's demographic profile of its working age population is similar to that of Japan around 1974, when Japan was also enjoying fast growth (Figure 11.1). However, Japan's working population ratio and economic growth peaked around 1989–1990, and subsequently the aging of the population has dragged down consumption, innovation and growth. For example, in 1974 Japan's savings rate was 37.3 percent of GDP. The savings rate has declined in 30 years to 27.6 percent of GDP, partly because of aging.

Second, exactly like the rest of Asia, political stability and the determination of the political leadership and the elite to drag China from an agricultural economy into the 21st century played a crucial role. The Chinese bureaucracy's skills learnt in managing central planning, but being open to the strengths of the market, made the transition in an orderly and stable manner. China was following the Asian model of 'managing the market'.

I first visited China in 1986, following the delegation led by the Malaysian Minister of Finance to examine China's opening up. At that time Malaysia's per capita GDP was US$1,753, significantly more than that of China's at US$275. In 1991 I started working on the World Bank project to aid the reform of China's financial system. My specific area was to help with China's payment system, under the supervision of the then Deputy Governor of the People's Bank of China, Mr Chen Yuan. We had the finest minds and specialists from the New York Fed, Bank of England, Bank of Japan, German Bundesbank and Swiss National Bank working on the project. Through the project I made many personal friends in China and learnt a lot about the complexities of the Chinese financial system. I also learnt the scale of the system because the economy was divided administratively into five levels of government: central, provincial, city, prefecture and county. This system has remained largely in place since the Qin Dynasty in 200 B.C.

Although I worked closely with Chinese officials and had visited China many times since I went from the World Bank to the Hong Kong Monetary Authority, most of my visits had been fleeting. However, since 1999 I had lectured twice a year on corporate governance and the importance of financial markets at the National School of Administration on corporate governance, arranged by my friend Nellie Fong, formerly Chairperson of PricewaterhouseCoopers (PwC). Senior executives of the state-owned enterprises made up my audience.

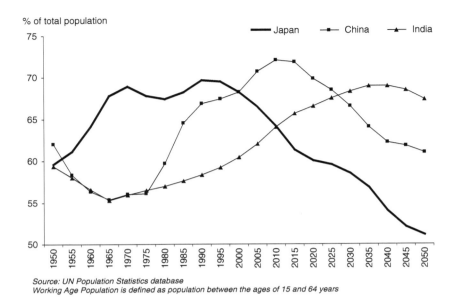

% of total population

Source: UN Population Statistics database
Working Age Population is defined as population between the ages of 15 and 64 years

Figure 11.1.   Working-Age Population as a Percentage of Total Population, 1950–2050

Through my conversations and discussions with these executives, I learnt to be humble in my understanding of the difficulties and challenges of managing enterprises that inherited obsolete equipment, huge social welfare burdens and staff that numbered over a million. Some of the largest enterprises had not only their own hospitals, but also universities and retirement homes. The transformation of the enterprise sector, and with them the banking system, was a daunting task. To someone like myself who had worked almost most of my career in banking reform, it was the mother of all bank reforms.

In 2000, after the Asian crisis was largely over, I travelled in China with my best friend, Dr Tan Tat Wai, an MIT-trained engineer and Harvard-trained economist who worked closely with me at Bank Negara Malaysia in the late 1970s and early 1980s. He currently runs one of the most innovative steel mills in Malaysia, with investments also in China. Both of us travelled with two purposes in mind. The first was to see first-hand some of the Chinese countryside. The second was to understand how China managed the transition to compete so strongly with the other Asian economies. As we travelled by train through the countryside, we discussed over tea and dumplings how this transformation was achieved. At the end of the trip, we came to the conclusion that the transformation was fundamental and irreversible, and that what was emerging was a formidable competitor. At the same time, the rise of China offered a huge opportunity for the rest of Asia, as here was a growing market with tremendous consumer power.

Perhaps because China had been so exploited and nearly completely colonized in the 19th century, the determination of the Chinese elite to transform the nation into a stable, industrialized and modern society was totally resolute but hard-nosed. They would listen to reason, logic and experience but would not totally believe theories. By comparison, although the Japanese character was also realistic, there was a romantic element in the spirit of Bushido, which would sometimes stake all in one defiant move.

In contrast to my own experience in working in bureaucracies in Malaysia, the World Bank and Hong Kong, the Chinese bureaucracy struck me as the most thorough and hard-nosed I have ever come across. An example was my first conversation with Mr Yang, a senior official in the State Planning Commission in 1991 during a World Bank conference on bank and enterprise reform. He asked me how foreign countries began the process of reform. I replied that they usually passed a new law that shaped the reform process. His answer floored me: how could we pass a law when no one, not even the reformers, had any experience with either the market or the law? In other words, they had to have faith and personal experience that the new law and the new policy would indeed bring benefits, instead of chaos and disorder.

This willingness to challenge theory and the unknown by reference to experience was a defining feature of Chinese pragmatism and realism. This characteristic was encapsulated in two famous dictums attributed mostly to Deng Xiaoping: 'It does not matter whether the cat is black or white, as long as it catches mice' and development and reform is like 'crossing the river by feeling the stones'. Of course, much of the realism stemmed back to Mao Zedong's dictum to 'seek truth from facts', reflecting the huge political struggle between Mao and the Comintern during the Long March of 1934–1937, when he had to convince his fellow party members that revolution in the countryside through guerrilla warfare was much more realistic than the urban revolution that was propounded by the Comintern and their followers.

I then realized that the Western approach to economic development took the whole Western institutional structure for granted as the universal 'natural' order of mankind. In other words, the whole basis of democracy, common law property rights, the Montesquieu Trinity of Executive, Parliament and Judiciary as mutual checks and balances against each other and individual freedom are the Utopia of all human societies. This was an assumption and a wish, not reality. Indeed, most emerging markets are far from this ideal. What if all these institutions, beliefs and processes, including the markets, do not exist? Is it possible to build these overnight simply by privatization or by political reform? The Chinese answer is that there is always a transition that takes time and that political reform comes gradually with economic reforms. Looking after society's basic economic needs, including social stability, comes first before all else.

The best example of not understanding the sequence of institutional failure was Gorbachev's experiment with political reform in the Soviet Union. To quote Susan Shirk, the author of a major study on the political lessons of economic reforms in China, 'The consequences of Gorbachev's bold strategy were political chaos and economic failure. Communist Party rule collapsed, ethnic conflicts erupted, the Soviet Union disintegrated, the command economy came to a standstill, and market reforms went nowhere'.[10]

China went the other route, because the Chinese leaders recognized that the Communist Party was the only viable institutional base strong and resilient enough to bring China through the difficulties of transition to a socialist market economy with Chinese characteristics, without massive chaos or instability. The political stability of basic one-party rule has brought stability for the transition in many Asian economies, including Japan (Liberal Democratic Party), Singapore (People's Action Party) and Malaysia (Barisan Nasional). Some economies such as those of South Korea, Taiwan, Thailand and Indonesia have transited to multiparty systems, but there is no doubt that in these countries a strong one-party system enabled the economic transition to be made before there were changes in the political framework. I do not suggest for one moment that this is necessarily desirable or feasible for all developing countries, but within the Chinese and so far the East Asian experience, this worked, even though it failed in the cases of North Korea and Myanmar.

Second to the question of political stability is the effectiveness of the bureaucracy. No reforms in the market place can be taken without a strong and effective bureaucracy. In this regard, 'crossing the river by feeling the stones' is not an empty slogan. There is methodology in the process of crossing the river. The process of economic reform is not a random process. Chinese officials study very carefully the benefits and costs of each reform, debate them intensely and study the international experience. Once the options are narrowed down, the pilot projects begin. They choose one or two cities or provinces in which to give the reforms a trial run and then

---

[10] Shirk (1993), 333.

assess the impact of the reforms. Leaders and experts would make personal study trips to the pilot projects and listen to everyone's views, including getting independent feedback from World Bank or academic experts, before making the next step of reform.

If the pilot project succeeds, then the reform is expanded nation-wide. If it fails, there is no hesitation to close down the pilot reform and start all over again. This discipline was carried out at every administrative level, over five-year cycles of planning. It reminded me of the Mao dictum in guerrilla warfare, 'When the enemy advances, we retreat; when they retreat, we harass and advance'. Reform measures were always pragmatic and flexible, reacting to the conditions on the ground, but the direction was always relentlessly forward, despite the difficulties of implementation, resources and bureaucratic opposition.

The process of reform was always widely debated, with an eye on resource constraints and the enormity of risks and opposing forces. But each reform was carefully weighed as to the benefits and the costs. I still remember my conversation with the Chairman of PetroChina, just before it listed on the Hong Kong stock market in 2000. They had to separate nearly one million workers and retirees, mostly in the welfare and social functions of the China National Petroleum Corporation, into a distinct group, in order to be able to identify the commercially viable part of PetroChina to enable it to list. To my question as to how this painful decision was made, he said that the reforms in the Northeast coal and iron mines and sunset industries had determined one clear result. Was it more expensive to keep the inefficient SOEs running at huge losses, or was it cheaper to close down the SOEs and retrench the staff, but give a social safety net for the transition? They concluded that the latter was the only solution, however painful the social adjustment and risks to social stability.

Three clear features came through the Chinese reform process. The first was prioritization. The Chinese reforms in the 1990s accepted the reality that banking reforms cannot be undertaken in isolation of reforms in the real sector. It is no coincidence that the method of banking transformation more or less mirrored the transformation in the enterprise sector. In the SOE sector China's pragmatic and gradualist approach followed a consistent, methodical and experimental approach towards 'corporatization'.

The solution was found in 'grab the large and let go of the small'; in other words, only the control of the thousand largest and strategically most important SOEs mattered, whereas the thousands of retail and small SOEs could be sold and privatized without material damage to state control.

Since the bulk of the SOEs were small to medium sized enterprises, the central government concentrated only on owning and transforming roughly one thousand large SOEs of national strategic importance and requested the provincial and municipal governments to rapidly sell or dispose of smaller, loss-making enterprises. The policy of 'privatization without official privatization' succeeded in raising the overall efficiency of the corporate sector, through a combination of opening up to FDI, allowing nonstate enterprises to acquire loss-making SOEs and then devoting energy and resources to transforming the giant SOEs. This policy played a major role in the turnaround of the banking system. By 2005 value added in the economy was contributed roughly one-third by the foreign sector, one-third by the state owned enterprises and one-third by the domestic private sector.

The second was to clarify property rights and change incentives through public listing. By getting the best and largest Chinese SOEs to list in Hong Kong and New York, the previously inward-looking institutions were forced to clarify their property rights, subject their accounts to audit according to international accounting standards and increase transparency. Also, raising salaries and giving options to key executives dramatically changed the incentives. Although the exercise was not cheap in terms of listing and restructuring fees and costs, the result was dramatic if not spectacular. By late 2007 three Chinese companies, PetroChina, Industrial and Commercial Bank of China (ICBC) and China Mobile, had joined the ranks of the world's top 10 corporations by market capitalization, with PetroChina overtaking Exxon-Mobil as the world's largest company in terms of market capitalization and ICBC overtaking Citigroup as the world's largest bank.[11] In addition, in the last decade the domestic stock market capitalization also grew by about 21-fold (Table 11.5).

Initially, in the mid-1990s, IPOs were seen as an objective in themselves and as a means of rescuing ailing SOEs. It quickly became clear that fundamental institutional transformation and improvement in the governance model was the precondition to successful listing and efficient operations. As eminent Professor Wu Jinglian incisively puts it, 'The root cause of the Big Four's problems lies in their poorly defined relations of property rights and lack of proper governance structure'.[12] This insight holds for all SOEs, including banks.

---

[11] *The Economist* (2007); Dyer (2007).
[12] Wu (2005), 231. The 'Big Four' is the four large Chinese banks: the Industrial and Commercial Bank of China, Bank of China, China Construction Bank and Agricultural Bank of China.

Table 11.5. *China: Stock Market Indicators*

	1996	1997	1998	1999	2000	2001	2002	2003	2004	2005	2006	2007
Shanghai Composite Index End of period	917	1,194	1,147	1,367	2,073	1,646	1,358	1,497	1,266	1,161	2,675	5,262
Shanghai Stock Exchange Price-earning ratio	–	–	–	–	–	37.7	34.4	36.5	24.2	16.3	33.3	59.2
Shenzhen SE Composite IX Index End of period	327.3	381.3	343.9	402.2	635.7	475.9	388.8	378.6	315.8	278.7	550.6	1,447
Shenzhen Stock Exchange Price-earning ratio	–	–	–	–	–	39.8	37.0	36.2	24.6	16.4	32.7	69.7
Stock market capitalization US$ billion	118.6	211.7	235.6	319.7	581.0	525.8	463.1	513.0	447.7	401.9	1,145.5	4,478.9

Sources: China Securities and Futures Statistical Yearbook, World Federation of Exchanges, Bloomberg and author's estimates

Dash means data not available

The third and most important feature of the Chinese reform process was to subject SOEs to international and domestic competition. By agreeing to WTO conditions to opening up trade and welcoming foreign direct investment, Chinese SOEs and banks were openly told that they would be increasingly subject to competitive threats. Thus, senior executives and SOE staff were all aware that there was no excuse and precious little time to prepare for open competition to global standards. Indeed, Dr Tan and I both observed that the greatest engine of Chinese SOE reform and growth was competition within China between provinces, cities and even towns. Peking University economist Dr Zhou Qiren first highlighted this point to me. Competition was fierce as each province or city pushed for higher efficiency and growth. There were many negative elements to the 'GDP fever' that were not evident in the headlong rush to growth, such as social inequality, environmental degradation, administrative abuses and financial crime, but that story would come later.

Dr Tan and I concluded that what had happened in addition to the wholesale arrival of modern technology through foreign direct investments in special economic zones, such as the Pearl River Delta (centred around Hong Kong and Guangzhou) and the Yangtze River Delta (centred on Shanghai), was the fact that Chinese SOEs were able to transform themselves through a whole series of virtuous circle of self-reinforcing fundamental changes.

The first advantage was the abundance of cheap labour that was dextrous and well educated, even by Asian standards. This was complemented by an abundant pool of good managers, engineers and technicians who were highly absorptive of new technology and management skills. Changing management culture and factory design was easy when you had flexible labour and management, eager to get rid of old machinery and obsolete practices.

The second advantage was that as China urbanized, the SOE factories were shifted to special industrial economic zones that offered cheaper land, better facilities and cluster effects of superior infrastructure, utilities and complementary supporting industries. Moreover, the SOEs were often able to sell their old factory sites to finance their reforms. This was a once-off advantage that could not be repeated after the 1990s.

The third advantage was that government policies, including the availability of foreign exchange, were supportive for exports. During the Asian crisis, many of the exporters in Thailand, Indonesia and Malaysia were hurt by the sharp rise in interest costs, exchange rate devaluations and exchange controls. Importers in the West realized that it was faster and cheaper to shift production and order processing to China, where the exporters were eager to fulfil such orders, without disruption. Once the order system shifted, it was difficult for the crisis countries to get them back from the Chinese exporters, even if there was a lower exchange rate. The reason was that in the Asian supply chain, devaluation might not confer such an advantage because much of the exports comprised imports that had to be bought and paid for just in time for assembly and final export.

The fourth advantage was one of scale and the large Chinese market. For multinational manufacturers, the large Chinese market was irresistible, as it offered additional insurance. In addition to cheap labour, multinational companies began to realize that China's domestic market, with a population of around 1.3 billion, offered an extra degree of risk hedge or opportunity. In the event of an export slowdown, China had its own large internal market that would grow larger as it becomes more prosperous. Thus, net FDI flows into China rose by almost 200 percent to about US$121.4 billion in 2007 from US$41.7 billion in 1997, making it one of the largest recipients of FDI in the world (Table 11.6).

Finally, in addition to forcing China to forge ahead with the reform of its economy on the domestic front, the decision not to devalue the RMB also proved beneficial to China on the external front. China enjoyed improving net external positions since the crisis and turned into a net creditor after 2003, mainly because of the continued increase in international reserves and a reverse in the net position of debt instruments since 1999.[13] Furthermore, China benefited from a massive inflow of FDI after the Asian crisis, a result of a major switch in the manufacturing of exports from Southeast Asian factories to production in China.

As China becomes a favoured destination for both FDI and portfolio investment, it would confront the same issue of too much net inflow, putting pressure on domestic liquidity and the exchange rate. As Chinese enterprises gain confidence, they will be making more investments abroad, but their corporate governance and international experience so far are limited. According to Chinese Ministry of Commerce data, between 2003 and 2006, Chinese FDI increased from US$2.9 billion to US$17.6 billion. By the end of 2006, more than 5,000 Chinese enterprises had invested in 10,000 companies abroad, with a stock total of US$90.6 billion. This was estimated at 2.7 percent and 0.85 percent, respectively, of the world's total FDI outflow and stock, respectively.

---

[13] For a more detailed discussion, see Sheng and Ng (2007).

Table 11.6. *China: Selected Foreign Capital Indicators*

					Capital Flows*							
	1996	1997	1998	1999	2000	2001	2002	2003	2004	2005	2006	2007
Net FDI flows US$ billion	38.1	41.7	41.1	37.0	37.5	37.4	46.8	47.2	53.1	67.8	60.3	121.4
Net portfolio investment flows US$ billion	1.7	6.9	−3.7	−11.2	−4.0	−19.4	−10.3	11.4	19.7	−4.9	−67.6	18.7
Net other flows, including bank credit US$ billion	0.2	−27.6	−43.7	−20.5	−31.5	16.9	−4.1	−5.9	37.9	−4.0	13.3	−69.7
Net total capital flows US$ billion	40.0	21.0	−6.3	5.2	2.0	34.8	32.3	52.8	110.7	58.9	6.0	70.4
Japanese net outward FDI flow to China US$ billion	2.3	1.9	1.3	0.4	0.9	2.2	2.6	4.0	5.9	6.6	6.2	6.2

	Other Indicators[†]											
---	1996	1997	1998	1999	2000	2001	2002	2003	2004	2005	2006	2007
Total foreign bank borrowings US$ billion	55.5	87.3	80.5	65.0	61.6	57.5	49.4	64.0	91.1	115.0	169.9	276.0
Short-term international bank loans[1] US$ billion	26.9	33.4	31.4	18.9	19.3	19.4	19.7	28.8	42.3	61.4	79.2	120.5
Japanese bank lending to China US$ billion	17.8	19.7	15.3	12.2	11.3	11.5	9.4	11.6	16.3	18.7	23.7	33.1
Net external wealth position[2,3] US$ billion	−122.9	−106.8	−88.1	−83.4	−45.8	−51.8	−0.4	26.7	292.8	422.6	662.1	–
Net external wealth position[2,3] % of GDP	−14.4	−11.2	−8.6	−7.7	−3.8	−3.9	0.0	1.6	15.2	18.8	25.0	–

Sources:
* ADB and Japan External Trade Organization (JETRO)
† China's State Administration of Foreign Exchange, BIS, Lane and Milesi-Ferretti (2006) and author's estimates
[1] Foreign currency denominated loans of up to and including one year
[2] Negative means net liabilities position; positive means net assets position
[3] From 1996 to 2003, data from Lane and Milesi-Ferretti (2006). From 2004 to 2006, net international investment position data from China's State Administration of Foreign Exchange web site at http://www.safe.gov.cn
Dash means data not available

According to the Net International Investment Position at the end of 2006 published by the State Administration for Foreign Exchange, total Chinese portfolio investment abroad was US$229.2 billion, of which equity investment was US$1.5 billion and the balance debt securities. Of the liability abroad of US$120.7 billion, US$106.5 billion was equity debt, which represented investments in Chinese stock markets and unlisted companies.

In sum, China demonstrated considerable courage and international confidence in its commitment to stability with an attractive package for foreign investment, including a stable exchange rate. China was able to maintain its export competitiveness after 1998 not from exchange rate devaluation but from productivity gains. This was maintained despite the fact that its export competitors in the crisis economies experienced currency devaluations ranging from 48 percent (Malaysia) to 85 percent (Indonesia).

In this regard, it is easy to conclude that China's rapid expansion and emergence, as a global magnet for FDI, is a bane to other Asian economies, especially those that have previously benefited from FDI inflows in 1970 and 1990s. Empirically, however, there is very little evidence to suggest that China's growth has been at the expense of other Asian economies. Many studies have found mixed results, with some even discovering that China's rapid growth and attraction as a destination for FDI has actually encouraged FDI inflows and export growth in other Asian countries, as if producers in these economies belong to a common supply chain.[14]

THE ROAD AHEAD

Recently a number of papers have questioned Chinese gradualism in reforms. There is no doubt that China is also facing the same transitional challenges that the other emerging Asian economies went through when they globalized. If emerging markets succeed through manufacturing exports and productivity gains, using a soft peg against the currency of their major trading partner, the United States, the Samuelson-Balassa effect almost guarantees that as they become more prosperous their real effective exchange will rise. If their nominal exchange rate remains unchanged, then there will be a danger of asset bubbles forming in the stock and real estate markets. The collapse of the asset bubbles will prove extremely painful for banking systems, as the 1997–1998 Asian crisis demonstrated. If the emerging market economies decide to run current account deficits to maintain their exchange

---

[14] See Sheng and Ng (2007).

rates, they run the risk of a Latin American–style financial crisis. There is no easy solution to the rise of emerging markets in the world.

The debate is already ongoing within China. As with other major stock markets around the world, however, the Chinese stock market rose sharply in 2006 and 2007, but suffered a meltdown in 2008. As of the end of 2008, the Shanghai A share Composite Index, which stood at its peak of 6,092 in October 2007, was down roughly 70 percent from its historical peak. Under tighter monetary policy, property prices have also started to decline in the major cities. With inflation rising to a peak of 8 percent in May 2008, with rising producer prices under the impact of higher energy and food prices, the challenge of China is to manage growth within an environment of slowing global growth.

The question whether China will face the same kind of financial crises as its Asian neighbours is not a trivial issue. Certainly, the macroeconomic conditions are strong, with tax revenue, foreign exchange reserves, balance of payments, bank profits and economic growth at historical highs. At the same time, regional and income disparities, high property prices, pollution and social stability are clearly issues that all need urgent attention. The risks are not small, but neither is the ability of the Chinese Government to tackle these issues, as was shown in the rescue efforts during the Sichuan earthquake in May 2008. How much should exchange rate policy play a role in addressing domestic inflation or the trade balance?[15] To what extent will the global economic slowdown affect China? Will there be a global financial meltdown that includes China? We do not have all the answers but do know from historical experience that all crises are inevitable – it is a matter of when and how serious. The evaluation of this issue is unfortunately beyond the scope of this book.

Taking an institutional development approach to financial sector reforms, I conclude that since it takes time to change institutions (the banks), the property rights infrastructure (the laws and judicial systems) and the regulatory framework, a gradualist way is the only way to reform with stability. The real difficulty lies in transforming existing or creating not only new institutions, systems and processes, but also incentives and mindsets. Many foreign analysts grossly underestimate the complexity and scale of Chinese banking institutions, thinking that large bureaucracies and institutional structures, particularly the complex five-level governance system, can be changed

---

[15] For an up-to-date survey, see Burdekin (2008).

overnight. By sheer scale this is not realistic. As Douglass North wrote in the *Wall Street Journal* on 7 April 2005:

The Chinese experience should force economists to rethink some of the fundamental tenets of economics as they apply to development. Two features stand out: 1) While the institutions China employed are different from developed nations, the incentive implications were similar; and 2) China has been confronting new problems and pragmatically attempting new solutions.[16]

To sum up, the Asian crisis gave China an opportunity to make another leap forward, which it seized. But its successes also reveal that as China becomes a larger and larger player in global trade, economy and finance, its global responsibilities and contributions will become heavier. In this regard, China still has a long road ahead in terms of its ongoing economic reform agenda.

As historian Ray Huang remarked, 'As the world enters the modern era, most countries under internal and external pressure need to reconstruct themselves by substituting the *mode of governance* rooted in agrarian experience with a new set of rules based on commerce'. The Asian crisis occurred because Asian nations were not able to manage the risks arising from globalization. Asia has benefited hugely from globalisation, but the region must also learn more about the risks of globalization, just as the global community must learn about Asian risks. It is not right just to blame the outside world for a nation's own crisis.

Next, we shall look at how the Asian crisis led to efforts at regional integration.

[16] North (2005a).

TWELVE

From Crisis to Integration

Empires wax and wane, states cleave asunder and coalesce.
~ Romance of the Three Kingdoms, *Chinese 15th-century novel*

How bad was the damage from the Asian crisis? This chapter looks at the damage incurred and the steps taken by Asia as a region to prevent the next crisis.

ASIA'S GROWING PAINS: NEVER AGAIN!

There are several ways to measure the damage of the Asian crisis, including the loss of annual GDP, wealth and jobs. Various studies suggest that the output loss was quite large, ranging from Japan (17.6 percent) to Malaysia (50.0 percent), South Korea (50.1 percent), Indonesia (67.9 percent) and Thailand (97.7 percent).[1]

In terms of wealth losses, Japan suffered the most, being the largest economy in Asia, and the deflation was the most long drawn. According to Nomura's Chief Economist Richard Koo, the Japanese economy lost ¥1,200 trillion in wealth because of the massive fall in asset prices between 1989 and 1998, equivalent to 2.7 times Japan's 1989 GDP. Most of the wealth loss resulted from the drop in land prices, with the price of land in six major cities falling by 85 percent.[2] American analyst Jim Rohwer was more blunt: 'Japan's financial problem in a nutshell was that from the beginning of 1990 to the end of 1998 around $4.5 trillion worth of wealth in the stock market, and $11.5 trillion worth in the property market, was destroyed without anyone – government, banks or companies – being prepared to recognize the losses.'[3]

[1] Laevan and Valencia (2008) and Table 4.3.
[2] Koo (2003).
[3] Rohwer (2001), 82.

According to PIMCO Japan specialist Koyo Ozeki,[4] 'Japanese banks had around 50 trillion yen (US$450 billion) in non-performing loans immediately after the burst of the bubble in 1993, which shot up to nearly 100 trillion yen (US$910 billion) by 1996'. This was an estimated 25–30 percent of GDP, whilst the value actually written off by financial institutions amounted to nearly ¥100 trillion (US$910 billion) or 20 percent of GDP. The large banks alone accounted for ¥75 trillion (US$680 billion) of this total. This exceeds the combined value of their net worth of ¥20 trillion (US$180 billion) and 14 years of net operating profits at ¥50 trillion (US$450 billion).

Ozeki's estimates are about the same as IMF estimates of the Japanese fiscal costs of recapitalization of the banking system at 24 percent of GDP (see Table 4.3). It is interesting to note that the bad debts turned out to be five times the banks' net worth. There is no standard way of calculating losses, because in addition to the fiscal costs of recapitalization, you would have to include the banks' own write-down of net worth, cut in net operating profits and the implicit subsidy provided by Japanese depositors as they received near zero deposit rates for more than 17 years.

In the period leading up to 2000, 110 deposit-taking institutions were wound down by the Japanese deposit insurance scheme. The losses of the largest banks, three international active banks and five regional banks, were staggering, accounting for 10.6 trillion yen of losses, equivalent to 9.9 times their capital.[5]

In rough terms, Ozeki estimated that the total wealth loss was around ¥800 trillion, comprising ¥500 trillion in land price deflation and ¥300 trillion in stock market losses. If the banking system absorbed roughly ¥200 trillion, it suggests that banks bore one-quarter of the wealth loss.

The wealth losses for the rest of Asia are a little more complicated to estimate. In terms of stock market capitalization, the Japanese market lost US$2.4 trillion between the peak in December 1989 and August 1998, whilst the crisis-hit Asian countries and Australia lost US$1.4 trillion between their individual bubble peaks in 1996–1997 and August 1998, broadly the trough of the Asian crisis (Table 12.1).

The losses in specific markets were severe. Like the Great Crash in the United States in 1929–1933, stock prices in Indonesia and Malaysia fell to as low as one-tenth of their peak values in U.S. dollar terms. On average, in terms of stock market losses, the region lost 66 percent of its 1997 GDP, whereas Japan lost nearly 55 percent of its 1997 GDP. The Japanese market

---

4   Ozeki (2008).
5   Nasako (2001), table 11, 61.

Table 12.1. *Loss in Stock Market Capitalization from Peak to Trough during the Asian Financial Crisis*

	Peak		Trough		Change		
	Month	Market Cap	Month	Market Cap	Value	%	% to 1997 GDP
Japan							
In billion yen	Dec 89	611,152	Sep 98	252,008	−359,144	−58.8	68.9
In billion US$	Dec 89	4,250	Aug 98	1,863	−2,387	−56.2	55.3

Non-Japan Asia (US$ billion)

	Peak		Trough		Change		
	Month	Market Cap	Month	Market Cap	Value	%	% to 1997 GDP
Australia	Sep 97	336	Aug 98	260	−76	−22.6	18.7
Hong Kong	Jul 97	595	Aug 98	253	−342	−57.5	196.9
Indonesia	Jun 97	107	Aug 98	10	−96	−90.4	40.7
Malaysia	Feb 97	356	Aug 98	46	−310	−87.1	309.4
Philippines	Jan 97	89	Aug 98	19	−70	−78.3	83.2
Singapore	Feb 97	155	Aug 98	63	−91	−59.2	95.8
South Korea	May 97	154	Jun 98	45	−109	−71.0	20.7
Taiwan	Jul 97	352	Aug 98	224	−127	−36.2	43.9
Thailand	Jan 96	155	Aug 98	17	−137	−88.8	91.1
Total					**−1,359**		**65.9**

Sources: IMF and WFE

Table 12.2. *Japan: Loss in Stock Market Capitalization from 1998 Trough to 2003 Trough*

	1998 Trough		2003 Trough		Change		% to 2003 GDP
	Month	Market Cap	Month	Market Cap	Value	%	
Japan							
In billion yen	Sep	252,008	Mar	232,862	−19,146	−7.6%	−3.8%
In billion US$	Aug	1,863	Mar	1,939	+75	4.0%	1.7%

Sources: IMF and WFE

continued to drift and lost another 3.8 percent of 2003 GDP in yen terms until it bottomed out in March 2003 (Table 12.2), but because of appreciation of the yen against the U.S. dollar, it actually rose by 1.7 percent.

Wealth losses in real estate for the Asian crisis-hit nations are even more difficult to estimate, because of a lack of common indices of property prices. IMF estimates[6] suggest that property prices probably dropped by two-thirds in Hong Kong from peak, by half in Thailand, by one-third in Malaysia and only modestly in South Korea. In Indonesia land prices actually rose in local currency terms because land was the only hedge against inflation, and it was difficult to realize collateral.

As described in Chapter 4, bank nonperforming loans grew, and real credit to the private sector fell. At the height of the crisis, private sector estimates of NPLs for Asian banks ranged from 30 percent for Malaysia to as high as 50–70 percent for Indonesia (see also Table 4.3). Real bank credit to the private sector was estimated to have contracted at an annual rate of 50 percent in Indonesia and 10–20 percent in the Philippines, Malaysia and Thailand.[7]

As a result of bank failures and consolidation, the number of banks in East Asia shrank considerably. In Malaysia the number fell from 23 in 1994 to 10 by 2005, in South Korea from 26 to 13 and in Indonesia from 240 to 131.[8] In Japan the number fell from 150 to 122. Finance companies were rapidly consolidated into banks in Malaysia and Thailand.

---

[6]   Collyns and Senhadji (2003).
[7]   Mohanty (2006).
[8]   Barton (2007).

Of course, foreigners also shared part of the losses. Estimates by the World Bank suggest that foreign market losses in the East Asian equity markets were somewhere between US$83.5 billion and US$166 billion,[9] whilst foreign bank loan losses in the region were roughly US$60 billion.[10] In addition, foreign creditors lost another US$50 billion. Hence, excluding losses from foreign investments in real estate, which were probably relatively small, foreign losses in the four crisis countries were probably as high as US$270 billion. This is small relative to domestic losses, but not insignificant by any measure. Foreign bondholders were also not spared. An unconfirmed IIF report estimated that the mark-to-market losses of Eurobonds in the region were roughly US$160 billion, but some of it would have recovered as risk spreads recovered to normal.

Perhaps the greatest damage, however, was the social distress the crisis cost Asia. After more than three decades of prosperity and stability, the East Asian region witnessed riots, looting and student demonstrations in Indonesia, strikes against layoffs in South Korea and public protests against IMF conditionality in Thailand. Ultimately, new governments emerged in Indonesia, South Korea and Thailand, whilst the political leadership in Malaysia became split. As the crisis grew deeper, it soon became clear that the costs of the crisis on the less socially privileged were the most severe. High inflation, unemployment and disruption of social services due to budget cuts had a severe impact on the poor.

Amongst the four worst crisis-hit economies, the country that paid the biggest price in terms of human costs was Indonesia. In tandem with its drastic fall in real GDP of 13.1 percent in 1998, Indonesia's real GDP per capita decreased 14.4 percent. In Thailand and Malaysia real GDP per capita decreased 11.6 percent and 9.5 percent, respectively. South Korea was the least affected, with a fall of 7.5 percent. The contraction in nominal GDP per capita in U.S. dollars terms was even more drastic because of the steep decline in the value of the affected Asian currencies vis-à-vis the dollar. Since its currency depreciated most against the U.S. dollar, Indonesia suffered a decrease in nominal GDP per capita of 56.4 percent in 1998, followed by South Korea (34.4 percent), Malaysia (30.0 percent) and Thailand (26.7 percent).

The unemployment rate jumped together with the sharp falls in GDP per capita levels between 1996 and 1998–1999. South Korea experienced the biggest jump in unemployment rate, from 2.1 percent in 1996 to a peak of

[9] Barth and Zhang (1999).
[10] Institute of International Finance, quoted in Barth and Zhang (1999).

7.0 percent in 1998. This was followed by Thailand (up by 2.9 percent to a peak of 4.4 percent in 1998), Indonesia (up by 1.5 percent to a peak of 6.4 percent in 1999) and Malaysia (up by 0.9 percent to a peak of 3.4 percent in 1999). Cumulatively the four worst crisis-hit economies witnessed an increase of approximately 3.5 million unemployed persons, or a 63.7 percent increase in the unemployed between 1996 and 1999.

A breakdown of the general unemployment figures showed that youths between 15 and 24 years old were one of the groups most severely affected by the crisis. Unemployment amongst this group in Indonesia hit a high of 19.0 percent in 1999, 15.9 percent in South Korea in 1998, 9.7 percent in Malaysia in 1999 and 7.7 percent in Thailand, also in 1999.[11] Women were the other group that was particularly hard hit. According to Nahid Aslanbeigui and Gale Summerfield, who studied the gender impact of the Asian crisis,[12] in Indonesia 46 percent of the unemployed between 1997 and 1998 were women, although they made up slightly more than one-third of the labour force. In Thailand women composed 50–60 percent of the unemployed because they made up 90 percent of the work force in the textile industries.[13]

The unemployment statistics of the four worst crisis-hit economies may nevertheless be underestimated for a couple of reasons. Between 1997 and 1998 South Korea suffered the highest declines of falls of 26.4 percent in construction and manufacturing employment.[14] But workers may have found jobs at lower pay in the agriculture or rural areas.

Second, these unemployment statistics also hide the impact of the crisis on migrant workers.[15] For instance, many migrant workers in Malaysia and South Korea were repatriated.[16] Singapore, Hong Kong and other economies also retrenched their migrant workers, thus hitting the labour-exporting economies of Thailand, Philippines and Indonesia particularly severely.

Higher inflation hurt real wages very badly. Inflation in Indonesia rose from 7.0 percent in 1996 to a staggering 58.0 percent in 1999. In the same 1996–1999 period, Thailand's inflation rate increased from 5.9 percent to 8.1 percent and South Korea's from 4.9 percent to 7.5 percent, whilst inflation in Malaysia rose from 3.5 percent in 1996 to 5.3 percent in 1998. As a result, in 1998, real wages fell by 44 percent in Indonesia, 9.8 percent in

[11] UN Millennium Development Goal indicators.
[12] Aslanbeigui and Summerfield (2000).
[13] Ching (1999).
[14] Fallon and Lucas (2002).
[15] See Fallon and Lucas (2002); UNESCAP (2002).
[16] Fallon and Lucas (2002), 30.

South Korea, 6.3 percent in Thailand and 2.7 percent in Malaysia.[17] The effects of inflation were particularly severe on the poor because many essential product prices rose, because of higher imported food prices and cuts in subsidies. For example, instant noodles, a main food staple for many poor Indonesians, increased substantially in price when the price of wheat went up because of the devaluation.

An interesting feature to note is that crisis economies with massive devaluation had higher inflation than Mainland China and Hong Kong, which maintained stable exchange rates (Table 12.3). Fixed exchange rate regimes, particularly in Hong Kong, squeezed out inflation and restored competitiveness, but the process was extremely painful. In China the authorities pushed through many reforms in order to maintain competitiveness under the stable exchange rate regime.

The twin effects of unemployment and inflation made a visible dent in the region's poverty reduction programmes because the crisis affected also the middle class. Former Philippines President Fidel Ramos lamented in December 1998, 'Millions of Southeast Asia's families – who had painfully pulled themselves up to middle-class status – are slipping back into abject poverty'.[18]

Based on a variety of sources, my rough estimates indicate that the crisis pushed an additional 15–17 million Asians below their respective national poverty lines between 1996–1997 and 1999. Indonesia was the worst casualty with its poverty rate increasing from around 18 percent in 1996 to a peak of 23 percent in 1999. Malaysia's poverty rate increased from 6.8 percent in 1997 to a peak of 8.5 percent in 1998, Thailand's increased from 11.4 percent in 1996 to a peak of 16.0 percent in 1999, whilst South Korea's urban poverty jumped from 4.3 percent in the fourth quarter of 1996 to a peak of 8.8 percent in the third quarter of 1998.

There was perhaps one silver lining amidst the gloom. First, the changes in overall income inequality amongst the crisis-hit nations between 1997 and 1998 appear to have been minor. Between 1997 and 1998, Malaysia's, Thailand's and South Korea's Gini coefficients increased slightly, from 0.496 to 0.498, 0.477 to 0.481 and 0.279 to 0.285, respectively, whilst Indonesia's Gini coefficients actually decreased slightly, from 0.380 to 0.370.[19] A cynic could say that the crisis was quite democratic in the reduction of wealth for everyone.

---

[17] Fallon and Lucas (2002), table 6, 32.
[18] Ramos (1998).
[19] Fallon and Lucas (2002), table 7, 35.

Table 12.3. Selected Asian Economies: Inflation (Annual % Change)

	1990	1991	1992	1993	1994	1995	1996	1997	1998	1999	2000
China	3.1	3.4	6.4	14.7	24.1	17.1	8.3	2.8	-0.8	-1.4	0.4
Hong Kong	10.3	11.3	9.5	8.8	8.8	9.0	6.3	5.8	2.8	-3.9	-3.7
Indonesia	7.8	9.4	7.5	9.7	8.5	9.4	7.0	6.2	58.0	20.7	3.8
Malaysia	3.0	4.4	4.8	3.6	3.7	3.2	3.5	2.7	5.3	2.7	1.6
South Korea	8.6	9.3	6.2	4.8	6.3	4.5	4.9	4.4	7.5	0.8	2.3
Thailand	5.9	5.7	4.2	3.3	5.1	5.8	5.9	5.6	8.1	0.3	1.6

Source: IMF

Cumulatively, all four crisis-hit nations suffered setbacks in their respective Human Development Index during the 1997–1998 period (Table 12.4).[20]

Ultimately, no statistical data can quantify the shame and trauma suffered by millions of Asians at the personal and professional levels. The resourcefulness and determination to survive of many were admirable. Each country had its own heroes, former high-flying professionals and businessmen turned street vendors or those who struggled to turn around bankrupt companies because they had faith in themselves and in their country. The humiliation of previously proud achievers drove solutions towards prevention of the next crisis.

FROM RECOVERY TO REGIONAL ECONOMIC INTEGRATION

By 1999 there were clear signs that the crisis had turned the corner. South Korea was on a strong recovery, aided by the reforms and recovery in exports. As the United States lowered interest rates to prevent a global slowdown, one by one the crisis economies pulled themselves out of the deflation. Up until 2000 there was a dot.com bubble, benefiting North Asia more because of the investments in year 2000 (Y2K) technology and the comparative strength of technology products. By April 2003 all the Asian economies and the markets had begun their strong recovery, driven partly by the rise of India and China that has carried on to the present day.

As Asian economies regained their strength and confidence, there was increasing awareness that the region has emerged almost naturally as the third area of economic integration, next to the EU and the NAFTA in terms of size and importance. Indeed, the idea of Asia as a third economic zone is not new. When Japan became the first Asian economy to reach global economic status in the 1980s, Japanese writers such as Kenichi Ohmae already pronounced that the world was a tripolar world – the Americas, led by the United States, Europe and Asia. Europe became a political union by 1992 via the Maastricht Treaty and a monetary union in 1999 through the launch of the Euro. NAFTA was formed in 1994.

The main driver of Asian regional economic integration is trade integration. Over the last quarter century (1980–2005), intra-Asian trade has risen steadily from about 35 percent to 55 percent of the region's total world trade.

---

[20] The Human Development Index measures a country's achievement in three basic dimensions of human development: a long and healthy life, as measured by life expectancy at birth; knowledge, as measured by the adult literacy rate and the combined primary, secondary and tertiary gross enrolment ratio; and a respectable standard of living, as measured by the log of GDP per capita at purchasing power parity in U.S. dollars.

Table 12.4. *Crises Economies: Human Development Index, 1997–1999*

Country	1997		1998		1999	
	Ranking	HDI Value	Ranking	HDI Value	Ranking	HDI Value
Indonesia	105	0.681	109	0.670	102	0.677
Malaysia	56	0.768	61	0.772	56	0.774
South Korea	30	0.852	31	0.854	27	0.875
Thailand	67	0.753	76	0.745	66	0.757

Source: UNDP, Human Development Reports, various years

This is lower than intraregional EU trade (66 percent) but higher than that of NAFTA (45 percent). By 2007 Asia had clearly become the global supply chain, with East Asia as the manufacturing supply chain, whilst India was asserting itself in the IT services and outsourcing industries.

Following the Asian crisis there has also been massive efforts to promote Asian financial integration. The regional financial cooperation efforts have led to five important initiatives with varying degrees of success:

1. *Chiang Mai Initiative (CMI)*, which as of May 2007, had 16 Bilateral Swap Arrangements, amounting to US$83.0 billion in resources.[21]
   The CMI was established in May 2000, when the ASEAN+3 (China, Japan and South Korea) Finance Ministers met in the northern city of Chiang Mai, Thailand. The CMI enhanced the ASEAN Swap Arrangements (ASA), which itself was strengthened in May 2000 by raising the swap resources to US$1 billion to include all ASEAN members. The ASA was enhanced by a Bilateral Swap Arrangement and Repurchase Agreement (BSA), through which the three non-ASEAN countries with larger reserves could support the ASA through bilateral swaps. This would increase the available funds to defend against speculative attacks. The timing of the release of funds would be linked to IMF conditionality.
   In May 2007, at the Kyoto Meeting, the ASEAN+3 leaders agreed to seek ways to multilateralize the present bilateral arrangements.
2. *Asian Bond Market Initiative (ABMI)*. This initiative has also caught regional and global attention. EMEAP has taken the lead on this, with

---

[21] Joint Ministerial Statement of the 10th ASEAN+3 Finance Minister's Meeting, Kyoto, Japan, 5 May 2007.

BIS providing technical support. The intention of ABMI is to (a) facilitate development of efficient and liquid debt markets in Asia and (b) further better utilization of Asian savings for Asian investments.

The ABMI comprises two packages:

- Asian Bond Fund I (ABF-1) issued in June 2003, comprising US$1 billion, invested in sovereign and quasi-sovereign U.S. dollar bonds issued by eight EMEAP members (excluding Australia, Japan and New Zealand) and
- Asian Bond Fund II (ABF-2) issued in December 2004 for US$2 billon, using private sector intermediaries and open to investment by the public. It involves two primary components:

    - Pan-Asian Bond Index Fund (PAIF), a single bond fund index investing in sovereign and quasi-sovereign local currency bonds issued by eight members and

    - Fund of Bond Funds, with eight-country subfunds, which is the retail element.

So far, the PAIF and five single-market Funds have been issued in Hong Kong, Malaysia and Singapore. A won-denominated bond and baht-denominated bonds, with partial guarantees by Japanese authorities, have also been issued. Much of the work were also assisted by the Asian Development Bank and the International Finance Corporation (IFC), which issued local currency bonds in Malaysia and Thailand and plan to do so in China. The ADB has also launched an Asian Bond Online web site (http://www.asianbondsonline.adb.org) to disseminate information on Asian bonds. Although both funds were launched with much fanfare, one must admit that more institutional and retail trading is necessary to provide a deep and liquid regional bond market.

3. *Monitoring of Short-Term Capital Flows*, agreed to in Honolulu in May 2001. The progress on this initiative has been uneven, as nations are still building up their database.

4. *Economic Review and Policy Dialogue (ERPD)*. This is conducted at the Ministerial level annually and twice a year at the Deputies level.

5. *ASEAN+3 Research Group*. This was proposed by Japan and agreed in August 2003. The research themes are Regional Financial Architecture and Regional Exchange Rate Arrangements. Recently the Group has been working on regional credit database and financial assistance to small and medium-sized enterprises.

Of late, the proposals for the Asian Monetary Fund have also surfaced in different forms. Furthermore, the 12th ASEAN Summit in the Philippines on 13 January 2007 agreed that the target date for creating the ASEAN Economic Community (AEC) be brought forward by five years to 2015.[22]

As East Asian trade and financial integration increases, the creation of an East Asian Free Trade Area (along the lines of NAFTA) would be a formidable third economic force globally, on par with the EU and NAFTA. However measured, such a grouping would account for roughly 20 percent of global output, 20 percent of world trade and over 50 percent of international foreign exchange reserves. The humiliation of subordination to external conditionality has led to the massive increase in the size of Asian foreign exchange reserves since 2000, with Asia's foreign reserves amounting to approximately US$4 trillion by the end of 2008.

However, despite recognizable progress in terms of Asian financial integration, the region's financial markets still remain small relative to global markets. Of the world's stock market capitalization of US$51 trillion in 2006, Asia accounted for US$12 trillion or 23 percent, when compared to the United States (US$20 trillion or 38 percent) and EU (US$13 trillion or 26 percent).[23] Also, the global equity market remains heavily dollar-based (about 55 percent), mainly because of the depth and size of the New York Stock Exchange and NASDAQ.[24] Furthermore, although BIS data suggest that the size of the Asian local currency bond market has increased by about 2.4 times from roughly US$4.6 trillion in 1997 to US$11.2 trillion in 2006, it is still not possible to say that Asia has deep and liquid bond markets. Most of the growth in the bond markets has been in the Korean and Chinese markets. Like the equity markets, in currency terms, the U.S. dollar and the Euro still dominate the international bond markets.

In addition, although growing in absolute terms and as a share of GDP, Asia's intraregional cross-border portfolio investment is relatively small. Asia's portfolio liabilities to other Asian countries amounted to only 2.25 percent of its GDP in 2004, less than one-third the liabilities to either NAFTA or the EU. A similar pattern holds for Asia's portfolio assets. Asian investments in either NAFTA or the EU – at almost 10 percent of Asia's GDP in each in 2004 – were roughly 4.5 times that within Asia.[25] In other

---

[22] The ASEAN Economic Community is the realization of a single market and production base in order to bolster ASEAN's competitiveness to meet the challenges of new global competition.

[23] International Monetary Fund (2007b), table 3, 139.

[24] Sheng and Kwek (2007).

[25] Cowen et al. (2006).

words, Asia continues to prefer to put its overseas investments in markets outside Asia, rather than within Asia, demonstrating the superiority of U.S. and European financial intermediation skills, as well as the weaknesses of Asian financial markets.

One would have thought that after such painful lessons, the Asian financial system would have transformed itself more radically and thoroughly. There is certainly no lack of official will because there are literally hundreds of task forces working on trade and financial integration. Furthermore, there is no shortage of money, because Asian domestic savings remain high. The mixed results from Asia's reform efforts, especially with regard to the financial sector since the 1997–1998 Asian crisis, seem to imply that the problems lay deeper than we all commonly realize. To me, the major stumbling block of Asian financial markets is in managing the process of change.

Change management is often slow and frustrating because it requires a paradigm shift in mindsets in both the public and private sectors. Also, there are usually too many vested interests and conflicting views on the outcomes of change. The forces of change must come from internal and external sources.

Globalization and the arrival of foreign financial institutions offer both opportunities and threats. According to IMF data, the average share of foreign financial institutions in total domestic bank assets globally was 23 percent, whereas East Asia had an average level of only 6 percent.[26] Foreign financial institutions offer five advantages – foreign funding, access to foreign markets, modern financial technology and products, training of local expertise to think out of the box and competition to local financial institutions by giving better quality service, often at lower risks. Whilst competition is always healthy, there is always the risk that those local institutions that cannot take competition will fail, thus posing some systemic risks that should be handled carefully. Of course, one must never underestimate the nationalist sentiment against foreign competition.

At the root of dealing with changes forced by globalization is the capacity and ability of the Asian bureaucracy to understand globalization and market forces. Having been groomed since independence to participate in mercantilist export growth, with fairly strong 'window guidance' towards integration with global markets, many Asian policymakers do not realize that the game has changed profoundly.

The more you protect domestic players, the more you risk that they cannot compete internationally and therefore face marginalization. If you do

---

[26] International Monetary Fund (2007a), table 3.2, 101.

not open up, your domestic players do not get the chance to learn and compete. Of course, there will be risks of contagion, but the longer you delay opening up, the larger the risks of marginalization. Therefore, regional cooperation is an intermediary step towards globalization.

STUMBLING BLOCKS TO ASIAN FINANCIAL INTEGRATION

Although the issue of Asian integration has been bandied about for years, much of the intellectual thinking and experience in regional cooperation stems from recent European history. The European path was first and foremost political,[27] with agreement between two key partners in continental Europe, France and Germany, to lock in economic security in exchange for peace in Europe. Despite missteps in the European Monetary System (EMS), the path was found to have a single currency (the Euro) as a prelude to a single market. But does greater financial integration for Asia make sense? Who benefits and who loses?

Even though currently there is no clear objective about a single market, single currency or monetary union in Asia, there is common awareness that there are possible gains from regional cooperation. Some Australian experts think that there are three major benefits towards integration. First, integration helps put internal and external pressure on much needed domestic reforms. Second, Asia has excess savings but financial markets that are inefficient. With integration Asian savings can be used more efficiently. Third, as a group, Asians would have more say on the global trade, political and economic discussions. The other advantages from regional cooperation (and progress towards integration) are the gains from a larger market through trade and possible mechanisms to prevent or minimize global shocks from outside the region.

Despite these possible advantages of regional financial integration, there are at least four major reasons why Asian integration will move slowly, unless there is fresh new impetus, such as another crisis, to push it forward.

First, no one has been able to define what an Asian bloc really means. Asia is politically divided into at least four leading economic groups, including Japan, China, ASEAN and India with Russia and the Middle East all having claims to Asian interests. Do we also include Australasia within Asia? Asians also do not think alike, and there is no historical sense of being 'Asian'.

Second, one of the major problems of Asian integration is the globalisation question: closed or open regionalism? This issue has three aspects

[27] Padoa-Schioppa (2004).

to it. First, although there are possible benefits of regional integration when viewed in terms of the region as a whole, the benefits to individual countries from further progress are not immediately obvious and measurable. For the smaller Asian countries, there is considerable anxiety that given the large size of Japan, China and India, the payoffs for the smaller economies may be less than the costs of adjustment to regionalism. Even for the larger countries in Asia, there are conflicting signals and objectives, because currently the bulk of trade of Japan and China (including their indirect trade through the Asian supply chain) is directed outside the Asian region. There are thus no obvious reasons why the benefits of a larger Asian market (less payoffs and costs associated with regionalism such as regional institutions) are larger than simple open globalism. In other words, the case is not proven at the individual country level whether bilateral bargaining, such as bilateral free trade agreements (FTAs), is not more fruitful and beneficial than bargaining as a cooperative bloc, especially because it is most cumbersome and slow in getting regional agreement.

The second aspect to the issue of closed or open regionalism is the reaction of both the G-10 industrial countries, which, excluding Japan, consists of the Americans and Europeans as well as the IFIs. The G-10 and the IFIs will almost definitely oppose closed regionalism and will not stand by idly if Asia attempts to go its own way politically and economically. Fred Bergsten, an iconoclast observer of global economics and security, voiced the following concerns:

An East Asian economic bloc could also, however, generate major problems for the world economy. It would inherently create substantial trade diversion, which would reduce US exports alone by about $25 billion per year immediately and much more as the group's dynamic effects kicked in. It could undermine rather than support the multilateral economic institutions, notably the World Trade Organization (WTO) and the International Monetary Fund (IMF), by creating a three-bloc world in which those institutions became largely irrelevant. Taken in conjunction with the evolution toward a Free Trade Area of the Americas, which is also slow and halting but likely to eventually succeed, it could draw a 'line down the middle of the Pacific' that would produce disintegration rather than integration of the Asia-Pacific region and a fundamental split between East Asia and the United States (and the rest of the Americas).[28]

Thus when Dr Mahathir Mohamad, former Prime Minister of Malaysia, first proposed the East Asian Economic Caucus (EAEC) group in the late 1980s without U.S. participation, there were two primary objections. One

---

[28] Bergsten (2005), 2.

was that it reminded many people of the Japanese Second World War concept of a Greater East Asian Co-Prosperity Sphere and the second was that the United States would not stand back to be excluded from any Asian regional cooperation. Hence, the Asia-Pacific Economic Co-operation (APEC) Group was established to include not only the United States, but also all the Pacific Rim economies. In addition, the idea of an Asian Monetary Fund of US$100 billion to try and stem the Asian crisis fizzled out partly because of immediate opposition from the IMF, the EU and the United States. Such objection coupled with the noncommitment of China and other Asian members caused the AMF idea to be dropped in favour of the Manila Framework in November 1997. The Manila Framework Group, which included participation from the United States, focused on enhancing regional surveillance and cooperation, but any regional funding would be used to complement and not supplement IMF's efforts.

The idea of the AMF, of course, did not completely die out, particularly in the minds of the Japanese Ministry of Finance. In October 1998 Japanese Finance Minister Miyazawa announced a New Initiative (sometimes called New Miyazawa Initiative or NMI) to 'assist Asian countries affected by the currency crisis in overcoming their economic difficulties and to contribute to the stability of international financial markets'. The NMI comprised essentially US$30 billion, of which half was for short-term needs and half for medium to long-term needs. Nevertheless, the IMF remained the core international financial institution coordinating efforts in the Asian crisis because, like the Manila Framework, the NMI funding role was to complement the needs of the IMF through the provision of bilateral aid to the crisis economies.

The third aspect of the issue of closed or open integration is Japan. As a key member of G-10, it will have to choose accordingly in the face of likely opposition to closed integration by the group.

One of the key differences, other than historical and institutional differences, between Asia and the EU is the degree of concentration of size. This difference between Asia and Europe is not often fully appreciated. As of 2006, the largest economy in Europe, Germany, accounts for about 21 percent of EU GDP and around 15 percent of total EU financial assets.[29] In Asia Japan alone accounts for 41 percent of total Asian GDP in 2006 and 53 percent of total Asian financial assets. This means that unlike Germany's position in Europe, Japan clearly dominates the Asian economic and financial landscape. This economic and financial dominance, currently overlooked

[29] International Monetary Fund (2007b), table 3, 139.

because observers tend to concentrate on the growing size of China and India, implies that even though Japan's influence has somewhat taken a back seat following its sputtering economic growth for the last 17 years, no Asian integration can occur without Japan. The choice made by Japan as to closed or open integration would thus be crucial, as it would clearly play a leading role in any regional cooperative efforts.

Third, any discussion of Asian integration has to take into consideration historical differences. Bitter memories of major conflict during the Second World War continue to be stirred up over visits to the Yasukuni shrine, a national monument where identified war criminals are enshrined. Unless there is common political agreement, further progress in regional integration will be limited, despite considerable achievements in the trade and financial side.

Fourth, and this is perhaps the most important point, the economic case for integration is simply not clear within Asia. European integration occurs because the EU is willing to pay 1 percent of its Gross National Income (GNI) towards integration. Under the 2007–2013 financial framework, the EU budget is around €120 billion annually, of which nearly half is distribution such as agricultural subsidies to EU members. As of 2006, EU has a combined GNI of roughly US$14 trillion, whereas Asia has a combined GNI of approximately US$10 trillion. Like Europe, which Asian economy would be willing to pay US$100 billion annually to finance Asian integration? Of course, smaller Asian economies are willing to receive benefits in exchange for greater cooperation.

Nevertheless, despite these stumbling blocks, leading thinkers and leaders in Asia, such as Haruhiko Kuroda, Japan's former Vice Minister of International Affairs and currently the President of the ADB, are optimistic that Asian integration will be built on four major pillars:[30]

- *Sub-regional Cooperation* – connecting through bridges, ports, roads and telecommunication networks, which would facilitate trade considerably.
- *Money and Finance* – through the CMI and ABF-1 & 2 described earlier.
- *Trade and Investment* – this is perhaps the most advanced area. Intraregional trade in Asia already accounts for 55 percent of the region's total trade, compared with only 35 percent in 1980. Competition within the region has resulted in at least 50 bilateral FTAs being signed which would eventually lead to a crude common Free Trade Region, with the possibility to extend towards a common customs union.

---

[30] Kuroda (2005).

- *Provision of Regional Public Goods* – in areas such as SARS, Avian flu and HIV/AIDS prevention and management, cross-border trafficking and environmental degradation. There is greater awareness that regional cooperation is key in these areas, but funding remains lacking.

The ADB thus in recent years has led the efforts in regional cooperation, with several major studies on the issues, including comparative lessons from the EU and NAFTA (ADB 2005). The Japanese Ministry of Finance web site (www.mof.go.jp) has also published material and research on these subjects.

ASIA'S OPTIONS ON ECONOMIC INTEGRATION

There are essentially four routes to economic integration: the political route, the trade route, through financial integration and through monetary integration.

The Europeans chose the political route, with monetary integration moving ahead of financial integration. Political union was possible because a politically unified Europe would avoid future wars. The Euro was created to enhance political, monetary and financial integration. Within Asia, however, the political route seems too remote because of major historical differences.

In the Americas the trade integration route was chosen, with the creation of NAFTA in the early 1990s. But after the 1994 Mexican crisis, the U.S. Congress would not allow the Fed to become the lender of last resort to Latin American economies. This means that the key currencies in America, the U.S. dollar, Canadian dollar, Mexican peso and others, float against each other, with the U.S. dollar having the most influence within the region. Dollarization seems to be out of favour.

Within Asia, although over 55 percent of the region's world trade is already intra-Asian, there is still insufficient intra-Asian demand for Asian final goods to create a strong domestic Asian market. Non-Asian exports remain the Asian engine of growth. Nevertheless, given its progress, the trade route may indeed be the best possible way towards Asian integration.

There are two possible routes to financial integration: through harmonization, which is the EU approach, or the mutual recognition approach, which is the U.K. preferred approach. Within Asia the mutual recognition approach is the softer approach to financial integration and may be the more pragmatic approach for a number of reasons.

First, there is great Asian diversity in terms of income, finance, politics and development. For example, the Chinese capital market still requires considerable time to resolve some of its structural issues before it is ready to play a regional role.

Second, currently, each market of the Asian financial centres remains too small and domestic oriented to take on the financial centre role that London plays for the European time zone and New York plays for the American time zone. Tokyo, for instance, being the largest financial market in Asia, needs to move from its domestic focus towards being a regional leader if the yen is to consolidate its role as a regional currency. In the last 17 years the number of non-Japanese listings in Tokyo stock exchange has actually declined. The huge savings in Japan could be channelled to meet the investment demand in parts of Asia outside Japan if the transaction costs in Tokyo are made more competitive.

Third, there are still too many regulatory, institutional and structural barriers towards the creation of an Asian regional financial market. For instance, it is easier for a Luxembourg-registered mutual fund to be licensed to be sold throughout Asia than for a Hong Kong fund to be licensed for sale in another Asian centre. Similarly, it is easier for a Dublin-listed bond to be traded throughout Asia than any bond issued in any Asian centre. In other words, transaction costs are lower for global financial institutions and funds to register (even instruments originating in Asia, such as pan-Asian funds) outside Asia and sell to Asians than it is for Asian financial institutions to sell to each other within Asia.

These practical anomalies are due to obsolete rules and regulations that must be changed before regional financial markets can take place. There is currently no institutional arrangement to examine and discuss these impediments. Securities regulators cannot deal with this on their own initiative, because legal and regulatory changes need the support of the other parts of the bureaucracy. But neither can central bankers nor ministries of finance manage such a complex task on their own. Individual silos cannot deal with cross-cutting issues that require political will, bureaucratic skills and a 'big push' to resolve. The matter is made even more complex with regional initiatives, which would involve ministries of foreign affairs, international trade and the private sector.

Despite these obstacles, however, the current initiatives on ABMI are steps in the right direction, but the deepening of Asian capital markets will require considerable leadership to take forward and time to bear fruit.

Finally, monetary integration could be achieved through either an Asian Currency Unit (ACU), consisting of a basket of Asian currencies, or a single currency along the lines of the Euro. The monetary integration route is very much in its infancy – although according to Eisuke Sakakibara, he 'would not be surprised to see the emergence of an Asian currency within the next 40 to 50 years'. Indeed, he has 'already given the name to the currency. It would be called ASEANA'.[31]

My personal opinion is that there are centripetal forces pushing for a regional currency, but its formation would have to await the full convertibility of the Chinese RMB. Nevertheless, since the depegging of the RMB and the Malaysian ringgit in July 2005, there has generally been an upward revaluation of a number of East Asian currencies, including the yen. There is some evidence that East Asian currencies are beginning to drift around broad parities with each other, in much the same way that they used to have broad parity before the crisis.

Political agreement will determine whether there will be a regional currency bloc. The economic case for a regional currency would become stronger if the Asian global supply chain becomes even more integrated. Much will depend on whether the leading currencies in that basket, particularly the RMB and the yen, can become strong currencies. This implies that these currencies will offer comparable property protection, long-term value creation and low transaction costs, relative to the U.S. dollar and the Euro. This further implies that the macroeconomic and financial policies for the larger members must be stable and consistent with each other. As experience with the EMS showed, this is a highly volatile road because misunderstanding and differences in fiscal and monetary policies, as much as differences in political approach, can be reflected in higher market volatility.

Financial integration and monetary integration are, in fact, not mutually exclusive paths, but are complementary to each other. One cannot move too far ahead of the other, with the understanding and willingness to discuss monetary integration reaching fruition when financial integration becomes deeper. This is not to say that monetary integration requires financial integration first. The European experience suggests that monetary integration can advance ahead of a full common market in financial services. Currently, European regulatory harmonization is still a work in progress.

PROSPECTS OF ASIAN FINANCIAL INTEGRATION

Talks about Asian financial or monetary integration arose from the region's insecurity after the Asian crisis. There is some feeling of common vulnerability as the different Asian currencies are individually vulnerable to greater

---

[31] Sakakibara (2007).

volatility in the global financial markets. This question arises whether the current global crisis will push efforts to greater regional integration. That remains to be seen.

Korean Professor Yung Chul Park recently analysed the future of regionalism in East Asia into three scenarios.[32] The first is that China and Japan will work together in developing a common political will in East Asia, like the role of France and Germany in Europe's integration process. This is the co-partnership role that could open up a closer working relationship that would speed up the integration process. In this balanced role, South Korea and ASEAN would play the role of middlemen in the process.

The second scenario involves China taking on a more aggressive leadership role in regional integration. If China emerges as the region's engine of growth over the longer term, it could take the lead in the monetary and trade integration issues, particularly once the RMB becomes fully convertible, because the Chinese capital market may then play a dominant role in the Asian capital markets. It is, however, realistic to assume that, without Japan, cohesiveness of the grouping may not be that strong, because ASEAN may prefer that there is no dominant member in the grouping.

A third scenario is to widen the group to ASEAN+6, including Australia, New Zealand and India. The East Asian Summit of leaders is already beginning to explore the feasibility of this grouping. It is by no means clear who would emerge as a leader in this grouping, because both India and Australia also have strong views on the matter.

The fourth and perhaps the most realistic scenario is one of present muddling through. Former Japanese Prime Minister Yasuo Fukuda, whose father, former Prime Minister Takeo Fukuda, enunciated the Fukuda doctrine of Asia for Asians, generally improved policy dialogue in the region, particularly for Sino-Japan relations. He resigned in September 2008, throwing open once again not only the leadership in Japan, but also dialogue within the region. However, there remain many thorny issues that need resolution, such as North Korea and Myanmar, as well as energy and water conservation, environmental degradation, potential terrorism and social inequalities. All these could torpedo any effort to integrate or, if another crisis emerges, generate further forces for integration.

Pragmatically speaking, views supporting Asian financial and monetary integration are still limited to a small circle of intellectuals and policy thinkers. Moreover, even if more Asians sign off on this bold vision on

---

[32] Park (2007).

the longer term, the steps necessary to achieve concrete integration will require tremendous understanding, cooperation and patience amongst the key players.

In my mind, Asian integration is a force that will only accelerate in the near future. The reason is that financial crisis globally will change the global balance of power. We shall explore this in the rest of this book.

THIRTEEN

The New World of Financial Engineering

Derivatives are financial weapons of mass destruction, carrying dangers that, while now latent, are potentially lethal.

We view them as time bombs, both for the parties that deal in them and the economic system.

~*Warren Buffett*

Although the benefits and costs of derivatives remain the subject of spirited debate, the performance of the economy and the financial system in recent years suggests that those benefits have materially exceeded the costs.
~*Alan Greenspan*

Now that we have completed an overview of how the Asian crisis evolved and the individual country stories, we are ready to review how that crisis created the conditions for the present global financial crisis.

History is a river of memory that runs from many streams, sometimes calm and other times cataclysmic. Like a decision tree chart, events fan out from turning points in history, setting the conditions for the next event. The factors that led to the Asian crisis were also the key reasons for the current crisis: globalization, technology, financial innovation and deregulation, but the last two factors were critical in the latter crisis. The build-up of leverage and globalization of trade and financial services could not have happened without financial innovation in new institutions and derivative products that changed the financial landscape. All these became possible because of financial deregulation.

In hindsight, we could see signs of the present crisis emanating from the Asian crisis. The lethal brew of large capital flows, high market volatility, leverage and investment banks were all there during the Asian crisis. Surely the current banking crisis looks very much like the dot.com plus Enron failures of 2000–2001 writ large? There were the same trading of complex derivatives, bad corporate governance, poor accounting, SIVs and fraud.

We shall now look at the changes in the structure of the financial services industry and the profound evolution of financial derivatives. In the next chapter we shall scrutinize the philosophy, structure and processes of financial regulation that tragically allowed the current credit crisis to emerge.

CONVERGING NETWORKS

Seen from the perspective of networks, the Asian crisis was a regional network event, a traditional banking cum currency crisis. But the crisis that erupted in 2007 was of a different order in terms of size and complexity. The reason is that the Western financial system had evolved through financial engineering into a more complex, interconnected network, which was supposed to disperse risks but ended up returning them to the commercial banks and bringing them down with a vengeance.

In 1933 the U.S. Congress concluded that mixing business, banking and securities was bad business. The Glass-Steagall Act first segregated commercial banking from securities business and prevented bank management from lending to businesses that they controlled. For example, JP Morgan & Co. spun off its investment banking arm into Morgan Stanley. The Act also created the Federal Deposit Insurance Corporation (FDIC) that guaranteed retail deposits, thus stopping the bank run against the smaller banks. In network terms Glass-Steagall set up firewalls between networks to prevent contagion between them. Repeal of the act in 1999 set the stage for complete network integration and therefore massive contagion.

But over the years, the network effect of economies of scale was such that the financial industry became more and more concentrated over time, with periodic financial crises eliminating smaller and weaker institutions. The main driver for consolidation, of course, was the high costs of technology for service delivery and specialist people skills, as well as the drive for capital efficiency. For example, from 1984 to 2003, FDIC data showed that the number of U.S. banks and deposit-taking institutions dropped by half from 15,084 to 7,842, with the exit of smaller institutions. The largest banks are also gaining more market share. At the end of 1999, the 50 largest bank holding companies in the United States accounted for 68 percent of all commercial bank assets, compared with 55 percent in 1990. This trend has been replicated all over the world. The Asian crisis eliminated many small financial institutions, and the remaining banks were merged into a smaller number of larger institutions.

The financial integration was not only horizontal (mergers of the same type of institutions) but also a vertical conglomeration of banking, securities, insurance and fund management businesses. Clustering economies of scale were achieved through merging and linking with other networks and offering different products and services by sharing common standards and common platforms. As a result of this, banks, insurance companies, securities broker-dealers and fund managers began to compete in each other's businesses. They increased their footprint domestically and globally. Everyone sought to become the global financial WalMart.

In one sense Karl Marx was correct to predict that the declining profits of traditional markets would cause capitalism to move to new markets through innovation. Banking interest rate spreads and profit margins declined relentlessly because of intense competition. For example, net interest rate margins for U.S. banks fell from 4 percent in 1990 to 3.4 percent in 2007, and the manufacturing and distribution fees in the mutual fund business fell over the same period from 183 basis points to 107 basis points.[1] Wall Street commissions declined from roughly one-third of revenue in the 1980s to 11 percent in 2007. Over the same period underwriting profits also declined from 12 percent to just over 5 percent. The combination of higher liquidity and 'chase for yield' drove risk spreads down, with spreads of junk bonds falling from 23 percentage points in October 2002 to four percentage points in June 2007. Over the same period risk spreads of emerging market bonds fell from 10 to less than two percentage points, clearly not reflecting true risks in the markets.

In the face of such competitive threats, the larger Western banks began to lend to emerging sovereign countries in search of better yield. In the late 1970s, then Citibank Chairman Walter Wriston was reputed to assert that 'countries can't go bankrupt'. Exposure to Latin American sovereign debt nearly brought some of these banks to failure in the late 1980s. Citibank under his successor John Reed then moved into consumer banking with great success, particularly in emerging markets.

All these factors drove the trend for financial conglomeration, with the Dutch taking the first steps to merge insurance companies and banks in 1991, when the Nationale-Nederlanden insurance group merged with the NMB Postbank Group to form ING. In 2000 the German Allianz insurance group bought into asset manager PIMCO and then Dresdner Bank. In 2001 Citigroup was formed from the merger of Citibank with the insurance company Travellers Group. Large commercial banks bought up investment banks

---

[1] Data compiled by McKinsey for Sheng (2008c).

or fund managers. Deutschebank bought up Morgan Grenfell and Banker's Trust. UBS was formed from the merger of Union Bank of Switzerland and Swiss Banking Corporation and had earlier absorbed investment banks SG Warburg, Dillon Read and Paine Webber. AIG also diversified into innovative financial products in 1987.

In 1999 pressure to follow the universal bank model led to the repeal of the Glass-Steagall Act by the Gramm-Leach-Bliley Act in the United States. Thereafter, there evolved four separate models of global financial services integration: the pure Glass-Steagall separation of banking from insurance, securities and asset management that still prevails in many emerging markets; the European Universal Bank, which could do all four types of business within the universal bank; the U.K. bank (holding) company with separate legal subsidiaries in insurance and other areas; and the financial holding company with separate banking, insurance, asset management and securities subsidiaries.

The advantages and disadvantages of financial services integration are fairly clear. On the plus side were economies of scale, capital efficiency and the concept of a financial supermarket that offered customers the whole range of financial services. On the minus side, there were conflicts of interest between the universal bank and its clients, and the risks of connected lending and contagion between the various businesses.

In essence, there was not only network integration, but also product integration and platform integration, as financial services became not just national, but regional and global in scale.

THE EMERGENCE OF FINANCIAL ENGINEERING

The drive towards large financial conglomerates was helped by the rise of financial engineering to meet the needs of portfolio investment and risk management. In the 1970s a number of financial engineers emerged, drawing from scientists and physicists who applied their technical and statistical skills to financial markets. They built on the powerful theoretical portfolio management models of Harry Markowitz, the Sharpe capital asset pricing model and the Black-Scholes and Robert Merton option pricing models to use in trading in markets. Very soon the first trading of financial futures and options began on the Chicago Mercantile Exchange and Chicago Board of Trade.

Using super-fast computers and global networks, the quantitative traders (or quants) were able to evolve dynamic trading strategies that traded faster and much more nimbly than traditional buy-and-hold retail investors or conservative pension fund managers. Computerized trading made possible automatic trading that build in stop losses and momentum trading, because computers pick up market trends faster than human traders. The 1987 stock market crash, when the Dow Index lost 22.6 percent on 19 October, was partly blamed on computerized trading. Quant traders also hedge their risks so that they can not only engage on complex long-short strategies, but also use proxy hedges and structured products to diversify their risks.

By the early 1990s a new generation of financial engineers and asset managers had spawned the hedge fund industry, drawing on their quantitative skills and working closely with investment banks and large commercial banks as their prime brokers. Today there are an estimated 9,000 hedge funds managing an estimated US$2 trillion in assets, compared with less than US$200 billion in 1999. Hedge funds arbitrage in a wide variety of markets, from equities, bonds, foreign exchange, commodities, real estate investment trusts and, of course, the derivative markets.

A fundamental condition for dynamic trading and use of quant technology is low transaction costs. This was made possible with brokerage fee deregulation in the 1990s and reduced fees and taxes by financial centres and exchanges to attract liquidity. However, the largest cost expense remained funding costs. Hence, the real boost to hedge funds and quantitative trading occurred with the carry trade, especially when the yen borrowing costs were reduced to almost zero in the 1990s. The supply of almost interest-free funding was effectively to subsidize the rise of financial engineering. The success of such carry trades was then applied and magnified through leverage and derivatives, a hallmark of the new investment banking and hedge fund class.

In Chapter 2 it was estimated that during the Asian crisis the yen carry trade was around $200–350 billion. By 2007 it was estimated that the global carry trade had risen to US$2 trillion, of which half is probably the yen carry trade. The estimate was based on net foreign banking assets of funding countries and net foreign banking liabilities of recipient countries.[2] The most visible yen carry trade is the yen–Australian dollar carry, which has given a spread of over 6 percent per annum for the investor. Today investors monitor the increase and reversal of carry trades to determine the ebb and flow of global financial trading.

But quants are not limited to hedge funds or investment banks. Increasingly, even conventional asset managers, pension funds and corporations have begun to use quantitative tools and derivatives to hedge

---

[2] Tim Lee (2008).

their risks. Hedging risks, of course, depended on good quality information, the use of derivative instruments and good risk management skills. As quant trading gathered momentum, it contributed significantly to market turnover as well as volatility. By 2007 it was estimated that quant trading accounted for as much as 70 percent of volume in New York and London markets and between 40–50 percent in Tokyo and other Far East markets.

The network effects of highly dynamic markets are such that only large financial institutions with specialist skills and computer technology were the winners. Between 2001 and 2007, 15 of the world's largest banks and investment banks (called large complex financial institutions or LCFIs)[3] accounted for more than two-thirds of transactions in financial derivatives. Between 2001 and 2007 these 15 LCFIs tripled their balance sheets and increased their leverage markedly. The true scale of their trading was even more dominant if one considered that many hedge funds comprised former staff of these LCFIs, which also acted as their prime brokers.

To sum up, the search for yield enabled the U.S. and European banking systems to evolve from their traditional retail-banking model (accept deposit and lend) to a new wholesale banking 'originate to distribute' model. Using the asset securitization and distributing such asset-based securities, the banks freed themselves from the constraints of limited domestic savings and could draw on global savings. They found their new pot of gold.

Unlike the 1997–1998 Asian crisis, which was essentially a traditional retail banking crisis together with a currency crisis, the present crisis was truly a wholesale banking crisis with huge derivative amplification effects. Because the Asian crisis was still a crisis at the periphery, its network effect was limited. But the present crisis is a crisis at the centre of global finance, and its amplification effect was therefore significantly larger and deeper.

To understand how the micro- fused with the macro-environment to create the crisis, we need to understand what the financial engineers did with the derivatives, coupled with what evolved in the financial industry as a whole. New securitized products were tailored to suit investor needs. All these pushed the banking system into higher and higher levels of leverage.

EXCESSIVE LEVERAGE – THE ACHILLES HEEL
OF FINANCIAL SYSTEMS

Rising leverage is a phenomenon of the 20th century. Under the twin trends of liberalization and financial/communications innovation, global financial

---

[3]   According to Bank of England, the 15 are 3 U.S. banks, 4 U.S. investment banks, 3 U.K. banks, 2 Swiss banks, 1 German, 1 French and 1 Belgium bank.

assets have grown nearly four times from 109 percent of global GDP in 1980 to 421 percent in 2007.[4] The IMF estimated that as of 2007, the total value of global financial assets, comprising banking assets, stock market capitalization and bond market value, amounted to US$230 trillion, four times the size of global GDP of US$55 trillion in 2007 (Table 13.1). In contrast, the total notional value of global derivatives amounted to US$596 trillion or roughly 11 times world GDP and 2.6 times the size of underlying financial assets.[5] Although the estimated gross market value[6] of derivatives is considerably smaller at US$14.5 trillion or 27 percent of global GDP, there is no doubt that the level of embedded leverage in derivative products has helped increase the liquidity in global markets.

The relationship between the conventional financial assets, such as bonds, equity and bank assets and financial derivatives, can be seen from Figure 13.1, constructed by David Roche (2006, 2007). He suggested that world liquidity is like an inverted pyramid that has grown exponentially, with derivatives accounting of 80 percent of liquidity. By defining traditional liquidity as high-powered money and broad money, he observed that since 1990 the proportion of traditional liquidity has been almost halved from 13.6 percent of total securitized debt and derivatives to 7.1 percent by 2006.

How Dangerous Are These Levels of Leverage?

In January 1999 Fed Chairman Greenspan, SEC Chairman Arthur Levitt and U.S. Treasury Secretary Robert Rubin endorsed the creation of a private Counterparty Risk Management Policy Group (CRMPG) formed by 12 internationally active commercial and investment banks. Goldman Sachs Managing Director E. Gerald Corrigan, former New York Fed President and one of the most eminent thinkers on market risk issues, chaired the Group. In its first report (CRMPG I), the Group made excellent suggestions as to improving transparency, credit practices, harmonization of standards and overall improvement of risk management. This focused on largely what the large commercial and investment banks should do to improve their own counterparty risk management practices.

Even in this first report, the complexity of defining and measuring leverage became evident. All these stemmed from the difficulties of standard

---

[4] 1980 estimate from Farrell, Key and Shavers (2005), 70.

[5] Calculated from data in IMF (2008), tables 3 and 4, 181 and 182.

[6] Calculated as the sum of the total gross positive market value of contracts and gross negative market value of contracts.

Table 13.1. *Global Financial Assets, 2007 (US$ Trillion unless Noted Otherwise)*

Region	GDP	Total Reserves (Excluding Gold)	Stock Market Cap	Debt Market	Bank Assets	Total Financial Assets	Total Financial Assets (% of GDP)	Total Financial Assets (% of World Total)
World	54.5	6.4	65.1	79.8	84.8	229.7	421.1	100.0
European Union	15.7	0.3	14.7	28.2	43.2	86.1	548.8	37.5
United States	13.8	0.1	19.9	29.9	11.2	61.0	441.8	26.6
Japan	4.4	1.0	4.7	9.2	7.8	21.7	495.7	9.5
Asia including Middle East	9.0	3.3	15.1	4.6	10.6	30.3	336.7	13.2
Rest of the world	11.6	1.7	10.7	7.9	12.0	30.6	263.8	13.3
Memo item								
Asia including Japan	13.4	4.0	19.8	13.8	18.4	52.0	388.0	22.6

Source: IMF (2008)

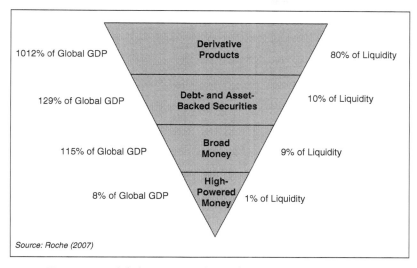

Figure 13.1. Global Leverage and Liquidity – The Unstable Pyramid

measures of market and liquidity risks. Given the considerable judgement and experience required to measure and assess such risks, the industry pushed for individual banks to adopt their own proprietary models, rather than accept any industry or regulatory-mandated models. This was at the heart of the problem of fallacy of composition, because every market participant would have their own perspective of what risks were, whilst the regulators could only take on trust that they knew what they were doing. The financial regulators had no standard to judge whether systemic leverage or individual institutional leverage was overstretched or not. By not digging further, the regulators were essentially taking financial stability on faith, rather than doing proper due diligence.

In 2005 the reconvened Counterparty Risk Management Policy Group (CRMPG II) studied the evolution of markets since 1999 and warned that the new financial products are complex and overall leverage of counterparties is difficult to monitor:

The market shift from a more qualitative and fundamental investment approach to a more quantitative, technical, model-driven approach has contributed to significantly higher overall trading volumes and shorter reaction periods, and has in turn contributed to the proliferation of new products, including CDS and numerous varieties of complex products. The design of these products allows risks to be divided and dispersed among counterparties in new ways, often with embedded leverage. Transparency as to where and in what form risks are being distributed among industry participants may be lost, as risks are fragmented and dispersed more widely. Associated hedging activities, especially with respect to the structured CDS market, tend to amplify liquidity measures.[7]

The problem is that even though the notional value of derivatives does not imply that all of it is leveraged, there is a considerable element of embedded leverage in many derivatives that can impact on the liquidity of the holders very fast. Derivatives are traded based on lines of credit provided by issuers or prime brokers to the buyer or investor. Moreover, the fact that traditionally nonleveraged mutual funds and pension funds have begun to buy hedging instruments to manage their portfolio risks means that they have also become leveraged, although not to the extent of risk traders. For example, if a pension fund or mutual fund adopts a 130/30 position neutral strategy (130 percent long and 30 percent short), both sides of the balance sheet are increased by 30 percent leverage.

The cumulative consequence of higher leverage (part of which is for hedging purposes) is that whenever such risk holders decide that they would sell off their derivative assets or hedges to reduce their exposure (through legitimate stop-loss trades), the reversal of derivative leverage can happen very fast and reduce liquidity substantially. This is known in the business as the 'crowded trade', as everyone rushes for the exit.

Thus, a fundamental problem with the world of financial derivatives is that neither regulators nor market participants have a good handle on how much true leverage exists in the system and consequently how much capital is necessary. The embedded leverage in many derivative products magnified the impact on market volatility.

Five elements of financial innovation and deregulation plus one black hole in regulation came together to create the toxic products that were at the root of the current crisis:

- The first was plain vanilla residential mortgages that were securitized into mortgage or asset backed securities (ABS) by government mortgage institutions such as Fannie Mae and Freddie Mac. Securitization meant that assets could be moved off-balance sheet into unregulated special investment vehicles (SIVs) that did not require capital.
- The second was to slice the mortgages into different tranches of credit quality, collateralizing each tranche with various guarantees or assets,

---

[7] CRMPG II (2005), 44.

to form 'structured' collateralized debt obligations (CDOs) that had AAA credit ratings.

- The third was that accounting and regulatory standards permitted such potential liabilities to be moved off the balance sheet so that the banks benefited from 'capital efficiency', meaning that leverage could increase using the same level of capital.
- The fourth was the use of insurance companies and the newly evolved credit default swap (CDS) markets to enhance credit quality of the underlying paper. If the underlying assets looked weak, the purchase of credit default swaps sold by triple A insurers such as AIG enhanced their credit quality.
- The fifth sweetener was the willingness of the credit rating agencies to give these structured products AAA ratings, for a fee.

The ABS market was central to the transformation of the banking sector from a 'lend/buy and hold' to 'originate-to-distribute'. Through this new business model, the banks gained capital efficiency, off-loaded assets and earned high origination fees, as well as income from proprietary trading. By taking origination fees up front, investment banks, rating agencies and mortgage originators made huge profits without anyone regulating the origination process.

The theory was that credit risks were transferred to holders of such ABS, such as pension funds, insurance companies, mutual funds and hedge funds and even retail customers. What these investors did not realize that these products carried embedded leverage that could unravel under certain circumstances.

In order to sell the CDOs and ensure their liquidity, the originating banks offered a 'conduit' or 'liquidity puts' that in effect provided the investors the right to sell them back to the bank if there was no market for such CDOs.

The CDOs looked attractive because they carried not only AAA ratings, but one could also hedge against the underlying paper by buying insurance from mono-line insurers or CDSs, again sold by the investment banks or insurance companies. Such CDSs underwrote the credit quality as a side bet. If the CDO failed for whatever reason, the buyer of the CDS collected from the seller.

Unfortunately, investors withdrew when doubts arose on the quality of the CDOs, banks had to buy these toxic assets back and valuations failed, causing a massive liquidity crunch for the banking system. The credit rating agencies did not help by downgrading such paper from AAA to junk status overnight.

If anyone wants an unexpurgated explanation of how the whole system worked, read Michael Lewis of *Liar's Poker* fame, who interviewed market participants on their views: 'What I learned from that experience was that Wall Street didn't give a s**t what it sold.'[8] As a financial regulator, I kicked myself that I had missed reading another insider account of the way investment banks unscrupulously packaged and sold derivatives to investors as early as the mid-1990s.[9] Since it was published in 1998, I was by then too preoccupied with the Asian crisis. These books should be compulsory reading for all business school graduates.

It looked too good to be true, even to the regulators, but they were assured when the market kept on growing. Time and again, Greenspan and others commented on the potential risks, but at the same time they remarked that risks were being distributed outside the banking system.

This 'black hole' in regulation was in practice the over-the-counter (OTC) market that originated from bilateral transactions between banks and their clients. The largest and most successful OTC market is the foreign exchange market. The advantage of the OTC market is that it is opaque to outsiders, including the regulators, but if the product is well understood, it can be a highly liquid market.

Derivatives in foreign exchange and interest rate derivatives were supported by central banks because it was thought that their evolution would enhance their monetary policy instruments, as well as enable the banks and their clients to hedge their market risks. That protection was so strong that even when Hong Kong, South Africa, Malaysia and others protested during the Asian financial crises that illiquid foreign exchange markets in emerging markets were often manipulated, these charges were dismissed. Too much vested interests were at stake. Emerging market supervisors were too weak to change this bastion of nonregulation, because the winners of superior financial innovation were Western banks.

This 'originate to distribute' banking model, plus the OTC market, formed what PIMCO fund manager Bill Gross[10] called a 'shadow banking' system (Figure 13.2). New York Fed President Tim Geithner[11] estimated that this dynamic 'shadow banking' system could be as large as US$10.5 trillion, comprising US$4 trillion assets of the large investment banks, US$2.5 trillion in overnight repos, US$2.2 trillion for SIVs and another US$1.8 trillion

---

[8]   Lewis (2008), 3.
[9]   Partnoy (1997).
[10] Gross (2008). In the film Jimmy Stewart saved his bank from a bank run because it was better capitalized than most banks today.
[11] Geithner (2008) actually called it a nonbank or parallel system.

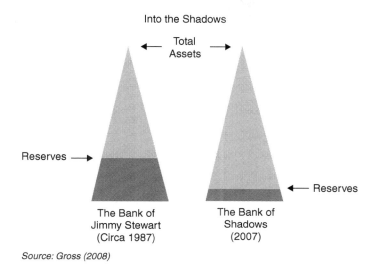

Figure 13.2. The Shadow Banking System: Securitizing and Moving Liabilities Off Balance Sheet, 1987 and 2007

in hedge fund assets. This compared with US$10 trillion in assets with the conventional U.S. banking system.

The shadow banking system is dangerous for two reasons. First, there was no way that any financial regulator could claim with a straight face to maintain financial stability when half the assets of the system were outside his purview and he had no knowledge and understanding what was going on inside. Second, the incentive structure was such that market participants would clearly prefer to move all trading away from regulation into the shadow area, which gave ample opportunity for fraud and other gray trading.

Why this was allowed was because the industry was making too much money and regulators may have found it too difficult to stir up a hornet's nest of vested interests defended by lobbyists and legislators. After all, many regulators also found lucrative jobs within the industry after they stepped down.

Throughout the last decade, central bankers would marvel at the phenomenal growth of the financial derivative markets. By December 2007 BIS data showed that the notional value of derivative markets had reached US$596 trillion. About two-thirds of this was relatively simple interest-rate derivatives, but nearly US$58 trillion was the rapidly growing CDS market.

The exchange-traded derivatives were US\$95 trillion in size. Together, these financial derivatives were 14 times global GDP, whereas conventional financial assets, comprising bonds, equities and bank assets were only four times GDP. Market traders reassured everyone that the gross market value of such derivatives were actually much smaller, being US\$14.5 trillion for the OTC derivatives.[12]

What the traders did not tell people is that although there is some bilateral netting between market participants, the bulk of the transactions remain on a gross basis, because there was no central clearing house to monitor and clear on a net basis, like an equity clearing house. Gross derivatives clearing and settlement (except where bilateral netting apply) could function only if the wholesale market remained highly liquid.

Because these markets are mostly bilateral trades, the OTC market works on a sophisticated and complex system of margin or collateral management. For each derivative trade, the primary dealer calls for margin, collateral and haircuts from the counterparty to protect itself from credit or market risks. In a rising market when risk spreads and volatility are narrowing, less and less collateral is required, thus pro-cyclically increasing liquidity. In other words, liquidity begets liquidity, a classic network effect.

Unfortunately, it also works the other way pro-cyclically, so that if volatility increases, the need to call margin and sell assets to realize liquidity would immediately worsen liquidity. This is because the counterparty would have to sell assets quickly to meet margin calls. Very likely, his best assets were already collateralized with the prime broker. Hence, any selling of secondary and illiquid assets would widen risk spreads, forcing further margin calls. As more and more selling occurs, the mark-to-market accounting of such collateral paper creates losses for the holders of such paper.

Since rating agencies monitored the CDS premia and risk spreads for indications of possible default, such widening could also result in a credit downgrading. Such downgrading would widen spreads more, forcing more selling or stop-loss action. More collateral would be called. This was experienced by LTCM in 1998, when it did not have enough liquid assets to meet margin calls. Any stop-loss selling of margin collateral at the highest point of volatility by its counterparties would immediately precipitate insolvency for LTCM. But this was not immediately transparent to other market players because no single player is fully aware of market positions in an OTC market. There is no single regulator or clearinghouse to monitor

---

[12] Bank of England (2008), Box 2: Counterparty credit risks in OTC-derivative markets.

counterparty positions. The opacity of the OTC market is both its strength as well as its Achilles' heel.

The reality was that instead of widely distributing derivative risks outside the banking system, much of the risks were concentrated within the banking system. According to BIS statistics, only 19 percent of OTC trades were with nonfinancial customers. In the CDS market 2006 British Bankers' Association data reported that the banks were 16 percent net buyers of CDS 'protection', whereas the net protection sellers comprised insurance companies 11 percent, hedge funds 3 percent and pension funds 2 percent. Since hedge funds were never risk holders, they would sell their risks back to the primary dealer at the first sign of trouble.

We now know that the shadow banking system grossly disguised the true level of leverage, grossly underestimated the liquidity required to support the market, grossly misunderstood the network interconnections in the global markets and enabled the key players to overtrade with grossly inadequate capital. For example, at the end of 2007 the five U.S. investment banks had total assets of US$4.3 trillion, but only equity of US$200.3 billion or a leverage of 21.3 times. However, together they had notional off-balance liabilities of US$17.8 trillion, implying further leverage of 88.8 times.

But, of course, they were allowed in 2004 by an SEC rule change to exempt their net capital caps of 15 times to value their derivatives according to their own sophisticated risk models, thereby opening up the leverage limit. In practice, perhaps only management fully understood their true leverage, because Bear Stearns had to be rescued despite the SEC Chairman protesting that it had capital adequacy even at the eleventh hour.

THE ILLUSION OF LIQUIDITY

Is the current crisis a liquidity crisis or solvency crisis? When the world was flush with liquidity, many forgot Keynes's insight that liquidity of the market as a whole may be ephemeral:

Of the maxims of orthodox finance none, surely, is more anti-social than the *fetish of liquidity*, the doctrine that it is a positive virtue on the part of investment institutions to concentrate their resources upon the holding of 'liquid' securities. *It forgets that there is no such thing as liquidity of investment for the community as a whole.* The social object of skilled investment should be to defeat the dark forces of time and ignorance which envelop our future. The actual, private object of the most skilled investment today is 'to beat the gun', as the Americans so well express it, to outwit the crowd, and to pass the bad, or depreciating, half-crown to the other fellow. (italics added)

Keynes understood that in complex markets, liquidity and valuation are subject to expectations that could change rapidly: 'A conventional valuation which is established as the outcome of the mass psychology of a large number of ignorant individuals is liable to change violently as the result of a sudden fluctuation of opinion due to factors which do not really make much difference to the prospective yield; since there will be no strong roots of conviction to hold it steady'.[13] It is the confidence in near term stability that make investments 'liquid' for the individual player, but changes in expectations can wipe out market liquidity very rapidly.

Was the excess liquidity of 2003–2006 due to market confidence, or the mistaken belief by market players that a Central Bank Put and Lender of Last Resort (LOLR) facility existed to bail investors out of their mistakes? In other words, the liquidity and leverage musical chairs can continue, as long as the market thinks, rightly or wrongly, that the central bank is there to pick up the tab when the music stops. As Professor Charles Goodhart[14] pointed out, bank liquid assets have moved from roughly 30 percent of total assets for British banks in the 1950s to current levels of 1 percent. He asked critically, 'Why should the banks bother with liquidity management when the Central Bank will do all that for them? The banks have been taking out a liquidity "put" on the Central Bank; they are in effect putting the downside of liquidity risk to the Central Bank'.

The imprecise definition of liquidity has caused some of the current confusion. Liquidity is not easy to define both conceptually and operationally. There are in fact two types of liquidity: asset liquidity, which is the ability to sell an asset easily without major loss, and funding liquidity, which is the ability to borrow funds easily without paying excessive interest rates. Both are contingent on the sentiment of the market, because buyers or borrowers may not be willing to pay or lend when markets get into highly volatile conditions. To make matters even more confusing, 'liquidity' in monetary economics sometimes refers to high-powered money.

Whatever the choice of definition, liquidity is an attribute that cannot be divorced from asset valuation, leverage and risks. Former United Bank of Switzerland (UBS) Risk Manager and a member of the CRMPG I, Robert Gumerlock, insightfully pointed out in his 2000 monograph that prices, valuation, capital and leverage are all relative and interrelated, depending on context and timing. In times of crisis, when market prices fluctuate wildly, what is fair value? The normal definition is that fair value is the price

---

[13] Keynes (1942) [1936], 154.
[14] Goodhart (2007).

between two willing parties under normal circumstances. In the ordinary course of events, asset liquidity or price is determined between one willing party and one neutral party. On the other hand, in a crisis event, price and liquidity is determined between one desperate party and one unwilling party. Consequently, to define fair value as 'mid-market' or 'price between two willing parties' systematically overstates true worth.

Moreover, from the funding view of liquidity, 'one measure of the liquidity of a financial instrument is to ask how much a creditor would be willing to lend against it. But an instrument's worth as collateral is intimately tied to its current valuation, and to the extent that valuation of collateral is increasingly tied to market prices, the stability of "collateralizing" financing is brought into question, particularly in moments of crisis when market prices are either not available or fluctuating wildly'.[15] Consequently, as discovered by Northern Rock, 'forced liquidation in a predator market virtually guarantees insolvency'.

So what is fair value? The Financial Accounting Standards Board (FASB) definition of fair value is 'an estimate of the price that could be received for an asset or paid to settle a liability in a current transaction between marketplace participants in the reference market for the asset or liability'. But in a crisis, all types of valuation may be questionable. If we have to use model valuation, and market prices diverge from model valuations, are fair values better represented by a mark-to-market or mark-to-model? If mark-to-model, which model should be used?

In other words, can fair value or model value be divorced from the risk profile of the borrower, because if we use the lowest available market price, the borrower may be insolvent? Gumerlock rightly pointed out that liquidity depends on the behaviour of market participants in a crisis event, and it could easily disappear in a crisis, because risks become impossible to measure, as prices would depend on the uncertain behaviour of counterparties.

After Northern Rock, the UK Financial Services Authority (FSA) issued a consultation paper that defined liquidity risk as 'risk that a firm, although balance-sheet solvent, cannot maintain or generate sufficient cash resources to meet its payment obligations in full as they fall due, or can only do so at materially disadvantageous terms'.[16] The trouble with this definition operationally is that the firm would have to maintain two sets of liquidity, one for normal conditions and one for 'tail events'. The two are not necessarily

---

[15] Gumerlock (2000).
[16] UK Financial Services Authority (2007), 8.

compatible in an environment in which the firms are trying to maximize capital efficiency.

The conundrum is that commercial banks are supposed to be first-line liquidity providers, but they have pushed their risk-return envelop to the limit by overrelying on central bank lender of last resort facilities. To remain as liquidity providers, they would need much higher levels of capital. We have an odd situation whereby in a world of abundant savings, we have banks that are illiquid because banks did not trust each other's solvency.

What Gumerlock and other experienced risk managers have observed is there are two sets of market conditions. Under normal market conditions, the first-order approximation of any market attribute, such as price, volatility, risk or liquidity, can be stable for it to be relatively distinct and measurable. However, in extreme market conditions, risk, liquidity and leverage become so interconnected that they are both unstable and immeasurable (at least by present models). In other words, under normal market conditions, we can differentiate between credit risk, market risk and liquidity risk, and measure and hedge such risks using statistical tools. However, under extreme market conditions, these risks become inseparable and immeasurable, so the only alternative is to exit at any price, and the devil takes the hindmost.

In short, financial engineering had built a market that was either a sandcastle or a Ponzi scheme. It could succeed only if prices continually went up or there were fresh investors to bring liquidity to the market. The minute sentiment turned, the system collapsed. To understand this, we need to go back to another Keynesian disciple, Hyman Minsky.

MINSKY FINANCIAL INSTABILITY HYPOTHESIS: 'STABILITY IS DESTABILIZING'

Minsky's Financial Instability Hypothesis holds that over a run of good times the financial structure evolves from being robust to being fragile. This hypothesis rests on the profitability of debt financing, given the term and risk class structures of interest rates in a robust financial structure and the way asset values can collapse whenever speculative and Ponzi financing units are forced to 'make position by selling out positions'.[17]

In other words, prolonged stability of values of risks, liquidity and prices may lull market participants into higher and higher levels of leverage until the system becomes completely unstable.

[17] Minsky (1992), 22–23.

For those economists who follow the more recent work of econophysicists and financial market modelling,[18] financial markets are seen as dynamic, evolving, adaptive ecosystems that go through periodic periods of instability, rather than mean-reverting, stable systems that go back to equilibrium. J. Doyne Farmer's pioneering study on agent-based modelling of financial markets suggests that Minsky's dictum 'stability is de-stabilizing' may be true. Using four types of agents, value investors, technical traders, liquidity traders and market makers, Farmer modelled the financial market using traditional economic assumptions such as random-walk behaviour.[19] By repeating the agent-based behaviour over a long period of time, he discovered that, initially, the market behaviour was as predicted by traditional economics. Prices converged and bid-ask spreads narrowed.

At some point in time, when the market became very stable, traders began to make larger and larger trades and bets, and

[the] market looked as if it were rapidly approaching perfect efficiency. But then, volatility suddenly exploded, and prices began to move chaotically. What had happened was this: as the technical traders became richer, their trades became larger, and the large trades started introducing their own movements into the price. These movements created opportunities for other technical traders to try to arbitrage the patterns created by their fellow technical traders – when the technical traders had finished lunching on the seasonal traders, they began feeding off each other![20]

Farmer's modelling results seem to ring a bell with what has happened in global markets since 2004–2005, when global credit risk and bond/equity spreads narrowed and volatility went down. Central bankers and regulators worldwide attributed this to the success of financial innovation to spread risks, forgetting that risks were in fact building up as quants started increasing their bets using leverage.

Khandani and Lo recently examined the implications of collective quant trading behaviour.[21] They examined the events of the week of 6 August 2007, when a number of quantitative long/short equity hedge funds experienced unprecedented losses. They hypothesized that the losses were initiated by the rapid unwinding of one or more sizeable portfolios, which caused larger and larger market movements, which suggested that systemic risk in the hedge fund industry might have increased in recent years. This suggests that the impact of quant trading feeding off each other into

---

[18]   This section is drawn largely from the work of Beinhocker (2006).
[19]   Farmer (2001).
[20]   Beinhocker (2006), 397.
[21]   Khandani and Lo (2007).

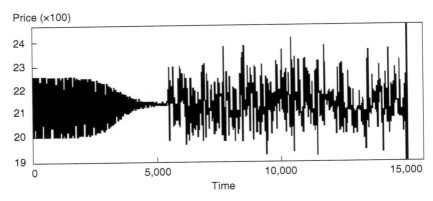

Price (×100)

Source: Farmer (2001)

Figure 13.3. Modelling of Financial Markets: Agent-Based Behaviour

larger and larger trades may have created volatile trade unwinds that have systemic implications. This fits neatly into the market pattern predicted by Farmer and the Minsky hypothesis that (prolonged) stability is destabilizing (Figure 13.3).

HOW DID THE MARKET MISS THESE RISKS?

But between 1999 and 2007, the derivative markets continued to grow at an exponential rate, especially the appearance of credit risk transfer instruments, notably the CDSs. The CDS market allows investors to bet on the chance of a debt default or protect themselves from that risk, without any understanding of the true credit risks. The protection buyer pays an annual fee to the seller with the promise that that they will be compensated in a default. The notional value of outstanding contracts in CDSs could be substantially larger than the underlying debt contract.

Proponents of the CDS market, such as the International Swaps and Derivatives Association (ISDA), which issues the contract that defines these products, argue that the market enables the pricing of credit risks and therefore its transfer to long-term holders. Critics of the derivative argue that the CDS market encourages lenders to exercise less credit discipline and due diligence because they feel comforted by the CDS protection. They also feel that because the CDS market is unregulated, it hides the true level of credit risk from the market.

In 2003 the BIS Committee on Payment and Settlement Systems commissioned a study on credit risk transfer and, indeed, pointed out that there were issues with transparency, lack of aggregate data, the role of rating agencies, diversification and concentration, contract design, risk management, accounting and their regulatory approach.

As a result of this report, the Financial Stability Forum asked the Joint Forum of banking, securities and insurance regulators to look at the credit transfer issue. The Joint Forum issued a report on credit risk transfer in March 2005. It noted that whilst there were benefits for market efficiency, there were urgent problems to be addressed in the risk management area by firms and regulators. The Report warned market participants that they need to understand the complex nature of the risks involved and 'not to rely solely on rating agency assessments'.[22]

Partly as response to market needs, the Counterparty Risk Management Policy Group II (CRMPG II) published a report in July 2005 entitled *Toward Greater Financial Stability: A Private Sector Perspective* that aimed at examining additional steps that the private sector could take to contribute towards global financial stability.[23] The Report noted that since 1999, the derivative markets had resiliently absorbed several stresses, such as the dot.com bubble and mild recession, 11 September, two wars and a wave of corporate scandals. The report presciently saw that very rare financial shocks could produce significant damage to the financial system and the real economy, and that the speed and complexity of unwinding could be worrisome. It worried about the 'perfect storm' and listed 10 fundamentals and potential points of vulnerabilities, the in-depth understanding of which could assist in the better anticipation of financial shocks and reduction of their severity. They are the following:

- 'First, credit risk, and in particular counterparty credit risk, is probably the single most important variable in determining whether and with what speed financial *disturbances* become financial *shocks* with potential systemic traits'.
- 'Second, the evaporation of market liquidity is probably the second most important variable in determining whether and at what speed financial disturbances become financial shocks with potentially systemic traits'.

---

[22] Joint Forum (2005).
[23] Counterparty Risk Management Policy Group II (2005).

- Third, the value of complex financial instruments, especially instruments having 'embedded leverage' can change rapidly 'even in a matter of hours or days'. 'The risk of rapidly changing prices can be of particular consequence with high complex instruments in an environment in which investor behaviour is influenced by the "reach for yield" phenomenon'.
- Fourth, the heavy reliance on complex proprietary models to value the many classes of financial instruments. The value of these instruments is difficult to determine even in normal circumstances. As such, 'the fact that many financial institutions use broadly similar analytical tools to model price changes in response to external events heightens the risk of precipitous price changes in the face of crowded trades. Because of this, final authority for valuations must be vested in a business unit that is fully independent of the revenue producing businesses'.
- Fifth, 'most statistically driven models and risk metrics such as value at risk (VaR) calculations fail to capture so called "tail events"'. 'As such, their use must be supplemented by a wide range of complementary risk management techniques such as stress tests and hybrid VaR measures that take into account market liquidity'.
- Sixth, 'the integrity and reliability of all elements of financial "infrastructure", including, for example, payments, settlement, netting and close out systems – as well as the smooth functioning of back offices, especially in times of stress – are critical risk mitigants and must be managed and funded accordingly'.
- Seventh, 'many classes of financial institutions including banks, investment banks and hedge funds now have sizeable investments in assets that are highly illiquid even in normal market conditions'.
- Eighth, the soundness of cost-benefit analysis of comprehensive risk and control-related functions of financial institutions, whereby 'if the operating costs of effective end-to-end risk management are seen as too high to bear, the logical conclusion may be that the risks are too great – a judgment that can only be made at the highest level of management'.
- Ninth, the restructuring process of troubled but viable companies and countries in the future may be more difficult due to the increasing use by primary creditors of the credit default swap market to dispose their credit exposure and who thus do not have as major a financial interest in the outcome of the restructuring as they used to in the past.
- Tenth, financial disturbances and even financial shocks will occur in the future, as no approaches to risk management or official supervision are fail-safe. Thus, it is necessary to preserve and strengthen the institutional arrangements whereby, at the point of crisis, industry groups and

industry leaders, as well as supervisors, are prepared to work together in order to serve the larger and shared goal of financial stability.

At the end of the day, the Report concluded, 'official oversight is not a substitute for the effective management of financial institutions, which is, and should remain, a private sector function. Yet here too there is a dilemma; namely, in a competitive marketplace it is very difficult for one or a few institutions to hold the line on best practices, much less for one or a few institutions to stand on the sidelines in the face of booming markets'.

Unfortunately, almost all the vulnerabilities identified came to pass in 2007–2008. The warnings were too late to stop the current global financial crisis. In December 2008 Alan Greenspan stated bluntly, 'global financial intermediation is broken'.[24]

We now need to turn to the issue why conventional risk management failed, despite advances in risk management in theory and practice.

THE CRISIS OF RISK MANAGEMENT

As described earlier, the whole world of financial engineering was based on the emergence of risk management as a science. Professor Avinash Persaud,[25] currently one of the most astute observers of the risk management game, commented aptly that many of the Markowitz models used for measuring and controlling risks (such as Value-at-Risk models) all made simplifying assumptions that when one sells or buys in a market, one is the only one doing so. In reality, one is buying with the herd and selling with the herd when everyone has more or less the same information or same models. In other words, *'far from diversifying risk, these tools will concentrate risk'*.

Moreover, the market assumes that risks could be shifted to long-term risk holders such as pension and insurance funds, who could hold the securitized debt. Unfortunately, hedge funds and short-term traders, who are risk traders and not risk absorbers, hold a considerable portion of ABS paper. As pension and insurance funds are also marked to market and are beginning to use the same quantitative investment models with hedging tools, they too behave with shorter time horizons. Thus, whenever price volatilities increase, everyone begins to sell the 'bad half-crown ABS' to stop loss, and their collective action adds to crowded trades, higher volatility and worsen market liquidity.

---

[24] Greenspan (2008b).
[25] Persaud (2007).

Persaud also pointed out that 'riskiness is *as much a characteristic of the investor, as the instrument*'. Current risk management models look more at the risk profile of instruments, and ignore the former.

The above defects of the current status of risk management and recommendations for correction were documented by the Institute of International Finance Report on the current crisis.[26] The Report firmly acknowledge that each firm should make clear that senior management, in particular the CEO, is responsible for risk management; the Board has an essential oversight role in risk management; and developing a risk culture that covers firm-wide activities. With respect to risk models and tools, the Report recommended that in a market environment that can produce unprecedented price moves, firms should do the following:

- Ensure that risk management does not rely on a single risk methodology, and analyze group-wide risks on an aggregate basis
- Ensure that metrics are calibrated appropriately to risk-appetite horizons
- Take into account the technical limitations of risk metrics, models, and techniques (such as Value-at-Risk, or 'VaR')
- Ensure that the appropriate governance structure that has been adopted is actually implemented in managing day-to-day activities.

Perhaps the best analysis of the failure of risk management was the confessions of an anonymous risk manager, published in *The Economist* in August 2008.[27] He acknowledged that 'no crisis comes completely out of the blue; there are always clues and advance warnings if you can only interpret them correctly'. In the area of CDOs, where risks were tranched, traders were deluded that the risks were in the non–investment-grade tranches, whereas when the CDO market collapsed, even prices of AAA tranches fell drastically. They 'made two assumptions which would cost us dearly. First, we thought that all mark-to-market positions in the trading book would receive immediate attention when losses occurred, because their profits were published daily. Second, we assumed that if the market ran into difficulties, we could easily adjust and liquidate our positions, especially on securities rated AAA and AA.'[28] Both assumptions proved false. They also made the mistake of trusting the rating agencies.

Surely self-interest should have been enough for bankers to manage their risks? As the above anonymous risk manager confessed, the pressure for

---

[26] Institute of International Finance (2008b).
[27] *The Economist* (2008b), 72–73.
[28] *The Economist* (2008b), 73.

risk managers to approve transactions was immense, because the business side, which was driven by huge bonuses, often leaned towards giving the benefit of the doubt to the risk takers. Through the drive for profits, the banks had built up a portfolio that appeared safe on the asset side and a liability structure that was unsustainable when liquidity disappeared. As Jacob Frenkel, Vice Chairman of AIG quipped, 'on the right hand side of the balance sheet, nothing looked right, and on the left hand side of the balance sheet, nothing was left'.

I did not fully appreciate the depth of greed until I read former Goldman Sachs and Morgan Stanley staff member Jonathan Knee's insider exposé of how investment bankers behave. He asked a profound question, 'Did greedy clients produce greedy bankers, or the opposite?'[29] Bankers are supposed to be giants of integrity, trust and fiduciary duty, fiercely guarding their professionalism for independent opinion and discretion. After the 1980s era of junk bonds and ruthless corporate raiders, the popular image of Wall Street bankers had deteriorated to the figure of Gordon Gecko, the unscrupulous smooth banker in the Hollywood movie *Wall Street*, who would stoop at nothing for a fast buck. Even the draconian Sarbanes-Oxley Act was not strong enough to stop the deterioration of banking values.

A senior Swiss banker who was remarkably objective provided the answer to me in private conversation. The reality of financial engineering, he said, is that investment bankers who were driven quarter by quarter to deliver improved financial results by investors had to create newer and newer products that allowed profits to be taken up front. If markets insisted that financial institutions deliver value in the form of higher and higher return on earnings (ROE), and huge bonuses were predicated on such delivery, are we surprised that investment bankers took short cuts, used every trick in the book, increased leverage, and ignored warning signals from risk managers in order to deliver what the market wanted? In taking proprietary positions, weren't investment bankers exploiting huge conflicts of interests? In the end, they even picked pennies in front of roller coasters.

In a bonfire of their own vanities, investment bankers burned their own reputations in the relentless search for profits.

In the next chapter, we have to look at how the current regulatory structure allowed the crisis to emerge.

---

[29] Knee (2006), xi.

FOURTEEN

What's Wrong with Financial Regulation?

Simply stated, the bright new financial system – for all its talented participants, for all its rich rewards – has failed the test of the market place.
~ Paul Volcker

The consistent complaint from the industry is that their supervisors do not adequately understand their business. And the consistent complaint from regulators is that senior management of financial institutions may not adequately understand the business for which they are responsible.
~ Martyn Hopper

What role did financial regulation play in this crisis?

I start by stating what I presume to be obvious: in today's democratic environment where the people expect governments to protect their savings, zero financial regulation is not an option. As FT columnist Martin Wolf shrewdly observed: 'The public, governments feel, must be protected from banks and banks must be protected from themselves. Finance is deemed far too important to be left to the market'.[1]

But financial regulation is not yet a science, even though much of it has been explained in economics that claims to be a science. When I first tackled the failure of deposit-taking cooperatives in Malaysia in the mid-1980s, the only book I could find of practical use in handling bank runs remained Walter Bagehot's *Lombard Street*. Even today, there are few books on financial regulation,[2] and it is scarcely taught in universities. Largely, it has been learnt on the job. Although there are now more books on bubbles and crises, a common theme running through them is the inadequacy of financial regulation that 'allowed' crises to happen.

[1] Wolf (2008a).
[2] Readers who are interested in good introductions to regulation should read Davies and Green (2008) and Barth, Caprio and Levine (2006).

If, however, financial regulators ever hope to regulate the markets, they must at least understand the nature of the beast, and they must understand themselves. As Chinese military strategist Sunzi said, 'Know your enemy and know yourself, a hundred battles will not be at risk.'[3]

The conventional definition of regulation[4] is government activity that is intended to affect directly the behaviour of private sector agents in order to align them with the 'public interest'. Since this chapter is written by an Asian financial regulator to explain crises, it may be easier for the reader to follow my conceptual approach that is summarized upfront as follows:

> The market is a social institution that is interactively shaped by individual and social behaviour. Every now and again the madness of crowds prevail. Financial regulation is necessary because enforcement of rules changes behaviour that harms society as a whole. As social change is a process, the conduct of financial regulation is also a process. To regulate effectively, you must understand the market, but also what you do not know, especially about yourself. The behaviour of regulators/policy makers and the market is reflexive.

Is the above so different from conventional wisdom? After working in China and delving into Chinese thinking about governance and regulation, I realized that there is a fundamental difference in approach. Western thinking uses a theoretical approach, seeking simplicity out of complexity. This is most helpful, but if the theory is wrong, huge policy mistakes can be made. Asian thinking takes complexity for granted, knowing that there is much that is not known or simply not knowable, and accordingly, moves forward in a search and experiment process. But this innate caution does not prepare them when the environment changes. Both approaches have their advantages and disadvantages. This chapter attempts to lay out a practical guide to think about the processes of regulation. But first, a quick survey of the conventional wisdom.

THREE PILLARS OF FINANCIAL STABILITY

As former BIS Economic Adviser William White perceptively pointed out, 'crisis prevention to date has largely been based on a bottom-up approach which tries to identify vulnerabilities with respect to each of the major pillars that make up the international financial system: financial institutions, markets and the supporting infrastructure.'[5] This approach is

---

[3] Author's translation.
[4] Chang (2003).
[5] White (2008).

a legacy from the institution-based regulation that was framed after the separation of commercial banking from the securities industry under the Glass-Steagall Act of 1933. The trouble is that despite profound changes in the financial industry, the regulatory structure worldwide remained largely institution based. It has the mindset of doctors rather than public health experts – as long as the health of individuals was fine, public health would be all right, forgetting that viral attacks could wipe out whole populations. We have to look at contagion from the perspective of interconnecting networks.

Out of the ashes of the Asian crisis, and in recognition of the multidimensional aspect of financial stability, the IMF and the World Bank embarked in 1999 on financial sector assessment programmes (FSAPs) for their members. The FSAPs[6] were the product of intensive cooperation between the Bretton Wood institutions, the BIS, international standard-setting bodies and national authorities. After nearly 10 years, nearly three-quarters of IMF and World Bank members have completed or requested FSAPs. It is notable that the United States, being at the centre of the current crisis, is not one of them.

The FSAPs start on the premise that 'the financial crises of the 1990s underscored the linkages between macroeconomic developments and financial system soundness. Indeed, weak financial institutions, inadequate bank regulation and supervision, and lack of transparency were at the heart of these crises'. The FSAP Handbook defines financial stability as

(a) 'An environment that would prevent a large number of financial institutions from becoming insolvent and failing; and

(b) Conditions that would avoid significant disruptions to the provision of key financial services such as deposits for savers, loans and securities to investors, liquidity and payment services to both, risk diversification and insurance services, monitoring of the users of funds, and shaping of the corporate governance of non-financial firms'.

Based on the above, the Bretton Wood institutions arrived at the view of Financial Stability as Three Pillars, comprising the following:

Pillar I – Macroprudential surveillance and financial stability analysis by the authorities to monitor the impact of potential macroeconomic and institutional factors (both domestic and external) on the soundness (risks and vulnerabilities) and stability of financial systems.

---

[6]   www.imf.org/external/np/fsap/fsap.asp.

Pillar II – Financial system supervision and regulation to help manage the risks and vulnerabilities, protect market integrity and provide incentives for strong risk management and good governance of financial institutions.

Pillar III – Financial system infrastructure:

- Legal infrastructure for finance, including insolvency regime, creditor rights, and financial safety nets
- Systemic liquidity infrastructure, including monetary and exchange operations, payments and securities settlement systems, and microstructure of money, exchange and securities markets
- Transparency, governance and information infrastructure, including monetary and financial policy transparency, corporate governance, accounting and auditing framework, disclosure regime and market monitoring arrangements for financial and nonfinancial firms and credit reporting systems.

All Three Pillars support financial stability at the institutional, national and global level. The FSAPs would review weaknesses in each of the Three Pillars and make recommendations to member countries to overcome the identified weaknesses. The underlying assumption is that effective surveillance of national financial systems by the Bretton Wood institutions, along with a harmonization and international convergence of financial policies, will help minimize risks, including the risk of cross-border spillovers of financial system disturbances, and will promote orderly development of the financial system.[7]

The design concept behind the above conventional wisdom of financial stability looks pretty complete, but the practice at ground level is much more messy. The underlying belief behind the FSAP model is that if only markets and infrastructure were complete, policies were rational and properly conceived and everyone obeyed international standards and rules, there would be financial stability. If only life were so simple.

In reality, there are no perfect policies, perfect institutional structures and perfect supervisory enforcement. Nevertheless, these imperfections cannot detract us from the fact that the weaknesses in any one of these Three Pillars can and do lead to financial instability.

To understand how current regulatory structures and processes failed to prevent the current global crisis, we need to go back to basics and start with

---

[7]   World Bank/IMF Financial Sector Assessment: A Handbook (2005).

the objectives of financial regulation, which flow from the fundamental objectives of social policy – to protect property rights equitably and fairly, to minimize transaction costs (including regulatory costs) and to have high levels of transparency so that members of society can look after their own interests.

The Group of Thirty has recently published a study on the structure of financial supervision,[8] which outlined the goals of financial regulation as '(a) safety and soundness of financial institutions, (b) mitigation of systemic risks, (c) fairness and efficiency of markets and (d) the protection of customers and investors', subject to 'minimum regulatory burden through efficiency and cost-effectiveness'. The Report identified four basic models of financial supervision: (a) the Institutional Approach, (b) the Functional Approach, (c) the Integrated Approach and (d) the Twin Peaks Approach. The first regulates institutions by legal unit. The second regulates the functions of individual institutions. The third covers both legal unit and functions through a super-regulator. The fourth divides the work between a prudential regulator and a conduct regulator, the latter largely on disclosure and market behaviour.

As is recognized by the Report, there is no 'one size fits all' optimal model for every country. Most markets (including the United States) are still in the Institutional category, whilst some are moving towards the other three. The Institutional Approach remains predominant because current laws that have not evolved with market change define financial institutions and regulation. The model Integrated Approach is the U.K. super-regulator, the FSA, whilst the model Twin Peaks approach that splits regulation into the Prudential function and another into the Conduct or Disclosure function is represented by the Australian and Dutch systems. Under the Twin Peaks approach, the Prudential Regulator (mainly the bank regulators) looks after the solvency, liquidity and governance of financial institutions according to the law, whereas the Conduct or Disclosure Regulator (usually the securities regulators) looks at the disclosure and market behaviour of market players, focussing on investor protection and market misconduct aspects. These approaches have converged in many countries, and the differences are not absolute but relative in degree.

The reality on the ground as practiced is that the present Institutional Approach is unable to cope with the changes in the business model of the financial industry. That said, it is also not obvious that for most emerging markets, the other three Approaches could cope, because the current

[8]   Group of Thirty (2008), 22.

'originate to distribute' wholesale banking model in advanced markets described in the last chapter is also seriously flawed.

We need a complete review of financial regulation, because the current global crisis occurred *despite* its major revamp after the Asian and dot. com crises. In the last 10 years financial regulatory structures, processes, accounting standards and even the machinery to coordinate financial stability issues globally – the Financial Stability Forum – were overhauled. Various central banks and the IMF have dedicated financial stability reports published regularly to warn about the risks. Most of the weaknesses exposed during the Asian and dot.com crises appear to have been addressed, such as lack of transparency and disclosure, unclear regulatory standards, bad corporate governance, lack of independence of auditors and rating agencies and the like.

In addition, no one can use under-resourcing of regulation as an excuse. After the corporate failures of Enron and Parmalat in 2001–2002, regulatory resources were strengthened worldwide. In the United States, studies at George Mason University estimated that real increase in regulatory spending was 31.6 percent between 2002 and 2005 and 21.1 percent between 1998 and 2001. Since 1999 Europe established a Council of Securities Regulators and strengthened its internal structures to coordinate financial regulation. A number of countries formed independent financial supervisory agencies. The accounting and auditing profession as well as global accounting standards have been reformed, adopting fair-value accounting, with convergence between the International Accounting Standards and U.S. accounting standards. The Basel Capital Accord underwent its second revision.

Consequently, it is perhaps less important to find out who to blame and concentrate on what to fix. No one understood this urgency better than U.S. Treasury Hank Paulson[9] when he pushed Congress to pass the US$700 billion bailout plan in September 2008: 'We can spend a lot of time talking about how it happened and how we got here. But we have to get through the night first'.

In May 2008, following an analysis by Nouriel Roubini,[10] Martin Wolf called for seven principles of regulation,[11] namely, coverage, cushions, commitment, cyclicality, clarity, complexity and compensation. He also added an eighth 'c', a reference to John Maynard Keynes's comment that capital

---

[9]   Paulson (2008), 17.
[10] Roubini (2008).
[11] Wolf (2008a).

would be ill served if the market behaves like a casino. But in 2007–2008, the market did behave like a casino.

WHAT WENT WRONG?

Although the unfolding of the current crisis will be considered in more detail in the next chapter, there is already consensus by the regulatory and academic profession on what broadly went wrong:

- First, the global excess liquidity that led to risk mispricing and 'search for yield'
- Second, the bubble in residential property, which was created by low interest rates, easy credit and lax credit due diligence
- Third, the securitization of residential mortgages into complex CDOs that were insured, rated AAA and backed by CDSs
- Fourth, the complexity and interconnectivity of financial derivatives that clearly went beyond the capacity of bank management, investors and financial regulators to comprehend
- Fifth, the accounting and regulatory standards that allowed such derivatives to be considered off-balance sheet, thus disguising the true leverage of the institutions
- Sixth, the inadequate levels of liquidity held by financial institutions that overrelied on wholesale funding, and ultimately central bank support
- Seventh, the fragmented regulatory structure that allowed regulatory gaps, inertia and arbitrage that weakened oversight of the industry
- Eighth, the regulatory capture and inherent moral hazard of central bank puts that weakened both regulatory and market discipline in the system
- Ninth, the incentive structure of compensation that rewarded short-term risk taking
- Tenth, the overreliance on credit rating agencies which gave risky structured products AAA ratings that were in hindsight not justified
- Eleventh, the need for anticyclical action, such as preventive regulation and dynamic provisioning, to stop risky procyclical behaviour by financial institutions.

I concur with these views, particularly the need for anticyclical action and dynamic provisioning. The point is that when the financial regulator bears a high profile taking tough action and warning against imprudent behaviour, the market participants will take heed. If the policeman is not seen proactively on the beat, are you surprised that crooks come out to play?

GETTING SIMPLICITY OUT OF COMPLEXITY

Before we proceed to discuss the above list of issues, it would be useful to address the fundamental issue of complexity and transparency. The Counterparty Risk Management Group,[12] which reconvened again in April 2008 to address the unfolding current crisis, commented in its third report in August on the complexity of modern derivative markets:

> Needless to say, the complexity factor is an issue as it pertains to the capacity of the international community of supervisors and regulators to discharge their responsibilities. The key issue here is not complexity per se but rather the extent to which complexity feeds on itself thereby helping to create or magnify contagion risk 'hot spots' that may have systematic implications. Thus, we are faced with the pressing need to find better ways to manage and mitigate the risk associated with complexity, a subject that will continue to challenge the best and the brightest among us.

We should appreciate that growing complexity is part of the evolution of all knowledge societies. Man is continuing to struggle with his lack of comprehension of the world around him as society evolves. Over two millennia ago, the Chinese Qin Dynasty Legalist Premier Shang Yang had already recommended that laws must be made clear, easily understood and properly defined, so that even the ordinary person can understand them and officials can implement them. He also recognized that laws and their enforcement must change with the times.

In today's environment, financial regulators have been trying to simplify complex rules-based regulation into principles-based regulation. Given a shortage of resources and concentrating on cost effectiveness, financial regulators have been moving towards objective-based regulation and risk-based regulation. But it keeps getting more complex.

For example, these objectives and principles were elegantly and simply embodied in the U.K. Financial Services and Markets Act of 2000, which was only 321 pages, compared with the more rule-based Hong Kong Securities and Futures Act of 2003 that was three times thicker. However, because of the industry's desire to have more clarity and detail, so as to avoid being sanctioned, the Act is now supported by an online FSA Handbook[13] that

---

[12] Counterparty Risk Management Policy Group III (2008), Introduction, 4.
[13] www.fsa.gov.uk.

comprises a Glossary, seven high-level standards, 11 prudential standards, 9 business standards, 5 regulatory processes, 9 specialists source books, 8 handbook guides and 6 regulatory guides. Like with the SEC rules and regulations, even an experienced regulator like myself had difficulty navigating and interpreting these detailed rules.

There are no easy answers to the growing complexity, because we are dealing with a constantly evolving multifaceted world of derivative finance, where even the leading practitioners are struggling to comprehend, let alone master.

Students of Benoît Mandelbrot would understand that the world is inherently complex, but it is the theories that are too simple and therefore inadequate. As Mandelbrot puts it: 'the implicit assumption in all this: If one knows the cause, one can forecast the event and manage the risk'.[14] In other words, if only we improve our knowledge, have faster computers to manage more data more accurately and apply better statistical techniques and models, we can manage our risks. Or can we?

TRANSPARENCY IS NECESSARY BUT NOT SUFFICIENT

One of the successful outcomes of the 1997–1998 Asian crisis was the call for transparency and the reform of international accounting and disclosure standards of corporations, financial institutions and governments. The need for transparency came from a fundamental flaw of financial markets – information asymmetry. Without good information, it is difficult to sensibly appraise risks and rewards and, consequently, to make good investment decisions or form sound policies. Misguided investment decisions and policies due to imperfect information in turn can lead to unforeseen systemic financial shocks, thereby posing a major threat to financial stability.

Information asymmetry comes in at three levels – first, the availability of information to make sound judgements; second, the ability or technology to analyze that information for risk management purposes; and third, the willingness to make tough decisions under uncertainty. Conventional risk management focuses on the first two levels, and much has been done to improve accounting and disclosure standards and to learn modern risk management techniques. But the third level needs experience and wisdom, because how one makes decisions under conditions of complexity, ambiguity and uncertainty is still more of an art than a science.

---

[14] Mandelbrot and Hudson, 2008, 8.

As someone who was and still is an advocate of higher transparency,[15] I now realize that what we reformed 10 years ago was on the supply side of information, in the sense that disclosure by market participants has become much better. However, we all underappreciated the demand side of transparency, that is, the level of understanding of complex products and transactions by the investor (retail or professional) or the regulator. We all suffer from selective memory or selective amnesia. We see what we choose to see or hear.

The current crisis has disproved the naive assumption that if the risks were fully disclosed by all issuers, the market would be more stable. The fallacy of composition, by which market participants erroneously assume that what they believe is true based on partial information is true for the market as a whole, was prevalent in both the Asian and current crises. Market participants acted on partial information, and their collective herd behaviour created market overshooting or undershooting.

Full disclosure is therefore necessary but not a sufficient condition for market stability, certainly if large parts of the market don't understand the risks or choose to ignore them because of greed, ignorance or self-interest.

Two examples will suffice. In the Asian crisis case, former Japanese Vice Minister of Finance Eisuke Sakakibara[16] and others have pointed out that pertinent information, including the real effective exchange rates, the private sector's short-term foreign debt, the current account balances and the banking sector's balance sheets, was largely available in the lead-up to 1997. In the current case, Bill White has cited how the BIS had laid out the dangers associated with credit risk transfer instruments in several reports before the crisis broke. 'Unfortunately, the risks identified were not thought significant enough by the private sector to elicit any real changes in behaviour'.[17]

At the level of theory, it is easy to fall into the trap of making assumptions about market behaviour that could be drastically wrong. Before the Asian crisis, both Asian policymakers and their Bretton Wood advisers assumed that as long as the public sector did not run large deficits and external borrowings, self-interest would constrain private sector debt. That turned out to be wrong. The same mistake was made about self-interest constraining bank behaviour.

The second mistake was to assume that risk management works on what is statistically measurable, but uncertainty is about events and new factors

---

[15] Group of Twenty Two, 'Report of Working Group on Transparency and Accountability', co-chaired by Mervyn King and Andrew Sheng, 1999.

[16] Sakakibara (1999a).

[17] White (2008).

that may not be statistically significant. In other words, rare events could have massive effects, and our present systems are not designed to cope with such 'long tail effects'. Mandelbrot, Nassim Taleb[18] and others have already proven how inadequate present risk management models are.

Third, the most relevant and material information, such as the size of the property bubble and the size of the systemic leverage, was not widely understood or even measured. At least, those responsible for systemic stability grossly underestimated the fragility of the system to a reversal of the bubble and the leverage.

In sum, Asian financial systems were simply not designed to cope with the network effects of the global financial system. They were essentially designed in the 1960s to mobilize domestic savings in order to achieve high growth. There was therefore no clear realization that high growth was achieved at high risk. Certainly, Asian policymakers never dreamt that their financial systems would be subject to huge exchange rate or capital flow shocks.

As former U.S. Defence Secretary Donald Rumsfeld aptly described it: 'there are also unknown unknowns. There are things we don't know we don't know'.[19]

Asian policymakers did not believe that the risks of unknown unknowns were serious. Thus, 10 years ago emerging Asia did not think very carefully about how to manage risks of growth on a national basis and in the context of one interdependent world. Crucially, the need for a robust financial system that effectively distributes risks within the economy to complement Asia's relatively strong export manufacturing sector was not given the adequate attention it demanded.

It could be argued the present national-based financial systems are not designed to absorb volatilities in global financial markets. In a simple engineering analogy, as with the LTCM model, the financial system was designed for four standard deviations of shocks. However, we had a 15-standard-deviation shock or power surge. Are we surprised that the system blew a fuse?

AN INSTITUTIONAL APPROACH TO FINANCIAL REGULATION

So far, we have looked at the problem of information asymmetry. But there is another flaw of markets – the principal-agent problem. Financial

---

[18] Taleb (2007).
[19] Rumsfeld (2002).

regulators are agents of society, so why is it that their structure, tools and processes did not prevent financial crises? This question is at the heart of the issue of regulation.

To begin with, we must accept that there can be no 'one-size fit all' approach for financial regulation, reform, crisis prevention or resolution. This is due to the different stages of development of markets, their different history as well as the experience and sophistication of the market participants, including the regulators and policymakers.

At most, we can arrive at both general principles and a general approach to the diagnosis and prognosis of each market, noting that they are networks that are increasingly interlinked with each other on a global scale. In the introductory chapter, we stated that financial markets are social institutions that help to trade and protect property rights, with four fundamental functions – resource allocation, price discovery, risk management and corporate governance. Hence, any problems with the markets could be examined from where they are misfunctioning.

But even in this simplistic view of the market as an institution, we recognize the critical role of the state in legislating and enforcing the rules and maintaining the property rights infrastructure, such as the judiciary and law enforcement. All too often, market failures are also due to the failure of the state to enforce rules or undue state intervention (including bad or obsolete regulations) that distort incentives. Consequently, crises are the interactive outcome of a combination of market failures and also regulatory failure. The two are like Siamese twins that are not separable.

There is therefore a purpose to regulation as a social tool. Society has given regulators the powers to safeguard its rights, but such power or authority is both a blessing and a curse. Just as financial institutions have fiduciary duty on behalf of their investors and clients, regulators can be said to be agents on behalf of the principal, which is society as a whole. The regulator therefore suffers as much from the principal-agent problem as corporate management. The interests of the regulators and the public may often diverge. How to align both interests is a crucial question of regulatory policy.

An example is the recent push for market-friendly regulations, particularly emphasizing the high cost of industry compliance to rules and regulations. Does market friendly mean friendly to the industry or the investors? If regulators are friendly to industry, then the interests of the investors are harmed. The present crisis demonstrates clearly that the additional costs of financial regulation are miniscule compared with the losses from the meltdown. Hence, one needs an objective view of how to balance such interests.

Table 14.1. *The SPISSPER Process Cycle of*
Financial Regulation

SPISSPER Process Cycle	Institutional Elements
Strategize	Information
Prioritize	Values
Incentivize	Incentives
Standardize	Standards
Structurize	Structure
Process design	Process
Execution	Property rights
Review	Dimensions

Source: See Introduction

CRISIS AND THE EIGHT ELEMENTS OF INSTITUTIONS

Taking change as a process, it struck me that the third century B.C. Chinese text the *Record of Rites* was spot on in recognizing that learning and doing form a feedback loop: 'Learn, Question, Reflect, Choose, Execute'. The Confucian scholars were trying to make sense out of the chaos of war, corruption and social decay during the period of the Warring States. What they appreciated was that in this world of increasing complexity and change, it might be impossible to arrive at even commonly agreed principles. The least we can do is to have a common process of searching, learning, doing and reviewing the whole process of social change.

To facilitate an analysis of the role of regulation in the Asian and current crises, I shall use the MBA tool of acronyms to break down the process review of policy and institutional change into the eight elements of the SPISSPER Process cycle (Table 14.1). The eight institutional elements have been described in the Introduction in Figure A. If financial regulators hope to adapt market institutions and themselves to environmental change, there is a process to Strategize, Prioritize, Incentivize, Structurize, Standardize, Process design, Execution and Review.

I should point out that these eight elements are not mutually exclusive and are, in fact, interdependent on each other. We can indeed start with any of these eight elements, but I have used strategy as a key way to begin, because strategic calculation of the context, based on reliable information, is normally where you begin the process of diagnosis. Martin Wolf, for example, started with Coverage, meaning that one must look system-wide and the regulatory net must cover the whole span of financial activities.

In the following discussion I use the SPISSPER Process to review what I consider to be wrong with the present regulatory regime. As former Chairman of the IOSCO Technical Committee and a financial regulator almost all my working life, I do not absolve myself from these shortcomings. I offer my insights in the hope that the system can change for the better.

The first two elements, *Strategizing* and *Prioritizing*, are about clearly understanding the values, options and constraints and picking realistic objectives that can be achievable. Many policies fail because the *incentives*, *structures* and *standards* do not exist for such policies to be implemented. If the strategy and options are to be of any use, they must be supported by the organizational structure, with implementing *processes, execution* and regular *review* as keys to success or failure. Hence, even before policy is made, strategic calculations will have to be made.

STRATEGIC CALCULATIONS – CONTEXT AND CLARITY

But before we begin even to strategize, we must have reliable, timely and accessible information to put the issues we confront in context. No policymaker can afford to take the institutional environment for granted and underestimate the ground conditions, vested interests and bottlenecks and constraints that all reformers and regulators face in the real world.

This is why I like to compare financial regulation with warfare. If we think only about normal conditions, we are not prepared for crises. In peacetime, prepare for war, and in war, prepare for the unexpected.[20] Military strategists appreciate that ground conditions are continually changing and that strategic resources cannot be stretched too thinly. For best effect, they must be concentrated and used against a chosen sector with the greatest effect. They remember all too clearly that it is most dangerous when all is quiet on the Western Front. Likewise, financial regulators have to learn to recognize that dangerously low-risk spreads and low volatilities, coupled with fast-rising markets, are usually precursors to crisis.

This analogy is also useful because in order to achieve effectiveness the military leader must make different components of his forces work together, which is precisely the problem in coordinating different parts of the regulatory machinery, such as central banks, financial regulators and ministries of finance, not excluding other parts of government, to prevent or tackle

---

[20] Sheng (2008b).

an impending financial crisis. I learnt from bitter experience in Hong Kong that no single regulatory agency could solve market problems on its own. The most important job of a leader in a regulatory agency is to knock heads within one's own organization and work closely with other regulatory agencies and government departments to achieve the common goal. All too often, too much emotional energy and resources are spent on turf battles and cover your ass action, rather than delivering results. It is clear that the fragmented nature of regulatory structure is a core issue in the current crisis.

But even if there is good leadership at individual organizations, my own experience is that, more often than not, a large part of the explanation of crisis arises from the weaknesses in the institutional structure, which is inextricably interconnected to the political economy of power, vested interests and values in each economy. What have made life much more complicated are the globalization of risks and the interactivity of mutually reinforcing behaviour between domestic participants and the rest of the world. The world has become networks through which chaos can be transmitted from one corner of the world to the next.

The circularity and interdependence of the SPISSPER process requires us to have a good assessment of the scale or dimensions of the problem before we strategize. Having a 30,000-feet system-wide view would help us appreciate what we are dealing with relative to our resources. All too often financial regulators are daily dealing with the urgent rather than the important. If we were to strategize and look objectively at the present system of regulation and the size of the problem before us, we would be struck by two significant facts.

First, the present fragmented system of financial regulation is completely outdated relative to the interwoven nature of modern finance. The present structure of underresourced institutional regulators in over 150 countries trying to figure out what global financial conglomerates are doing is somewhat comic, if not tragic. The top largest 15 financial institutions control resources larger than most countries' GDP. Each regulator would be like pygmy Lilliputs trying to tie down the giant in *Gulliver's Travels*. When powerful investment banks backed by very expensive lawyers and political lobbyists are skirting the regulatory ice in complex derivatives, it is a brave regulator who dares to show up his own ignorance by asking obvious questions.

Second, despite the central role that the property bubble played in the Asian crisis, U.S. and Europeans financial regulators and central bankers did not pay enough attention to the dangers of the leverage in the financial institutions' balance sheets arising from mortgages. Since real estate is usually the largest and lumpiest component of private sector assets and the major collateral for bank lending, this lack of attention is surprising. Relatively few national statistical agencies publish data on real estate values for balance sheet analysis purposes. Worse, insufficient stress tests were done to examine what would happen to bank balance sheets should real estate values decline.

A fundamental similarity between the Asian and the current crisis is that both were balance sheet crisis, in the sense that the net worth of financial institutions was hurt badly because of the deflation of the real estate bubble. The balance sheet effect of this deflation is not difficult to see. The U.S. private sector holdings of real estate amounted to 225 percent of U.S. GDP in 2007. In Japan real estate values were roughly half of total national wealth. When Japanese real estate prices declined roughly 60 percent after the bubble, causing a wealth loss estimated at 500 trillion yen, and Japanese bank credit to the private sector was 773 trillion yen or 180 percent of GDP,[21] it would not take a genius to see that the decline in property prices would hurt the banks badly.

For strategy to be effective, strategic objectives must have clarity. All too often, financial regulators are saddled with conflicting objectives. Once they are burdened with dealing with social inequities that are rightly the goal of other government agencies, then financial stability concerns are compromised. Hence, given limited resources and set targets, prioritization of objectives and choice of tools is step two.

PRIORITIZATION WITHIN RESOURCE CONSTRAINTS

In a situation of asymmetric information and limited resources, all financial regulators are limited by 'bounded rationality' and must make difficult policy choices. Such choices are obviously shaped by the values embedded in the institution. For example, the liberal regulator who has the mindset of 'market knows best' may easily omit the 'trust but verify' due diligence crucial to enforcing regulatory discipline. Regulators with more recent experience with crisis are more inclined to be tougher on regulation because they understand the costs of underregulation.

Prioritization is exactly what Harvard regulation professor Malcolm Sparrow called 'pick important problems, fix them and tell everyone'.[22] Sparrow argues that financial regulators must be results oriented, looking for outcomes, rather than just objectives. The currently fashionable

---

[21] Ozeki (2008).
[22] Sparrow (2000), 132.

risk-based regulation uses sophisticated tools to identify risks in individual institutions, rating them and applying the appropriate regulatory resources. This type of approach is not inherently wrong, so long as the regulator understands that (1) the information he used may be wrong, (2) the regulated firm itself may not know their own risks, (3) the current generation of risk models are flawed and (4) the regulator also has blind spots, due to lack of training or experience. This is why all financial regulators need to take regularly a strategic, holistic and coldly objective view of what is happening in the markets, what they are doing and where they may be missing the big picture.

Given rapidly changing market conditions, in which the market relentlessly adopts regulatory arbitrage practices, a continual Strategizing and Prioritizing of regulatory options is part of each financial regulator's tool kit. No theory is adequate to guide him under complex multidisciplinary and contextual changes. Financial regulators have to constantly engage the market through dialogue, inspection and enforcement action in order to understand and experience for themselves what is really happening on the ground. Indeed, given the inherent 'fallacy of composition' of partial information of market participants, the financial regulator may be the only person with access to system-wide information, if only he is willing to look for it. Hence, prioritization is determined by values, commitment and incentives.

THE WRONG INCENTIVES

Getting market incentives right is an area that most financial regulators tend to underestimate. The current debate around incentives centres around two issues – banker compensation and moral hazard. But there is a third: how to align regulators' incentives to do their job.

In the current crisis there is almost unanimous agreement that bankers' compensation was wrongly skewed towards rewarding short-term risktaking at the expense of long-term shareholders' value. This is a challenge that the Institute of International Finance, the representative of major international banks, promised to review in their response to the recent credit crisis.[23] Now that many of the large banks have been nationalized, bankers' pay has already been scaled back, and there are many suggestions how to tie performance to long-term value creation, by deferring compensation and strengthening teamwork.

---

[23] Institute of International Finance (2008a and 2008b).

The theory again is that those who have large stakes in the stability of the system are unlikely to destroy their own rice bowls. Obviously bankers that have no stake in the securitized and sold mortgages are not committed to their quality. After the Asian crisis, every borrower understood that if you owed the bank $1 million, you are in trouble. But if you owed the bank $1 billion, the bank is in trouble. Hence, commitment to credit culture is related to ownership and leverage. The higher the leverage, the greater the moral hazard.

Moral hazard is inherent in nature of leverage. The common insurance definition of moral hazard is the risk that the presence of a contract will affect the behaviour of one or more parties. But in the case of an explicit or implicit social contract (such as deposit insurance), moral hazard behaviour can occur if the government does not constantly remind the public that moral hazard behaviour will not be rewarded. This has to occur through either regulatory action against bad financial institution behaviour or the central bank refusing to exercise the central bank put (in other words, bail out investors who assume that the central bank will always lower interest rates to keep the stock or bond market buoyant).

During the Asian crisis, most commentators focused on the moral hazard issues of implicit guarantees on bank deposits. It was assumed that Asian borrowers took huge risks, condoned by bankers, because the state underwrote the banking system. We now know from the present crisis that the state eventually had to underwrite all the mistakes of the financial engineers.

Moral hazard occurs in insurance contracts because of hidden action, which is the deliberate action taken by the insured not to disclose risks or to benefit from the insurance. An insurance policy can be voided if the policyholder deliberately acts to benefit from hidden action. However, a central bank or even society cannot avoid moral hazard consequences when a segment of society decides to socialize their losses. In other words, whenever a borrower becomes insolvent, his losses are passed to his lenders, and if these lenders fail, society will bear the residue losses. Consequently society must control excess leverage in any part of society, knowing full well that ultimately such losses would be borne, voluntarily or involuntarily, by the state. This is the rationale of financial regulation. Unfortunately, the current regulatory framework totally lost the plot. Through lack of transparency in highly complex derivative transactions, neither the market participants nor the regulators understood the degree of leverage and therefore moral hazard risks.

Note that the risk creating moral hazard behaviour of the market participants is one sided, in the sense that as long as the central bank and the regulators do not say *explicitly* what behaviour is frowned on and explicitly that there is no 'central bank put', the market can merrily behave as if everything is permissible and that increasing leverage is fine. In other words, if the market assumes that the central bank put exists (even if in the mind of the central bank and the regulator it does not), the moral hazard risk is real and material. Hence prevention of moral hazard is not a one-off action.

The regulator or the central bank has to continually remind the market through regulatory action that financial institutions or investors that behave irresponsibly will be sanctioned. I totally agree with Charles Goodhart: 'the time to worry about moral hazard is in the boom. The first priority is to get out of the present hole. Worrying about moral hazard in current circumstances is rather like refusing to sell fire insurance just after the Great Fire of London for fear of adversely affecting future behaviour'.[24]

We turn now to the alignment of regulatory incentives to their own performance. The problem of incentivizing financial regulators is common to all public service. If public servants are underpaid and not rewarded for risk taking, are we surprised by the common complaint that they are bureaucratic, inefficient and focused on process and compliance rather than outcomes? During the post-Asian crisis reforms, the accusation was that Asian regulators were 'over-regulating and under-enforcing', meaning that the incentives were to regulate in order to extract rents or favours from approvals, whereas no one wanted to do the dirty and unpleasant work of enforcing the rules.

In contrast, the Western approach under free markets is to trust that the bankers knew what they are doing. Former Fed Chairman Greenspan admitted as much, when he pleaded that 'those of us who have looked to the self-interest of lending institutions to protect shareholders' equity, myself included, are in a state of shocked disbelief'.[25] It was right to trust, but regulators must verify.

The reality is that in an environment when public opinion is all for market-friendly regulation, it is grossly unpopular for a single regulator to put a stop to egregious behaviour, especially when the industry can finance media campaigns and lobby action against tough regulatory action and reform. In an open democratic environment, the public will back tough regulatory action only if they feel that such action is to protect its interests. But if financial regulators have asymmetric incentives where they are chided for taking tough action and applauded for the light touch or looking

---

[24] Goodhart (2008c), 13.
[25] Scannell and Reddy (2008), A15.

the other way (safe harbour or no action clauses), are we surprised that the law is not enforced?

The issue of aligning regulatory incentives with social outcomes is so important within the current context that this is discussed in the next chapter.

STANDARDS, PRINCIPLES AND RULES – THE NEED FOR SIMPLICITY

In order to assess performance and behaviour, we must have standards and commonly agreed-on rules or codes. The Asian crisis occurred at a time where there were differing accounting standards, without agreed-on standards of corporate governance and the like. Thanks to the work of the Financial Stability Forum (FSF) and the global standard setters, there was a complete review of standards and codes (ROSC), with convergence in accounting standards and greater clarity in regulatory and disclosure standards, undertaken in conjunction with FSAPs.

Since then, the Asian economies have embarked on a massive programme of adopting these standards, together with technical assistance from the development banks and aid donors. By and large, progress has been made in raising standards, but the gaps with best practice are still considerable. A recent study on the implementation of international standards in East Asia concluded,

In the East Asia context, the low priority afforded to prudential regulation in the past became very dangerous and threatened the viability of national development strategies. However, the idea that the creation of independent regulatory agencies, applying and enforcing Western-style standards, would be considered necessary and sufficient to achieve this objective was at best naive. In practice, it has sometimes simply allowed politicians and associated vested interests to pursue the form but not the substance of compliance.[26]

This is not an unfair comment, but it applies equally to the current crisis.

There are three observations that one can make about standards. First, some standards have now reached the level of theology, forgetting that all standards are relative and not absolute. For example, few people would disagree with the idea of fair value accounting, especially the standard of marking to market, because market prices are determined by many buyers and sellers. However, when bubbles hugely inflate the market, would

---

[26] Walter (2008), 3.

marking to market be realistic? There is no simple answer to this, and it is gratifying to know that the International Accounting Standards Board has recently taken on board some of the circumstances when marking to market is not appropriate. Recently Avinash Persaud and others[27] have pushed for the idea of 'marking to funding', as a way to avoid 'marking to market' creating pro-cyclical behaviour. My personal preference is for consistent application of standards and not to change when standards are found to be inconvenient. The basis of valuation should be fully disclosed, so that if one used 'mark to funding', then the differences with mark to market should be disclosed.

Second, the trend towards harmonization of standards whereby everyone begins to adopt one standard is inherently unhealthy. Avinash Persaud has perceptively pointed out that if the whole market used the same risk management standards, the market would herd only one way.[28] The market is more likely to be stable if there is heterogenic opinion about the direction of the market. Competition between standards is healthy. The market will make the choice between competing technology standards like HDVD versus Blu-ray and equipment that can read multiple standards. There should be adequate disclosure of the differences in outcomes and treatment should different standards be used. We should let the market decide, rather than mandating a universal standard.

Third, standards should be simple, clear and understandable. Complex standards, rules and regulations add costs to the market, so that there are either huge regulatory arbitrages or huge regulatory gaps and black holes.

STRUCTURE AND COVERAGE

Management guru Peter Drucker taught that (organizational) structure follows strategy. At the national level, strategies are embodied in macro-economic policies and are implemented by the entire government and bureaucratic structure. The best policies do not get implemented if the bureaucracy is weak, corrupted, disinterested or captured. Whether you get good outcomes would depend on the incentive structures built into the system or the political will to make the necessary reforms.

The key structural problem faced by the Asian economies is the legacy of a relatively closed top-down silo governance structure faced with an open, rapidly evolving and complex global market. In network architecture terms,

---

[27]   Brunnermeir et al. (2009).
[28]   Persaud (2000).

this is the competition between a single star network, with a rigid hub controlling all links, versus a flat, open architecture of the Internet. Single-star hubs are efficient but not resilient, in the event of the failure of the hub. On the other hand, the Internet had multiple hubs and is much more resilient and adaptable to change.

These structural conflicts arose partly due to the way Asian economies evolved and partly due to the fact that policy making, laws and market practice are still national-centric, whereas globalization has created a borderless market space. Financial markets, on the other hand, have already adapted to a matrix form of management, so that functions and responsibilities report to different parts of the organization for better checks and balances.

The network effects of the global network economy thus bear two important implications in terms of risk management. First, we need to focus on managing risk as one world, taking into account risk management at the individual level, the corporate or institution level, the sectoral level and finally the national, regional and global levels. Second, risk management can no longer be static and nation-centric, but dynamic, global and interactive. Essentially, this means that we cannot look at an economy as an isolated island, but part of the global network where shocks can be transmitted through contagion. We can no longer work in silos, but must knock heads so that everyone works towards a common purpose of financial stability.

From this perspective, the domestic economy must therefore be designed to withstand shocks that come from within and without its borders, with the most dangerous shock being the one which we cannot see, have never experienced and cannot foresee. However, in practice, no economy is designed that way – each evolves through its own experience and historical and social environment. If an economy did not have a crisis, it would not evolve policies and institutions to deal with such a crisis. In this sense, crisis is an inevitable price of growing up.

PROCESS, EXECUTION AND REVIEW

Using the military analogy once again, once a general has his strategy, priorities, incentives, standards and structures in place, the rest is tools or processes, execution and review. As Napoleon used to say, It's all in the execution. As every regulator learns to his cost, the best regulation is useless if there is no strict enforcement. Enforcement is hard work, but only through detailed examination, routine or forensic, can evidence be gathered on the problems of the market. The bank examiner is like a CSI investigator, constantly sifting partial information from many sources to build a composite picture of what happened and why. Because of the new paradigm of interconnectivity, we can no longer look at a single institution for problems, but whether a seemingly benign 'plain vanilla' product has evolved through financial engineering into a toxic virus that can bring down whole populations.

How is it that the leading financial regulators missed the fragilities in the current crisis? As late as September 2007, a senior European regulator confessed to me that until midsummer SIVs and conduits were not on his radar screen.

My own observation is that currently applied practice of increased levels of off-site surveillance and on-site examination of the same institutions by the same teams would yield very little new information. The first rule of bureaucracy, at both the regulated firms and the regulator, is to stick to known knowns.

The approach of looking at risks from the eyes of bank management (using their database and stress tests) is of limited value, because the regulated firm may not know where it is blind. What would be more effective is to take a system-wide view and conduct end-to-end examinations in a forensic manner for a single product across different institutions. The examination should be conducted from the beginning in origination to distribution, trading and end investor. This cross-institutional examination is not for fault finding, but to examine whether at each stage of the evolution of the product, financial institutions, dealers, custodians and investors have done their due diligence and understand their risks. This type of 'cross-sectional' examination is commonly adopted in auditing to 'follow the money'. Unfortunately, because traditional financial supervision is institution based, very few regulators have adopted this to verify the risks of financial innovation in practice.

In other words, because financial markets are interconnected through complex processes and products, it is important for regulators to have an understanding of the level of controls and due diligence at all levels of the processes across different institutions to find out where the weak links are. You only understand the contagion if you examine the process from end to end.

Similarly, stopping the detailed examination at a single bank level, without looking at how its products are originated and distributed by its counterparties would yield little new information for the system as a whole, nor where the risks of 'interconnectedness' lie. An end-to-end examination of subprime mortgages would have quickly revealed that insufficient due diligence was being done at the origination level, and certainly not enough due diligence was conducted by the primary dealers when they packaged such mortgages into CDOs and other structured products. A forensic examination of investors might have revealed that their own due diligence and risk controls were inadequate. Since pension funds and insurance companies were not subject to such inspections on a random basis, the lines of defence against fraud and risks failed miserably.

Finally, two critical elements of the regulatory cycle are the enforcement and review processes. Execution can never be separated from constant review. The results of examination cannot be left to inexperienced and undertrained examiners, because the structure and process must allow for constant feedback and dialogue between expertise in different parts and different levels of the regulatory organization. Review of different pieces of information, from off-site surveillance, on-site examination, market dialogue, whistle blowers, media and analyst reports and sheer gut-feel, will tell the experienced regulator that something does not smell right. I remember that Bill Taylor, the Fed examiner who later became Chairman of the Federal Deposit Insurance Corporation (FDIC), used to remind me that any bank that doubled its loan book over three years should be examined for problems. Northern Rock would not have passed this simple rule of thumb.

Constant review of market indicators would also call for anticyclical regulatory action. Probably because of the free market philosophy, for quite a while the mood among leading financial regulators was not to take anticyclical action. Indeed, when the Bank of Spain decided to require dynamic loan provisioning for Spanish banks as property prices rose, the accounting treatment had to be disclosed, because there were views from disclosure regulators that such provisioning may not be fair to investors as a departure from fair value accounting. Only after the pain of crisis did many financial regulators concede that dynamic provisioning might not be a bad idea after all. At the execution level, suffice to repeat that regulation is ineffective without enforcement, which must be speedy and outcome oriented. Without quick enforcement action, the market will think that the regulator is either turning a blind eye to misbehaviour or has implicitly allowed such action through 'no action'.

This is precisely why the regulatory cycle must include constant reviews of outcomes against objectives. These reviews must examine how the strategy, priorities, incentives, standards, structures, processes and execution have been done in the right dimensions and context. Unless such reviews are done, and done independently by either the Board responsible for the regulatory authority or an independent body, it is likely that the regulator will easily slip into a compliance mode of operation that misses the big picture. A routine execution of current processes without examining outcomes is likely to lead to process for process' sake. It is the ultimate red tape that can only be exposed through crisis. Those who regulate by the [outdated] book will see their reputations destroyed by the book.

Having surveyed the industry and the regulatory framework, we can now embark on a ride through the recent crisis.

FIFTEEN

The Global Financial Meltdown

International financial crises, I might even say domestic financial crises, are built into the human genome. When we map the whole thing, we will find something there called greed and something called fear and something called hubris. That is all you need to produce international financial crises in the future.
~ Paul Volcker

The end of a journey always comes back to its beginning. Why do financial crises occur? Do they have the same root causes? Are the solutions the same? Ten years after the Asian crisis ended, the U.S. subprime crisis by Christmas 2008 had plunged the world into a deep recession that is still unfolding. Future historians will no doubt compare the 2008 crisis with the Great Depression of the 1930s, which led up to the Second World War and changed the financial landscape for nearly 80 years. Similarly, the present crisis is likely to induce profound changes in economic theory, philosophical outlook and institutional structure.

The famous Mr Yen, Dr Eisuke Sakakibara, pronounced in 1999, after he stepped down as Vice Minister of Finance for International Affairs, that the Asian crisis was not 'Asian', but 'a crisis of global capitalism'.[1] Even then, he understood the inherent instability of liberalised capital markets where sudden reversals of market confidence cause periodic panics of differing magnitudes and durations. Former U.S. Treasury Secretary Larry Summers already recognized as early as February 1998 that 'It is important to recognize that this is a distinct kind of crisis. It has a common element with almost all financial crises: money borrowed in excess and used badly. But it is also profoundly different because it does not have its roots in improvidence: excessive budget deficits, excess rates of inflation or insufficient rates of saving'.[2]

---

[1] Sakakibara (1999b), 181.
[2] Summers (1998).

How different is it this time from the Asian crisis? Was the Asian crisis a pre-cursor to the current crisis?

Seen from a longer historical perspective, there is no doubt that there are similarities. In terms of the apparent causes, most analysts would list the usual suspects: the existence of asset bubbles, excessive liquidity and leverage, large capital flows, inadequate financial supervision over complex financial products, bad monetary policy and bad banking all came together to create the subprime crisis, just as they did during the Asian crisis.

As indicated earlier, the Asian crisis was a regional crisis, but the current crisis was of a different order of magnitude because it emanated from the center of global power. The crisis was amplified by the global interconnectivity woven together by financial engineers through new institutions, new instruments and higher levels of leverage.

In the one month following the failure of Lehman Brothers on 15 September 2008, the world's banking system nearly collapsed like a domino, with stock markets almost seeing meltdown. Banks in the United States and Europe were partly nationalized, and investment banks disappeared as a separate unit in the United States. An estimated US$27 trillion or over 50 percent was wiped from global stock markets in 2008. On 10 October the Dow Jones Index dropped a record 7.7 percent to hit an intraday low of 7,773, just over half of its peak a year before. The Bank of England has estimated that the mark-to-market losses in bond and credit securities would be in the region of US$2.8 trillion. This was equivalent to 85% of global banks' tier 1 capital of US$3.4 trillion.[3] If estimated declines in real estate prices were to be included, the decline in global wealth could be on the order of 100 percent of global GDP.

Furthermore, between April and October 2008, various central banks and governments had provided implicitly or explicitly US$8 trillion of funding for their wholesale markets to prevent total seizure, equivalent to 15 percent of global GDP. Interest rate cuts were made across the board. To combat the deflation, the Fed had cut the Fed Funds rate by 100 basis points in 2007 and another 425 basis points back to 0–0.25% per annum by 16 December 2008.

In moving to a zero interest rate policy, there is an immediate parallel between the present U.S. policy and the way Bank of Japan dealt with the 1990 Japanese bubble crisis, except that the United States achieved this within one year, whereas Japan took 10 years.

---

[3]　Bank of England (2008).

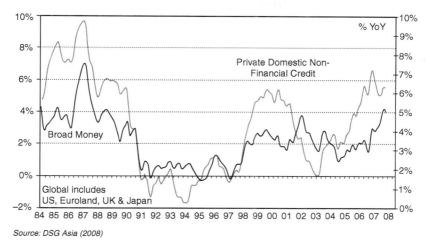

Figure 15.1. Global Real Money and Credit Growth, 1984–2008

EXCESS LIQUIDITY

Just like the Roaring 1920s that preceded the Great Depression, it was the long period of prosperity in the early years of the 21st century that gave rise to the excesses of 2007–2008. Western economists, led by Fed Chairman Ben Bernanke,[4] blamed the Savings Glut in East Asia for the excessive low interest rates and high liquidity that provided conditions for the asset bubble and subsequent deterioration in credit quality. I find this argument disingenuous because it smacks of a banker blaming his excess liquidity on the thriftiness of the depositors. What the banker did with his balance sheet was the banker's responsibility, over which the depositors had little say.

Figure 15.1 shows the growth in broad money and credit to the nonfinancial sector in the major economies, including the United States, Europe and Japan. There were two cycles of strong growth, 1997–1999 and the end of 2002 to end of 2006. The first period was to combat the negative effects of the Asian crisis, and the second to combat deflation in the United States after the bursting of the dot.com bubble. Throughout this period Japanese monetary policy was deliberately loose to combat its own deflation, whilst European monetary policy was broadly neutral. U.S. monetary policy therefore played a major role in stimulating both domestic liquidity and global liquidity. Specifically, between December 2000 and June 2003, in a series of

---

[4]   Bernanke (2005).

steps, the Fed Funds rate was lowered to 1 percent per annum, the lowest in over 40 years, bringing the real rate into negative territory from 2002 to 2005. During this period of growth and low inflation, there was an abundance of global liquidity.

The high savings rate in the emerging markets was primarily a combination of at least four factors. The first is the high level of consumption in the United States that boosted exports and hence the exporters' income levels. The second is the demographic endowment factor. Because emerging markets are still relatively young in population age, their savings rate will go through a bulge before aging would naturally bring down their savings. Third, net savings grew because of inflows of FDI, improvements in governance and technology and higher fiscal savings. In China and India higher profitability of the corporate sector accounted for the increase in net savings. Fourth, the savings glut also reflected an 'investment gap', because East Asian economies cut back drastically their social investments as the direct result of the Asian crisis.

By 2006 the global imbalance became a major policy debate as the large U.S. current account deficit had grown to US$720 billion or 5.2% of GDP. In 2007 it was estimated that the United States had to import about US$1 trillion foreign capital annually to finance its deficits or roughly US$4 billion per working day. The net international position of the United States had deteriorated continually from a surplus position of 5.8 percent of GDP in 1970 to a deficit position of 20.4 percent of GDP by 2006.[5] U.S. gross savings had fallen by 2007 to 14% of GDP and net savings to 1.7% of GDP, compared with over 30 percent for Asian economies.

Similarly, the Euro area also had a net international deficit position of 13.5 percent of GDP. The counterparty net surplus external positions (excluding gold) were mainly Japan (42 percent of GDP), China (20.3 percent) and Saudi Arabia (100 percent).

The tables had clearly turned. For the first time in recent history, the emerging markets had shifted from net borrowers to large creditors to the developed markets.

Clearly this deficit was unsustainable. The IMF staff estimated that if nothing was done, the U.S. net international deficit could reach 45 percent of GDP by 2012. Note that when East Asian countries' net international position reached 50 percent of GDP in 1997, they went into crisis. The scenario building showed that if four major conditions were met, the U.S. position might stabilize at around 30–35 percent of GDP by 2012. The

---

[5]   IMF (2007b).

four conditions were (1) increased exchange rate flexibility and higher consumption in emerging Asia, (2) fiscal adjustment in the United States, particularly a gradual reduction in the federal budget deficit by about one-half percentage point of GDP per annum, (3) structural reforms in Japan and the Euro area, and (4) additional spending by oil exporters. By the end of 2008 the Chinese RMB had appreciated by roughly 18 percent against the rate in July 2005, whilst the U.S. dollar had depreciated by about 20 percent in real effective exchange rate terms. In 2007 the U.S. current account deficit had begun to moderate. But by this time, the asset bubbles had already formed, and crisis was unravelling the imbalance.

BUBBLY BUBBLES

The excess liquidity described above had its manifestations common to both crises: asset bubbles in stock and real estate markets. In a seminal study of financial crises, Kaminsky and Reinhart found that run-ups in equity and housing prices are the best leading indicators of crisis in countries experiencing large capital inflows.[6] These bubbles had a multitude of origins, but excess liquidity, large capital inflows, rapid expansion of bank and nonbank credit, plus excessive investments in capital stock and premature capital account liberalization, all created vulnerable conditions for crisis. The Japanese bubble coined a phrase of three excesses – excess capacity, excess borrowing and excess exuberance. This was true during the Asian crisis and certainly true in the present crisis.

These asset bubbles were the products of the contradictions between monetary policy and exchange rate policy. Common to the Japanese bubble, the Mexican crisis, as well as the Asian financial crisis was the role of easy monetary policy that stemmed partly from attempts to limit exchange rate appreciation in the face of large capital inflows.[7] Taiwan suffered similar asset bubbles in the late 1980s,[8] which led to subsequent stock market price support activities. In 2006–2007 the spectacular bubble in Chinese stock prices, which subsequently collapsed by more than 70 percent, originated from a similar confluence of forces.

Recently Reinhart and Rogoff[9] found stunning qualitative and quantitative parallels between the subprime crisis and 18 post–World War II banking crises in the industrial countries, particularly the Big Five crises: Spain (1977),

[6] Kaminsky and Reinhart (1999).
[7] I am grateful for an anonymous referee for pointing out these relationships.
[8] Chen (2001).
[9] Reinhart and Rogoff (2008).

Norway (1987), Finland (1991), Sweden (1991) and Japan (1992). The increase in real housing prices in the United States over the four years before the crisis was over 30 percent, double those on average for banking crises countries in advanced economies and roughly half higher than those of the Big Five: 'Using the S&P/Case-Schiller national index, US house prices peaked in 2006 after rising over 134 percent in the decade 1996–2006. The problem is that "the unprecedented global housing boom of 1995–2006 is now unwinding'.[10]

Asset bubbles are damaging to the real economy because sooner or later they implode, hurting the real wealth of households and corporations and thereby reducing consumption, employment and incomes. In the United States, the proportion of real estate (worth US$20.5 trillion) in households' net worth was 29.5 percent at the end of 2006.[11] Home mortgages, amounting to US$9.8 trillion, amounted to 47.9 percent of residential real estate, but 73.2 percent of household liabilities. Household ownership of equity or shares in the United States is US$6.3 trillion or 9.1 percent of households' net worth. If one were to include mutual fund holdings (US$4.6 trillion), pension fund and life insurance reserves, the proportion rises to 34.7 percent. Since the funds, such as pension, life and mutual funds, also hold a large proportion of equity, any fall in stock prices would have an impact on household net worth, but the impact would be less direct than the fall in house prices.

How did the housing boom occur? It was no doubt due to easy credit conditions and the belief that home ownership is fundamental to democracy. Former U.S. Treasury Under-Secretary for International Affairs John Taylor attributed this to the overly low interest rate policy by the Federal Reserve.[12] In 2001 the Fed reduced the Fed Funds rate 11 times from 6.5 percent to 1.75 percent per annum, partly to counteract the recession post-dot.com bubble of 2000 and the terrorist shock of 9/11. By June 2003 it was lowered to a historically low level of 1 percent. The unintended consequence was rising house prices, as lower interest rates made property more affordable to borrowers.

By 2004 the U.S. homeownership rate had peaked at an all-time high of 69.2 percent. During the housing boom of 2001–2005, banks began to lend freely and loosely, including to house buyers who did not satisfy normal prudential credit standards. Housing affordability was increased by giving

---

[10]   Renaud and Kim (2007), 153.
[11]   Board of Governors of the Federal Reserve System (2007), table B.100.
[12]   Taylor (2007).

interest-only mortgages or by totally relaxing lending standards. Some of borrowers were termed NINJAs: no-income, no-job assets. They bought houses in the hope that house prices would continue to increase over the medium term.

The increase in house prices not only created an illusion of growing wealth, but also encouraged consumption and leverage. It stimulated home construction, creating jobs in the construction industry. The Fed estimated that in 2005 U.S. households extracted US$750 billion in home equity, spending two-third on personal consumption. My view is that allowing the housing bubble to occur was a grave policy error, because the Fed grossly underestimated what the bubble could do to the financial system through high and unseen leverage. From the Asian and Japanese experience, housing bubbles are fed by excess bank credit, and these could be restrained partly through tighter monetary policy and partly through prudential measures, such as lower loan-to-value ratios and higher capital requirements. None of these prudential measures were taken by either the Fed or the other bank regulators.

But no one expected that over two years between June 2004 and June 2006 the 17 step increases in the Fed Fund rate of 425 basis points by the Fed from the low of 1% to a peak of 5.25% would be followed not only by a decline in property prices, but also a near collapse of the U.S. and European banking systems. In February 2007, when the subprime mortgage default rate rose from around 10 percent to about 15 percent, everyone thought that since the outstanding amount was only US$757 billion, of which losses were estimated at US$150 billion or roughly 1% of U.S. GDP,[13] the matter was manageable. No one realized that it was the tip of the iceberg.

Matters became dramatic in April 2007, when New Century Financial, the largest of the subprime lenders, declared bankruptcy. In June 2007 two hedge funds investing in subprime assets run by Bear Stearns, the fifth largest investment bank in the United States, failed. In August 2007 the world was caught by surprise when the Fed and the European Central Bank had to inject over US$300 billion of liquidity to prevent a seizure of the interbank market due to the collapse of the asset-backed securities (ABS) market.

What had happened was the spread of risks through securitization of mortgages and other credit assets to investors outside the United States, particularly in Europe. In a world flush with liquidity, investors engaged in a frantic 'search for yield'. As described in Chapter 13, the financial engineers obliged by packaging new structured products mixed assets of

---

[13] Bank of England (2007), box 1, 20.

different credit quality into collateralized debt obligations (CDOs). By July 2007 several German regional banks that invested in such CDOs began to require heavy liquidity support, as their own liquidity dried up as CDO prices fell. The problem escalated in mid-August, when Northern Rock, the largest specialist mortgage lender in the United Kingdom, needed liquidity support, and in September it suffered bank runs, the first in the country for over a century. It took a U.K. Government blanket guarantee on Northern Rock's deposits to stop the runs.

From then on, the subprime crisis continued to unwind, with more and more commercial banks and investment banks announcing greater provisions against the toxic products that they held. This also meant that they needed more capital injection. The market began to focus on the quality of their asset holdings, divided into three levels. Level 1 assets were those that are marked to liquid market prices. Level 2 assets were marked partly to market and partly to model, and Level 3 assets were marked to either model or management judgement, or as some cynics claimed, marked to myth.

The scale of the shrinkage of the ABS market can be judged by the fact that from August to year-end 2007, the market size shrank by US$447 billion, or nearly one-third.[14] In January 2008 the world's largest bank, Citigroup, reported a US$10 billion quarterly loss, due mostly to write-down of $18.1 billion related to subprime mortgage investments. It had to receive a US$12.5 billion capital infusion from key strategic investors. Share prices of financial stocks fell continuously in 2008.

Global markets were shaken badly on 14 March 2008, when the Federal Reserve Bank of New York helped to negotiate a deal whereby JP Morgan bought the fifth largest investment bank, Bear Stearns, for US$2 per share, compared with a peak price of US$169 in 2007. Bear Stearns had admitted that it owned US$48 billion in subprime debt, of which US$17 billion was difficult to value. The New York Fed undertook to provide US$30 billion to JP Morgan against the value of Bear Stearns assets.

On 17 March 2008, the Fed made an unprecedented interest rate cut of 75 basis points, bringing the Fed Funds rate to 2.25 percent, the level it had been at in December 2004. Although it was estimated that two million mortgages, valued at between US$700 and US$1,000 billion, will have their interest rates reset to market levels, the effect of the rate cut was to avoid the resets to levels that would cause more subprime defaults. The Fed also announced that it would provide a new US$200 billion emergency loan facility.

---

[14] Hale (2008).

The summer of 2008 will go down in history as a period of central banking schizophrenia. On the one hand, inflation was clearly on the rise. Oil and commodity prices rose relentlessly until Brent oil crude peaked at US$147 per barrel on 3 July. But at the same time, interbank liquidity dried up, whilst banks frantically sought to increase capital from around the world, particularly from sovereign wealth funds.

MELTDOWN

On 11 July the U.S. Treasury announced plans to rescue Fannie Mae and Freddie Mac, the two largest agencies lending to the mortgage market. For years the publicly listed Government-Sponsored Enterprises (GSEs) were anomalies, fully privately owned but carrying an implicit guarantee of the government. They accounted for over US$5 trillion of mortgage-backed securities, nearly half of which was owned by foreigners. They were lightly regulated and had political clout, resisting for years calls for changes to bad governance and shaky accounting. The U.S. Congress consistently backed the idea of home ownership, and these GSEs provided the lion's share of financing. By 7 September the share prices of both GSEs had fallen so much with widening CDS spreads that the U.S. Treasury had to place both into conservatorship, promising to take enough shares to keep them with positive net worth. They were in effect nationalized.

In hindsight, Congress did not ideologically like the idea of government intervention, so after the rescue of the two GSEs, it became politically impossible to rescue the next failing institution, exactly the reason the United States could not help Asia in 1997 after Congress objected to help for Mexico in 1994.[15] On 15 September the fateful decision was taken to allow the fourth largest investment bank, Lehman Brothers, to fail. The U.S. Government stated that there was no legal authority to rescue the firm, but it did later inject capital to stop other banks from failing.

That failure will go down in history as the trigger that set off the systemic crisis worldwide. Although it had only US$620 billion in assets, regulators grossly underestimated that at the time of failure Lehman had a total of US$1.6 trillion worth of counterparty positions that became frozen. Since Lehman accounted for nearly 14 percent of trading in equities on the London Stock Exchange and 12 percent of fixed income in New York and it also managed client assets for hedge funds and investor clients, the liquidity of its counterparties was immediately impaired on default.

---

[15] See Chapter 5.

The default of Lehman also triggered huge increases in CDS premia, which meant that those who sold protection had to offer immediately greater collateral. AIG, which had US$441 billion of CDS positions, had to provide US$14.5 billion to bring total collateral posted to US$31 billion in a matter of days. If AIG had not been nationalized by an US$85 billion loan in exchange for 79.9 percent of its equity by the Fed, its failure would have set off contagion failure beyond imagination.

The default on Lehman bonds also caused money market funds to fall below their US$1 par value, so that there were immediate withdrawals from the US$3.4 trillion money market fund sector. If that sector had collapsed, the liquidity crunch in the United States would have been catastrophic.

The irony of the Lehman failure was that it was an effort by the high priests of free market fundamentalism to demonstrate to everyone that they were acting against moral hazard, to demonstrate that no investment bank is too large to fail. The decision had an opposite effect – it triggered the panic that almost broke the markets. In demonstrating that those who practice bad behaviour can be allowed to fail, the effect was to tell the market that another and another may also be allowed to fail, so that the best strategy to protect oneself is to cut and run. Perhaps the middle of a crisis is not the appropriate time to prove a philosophical point. The correct anti–moral hazard action is during normal times, to be exercised dynamically in scale as financial risks escalate. With Lehman, a massive deleveraging operation began and unfettered finance began to implode.

The Lehman shock was like a tsunami that cascaded across the globe in ever-widening circles. It was as if a brownout in New York shut down half the European grid, because European banks shared nearly half of the losses. The sharp retrenchment in interbank lending became rapidly a global affair, spreading to emerging markets. The Mexican peso and Brazilian real had to be defended against sharp depreciation, and Indonesia closed its stock market for three days. Hong Kong and Singapore faced investor protests against the default of Lehman minibonds. A number of countries had to fully guarantee their bank deposits. Oil prices collapsed back to just over US$60 compared with US$146 per barrel in July 2008. The Australian and New Zealand dollars sharply depreciated as the yen carry trade unwound. Commodity prices began to unravel.

From an institution that six months ago faced almost no new lending, the IMF suddenly found itself once again lending to Iceland (US$2.1 billion), Hungary (€12.5 billion) and Ukraine (US$16.5 billion) and credit negotiations with Belarus and Pakistan. As various emerging markets got into payment problems, the IMF created a short-term lending facility amounting to US$100 billion.

After the failure of Lehman, the financial rescue plans were the largest in history, in total some US$3.4 trillion, the largest being the United States (US$700 billion), United Kingdom (£400 billion) and Germany (€515 billion). On 3 October the U.S. Congress passed the Troubled Assets Relief Programme (TARP) that allowed the Treasury to buy toxic assets and remove them from the books of the banks. The Treasury instead used US$250 billion to inject capital to the largest banks. By November the Chinese Government announced a RMB 4 trillion (US$586 billion) fiscal stimulus package to protect the economy against an expected slowdown. Japan and Europe fell into recession after two quarters of negative growth, and the U.S. statistical authorities announced that the U.S. economy had been in recession since December 2007.

The idea that emerging markets could decouple from the major markets proved to be a myth. As exports plunged throughout East Asia to negative growth levels, even the fastest growing region in the world was planning for recession. The World Bank announced world trade might decline by 2 percent in 2009, the first time it had shrunk since 1982.

WHAT WENT WRONG?

The complexity of the 2007–2008 crisis is such that we need to examine the current credit crisis from at least three perspectives – that of history and macro- and micro-economic conditions.

The analysis from the longer historical perspective will be deferred to the last chapter, but the more recent origins of the current crisis can be traced to four major mega-trends. The first was the appearance in 1989 of a 3 billion member labour force in the market economies following the end of the Cold War, which gave rise to a global flood of cheap goods and low inflation for nearly two decades.

The second was the monetary policy responses to the Japanese bubble/deflation following 1990, which gave rise to over two decades of almost interest-free yen loans globally, creating the famous yen carry trade. Recent estimates of the global carry trade, essentially the arbitraging of differences in national interest rates and exchange rates, amounted to US$2 trillion, of which half is probably the yen carry trade.[16] The supply of almost interest-free funding was effectively to subsidize the rise of financial engineering, which was applied with great effect in the Asian crisis period. The success of such carry trades was then applied and magnified through leverage and derivatives, a hallmark of the new investment banking and hedge fund class.

[16] Lee (2008).

The increase and reversal of carry trades using low interest rate currencies added to volatility and volume of global financial trading and flows.

The third therefore was the emergence of financial engineers, described in Chapter 13. Underlying their sophisticated risk management models was one fatal flaw, that the world of risk was a bell-shaped statistical curve that ignored the long-tailed black swan risk. It was the underestimation of once-in-400-year risks that proved their undoing.

The fourth was the phase of global deregulation of markets, described in the previous chapter.

Essentially, these mega-trends were four arbitrages that created converging globalization – wage arbitrage, financial arbitrage, knowledge arbitrage and regulatory arbitrage.

At the policy level, the failure of state planning also saw the ebb tide of Keynesian economics, which called for greater government intervention in the economy. The dominance of Friedmanite free market capitalism unfortunately overemphasized the use of monetary policy tools and the importance of central banks. Fiscal policy was relegated back to minimizing fiscal deficits, whilst elegant monetary targeting theories were propounded based on consumer prices that ignored the crucial role of asset prices. Worse, both regulators and central banks chose not to act anticyclically, allowing the bubbles to inflate.

It was a grave intellectual blind spot that the endowment effect of cheap labour entering into the world economy deluded many Western central bankers that their monetary policy was working wonders on global inflation.

In hindsight, that intellectual blind spot was minor compared to the macroeconomic policy mistake to ignore the bubble in real estate prices. The naive belief that widespread home ownership was good for long-term social stability irrespective of affordability and supply constraints had the unintended consequence of creating social expectations that house prices would rise and never drop. The central importance of housing within household balance sheets is often taken for granted. However, real estate accounts for the bulk of assets of households and is certainly the most important collateral asset of the banking system. In many countries the desire for greater home ownership was not backed by sufficient supply side responses, so that larger and more lending for housing created an upward price push that became self-fulfilling. Between 2003 and 2007 real estate assets of U.S. households rose by US$6 trillion, but household liabilities increased by US$4.5 trillion, implying that households consumed a large part of the increase in house prices.

This was made possible because the financial system pushed loans to the consumer sector. Mortgage loan-to-value (LTV) ratios rose to as high as 100 percent for some house buyers, and credit evaluation deteriorated by lending to subprime borrowers. Unlike mortgage markets around the world, these U.S. mortgages were without recourse, meaning that the borrower could default and hand house price losses back over to the lender. These subprime mortgages were then sliced and diced into packaged derivatives by the financial engineers without supervision of the regulators and sold to the financial markets that were hungry for yield during the low-interest environment from 2003 to 2007.

The above macroeconomic question is crucial to understanding the current world financial crisis, because it was the ability to finance external deficits that was the basis for the emergence of the current 'originate to distribute' structure of the U.S. banking system. In other words, the U.S. and European banking system evolved from the traditional retail banking model (accept deposit and lend) to the new wholesale banking model because they were no longer constrained by limited domestic savings, but could draw on global savings through the securitization channel. Microweaknesses were then amplified to become global imbalances. It was an accident waiting to happen.

The inevitable question becomes: who is to blame?

WHO IS TO BLAME?

The more I read books and articles about financial crises, the more I am struck by the truth of the Chinese saying 'The bum pushes the brain' or 'Your viewpoint depends on where you sit'. Western views fall into two broad schools: 'It's all the fault of Asians' or 'It's the international architecture'. Asians' views range from denial to 'Blame the foreigners, including the IMF'. Political scientists tend to blame domestic politics, economists tend to blame faulty policies and investors tend to blame bad corporate governance and lack of transparency. Our own education system seems at fault, because all of us seem to seek 'the magic bullet' of one single most important cause and look for a 'one size fits all' solution. The globalized world has become too complex for that.

What was amazing was the crisis breached four lines of defence for financial stability. The first line is at the Board level of corporate governance, internal audit and controls, a matter of self-discipline. The second line is at the level of external auditors and external advisers, such as investment banks, corporate lawyers and consultants. The third line is the rating agencies, market analysts and the media, who provide the market discipline of sunshine. The fourth line is the regulatory discipline provided by the multiple financial regulators and the criminal enforcement agencies. None worked to stop the crisis.

Sir Howard Davies in his tour de force *The Future of Regulation*[17] raised the classic blame game: 'Politicians and others have raised serious questions about the adequacy of market regulation. Could the crisis not have been prevented? Were the regulators asleep at the wheel?' This is not a trivial question. Asians who suffered through the Asian crisis could at least hide behind the excuse that they were less sophisticated, they did not know better and they had weak governance, poorer supervision and bad transparency. But why did the subprime crisis occur in the most sophisticated of markets and advanced market regulation?

In the previous chapter I have already alluded to the technical mistakes that were made at the level of monetary policy and regulatory techniques employed, but my personal view is that the mistake at the philosophical level was deeper and more damaging.

Unfortunately, the ideology that markets are self-equilibrating created complacency amongst those responsible bordering on irresponsibility. It could be said that in the Asian crisis the authorities interfered in the market too much. In this crisis they intervened too little, too late. Worse, they assumed that someone else was watching the shop.

Former Fed Chairman Greenspan[18] has begun to defend his record and views in his autobiography and in a series of articles. In 2002 he reasoned why the central bank did not tackle the emerging bubble:

We at the Federal Reserve considered a number of issues related to asset bubbles – that is, surges in prices of assets to unsustainable levels. As events evolved, we recognized that, despite our suspicions, it was very difficult to definitively identify a bubble until after the fact – that is, when its bursting confirmed its existence. Moreover, it was far from obvious that bubbles, even if identified early, could be preempted short of the central bank inducing a substantial contraction in economic activity – the very outcome we would be seeking to avoid.[19]

I beg to disagree. There is never perfect information, and certainly in the real world leaders are paid to make judgements, however difficult they are. The toughest part of being a leader is to do the most unpopular task, such

---

[17]   Davies (2008).
[18]   Fleckenstein and Sheehan (2008); Blake (2008).
[19]   Greenspan (2002).

as taking away the punch bowl when the party gets interesting. The easiest part of bureaucratic life is not to do anything and simply wait and see, but the consequences could be catastrophic. A more nuanced approach would be to tighten the regulatory side to prevent excesses in financial sector, a move that would have been unpopular with the industry, but it would have been prudent for society as a whole.

To be fair to the loose monetary policy, no one can deny that the period from August 2003 to December 2007 created 8.25 million jobs in the United States, generating prosperity throughout the world.[20]

But what about the property market? In his autobiography Greenspan described his judgement call on the property bubble:

I was aware that the loosening of mortgage credit terms for subprime borrowers increased financial risk, and that subsidized home ownership initiatives distort market outcomes. But I believed then, as now, that the benefits of broadened home ownership are worth the risk. Protection of property rights, so critical to a market economy, requires a critical mass of owners to sustain political power.[21]

On the day that the Bear Stearns' takeover was announced on 17 March 2008, Greenspan wrote an article in the *Financial Times* blaming current risk models and econometric models: 'as complex as they have become, are still too simple to capture the full array of governing variables that drive global economic reality'.[22] As a traditional central banker, I personally find it unconvincing that just because it is difficult to call the existence of a bubble, a central bank should not take preventive action. If a central bank is not there to safeguard a financial system from financial crisis and to make a judegment call on threats to financial stability, what is it there for?

As Clive Crook perceptively commented on Greenspan's views, the fundamental problem was

moral hazard (operating at multiple levels); a gross failure of regulation in mortgage lending (for which Greenspan is substantially responsible: remember that he was a cheerleader for the subprime lending business); a structure of finance-industry incentives that rewarded greed and recklessness indulged at other's expense (itself a failure of regulation); and last but not least the most credit-friendly tax regime in the world.[23]

---

[20]   Giles (2008).
[21]   Greenspan (2007), 233.
[22]   Greenspan (2008a), 9.
[23]   Crook (2008).

REGULATORY IMPLICATIONS FROM SUBPRIME

By mid-2008 there was a rush of papers by regulators and industry associations alike on the regulatory fallout from the subprime crisis. In December 2007 the U.K. FSA[24] was quick to conclude after Northern Rock, inter alia, that there is a need to improve stress testing, there should be more consistent liquidity regulation internationally and there should be a closer look at securitization, the role of credit rating agencies and improved transparency about who is carrying risk, especially off-balance sheet exposures.

In March 2008 the Senior Supervisors Group,[25] comprising eight developed market supervisors, had already identified both the strengths and weaknesses of the risk management practices of the major market participants. A few days later the U.S. President's Working Group on Financial Markets made a report on the subprime crisis,[26] identifying the principal causes of the credit crisis as a breakdown in underwriting standards for subprime mortgages, significant erosion of market discipline in the securitization process, from originators to rating agencies to investors, flaws in credit rating agencies' assessment of subprime securities and risk management weaknesses at financial institutions and regulatory policies, including capital and disclosure requirements that failed to mitigate risk management weaknesses.

To deal with the problems identified, the Group made the following recommendations:

- Reform key parts of the mortgage origination process, including stronger licensing standards for mortgage brokers, oversight of originators and stronger consumer protection rules
- Enhance disclosure and market practices to impose greater market discipline, such as greater oversight of institutional investors, requiring originators to provide more information about the underlying risk profiles of structured products
- Reform the credit rating agencies' processes
- Improve global financial institutions' risk management practices and
- Ensure that prudential regulatory policies would strengthen such risk management.

By April 2008 the Institute of International Finance (IIF), the de facto association representing global financial institutions, had already made an

---

[24] UK HM Treasury, Financial Services Authority and Bank of England (2008).
[25] Senior Supervisors Group (2008).
[26] US President's Working Group on Financial Markets (2008).

Interim Report on Market Best Practices[27] that also identified risk management weaknesses that had led to the subprime turmoil. The IIF Committee noted that for global markets to work efficiently, particularly the 'originate-to-distribute' model, there had to be better management standards at all levels, from originator, broker and rating agency to the investor. Significantly, the IIF Committee requested that the fair-value accounting and Basel II Accord standards be reviewed with respect to their procyclical effects.

It is hard to see how the rating agencies would be able to avoid severe regulation after their performance in rating CDOs. After the Enron, Parmalat and dot.com crises, IOSCO tried to impose more regulation on them beyond voluntary codes of conduct, but the rating agencies were able to hide behind the argument that they were members of the press and therefore subject to the protection of the First Amendment that protected their freedom.[28]

THE PROBLEM OF REGULATORY CAPTURE

The real issue has to be asked. Since Western regulators all had increased resources, perceived independence of action and technical tools all in place, how did financial crisis still occur? As Sherlock Holmes used to say, when you have excluded the impossible, whatever remains, however improbable, must be the truth.

I can only conjecture that it was because the regulatory community as a whole, rather than any individual, became captive to the lobbying power of the financial industry. There is a deafening silence in the debate on this subject, because during the Asian crisis, the close relationship between business interests and their regulators was labelled 'crony capitalism'. But it is a fact that many leading financial institutions hire former regulators to lobby for their interests. The close interconnectivity between the regulatory community and their regulated institutions is a matter that deserves greater public debate.

No financial regulator is independent from the market that he or she is trying to regulate. Stigler (1971), Posner (1974) and others identified the problem of regulatory capture, whereby vested interests lobby or influence the regulator to behave in ways that are favourable to the vested interests.

Alan Greenspan's remark during his interrogation by a hostile Banking Committee that he was 'often following the "will of Congress"' during this

---

[27] Institute of International Finance (2008a).
[28] Grais and Katsiris (2007).

long tenure and did 'what I am supposed to do, not what I'd like to'[29] illustrated the frustration of central banks and financial regulators facing hostile politicians who want the bureaucracy only to follow what is politically expedient, but what could be morally and strategically wrong in the long term.

In December 2008 the news broke of a paragon of New York society, a former chairman of NASDAQ no less, Bernard Madoff, confessing to a Ponzi scheme of up to $50 billion. This happened despite several tipoffs to the SEC since as early as 1999 that something was amiss.[30] Mr Madoff's niece was his compliance officer and subsequently married a former SEC attorney. Members of the Madoff family served on various regulatory advisory bodies. In June 2009, Madoff was sentenced to 150 years imprisonment, the maximum period allowed.

The contradiction between the regulator and the regulatees is one of both cooperation and conflict of interests. In order to regulate well, the regulator should enforce the law fairly and independently. And yet, to be effective, the regulator must have support and cooperation from the market and the legislature, and because they comprise different competing interests, the regulator can either be subject to regulatory capture or try to engage interactively and independently to change public opinion, so that the regulatory objectives are met. Given the dynamic, reflexive and evolving game that is played between the regulator and the regulated, it is not surprising that outcomes are neither ideal nor anywhere near optimal.

The problems of the specialized financial regulator are almost identical to those faced by central banking. It is now widely accepted that for the central bank to conduct its monetary policy well, it must be operationally independent from the government, and ideally from political influence, so that the central bank is able to conduct its monetary policy objectively and in the best interest of society.[31] Where independent regulators and central banks report directly to the legislature, they become captive to the political debate. Where they become too market friendly, they become captive to industry.

However, there is the difference between operational independence and policy independence.[32] A central bank is independent within government, but not of (the wider functions of) government. Similarly, a regulator must have operational independence, but its actions ultimately cannot be independent from the rest of government.

---

[29] Scannell and Reddy (2008), A1.
[30] Zukerman and Scannell (2008).
[31] See Cuikerman (2008); Sargent (1993).
[32] Goodhart, Per Jacobsen Lectures 2004.

These thorny issues of regulatory and central bank independence have resurfaced with the current crisis. There is no free lunch and there is no such thing as absolute independence. Once central bankers become independent in law, they become hostage to influences through the media, through lobbyists and through comments or calls for accountability by the legislature, in addition to budgetary influence from public auditors or ministries of finance. Because it is popular to allow a market boom to proceed and to intervene through reducing interest rates when markets fall, central banks are accused of inducing moral hazard through what is known as the 'central banking put'. This is the option open to central banks to bail out bad market investment decisions by either injecting liquidity or lowering interest rates.

In contrast to central bankers, which have the optional ability to exercise puts, financial regulators are subject to calls. This is the option of the public to blame the regulator for every instance of market failure, to call the regulator to account in public enquiry and to ultimately fire the regulator or at least its chairman or chief executive. Republican candidate John McCain openly said that he would fire SEC Chairman Christopher Cox. The regulator's job is not a popular one and is probably best taken as a pre-retirement job, because it is difficult to be a popular regulator if one is to do one's job effectively. I have personally seen how Brooksley Born, Chairperson of the U.S. Commodity Futures Trading Commission, bravely called for the regulation of OTC financial derivatives in 1998, in the light of experience with derivative losses in the Asian crisis and Orange County.[33] Because that view was unpopular with industry and the other regulators, she stepped down in June 1999. I believe that her stand has been vindicated.

Second, to do their job properly, the financial regulator must also be an institutional reformer, continually changing the rules, products, processes and institutions so that markets function effectively and robustly. Such activity will inevitably rouse the opposition of vested interests who are likely or believe themselves victims of any changes. Unfortunately, financial regulators have little compensatory power, such as the ability of central banks to provide lender of last resort facilities. Indeed, any exercise of compensatory powers, such as lax licensing, is likely to reflect badly on the regulator.

Indeed, sometimes one of the most difficult tasks of financial regulators is to resist calls for regulatory relaxation and forbearance. An example is the relaxation of the Net Capital Rule 15c3-1 for securities broker/dealers under the Securities Exchange Act (1934) made in 2004.[34] The old

---

[33] Born (1998).
[34] Labaton (2008).

capital rule basically capped liabilities at 15 times net capital. After searching through 232 pages of the rule,[35] looking carefully at the exemptions to the basic caps and appendices E to the rule, I finally uncovered that the net effect of the exemption for large investment banks of more than $5 billion in equity was to allow them to use their own risk management models to calculate their own net capital. This in effect meant that there were no more limits to their leverage. It also explained why the investment banks were so vehemently against the use of any crude net capital caps.

But the net result of the removal of any crude capital limit was that their excess leverage and almost complete dependence on wholesale interbank funding blew up the investment banking industry in 2008. It was ironic to note that Hank Paulson was head of Goldman Sachs when the rule change was requested and made, whilst he had to deal with the consequences of the regulatory change in 2008 as Secretary of the Treasury.

The moral of this story is that modern financial regulators constantly must use their persuasive powers to argue for the higher moral ground and appeal for public support. The regulators must transparently explain their actions, accountability and performance. Without public support, financial regulators are the first scapegoats for any market failure. Sacking a financial regulator is often an excuse for not undertaking any fundamental changes that would prevent recurrence of factors that gave rise to the market failure. Financial regulators therefore need to be constantly vigilant as to the consequences of being effective regulators. Market events are often outside the control of even the best of regulators. Moreover, the regulator cannot afford to ignore the law of unintended consequences in what appears to be small steps of deregulation that open up huge holes of nonregulation.

Once we realize that financial regulation is tied up with the political economy of policy choice, we begin to see clearly why market failures are not divorced from policy and regulatory failures. The market interactively arbitrages regulatory action or inaction, which are also shaped by market lobbying and vested interests. These all add to the complexity of regulatory timing, sequencing of policies and reform design and processes. Keynes was perhaps the first to quip that the psychology of policymakers to be popular did make bold decisions against the market consensus easy, because 'worldly wisdom teaches that it is better for reputation to fail conventionally than to succeed unconventionally'.[36]

---

[35] www.finra.org.
[36] Keynes (1942) [1936], 158.

We come back to the purpose of financial regulation, which is to safe-guard the interests of society as a whole through supervision of the activities of the financial market participants. In one sense, financial regulation and supervision can be likened to an insurance policy. If we know that in every economic cycle there is likely to be a financial crisis that causes a certain amount of losses to society, then the annual costs of financial regulation, supervision and enforcement are equivalent to the annual insurance premium that society pays for either prevention or amelioration of the losses from a financial crisis. It may very well that we can never remove crises losses, but if the discounted present value of annual regulatory costs is lower than the costs saved or ameliorated through supervision during the crisis, then the costs are worth it. Clearly, if the reverse is true, we have overregulated.

John Kenneth Galbraith, author of *The Great Crash 1929,* puts the question elegantly:

But now, as throughout history, financial capacity and political perspicacity are inversely correlated. Long-run salvation by men of business has never been highly regarded if it means disturbance of orderly life and convenience in the present. So inaction will be advocated in the present even though it means deep trouble in the future. Here, at least equally with communism, lies the threat to capitalism. It is what causes men who know that things are going quite wrong to say that things are fundamentally sound.

If Asia and the world are to survive this and the next financial crisis, we will need wise men, central bankers or financial regulators, who not only will have the courage to say when things are going wrong, but to do something about them.

SIXTEEN

A Crisis of Governance

Yesterday's world order is going fast, while tomorrow's world has yet to emerge. We are not in fact facing the 'new world order' today's politicians so constantly invoke. Rather we are facing a new world disorder *– no one can know for how long.*
                    - Peter Drucker

We now come to the key lessons that we can draw from the Asian and current crises.

RITES OF PASSAGE

The Asian crisis was like a drama where we can blame the actors (Asians versus foreigners), the stage (weak domestic architecture versus faulty international architecture) or the script (bad domestic policies versus wrong international medicine). What made the Asian crisis even more fascinating is that it was not a case of the collapse of failed or failing states, but the crisis of previously highly successful states.

The more I reflect on the Asian crisis, the more convinced I am that the crisis was a clash of mindsets between the political economy of domestic economies and the rise of globalization. This clash of mindsets was inevitable, as the world becomes more and more interconnected and interactive. The Asian systems of public and private governance that worked and succeeded spectacularly in the Asian Miracle period proved to be fragile and vulnerable under the shocks of global capital flows.

Similarly, more than a decade later, the global crisis erupted because no economy is now an island to itself. A chain of domestic events, each apparently harmless or benign in itself, can be catastrophic when linked globally. The crisis was a network crisis where no one was looking at the whole. In short, it was a crisis of national and global governance in a networked world.

American banker Richard O'Brien, writing in 1995 on 'Who Rules the World's Financial Markets', posed the problem presciently: 'In this fast-paced environment, regulators are entrusted with preserving a system they no longer thoroughly control but also with controlling a system that neither they nor the players thoroughly understand.'[1] In reality, the world is changing so fast that current economic theory and analysis cannot cope with understanding it properly. The four mega-trends of the 21st century – globalisation, financial innovation, liberalisation and technological advancement – tested the quality of governance of the corporate, national and international economic and financial architecture. At the very least, they all came out with pretty bad marks.

Put in another way, the Asian crisis was the growing pains of Asian economies transiting to become middle-income global economies that were not psychologically, organizationally or technically prepared for the risks of globalization. The crisis was the price Asia paid for its rites of passage. Ironically, the current crisis may also be the price that the world is paying to transit into the next stage of globalization.

From that perspective, 2007–2008 clearly marked an important turning point in the global market economy. We must pose three significant questions. First, does this mark the peak of global capitalism?

One thing at least is certain: the crisis put a question mark on the American dream – that every individual, through his or her own labour and creativity, can have all that he or she wants. This could be true, for individual Americans, who number less than 5 percent of world population, account for 25 percent of global GDP and are able to consume annually net external resources equivalent to 6 percent of GDP. Unfortunately, the global resource environment cannot support that American dream for average Chinese and Indians, who together number 37 percent of the world population. The problems of global resources and the environment were not constraints to emerging markets during the Great Depression, but fast-growing countries like China and India must address global warming and environmental sustainability not only for their own health, but also for mankind as a whole.

It is easy to forget that the Great Stability occurred in a period of global warming, when good weather produced good harvests. As we have been reminded by Mother Earth, drought in Australia, earthquake in China, avian and swine flu and water stress elsewhere are all symptoms that global weather and natural disasters may change the whole growth equation. Environmental sustainability is probably the most important global issue

---

[1] O'Brien (1995), 149.

for which current theory and governance models are not equipped to cope. When the earth is stressed, human society is stressed, with terrorism, crime and fundamentalism creating social alienation and polarization.

But this issue is profound. My own conjecture is that Asians will have to find their own model of growth, in which we discard GDP fever (the mad rush for fast growth) and look for a more sustainable pace of growth that provides employment without destroying our environment.

The second macro-history trend is that if India and China are both growing at more than 8 percent per year, whilst G-3, the United States, Europe and Japan are growing at less than 2 percent per year, the relative power between the mature economies and the emerging markets will change dramatically. Angus Maddison[2] has projected that by 2018, China will overtake the United States as the largest economy in the world, with India as number 3. By 2030 he estimates that Asia (including Japan) will account for 53 percent of world GDP, whereas the United States and Europe will account for only 33 percent. If this were the case, the global financial architecture would be significantly different from the present.

Already by 2007 Asia accounted for 66.8 percent of world official reserves, 55 percent of the world population, 24.5 percent of world GDP, but only 16 percent of IMF quotas, equivalent to its voting power in the Bretton Wood institutions. My own crude calculations suggest that Asian financial markets will be the largest in the world within the next 10 years, assuming that financial deepening in Asia continues to improve and Asian currencies appreciate relative to the U.S. dollar and Euro. This means that either one Asian currency or Asian currencies as a group will very likely play a role as a global reserve currency by that time.

Thirdly, is Asia ready to play that role? Not by far. In the past, emerging markets were dependent on the advanced economies for markets and financing. Asia's surplus role has been too recent for the fact to sink in.

Asia had to put its excess savings in the West precisely because its own financial system is not ready to intermediate such savings. Its regulatory structure is still evolving, and most Asian bureaucrats are neither internationally minded nor prepared psychologically to act in the international monetary order. In the last 10 years, the number of Asian bureaucrats in the Bretton Wood institutions has declined not just because of better career prospects at home, but also because they see little future for themselves in these institutions. There are hardly any think tanks in Asia dedicated to thinking about the international financial order.

---

[2] Maddison (2007).

THE IMMEDIATE LESSONS

The speed at which the entire financial system in the United States and Europe began to unwind showed how networked the financial systems have become as a result of two decades of deregulation.

There is every likelihood that the Web of Debt,[3] as Ellen Hodgson Brown so elegantly puts it, will unwind. Global deleveraging will continue until the excesses are worked out. Globally important banks will all have to cut their loans materially because of undercapitalization. Nationalized banks would also act much more prudently than private ownership. But the real sector adjustment has only just begun. At the heart of the adjustment is the U.S. savings gap, manifested in its current account deficit. If it were to adjust back to 3 percent of GDP, it would cut back exports to the United States to the order of roughly US$320 billion annually or roughly 13.5 percent fall in imports. This is already beginning to have major negative multiplier effects on Asia.

Whilst the amount of subprime-related paper held by Asians is limited, the amount of financial paper denominated in U.S. dollars and Euros by official reserves, banks and sovereign wealth funds remains substantial. Hence, Asians will not only be hurt by the global financial crisis through the trade channel, but as well as through wealth loss from either currency devaluation or a fall in asset prices. In addition, those countries such as Korea and others that relied heavily on global interbank borrowing will be subject to tighter liquidity and higher borrowing costs.

There are many lessons to be learnt, but I feel six deserve highlighting because of their significance.

BACK TO BASICS

The first is that crisis is the natural outcome of human excesses. It is the most Darwinian of collective human action – it creatively destroys the irrational exuberance and brings everyone back to the reality that there is no free lunch. Schumpeter was right to say that out of crisis comes rejuvenation. Crisis actually accelerates the exit of weak and fraudulent institutions that should have been the function of effective regulation over a normal period of time. Accordingly, we cannot forget that crisis is an event, whereas reform, restructuring and regulation are continuous processes.

Crisis concentrates the mind on only what we need to do to fix what is wrong with society and the economy and what we did not do or could

[3]   Hodgson Brown (2007).

not do because of vested interests. There is, in fact, only a short window of opportunity of reform before memory fades and vested interests again capture the need for reform. If we do not reform whilst the sun is shining, crisis, like the next tsunami, is an inevitable consequence.

The second is that derivatives carry leverage and therefore risks. Risks are transferred but do not disappear. Indeed, not understanding the nature of derivatives is itself a major risk.

Basic finance theory will tell you that a derivative is a representation of an underlying asset that is essentially linked through leverage. The advantage of derivatives is that one can easily subdivide an indivisible underlying asset (such as a large piece of immovable land) and make the property right transferable at lower transaction costs. Real products require labour and real assets to make. Financial derivatives require imagination. There can be multiple derivation of the same underlying asset. As we see from experience, if the underlying asset gets into trouble, the derivative pyramid can come crumbling down very rapidly.

The instability of the financial pyramid is precisely why finance should be fettered or regulated heavily. Left to pure market forces and no constraints, the financial derivative game can be exploited at great moral hazard – increase leverage and opacity for private gain at eventual social cost. At the purest conceptual level, there is therefore no principal difference between state planning and unfettered finance – both consume or waste at great social loss. The crux is the golden mean – how to utilize the efficiencies of market forces and yet regulate them to prevent excesses and instability. Herein lies the uncomfortable relationship between the government and the market. Too much government is bad, and too much unfettered markets is also bad.

The third fundamental is that if finance is a derivative of the real economy, no financial structure is strong unless the real economy is strong. We cannot allow monetary theory to dazzle us away from the common sense fact that finance must serve the real economy, rather than drive it. If this is so, then it does not make sense that Wall Street should be paid more than Main Street. We must ensure that the incentive structure is even-handed – financial wizardry cannot be rewarded irrespective of performance. The corporate governance structure must be transformed so that there can be no golden parachutes, and pay must be aligned with long-term performance.

Focusing on the real sector means that greater attention will have to be paid to the housing market as one of the key pillars of social stability, to ensure via appropriate government policy that there is adequate supply and that housing is affordable to the majority of the population on a sustainable and equitable basis. The mistake in the Basel Accord was to exercise social policy through regulatory forbearance, by giving credit to housing a lower than appropriate capital weighting. We must have dynamic credit provisioning and better use of loan-to-value ratios in preventing credit excesses to finance real estate bubbles.

For emerging markets, I draw two immediate conclusions from the current crisis. The first is that the universal banking model has serious problems for two fundamental reasons. One is that you cannot mix the culture of investment banking (where risk taking is key) and commercial banking (where prudence is vital) under one roof. Glass-Steagall was not fundamentally wrong. The other is that not every banking system can become totally wholesale: the bulk of the banking system must remain retail and therefore concentrate on what Main Street banking does or should do well – protect the interest of depositors and serve the bulk of the corporate sector, especially small and medium-sized enterprises that provide mainstream employment in the real economy. It is no longer about quick money, but long-term returns on a safe and steady basis.

The fourth key lesson is that even though unregulated financial innovation was at the heart of the current crisis, we cannot conclude simply that all financial innovation is bad. The plain vanilla types of mortgages and mortgage-backed securities are performing relatively well in the United States and markets such as Hong Kong and Malaysia. In fact, the covered bond *Pfandbrief* market remains vigorous in Germany because the originating bank still bears responsibility for asset quality. Asset securitization can become the backbone of a robust corporate bond market in Asia as well as a means of reducing the maturity mismatch of the banking system when it finances home ownership. Just as there is a national drug administration to vet and approve new drugs, there is no inherent reason why financial regulators should not examine, approve and exercise proper due diligence on new financial products. As long as such products do not have systemic implications, they can be traded on an over-the-counter basis. But once these products reach a certain level of scale, these should be moved onto net clearing arrangements with centralized counterparty arrangements to monitor counterparty risks and levels of leverage. Opacity is fine for private modesty, but where public health is concerned, transparency and regulation are necessary.

Fifth, the whole philosophy of financial regulation and the way it functions within the financial stability policy function needs to be examined. The recent trend towards creation of financial super-regulators was due to the concentration and conglomeration of the financial industry itself.

The present institutional basis of financial regulation created multiple regulators, making the coordination and enforcement of supervision complex, costly and less effective. One of the arguments for super-regulators was that costs to the industry were too high. The answer is now obvious. Higher costs of regulation to LCFIs were still cheaper than the costs of crisis to the public. Hence, it is not the cost of regulation to the industry that counts, but the total social costs (including prevention of innovation and crisis) that matter.

Note that even in countries with super-regulators, you cannot avoid tripartite coordination between the super-regulator, the central bank and the ministry of finance. Hence, the fundamental problem of financial stability is that appropriate government policy must be coordinated and enforced in order to achieve stability. This cannot be the function of financial regulators alone. If this is complicated at the national level, it is even worse at the global level.

Financial regulators need to think strategically on how to regulate effectively over the whole economic cycle. The current Basel-type approach has assumed peacetime conditions as normal, whereas financial regulators need to deal with and prepare for crisis conditions as bubbles emerge. Anticyclical mentality needs to be built into the work process, including the necessary budgetary resources. As Churchill used to say, in peace, prepare for war, and in war, prepare for peace.

Finally, we cannot allow theory and wishful thinking to advance way ahead of practice and reality. The Europeans did not expect that the U.S. subprime crisis would hit them so badly, until they realized that it was their less-sophisticated parts of the banking system that had purchased large amounts of toxic products and that some of them had become overdependent on external and wholesale financing. For example, it was the weaker regional German banks and British building societies that had to be rescued from their follies. Clearly, even though there was massive restructuring of European financial oversight and regulation, the sectors that were local and not subject to clear oversight became the most vulnerable to external shocks.

In many emerging markets, the reality on the ground is that commercial banks are still struggling with their basic function of serving retail customers and credit to enterprises, let alone moving to wholesale banking. Emerging market regulators, central banks and ministries of finance are still focused on their daily domestic turf battles rather than understanding that the global game of finance is changing. Global interconnectivity is reality, but mindsets and social and financial institutions are still local.

The reality is therefore that it will take time to change mindsets and institutional structures to fit the new world of financial interconnectivity.

THE LONGER VIEW

Now that the financial crisis phase is passing, the world has moved into the crisis management and resolution phase. The U.S. and Europe will do whatever it takes to restore order. They will recapitalize banks, use fiscal policy to stimulate the economy, stop the foreclosure of mortgages, engage in regulatory reforms and then start talking about the global architecture. President Bush called the Group of 20 Leaders' meeting on 14–15 November 2008 in Washington, DC, to discuss the crisis. The communiqué that followed made all the right noises. At the London G20 Summit in April 2009, the leaders committed to treble the resources of the IMF to US$750 billion, raise concerted fiscal expansion to US$5 trillion and reform the global financial architecture. Significantly, the Financial Stability Forum will be succeeded by a Financial Stability Board, with all G20 members, Spain and the European Commission.

Are we addressing the right issues, or are we just wrapping duct tape on the broken international order and hoping that it will still work?

We come back to the structural issue of how we got to where we are – a financially interconnected world with no global monetary authority and financial regulator that was not able to manage the risks of global imbalances.

To paraphrase Rousseau, markets are born free, but everywhere they are in silos. Globalization has made the world a more integrated network of markets, and yet, monetary and fiscal policies, regulation and supervision of different parts of the market are divided into national and jurisdictional silos that are obsolete, inefficient and counterproductive. For domestic political reasons, every government looked only at their own national interests, but not necessarily the externalities or impact on the rest of world. The more powerful the nations, the greater the externalities. Because no one looked at the market as a whole, nor traced the interactions and interlinkages between markets, institutions and products, liquidity, leverage, greed and fear came together to create the perfect storm of financial shocks.

Going back to the eight elements of institutions, we need to think through whether the strategy, values, incentives and structures are right. Having rejected Friedmanite policies, we have returned to Keynesian pump-priming with a vengeance, with the Obama Administration committing as much as US$775 billion to revive the U.S. economy.

As this book has shown, Japan was the first major economy in the post-war period to have gone through a balance sheet bubble and deflation. After massive pump-priming and more than 17 years of deflation and low growth, it replaced a stock market and property bubble with a public debt bubble of 195 percent of GDP and has still not solved many of its structural issues. The zero interest rate policy has become necessary if only to keep the fiscal position sustainable, because raising interest rates would cause a debt market implosion and further pressure on the yen. Ironically, zero interest rates are forcing a nation of aging high savers to hold back on consumption. I have tried to show how financial engineers and the yen carry trade have made global markets more leveraged, volatile and risky.

We now have the Japanese zero interest rate policy (ZIRP) duplicated in the United States, and presumably, other countries will rapidly follow. As the Japanese learnt from bitter experience, when you fix the price of money at zero, then all other adjustments in the economy are quantitative or through other prices, such as exchange rates. No country can now run independent monetary policy without some exchange controls, because there will be huge carry trades to arbitrage out any attempts to raise interest rates as part of monetary policy.

The implications on exchange rate policy under ZIRP are huge. We are entering uncharted waters, because if everyone tries to use flexible exchange rates to pass adjustment costs to neighbours, then the world will enter into a deflation trap exactly like the 1930s.

Will the United States and other governments, using the same tools of zero interest rates and fiscal pump-priming to reflate their economies back to the old model, repeat Japan's mistakes? Can we sort out one set of distortions with another, or should we reexamine whether the old model is broken and what we should be doing to move to the new model?

Even though Keynesian thinking hugely influences me, I would be dishonest if I do not point out that the context for Keynesian thinking is vastly different from the problems of today. Keynesian economics evolved in a situation in which there were no natural resource or environmental constraints. It is my conjecture that the commodity bubble of 2008 reflected the first serious signs of the environmental limits of the present 'growth for growth's sake' model. It did not take more than a drought in Australia to affect global price of rice. What would happen to food prices globally if there was a prolonged drought, exactly like the long drought that destroyed the Mayan civilization in the ninth century? We have been lulled by the good years of global warming to think that good weather conditions will last forever, exactly like thinking that stock market and real estate prices will rise forever.

From an incentive point of view, printing money to keep the present asset bubbles from deflating is rewarding exactly the greed, excess consumption and leverage that created the bubbles in the first place and encouraging nonsustainable growth. Ironically, the poor did not benefit that much from the bubbles, and if Asian experience is anything to go by, they will pay considerably towards the costs of crises.

Huge structural adjustments lie ahead. Job creation in the West will mean that protectionism will be on the rise, as manufacturing jobs are brought home and new services and knowledge industries will be promoted. For the Asians, it took more than 30 years to build the global supply chain, and if demand for its products is unwound rapidly, there will be massive unemployment. Designed to supply fundamentally the developed markets, the supply chain now faces serious realignment to switch to production for domestic or regional consumption. But to ask Asians to consume the same quality and quantity of products as Western markets to reflate the present bubble is also unrealistic. There is therefore a colossal structural adjustment required in the global supply chain, which may have further multiplier effects on Asia and the rest of the world.

The second set of structural issues is the robustness of current financial systems to absorb such shocks. What is the right level of bank capital adequacy under modern-day volatile market conditions? According to FDIC data quoted by Greenspan,[4] U.S. bank capital in 1840 was more like 60 percent of assets, falling to only 20 percent by 1900 and less than 10 percent by the end of the century. If market volatility is likely to remain high as in recent years, bank capital cannot afford to be maintained at 8 percent and may have to be dynamically adjusted upward as risks increase.

The third significant challenge for domestic governance, more acute in the case of Asia, is the inherent conflict between rigid traditional top-down bureaucracies and modern organizations that must respond quickly and flexibly to multidimensional changes in markets and social needs.

At the heart of the debate on the crucial role of institutions in national and global development is the complex interaction between the role of government and the role of markets. When markets are immature, institutions are young and society is closed, the role of government as the dominant force in society commanding all the levers of expertise and power to allocate scarce resources to gain maximum efficiency is understandable. Unfortunately, without checks and balances, any authoritarian regime, however benevolent, may eventually make large mistakes that could lead

---

[4] Greenspan (2008b).

to crisis and loss. Concentration of power and knowledge brings inequalities that reduce social stability (or robustness), hence the need to be more diverse and 'flat' in governance. In network terminology, the market as a network has 'winner take all' effects, which concentrate wealth and knowledge in fewer and fewer hands. This increases social tension, and there is a countervailing force seeking justice and equality that only effective governments can deliver.

In political scientist Mancur Olson's[5] terminology, this requires change into a *market-augmenting government*. It is this change in governance model and mindset (that elites no longer have full control in a global economy) that is the most difficult to achieve without the trauma of crisis.

As a recent OECD[6] study on modernizing government showed, we all want open, transparent, accessible and consultative governments that are legitimate, responsible and responsive. One consequence of the present crisis is that the difference between Asian and Western governments has narrowed considerably after the nationalization of banks and aid to industry. All governments have now become sovereign wealth funds, owning significant parts of the economy.

The differences that remain are whether one is running a *market-augmented government* or a *government-augmented market*.

For example, Asia has always run the latter type of model. Although Asian governments bore the brunt of responsibility for policy mistakes and lack of enforcement, it is quite clear that the Asian corporate sector created most of the risks that led to failure. It was the Asian corporate drive for growth and market share that drove their high leverage ratios and reliance on foreign borrowing. Asian governments supported that drive and paid the price. One could interpret the Western governments' unwillingness to restrain their banking systems' drive for market growth that similarly exposed their economies to excessive leverage and risks. As explained in the previous chapter, the cosy relationship between the policymakers and the risk takers was a common element in both crises.

THE BEAM IN OUR EYES

In 1999 the World Bank undertook a review of its famous 1993 study on the Asian Miracle. Amongst other things, it concluded that 'in spite of the severity of the crisis, mindsets and the culture of business had changed very

---

[5] Olson (2000).
[6] OECD (2005).

little … with many waiting to go back to business more or less as usual'.[7] This is precisely the danger of fighting tomorrow's problems with yesterday's mindset.

For example, if the United States were to go back to the same tools that were used in the U.S.-Japan relationship in pressurizing China to rapidly adjust its exchange rates, then China may risk exactly the same bubble deflation that Japan suffered. The consequences for global stability are unthinkable.

The Asian experience with globalization posed a curious dilemma: initially, the more you open up, the more you gain; conversely, the more you close, the more you lose. China and India are vivid examples of the countries that benefited from the opening up strategy. Myanmar and North Korea are classic examples of closed states that failed without learning from their neighbours. However, the current crisis demonstrated the opposite dilemma: the more you open up, the more the risks of contagion. Clearly, the forces of vested interests that are hurt by globalization will rally under nationalism, cultural identity and fundamentalism. These are powerful forces that cannot be underestimated.

Mancur Olson was surely right in saying that development is the outcome of negotiations between different vested interests. The early capital-intensive opening-up strategies benefited Asian elites and created growth and employment. At the same time, much of the growth that was generated occurred at the expense of the environment and the underfunding of retirement and social protection systems. As Asian economies age and society becomes more middle class in prosperity and outlook, the demands for openness and transparency, environmental sustainability, service quality and social choice will become much more diverse and complex. Inevitably, the institutional side of Asia must change to fit the age of globalization, technology and the knowledge society.

Therefore, what Asia needs is a set of second generation reforms to manage the region's transition from middle- to higher-income economies that play their rightful role in global affairs, alongside Europe and the Americas. The second-generation reforms involve fundamental institutional change that is not captive to only one set of market players.

To do this, we must first go back to basic principles of political economy and admit that in order to move forward, we have to start with building effective bureaucracies in Asia that understand how to balance the government's role in a market economy, a role that can simultaneously

---

[7] de Silva and Yusuf (1999).

educate, regulate, lead and motivate change. Once the need to build effective Asian bureaucracies is recognized, the next step is to strengthen and motivate the bureaucracy to effectively exercise the core function that only governments can provide. In today's global economy, this core function is to complement and facilitate the building of effective markets, including addressing market failures, such as social inequality, terrorism, natural disasters and environmental degradation, together with civil society.

But herein are the horns of the institutional dilemma. It is a fact that in emerging markets many public bureaucracies are underpaid, undermotivated and undermanaged. Why should they help facilitate change when all it does is to appear to benefit the private sector? If the existing bureaucracies are unwilling or unable through under-resourcing, inertia, ignorance, corruption or lack of incentives to move effectively to make the necessary social, institutional and policy changes, then these market failures will not be tackled. And if the bureaucracies cannot change, the market cannot change and perform effectively.

More importantly, we need to ask what set of values should imbue the new equitable, environmentally sustainable society and related financial system. There is no doubt that the greedy rush for 'we want it now' short-termism that has characterized the bubbles of the last decade is neither fair nor environmentally or financially sustainable. In a period of plenty, we have witnessed blatant abuse of public interest for private gain. Nowhere was this more evident than in the financial markets. Nationalization of large parts of the financial system has been the consequence. The incentive structure will need to be rebuilt to change social values towards greater social responsibility and over a longer time horizon.

All this means that the changes in the way we think and measure our quality of life will be very different. Current quantitative measures of income and wealth have proven grossly inadequate, if not distortive, for a better quality of life. The GDP fever in many emerging markets has resulted in asset bubbles, huge waste and inefficiencies and massive destruction of our environment. Even mark-to-market accounting will have to change from an instant price for everything into valuation in its proper time perspective. Mark-to-funding, which Avinash Persaud is advocating, is an attempt in that direction. Unfortunately, we do not have as yet a system of values that readily replace the current market system. Because social science has become too complex, we lack a modern Adam Smith or Keynes to give us the philosophical basis to comprehend the new world.

Peter Drucker sees the postcapitalist society as a knowledge society, in which knowledge is valued much higher than materialist goods that we currently consume. He has come to the same conclusion as ancient Asians, who were able to find balance between inner peace, self and social responsibility. We move forward by going back to the roots of our cultural and natural heritage.

CONCLUSION

This survey brings me to the conclusion that crisis is ultimately political in nature. Even if it erupts as a financial crisis, its resolution would inevitably be political because the distribution of losses would be highly arbitrary and controversial. Ultimately, all financial crises are crisis of governance. Financial crises prove that financial engineering cannot create perpetual prosperity. It takes good governance, at the corporate, financial and social levels, to generate long-run sustainable stability. All crises have to be solved by governments, and if not satisfactorily, by the next government.

To sum up, the Asian crisis revealed that the Tokyo Consensus, the Japanese view that industrial policy will generate growth and prosperity, was not sustainable. In addition, the Washington Consensus was put to a stress test and found to be wanting. So far, it is not clear whether there is a Beijing Consensus.

Asia has now emerged into the world as a third force, but how it globalises and how the world is influenced by Asia will precisely bring about the interactive forces of competition and cooperation that will make the world move towards peace or war. Much of it will also require leadership at all levels, political, business, social and even religious, which can bring about the necessary changes in structures and mindsets that will make the world a safer, healthier, prosperous and more just place to life in. During this period, we will witness truly the clash of civilizations, cultures and beliefs that will require enormous statesmanship, vision, mission, resources and the determination to manage. Who in Asia has the vision, mission and will to make that change is a question that is beyond the scope of this book.

Perhaps the real lesson from the Asian crisis is that no one can predict how Asia can advance to a more stable and sustainable stage of development without greater volatility or another crisis. But that precisely is the price of growing up. Nevertheless, one thing is clear – as Asian economies emerge to become economic powers in their own right, there will be no one else to blame the next time around except ourselves.

From Asian to Global Crisis: Chronology
of Notable Events

Late 1970s   Japan begins to build the Asian global supply chain.

October 1983   Hong Kong dollar is pegged at HK$7.80 to the U.S. dollar.

1985   U.S. current account deficit with Japan hits record of approximately US$46 billion.

September 1985   Yen hovers around ¥240 to the U.S. dollar.

22 September 1985   Plaza Accord. Yen appreciates against U.S. dollar.

January 1986–February 1987   Bank of Japan cuts interest rates five times from 5 percent to 2.5 percent.

1986   Japan's asset price bubble begins to emerge.

February 1987   Yen hovers around ¥153 to the U.S. dollar.

19 October 1987   U.S. stock market crashes. Dow Jones Industrial Average falls by 23 percent.

December 1988   Yen peaks at around ¥123 to the U.S. dollar and begins to depreciate.

May 1989–August 1990   Bank of Japan raises interest rates five times from 2.5 percent to 6 percent.

1989–1990   Japan's asset price bubble begins to burst.

29 December 1989   Japanese stock Nikkei 225 Index reaches all-time high of 38,957.

1 January 1990   Kuala Lumpur Stock Exchange operates as an independent exchange following the delisting of Malaysian-incorporated companies from the Stock Exchange of Singapore and the delisting of Singapore-incorporated companies from the KLSE.

2 January 1990   Singapore launches the Central Limit Order Book, a new OTC market for Malaysian stocks and six other foreign stocks.

April 1990   Yen bottoms at ¥160 to the U.S. dollar and begins to appreciate.

1990   Indonesia's Bank Duta is bailed out.

1991   Japan enters into recession. GDP growth rate falls from 5.2 percent in 1990 to 3.4 percent.

July 1991–September 1993   Bank of Japan cuts interest rates seven times from 6 percent to 1.75 percent.

December 1992   Indonesia's Bank Summa fails.

1993   U.S. current account deficit with Japan increases sharply to US$51 billion from US$38 billion in 1992. Yen appreciates sharply. Japan further increases economic linkages with other Asian countries.

Thailand establishes the Bangkok International Banking Facilities.

World Bank publishes the report *The East Asian Miracle: Economic Growth and Public Policy*.

1 January 1994   NAFTA between Canada, Mexico and the United States comes into effect.

China unifies its 'dual' exchange regime into a single one.

April 1994   Mexico joins the OECD.

9 December 1994   Japan's Tokyo Kyowa and Anzen credit cooperatives fail.

20 December 1994   Mexico devalues the peso.

1994   IMF begins to recommend that Thailand relax its foreign exchange policy.

Mid-January 1995   Speculative attack on the Thai baht as well as other ASEAN currencies following Mexican peso crisis.

17 January 1995   Earthquake hits Kobe, Japan.

1 February 1995   IMF announces Mexico rescue package totaling around US$50 billion from the IMF, United States, BIS and other commercial banks.

Mid-March 1995   Mexican peso loses about 50 percent of its value since December 1994.

14 April 1995   Bank of Japan cuts interest rates from 1.75 percent to 1 percent.

19 April 1995   Yen peaks at ¥80 to the U.S. dollar and begins to depreciate.

July 1995   Japan's Cosmo Credit Cooperative suspends operations.

August 1995   Japan's Kizu Credit Cooperative and Hyogo Bank fail.

8 September 1995   Bank of Japan cuts interest rates from 1 percent to 0.5 percent.

September 1995 Japan's Daiwa Bank announces loss of US$1.1 billion due to fraud at its New York branch.

December 1995 Yen continues to depreciate and hovers around ¥101 to the U.S. dollar.

March 1996 Japan's Taiheiyou Bank fails.

28 April 1996 Indonesia's President Suharto's wife, Siti Hartanah, passes away.

May 1996 Thailand's Bangkok Bank of Commerce is taken over because of a bad loan.

Mid-July 1996 Thailand's Bangkok Metropolitan Bank is ordered by U.S. regulators to close operations in U.S. markets.

27 July 1996 Riots erupt in Jakarta, Indonesia, following the burning of the headquarters of the Indonesian Democratic Party. Indonesian rupiah comes under pressure.

Late July 1996 First major speculative attack on the Thai baht after the Mexican peso crisis.

3 September 1996 Moody's downgrades Thailand's short-term debt credit rating.

October 1996 Dow Jones Industrial Average breaks 6,000, Alan Greenspan makes 'irrational exuberance speech'.

November 1996 Japan's Hanwa Bank is ordered to suspend operations.

12 December 1996 South Korea joins the OECD.

December 1996 Yen depreciates to ¥113 to the U.S. dollar.

Bank Indonesia, the Indonesian central bank, proposes the closure of seven small commercial banks. President Suharto turns down the proposal.

China makes the RMB convertible for current account transactions.

1996 Japan shows signs of recovery. Annual GDP growth rate increases from 1.9 percent in 1995 to 2.6 percent.

23 January 1997 South Korea's Hanbo Steel, the 14th largest *chaebol*, fails.

January–February 1997 Second major speculative attack on the Thai baht after the Mexican peso crisis.

5 February 1997 Thailand's Samprasong becomes the first large Thai company to miss payments on foreign debt.

March 1997 South Korea's Sammi Steel, the 26th largest *chaebol*, fails.

IMF urges Thailand to introduce greater exchange rate flexibility promptly.

Bank of Thailand, the Thai central bank, orders 10 finance companies in Thailand to increase their capital.

1 April 1997   Japan's Nippon Credit Bank experiences funding problems and announces its restructuring plan.

April 1997   Japan raises value added tax from 3 percent to 5 percent. Japanese economy, already fragile, enters into a slump. Yen depreciates to ¥127 to the U.S. dollar.

South Korea's Ssangyong automobile group, the 6th largest *chaebol*, experiences financial difficulties.

South Korea's Jinro Group, distillers of beer and liquor, the 19th largest *chaebol*, experiences financial difficulties.

Indonesia's President Suharto approves but delays the proposal by Bank Indonesia to close seven Indonesian banks.

Early May 1997   Japan hints that interest rates may be raised to defend the yen. Yen begins to strengthen.

Finance One, largest Thai finance company, collapses.

8–15 May 1997   Third major speculative attack against the Thai baht after the Mexican peso crisis.

Mid-May 1997   First major speculative attack on the Malaysian ringgit in 1997.

20 May 1997   IMF recommends that Thailand devalue the baht by about 10–15 percent accompanied by a float.

24 May 1997   Meeting of Deputy Governors of Asian central bankers to discuss Thai baht crisis.

Late May 1997   South Korea's Dainong Group, a retail chain, experiences financial difficulties.

19 June 1997   Thailand's Finance Minister, Amnuay Viravan, resigns, with Thailand's Prime Minister declaring that Thailand 'will never devalue the baht'.

27 June 1997   Bank of Thailand suspends operations of 16 insolvent and liquidity-strapped finance companies.

Hong Kong's Hang Seng Index peaks at 15,196 before the handover of Hong Kong to China.

Early July 1997   South Korea's Kia, an automotive group, eighth largest *chaebol*, experiences financial difficulties.

1 July 1997   Hong Kong returns to China after 156 years of British colonial rule.

2 July 1997   Bank of Thailand announces floatation of Thai baht.

Philippine peso is savagely attacked.

8 July 1997   Second major speculative attack on the Malaysian ringgit in 1997. Bank Negara Malaysia, Malaysia's central bank, intervenes to defend the ringgit.

11 July 1997   The Philippines allows the peso to float and requests assistance from the IMF.

Indonesia widens its trading band for the rupiah from 8 percent to 12 percent.

14 July 1997   Bank Negara Malaysia allows the ringgit to freely depreciate.

18 July 1997   The IMF announces about US$1 billion worth of financial assistance to the Philippines.

24 July 1997   Malaysian Prime Minister Dr Mahathir Mohamad attacks 'rogue speculators'. Currency pressure on baht, rupiah, ringgit and peso.

25 July 1997   Second EMEAP Governors' Meeting in Shanghai, China.

Malaysia and Thailand seek Japan's help in the creation of a regional rescue fund.

26 July 1997   Dr Mahathir accuses hedge fund manager George Soros of leading the speculative attack on Southeast Asian currencies.

28 July 1997   Thailand calls in the IMF.

5 August 1997   The Bank of Thailand suspends 42 additional finance companies as part of the IMF-guided rescue plan.

7 August 1997   Hong Kong's Hang Seng Index peaks at 16,673 after the return of Hong Kong to China.

11 August 1997   IMF convenes meeting in Tokyo to discuss Thailand's economic woes.

13 August 1997   Indonesian rupiah hits historic low of Rp 2,682 to the U.S. dollar.

14 August 1997   Indonesia abandons the rupiah's trading band and allows the currency to float freely.

New Taiwan dollar comes under speculative attack.

15 August 1997   Hong Kong dollar comes under speculative attack. The Hong Kong Monetary Authority raises interest rates sharply.

19 August 1997   Hang Seng Index falls 620 points to close at 15,477.

20 August 1997   IMF announces Thailand rescue package totalling around US$17 billion from the IMF, Asian nations and other multilateral agencies.

28 August 1997   KLSE designates the 100 component stocks of the KLCI and suspends regulated short selling.

17–25 September 1997   52nd joint Annual Meetings of the World Bank and the IMF in Hong Kong.

Japan proposes the creation of an Asian Monetary Fund at the G7-IMF meetings.

October 1997   South Korea discovers that Korean banks have unreported offshore short-term borrowings of more than US$60 billion.

8 October 1997   Indonesia calls in the IMF.

13 October 1997   Thailand's Chairman of the Committee to Supervise Mergers and Acquisitions of Financial Institutions, Amaret Sila-on, resigns.

17 October 1997   Taiwan allows New Taiwan dollar to float.

19 October 1997   Thailand's Finance Minister, Thanong Bidaya, resigns.

20 October 1997   Hong Kong dollar comes under speculative attack. Hang Seng Index suffers four consecutive days of losses.

23 October 1997   Hong Kong's 'Black Thursday'. Overnight interest rates rise to 280 percent briefly. Hang Seng Index falls by 1,211 points or 10.4 percent to close at 10,426.

Korean won begins to weaken.

24 October 1997   Thailand establishes the Financial Sector Restructuring Authority to review the rehabilitation plans of the 58 finance firms that were suspended.

Standard & Poor's downgrades South Korea's foreign currency long-term sovereign debt rating from AA− to A+.

27 October 1997   DJIA falls by 554 points or over 7 percent to close at 7,161.

31 October 1997   Indonesia signs the first IMF Letter of Intent. A highly publicised impasse between President Suharto and the IMF begins.

November 1997   Thailand establishes an Asset Management Corporation to act as a bidder of last resort for the impaired assets of the finance companies auctioned by the FRA.

1 November 1997   Indonesian government closes 16 banks, including three connected with the President's family – Bank Andromeda, Bank Industri and Bank Jakarta.

Moody's downgrades credit ratings of four major Korean banks.

3 November 1997   Thailand's Prime Minister, Chavalit Yongchaiyudh, resigns.

A medium-sized Japanese securities house, Sanyo Securities, suspends operations.

5 November 1997   IMF announces Indonesian rescue package totalling around US$23 billion from the IMF, Asian nations, other multilateral agencies and Indonesia's own external assets.

5–8 November 1997   KOSPI falls by about 10 percent.

10 November 1997   Korean won nearly breaks the W 1,000 to the U.S. dollar barrier. South Korean government pledges to hold the won at 1,000.

Mid-November 1997   A bailout between two Malaysian public listed conglomerates, United Engineers Malaysia and the Renong Group, is arranged.

16 November 1997   Michel Camdessus, Managing Director of IMF, secretly visits Seoul for discussions with the Korean Minister of Finance and Economy and the Bank of Korea Governor.

17 November 1997   Japan's Hokkaido Takushoku Bank collapses under the weight of bad loans. First of Japan's big banks to fail.

Bank of Korea abandons efforts to defend the won from breaking the W 1,000 to the U.S. dollar barrier.

18 November 1997   South Korea's National Assembly fails to pass a package of financial reform bills.

19 November 1997   Korean Finance and Economy Minister, Kang Kyong Shik, and the President's Chief Economic Secretary, Kim In Ho, resigns.

20 November 1997   South Korea seeks financial support from the U.S. and Japanese governments.

Bank of Korea widens the daily exchange rate band for the Korean won from 2.25 percent to 10 percent.

21 November 1997   South Korea calls in the IMF.

22 November 1997   Standard & Poor's downgrades South Korea's foreign currency long-term sovereign debt rating from A+ to A−.

23 November 1997   Indonesia's President Suharto's son buys a small bank and starts its banking business from the old premises of Bank Andromeda.

24 November 1997   South Korea's 'Black Monday'. Korean won slides and KOSPI closes at a 10-year low at 451.

Japan's third largest broker of stocks and securities, Yamaichi Securities, collapses.

25 November 1997   Japanese yen falls to ¥127.45 to the U.S. dollar. Nikkei-225 plunges by 5.1 percent to close at 15,868.

Hong Kong experiences a 'cake run'. Panic also spreads to the amusement arcades.

26 November 1997   Japan's Tokuyo City Bank fails. Finance Minister Hiroshi Mitsuzuka and Bank of Japan Governor Yasuo Matsushita jointly appeal for calm.

2 December 1997   South Korea suspends nine technically insolvent merchant banks.

4 December 1997   IMF announces Korean rescue package totalling around US$55 billion from the IMF, other multilateral agencies and bilateral sources.

5 December 1997   Indonesia's President Suharto begins an unprecedented 10-day rest period. Rumours that he is gravely ill begin to circulate.

8 December 1997   South Korea's 12th largest conglomerate, Halla Group, which is involved in heavy industry, fails.

Korean press reports, citing leaked IMF report, claim that South Korean foreign reserves declined to a mere US$5 billion in the previous week.

Thailand announces that 56 of the 58 suspended financial institutions ordered closed.

9 December 1997   South Korea suspends the operation of five additional insolvent merchant banks, bringing the total suspended to 14, and takes majority stakes in Korea First Bank and Seoul Bank.

11 December 1997   Moody's downgrades South Korea's sovereign debt rating from A3 to Baa2. Moody's also downgrades the credit ratings of 31 Korean issuers.

Standard & Poor's downgrades South Korea's foreign currency long-term sovereign debt rating from A– to BBB–.

Kim Dae-Jung, the leading presidential candidate, hints that he might renegotiate a deal with the IMF.

12 December 1997   Indonesia's President Suharto cancels plans to attend the ASEAN summit in Kuala Lumpur.

11–12 December 1997   Korean won falls by its daily limit of 10 percent against the U.S. dollar.

13 December 1997   KOSPI closes at 360, 17 percent lower than the previous week's close on 6 December of 436.

16 December 1997   South Korea allows Korean won to float.

17 December 1997   Japan's Prime Minister Ryutaro Hashimoto announces a special ¥2 trillion (US$15.7 billion) cut in personal incomes taxes to boost faltering economy.

18 December 1997   Kim Dae Jung is elected President of South Korea.

19 December 1997   Japan's Toshoku Ltd., a foodstuffs trader, fails. One of the country's largest postwar bankruptcies.

President Kim Dae Jung reaffirms that South Korea will abide by agreements with IMF.

22 December 1997   Moody's downgrades the long-term sovereign debt ratings of Indonesia, South Korea and Thailand to below investment grade.

Standard & Poor's downgrades South Korea's foreign currency long-term sovereign debt rating to below investment grade.

23 December 1997   South Korea won breaks through the W 2,000 to the U.S. dollar psychological barrier, KOSPI closes at 366, down by more than 7 percent from the previous day close, and market interest rates shoot up to as high as 40 percent.

24 December 1997   IMF, World Bank and ADB agree to make an early payment of US$10 billion in loans to South Korea by early January 1998.

29–30 December 1997   G-10 banks agree to roll over short-term loans to South Korean banks.

1 January 1998   Malaysia strengthens prudential regulations. Thailand appeals to the IMF to ease fiscal tightening.

6 January 1998   Indonesia's President Suharto announces an expansionary budget that is contrary to IMF demands for a budget surplus.

7 January 1998   Malaysian ringgit falls to its lowest point of RM 4.88 to the U.S. dollar, lowest since the crisis began. National Economic Action Council is formally established.

8 January 1998   Rupiah breaks the Rp 10,000 to the U.S. dollar psychological level. Jakarta Composite Index falls sharply. Riots break out in Jakarta.

12 January 1998   Hong Kong investment bank, Peregrine Investments, fails because of loan exposure in Indonesia.

15 January 1998   Indonesia's President Suharto personally signs second Letter of Intent with the IMF. The publication of a picture showing Michael Camdessus standing like a school master over President Suharto causes public outcry.

19 January 1998   President Suharto emphasizes that the National Car Project and plan to develop an Indonesian jet plane will continue without state funding or assistance.

Hong Kong's CA Pacific Securities, a midsized stockbroker, goes into voluntary suspended operations.

20 January 1998 Malaysia announces blanket guarantee for bank deposits.

26 January 1998 Indonesia Bank Restructuring Authority is established. A blanket guarantee for all liabilities and assets of banks incorporated in Indonesia is introduced.

29 January 1998 South Korea closes 10 merchant banks because of insolvency.

31 January 1998 South Korean government recapitalizes Korea First Bank and Seoul Bank, taking effective control.

January–February 1998 Indonesia's President Suharto toys with the idea of a currency board system.

13 February 1998 Riots break out in Indonesia, due to rising prices.

14 February 1998 54 Indonesian banks are brought under IBRA.

17 February 1998 Indonesia's President Suharto informs the central bank governor of his dismissal through a presidential decree on 11 February 1998.

19 February 1998 Students from the University of Indonesia stage their first demonstration.

23 February 1998 Riots continue in Indonesia.

2 March 1998 Indonesia's President Suharto claims that the implementation of structural reforms under the IMF programme is incompatible with Indonesia's constitution.

10 March 1998 Indonesia's President Suharto reelected as president.

14 March 1998 Indonesia's President Suharto's new cabinet sworn into office.

19 March 1998 China's Prime Minister, Zhu Rongji, states that Beijing will defend the Hong Kong currency's link to the U.S. dollar at any cost.

25 March 1998 Malaysia announces program to consolidate finance companies and restructure banks.

31 March 1998 Philippines agrees to a three-year Standby Arrangement with IMF.

April 1998 Japan unveils a ¥16 trillion (about US$120 billion) fiscal pump-priming package to revive domestic economy.

Indonesia closes seven small banks, and IBRA takes over seven banks.

4 April 1998   South Korea successfully launches its first international bond issue since the crisis.

Early May 1998   Indonesia's President Suharto announces fuel price increases.

12 May 1998   Four students from Trisakti University are shot dead by Indonesia security forces during a confrontation.

13–16 May 1998   Widespread riots in Indonesia and rupiah falls.

21 May 1998   Indonesia's President Suharto resigns after 32 years in power.

27 May 1998   Russian financial system shows increasing signs of real trouble.

27–28 May 1998   South Korea experiences a two-day nationwide strike by union workers to protest growing unemployment.

June 1998   New Taiwan dollar falls to an 11-year low.

Indonesian rupiah falls to its lowest point since the crisis began.

Hong Kong dollar comes under speculative attack.

12 June 1998   Japan announces that its economy is contracting for the first time in 23 years.

17 June 1998   Yen depreciates to levels near ¥144 to the U.S. dollar. U.S. and Japan intervene to support the yen.

24 June 1998   Indonesia and the IMF sign a fourth agreement to rescue the economy.

June–July 1998   Latin American countries are forced into a series of knock-on currency devaluations.

12 July 1998   Japanese Prime Minister Hashimoto loses power.

13 July 1998   Malaysia announces a RM7 billion fiscal stimulus package to boost economic growth.

23 July 1998   Malaysia unveils its National Economic Recovery Plan.

28 July 1998   IMF announces that it will ease conditions on US$55 billion aid package to South Korea.

3 August 1998   Dow Jones Industrial Average plunges by about 300 points.

Early August 1998   Yen further depreciates to around ¥150 to the U.S. dollar levels.

Hong Kong dollar comes under speculative attack again.

3 August 1998   Malaysia officially establishes Danamodal, the agency for the recapitalization of banks.

5 August 1998   Malaysian parliament passes the bill to establish Danaharta, the national asset management corporation.

14 August 1998   Hong Kong government intervenes in the Hong Kong Stock Exchange.

17 August 1998   Russia devalues the ruble.

Malaysia establishes the Corporate Debt Restructuring Committee.

19 August 1998   Russia officially defaults on its Treasury Notes.

21 August 1998   Russia's economic crisis shakes world markets.

26 August 1998   Bank Negara Malaysia's Governor, Ahmad Don, and his Deputy, Fong Weng Phak, resign.

31 August 1998   Dow Jones Industrial Average plunges by more than 500 points.

1 September 1998   Malaysia introduces capital controls. KLCI plunges to 262.7 points, its lowest point since 2 July.

2 September 1998   Malaysian ringgit is pegged at RM3.80 to the U.S. dollar.

Anwar Ibrahim is sacked as Malaysia's Deputy Prime Minister and Finance Minister.

Long Term Capital Management announces huge losses. World markets shaken.

4 September 1998   U.S. Federal Reserve Chairman Alan Greenspan says that the United States is ready to cut interest rates.

18 September 1998   Anwar Ibrahim is arrested and subsequently charged and convicted of corruption and sodomy. In 2004 the Malaysian Federal Court acquits Anwar on the sodomy charge.

23 September 1998   Federal Reserve of New York puts together a US$3.75 billion bailout package for LTCM.

Indonesia's bilateral external debt refinanced.

September 1998   Brazil goes into crisis.

Indonesia merges four largest state banks into Bank Mandiri.

3 October 1998   Japan announces first stage of the New Miyazawa Initiative, a US$30 billion financial package to help the region recover from recession.

G-7 ministers create a rescue plan for Brazil.

October 1998   The Exchange Fund Investment Limited is established to advise the Hong Kong government on the orderly disposal of the substantial portfolio of Hong Kong shares it acquired in August 1998.

Late 1998   Japan begins to systematically manage its banking crisis. Asian Crisis shows signs of abating.

15 January 1999   The Brazilian government allows the real to float freely.

February 1999   Japan operates in a zero interest rate policy environment. Malaysia begins to gradually relax the capital controls introduced in September 1998.

29 March 1999   Indonesia closes 38 banks, and IBRA takes over another seven.

Dow Jones Industrial Average closes above the 10,000 level for the first time in its history.

6 April 1999   Malaysia releases a white paper on the Malaysian crisis.

May 1999   Second stage of the new Miyazawa Initiative.

July–August 1999   South Korea's Daewoo group, the fourth largest *chaebol*, collapses.

November 1999   The Tracker Fund of Hong Kong, an Exchange Traded Fund, is launched as the first step of the Hong Kong government's plans in disposing of the stocks it acquired in August 1998.

1999   Crisis-hit countries experiences positive GDP growth rates.

10 March 2000   All-time high of NASDAQ Composite Index of 5,132, marking peak of dot-com stock market bubble.

23 August 2001   South Korea fully repays its loan to the IMF.

25 June 2003   U.S. Fed Funds rate reduced to 1 percent per annum.

28 July 2003   The Independent Evaluation Office of the IMF releases its evaluation report on the IMF's handling of the crises in Indonesia, South Korea and Brazil.

31 July 2003   Thailand fully repays its loan to the IMF.

21 July 2005   China announces that the RMB will be allowed to operate in a managed float.

Malaysia announces that the ringgit will be allowed to operate in a managed float.

Summer 2005   Between 1997 and 2006, U.S. house prices rise roughly 120 percent. House prices begin to peak in late summer 2005, as the Fed raises the Fed Funds rate by 5 steps of 25 bps in 2004 and 8 steps of 25 bps in 2005, bringing the Funds rate to 4.25 percent at the end of 2005.

29 June 2006   Fed Funds rate is raised to recent peak of 5.25 percent.

12 October 2006   Indonesia fully repays its loan to the IMF.

December 2006   Dr Mahathir and Soros publicly make up.

5 March 2007   HSBC reports loss of US$1.8 billion on portfolio of subprime loans.

First Quarter 2007   S&P/Case-Shiller house price index records first-ever U.S. nationwide price decline since 1991.

March–2 April 2007   More than 25 subprime lenders file for bankruptcy, including New Century Financial, the largest.

14–22 June 2007   Two Bear Stearns–managed hedge funds announce losses of US$1.4 billion in subprime loans.

10–12 July 2007   Credit rating agencies downgrade subprime mortgage bonds and CDO tranches.

30 July–1 August 2007   Germany's IKB announces losses. KfW, its main shareholder plus other banks put up €3.5 billion rescue fund.

31 July–9 August 2007   American Home Mortgage Investment Corporation announces and files for Chapter 11. BNP Paribas freezes redemption for three investment funds, due to impossibility to value.

9–10 August 2007   ECB injects €95 billion to fund overnight liquidity in European banks, and Federal Reserve injects US$38 billion into U.S. banks.

13–17 September 2007   U.K. mortgage lender Northern Rock suffers liquidity problems, then a bank run (first in 140 years in the U.K.) and requires deposit guarantee by U.K. Treasury. U.S. Fed cuts interest rates by 50 basis points.

9 October 2007   Dow Jones Industrial Average peaks at 14,164.

11–19 October 2007   Rating agencies downgrade subprime bonds.

On 16 October, Shanghai A-share Composite closes at peak of 6,092.

September–December 2007   Banks reveal large credit losses. Merrill Lynch announces credit losses of US$8.4 billion. Merrill CEO and Citigroup CEO step down.

12 December 2007   Central banks from five currency areas announce measures to provide liquidity for financial institutions for year-end.

2 January 2008   Crude oil price rises above US$100 per barrel.

15 January 2008   Citigroup announces fourth quarter loss of US$9.8 billion due to write-down of US$18.1 billion on subprime-related exposures, then raises US$12.5 billion of convertible preferred capital.

21–31 January 2008   Federal Reserves cuts 75 bps and 50 bps, respectively, within 10 days, citing weaknesses in markets.

24 January 2008   Societe Generale, one of the largest French banks, announces loss of €4.9 billion (US$7.2 billion), due to a rogue trader, requiring a capital call of €5.5 billion or US$8 billion.

17 February 2008   U.K. Treasury announces nationalization of Northern Rock.

16 March 2008   Bear Stearns runs into liquidity problems and is sold to JPMorgan, with New York Fed backing loans of up to US$29 billion. Fed establishes Primary Dealer Credit Facility.

Gold price hits peak US$1,011.25 per ounce on 17 March.

1 April 2008   UBS Chairman steps down after write-down of US$19 billion, on top of write-down of US$10 billion in December 2007.

8 April 2008   IMF Global Financial Stability Report estimates that worldwide credit losses may total as much as US$945 billion.

30 April 2008   U.S. Fed Funds rate lowered to recent low of 2 percent.

3 July 2008   Oil price hits peak of US$146 per barrel (Brent Crude).

11 July 2008   U.S. Treasury announces plan to rescue Fannie Mae and Freddie Mac, the two largest agencies that own or gurantee about 45 percent of US$12 trillion mortgage market in the United States.

Late July 2008   Institute of International Finance estimates that in the year up to June 2008, global financial system suffered US$476 billion in credit losses and raised US$354 billion in new capital.

7 September 2008   U.S. Government places Fannie Mae and Freddie Mac in conservatorship, with Treasury promising to take enough shares to keep the two GSEs with positive net worth.

8 September 2008   Global stock markets react favourably to Fannie Mae bailout, but computer problems shut down London Stock Exchange on Monday, 8 September, causing funds to not being able to exit their positions.

10 September 2008   Korean Development Bank pulls out of talks to invest in Lehman Brothers, causing Lehman shares to plunge 30 percent.

12 September 2008   U.S. Senate discloses that several large investment banks and brokerages, including Morgan Stanley, Lehman Brothers, Citigroup and Merrill Lynch, marketed allegedly abusive transactions that helped foreign hedge fund investors avoid billions in U.S. taxes. Lehman shares fall more than 50 percent since Monday.

13 September 2008   Barclays Bank backs away as a buyer for Lehman.

People's Bank of China cut rates for first time in six years.

14 September 2008 (Sunday)   Global consortium of banks announces a US$70 billion pool of funds to help troubled financial institutions.

Bank of America takeover of Merrill Lynch at US$29 per share, a premium of US$17.05 at market close on Friday, 12 September, but less than one-third of US$100 a share in early 2007.

15 September 2008   158-year-old investment bank Lehman Brothers (fifth largest in United States) files for Chapter 11 bankruptcy protection, partly because of US$30 billion in toxic real estate. Total debt amounts to US$613 billion.

Fed provides largest U.S. insurer AIG US$85 billion support, in exchange for warrants for 79.9 percent equity stake. AIG CEO Willumstad is replaced. AIG's share price drops over 95 percent to just $1.25, from a 52-week high of $70.13. AIG had provided market with $446 billion of credit default swaps.

U.S. stocks suffer biggest one-day decline since 11 September 2001.

17 September 2008   Goldman Sach's earnings declines 70 percent in third quarter earnings.

Russian shares fall 20 percent in one day, and oil price falls to $90 per barrel.

Panic grips markets as investors flee to safety.

Putnam announces closure of a large money market fund because of heavy redemptions. U.S. money markets funds are $3.4 trillion business.

18 September 2008   Central banks continue to flood markets with liquidity support in wake of stock market slide globally. Fed boosts its U.S. dollar swap line with foreign central banks by $180 billion as financial shares drop.

SEC and FSA ban short selling of financial shares until January 2009.

HBOS, one of the largest U.K. mortgage lenders, is rescued by takeover by Lloyds TSB, a large U.K. bank.

19 September 2008   China cuts stamp tax and Central Huijjin will buy back shares in large banks, as A-share index falls 70 percent since beginning of the year.

Russian Government pledges $20 billion to prop up stock market.

U.S. Treasury moves to increase capital of Fed as, out of $888 billion in assets, some $380 billion are committed to mortgage rescue operations. Fed holdings of Treasuries have dwindled to under $480 billion from $800 billion a year before.

U.S. Government pledges $50 billion to guarantee money-market funds.

20–21 September 2008   U.S. Treasury Secretary proposes $700 billion rescue fund to buy toxic residential and commercial mortgage-based assets from banks. Troubled Asset Relief Program (TARP) would be subject to legislative approval.

Fed approves transformation of Goldman and Morgan Stanley into bank holding companies, ending era of investment banks.

22 September 2008 Japanese bank Mitsubishi UFJ buys 10–20 percent stake in Morgan Stanley for $8.39 billion.

Nomura Securities pays $225 million for Asian operations of Lehman Brothers.

Shinsei Bank forecasts net loss for fiscal first half due to provisions for exposure to Lehmans and European asset-backed securities.

25 September 2008 Bank run on Bank of East Asia in Hong Kong (BEA), a reflection of nervousness in Asia arising from credit crisis fallout. Investors in Hong Kong and Singapore have lost money because they bought Lehman Brothers' minibonds through banks. Moody's downgrades BEA from stable to negative after the bank announces an investigation into a HK$93 million trading loss on equity derivatives on 18 September. The bank also had exposures to Lehman Brothers and AIG of HK$423 million and HK$50 million, respectively.

President Bush speaks to the nation on financial crisis.

26 September 2008 Washington Mutual, the largest U.S. savings and loan with US$307 billion in assets, is sold to JPMorganChase for $1.9 billion. Depositors will still be insured, but shareholders will lose their money.

Warren Buffet invests $5 billion in Goldman Sachs.

Governments of Belgium, Netherlands and Luxembourg rescue Fortis, the Belgian-Dutch banking and insurance group. It has €871 billion in assets at end of 2007 and paid €24 billion to buy ABN-Amro's retail operations.

29 September 2008 Citigroup takes over Wachovia.

Bradford and Bingley is nationalized by the United Kingdom.

Germans bail out Hypo Real Estate, a property finance company.

The Iceland Government takes control of Glitnir, the country's third largest bank.

Dow Jones falls 777 points, one of the largest falls ever to 10,365.45.

30 September 2008 Rescue of Belgium bank Dexia.

Ireland guarantees all deposits of its six largest banks, followed by other governments.

3 October 2008 U.S. Congress approves US$700 billion rescue plan, after initial rejection on 29 September.

Dutch Government acquires Fortis Nederland.

6 October 2008   German Government rescues Hypo Real Estate.

BNP Paribas takes over Fortis operations in Belgium and Luxembourg.

7 October 2008   Icelandic Government takes control of Glitner and Landsbanki.

8 October 2008   U.K. Government announces provision of capital to U.K. incorporated banks.

Coordinated interest rate cut of 50 bps by Fed, ECB and Bank of England.

13 October 2008   European governments announce measures to inject capital into European banks of up to €1 trillion.

United States announces $250 billion injection into nine largest banks, leading to the Dow Jones Industrial Average soaring by 11 percent for the largest point gain ever.

19 October 2008   Dutch Government injects €10 billion into ING.

21 October 2008   Fed creates Money Market Investor Funding Facility.

24 October 2008   U.S. House Oversight Committee questions Alan Greenspan, who admits to partial error.

4 November 2008   Barack Obama elected President of the United States.

11 November 2008   China announces RMB4 trillion (US$586 billion) stimulus package.

12 November 2008   U.S. Government increases aid to AIG to $150 billion, including $40 billion equity stake.

15 November 2008   G20 leaders meeting in Washington, DC.

18 November 2008   Citigroup announces layoff of 52,000 staff.

4 December 2008   Bank of England slashes interest rate by 1 percent to 2 percent, the European Central Bank cuts by 75 basis points, the largest ever, to 2.5 percent after the Swedish central bank cuts rates by 175 basis points.

9 December 2008   S&P downgrades Russia from BBB+ to BBB.

11 December 2008   Bernard Madoff is charged with running a Ponzi scheme where losses could amount to US$50 billion. Investors include banks, charities, hedge funds and funds of funds.

16 December 2008   Fed cuts interest rate to historical low of 0 to 0.25 percent. Yen hits a 13-year high of 87.26 against the U.S. dollar, whilst the Euro rises to 1.4720.

19 December 2008   Crude oil hits four-year low of $35 per barrel, despite OPEC cutting production by 2.2 million barrels per day.

Abbreviations and Acronyms

ABF-1	Asian Bond Fund 1
ABF-2	Asian Bond Fund 2
ABMI	Asian Bond Market Initiative
ABN-AMRO	former Dutch Bank formed from merger of Amsterdam-Rotterdam (AMRO) Bank and ABN
ABS	Asset-Backed Security
ADB	Asian Development Bank
AEC	ASEAN Economic Community
AMF	Asian Monetary Fund
APEC	Asia-Pacific Economic Cooperation
ASA	ASEAN Swap Arrangement
ASEAN	Association of Southeast Asian Nations
BCCI	Bank of Credit and Commerce International
BIBF	Bangkok International Banking Facility
BIS	Bank for International Settlements
BLBI	*Bantuan Likuiditas Bank Indonesia* (Bank Indonesia Liquidity Support)
BNM	Bank Negara Malaysia
BoJ	Bank of Japan
BoT	Bank of Thailand
BSA	Bilateral Swap Arrangement and Repurchase Agreement
BSP	*Bangko Sentral ng Pilipinas* (Central Bank of the Philippines)
CDO	Collateralized Debt Obligation
CEO	Chief Executive Officer
CFTC	Commodity Futures Trading Commission
CLOB	Central Limit Order Book

CMI	Chiang Mai Initiative
COSMAFI	Committee to Supervise Mergers and Acquisitions of Financial Institutions
CPSS	Committee on Payment and Settlement Systems
CRMPG	Counterparty Risk Management Policy Group
DJIA	Dow Jones Industrial Average
EAEC	East Asian Economic Caucus
EFIL	Exchange Fund Investment Limited
EMEAP	Executives' Meeting of East Asia-Pacific Central Banks
EMS	European Monetary System
EPF	Employees Provident Fund
ERM	Exchange Rate Mechanism
ERPD	Economic Review and Policy Dialogue
EU	European Union
FASB	Financial Accounting Standards Board
FCC	Forward Commitment Capacity of the IMF
FDI	Foreign Direct Investment
FDIC	Federal Deposit Insurance Corporation
FPI	Foreign Portfolio Investment
FRA	Financial Sector Restructuring Authority
FSA	Financial Services Authority
FSAP	Financial Sector Assessment Program
FSF	Financial Stability Forum
FTA	Free Trade Agreement
G-7	Group of Seven
G-8	Group of Eight
G-10	Group of 10
G-22	Group of 22
G-30	Group of 30
GDP	Gross Domestic Product
GITIC	Guangdong Investment and Trust Company
GNI	Gross National Income
GNP	Gross National Product
HIBOR	Hong Kong Interbank Offered Rate
HKCEC	Hong Kong Convention and Exhibition Centre
HKMA	Hong Kong Monetary Authority
HKSAR	Hong Kong Special Administrative Region
HLI	Highly Leveraged Institution
HSBC	Hong Kong and Shanghai Bank Corporation
HSI	Hang Seng Index

IAAS	International Accounting and Auditing Standards
IBRA	Indonesian Bank Restructuring Agency
IEO	Independent Evaluation Office of the IMF
IFC	International Finance Corporation
IFI	International Financial Institution
IFRS	International Financial Reporting Standards
IIF	Institute of International Finance
IMF	International Monetary Fund
IOSCO	International Organization of Securities Commissions
IPO	Initial Public Offering
IT	Information Technology
JCI	Jakarta Composite Index
JETRO	Japan External Trade Organization
KAMCO	Korean Asset Management Corporation
KLCI	Kuala Lumpur Composite Index
KLSE	Kuala Lumpur Stock Exchange
KOSPI	Korea Composite Stock Price Index
LOI	Letter of Intent
LOLR	Lender of Last Resort
LTCM	Long-Term Capital Management
MIT	Massachusetts Institute of Technology
MITI	Ministry of International Trade and Industry
MoF	Ministry of Finance
MSCI	Morgan Stanley Capital International
NAB	New Arrangements to Borrow
NAFTA	North American Free Trade Agreement
NEAC	National Economic Action Council
NERP	National Economic Recovery Plan
NIEs	Newly Industrializing Economies
NIIP	Net International Investment Position
NPL	Non-Performing Loan
NYSE	New York Stock Exchange
OECD	Organisation for Economic and Co-operation and Development
OTC	Over the Counter
PAIF	Pan-Asian Bond Index Fund
PBoC	People's Bank of China
PDI	Indonesian Democratic Party
PE	Price-to-Earnings Ratio
PSI	Private Sector Involvement

RBS	Royal Bank of Scotland
RMB	Renminbi
ROSC	Review of Standards and Codes
RTGS	Real Time Gross Settlement
SAFE	State Administration of Foreign Exchange, People's Bank of China
SEACEN	Southeast Asian Central Banks
SEC	Securities and Exchange Commission
SEHK	Stock Exchange of Hong Kong
SES	Stock Exchange of Singapore
SFCHK	Hong Kong Securities and Futures Commission
SIV	Special Investment Vehicle
SOE	State-Owned Enterprise
TARP	Troubled Assets Relief Programme
TTRS	Two-Tier Regulatory System
UBS	Union Bank of Switzerland
VaR	Value at Risk
WTO	World Trade Organization

Bibliography

Abdelal, Rawi, and Laura Alfaro. 2003. Capital and Control: Lessons from Malaysia. *Challenge*, July/August, 26–53.

Abdulgani-Knapp, Retnowati. 2007. *Soeharto: The Life and Legacy of Indonesia's Second President*. Singapore: Marshall Cavendish Editions.

Aglioby, John, et al. 2006. Most Analysts Doubt Rest of Region Will Copy Bangkok. *Financial Times*, 20 December, 5.

Akaba, Yuji, Florian Budde and Jungkiu Choi. 1998. Restructuring South Korea's Chaebol. *McKinsey Quarterly*, no. **4**, 68–79.

Akamatsu, Kaname. 1961. A Theory of Unbalanced Growth in the World Economy. *Weltwirtschaftliches Archiv*, Hamburg, **86**, 196–217.

Akyuz, Yilmaz. 2006. Reforming the IMF: Back to the Drawing Board. Third World Network, Global Economy Series, no. 7, Penang.

Adelman, Irma, and Song Byung Nak. 1999. The Korean Financial Crisis. *CUDARE Working Paper Series*, University California at Berkeley.

Allen, Roy E., ed. 2004. *The Political Economy of Financial Crises*. Vol. I. Cheltenham: Edward Elgar.

Amyx, Jennifer A. 2000. Political Impediments to Far-Reaching Banking Reforms in Japan: Implications for Asia. In Gregory W. Noble and John Ravenhill, eds., *The Asian Financial Crisis and the Architecture of Global Finance*, 132–151. Cambridge: Cambridge University Press.

Arrow, Kenneth, J. 1974. On the Agenda of Organization. In R. Marris, ed., *The Corporate Society*, 214–234. London: Macmillan.

Asia-Pacific Economic Cooperation Study, University of Hong Kong and China Centre for Economic Research. 2000. *Asian Financial Crisis: Causes and Development*. Hong Kong: Hong Kong Institute of Economics and Business Strategy, University of Hong Kong.

Asian Development Bank. 1998. *Asian Development Outlook*. Manila: ADB.

2000. *Asia Economic Monitor*. March. Manila: ADB.

2007. *Asian Development Outlook: Change amid Growth*. Manila: ADB.

Asian Policy Forum. 2000. *Policy Recommendations for Preventing Another Capital Account Crisis*. Asian Development Bank Institute, Tokyo, July.

Asiaweek. 1998. The Evolution of a Crisis. *Asiaweek*, 17 July. Available at http://cgi.cnn.com/ASIANOW/asiaweek/98/0717/cs_3_evolution.html.

1999. Passage. *Asiaweek*, 3 September. Available at http://www-cgi.cnn.com/ASIANOW/asiaweek/magazine/99/0903/passage.html.

Aslanbeigui, Nahid, and Gale Summerfield. 2000. The Asian Crisis, Gender and the International Financial Architecture. *Feminist Economics*, **6**(3), 81–103.

Asra, Abuzar. 2000. Poverty and Inequity in Indonesia: Estimates, Decomposition and Key Issues. *Journal of Asia Pacific Economy*, **5**(1/2), 91–11.

Athukorala, Prema-Chandra. 2000. Capital Account Regimes, Crisis and Adjustment in Malaysia. *Asian Development Review*, **18**(1), 17–48.

    2003. Foreign Direct Investment in Crisis and Recovery: Lessons from the 1997–1998 Asian Crisis. *Australian Economic History Review*, **43**(2), 197–213.

    2007. The Malaysian Capital Controls: A Success Story? Australian National University Working Papers in Trade and Development, 2007/07, July.

Auster, Amy, Jasmine Robinson and Katie Dean. 2006. The Fallout from Thailand's Capital Controls. *Economics@ANZ*, 20 December. Available at http://www.anz.com/documents/economics/FalloutfromThailandscapitalcontrols-20Dec06.pdf.

Bacani, Cesar. 1998. Expensive City. *Asiaweek*, 7 August, 50–53.

Backman, Michael. 2001. *Asian Eclipse: Exposing the Dark Side of Business in Asia*. Revised edition. Singapore: John Wiley & Sons (Asia).

Bagehot, Walter. 1991 [1873]. *Lombard Street: A Description of the Money Market*. Philadelphia: Orion Editions.

Baker-Said, Stephanie, and Logutenkova, Elena. 2008. The Mess at UBS. *Bloomberg Markets*, July, 36–50.

Bank for International Settlement. 1999. The Yen Carry Trade and Recent Foreign Exchange Market Volatility. *BIS Quarterly Review*, March, 33–37.

    2008. *78th Annual Report*. Basel, 30 June.

    2008. Financial System and Macroeconomic Resilience. BIS Papers, no. 41, July. Available at http://www.bis.org.

Bank Negara Malaysia. 1998. *Annual Report 1997*. March. Kuala Lumpur: Bank Negara Malaysia.

    1999. *The Central Bank and the Financial System in Malaysia: A Decade of Change (1989–1999)*. Kuala Lumpur: Bank Negara Malaysia.

    2005. Malaysia Adopts a Managed Float for the Ringgit Exchange Rate. Press release, Kuala Lumpur, 21 July.

Bank of England. 2007. *Financial Stability Report*. London, October.

    2008. *Financial Stability Report*. London, October, issue no. 24.

Bank of Japan. 1997. Statement by Governor. Tokyo, 17 November.

Bank of Korea. 1998. *Bank Restructuring in Korea, Bank Analysis Office*. Banking Department, Bank of Korea, December.

Bank of Thailand. 2000. *Supervision Report*. Bangkok: Bank of Thailand.

Banker, The. 1996. Jakarta Upheavals Highlight Riots, Risks and Returns. *The Banker*, September, 85.

Barth James R., and Zhang Xin. 1999. Foreign Equity Flows and the Asian Crisis. In Alison Howard, Robert Litan and Michael Pomerleano, eds., *Financial Markets & Development: The Crisis in Emerging Markets*, 179–218. Washington, DC: Brookings Institution Press.

Barth, James R., Gerard Caprio, Jr. and Ross Levine. 2006. *Rethinking Bank Regulation: Till Angels Govern*. Cambridge: Cambridge University Press.

Barton, Dominic. 2007. The Asian Financial System: Recovered and Ready to Play a Significant Global Role. Speech to the Federal Reserve Bank of San Francisco, 6 September.

Barton, Dominic, Roberto Newell and Gregory Wilson. 2003. *Dangerous Markets: Managing in Financial Crises*. Hoboken, NJ: John Wiley & Sons.

Basel Committee on Banking Supervision. 2008. Principles for Sound Liquidity Risk Management and Supervision. Bank for International Settlements, Basel, 17 June.

Beck, Thorsten, Asli Demirgüç-Kunt and Ross Levine. 2000. A New Database on Financial Development and Structure. *World Bank Economic Review*, **14**, 597–605.

Beinhocker, Eric. 2006. *The Origin of Wealth: Evolution, Complexity and the Radical Remaking of Economics*. London: Random House Business Books.

Beja, Edsel, Jr. 2007. Unchained Melody: Economic Performance after the Asian Crisis Working Paper Series, no. 139, Political Economy Research Institute, University of Massachusetts, Amherst, June.

Bergsten, Fred. 1998. Japan and the United States in the World Economy. *Speech given at the Conference on Wisconsin-US-Japan Economic Development, Sponsored by Kikkoman Foods*, Lake Geneva, WI, 19 June.

Bergsten, Fred, and Park Yung Chul. 2002. Toward Creating a Regional Monetary Arrangement. ADBI Research Paper Series, no. 50, Asian Development Bank Institute, Tokyo, December.

Bernanke, Ben. 2005. The Global Savings Glut and the US Current Account Deficit. Remarks by the Governor of the Federal Reserve Board at the Sandridge Lecture, Virginia Association of Economics, Richmond, VA, 10 March.

2006. The Chinese Economy: Progress and Challenges. Remarks by the Chairman of the U.S. Federal Reserve Board at the Chinese Academy of Social Sciences, Beijing, China, 15 December.

2008. Reducing Systemic Risks. Speech by the Chairman of the U.S. Federal Reserve Board at the Federal Reserve Bank of Kansas City's Annual Economic Symposium, Jackson Hole, WY, 22 August.

Bhattacharya, Anindya K. 2001. The Asian Financial Crisis and Malaysia Capital Controls. *Asia Pacific Business Review*, 7(3), 181–193.

Bidaya, Thanong. 2007. No Choice, but No Regrets Either. *Bangkok Post 2007 Mid Year Economic Review*. Available at http://www.bangkokpost.com/economicmid-year2007/Thanong.html.

Bisignano, Joseph R., William C. Hunter and George G. Kaufman, eds. 2001. *Global Financial Crises: Lessons from Recent Events*. Boston: Kluwer Academic.

Blake, David. 2008. Greenspan's Sins Return to Haunt Us. *Financial Times*, 19 September, 13.

Bloom, David, and Jeffrey Williamson. 1998. Demographic Transitions and Economic Miracles in Emerging Asia. *World Bank Economic Review*, **12**(3), 419–455.

Board of Governors of the Federal Reserve System. 2007. Flow of Funds Accounts of the United States. *Federal Reserve Statistical Release*, Washington, DC, 6 December.

Boediono. 2005. Managing the Indonesian Economy: Some Lessons from the Past. *Bulletin of Indonesian Economic Studies*, **41**(3), 309–324.

Booz, Allen and Hamilton. 1997. Revitalizing the Korean Economy toward the 21st Century. Sponsored by Vision Korea Execution Committee, Maeil Business

Newspaper, Maeil Economic Research Institute and Korea Development Institute, Seoul, South Korea, October.

Born, Brooksley. 1998. Testimony Concerning the Over-the-Counter Derivatives Market, 24 July, U.S. House of Representatives Committee on Banking and Financial Services.

Bowers, Tab, Greg Gibb and Jeffrey Wong. 2003. *Banking in Asia: Acquiring a Profit Mindset*. 2nd ed. Singapore: John Wiley & Sons (Asia).

Breedon, Francis. 2001. Market Liquidity under Stress: Observations from the FX Market. *BIS Papers*, no. 2, April, 149–151.

Bruell, Steven. 1994. Japan Rescues Thrifts with Public Funds. *International Herald Tribune*, 10 December.

Brunnemeier, Markus, Andrew Crockett, Charles Goodhart, Avinash Persaud and Hyun Shin. 2009. The Fundamental Principles of Financial Regulation. Geneva Reports on the World Economy, no. 11, International Center for Monetary and Banking Studies, Centre for Economic Policy Research, January.

Buffet, Warren. 2003. Chairman's Letter to Shareholders. *Berkshire Hathaway Inc. 2003 Annual Report*, 8 March.

2006. Chairman's Letter to Shareholders. *Berkshire Hathaway Inc. 2006 Annual Report*, 3–24.

Burdekin, Richard. 2008. *China's Monetary Challenges: Past Experiences and Future Prospects*. New York: Cambridge University Press.

Cabellero, Ricardo J. 2006. On the Macroeconomics of Asset Shortages. NBER Working Paper, no. 12753, December.

Callen, Tim, and Jonathan D. Ostry, eds. 2003. *Japan's Lost Decade: Policies for Economic Revival*. Washington, DC: International Monetary Fund.

Camdessus, Michel. 1995. Drawing Lessons from the Mexican Crises: Preventing and Resolving Financial Crises – The Role of IMF. Address at the 25th Washington Conference of the Council of the Americas on Staying the Course: Forging a Free Trade Area in the Americas, Washington, DC, 22 May.

1997. Global Capital Flows: Raising the Returns and Reducing Risk. *Address at the World Affairs Council of Los Angeles, California*, 17 June.

1998. The IMF and Its Programs in Asia. *Remarks at the Council on Foreign Relations*, New York, 6 February.

Caprio, Gerard, Jr. 1998. Banking on Crisis: Expensive Lessons from Recent Financial Crisis. World Bank Working Paper, no. 1978, Washington, DC.

Caprio, Gerard, Jr., and Daniela Klingebiel. 2003. *Episodes of Systemic and Borderline Financial Crises*. World Bank dataset. Available at http://go.worldbank.org/5DYGICS7B0.

Carr, Caleb, ed. 2000. *The Book of War: Sun-tzu The Art of Warfare & Karl von Clauswitz on War*. New York: Modern Library.

Casserley, Dominic, et al. 1999. *Banking in Asia: The End of Entitlement*. Singapore: John Wiley & Sons (Asia).

Castells, Manuel. 2000. *The Rise of the Network Society: Economy, Society and Culture*. Oxford: Blackwell Publishing.

Chakkaphak, Pin. 2007. Not Again, Please. *Bangkok Post 2007 Mid Year Economic Review*. Available at http://www.bangkokpost.com/economicmidyear2007/Pin.html.

Chalmers, Johnson. 1998. Economic Crisis in East Asia: The Clash of Capitalisms. *Cambridge Journal of Economics*, **22**(6), 653–661.

Chancellor, Edward. 2007. Ponzi Nation. *Institutional Investor, International Edition*, **32**(1), 71–78.

1999. *Devil Take the Hindmost: A History of Speculation*. New York: Farrar, Straus and Giroux.

Chang, Ha-Joon. 1998. The Hazard of Moral Hazard. *Financial Times*, 7 October, 11.

2003. *Globalization, Economic Development and the Role of the State*. New York and Penang, Malaysia: Zed Books and Third World Network.

2006. *The East Asian Development Experience: The Miracle, the Crisis and the Future*. New York and Penang, Malaysia: Zed Books and Third World Network.

Chemko, Victoria. 2002. The Japanese Yakuza: Influence on Japan's International Relations and Regional Politics (East Asia and Latin America). Available at http://conflicts.rem33.com/images/yett_secu/yakuza_chemko.htm.

Chen Nan-Kuang. 2001. Asset Price Fluctuations in Taiwan: Evidence from Stock and Real Estate Prices 1973 to 1992. *Journal of Asian Economics*, **12**(2), 215–232.

Chen, Shaohua, and Martin Ravallion. 2007. *Absolute Poverty Measures for the Developing World, 1981–2004*. Washington, DC: Development Research Group, World Bank.

China Daily. 1998. Zhu Charts Development Course. *China Daily*, 20 March.

Ching, Frank. 1999. Social Impact of the Regional Financial Crisis. In *The Asian Economic Crisis: Policy Choices, Social Consequences and the Philippines Case*. New York: Asia Society, February. Available at http://www.asiasociety.org/publications/update_crisis_Ching.html.

Chun Chang. 2000. The Informational Requirement on Financial Systems at Different Stages of Economic Development: The Case of South Korea. Working Paper, University of Minnesota.

City of London. 2007. *The Global Financial Centres Index: Executive Summary*. September. London: City of London.

Claessens, Stijn, Simeon Djankov and Larry Lang. 1998. East Asian Corporates: Growth, Financing and Risks over the Last Decade. World Bank Policy Research Working Paper, November.

Claessens, Stijn, Ayhan Kose and Marco Terrones. 2008. What Happens during Recessions, Crunches and Busts? IMF Working Paper, August.

Collyns, Charles, and Abdelhak Senhadji. 2003. Lending Booms, Real Estate Bubbles, and the Asian Crisis. IMF Working Paper, WP/02/20, January.

Commission Tasked with Making Recommendations to Improve the Efficiency and Management of Thailand's Financial System. 1998. *The Nukul Commission Report: Analysis and Evaluation of the Facts behind Thailand's Economics Crisis*. English translation. Bangkok: Nation Multimedia Group.

Corrigan, E. Gerald. 2008. The Credit Crisis: The Quest for Stability and Reform. William Taylor Memorial Lecture, Washington, DC, 12 October.

Counterparty Risk Management Policy Group. 1999. Improving Counterparty Risk Management Practices. New York, June.

2005. Toward Greater Financial Stability: A Private Sector Perspective. 27 July. Available at http://www.crmpolicygroup.org.

2008. Containing Systemic Risk: The Road to Reform. Report of the CRMPG III. 6 August. Available at http://www.crmpolicygroup.org.

Cowen, David, Ranil Salgado, Hemant Shah, Leslie Teo and Alessandro Zanello. 2006. Financial Integration in Asia: Recent Developments and New Steps. IMF Working Paper, WP/06/06, August.

Cox, Christopher. 2008. Testimony Concerning Turmoil in US Credit Markets. Senate Committee on Banking, Housing and Urban Affairs, 23 September. Available at www.sec.gov.

Crook, Clive. 2008. The View from Mount Greenspan. *The Atlantic*, 17 March. Available at http://clivecrook.theatlantic.com/archives/2008/03/the_view_from_mount_green-span.php?ref=patrick.net.

Cukierman, Alex. 2007. Central Bank Independence and Monetary Policy Making Institutions – Past Present and Future. Available at http://ideas.repec.org/p/cpr/ceprdp/6441.html.

Cull, Robert, and Maria Soledad Martínez Pería. 2007. Foreign Bank Participation and Crises in Developing Countries. World Bank Policy Research Working Paper, no. 4128, February, Washington, DC.

Damuri, Yose Rizal, Raymond Atje and Arya B. Gaduh. 2006. Integration and Trade Specialization in East Asia. Centre for Strategic and International Studies (CSIS) Working Paper Series, WPE 094, March.

D'Arista, Jane. 2008. Broken Systems: Agendas for Financial and Monetary Reform. Levy Economics Institute, Bard College, New York, 17 April.

Davies, Howard. 1999. The Changing Face of International Financial Regulation. Speech by Chairman of the Financial Services Authority, UK, to the Japan Banker Federation, Tokyo, Japan, 11 November.

2008. The Future of Financial Regulation. Oxonia Lecture, Economics Department, Oxford University, 15 January.

Davies, Howard, and David Green. 2008. *Global Financial Regulation: The Essential Guide*. Cambridge: Polity Press.

Davies, Simon. 1997. HSBC in the Firing Line as It Backs Support of Currency. *Financial Times*, 24 October, 20.

Davies, Simon, and Edward Luce. 1997. Asian Ratings Downgraded to Junk Bond Status. *Financial Times*, **23** December, 17.

De Jonquieres, Guy. 2006. Talk of an East Asian Renaissance Is Premature. *Financial Times*, 12 October, 13.

De Juan, Aristobulo. 2003. From Good Bankers to Bad Bankers: Ineffective Supervision and Management Deterioration as Major Elements in Banking Crisis. *Journal of Banking Regulation*, **4**, 237–246.

de Meyer, Arnoud, Pamela Mar, Frank-Jurgen Richter and Peter Williamson. 2005. *Global Future: The Next Challenge for Asian Business*. Singapore: John Wiley & Sons (Asia).

De Nicolò, Gianni, and Elena Loukoianova. 2007. Bank Ownership, Market Structure and Risk. IMF Working Paper, WP/07/215, September.

de Rato, Rodrigo. 2007. Ten Years after the Asian Currency Crisis: Future Challenges for the Asian Economies and Financial Markets, Speech by the Managing Director of the International Monetary Fund at the Bank of Japan Symposium. Tokyo, Japan, 22 January.

de Silva, Migara, and Shahid Yusuf. 1999. *Summary Proceedings of the World Bank Workshop on Rethinking the East Asian Miracle.* San Francisco, CA, 16–17 February.

de Brouwer, Gordon. 1999. *Capital Flows to East Asia: The Facts. Conference Held at the H. C. Coombs Centre for Financial Studies,* Kirribilli, Australia, 9–10 August.

2001. *Hedge Funds in Emerging Markets.* Cambridge: Cambridge University Press.

Delhaise, Philippe F. 1998. *Asia in Crisis: The Implosion of the Banking and Finance Systems.* Singapore: John Wiley & Sons (Asia).

Desai, Padma. 2003. *Financial Crisis, Contagion, and Containment: From Asia to Argentina.* Princeton, NJ: Princeton University Press.

Desvaux, Georges, Michael Wang and David Xu. 2004. Spurring Performance in China's State-Owned Enterprises. *McKinsey Quarterly,* Special Edition, 96–195.

Deutsche Bank Research. 1998. Can the Gathering Financial Crisis Be Stopped in Japan? *Emerging Markets,* August.

2006. China's Banking Sector: Ripe for the Next Stage? *Current Issues,* China Special, December. Available at http://www.dbresearch.com/PROD/DBR_INTERNET_EN-PROD/PROD0000000000204417.pdf.

Diaz-Alejandro, Carlos. 1985. Goodbye Financial Repression, Hello Financial Crash. *Journal of Development Economics,* **19**, 1–24.

Dick, Kathryn. 2008. Testimony before Senate Subcommittee on Securities, Insurance and Investment, Comptroller of the Currency, Washington, DC, 9 July.

Djiwandono, Soedrajad J. 2000. Bank Indonesia and the Recent Crisis. *Bulletin of Indonesian Economic Studies,* **36**(1), 47–72.

2004. Liquidity Support to Banks during Indonesia's Financial Crisis. *Bulletin of Indonesian Economic Studies,* **40**(1), 59–75.

2005. *Bank Indonesia and the Crisis: An Insider's View.* Singapore: Institute of Southeast Asian Studies.

Dobson, Wendy, and Anil K. Kashyap. 2006. The Contradiction in China's Gradualist Banking Reforms. Paper prepared for the Brookings Panel on Economic Activity, Washington, DC, October.

Dollar, David, and Mary Hallward-Driemeier. 2000. Crisis, Adjustment, and Reform in Thailand's Industrial Firms. *World Bank Research Observer,* **15**(1), 1–22.

Dombey, Daniel. 2006. The Billion Dollar Memory Lapse: George Soros Has Moved on to Higher Things since Black Wednesday 1992, When He Broke the Bank of England and Made a Fortune – or Was It a Thursday? *Financial Times,* 5 August, 14.

Dominguez, Kathryn M. 1999. The Role of the Yen. In Martin Feldstein, ed., *International Capital Flows,* 133–168. Chicago: University of Chicago Press.

Dooley, Michael, Peter Garber and David Folkerts-Landau. 2004. An Essay on the Revived Bretton Woods System. *International Journal of Finance & Economics,* **9**, October, 307–313.

Drucker, Peter. 1993. *Post-Capitalist Society.* New York: Harper Business.

Drucker, Peter, and Isao Nakauchi. 1997. *On Asia.* London: Butterworth/Heinemann.

DSG Asia. 2008. *Asia's Economic and Financial Market Landscape – 2008.* 7 January.

Dyer, Geoff. 2007. Fuelling the Chinese Boom in Equities. *Financial Times,* **6** November, 26.

Eatwell, John, and Avinash Persaud. 2008. Fannie Mae and Freddie Mac: Damned by a Faustian Bargain. *Financial Times,* 17 July. Available at http://www.ft.com/cms/s/0/642d7dd2-5409-11dd-aa78-000077b07658.html?nclick_check=1.

Eatwell, John, and Lance Taylor. 2000. Capital Flows and the International Financial Architecture. A Paper from the Project on Development, Trade and International Finance, Council on Financial Relations, July 1998. Available at http://www.cfr.org/publication/8717/capital_flows_and_the_international_financial_architecture_a_cfr_paper.html.

The Economist. 1993. Japanese in Asia: Branching Out. *The Economist,* 7 August, 69.

1995. Jittery Japan. *The Economist,* 22 April, 15–16.

1997a. Horrible Truth Revealed. *The Economist,* 25 January, 65–68.

1997b. Run, Run, Run. *The Economist,* 29 November, 80.

1998. The Hong Kong Dollar: Off the Peg? *The Economist,* 14 February, 77.

2007. Stir Fry Capitalism. *The Economist,* 1 September, 77.

2008a. Paradise Lost, A Special Report on International Banking. *The Economist,* 17 May, Suppl., 1–26, 58ff.

2008b. Confessions of a Risk Manager. *The Economist,* 9 August, 72–73.

Edwards, Sebastian. 1998a. The Mexican Peso Crisis: How Much Did We Know? When Did We Know It? *World Economy,* **21**(1), 1–30.

1998b. Barking Up the Wrong Tree. *Financial Times,* 7 October, 10.

1999. On Crisis Prevention: Lessons from Mexico and East Asia. NBER Working Paper Series, no. 7233, July.

Eichengreen, Barry. 2007. *Global Imbalances and the Lessons of Bretton Woods.* Cambridge, MA: MIT Press.

Eichengreen, Barry, and Tamim Bayoumi. 1996. Is Asia an Optimum Currency Area? Can It Become One? Regional, Global and Historical Perspective on Asian Monetary Relations. *Centre for International and Development Economics Research (CIDER) Working Paper,* no. C96–081, December.

Eichengreen, Barry, and Donald Mathieson. 1999. Hedge Funds: What Do We Really Know? *IMF Economic Issues,* no. **19**, September.

Einzig, Paul. 1935. *World Finance 1914–1935.* London: K. Paul, Trench, Trubner.

El-Erian, Mohamed. 2008. *When Markets Collide: Investment Strategies for the Age of Global Economic Change.* New York: McGraw-Hill.

EMEAP. 1997. Closer Cooperation and Coordination among EMEAP Members. Press Release of the Second EMEAP Governors Meeting, Shanghai, China, 27 July.

Emerging Markets Monitor. 2006. The Growing Need for Capital Market Reform. *Emerging Markets Monitor,* **12**(2), 26 June, 3–4.

2007a. Scenario Test: Hard Landing in China. *Emerging Markets Monitor* **12**(39), 22 January, 1–2.

2007b. China: Political Implications of Hard Landing. *Emerging Markets Monitor* **12**(40), 29 January, 1–2.

2007c. Asia: Beyond the Correction, Solid Fundamentals Will Prevail. *Emerging Markets Monitor,* 12(45), 5 March, 8.

Ernst, Dieter. 2004. Global Production Networks in East Asia's Electronic Industry and Upgrading Perspectives in Malaysia. In Shahid Yusuf, Anjum Altaf and Kaoru Nabeshima, eds., *Global Production Networks and Technological Innovation in East Asia,* 89–158. Washington, DC: World Bank.

Faber, Marc. 2002. *Tomorrow's Gold: Asia's Age of Discovery.* Hong Kong: CLSA Books.

Fallon, Peter, and Robert Lucas. 2002. The Impact of Financial Crises on Labor Markets, Household Incomes, and Poverty: A Review of Evidence. *World Bank Research Observer,* **17**(1), 21–25.

Fallows, James. 1995. *Looking at the Sun: The Rise of the New East Asian Economic and Political System*. Reprint edition. New York: Vintage Books.

Fan, Joseph P. H., and Yupana Wiwatanakantang. 2006. Bank Ownership and Governance Quality in Four Post-Crisis Asian Economies. In Sang-Woo Nam and Chee Soon Lum, eds., *Corporate Governance of Banks in Asia*, 75–106. Tokyo: Asian Development Bank Institute.

Farmer, J. Doyne. 2001. Toward Agent-Based Models for Investment. In *Benchmarks and Attribution Analysis* (the Association for Investment Management and Research), 61–70.

Farrell, Diana, Aneta Key and Tim Shavers. 2005. Mapping the Global Capital Markets. McKinsey Quarterly, Special Edition, 38–47.

Federal Reserve Bank of Kansas City. 2008. Jackson Hoel Economic Symposium. Available at www.kc.frb.org/publicat/sympos/symmain.htm.

Ferguson, Niall. 2008. *The Ascent of Money: A Financial History of the World*. London: Allen Lane.

Feridhanusetyawan, Tubagus, and Mari Pangestu. 2003. Managing Indonesia's Debt. *Asian Economic Papers*, **2**(3), 128–154.

Financial Services Authority. 2008. *FSA's Supervisory Enhancement Programme in Response to the Internal Audit Report on Supervision of Northern Rock*. FSA, London, 26 March.

Financial Services Bureau. 1998. *Report on Financial Market Review*. April. Hong Kong: Government of Hong Kong Special Administrative Region.

Financial Times. 2006. Yeah Baht, No Baht. *Financial Times*, 20 December, 16.

2007. Lessons from Asia: China's Rise Means ASEAN Never Full Recovered from 1997. *Financial Times*, 14 May, 14.

Fisher, Peter. 1997. Global Currency Market Risks and Rewards. Remarks by Executive Vice President of the Federal Reserve Bank of New York at the 19th Asia Pacific Financial Markets Assembly, Hong Kong, 28 November.

Fischer, Stanley. 1998a. The Asian Crisis: A View from the IMF. *Address by First Deputy Managing Director of the International Monetary Fund at the Midwinter Conference of the Bankers' Association for Foreign Trade*, Washington, DC, 22 January.

1998b. The Asian Crisis and the Changing Role of the IMF. *Finance & Development*, **35**(2), 2–6.

2002. The Asian Crisis: Lessons for the Future. Fifth Hong Kong Monetary Authority Distinguished Lecture, Hong Kong, 21 May.

Fleckenstein, William, and Fred Sheehan. 2008. *Greenspan's Bubble: The Age of Ignorance at the Federal Reserve*. New York: McGraw-Hill.

Flemming, Marcus. 1962. Domestic Financial Policies under Fixed and under Floating Exchange Rates. *IMF Staff Papers*, **9**(3), 369–379.

Fligsten, Neil. 2001. *The Architecture of Markets: An Economic Sociology of Twenty-first-Century Capitalist Societies*. Princeton, NJ: Princeton University Press.

Folkerts-Landau, David, and Alfred Steinherr. 1994. The Wild Beast of Derivatives: To Be Chained Up, Fenced in or Tamed? In *Amex Bank Review Prize Essays: Finance and International Economy*, vol. 8, 8–27. New York: Oxford University Press for American Express Bank.

Frécaut, Olivier. 2004. Indonesia's Banking Crisis: A New Perspective on $50 Billion of Losses. *Bulletin of Indonesian Economic Studies*, **40**(1), 37–57.

Freedman, Craig, ed. 1999. *Why Did Japan Stumble? Causes and Cures*. Cheltenham: Edward Elgar.

Friedman, Alan. 1997. Soros Calls Mahathir a "Menace" to Malaysia. *International Herald Tribune*, 22 September.

Friedman, Milton. 1998. The Hong Kong Experiment. *Hoover Digest*, no. 3. Available at http://www.hooverdigest.org/983/friedman.html.

Fukuyama, Francis. 1998. Asian Values and Civilisation. *ICAS Fall Symposium*, Institute for Corean-American Studies. Available at http://www.icasinc.or/1998/frff1998. html.

G-20 Secretariat. 2003. *Economic Reform in this Era of Globalization: 16 Country Cases*. New Delhi: G-20.

2005. *Institution Building in the Financial Sector*. New Delhi: G-20.

Galbraith, John Kenneth. 1954. *The Great Crash 1929*. 1975 edition. London: Penguin Group.

1983. *The Anatomy of Power*. London: Corgi Books.

Gan Wee Beng, and Ying Soon Lee. 2003. Current Account Reversal during a Currency Crisis: The Malaysian Experience. *ASEAN Economic Bulletin*, **20**(2), 128–143.

Gapper, John. 2008. The Cost of a Wrong Turn, Part 2, Future of Banking. *Financial Times*, 4 August. Available at http://us.ft.com/ftgateway/superpage.ft?news_id= fto080420081458393864.

Geithner, Timothy. 2008. Reducing Systemic Risk in a Dynamic Financial System. Speech at the Economic Club of New York, 9 June.

Gieve, John. 2008. Coping with Financial Distress in a More Markets-Oriented Environment. BIS Papers, no. 41.

Giles, Chris. 2008. Into the Storm. *Financial Times*, 14 November, 10.

Gill, Indermit, Yukon Huang and Homi Kharas, eds. 2007. *East Asia Visions: Perspectives on Economic Development*. Washington, DC, and Singapore: World Bank and Institute of Policy Studies, Singapore.

Girishankar, Navin. 2001. *Evaluating Public Sector Reform: Guidelines for Assessing County-Level Impact of Structural Reform and Capacity Building in the Public Sector*. Washington, DC: World Bank.

Godement, François. 1999. *The Downsizing of Asia*. London: Routledge.

Goh, Chok Tong. 1999. The Asian Crisis: Lessons and Responses. Speech by the Prime Minister of Singapore at the Argentine Institute of International Relations, Buenos Aires, Argentina, 2 June.

Goldstein, Morris. 1998. The Asian Financial Crisis: Causes, Cures, and Systemic Implications. IMF Policy Analyses in International Economics, no. 55, Washington, DC.

Gomez, Terence, ed. 2002. *Political Business in East Asia*. London: Routledge.

Goodhart, Charles. 2000. The Organisational Structure of Banking Supervision. FSI Occasional Papers, no. 1, November, Financial Stability Institute Bank for International Settlements, Basel.

2007. Liquidity Risk Management. LSE Financial Markets Group's Special Paper, no. 175, October.

2008a. The Regulatory Response to the Financial Crisis. Financial Markets Group, London School of Economics.

2008b. Lessons from the Crisis for Financial Regulation: What We Need and What We Do Not Need. Background Paper to the Financial Markets Reform Task Force Meeting 2008, University of Manchester, 1–2 July.

2008c. Now Is Not the Time to Agonize over Moral Hazard. *Financial Times* Comment, 19 September. Available at http://www.ft.com/cms/s/0/62db6730–85-e3–11dd-a1ac-0000779fd18c.html.

Goodhart, Charles, and Philipp Hartmann. 1998. *Financial Regulation: Why, How and Where Now?* New York: Routledge.

Goodhart, Charles, and Dai Lu. 2003. *Intervention to Save Hong Kong: The Authorities' Counter-Speculation in Financial Markets.* Oxford: Oxford University Press.

Goodhart, Charles, and Avinash Persaud. 2008. How to Avoid the Next Crash. *Financial Times*, 30 January, 9.

Goodstadt, Leo. 2007. *Profits, Politics and Panic: Hong Kong's Banks and the Making of a Miracle Economy, 1935–1985.* Hong Kong: Hong Kong University Press.

Gourinchas, P.-O., and Rey, H. 2006. From World Banker to World Venture Capitalist: U.S. External Adjustment and the Exorbitant Privilege. NBER Working Paper, no. 11562.

Government of Malaysia. 1999. *White Paper: Status of the Malaysian Economy.* 6 April. Available at http://www.epu.jpm.my.

Grais, David J., and Kostas D. Katsiris. 2007. Why the First Amendment Does Not Shield the Rating Agencies from Liability for Over-rating CDOs. *Bloomberg Law Reports*, November. Available at http://www.graisellsworth.com/Rating_Agencies.pdf.

Greenspan, Alan. 1996. *Remarks by Chairman of the US Federal Reserve Board at the Annual Dinner and Francis Boyer Lecture of the American Enterprise Institute for Public Policy Research*, Washington, DC, 5 December.

1997. Turbulence in World Financial Markets. Testimony of the Chairman of the US Federal Reserve Board before the Joint Economic Committee, U.S. Congress, 29 October.

1998a. Risk Management in the Global Financial System. Remarks before the Annual Financial Markets Conference in the Federal Reserve Bank of Atlanta, Miami Beach, FL, 27 February.

1998b. The Current Asia Crisis and the Dynamics of International Finance. Testimony of the Chairman of the US Federal Reserve Board before the Committee on Agriculture, U.S. House of Representatives, 21 May.

1998c. International Economic and Financial Systems. Testimony of the Chairman of the U.S. Federal Reserve Board before the Committee on Banking and Financial Services, U.S. House of Representatives, 16 September.

1998d. The Crisis in Emerging Market Economies. Testimony of the Chairman of the U.S. Federal Reserve Board before the Committee on Budget, U.S. Senate, 23 September.

1998e. Private-Sector Refinancing of the Large Hedge Fund, Long-Term Capital Management. Testimony of the Chairman of the U.S. Federal Reserve Board before the Committee on Banking and Financial Services, U.S. House of Representatives, 1 October.

1999a. Lessons from the Global Crisis. Address before the World Bank Group and IMF Program of Seminars, Washington, DC, 27 September.

1999b. Do Efficient Financial Markets Mitigate Financial Crises? 1999 Financial Markets Conference of the Federal Reserve Bank of Atlanta, Sea Island, Georgia, 19 October.

2002. Economic Volatility. Remarks by Chairman of the U.S. Federal Reserve Board at a Symposium sponsored by the Federal Reserve Bank of Kansas City, Jackson Hole, WY, 30 August.

2003. Speech to Conference on Bank Structure and Competition, Federal Reserve Bank of Chicago, 8 May.

2007. *The Age of Turbulence.* New York: Penguin Press.

2008a. We Will Never Have a Perfect Model of Risk. *Financial Times,* 17 March, 9.

2008b. Banks Need More Capital. *Economist,* Economic Focus, 20 December, 122.

Grenville, Stephen. 1998. The Asian Economic Crisis. Talk to the Australian Business Economists and the Economic Society of Australia (NSW Branch), Sydney, Australia, 12 March.

2004a. The IMF and the Indonesian Crisis. *Bulletin of Indonesian Economic Studies,* **40**(1), 77–94.

2004b. What Sort of Financial Sector Should Indonesia Have? *Bulletin of Indonesian Economic Studies,* **40**(3), 307–327.

Griffith-Jones, Stephany. 2008. Criteria for Financial Regulation after the Current Crisis. Background Paper to the Financial Markets Reform Task Force Meeting 2008, University of Manchester, 1–2 July.

Gross, Bill. 2008. Pyramids Crumbling. *PIMCO Investment Outlook,* January. Available at www.pimco.com.

Group of Thirty. 2008. The Structure of Financial Supervision: Approaches and Challenges in a Global Marketplace. Washington DC. Available at www.group30.org.

Gumerlock, Robert. 2000. Valuation, Liquidity and Risk. IFRI Risk Management Roundtable, mimeo, 6 April.

Gyohten, Toyoo. 1999. Two Lessons of the East Asian Financial Crisis. Remarks to the Trilateral Commission, Institute for International Monetary Affairs. Available at http://www.trilateral.org.

Hale, David. 1997a. The East Asian Financial Crisis and the World Economy. Testimony before the House Banking Committee, U.S. Congress, 13 November.

1997b. How Did Thailand become the Creditanstalt of 1997? *The Zurich Group's Global Economic Observer,* 23 December.

1998a. The IMF after the Asia Crisis. Presentation before the Bretton Woods Committee, Washington, DC, 13 February.

1998b. Indonesia's Currency Board. *The Zurich Group's Global Economic Observer,* 3 March.

1998c. Will Asia Force the U.S. to Create a Bubble Economy? *The Zurich Group's Global Economic Observer,* 13 April.

1998d. Developing Country Financial Crises during the 1990's: Will Mexico's Recovery from the 1995 Peso Crisis Be a Role Model for Asia? *The Zurich Group's Global Economic Observer,* June.

1998e. Can the G-7 Restrain Global Deflation without a Recovery in Japan? *The Zurich Group's Global Economic Observer,* 17 July.

1998f. Will Russia's Default Produce a Global Recession? *The Zurich Group's Global Economic Observer,* 8 October.

2008. 2008 Economic Forecast. Chicago: Hale Advisers. January.

Hale, Gillian. 2007. Prospects for China's Corporate Bond Market. Federal Reserve Bank of San Francisco Economic Letter, 16 March.

Hamilton, David P. 1998. Global Cry Urges Japan to Fix Economy: Country's Leaders Take a Restrained Approach as the Problems Spread. *Asian Wall Street Journal*, 17 June.

Hanke, Steve H. 1996. Anything in Asia but Japan. *Forbes*, 16 December, 394.

2002. On Dollarization and Currency Boards: Error and Deception. *Policy Reform*, 5(4), 203–222.

Hanke, Steve H., and Alan A. Walters. 1993. Yen Bashing. *Forbes*, 12 April, 64.

Hansakul, Syetam. 2006. China's Banking Sector: Ripe for the Next Stage? *Deutsche Bank Research*, 7 December.

Hartcher, Peter. 1998a. *The Ministry: How Japan's Most Powerful Institution Endangers World Markets*. Cambridge, MA: Harvard Business School Press.

1998b. Can Japan Come Back? *The National Interest*, no. 54, Winter, 32–39.

Harvie, Charles, and Hyun-Hoon Lee. 2003. Export-Led Industrialisation and Growth: Korea's Economic Miracle, 1962–1989. *Australian Economic History Review*, 43(3), 256–286.

He Huang, Richard, and Gordon Orr. 2007. China's State-Owned Enterprises: Board Governance and the Communist Party. *McKinsey Quarterly*, 1, 108–111.

Healy, Tim, and Julian Gearing. 1996. Didn't You See It Coming? Laying the Blame for the Bangkok Bank of Commerce Troubles. *Asiaweek*, 7 June. Available at http://www-cgi.cnn.com/ASIANOW/asiaweek/96/0607/biz3.html.

Hodgson Brown, Ellen. 2007. *Web of Debt*. Chippenham: Third Millennium Press.

Holzhausen, Arne, ed. 2001. *Can Japan Globalize?: Studies on Japan's Changing Political Economy and the Process of Globalization in Honour of Sung-Jo Park*. Heidelberg: Physica-Verlag.

Hong Kong Monetary Authority. 1997. *Annual Report*. Hong Kong: Hong Kong Monetary Authority. Available at www.hkma.gov.hk.

1998. *Annual Report*. Hong Kong: Hong Kong Monetary Authority.

2005. *Hong Kong's Linked Exchange Rate System*. November. Hong Kong: Hong Kong Monetary Authority.

Hong Kong SAR Government. 1998. *Hong Kong Yearbook*. Hong Kong: Hong Kong SAR Government.

Hookway, James. 2007. Politics and Economies: Thai Plan Worries Foreign Investors. *Wall Street Journal*, Eastern Edition, 9 January.

Horsley, Nicholas. 1997. Asia Needs a New Model. *Asian Wall Street Journal*, 9 December.

Huang, Ray. 1982. 1587, *A Year of No Significance: The Ming Dynasty in Decline*. Reprint edition. New Haven, CT: Yale University Press.

1998. *China: A Macro History*. New York: M. E. Sharpe.

1999. *Broadening the Horizon of Chinese History: Discourses, Syntheses and Comparisons*. New edition. Armonk, NY: M. E. Sharpe.

Hufbauer, Gary Clyde. 1998. Reshaping the Global Financial Architecture. Peterson Institute for International Economics, 5–6 November.

IMF Staff. 1998. The Asian Crisis: Causes and Cures. *Finance & Development*, 35(2), 18–21.

Independent Evaluation Office. 2003. The IMF and the Recent Capital Account Crises: Indonesia, Korea, Brazil. Evaluation Report, Washington, DC: International Monetary Fund. July.

Institute for International Monetary Affairs. 2003. Preventing Future Financial Crises: Lessons from Asian and Latin American Countries and the Role of IMF. Occasional Paper, no. 13, Tokyo. September.

Institute of International Finance. 2008a. Interim Report of the IIF Committee on Market Best Practices. Washington, DC, 9 April.

2008b. Final Report of the IIF Committee on Market Best Practices: Principles of Conduct and Best Practice Recommendations – Financial Services Industry Response to the Market Turmoil of 2007–2008. Washington, DC, 25 July.

International Monetary Fund. 1997a. IMF Approves Extension and Augmentation of EFF for the Philippines. Press Release, 97/33, Washington, DC, 18 July.

1997b. IMF Approves Stand-by Credit for Thailand. Press Release, 97/38, Washington, DC, 20 August.

1997c. IMF Approves Stand-by Credit for Indonesia. Press Release, 97/50, Washington, DC, 5 November.

1997d. International Capital Markets: Developments, Prospects and Key Policy Issues. Washington, DC, November.

1997d. World Economic Outlook – Interim Assessment. Washington, DC, December.

1998a. World Economic Outlook. Washington, DC, May.

1998b. International Capital Markets: Developments, Prospects and Key Policy Issues. Washington, DC, September.

1998c. World Economic Outlook. Washington, DC, October.

1998d. Thailand: Statistical Appendix. IMF Staff Country Report, no. 98/119, Washington, DC, October.

1998e. World Economic Outlook and International Capital Markets – Interim Assessment. Washington, DC, December.

1999a. World Economic Outlook. Washington, DC, May.

1999b. IMF Supported Programs in Indonesia, Korea, and Thailand: A Preliminary Assessment. IMF Occasional Paper Series, no. 178, Washington, DC.

1999c. Malaysia: Selected Issues. IMF Staff Country Report, no. 99/86, Washington, DC, August.

2000. Recovery from the Asian Crisis and the Role of the IMF. IMF Issues Brief, no. 00/05, Washington, DC, June.

2001. People's Republic of China – Hong Kong Special Administrative Region: Selective Issues and Statistical Appendix. IMF Country Report, no. 1/146, Washington, DC, August.

2003. Global Financial Stability Report. Washington, DC.

2006a. People's Republic of China: 2006 Article IV Consultation – Staff Report; Staff Statement; and Public Information Notice on the Executive Board Discussion. IMF Country Report, no. 06/394, Washington, DC, October.

2006b. Global Financial Stability Report. Washington, DC, September.

2007a. Global Financial Stability Report. Washington, DC, April.

2007b. Staff Report on the Multilateral Consultation on Global Imbalances with China, the Euro Area, Japan, Saudi Arabia, and the United States. Washington, DC, June 29.

2007b. Global Financial Stability Report. Washington, DC, October.

2008. Global Financial Stability Report. Washington, DC, April.

Ishigaki, Kenichi, and Hiroyuki Hino, eds. 1998. *Towards the Restoration of Sound Banking Systems in Japan – The Global Implications*. Kobe: Kobe University Press and International Monetary Fund.

Ito, Takatoshi. 1996. Japan and the Asian Economies: A 'Miracle' in Transition. *Brookings Papers on Economic Activities*, no. **2**, 205–260.

2007. Asian Currency Crisis and the International Monetary Fund, 10 Years Later: An Overview. *Asian Economic Policy Review*, **2**, 16–49.

Iwai, Koichi. 1998. Capital Flows, Capital Market Trends: A Monthly Guide to Investment in Japan. Nomura Research Institute, August.

Jackson, Karl D., ed. 1999. *Asian Contagion: The Causes and Consequences of a Financial Crisis*. Boulder, CO: Westview Press.

Jaimovich, Dany, and Ugo Panizza. 2006. Public Debt around the World: A New Dataset of Central Government Debt. Inter-American Development Bank Working Paper, no. 561, March.

Jao, Y. C. 1998. The Real Lessons of 'Black Thursday'. *HKMA Quarterly Bulletin*, August, 43–45.

2001. *The Asian Financial Crisis and the Order of Hong Kong*. Westport, CT: Quorum.

Joint Forum. 2005. Credit Risk Transfer, Basel Committee on Banking Supervision. March. Available at www.bis.org.

Jomo, K.S. 2005. Malaysia's September 1998 Controls: Background, Context, Impacts, Comparisons, Implications and Lessons. UNCTAD G-24 Discussion Paper Series, no. 36, March.

Jomo, K.S., et al. 1997. *Southeast Asia's Misunderstood Miracle: Industrial Policy and Economic Development in Thailand, Malaysia and Indonesia*. Denver, CO: Westview Press.

Jopson, Barney. 2003. Funding Gap in Japanese Pensions. *Financial Times*, 9 September, 28.

Kaminsky, Graciela, and Carmen M. Reinhart. 1999. The Twin Crises: The Causes of Banking and Balance of Payments Problems. *American Economic Review*, **89**, 473–500.

Kaminsky, Graciela, and Sergio Schmukler. 1999. What Triggers Market Jitters: A Chronicle of the Asian Crisis. *U.S. Federal Reserve International Finance Discussion Papers*, no. 634, April.

Kanaya, Akihiro, and David Woo. 2000. The Japanese Banking Crisis of the 1990s: Sources and Lessons. IMF Working Paper, no. WP/00/7.

Kane, Edward J. 2000. The Dialectical Role of Information and Disinformation in Regulation-Induced Crises. *Pacific Basin Financial Journal*, **8**, 285–308.

Kang, Tae Soo, and Guonan Ma. 2007. Recent Episodes of Credit Card Distress in Asia. *BIS Quarterly Review*, June, 55–68.

Kattoulas, Velisarios. 2002. Japan: The Yakuza Recession. *Far Eastern Economic Review*, 165(2), 17 January, 12–19.

Kaufman, Henry. 1998. A Lack of Leadership. *Financial Times*, 7 October, 11.

Kaufmann, Daniel, Aart Kraay and Massimo Mastruzzi. 2006. Governance Matters V: Aggregate and Individual Governance Indicators 1996–2005. World Bank Policy Research Working Paper, no. 4012, September.

Kawai, Masahiro. 2002. Bank and Corporate Restructuring in Crisis-Affected East Asia: From Systemic Collapse to Reconstruction. In Gordon de Brouwer, ed., *Financial Markets and Policies in East Asia*, 82–121. London: Routledge.

2003. *Japan's Banking System: From the Bubble and Crisis to Reconstruction*. Tokyo: Institute of Social Science, University of Tokyo.

Kawai, Masahiro, Richard Newfarmer and Sergio Schmukler. 2005. Financial Crises: Nine Lessons from East Asia. *Eastern Economic Journal*, 31(2), 185–207.

Kay, John. 2004. *The Truth about Markets: Why Some Nations Are Rich but Most Remain Poor*. London: Penguin Books.

Keown, Deidre. 2007. China: Land of Opportunities. *Money Management*, 16–18.

Keynes, John Maynard. 1942 [1936]. *The General Theory of Employment, Interest and Money*. 1942 reprint. London: Macmillan.

Khandani, Amir E., and Andrew W. Lo. 2007. What Happened to the Quants in August 2007? Massachusetts Institute of Technology, Cambridge, MA, September.

Kim, Dong Hwan. 2005. Cognitive Maps of Policy Makers on Financial Crises of South Korea and Malaysia: A Comparative Study. *International Review of Public Administration*, 9(2), January, 31–39.

Kim, Kihwan. 2000. The Korean Financial Crisis: Causes, Response and Lessons. In Joseph R. Bisignano, William C. Hunter and George G. Kaufman, eds., *Global Financial Crises: Lessons from Recent Events*, 201–208. Boston: Kluwer Academic.

2006. The 1997–98 Korean Financial Crisis: Causes, Policy Response and Lessons. Presentation at the High-Level Seminar on Crisis Prevention in Emerging Markets Organised by the International Monetary Fund and the Government of Singapore, Singapore, 10–11 July.

Kindleberger, Charles. (1996) [1978]. *Manias, Panics and Crashes: A History of Financial Crises*. 3rd ed. London: Macmillan.

King, Mervyn. 2006. Reform of the International Monetary Fund, Speech by the Governor of the Bank of England at the Indian Council for Research on International Economic Relations (ICRIER), New Delhi, India, 20 February.

2007. Monetary Policy Developments. Speech at the Northern Ireland Chamber of Commerce and Industry, Belfast, Ireland, 9 October.

Kirk, Don. 1998. Vague Charges Accuses Korean Officials of Letting Economy Fall: From Finance Ministry to Cell No. 3. *International Herald Tribune*, 21 July.

1999. In South Korea, Big Investment Firms Are Banking on Bad Loans. *International Herald Tribune*, 29 June.

Kissinger, Henry. 1998. The Asian Collapse: One Fix Does Not Fit All Economies. *Washington Post*, 9 February.

Kittiprapas, Sauwalak. 2002. Social Impacts of Financial and Economic Crisis in Thailand. *EADN Regional Project on the Social Impact of the Asian Financial Crisis*, January.

Knee, Jonathan A. 2006. *The Accidental Investment Banker*. New York: Random House Trade Paperbacks.

Knowles, James C., Ernesto M. Pernia and Mary Racelis. 1999. Social Consequences of the Financial Crisis in Asia: The Deeper Crisis. *Asian Development Bank Economics and Development Resource Centre (ADB EDRC) Briefing Notes*, no. 16.

Kobayashi, Masaki. 1997a. Recent Trends of the Japanese Direct Investment Abroad – Increasing Focus on Manufacturing Sector and Asia. *Nomura Asia Focus Quarterly*, Nomura Research Institute, Summer 1997, 2–5.

    1997b. Expansion of Japanese Businesses into Asia – Contributing Factors and Future Outlook, *Nomura Asia Focus Quarterly*, Nomura Research Institute, Summer 1997, 6–14.

Koh, Winston T. H., et al. 2004. Bank Lending and Real Estate in Asia: Market Optimism and Asset Bubbles. Wharton-SMU Research Centre, 10 January.

Kohn, Donald L. 2007. Financial Stability – Preventing and Managing Crises. Remarks by Vice Chairman of the Board of Governors of the US Federal Reserve System at the Exchequer Club Luncheon. Washington, DC, 21 February.

Kondo, M. James, William W. Lewis, Vincent Palmade and Yoshinori Yokohama. 2000. Reviving Japan's Economy. *McKinsey Quarterly*, Special Edition, 4, 19–37.

Koo, Richard. 1998. Overview, *Capital Market Trends: A Monthly Guide to Investment in Japan*. Nomura Research Institute, August.

    2003. *Balance Sheet Recession: Japan's Struggle with Uncharted Economics and Its Global Implications*. Singapore: John Wiley & Sons (Asia).

Kristof, Nicholas D., and Sheryl WuDunn. 2001. *Thunder from the East: Portrait of a Rising Asia*. New York: Vintage Books.

Krueger, Anne O. 2004. Lessons from the Asian Crisis. *Keynote Address by the First Deputy Managing Director of the International Monetary Fund at the SEACEN Meeting*, Colombo, Sri Lanka, 12 February.

Krueger, Anne O., and Aaron Tornell. 1999. The Role of Bank Restructuring in Recovering from Crises: Mexico 1995–1998. NBER Working Paper, no. 7042, March.

Krugman, Paul. 1994. The Myth of Asia's Miracle. *Foreign Affairs*, **73**(6), 62–79.

    1998a. *What Happened to Asia*. Unpublished Manuscript, Massachusetts Institute of Technology, Cambridge, MA, January. Available at http://web.mit.edu/krugman/www/DISINTER.html.

    1998b. Will Asia Bounce Back? Speech at Credit Suisse First Boston, Hong Kong, March.

    2000. *The Return of Depression Economics*. Revised edition. London: Penguin Books.

Kuper, Simon. 1997. Korean Won Hits 999 against Dollar. *Financial Times*, London Edition, 11 November, 33.

Kuroda, Haruhiko. 2002. Japan in the Global Economy: A Personal View. Speech before Chatham House, London, 17 June.

    2005. Towards a Borderless Asia: A Perspective on Asian Economic Integration. *Speech by the President of the Asian Development Bank at the Emerging Markets Forum*, Oxford, UK, 10 December.

Kwan, C. H. 1997. Deepening Asia-Japan Economic Interdependence – The Impact of the Yen's Appreciation. Nomura Research Institute, Tokyo, April.

    1998. Asian Currency Crisis: From the Viewpoint of Japanese Yen and Chinese Yuan. Nomura Research Institute, Tokyo.

Labaton, Stephen. 2008. How US Regulators Laid the Groundwork for Disaster. *International Herald Tribune*, 3 October. Available at http://www.nytimes.com/2008/10/03/business/worldbusiness/03iht-03sec.16660424.html?_r=1.

Laevan, Luc, and Fabian Valencia. 2008. *Systemic Banking Crises: A New Database*. IMF Working Paper, WP/08/24, November.

Lamfalussy, Alexandre. 1998. Asian Debt: The Signs Were There for All to See. *Financial Times*, 13 February, 24.

Lane, Philip R., and Gian Maria Milesi-Ferretti. 2001, The External Wealth of Nations: Measures of Foreign Assets and Liabilities for Industrial and Developing Countries. *Journal of International Economics*, **55**, 264–294.

2006. The External Wealth of Nations Mark II: Revised and Extended Estimates of Foreign Assets and Liabilities, 1970–2004. IMF Working Paper, WP/06/99, March.

Langley, Monica, Deborah Solomon and Mathew Karnitschnig. 2008. A Wave Engulfing Wall Street Swamps the World's Largest Insurer. *Wall Street Journal*, 19–21 September.

Lardy, Nicholas. 1998. *China's Unfinished Economic Revolution*. Washington, DC: Brookings Institution Press.

Lee, Kuan Yew. 1998. Melt Down in East Asia. East Lecture Series: The James A. Baker III Institute for Public Policy, Rice University, Houston, Texas, 23 October.

2000. *From Third World to First – The Singapore Story: 1965–2000*. Singapore: Times Media.

Lee, Phil-Sang. 2000. Economic Crisis and Chaebol Reform in Korea. APEC Study Centre Discussion Paper, no. 14, Columbia University, October.

Lee, Tim. 2008. The Currency Carry Trade and Emerging Markets – The Next Phase of the Global Crisis. July-August. Available at www.pieconomics.com.

Leekpai, Chuan. 1998. Lessons from East Asian Financial Crisis. Speech by the Prime Minister of Thailand at the Council of Foreign Relations and Asia Society, New York, 11 March.

Lewis, Michael. 2008. The End, December. Available at http://www.portfolio.com/news-markets/national-news/portfolio/2008/11/11/The-End-of-Wall-Streets-Boom.

Liker, Jeffrey. 2004. *The Toyota Way: 14 Management Principles from the World's Greatest Manufacturer*. New York: McGraw-Hill.

Linden, Eugene. 1997. How to Kill a Tiger. *Time*, Australia/New Zealand Edition, 3 November.

Lindsey, Richard R. 1998. Hedge Funds Activities in the U.S. Financial Markets. Testimony of the Director, Division of Market Regulation, U.S. Securities and Exchange Commission before the Committee on Banking and Financial Services, U.S. House of Representatives, 1 October.

Lipsey, Phillip Y. 2003. Japan's Asian Monetary Fund Proposal. *Stanford Journal of East Asian Affairs*, **3**(1), 93–104.

Lipsky, John. 1998. Asia's Crisis: A Market Perspective. *Finance & Development*, **35**(2), 10–13.

Liu, Olin. 2001. Overview. In Kanitta Meesok et al., *Malaysia: From Crisis to Recovery*. IMF Occasional Papers, no. 207, August. Available at http://www.imf.org/external/pubs/nft/op/207/index.htm.

Liu, Shiyu, Wu Yi and Liu Zhengming. 2006. The Lessons Learnt from the Development and Reform of China's Banking Sector. BIS Papers, no. 28, August, 181–187.

Lou, Ji Wei. 2006. Speech to University of Edinburgh. Chinese version only. Published in Chinese as 'Reflection on China's Economic Reform'. In Wu Jinglian (ed.), *Comparative Studies–23*. Beijing: China CITIC Press. 2006.

Lukauskas, Arvid John, and Francisco L. Rivera-Batiz, eds. 2001. *The Political Economy of the East Asian Crisis and Its Aftermath: Tigers in Distress*. Cheltenham: Edward Elgar.

Maddison, Angus. 2007. *Contours of the World Economy 1–2030 AD: Essays in Macro-Economic History*. New York: Oxford University Press.

Mahbubani, Kishore. 1999. *Can Asians Think? Understanding the Divide between East and West*. Singapore: Times Media.

———. 2008. *The New Asian Hemisphere: The Irresistible Shift of Global Power to the East*. New York: Public Affairs, Perseus Books.

Makin, John H. 2006. Does China Save and Investment Too Much? *Cato Journal*, 22(2), 307–315.

Mandelbrot, Benoît B., and Richard L. Hudson. 2008. *The Misbehaviour of Markets*. London: Profile Books.

Margolis, Richard, and Xu Xiaonian. 1998. The Myth of China's 'Devaluation'. *Asian Wall Street Journal*, 19 January.

Martinez, Guillermo Ortiz. 1998. What Lessons Does the Mexican Crisis Hold for Recovery in Asia? *Finance & Development*, 35(2), 6–9.

Martinez-Diaz, Leonardo. 2006. Pathways through Financial Crisis: Indonesia. *Global Governance*, 12, 395–312.

Mayhew, David, and Martyn Hopper. 2008. *The Future of Financial Regulation, with Howard Davies and Martin Wolf*. Herbert Smith, London, November.

McCauley, Robert. 2001. Financial Instability and Policy. APEC Economic Committee, Proceedings, Hong Kong.

McKibbin, W., and Tim Callen. 2003. The Impact of Japanese Economic Policies on the Asia Region. In T. Callen and J. Ostry, eds., *Japan's Lost Decade: Policies for Economics Revival*, 251–271. Washington, DC: International Monetary Fund.

McKinnon, Ronald I. 2005. *Exchange Rates under the East Asian Dollar Standard: Living with Conflicted Virtues*. Cambridge, MA: MIT Press.

McKinnon, Ronald I., and Kenichi Ohno. 2005. Japan's Deflation and the Syndrome of the Ever-Higher Yen, 1971–1995. In Ronald I. McKinnon, ed., *Exchange Rates under the East Asian Dollar Standards: Living with Conflicted Virtues*, 77–102. Cambridge, MA: MIT Press.

McKinnon, Ronald I., and Günther Schnabl. 2005. Synchronized Business Cycles in East Asia and Fluctuations in Yen/Dollar Exchange Rate. In Ronald I. McKinnon, *Exchange Rates under the East Asian Dollar Standard: Living with Conflicted Virtues*, 53–76. Cambridge, MA: MIT Press.

McKinsey Global Institute. 2006. *Putting China's Capital to Work: The Value of Financial System Reform*. San Francisco: McKinsey & Company.

———. 2007. *Banking in Changing World*. San Francisco: McKinsey & Company.

Meesok, Kanitta, et al. 2001. Malaysia: From Crisis to Recovery. *IMF Occasional Paper*, no. 27, August.

Meigs, James A. 1998. Lessons for Asia From Mexico. *Cato Journal*, 17(3), 315–322.

Mera, Koichi, and Bertrand Renaud, eds. 2000. *Asia's Financial Crisis and the Role of Real Estate*. Armonk, NY: M. E. Sharpe.

Meyer, Laurence H. 1999. Lessons from the Asian Crisis: A Central Banker's Perspective. *Levy Economics Institute Working Paper*, no. 276, April.

Mikitani, Riyoichi, and Adam S. Posen, eds. 2000. *Japan's Financial Crisis and Its Parallels to US Experience*. Washington, DC: Institute for International Economics.

Min, Byung S. 1999. South Korea's Financial Crisis in 1997: What Have We Learned? *ASEAN Economic Bulletin*, **16**(2), 175–189.

Ministry of Finance, Japan. 1999. *Internationalization of the Yen for the 21st Century – Japan's Response to Changes in Global Economic and Financial Environments.* Council on Foreign Exchange and Other Transactions, Ministry of Finance, Tokyo, April.

Minsky, Hyman P. 1982. The Financial-Instability Hypothesis: Capitalist Processes and the Behaviour of the Economy. In Charles P. Kindleberger and Jean-Pierre Laffargue, eds., *Financial Crises: Theory, History and Policy*, 13–139. Cambridge: Cambridge University Press.

   1992. The Capital Development of the Economy and the Structure of Financial Institutions. Jerome Levy Economics Institute of Bard College Working Paper, no. 72, January.

Mishkin, Frederic S. 1999. Lessons from the Asian Crisis. NBER Working Paper, no. 7102.

Miyazawa, Kiichi. 1999. Beyond the Asian Crisis. Speech on the Occasion of the APEC Finance Ministers Meeting, Langkawi, Malaysia, 15 May.

Mohamad, Mahathir. 1984. Speech by the Prime Minister of Malaysia at a Luncheon Meeting with Italian Industrialists and Businessmen. Rome, Italy, 24 September.

   1997a. The Opening of the 30th ASEAN Ministerial Meeting. Speech by the Prime Minister of Malaysia at the 30th ASEAN Ministerial Meeting, Petaling Jaya, Malaysia, 24 July.

   1997b. Asian Economies: Challenges and Opportunities. Speech by the Prime Minister of Malaysia at the 1997 IMF-World Bank Program of Seminars, Hong Kong, 20 September.

   1999a. Financial Stability through Exchange Controls: Malaysia's Experience. Speech by the Prime Minister of Malaysia at the Asia Society Dinner, New York, 27 September.

   1999b. Asia's Road to Recovery: The Challenge of Pragmatism. Speech by the Prime Minister of Malaysia at the World Economic Forum, 10 October, Singapore.

   1999c. The 1999 Budget Speech. Speech by the Prime Minister/Minister of Finance before the Dewan Rakyat, 23 October.

Mohamed, Mustapa. 1998. Malaysia: Measures for Economic Recovery. Speech by the Second Minister of Finance of Malaysia at the 1998 IMF-World Programme of Seminars, Washington, DC, 4 October.

Mohanty, Madhu. 2006. Banks and Financial Intermediation in East Asia: What Has Changed? Presentation at the OECD-ADBI Eighth Roundtable on Capital Market Reforms, Tokyo, Japan, 1 October.

Monetary Authority of Singapore. 1998. The Impact of the Asian Crisis on China: An Assessment. Monetary Authority of Singapore Occasional Paper, no. 8, October.

Moody's. 2007. Stress-Testing the Modern Financial System. *International Policy Perspectives*, September.

Moreno, Ramon. 2006. The Changing Nature of Risks Facing Banks. *BIS Papers*, no. 28, August, 67–98.

Moreno, Ramon, Gloria Pasadilla and Eli Remolona. 1998. Asia's Financial Crisis: Lessons and Policy Responses. Pacific Basin Working Paper Series, no. PB98-02, Pacific Basin Monetary and Economic Studies, Economic Research Department, Federal Reserve Bank of San Francisco.

Moreno, Ramon, and Agustin Villar. 2005. The Increased Role of Foreign Bank Entry in Emerging Markets. *BIS Papers*, no. **23**, 9–16.

Mundell, Robert. 1961. A Theory of Optimal Currency Areas. *American Economic Review*, **51**(4), 657–665.

Mussa, Michael, ed. 2006. C. Fred Bergsten and the World Economy. Peterson Institute for International Economics, Washington, DC.

Myrdal, Gunnar. 1968. *Asian Drama: An Inquiry into the Poverty of Nations*. Volume 1. Middlesex: Penguin Books.

Nakaso, Hiroshi. 2001. The Financial Crisis in Japan during the 1990s: How the Bank of Japan Responded and the Lessons Learnt. *BIS Papers*, no. 6, October.

Namekawa, Masashi. 1998. *Thailand's Monetary and Currency Crisis*. National Institute for Research Advancement Review, Tokyo, Spring. Available at http://www.nira.or.jp/past/publ/review/98spring/namekawa.html.

Nasution, Anwar. 2000. The Meltdown of the Indonesian Economy: Causes, Responses and Lessons. *ASEAN Economic Bulletin*, **17**(2), 148–161.

The Nation. 1998. Thai Tycoons: Winners & Losers in the Economic Crisis. Mid-Year Review, July, 27. Available at http://books.google.com/books?id=TLToo6osHS4C&pg=PA63&dq=THAI+TYCOONS+WINNERS+%26+LOSERS+IN+THE+ECONOMIC+CRISIS&ei=WLYSSr-CNp-OkASFl4HJAw&hl=zh-CN.

National Economic Action Council. 1998. *National Economic Recovery Plan: Agenda for Action – Synopsis*. Kuala Lumpur, Malaysia. August.

Neiss, Hubert. 1999. Lessons from the Asian Crisis. Paper prepared for the Cato Institute's Annual Monetary Conference co-sponsored with *The Economist*, Washington, DC, 22 October.

New York Times. 1996. Bank in Thailand Told to Shut U.S. Operations. *New York Times*, 26 July.

Nier, Erlend, and Lea Zicchino. 2008. Bank Losses, Monetary Policy and Financial Stability – Evidence on the Interplay from Panel Data. Working Paper, no. 08/232, 1 September.

Nimmanhaeminda, Tarrin. 2007. We Need to Manage Better. *Bangkok Post 2007 Mid Year Economic Review*. Available at http://www.bangkokpost.com/economicmidyear2007/Tarrin.html.

Noble, Gregory W., and John Ravenhill, eds. 2000. *The Asian Financial Crisis and the Architecture of Global Finance*. Cambridge: Cambridge University Press.

Noland, Marcus. 1996. Restructuring Korea's Financial Sector for Greater Competitiveness. APEC Working Paper, no. 96–14, Peterson Institute for International Economics, Washington, DC.

North, Douglass. 2005a. The Chinese Menu (for Development). *Wall Street Journal*, Eastern Edition, 7 April.

2005b. *Understanding the Process of Economic Change*. Princeton, NJ: Princeton University Press.

Noy, Ilan. 2005. Banking Crises in East Asia: The Price Tag of Liberalization. *Analysis from the East-West Centre*, no. 78, November.

O'Brien, Richard. 1995. Who Rules the World's Financial Markets? *Harvard Business Review*, March-April, 144–151.

OECD. 2005. *Modernising Government: The Way Forward*. Organisation for Economic Co-operation and Development, Paris.

Ohmae, Kenichi. 1982. *The Mind of the Strategist: The Art of Japanese Business.* New York: McGraw-Hill.

2008. America Must Seek Aid for a Global Credit Line, Comment. *Financial Times,* 1 October, 13.

Ohno, Kenichi. 1995. The Syndrome of the Ever-Higher Yen and the Japan-US Transfer Problem: Endaka Fukyos, Bubbles, and Credit Crunches. Paper prepared for the Fifth Seminar on International Finance, Asian Development Bank, Hong Kong, 27–29 September.

Olson, Mancur. 2000. *Power and Prosperity.* New York: Basic Books.

Ozawa, Terutomo. 2006. Asia's Labour-Driven Economic Development, Flying-Geese Style: An Unprecedented Opportunity for the Poor to Rise? UNU-WIDER Research Paper, no. 2006/59, June.

Ozeki, Koyo. 2008. Responding to Financial Crises: Lessons to Learn from Japan's Experience, Japan Credit Perspectives, PIMCO, August. Available at www.pimco.com.

Padoa-Schioppa, Tommaso. 2004. Regional Economic Integration in a Global Framework. In Julie McKay, Maria Oliva Armangol and Georges Pineau, eds., *Regional Economic Integration in a Global Framework: G-20 Workshop Organised by the People's Bank of China and European Central Bank, Beijing, 22–23 September 2004,* 27–34. Frankfurt: European Central Bank.

Pangestu, Mari. 1998. Briefing Notes for the World Economic Forum. 12 October. Available at http://kolom.pacific.net.id/ind/mari_pangestu.

2003. The Indonesian Bank Crisis and Restructuring: Lessons and Implications for Other Developing Countries. UNCTAD G-24 Discussion Paper Series, no. 23, November.

Park, Jae-Joon. 1998. Causes and Solutions to the Economic Crisis. *Business Korea,* October, 54–58.

Park, Yung Chul. 1998. The Financial Crisis in Korea and Its Lessons for Reform of the International Financial System. In Jan Joost Teunissen, ed., *Regulatory and Supervisory Challenges in a New Era of Global Finance,* 25–69. The Hague: FONDAD.

2007. Monetary and Financial Cooperation and Integration in East Asia: Recent Developments and Prospects. ISIS-FONDAD Conference on Globalization, Asian Economic Integration and National Development Strategies: Challenges to Asia in a Fast-Changing World, Kuala Lumpur, Malaysia, 14–15 August.

Patrick, Hugh. 2007. Comment on 'Japan's Lost Decade: What Have We Learned and Where Are We Heading?' *Asian Economic Policy Review,* **2**, 204–205.

Paulson, Henry, Jr. 2008a. Interview with *Fortune* Magazine: *Paulson to the Rescue. Fortune,* 29 September, 53.

2008b. Quoted in 'The Captain in the Street'. *Newsweek,* 29 September, 17.

Pei, Minxin. 2006. The Dark Side of China's Rise. *Foreign Affairs,* 153, March/April, 32–40.

People's Bank of China. 2005. Reforming the RMB Exchange Rate Regime. Public announcement, 21 July.

Persaud, Avinash D. 2000. Sending the Herd Off the Cliff Edge: The Disturbing Interaction between Herding and Market-Sensitive Risk Management Practices. eRisk.com, December.

2007. Risky Business: Why the Risk-Transfer Model Frequently Championed by Investment Banks, Credit Rating Agencies and Regulators Creates Liquidity Black Holes. London Business School Lecture, London, 29 October.

Phuvanatnaranubala, Thirachai. 2005. Globalisation, Financial Markets and the Operation of Monetary Policy: The Case of Thailand. BIS Papers, no. 23, May, 269–274.

Pilling, David. 2007. Weak Yen Gives Lift to Dynamic Exports. *Financial Times*, 6 June, 12.

Pitsuwan, Surin. 1998. Thailand's Foreign Policy during the Economic and Social Crises. Keynote Address by the Minister of Foreign Affairs of Thailand at the Seminar in Commemoration of the 49th Anniversary of the Faculty of Political Science, Thammasat University, Bangkok, Thailand, 12 June.

2000. Keynote Address by the Minister of Foreign Affairs of Thailand at the Ceremony in Commemoration of the 100th Anniversary of the German Asia-Pacific Business Association, Hamburg, Germany, 3 March.

Plender, John. 2008. Capitalism in Convulsion. *Financial Times*, 21 September, 12.

Pomerleano, Michael. 2002. Back to Basics: Critical Financial Sector Professions Required in the Aftermath of an Asset Bubble. *Appraisal Journal*, **70**, April, 173–181.

2007. Corporate Financial Restructuring in Asia: Implications for Financial Stability. *BIS Quarterly Review*, 3 September, 83–93.

Prestowitz, Clyde V. 2005. *Three Billion New Capitalists: The Great Shift of Wealth and Power to the East*. New York: Basic Books.

Prieb, Woody. 2004. *Dharmodynamics*. Bangkok: Asia Books.

Rajan, Raghuram G. 2006. Global Imbalances and Financial Reform with Examples from China. *Cato Journal*, **26**(2), 267–273.

Ramaswamy, Ramana, and Hossein Samiei. 2003. The Yen-Dollar Rate: Have Interventions Mattered? In Tim Callen and Jonathan D. Ostry, eds., *Japan's Lost Decade: Policies for Economic Revival*, 224–248. Washington, DC: International Monetary Fund.

Ramos, Fidel Valdez. 1998. The East Asian Crisis and Its Social Implications. Remarks to the Asia Society, Melbourne, 2 December.

Ramos, Roy. 1998. Banks: A Critical Ingredient to Recovery for Asia. *World Bank-Asian Development Bank Senior Policy Seminar*, Manila, Philippines, March.

Reading, Brian. 2007. The Bears Zero in on Goldilocks. *Euromoney*, **38**(453), 88–97.

Reinhart, Carmen M., and Kenneth S. Rogoff. 2008. Is the 2007 U.S. Subprime Financial Crisis So Different? An International Historical Comparison. AEA Session on New Perspectives on Financial Globalization, New Orleans, 6 January. Available at http://www.aeaweb.org/annual_mtg_papers/2008/2008_578.pdf.

Reisen, Helmut. 1999. After the Great Asian Slump: Toward a Coherent Approach to Global Capital Flows. OECD Development Centre, Policy Brief no. 16.

Renaud, Bertrand. 2003. Speculative Behaviour in Immature Real Estate Markets, Lessons of the 1997 Asia Financial Crisis. *Urban Policy and Research*, **21**(2), 153–173.

Renaud, Bertrand, and Kyung-Hwan Kim. 2007. The Global Housing Boom and Its Aftermath. *Housing Finance International*, 21, December, 3–15.

Richardson, Michael. 1997. Indonesia Signals It Is Firm on Closing 16 Banks. *International Herald Tribune*, 8 November.

Roach, Stephen. 2007. 'The Great Unraveling'. Morgan Stanley. *Global Economic Forum*, 16 March. Available at: http://www.morganstanley.com/views/gef/archive/2007/20070316-Fri.html.

Roche, David. 2007. The Global Money Machine. *Wall Street Journal*, 17 December.

Roche, David, and Bob McKee. 2007. *The New Monetarism*. Chelsea, London: Independent Strategy.

Rodrik, Dani. 2008. A Washington Consensus I Can Live With. 12 June. Available at http://rodrik.typepad.com/dani_rodriks_weblog/development_debates.

Rogoff, Kenneth. 2003. The IMF Strikes Back. *Foreign Policy*, **134**, January/February, 38–46.

Rohwer, Jim. 2001. *Remade in America: How Asia Will Change because America Boomed*. New York: John Wiley and Sons.

Roubini, Nouriel. 2008. *Ten Fundamental Issues in Reforming Financial Regulation and Supervision in a World of Financial Innovation and Globalization*. Available at www.rgemonitor.com.

Roubini, Nouriel, and Brad Setser. 2004. The U.S. as a Net Debtor: The Sustainability of the U.S. External Imbalances. Stern School of Business, New York University.

Rubin, Robert E. 1998. Strengthening the Architecture of the International Financial System. Remarks to the Brookings Institution, Washington, DC, 14 April.

2008. Rubin: Don't Blame Me. *Bloomberg Markets*, September, 46.

Rubin, Robert E., and Jacob Weisberg. 2003. *In an Uncertain World: Tough Choices from Wall Street to Washington*. New York: Random House.

Rumsfeld, Donald. 2002. Press Conference at the NATO Headquarters. Brussels, Belgium, 6 June.

Russell, Bertrand. 1948. *Authority and the Individual*. London: Unwin Books.

Sachs, Jeffrey D. 1997. International Monetary Failure? The IMF's Prescriptions Might Actually Make Asia's Financial Turmoil Worse. *Time*, **8** December.

2005. *The End of Poverty*. New York: Penguin Books.

Sadli, Mohammad. 1998. The Indonesian Crisis. *ASEAN Economic Bulletin*, **15**(3), 272–280.

Sakakibara, Eisuke. 1998. Academic Economists Reveal Vacuum of Thinking on Japan's Problems. *Financial Times*, **30** October, 18.

1999a. The Lessons of the Financial Crises of 1994 to 1998. Paper presented at the Round Table on Securities Market Reforms in the Face of the Asian Financial Crisis, 8 April.

1999b. From the Washington Consensus to the New International Financial Architecture. In David Gruen and Luke Gower, eds., *Capital Flows and the International Financial System*, 181–188. Sydney: Reserve Bank of Australia.

2000. US-Japanese Economic Policy Conflicts and Coordination during the 1990s. In Riyoichi Mikitani and Adam S. Posen, eds., *Japan's Financial Crisis and Its Parallels to US Experience*, 167–183. Washington, DC: Institute for International Economics.

2003. *Structural Reform in Japan: Breaking the Iron Triangle*. Washington, DC: Brookings Institution Press.

2007. Regional Cooperation in Asia after the East Asian Crisis. Speech by Former Vice Minister of Finance for International Affairs, Japan at the Conference on Trends in Financial Sector Organised by the Federal Reserve Bank of San Francisco, San Francisco, CA, 20 June.

Sakakibara, Eisuke, and Sharon Yamakawa. 2003. Regional Integration in East Asia: Challenges and Opportunities, Parts I and II. World Bank Policy Research Working Papers, no. 3078 and 3079, June.

Saludo, Ricardo, and Antonio Lopez. 1997. Eye of the Storm: As Speculators Reign Supreme, How Safe Is Your Country's Money? *Asiaweek*, 25 July.

Sargen, Nicolas. 2006. Reflections on Emerging Market Debt. Fort Washington Investment Advisors Inc., November.

Sargent, Thomas. 1993. *Rational Expectations and Inflation*. 2nd ed. New York: Harper & Row.

Scannell, Kara, and Sudeep Reddy. 2008. Greenspan Admits Errors to Hostile House Panel. *Wall Street Journal*, 24 October.

Schmidt, Johannes D. 2002. Political Business Alliances: The Role of the State and Foreign and Domestic Capital in Economic Development. In Terence Gomez, ed., *Political Business in East Asia*, 62–82. London: Routledge.

Schumpeter, Joseph A. 1954. *History of Economic Analysis*. London: George Allen & Unwin.

Sell, Friedrich L. 2001. *Contagion in Financial Markets*. Cheltenham: Edward Elgar.

Senior Supervisors Group. 2008. Observations on Risk Management Practices during the Recent Market Turbulence. New York, 6 March. Available at http://www.newyorkfed.org/newsevents/news/banking/2008/SSG_Risk_Mgt_doc_final.pdf.

Sesit, Michael R., and Laura Jereski. 1997. Traders Burnt in Thailand's Battle of Baht. *Wall Street Journal*, Eastern Edition, 22 May.

Setser, Brad. 2006. The Chinese Conundrum: External Financial Strength, Domestic Financial Weakness. *CESifo Economic Studies*, **52**(2), 364–395.

Setser, Brad, and Nouriel Roubini. 2005. How Scary Is the Deficit? *Foreign Affairs*, July/August. Available at www.foreignaffairs.org/20050701faresponse84415/brad-setser/how-scary-is-the-deficit.html.

Shanmugam, M. 2005. A RM23 Billion Bill. *The Edge*, 20 November.

Sheng, Andrew. 1996. *Asian Money: Its Dynamics and Prospects*. Unpublished manuscript, Hong Kong and Tokyo, 5 April.

1997a. Asian Currencies in Global Perspective. Speech at the Seminar on Business and Finance, Sandakan, Sabah, Malaysia, 10 August.

1997b. Regulatory and Development Issues in the East Asian Region. Speech at the KPMG Asia Pacific Banking and Finance Conference and Training on Balancing Risk and Reward in the World's Fastest Growing Market, Kuala Lumpur, Malaysia, 26 August.

1997c. Financial Stability in Emerging Market Economies. Speech at the APEC Working Level Symposium on Strengthening Financial Systems in APEC Economies, Federal Reserve Bank of San Francisco, 4–5 September.

1997d. Housing Finance and Asian Financial Markets: Cinderella Coming to the Ball. Speech at the 22nd World Congress of the International Union for Housing Finance, Bangkok and Phuket, Thailand, 24–30 October.

1997e. Asset Prices, Capital Flows and Risk Management. Speech at the Asian Securities Analysts Federation Conference, Bangkok, Thailand, 16–17 November.

1998. The Crisis of Money in the 21st Century. Guest Lecture at the City University of Hong Kong, Hong Kong, 28 April.

1999a. East Asia and the New Economy. Breakfast Briefing at the Council on Foreign Relations, New York, 19 March.

1999b. The Role of Yen in the Asian Financial Crisis. Unpublished Manuscript, Hong Kong, 15 April.

1999c. Accountability and Transparency in the Age of Global Markets. Speech at the American Chamber of Commerce Financial Services Luncheon Meeting, Hong Kong, 14 May.

1999d. Conclusion: An Asian Perspective on the Asian Crisis. In Alison Harwood, Robert E. Litan and Michael Pomerleano, eds., *Financial Markets and Development: The Crisis in Emerging Markets*, 413–420. Washington, DC: Brookings Institution.

1999e. The Framework for Financial Supervision: Macro and Micro Issues. BIS Policy Papers, no. 7, October, 154–166.

1999f. The Future of Prudential Regulation in Asia & South East Asia. Keynote Address at the Conference on The Future of Commercial and Central Banking, Hong Kong, 9 November.

2000a. Technology. Markets and Governance. Speech at the Asia Pacific Governance 2000: Ethics, Law, Management, Politics, Key Centre for Ethics, Law, Justice and Governance and Griffith Asia Pacific Council, Griffith University, Brisbane, Australia, 27–28 April.

2000b. Transparency, Accountability and Standards in Global Markets. Luncheon Address at the Second OECD/World Bank Asian Corporate Governance Roundtable, Hong Kong, 31 May–2 June.

2000c. The Importance of Risk Management. In Eric S. Rosengreen and John S. Jordan, eds., *Building an Infrastructure for Financial Stability*, 237–242. Boston: Federal Reserve Bank of Boston.

2001. Securing the Third Zone of the Global Markets. Speech at the Asian Securities Analysts Federation Conference, Hong Kong, 3–4 December.

2002. The Future of Capital Market Development in East and South East Asia. Paper presented at the 10th SEC Thailand Anniversary Seminar on How Can NBFIs Play a Greater Role in a Bank-Based Economy, Bangkok, Thailand, 6 September.

2003. The Future of Capital Markets in East Asia: Implications for China's Equity Markets. Stanford Centre for International Development Working Paper, no. 192, November.

2006a. The Art of Reform: Applying Lessons from Suntze to Asia's Financial Markets. *Finance and Development*, **43**(2), 20–23.

2006b. ASEAN Integration to Meeting Global Challenges. Unpublished manuscript, Kuala Lumpur, August.

2006c. Building National and Regional Financial Markets: The East Asian Experiences. Paper presented at the 2006 Global Meeting organised by the Emerging Markets Forum, Jakarta, Indonesia, 21 September.

2007a. China's Banking Reforms: Towards a Robust Financial Structure. Paper presented at the John Hopkins University School of Advanced International Studies (SAIS) Conference on China's Banking Reform and Governance, Washington, DC, 16 April.

2007b. The Asian Network Economy in the 21st Century. In Indermit Gill, Yukon Huang and Homi Kharas, eds., *East Asia Visions: Perspectives on Economic Development*, 258–284. Washington, DC: World Bank and Institute of Policy Studies.

2008a. Lessons for Banking and Market Regulation in Asia. In David Mayes, Michael Taylor, and Robert Pringle, eds., *New Frontiers in Oversight and Regulation of the Financial System*, 377–386. London: Central Banking Publications.

2008b. Regulatory Action in Financial Crises: A Parallel with Military Command. In David Mayes, Michael Taylor, and Robert Pringle, eds., *New Frontiers in Oversight and Regulation of the Financial System*, 125–138. London: Central Banking Publications.

Sheng, Andrew, and Xiao Geng. 2002. Japan's Economic Deflation: Lessons for China. Unpublished manuscript, Hong Kong.

Sheng, Andrew, and Tan Gaik Looi. 2003. Is There a Goodhart's Law in Financial Regulation? In Paul Mizen, ed., *Monetary History, Exchange Rates and Financial Markets*. Volume II, 234–249. Cheltenham: Edward Elgar.

Sheng, Andrew, and Allen Ng. 2006. The External Wealth of Malaysia: An Analysis Using the International Balance Sheet Perspective. Paper based on the 19 May 2006 Tun Ismail Lecture by Andrew Sheng, Kuala Lumpur, Malaysia, June.

2008. The External Wealth of China: An Investigation from the International Balance Sheet Perspective. HKIMR Working Paper, no. 1/2008, Hong Kong.

Sheng, Andrew, and Kwek Kian Teng. 2007. East Asian Capital Markets Integration: Steps beyond ABMI. Paper presented at the ANU-MOF Conference on Advancing East Asian Economic Integration, Bangkok, Thailand, 22–23 February.

Sheng, Andrew, Kwek Kian Teng and Tan Wai Kuen. 2007. A Framework for Developing Capital Market: Process, Sequencing and Options. Third APEC Policy Dialogue Workshop on Financial Sector Reform, Melbourne Australia, 9 May.

Sherer, Paul M. 1997. Thailand Shuffles Cabinet, Promises Elections in Early '98 to Defuse Crisis. *Wall Street Journal*, Eastern Edition.

Shirai, Sayuri. 2007. Promoting Tokyo as an International Financial Centre. Groupe d'Economie Mondiale (GEM) Sciences Po Working Paper, Paris, November.

Shirk, Susan. 1993. *The Political Logic of Economic Reform in China*. Berkeley: University of California Press.

Siamwalla, Ammar. 2000. *Anatomy of the Thai Economic Crisis*. Bangkok: Thailand Development Research Institute.

Sidel, John. 2006. *Riots, Pogroms Jihad: Religious Violence in Indonesia*. Ithaca, NY: Cornell University Press.

Sila-on, Amaret. 1998. The FRA and the Financial Crisis. *TDRI Quarterly Review*, 13(3), 3–6.

Smith, Adam. 1976 [1776]. An Inquiry into the Nature and Causes of the Wealth of Nations. In A. S. Skinner et al., *The Glasgow Edition of the Works and Correspondence of Adam Smith*. Volume II. Oxford: Oxford University Press.

Solomon, Jay. 1998. Salim's Big Indonesian Bank Put under Government Control. *Wall Street Journal*, Eastern Edition, 29 May.

Solomon, Robert. 1981. The Elephant in the Boat. *Foreign Affairs*, 60(3), 573–592.

Sonakul, Chatu Mongol. 1999. Thailand: What Happened and Has Anything Really Changed. Speech at the ASEM Conference, Copenhagen, Denmark, 8–9 March.

Song, Jung A. 1999. Heart Ache and Hope. *Far Eastern Economic Review*, 21 October, 50.

Soros, George. 1994. The Theory of Reflexivity. MIT Department of Economics, 26 April.

1998a. Capitalism's Last Chance? *Foreign Affairs*, **113**, Winter, 55–66.

1998b. *The Crisis of Global Capitalism: Open Society Endangered*. New York: Public Affairs.

South China Morning Post. 1998. Intervention Averted Disaster, Claims Tsang. *South China Morning Post*, 8 September.

Sparrow, Malcolm. 2000. *The Regulatory Craft: Controlling Risks, Solving Problems and Managing Compliance*. Washington, DC: Brookings Institution.

Spence, Michael. 2008. The Growth Report: Strategies for Sustained Growth and Inclusive Development. Commission on Growth and Development, Washington, DC, June.

Stern, Gary. 2000. *Thoughts on Designing Credible Policies after Financial Modernization: Addressing Too-Big-to-Fail and Moral Hazard*. Federal Reserve Bank of Minneapolis, September.

Stiglitz, Joseph E. 1998a. More Instruments and Broader Goals: Moving towards the Post-Washington Consensus. 1998 WIDER Annual Lecture, Helsinki, Finland, 7 January.

1998b. Sound Finance and Sustainable Development in Asia. Keynote Address to the Asia Development Forum, Manila, Philippines, 12 March.

2000. The Insider: What I Learned at the World Economic Crisis. *New Republic*, 17–24 April, 55–60.

2002. *Globalization and Its Discontents*. New York: W. W. Norton.

2003. *The Roaring Nineties: Seeds of Destruction*. London: Penguin.

2008. The Way Out. How the Financial Crisis Happened, and How It Must Be Fixed. *Time*, 17 October. Available at http://www.time.com/time/business/article/0,8599,1851739,00.html.

Stiglitz, Joseph E., and Shahid Yusuf, eds. 2001. *Rethinking the East Asian Miracle*. New York: Oxford University Press.

Strauss-Kahn, Dominique. 1998. Personal View: Six of the Best. *Financial Times*, 16 April, 16.

Studwell, Joe. 2007. *Asian Godfathers: Money and Power in Hong Kong and Southeast Asia*. Boston: Atlantic Monthly Press.

Summers, Lawrence H. 1998. Riding to the Rescue. *Newsweek*, 2 February, 39.

2007. History Holds Lessons for China and Its Partners. *Financial Times*, 26 February, 17.

Sundararajan, V., and Tomas J. T. Balino, eds. 1991. *Banking Crises: Cases and Issues*. Washington, DC: International Monetary Fund.

Suryodiningrat, Meidyatama. 2007. Living Diversity in Indonesia. *Jakarta Post.com*, 13 April.

Suzuki, Kenji. 2001. Effect of Amakudari on Bank Performance in the Post-Bubble Period. Stockholm School of Economics Working Paper, no. 136, November.

Suzuki, Yoshio. 1994. Financial Reform in Japan and Global Economic Stability. *Cato Journal*, 13(3), 447–451.

Taleb, Nassim Nicholas. 2007. *The Black Swan: The Impact of the Highly Improbable*. New York: Random House.

Taville, Suzanne. 2007. Hot Money Could Leave Us Cold. *Money Management*, 22 March, 16–17.

Taylor, John. 2007. Housing and Monetary Policy. NBER Working Paper, no. 13682, December.

Teranishi, Juro, and Yutaka Kosai. 1993. Introduction: Economic Reform and Stabilization in Postwar Japan. In Juro Teranishi and Yutaka Kosai, eds., *The Japanese Experience of Economic Reforms*, 1–27. New York: St. Martin's Press.

Tett, Gillian. 2008. A Year That Shook Faith in Finance, Part 1: How It Happened. *Financial Times*, 4 August, 11.

Tourres, Marie-Aimee. 2003. *The Tragedy That Didn't Happen: Malaysia's Crisis Management and Capital Controls*. Malaysia: Institute of Strategic and International Studies.

Trichet, Jean-Claude. 2007. Reflections on the International Financial Architecture, Keynote address by the President of the European Central Bank at the 2007 Salzburg Seminar on 'Challenges to the International Monetary System: Rebalancing Currencies, Institutions and Rules', Salzburg, Austria, 29 September.

Tsang, Donald. 1999. Unfinished Business. *Asiaweek*, 19 November.

Tsang, Shu-ki. 1998. The Hong Kong Economy in the Midst of the Financial Crisis. Hong Kong Journalists Association Regional Conference on the Financial Crisis, Hong Kong, 26 September.

Tuckett, David, and Richard Taffler. 2008. Phantastic Objects and the Financial Market's Sense of Reality: A Psychoanalytic Contribution to the Understanding of Stock Market Instability. *International Journal of Psychoanalysis* **89**, 389–412.

Tully, Shawn. 2007. Risk Returns with a Vengence. *Fortune*, 3 September, 31–36.

Turner, Philip. 2007. Are Banking Systems in East Asia Stronger? *Asian Economic Policy Review*, **2**, 75–95.

Ueda, Kazuo. 1998. The East Asian Economic Crisis: A Japanese Perspective. *International Finance*, **1**(2), 327–338.

  1999. The Japanese Banking Crisis in the 1990s. *BIS Policy Papers*, no. 7, October, 251–262.

UK Financial Services Authority. 2007. Review of Liquidity Requirements for Banks and Building Societies. FSA Discussion Paper, 07/7, December.

UK HM Treasury, Financial Services Authority and Bank of England 2008. Financial Stability and Depositor Protection: Strengthening the Framework. Consultation Document, CM7308, London, January.

UK House of Commons Treasury Committee. 2008. *The Run on the Rock*. Volume I. London, 26 January.

Underhill, Geoffrey. 2007. Global Financial Architecture, Legitimacy and Representation: Voice for Emerging Markets, Garnet Policy Brief, no. 3, January. Available at www.garnet-eu.org.

UNESCAP. 2002. *Protecting Marginalized Groups during Economic Downturns: Lessons from the Asian Experience*. Bangkok: United Nations Economic and Social Commission for Asia and the Pacific.

U.S. Department of the Treasury. 2008. Report on Foreign Portfolio Holdings of US Securities, as of June 30, 2007. Washington, DC, April.

U.S. President's Working Group on Financial Markets. 2008. Policy Statement on Financial Market Developments. Department of the Treasury, Washington, DC, 13 March.

Vijayaledchumy, V. 2003. Fiscal Policy in Malaysia. *BIS Papers*, no. 20, October, 173–179.

Visser, Hans, and Ingmar van Herpt. 1996. Financial Liberalisation and Financial Fragility: The Experiences of Chile and Indonesia Compared. In Neils Herman and Robert Lensink, eds., *Financial Development and Economic Growth: Theory and Experiences from Developing Countries*, 287–309. 2001 reprint. London: Routledge.

Vittas, Dimitri, and Bo Wang. 1991. Credit Policies in Japan and Korea: A Review of the Literature. *World Bank Policy Research Working Paper Series*, no. 747, August.

Vogel, Ezra F. 1986. Pax Nipponica? *Foreign Affairs*, **64**(4), 752–767.

Volcker, Paul A. 1998a. Emerging Economies in a Sea of Global Finance. Charles Rostov Lecture, Paul H. Nitze School of Advanced International Studies, John Hopkins University, Baltimore, MD, 9 April.

1998b. Can We Bounce Back? *Financial Times*, 7 October, 10.

1999. A Perspective on Financial Crisis. In Jane Sneddon Little and Giovanni P. Olivei, eds., *Rethinking the International Monetary System*, 264–268. Federal Reserve Bank of Boston Conference Series, no. 43, June.

2008. Speech to Economic Club of New York, 8 April.

Wade, Robert. 1998. The Asian Debt-and-Development Crisis of 1997–?: Causes and Consequences. *World Development*, **26**(8), 1535–1553.

Wade, Robert, and Frank Veneroso. 1998. The Asian Crisis: The High Debt Model vs. the Wall Street-Treasury-IMF Complex. *New Left Review*, **228**, 3–23.

Wessel, David. 1995. Rubin Says U.S. Is "Fully Committed" to Policies Needed for a Strong Dollar. Wall Street Journal, Eastern Edition, 10 March.

White, William. 2008. International Governance for the Prevention and Management of Financial Crisis. Bank of France International Monetary Seminar on Liquidity Crisis, Capital Crisis, Paris, 10 June.

Williamson, John. 2002 [1990]. What Washington Means by Policy Reform. Peterson Institute, Washington, DC, November. Originally published in John Williamson, ed., *Latin American Adjustment: How Much Has Happened?* chapter 2. Washington, DC: Institute of International Economics.

2008. Crises and International Policy Coordination. Peterson Institute, Washington, DC, 19 March.

Winters, Jeffrey A. 1997. The Dark Side of the Tigers. *Asian Wall Street Journal*, 12 December.

Wolf, Martin. 1998a. Capital Punishment: The Emerging Washington Consensus on the Lessons from the Asian Crisis Is Not Wrong, but It Is Too Limited. *Financial Times*, 17 March, 22.

1998b. Supporting a House of Cards. *Financial Times*, 16 September, 17.

2007a. The Lessons Asians Learnt from Their Financial Crisis. *Financial Times*, 23 May, 17.

2007b. Unfettered Finance Is Fast Reshaping the Global Economy. *Financial Times*, 18 June, 1.

2008a. Seven Habits That Finance Regulators Must Acquire. *Financial Times*, 7 May, 11.

2008b. America's Housing Solution Is Not a Good One to Follow. *Financial Times*, 10 September, 9.

2008c. The End of Lightly Regulated Finance Has Come Far Closer. *Financial Times*, 17 September, 13.

2008d. Why Paulson's Plan Was Not a True Solution to the Crisis. *Financial Times*, 24 September, 13.

Woo, Wing Thye, Jeffrey D. Sachs and Klaus Schwab, eds. 2000. *The Asian Financial Crisis: Lessons for a Resilient Asia*. Cambridge, MA: MIT Press.

World Bank. 1993. *The East Asian Miracle: Economic Growth and Public Policy*. Oxford: Oxford University Press.

2006. *Making the New Indonesia Work for the Poor*. Jakarta: World Bank Office of Jakarta.

2007a. *10 Years after the Crisis*. East Asia & the Pacific Update.

2007b. Indonesia's Debt and World Bank Assistance. Note Prepared by World Bank Office Jakarta, 24 July. Available at http://go.worldbank.org/OCKV5444A0.

2007c. Will Resilience Overcome Risk? East Asia and Pacific Update, November.

Wright, Chris. 2007. Thailand: An Accidental Pariah. *Euromoney*, March, 1.

Wu, Jinglian. 2005. *Understanding and Interpreting Chinese Economic Reform*. Mason: Thomson/South-Western.

Xafa, Miranda. 2008. Global Imbalances and Financial Stability. IMF Working Paper, no. WP/07/111, April.

Yam, Joseph. 1998a. The Hong Kong Dollar Link. Keynote Speech at the Hong Kong Trade Development Council Financial Roadshow, Tokyo, Japan, 3 March.

1998b. Why We Intervened. *Asian Wall Street Journal*, 20 August.

1998c. Defending Hong Kong's Monetary Stability. Address at the Hong Kong Trade Development Council Networking Luncheon, Singapore, 14 October.

1998d. Coping with Financial Turmoil. Inside Asia Lecture organised by *The Australian*, Sydney, Australia, 23 November.

1999a. Causes of and Solutions to the Recent Financial Turmoil in the Asian Region. Speech at the symposium in commemoration of 50 years of central banking in the Philippines organised by the Bangko Sentral ng Pilipinas, Manila, Philippines, 5 January.

1999b. Hong Kong: From Crisis to Recovery. Address at the HKMA Luncheon, London, 28 September.

Yashiro, Masamoto. 2005. Why Japan Failed to Deal with the Post-Bubble Problems, Keynote address at the Wharton Global Alumni Forum, Singapore, 27 May. Available at http://www.insead.edu/alumni/newsletter/June2005/printedversion-final.pdf.

Yellen, Janet L. 2007. The Asian Crisis Ten Years Later: Assessing the Past and Looking to the Future. Speech to the Asia Society of Southern California, Los Angeles, 6 February.

Yoshitomi, Masaru. 1999. Capital Flows to East Asia. In Martin Feldstein, ed., *International Capital Flows*, 182–186. Chicago: University of Chicago Press.

2005. Applying Key Lessons from the Asian Crisis to China in an Era of Asian Integration and Global Imbalances. Speech at the UNU-WIDER Jubilee Conference: WIDER Thinking Ahead – The Future of Development Economies, Helsinki, Finland, 17–18 June.

Yue, Chia Siow, and Shamira Bhanu. 1998. The Asian Financial Crisis: Human Security Dimensions. Background Paper for the International Dialogue on Building Asia's Tomorrow organised by the Japan Center for International Exchange, Tokyo, 2–3 December.

Yusuf, Shahid, Anjum Altaf and Kaoru Nabeshima, eds. 2004. *Global Production Networking and Technological Change in East Asia*. Washington, DC: World Bank.

Zainal Abidin, Mahani. 2000. Implications of the Malaysian Experience on Future International Financial Arrangements. *ASEAN Economic Bulletin*, 135–147.

Zoellick, Robert B. 1998a. Statement before the Committee on Banking and Financial Services, U.S. House of Representatives, 14 September.

1998b. The Political and Security Implications of the East Asian Crisis. *NBER Analysis on The East Asian Crisis – Implications for U.S. Policy*, 9(4), 5–29.

Zukerman, Gregory, and Kara Scannell. 2008. Madoff Misled SEC in '06. *Wall Street Journal*, 19–21 December.*Bibliography*

Index

6718350R00278

Printed in Great Britain
by Amazon.co.uk, Ltd.,
Marston Gate.